HUMAN RIGHTS WATCH WORLD REPORT 2001

Featured in World Report 2001

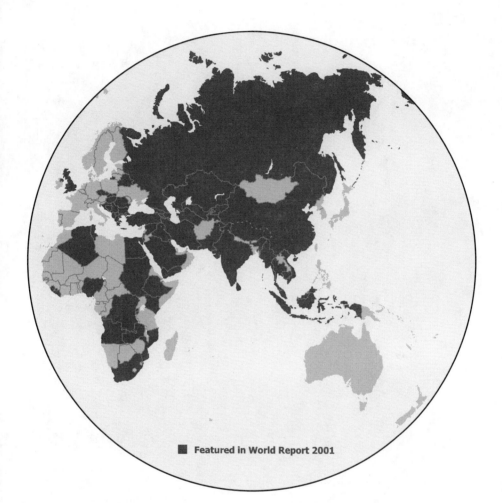

■ Featured in World Report 2001

HUMAN RIGHTS WATCH WORLD REPORT 2001

Events of 2000
(November 1999-October 2000)

New York • Washington • London • Brussels

ISBN 1-56432-254-8
ISSN 1054-948X
Library of Congress Catalog Card Number: 00-110682

Cover photograph ©2000 Laurent Van der Stockt
A Chechen fighter runs along a wall that shows the impact of the bitter
conflict being fought in Chechnya.
Cover design by Rafael Jiménez.

Human Rights Watch
350 Fifth Avenue 34th Fl.
New York, NY 10118-3299
Tel: (212) 290-4700
Fax: (212) 736-1300
E-mail: hrwnyc@hrw.org

Human Rights Watch
1630 Connecticut Avenue, N.W., Suite 500
Washington, DC 20009
Tel: (202)612-4321
Fax: (202)612-4333
E-mail: hrwdc@hrw.org

Human Rights Watch
33 Islington High Street
N1 9LH London
United Kingdom
Tel: (44171) 713-1995
Fax: (44171) 713-1800
E-mail: hrwatchuk@gn.apc.org

Human Rights Watch
15 Rue Van Campenhout
1000 Brussels, Belgium
Tel: (322) 732-2009
Fax: (322) 732-0471
E-mail: hrwbe@hrw.org

Website Address: http://www.hrw.org
Listserv address: To subscribe to the list, send an e-mail message to
majordomo@igc.apc.org with "subscribe hrw-news" in the body of the
message (leave the subject line blank).

HUMAN RIGHTS WATCH

Human Rights Watch conducts regular, systematic investigations of human rights abuses in some seventy countries around the world. Our reputation for timely, reliable disclosures has made us an essential source of information for those concerned with human rights. We address the human rights practices of governments of all political stripes, of all geopolitical alignments, and of all ethnic and religious persuasions. Human Rights Watch defends freedom of thought and expression, due process and equal protection of the law, and a vigorous civil society; we document and denounce murders, disappearances, torture, arbitrary imprisonment, discrimination, and other abuses of internationally recognized human rights. Our goal is to hold governments accountable if they transgress the rights of their people.

Human Rights Watch began in 1978 with the founding of its Europe and Central Asia division (then known as Helsinki Watch). Today, it also includes divisions covering Africa, the Americas, Asia, and the Middle East. In addition, it includes three thematic divisions on arms, children's rights, and women's rights. It maintains offices in New York, Washington, Los Angeles, London, Brussels, Moscow, Dushanbe, and Bangkok. Human Rights Watch is an independent, nongovernmental organization, supported by contributions from private individuals and foundations worldwide. It accepts no government funds, directly or indirectly.

The staff includes Kenneth Roth, executive director; Michele Alexander, development director; Reed Brody, advocacy director; Carroll Bogert, communications director; Barbara Guglielmo, finance director; Jeri Laber special advisor; Lotte Leicht, Brussels office director; Michael McClintock, deputy program director; Patrick Minges, publications director; Maria Pignataro Nielsen, human resources director; Jemera Rone, counsel; Malcolm Smart, program director; Wilder Tayler, general counsel; and Joanna Weschler, United Nations representative. Jonathan Fanton is the chair of the board. Robert L. Bernstein is the founding chair.

The regional directors of Human Rights Watch are Peter Takirambudde, Africa; José Miguel Vivanco, Americas; Sidney Jones, Asia; Holly Cartner, Europe and Central Asia; and Hanny Megally, Middle East and North Africa. The thematic division directors are Joost R. Hiltermann, arms; Lois Whitman, children's; and Regan Ralph, women's.

The members of the board of directors are Jonathan Fanton, chair; Lisa Anderson, Robert L. Bernstein, David M. Brown, William Carmichael, Dorothy Cullman, Gina Despres, Irene Diamond, Adrian W. DeWind, Fiona Druckenmiller, Edith Everett, Michael E. Gellert, Vartan Gregorian, Alice H. Henkin, James F. Hoge, Stephen L. Kass, Marina Pinto Kaufman, Bruce Klatsky, Joanne Leedom-Ackerman, Josh Mailman, Yolanda T. Moses, Samuel K. Murumba, Andrew Nathan, Jane Olson, Peter Osnos, Kathleen Peratis, Bruce Rabb, Sigrid Rausing, Orville Schell, Sid Sheinberg, Gary G. Sick, Malcolm Smith, Domna Stanton, John J. Studzinski, and Maya Wiley. Robert L. Bernstein is the founding chair of Human Rights Watch.

ACKNOWLEDGMENTS

A compilation of this magnitude requires contribution from a large number of people, including most of the Human Rights Watch staff. The contributors were:

Fred Abrahams, Marcia Allina, Haizam Amirah-Fernandez, Betsy Andersen, John Anderson, William Arkin, Monisha Bajaj, Suliman Baldos, Vikram Barekh, Joshua Barker, Tobie Barton, Adam Bassine, Jo Becker, Kate Beddall, Clarisa Bencomo, Rachel Bien, Michael Bochenek, Sebastian Brett, Reed Brody, Widney Brown, Bruni Burres, Sheila Carapico, James Cavallaro, Cassandra Cavanaugh, Anne-Gaelle Claude, Sara Colm, Allyson Collins, Lance Compa, Manuel Couffignal, Zama Coursen-Neff, Tzeitel Cruz, Sam David, Rachel Denber, Alison DesForges, Richard Dicker, Kinsey Dinan, Julia Duchrow, Corrine Dufka, Maura Dundon, Elizabeth Eagen, Matt Easton, Jamie Fellner, Janet Fleischman, Theresa Freese, Anne Fuller, Arvind Ganesan, Erika George, Pamela Gomez, Stephen D. Goose, Patricia Gossman, Judith Greene, Jeannine Guthrie, Julia Hall, Jason Halperin, Rebecca Hart, Malcolm Hawkes, Jill Hedges, Elahé Sharifpour-Hicks, Ethel Higonnet, Joost R. Hiltermann, Mark Hiznay, Ernst Jan Hogendoorn, Elizabeth Hollenback, Andrea Holly, Jonathan Horowitz, International Gay and Lesbian Human Rights Commission (IGLHRC), Bogdan Ivanisevic, Mike Jendrzejczyk, LaShawn Jefferson, Tejal Jesrani, Jesuit Refugee Service (JRS), Sidney Jones, Thomas Jonsson, Bianca Karim, Juliane Kippenberg, Robin Kirk, Diederik Lohman, Andre Lommen, Alex Lupis, Chirumbidzo Mabuwa, Kelli Maddell, Joanne Mariner, Bronwen Manby, Joanne Mariner, Mavis Matenge, Michael McClintock, Hanny Megally, Patrick Minges, Lisa Misol, Hasan Mujtaba, Hania Mufti, Smita Narula, Binaifer Nowrojee, Hannah Novak, Isis Nusair, Tatjana Papic, Vikram Parekh, Christine Parker, Carol Pier, Maria Pulzetti, Sara Rakita, Regan Ralph, Rachael Reilly, Gary Risser, Jemera Rone, Indira Rosenthal, Kenneth Roth, Shalu Rozario, Tamar Satnet, Joe Saunders, Erin Sawaya, Virginia Sherry, Acacia Shields, Jennifer Schmidt, Malcolm Smart, Joel Solomon, Mickey Spiegel, Rebecca Stich, Joe Stork, Marie Struthers, Brigitte Suhr, Jonathan Sugden, Judith Sunderland, Peter Takirambudde, Tony Tate, Cynthia Totten, Lee Tucker, Martina Vandenberg, Smita Varia, Jan van der Made, Alex Vines, José Miguel Vivanco, Ben Ward, Sinead Walsh, Yiong van Walsum, Mary Wareham, Liz Weiss, Lois Whitman, Anna Wuerth, Charli Wyatt, Julia Zuckerman, and Saman Zia-Zarifi

Michael McClintock and Malcolm Smart edited the report, with layout and production assistance by Patrick Minges and Jonathan Horowitz. Various sections were reviewed by Lotte Leicht, Rachael Reilly, and Joanna Weschler. Andrew Ayers, Mickael Bochenek, Elizabeth Eagan, Jonathan Horowitz, Michael McClintock, Rona Peligal, Evan Weinberger, and Saman Zia-Zarifi proofread the report.

CONTENTS

ASIA

CHILDREN'S RIGHTS

EUROPE AND CENTRAL ASIA

MIDDLE EAST AND NORTH AFRICA

SPECIAL ISSUES AND CAMPAIGNS

APPENDIX

INTRODUCTION

The scope of today's global human rights problems far exceeds the capacity of global institutions to address them. The problem is most acute in the global economy, where a disturbing institutional void frequently leaves human rights standards unenforced. But the problem also arises as the world struggles to stop mass atrocities, protect the victims of these crimes, rebuild their countries, and bring their persecutors to justice. In each case, a more interconnected and seemingly smaller world rightfully feels a greater responsibility to respond. Yet the capacity to meet these demands has not kept up with the challenges. A reinforced global architecture is needed.

This introduction to Human Rights Watch's annual World Report describes this weakness in the institutional capacity to address the global human rights challenges of our time. It highlights the enforcement gap for issues of human rights in the global economy. It discusses the inadequate resources given to the United Nations to assume its assigned tasks of keeping the peace and assisting war-torn nations with national reconstruction. And it describes the recent strides taken toward a new institutional justice system for the world's worst human rights criminals but laments the U.S. government's persistent refusal to countenance U.S. nationals being held to the same standards as the rest of the world.

This report—Human Rights Watch's eleventh annual review of human rights practices around the globe—covers developments in seventy countries. It is released in advance of Human Rights Day, December 10, 2000, and describes events from November 1999 through October 2000. Most chapters examine significant human rights developments in a particular country; the response of global actors, such as the European Union, Japan, the United States, the United Nations, and various regional organizations; and the freedom of local human rights defenders. Other chapters address important thematic concerns.

Highlights of the year include, on the positive side, the popular rebellion against the Milosevic regime in Yugoslavia, the conclusion of a treaty barring the use of children as soldiers, and the U.N. Commission on Human Rights's first formal criticism of a permanent member of the U.N. Security Council (Russia, for its abuses in Chechnya). On the negative side, the U.N. Human Rights Commission refused yet again to condemn China for its relentless suppression of political opposition, the U.S. government failed to abide by conditions included in a major military aid package to Colombia that would have required the Colombian army to sever its ties with paramilitaries, and there was a growing crisis in the world's response to refugees and asylum-seekers and persistently inadequate protection for the internally displaced.

This report reflects extensive investigative work undertaken in 2000 by the Human Rights Watch research staff, usually in close partnership with human rights activists in the countries in question. Human Rights Watch reports, published throughout the year (see http://www.hrw.org), contain more elaborate accounts of the brief summaries collected in this volume. The chapters here also reflect the work of the Human Rights Watch advocacy staff, which monitors the policies of governments and institutions with influence to curb abusive human rights conduct.

As in past years, this report does not include a chapter on every country where Human Rights Watch works, nor does it discuss every issue of importance. The failure to include a particular country or issue often reflects no more than staffing limitations and should not be taken as commentary on the significance of the problem. There are many serious human rights violations that Human Rights Watch simply lacks the capacity to address. Other factors affecting the focus of our work in 2000 and hence the content of this volume include the severity of abuses, access to the country and the availability of information about it, the susceptibility of abusive forces to outside influence, the importance of addressing certain thematic concerns, and the need to maintain a balance in the work of Human Rights Watch across various political divides.

The Global Economy

After street protests over the past year in Seattle, Prague, Washington, and elsewhere, proponents of the global economy seem on the defensive. Globalization—the increased international flow of trade, capital, information, and people—has delivered undeniable wealth and opportunity and created millions of jobs. But there is widespread unease at some of the associated and parallel ills. Income inequality is growing, as are the number of people in abject poverty. The much-criticized "race to the bottom" seems to stymie certain attempts at social and economic betterment. Resource extraction—the business of oil, minerals, and metals—often proceeds without regard to the rights of local residents. Governments depend on migrant workers to take on less desirable jobs but frequently deny them legal protection. Trafficking in people has flourished.

Despite these problems, the current system to regulate global commerce leaves little or no room for human rights and other social values. Relevant international human rights standards exist but are not uniformly ratified, effectively enforced, or adequately integrated into the global economy.

The debate about solving these problems has been unhelpfully polarized. Advocates of unfettered trade and capital flow tend to see commerce itself as a panacea. Pointing to the immense wealth generated by the global economy, they frequently resist any governance regime that might constrain globalization by attention to other social values. More and freer commerce, in their view, is the best route to social as well as economic betterment.

But as Human Rights Watch has repeatedly found, a world integrated on commercial lines does not necessarily lead to human rights improvements. In China, increased international trade has not lessened the government's determination to snuff out any political op-position. In Sudan, oil revenue made possible by international investment has allowed the government in only two years nearly to double the defense budget for its highly abusive war. In Central Asia, after the collapse of the Soviet Union, international investment in oil and gas exploration and production has only reaffirmed the new governments' resolve to cling to power at all costs while their people plunge into poverty. In Sierra Leone and Angola, international trade in diamonds has fueled deadly civil wars. The number of migrant workers and trafficking victims has grown with international commerce, yet abuses against them remain largely ignored. Experience shows that global economic integration is no substitute for a firm parallel commitment to defending human rights.

Opponents of globalization highlight the fate of the millions of people who are excluded from the benefits of the global economy or are forced to accept it on unsatisfactory terms. They argue that globalization mainly benefits the wealthy and that it aids the poor too slowly or actually contributes to their plight. Some opponents would simply shut down the process of globalization, convinced that its benefits are not worth the price. They include those who have used violence against institutions they see as supporting globalization. Others focus more constructively on reshaping the global economy to better serve social values. Many reforms have been discussed but none has gained a consensus.

Some of the firmest defenders of unfettered global commerce come from the developing countries in whose name the opponents of globalization claim to speak. Both governments and nongovernmental organizations (NGOs) in these countries fear that linking trade or investment to respect for social values, however well intentioned, will end up serving protectionist interests in the industrialized world and shutting off developing countries from the benefits of global commerce. They are particularly wary of the efforts of some activists to prescribe a "living wage" on a national basis for fear of being deprived of their principal competitive advantage—cheap labor. They also object to efforts by the global North to enforce selected social and economic values in the global South when it serves Northern interests, while neglecting more costly obligations to help achieve other important social and economic goals such as alleviating poverty or improving health care or education.

A Human Rights Framework

In this divisive debate, human rights offer a promising framework to address many of the problems of globalization, including the tendency of some governments and corporations to compete by profiting from repression. Some of the most alarming by-products of globalization are clear violations of rights enshrined in international treaties. By the same token, upholding these rights provides the basis for solving many of the ills associated with globalization in a way that need not shut down global trade or benefit the world's richer countries at the expense of the poor.

Within the workplace, for example, human rights speak directly to the problems of exclusion. Factory workers often face poor wages, abysmal working conditions, sexual abuse, no social safety net, and no legal protection. Respect for freedom of association would allow workers to join together—in trade unions should they choose—to improve wages and working conditions. The prohibition against discrimination on such grounds as gender, race, or ethnicity ensures that historically marginalized people enjoy the fruits of their labor on the same terms as others. The prohibition of forced or abusive child labor and the ban on arbitrary violence require employers to negotiate with adult free-agents.

On a societal level, respect for civil and political rights, including the right to elect one's government, allows the disadvantaged to have a voice in the direction of their nation's social and economic development. These rights permit citizens to press their government to take on such issues as increasing the minimum wage, protecting union activists from retaliation, enforcing prohibitions on discrimination, regulating extraction indus-

tries, or ensuring that investments are made with social values in mind. They also promote the transparency and accountability in national governments and international institutions that are prerequisites to making them responsive to popular concerns.

In addition, respect for these basic freedoms helps to encourage governments of the industrialized and developing world to take seriously their obligations to uphold economic, social, and cultural rights. It allows people to urge governments to ratify the leading treaty safeguarding these rights and to adopt reasonable plans to realize these rights progressively, including in the regulation of trade and investment. It also permits popular input into the choice among alternative routes to fulfill economic and social rights, such as the amount of investment to put into education or health care, the level of restrictions to place on industries that cause environmental damage or social disruption, or the type of social welfare programs needed to temper the shock of trade liberalization and structural adjustment policies.

This emphasis on rights may not guarantee particular wage levels, working conditions, or regulatory policies. Nor does it eliminate inequalities in bargaining power or eradicate all forms of social exclusion. But by allowing an unfettered civil society to make its views heard, a rights approach permits workers and citizens to have a say in these important matters.

A rights approach also discourages the tendency of some governments and multinational corporations to gain a competitive advantage by suppressing workers' demands for better treatment or society's pursuit of such goals as a clean environment. Corporations might still seek lower production costs by moving to lower-wage or less socially demanding countries. Governments might still seek a competitive advantage by restricting taxes, wages, regulations, or social benefits. But competition through repression—the most nefarious aspect of the "race to the bottom"—would be significantly constrained.

A rights approach would give developing countries a legal basis to broaden discussions of trade and investment policy to include the need for reciprocal benefits and concessions from the industrialized world to facilitate the realization of economic and social rights. Such demands would have more resonance because they would be grounded in legally binding international human rights treaties rather than more malleable and selective economic theories. A rights approach would thus serve as a useful supplement to development models that are premised on market liberalization but pay insufficient attention to attendant social and economic problems.

At the same time, a rights approach should prove acceptable to proponents of "free trade." It does not seek to shut down global trade and investment, only to invoke broadly accepted rights to define the limits within which commerce should proceed. It does not raise the drawbridge against global competition, but insists that the market be grounded in respect for international human rights law.

Finally, a rights approach would help develop international solutions to problems arising from the global movement of people, such as the lack of protection for migrant workers and trafficking victims. Many industrialized countries erect barriers to legal immigration from developing countries but tacitly accept undocumented migrants, or migrants with strict legal limits on their presence, to perform undesirable work. Many developing countries also export workers, some with documentation and some without, to earn foreign exchange through remittances. Lacking legal protection, these workers have little recourse in the face of such problems as sexual abuse, dangerous working conditions, and violations of the right to organize. In addition, many governments wrongly equate the smuggling used to infiltrate undocumented migrant workers with human trafficking—transport based on deception or coercion—thereby denying trafficking victims the protection they need.

The Need for Stronger Institutions

The advantages of a rights approach remain theoretical without broad governmental ratification of the relevant human rights treaties and a reliable means of enforcement. Stronger institutions are needed to insist that governments and corporations respect human rights in their global dealings. The United Nations and the International Labour Organization have played an important role in establishing human rights standards, including the U.N.'s international covenants and the ILO's core labor standards. But these institutions lack adequate enforcement powers. Except in extraordinary circumstances, the most they can do is encourage treaty ratification and condemn abusive conduct. The U.N. has been more effective because its special rapporteurs and working groups have more latitude to use public shaming to encourage compliance. The tripartite nature of the ILO —combining representatives of government, business, and labor—often leaves the organization paralyzed when it tries to uphold rights in contentious situations.

Meanwhile, the World Trade Organization, which does have enforcement powers, focuses on promoting global trade, sometimes at the expense of international human rights norms. The proposal to add a "social clause" to its mandate has been controversial in part because the WTO has no expertise, culture, or tradition of protecting rights. Moreover, many Southern governments and NGOs fear that sanctions under a social clause would be applied against only developing countries, not against comparable abuses in the industrialized world.

At a regional level, the Council of Europe has established clear rights standards in the European Convention on Human Rights, enforced by the European Court of Human Rights, and the European Social Charter. At the same time, the European Union has established an institutionalized "social dialogue" procedure among employers and unions, set forth in its Maastricht Social Protocol and Agreement, and an international court, the European Court of Justice, with a proven track record of protecting employment rights. However, the commitment to integration that made this model possible is peculiar to Europe. It is not clear whether the model can be applied elsewhere.

At a national level, labor rights have been promoted through trade conditionality, such as the linkage between respect for core labor rights and access to preferential trade benefits (Generalized System of Preferences) that exists in U.S. and E.U. legislation. But this conditionality is limited geographically and applied irregularly. It should be broadened, made justiciable, and applied more consistently.

Voluntary Codes of Conduct

The institutions noted above can at least call attention to governmental misbehavior, but multinational corporations have largely been left to police themselves, with occasional prodding from human rights and labor organizations. In recent years, progress has been made in increasing corporate attention to human rights, but more is needed.

Only several years ago, many corporations treated human rights as outside their legitimate concerns. They claimed their role was only to maximize profits for shareholders, that human rights concerns were best left to governments.

Today, after a series of exposés of corporate complicity in human rights abuse, the response is often quite different. Corporate leaders increasingly recognize that they must pay attention to human rights or risk consumer pressure, a tarnished corporate image, and problems with employee recruitment and morale. The 1997 Asian economic crisis provided other economic reasons to be sensitive to human rights. As a result, many corporations have adopted voluntary codes of conduct, pledging to abide by specified principles on human rights and other social concerns. These corporations include not only consumer-oriented companies in apparel, footwear, toys, and appliances but also major oil companies and other extraction industries.

These codes have been effective in changing some corporations' conduct, but they have shortcomings. They are typically written without consultation with the workers most affected, many of whom are not even aware of their company's code. They are usually written in vague language which looks good in corporate brochures but avoids some of the stickier human rights issues, such as how to do business in a country that bars labor unions, restricts the rights of women, guards company facilities with abusive soldiers, or uses joint-venture revenue to fund military abuses. With notable exceptions, the codes generally give independent organizations no formal role in monitoring compliance. They commonly address only workplace issues and the conduct of subcontractors, not broader societal concerns.

And, of course, the codes are voluntary. They contain no enforcement mechanism, nothing to fill the institutional gap in rights protection. Indeed, that these codes are unenforceable is one of their principal allures for corporations and governments that lack a firm rights commitment. It is thus left to human rights groups, labor organizations, and others in civil society to expand the number of corporations adopting these codes, encourage compliance, and promote improvement. These efforts can be effective, but they are ad hoc, under-funded, and not enough.

The United Nations took a potentially useful step in July by launching a "Global Compact" of business, labor, and civil society to promote social responsibility in the global economy. Its reporting requirements, though minimal, may make member corporations more accountable for their conduct. Its breadth —engaging companies based not only in Europe and North America but also in Africa, Asia, and South America—demonstrates that the demand for corporate responsibility is not limited to companies from industrialized countries. This scope also helps to refute the argument sometimes heard from U.S. companies that they are put at a competitive disadvantage by being asked to bear the brunt of concern with corporate responsibility themselves. Still, the Global Compact is also only a voluntary endeavor. It attempts to back voluntarism with a degree of social pressure, but has shown no sign of moving toward mandatory compliance. Its failure to require probing public reports, independent monitoring, and an enforceable legal regime has left it short of its potential.

There is no single prescription for filling this enforcement gap, whether for governments or multinational corporations. Among the ideas advanced so far have been giving the ILO real enforcement powers; linking the ILO with the WTO, so that the ILO's more rights-oriented culture might join with the WTO's enforcement powers; or creating an intermediate institution that might be free of both the WTO's exclusive trade orientation and the ILO's paralyzing tripartite system. Movement in any of these directions would be useful, but they are not the only options or necessarily the most productive. Below we outline three other possible approaches, all drawn from recent governmental or institutional practices. None of these is a panacea either. Indeed, none standing alone can address all of the problems associated with globalization. But they illustrate the kinds of steps that must be taken if rights in the global economy are to move from exhortation to enforcement.

The OECD Anti-Corruption Model

One approach could be modeled on the response of the Organization for Economic Cooperation and Development to the problem of corporate bribery of government officials. Such corruption once also had a "race to the bottom" dynamic. Governments were reluctant to prohibit it for fear of putting their corporations at a competitive disadvantage. In 1997, the OECD decided that a collective approach was required. It adopted anti-corruption standards and mandated that all OECD governments—the principal industrialized governments—criminalize violations. A special OECD working group was assigned responsibility for monitoring and reporting on governmental compliance. By setting a common, enforceable standard, the OECD helped undercut fears that bribery of foreign officials was necessary for corporations to keep up with the competition.

A similar global approach could help enforce human rights in the global economy.

National governments could be asked to adopt a prescribed enforcement regime to ensure that all corporations operating in or from their territory avoid complicity in serious rights violations. Such a regime would allow corporations and governments from the North and South to respect these rights in the commercial realm without fear of placing themselves at a competitive disadvantage, thus undercutting the "race to the bottom." (The OECD in June adopted voluntary Guidelines for Multinational Enterprises, but these lack the compulsory nature of its anti-corruption regime.)

The U.S.-Jordan Trade Pact

Another promising option can be found in the U.S.-Jordan Free Trade Agreement, concluded in October. Rather than uncritically endorsing national standards or relegating labor rights to a side accord, as does the North American Free Trade Agreement, the U.S.-Jordan accord incorporates core international labor rights standards in its body and insists that domestic laws uphold them. The parties explicitly recognize that "it is inappropriate to encourage trade by relaxing domestic labor laws" and vow not to do so. The agreement establishes consultative and adjudicative processes to address violations and allows unilateral sanctions in the event of breaches. But sanctions can be applied only if a violation of the accord "severely distorts the balance of trade benefits" or "substantially undermines the fundamental objectives" of the agreement—both quite high bars. The agreement also precludes judicial remedies for breaches, leaving it exclusively to governments to challenge violations.

International Financial Institutions

The international financial institutions should also help integrate human rights into the global economy by promoting the creation of national institutions to enforce rights and insisting on progressive improvement in respect for rights as part of loan packages. Their frequent failure to play this role has made the World Bank and the International Monetary Fund the focus of much of the protest against globalization.

These protests are understandable because, until recently, these institutions pursued a conception of economic development that was largely insensitive to human rights. For years, Nobel Prize economist Amartya Sen and others have demonstrated that abuse of human rights impedes economic development—that unaccountable governments are more likely to indulge corruption or misguided economic projects and less likely to distribute the benefits of development to those most in need. Yet the World Bank and the IMF insisted that human rights were a purely "political" matter outside their economic mandates. Because of the influence of these institutions, governments and private investors often followed suit. The funds they plowed into authoritarian governments were frequently wasted or misspent, while debts piled up that now thwart successor governments' efforts to lift their people from poverty.

Many of these problems remain today. But the World Bank in particular has begun to change this sorry legacy. Under the leadership of James Wolfensohn, the bank's efforts to combat corruption, reduce poverty, and promote good governance and the rule of law have led it, in some countries, to show greater sensitivity to human rights. Yet much of this attention is ad hoc. Additional progress is needed to institutionalize human rights as an essential foundation of the bank's development work if the bank is to help enforce human rights in the global economy.

The bank's approach to Zambia, Indonesia, and other countries in Asia illustrate some of the positive steps it took in 2000 to address human rights issues:

In advance of the World Bank-convened donors conference for Indonesia in October, Wolfensohn sent a personal letter to Indonesian President Abdurrahman Wahid urging action to halt the violence in West Timor. Without directly threatening to suspend funding, he warned that donors would raise this issue at the conference.

The donors conference convened in Zambia in July was the first in Africa to be wholly transparent. All deliberations were open to independent human rights activists and other representatives of civil society, and the human rights performance of the government was freely discussed as an integral part of development plans.

In Asia, civil society input on bank projects and at donors conferences was actively sought in Cambodia, Indonesia, East Timor, and elsewhere. However, during the bank's consultative process in Kyrgyzstan, the government excluded NGOs seen as linked to the political opposition, suggesting the need for rules based on international human rights standards to ensure participation by all elements of civil society.

In fighting corruption, the World Bank has also begun to pay more attention to human rights-related concerns. It has promoted greater transparency in bank projects and encouraged civil society to scrutinize these transactions. But it could still do more to support whistle-blowers, journalists, and nongovernmental monitors who are arrested or abused for exposing corruption. It should also do more to promote the basic legal and judicial reform needed to achieve access to justice for all. This would help to root out and prosecute corrupt police and public officials—steps that would improve official accountability for all sorts of human rights abuse.

The IMF, for its part, under the new leadership of Horst Köhler, has also begun slowly to change in ways that will help integrate human rights in the global economy. It was at its most innovative in Angola, where it secured the government's agreement to allow World Bank monitoring of oil revenues to ensure that they went toward development needs and were not mismanaged. It began negotiations for a similar audit of diamond revenues. Such transparency, coupled with stringent auditing, could become a model for extraction industries operating in countries ruled by abusive governments, such as Sudan, Turkmenistan, or Burma. Until now, the vast government revenues generated meant that these companies almost inevitably risked complicity in serious abuse by funding the machinery of repression. This new model of transparency should become a minimum requirement for companies entering into substantial revenue-producing joint ventures with repressive governments.

Yet the international financial institutions were hardly uniform in their attention to human rights. At the height of Russia's atrocities in Chechnya, the World Bank advanced Moscow U.S. $450 million in structural adjustment loan payments without any linkage to Russian conduct in the breakaway republic. The IMF continues to freeze new loans to Russia, but it denies Russian claims that Chechnya is the reason and insists that the only cause is the slow pace of economic reform. The World Bank gave U.S. $1.6 billion loans to China in fiscal year 2000 despite rampant corruption and restrictions on basic freedoms that made any genuine consultation with people affected by projects close to impossible. The bank vowed to expand the role of civil society in China's development but its intervention on human rights cases was selective.

The international financial institutions' new openness to incorporating human rights into their mandates at least sometimes has produced an ironic new problem of appearing impermissibly "political." The problem arises not because of these institutions' attention to human rights—a natural focus of their development work—but because of their inconsistency. A steadier commitment to human rights is needed.

A useful model might be the European Bank for Reconstruction and Development. Founded in 1991 to assist the countries of Eastern Europe and the former Soviet Union, it operates under a charter that reflects recognition of the link between governance and development. The charter permits assistance only to governments that are "committed to and applying the principles of multiparty democracy, pluralism, and market economics." In 2000, the EBRD cut off public sector lending to Turkmenistan in part because "there has been no progress towards a pluralist or democratic political system." However, the bank's enforcement of its charter has also been uneven. Moreover, its options should include not only suspending assistance but also aiding in the development of institutions to protect human rights.

From Voluntarism to Enforcement

There is no single way to ensure respect for human rights and other social values in the global economy. Any viable approach must move beyond simply articulating standards and hoping for good-faith compliance. The stakes are too high to rely on voluntarism alone. Enforcement is needed. The contours of an enforcement regime—its national or international focus, its institutional home—remain to be defined. But until there is a consistent commitment to enforce rather than simply pronounce international standards, the global economy is likely to fall short of its potential to serve all people rather than just the fortunate few. An urgent global dialogue is needed to fill this enforcement gap.

The United Nations

One would be hard-pressed to devise a surer recipe for failure: assign an institution responsibility for managing the world's most intractable problems, then deprive it of funds, give it a skeletal staff, overload the organization with peripheral tasks, and insist on its using large numbers of temporary personnel frequently offered less for their skills than for geographic balance or their government's desire to collect hard currency. Yet this is how the international community treats the United Nations. For some, this setup-for-failure is by design. For others, it reflects a lack of commitment—an eagerness to pass off problems without providing the means to address them. In Kofi Annan, the U.N. has a secretary-general of unusual vision, courage, skill, and dedication. But the world's refusal to give him the tools necessary to the tasks at hand has created an institutional crisis. It is time to stop treating the U.N. as the dumping ground for global problems without giving it the capacity to address them.

To highlight this institutional crisis is not to disparage the many parts of the U.N. that do work. The U.N. human rights staff, based in Geneva and led by Mary Robinson as high commissioner for human rights, has grown significantly in recent years in professionalism and impact. Despite woefully inadequate resources, it has made steady progress in overcoming the ocean that was deliberately put between it and the New York-based bodies that make the U.N.'s most important political decisions. The U.N. working groups and special rapporteurs, again established through Geneva, produce many first-rate accounts of serious human rights problems, even though the governments on the politicized U.N. Human Rights Commission routinely create new and often peripheral mandates to be carried out "within existing resources." Officials in New York at the U.N.'s Departments of Political Affairs and Peacekeeping also attempt to address problems of immense complexity with ridiculously small staffs.

Today, after several years of steady reform, the U.N.'s main problem is less the skill or dedication of its officials than the dire lack of capacity that the nations of the world are willing to permit it. Many of these institutional shortfalls are well described in a report on U.N. peace operations issued in August by a commission led by former Algerian Foreign Minister Lakhdar Brahimi. It describes a world body asked to take on immense challenges with paltry resources and half-hearted political backing. Earlier U.N. reports, issued in November and December 1999 on the inexcusable failure to respond to genocide in Srebrenica and Rwanda, highlight the tragic consequences of this neglect. Rare among most governments, this candid self-scrutiny is admirable. The time has come to act on these insights. If the U.N. is to remain a viable resource for addressing the world's most complex problems, the nations of the world must make an immediate and genuine commitment to remove the straitjacket of institutional weakness that they have imposed.

Sierra Leone

The tragedy of Sierra Leone highlights the consequences—for the U.N. and for people in need—of the international community trying to buy peace on the cheap. For years, the country was plagued by a vicious civil war in which the rebel Revolutionary United Front and its allies terrorized the population with murder, rape, and the signature atrocity of chopping off human limbs. The government clung to power with the help of a Nigerian-led West African military force known as ECOMOG. But Nigeria threatened to withdraw its troops, in part because the international community refused to help cover its expenses. Eager to diffuse public pressure to respond to the crisis, the U.S. government, backed by Britain, the U.N., the Organization of African Unity, and a group of West African states, brokered a power-sharing arrangement with the RUF in the guise of a peace accord. With its economy devastated and the international community unwilling to commit the required troops, Sierra Leone was forced to accept a peace agreement that was tantamount to political surrender.

This July 1999 accord gave the RUF and all other forces amnesty for their atrocities, awarded the RUF leader, Foday Sankoh, a status equivalent to vice president, and appointed him chairman of the commission that oversees exploitation of the nation's vast diamond fields and mineral wealth. When the amnesty was greeted by protests, the U.N. secretary-general insisted at the last minute that a provision be inserted denying international, as opposed to national, recognition of it. But the international community took no action on this disclaimer by moving to prosecute these criminals. The lesson was clear: the RUF would pay no price—indeed, would be rewarded—for its ruthlessness.

It took the RUF little time to apply this lesson. Its depredations continued unabated, and no one did anything to stop them. Then, in early May 2000, as U.N. peacekeepers drawn exclusively from developing countries replaced ECOMOG forces, the RUF killed several peacekeepers and took five hundred hostage. The badly equipped, poorly led U.N. force put up little or no resistance.

Even as the year progressed, the U.N. was left under-equipped. Elite British troops flown in on an emergency basis gave the peacekeepers the added muscle they needed to push the rebels back from the capital Freetown. Gradually, the hostages were freed. But even Britain would not subject its troops to U.N. command, and no other Western government volunteered its troops to lend a hand. The absence of governments with high-tech militaries willing to put their soldiers at risk in a dangerous conflict in Africa left the U.N. force significantly handicapped as it tried to contain the ruthless rebels. A stronger mandate—to provide meaningful protection for civilians throughout Sierra Leone—remained out of the question. Other aspects of the U.N. presence, including its in-country leadership, reflected a similar lack of international commitment.

East Timor and Kosovo

The international community fared only slightly better in East Timor and Kosovo—the two other most challenging situations it handed the United Nations in 1999 and 2000. Forced in each case to assemble personnel on an ad hoc basis, with no ready reservoir of experienced professionals, the U.N. operated under severe handicap.

In September 1999, immediately following an overwhelming vote in East Timor for independence, Indonesian-backed militia left the territory a charred ruin. An Australian-led military forced initially secured the territory, but by late 1999 the new country was handed over to a U.N.-led operation. The U.N. was given painfully inadequate tools for such large tasks as addressing past abuses, preventing new ones, and building basic governmental institutions from scratch. The international civilian police were recruited at an agonizingly slow pace and showed up poorly trained for short, three-month tours of duty. Their inadequacy, combined with divisions within U.N. operations, slowed investigations into the September 1999 violence and contributed to vigilante attacks and summary justice, as Timorese despaired of the U.N. police guaranteeing law and order.

In Kosovo, the U.N. again was asked to take over a territory that was virtually bereft of governmental institutions. Reconstruction was hampered by the Yugoslav government's history of repressing the ethnic Albanian majority, the institutional and legal void it left after its sudden withdrawal in June 1999 following the war with NATO, and the lack of clarity about the territory's future relationship with Yugoslavia. Under the circumstances, progress was made creating a new criminal justice system and civilian police force. But the justice system, inadequately supervised, fell far short of international human rights standards and showed a disturbing pattern of bias against ethnic Serbs. The international civilian police force, under equipped and poorly trained, was sometimes unwilling to arrest former Kosovo Liberation Army members and other ethnic Albanians who were responsible for violence against ethnic Serbs and other minorities, as well as against ethnic Albanian political rivals. A lack of investigative capacity and poor cooperation by the local population were also obstacles. These shortcomings meant that NATO troops sometimes had to assume sensitive law enforcement tasks for which they were unprepared. The violence against minorities persisted, meaning that virtually no ethnic Serbs participated in the October 2000 municipal elections.

Embargoes

U.N. attempts to curb conflicts through embargoes suffered from a similar lack of will and resources to ensure implementation. A U.N. panel found widespread breaches of a Security Council-imposed embargo on trade in arms or diamonds with Angola's murderous rebel group UNITA. The report, spearheaded by Canada's then U.N. Ambassador Robert Fowler, was remarkable for naming the companies and countries, including heads of state, involved in sanctions busting. But through October, the Security Council had taken no further action to enforce its lofty pronouncement of an embargo. No serious effort was made to sanction the embargo breakers or to monitor the flow of goods at borders and airports. An embargo on arms trading with Sierra Leone and Liberia fared no better.

North-South Collusion

That the U.N. is so handicapped in its capacity to address global problems is the product of an unfortunate congruence of interests between governments of the North and South, often against the interests of their people. Many governments of the industrialized world, particularly the United States, appreciate the U.N. as a place to hand difficult problem countries but distrust the global body too much to allow it the capacity to resolve these problems. The frequent result is the deployment of personnel who are starved of the resources needed to accomplish urgent tasks. Many governments of the developing world also do not like these political deployments. Rather than stand in solidarity with the people of the South whose calls for help might be answered, these governments see a U.N. emergency capacity as a diversion of resources from the U.N. development projects they most cherish and a threat to their own political latitude.

Solutions

It may be difficult to muster the political will to address these problems, but it is not difficult to identify solutions. Some of the changes are doctrinal, many described in the Brahimi report. For example, the U.N. must abandon its reflexive neutrality when circumstances call for protecting civilians from slaughter. Even when the U.N. enters dangerous situations consensually, it must do so with a sufficiently robust mandate and military capacity to protect U.N. personnel and the civilians they have come to serve. The Security Council must stop treating human rights as an unwelcome irrelevancy best left in its Geneva exile. Instead, drawing on the U.N.'s significant human rights expertise, the council must begin to recognize that human rights abuses are the cause of many conflicts and that ending these abuses is a critical element of lasting peace. In particular, accountability for the most heinous human rights crimes must be seen less as an obstacle to peace than as an essential building block—a

goal worth embracing for pragmatic as well as principled reasons.

Other changes are structural. It makes no sense for the U.N. to squander months at the outset of each new emergency desperately searching the world for qualified personnel and begging national governments to spare them. The U.N. needs a standby capacity – not the caricature of troops drilling on U.N. grounds in New York, but a reserve of personnel that governments would make available on short notice for emergency U.N. service. This reserve should include not only specially trained troops but also police, judicial, legal, human rights, development, and administrative personnel – and the leadership to deploy them effectively.

The U.N. Secretariat in New York must also be bolstered. At current staffing levels, it is designed to be solely reactive. Even when it does respond, it is grossly understaffed to manage complex emergencies. The political and peacekeeping departments do not begin to have the requisite capacity. Preventive work, for example, is impossible in an institution whose limited staff is overburdened with far less significant work. The answer requires not only a substantial increase in the staff of the political and peacekeeping departments but also a cultural change. The nations of the U.N. must accept the need to identify, name, and address problem areas before they explode. They must stop diverting the U.N. from more pressing problems with demands for unread reports delivered to forgotten committees. They must transcend the zero-sum logic that every dollar spent on political or peacekeeping affairs is a dollar less for development and recognize that ending abusive conflict is a prerequisite to development for the countries, and often the regions, involved.

The U.N. is fortunate to have a secretary-general who understands and embraces these truths. But he cannot lead alone. If the U.N. has any prospect of meeting its potential, the nations of the world must accept and support the organization's transformation.

International Justice

The greatest strides toward an enhanced global architecture have been taken in the area of international justice. Less than a decade ago, impunity for tyrants was the rule. The world's most heinous human rights criminals committed atrocities knowing that they could use intimidation and violence to fend off accountability. This impunity was an affront to the victims and an encouragement of further atrocities.

Today, the world is a far smaller place for tyrants because there are fewer places to escape justice. New international tribunals are being launched. These tribunals, in turn, have catalyzed national prosecutorial efforts, demonstrating that international justice serves to reinforce rather than replace national justice. Moreover, the actions of several Southern governments have made clear that justice for the worst human rights offenders is hardly an exclusively Northern concern. The most pronounced sour note in this steady progress has been the U.S. government's persistent opposition to having its citizens held to the same legal standards as the rest of the world.

International Tribunals

The movement to create international institutions of justice took several steps forward in 2000. Most significant was the progress toward the establishment of the International Criminal Court—the first global tribunal for genocide, war crimes, and crimes against humanity. A treaty to establish the court was adopted in Rome in July 1998. Despite the many legal complexities involved, twenty-two governments had already ratified the treaty by the end of October 2000 (of the sixty needed to launch the court) and another ninety-three governments had signed it. This broad embrace suggests that the court will be up and running soon—conceivably as early as 2002.

Because the ICC will not have retroactive jurisdiction, the world continues to rely on country-specific international tribunals for the most heinous crimes of the past and present. Political changes in Croatia and Yugoslavia show how international tribunals

have changed the long-term prospects of even seemingly secure human rights offenders. The death of Franjo Tudjman in December 1999 opened the way to the election of Croatia's new president, Stipe Mesic, who has been far more cooperative with the International Criminal Tribunal for the Former Yugoslavia, handing over evidence and suspects and opening the country's borders to investigators. The September 2000 electoral loss of Slobodan Milosevic to Yugoslavia's new president, Vojislav Kostunica, has also opened up new possibilities for cooperation. Kostunica at first insisted that he would not surrender Milosevic to the Hague, where the tribunal has indicted him for crimes against humanity committed in Kosovo. But Kostunica's later comments were more equivocal, suggesting that cooperation with the tribunal and even the eventual surrender of Milosevic remain possibilities. At stake is also the fate of former Bosnian Serb military leader Ratko Mladic, who has taken refuge in Serbia after his indictment by the tribunal for genocide and other crimes in Bosnia.

Meanwhile, as of late October, the U.N. Security Council was moving toward the creation of a hybrid national-international tribunal for Sierra Leone. The tribunal will effectively overturn the July 1999 amnesty and make possible the prosecution of those behind the horrendous crimes that have characterized the country's civil war. The hybrid nature of the court will be precedent-setting—an international prosecutor and judges in a dominant role to ensure the court's independence, but a significant role for Sierra Leonean judges and prosecutors to help them begin reconstructing their devastated legal system. However, certain issues remain to be worked out, including the power of the court to compel cooperation, the time period on which the court will focus, the court's treatment of juvenile offenders, and the extent of witness protection.

Unfortunately, a proposed hybrid tribunal for Cambodia has fared less well. Unlike Sierra Leone, the Cambodian government has insisted that Cambodians have a dominant role. The U.N. at first resisted because of the Cambodian government's long history of manipulating its legal system. But the U.N. was later forced to acquiesce when the U.S. government brokered a deal largely on Cambodian terms. Still, as of late October, the Cambodian government was dragging its feet in seeking the necessary parliamentary approval, raising doubts about the court's prospects.

National Justice Efforts

Some have questioned whether it is appropriate for international prosecutions to replace national justice systems. But that concern reflects a misunderstanding. The purpose of creating an option of international justice is to establish a backstop for national efforts. By making clear that violence or intimidation aimed at national judges and prosecutors no longer guarantees impunity, the option of international justice bolsters national justice systems. The International Criminal Court was built explicitly on these terms, and events in 2000 showed that the emergence of international tribunals has had precisely this catalyzing effect.

Britain's October 1998 arrest of former Chilean dictator Augusto Pinochet would almost certainly not have taken place before the ICC treaty changed the environment for international justice. In March 2000, the British government released Pinochet on health grounds after almost seventeen months in detention. He returned to a Chile that had been transformed by his arrest. In August, in a step that would have been unthinkable before his detention in Britain, the Chilean Supreme Court stripped him of his parliamentary immunity, allowing prosecution to proceed for his role in a notorious episode of execution and "disappearance" immediately following his 1973 coup.

Similarly, after the September 1999 rampage of Indonesian-backed militia in East Timor, the U.N. launched a commission of inquiry. In January 2000, the commission recommended the establishment of an international tribunal. Kofi Annan declined to endorse this recommendation so long as the Indonesian government upheld its vow to bring the abusers to justice on its own—a step it had no previous history of taking. In August, U.N. High Commissioner for Human Rights Mary Robinson reminded Jakarta that she would call for an international tribunal if it did not proceed with prosecutions. In September, the government published a list of nineteen suspects involved in the East Timor rampage, though by late October the prospect of actual prosecutions remained distant.

Interestingly, in one case a nationally based prosecutorial effort may precede action by an international tribunal, suggesting a complementary relationship. The international war crimes tribunal for Rwanda has jurisdiction not only over atrocities associated with the 1994 genocide but also over crimes committed at the time by the Rwandan Patriotic Front—the dominant force in the current Rwandan government. The RPF's military victory in June 1994 ended the genocide, but the Tutsi-led force committed serious abuses in the process. The Rwanda tribunal has issued no indictments for the RPF's crimes—a failure that is often attributed to its need to maintain good relations with the Rwandan government so it can retain access to the country to conduct investigations and secure witnesses for the genocide trials. In August 2000, a Belgian prosecutor began investigating a complaint of war crimes and crimes against humanity filed against the RPF by a group of Rwandans. This initiative may hasten similar action by the Rwanda tribunal.

Southern Initiatives

Some critics of efforts to hold human rights abusers accountable for their crimes have suggested that justice is a parochial concern of Northern governments which is imposed on the people of the South. But the events of 2000 demonstrated that Southern governments are also eager to pursue the most heinous human rights criminals—that the quest for justice does not break down on hemispheric lines.

In February, in an echo of the Pinochet case, a Senegalese court, acting at the request of Chadian victims, indicted former

Chadian dictator Hissène Habré for torture and ordered his arrest. Habré had taken refuge in Senegal following the fall of his dictatorship in 1990. In July 2000, in a blow to judicial independence, an appellate court dismissed the indictment after the new Senegalese government of President Abdoulaye Wade removed the judge investigating the case and promoted the head of the judicial chamber that issued the reversal ruling. The dismissal is on appeal to the country's Supreme Court.

In October, an Argentine judge asked Chile to extradite Pinochet and others for the 1974 assassination of General Carlos Prats and his wife, Sofia Cuthbert. Prats, the former commander-in-chief of the Chilean armed forces, had opposed Pinochet's 1973 coup and taken refuge in Buenos Aires with his family. The judge also sought the extradition of other Chileans in the case, including the former chief of Chile's secret police, Manuel Contreras Sepúlveda, who is in prison in Chile for having carried out a 1974 car-bombing in Washington that took the life of another coup opponent, former Chilean Foreign Minister Orlando Letelier, and his assistant, Ronni Moffitt.

Also in October, Vladimiro Montesinos, the shadowy intelligence figure behind the authoritarian government of Peruvian President Alberto Fujimori, unsuccessfully sought political asylum (effective amnesty) in Panama. Panama had evidently tired of being the world's dumping ground for deposed dictators and their accomplices. Montesinos, who had been responsible for forming and supervising a death squad in the early 1990s among other abuses, beat a hasty retreat to Peru.

In August, acting upon a Spanish request, Mexico arrested Ricardo Miguel Cavallo, an accused torturer for the 1976-83 Argentine military junta. Cavallo had been living in Mexico.

These and other cases demonstrate an increasingly global effort—involving governments of the North and South—to bring abusive officials to justice. The trend is still at a rudimentary stage, but it is clearly working against the impunity that so many ruthless officials enjoyed. This smaller world may make tomorrow's dictators think twice before embarking on the path of slaughter taken by their predecessors.

Disappointments

However, the news in 2000 was not all rosy on the justice front. The most glaring failure was the international community's refusal to put serious pressure on Russia to bring to justice the commanders who had been responsible for massacres, torture, and indiscriminate slaughter in Chechnya. With Russia wielding a veto on the U.N. Security Council, a council-created international tribunal was not an option. The U.N. Commission on Human Rights did criticize Russia's actions and urge prosecution—the first such resolution against a permanent member of the Security Council. The Parliamentary Assembly of the Council of Europe also suspended the Russian delegation's voting rights. But there was little follow-up on these initiatives, and no insistence that Russia apply the rule of law to its troops in Chechnya as a condition of receiving the large international assistance that continued to be sent its way.

Also disappointing was the lack of international attention to justice in Central Africa—particularly Burundi and the Democratic Republic of Congo. This failure is especially unfortunate in the Congo because the government of President Laurent Kabila effectively blocked an earlier U.N. commission of inquiry established to examine atrocities committed on Congolese soil during Kabila's rise to power in 1996-97. The war fought in Congo since 1998 has also been plagued by widespread atrocities. So far, the international community has taken no steps to end the impunity that helps drive these abuses.

Despite a clear mandate, NATO made no effort through October to arrest Radovan Karadzic, the former Bosnian Serb political leader who has been indicted for genocide and other crimes in Bosnia. Throughout all or most of 2000, he was reported still to be in Bosnia and hence in territory where NATO had permission to operate.

A Selective U.S. Vision of Justice

Perhaps the greatest disappointment was the persistently selective view of international justice adopted by the U.S. government. Washington has been an active supporter of country-specific tribunals insofar as they apply to others, but it has stood in the way of efforts to establish a more universal system of justice that might apply to U.S. citizens as well.

This attitude was evident in the cries of protest heard in Washington when the prosecutor for the Yugoslav war crimes tribunal, Carla del Ponte, dared even to consider opening an investigation of NATO's conduct during the 1999 air war with Yugoslavia. The tribunal has jurisdiction over war crimes committed in the territory of the former Yugoslavia, whether by residents of the territory or outside forces. The prosecutor's scrutiny of the NATO air campaign was entirely appropriate, given that, according to a Human Rights Watch study released in February, up to a half of the roughly 500 civilian deaths during the bombing campaign were attributable to possible NATO violations of international humanitarian law. Although the prosecutor ultimately decided against launching an investigation, Washington thought it an outrage that she would even contemplate holding NATO to the same standards as other forces. Indeed, NATO failed to turn over specific information requested by investigators.

In March, the U.S. government again fell short of its international justice obligations. Tomás Ricardo Anderson Kohatsu, a one-time major in Peru's Army Intelligence Service, was credibly accused of participating in the 1997 brutal torture of a woman who was beaten, burned, raped and electrically shocked in such a manner that she was rendered paraplegic. The U.S. State Department itself had described the case in its annual human rights reports for 1997 and 1999. Anderson Kohatsu came to Washington in March 2000 to testify on Peru's behalf at a hearing before the Inter-American Commission on Human Rights, part of the Organization of American States. At the request of the U.S. Justice Department, which had been alerted to his presence, he was detained while changing planes in Houston. Anderson Kohatsu was not on Peruvian government business and was not carrying a diplomatic passport. Nonetheless, without allowing the courts to consider the matter, Acting Secretary of State Thomas Pickering ordered his release on the dubious theory that he was entitled to diplomatic immunity because he had participated in official business of the OAS. Pickering's actions reflected an administration far more concerned with avoiding political problems with Peru than with carrying out international legal obligations to arrest and prosecute the worst human rights offenders.

Perhaps most troubling is the U.S. government's continued refusal to accept the International Criminal Court. With the help of the United States, the court already has extensive safeguards against unjustified prosecutions. Moreover, under the court's "principle of complementarity," any government can spare its nationals ICC prosecution by conducting its own good-faith investigation and, if appropriate, prosecution. Yet the U.S. government is determined to shut off even the theoretical possibility that its citizens would have to appear before the court. Washington maintains this stance even though an exception to the court's universal reach would undermine the court's legitimacy and effectiveness.

Because the U.S. government has no intention of ratifying the court's treaty anytime soon, it has focused on the supposed outrage that the court would have jurisdiction over the citizens of a state that has not ratified the treaty. But it is common practice for a government to prosecute a foreign national for crimes committed on its territory without first seeking permission of the foreigner's government. The jurisdiction of the ICC amounts to no more than a delegation of this widely accepted power for the most serious human rights crimes. Indeed, Washington itself routinely exercises far more expansive jurisdiction in unilaterally pursuing alleged terrorists or drug traffickers even when their crimes were not committed on U.S. soil.

Still, the U.S. government has advanced one scheme after another to shield U.S. citizens from the court's reach. The latest idea, floated in October, would exempt the citizens of any government that has not ratified the court, so long as the government could show that it "acts responsibly" and is "generally" willing to prosecute its own serious human rights offenders. But these requirements are not in the ICC treaty. Adding them would fundamentally revise the treaty and upend a whole series of carefully crafted compromises made in Rome to secure the court's broad support. Moreover, the principle of complementarity as framed in the treaty permits a government to avoid ICC prosecution of a citizen only by pursuing the specific suspect in question. Washington wants to weaken this rule by requiring only a "general" willingness to prosecute criminals of this nature—something a country could presumably establish once and for all and thereafter preclude the risk of ICC prosecution for any of its citizens. That is hardly a goal worth endorsing.

The best antidote to this U.S. exceptionalism is for the many governments supporting the court to reject all such schemes out of hand and proceed as rapidly as possible toward the sixty ratifications of the treaty needed to establish the court. The sooner the court is up and running, the sooner Washington will recognize the futility of its quest to carve out an exemption for its citizens. Ultimately, Washington will realize that its best defense against unfair (as opposed to legitimate) prosecutions of Americans is to help create a culture within the ICC that is deeply respectful of individual rights and the rule of law. The U.S. contribution to that culture will be far more effective if the United States joins the court—or at least becomes a friendly supporter of it—than if it persists in attacking the court from the outside.

Conclusion

An increasingly interconnected world is generating human rights problems of a global dimension. From regulating the global economy to rebuilding war-torn societies to bringing the most heinous criminals to justice, global solutions are needed to these global problems. A nation would never willingly address its most complex national problems with handicapped national institutions. So the world needs to enhance its institutional capacity on a global level to address the most serious human rights problems that transcend national borders. Some progress is being made in each of these areas, but far more needs to be done. The challenge today is to build a global institutional capacity commensurate with the complexity and importance of these global problems.

Over fifty years ago, as World War II ended and a new era began, the international community created a new set of institutions to address the challenges of the future. What emerged were such landmark organizations as the United Nations and the Bretton-Woods institutions. Similar vision is needed today. To manage the global economy, stronger institutions are needed to ensure respect for human rights. To assist war-torn nations, the United Nations must be bolstered substantially. To build an international system of justice, the International Criminal Court must be launched and supported. These are major steps requiring foresight and commitment. Complacency can no longer be tolerated. It is time to act.

HUMAN RIGHTS DEFENDERS

The international community took important actions in 2000 aimed at protecting those who are risking their lives to fight for human rights. During its annual session, the United Nations Commission on Human Rights voted to establish the post of a special representative of the secretary-general on the situation of human rights defenders. After a worldwide search, in August, the secretary-general appointed Hina Jilani, a Pakistani human rights lawyer (and a human rights monitor honored by Human Rights Watch in 1991 at our annual monitors' celebration) for the post. The special representative will be able to press for the implementation of the 1998 Declaration on Human Rights Defenders and intervene in cases of threats to and harassment of human rights defenders worldwide.

Five humanitarian workers were murdered in 2000 while aiding refugees. In West Timor, United Nations High Commissioner for Refugees (UNHCR) staff Samson Aregahegn, Carlos Caceres, and Pero Simun were killed on September 6. In Guinea, UNHCR head of office Mensah Kpognon was killed on September 17. In Burundi, Brother Antoine Bargiggia of the Jesuit Refugee Service (JRS) was killed on October 3. Their tragic deaths prompted a global protest and highlighted the dangers for humanitarian workers world wide. The murders also posed a serious threat to the protection of refugees as UNHCR responded by withdrawing all staff from West Timor and the border areas of Guinea, leaving refugees there almost completely unprotected. The Jesuit Refugee Service continued to serve refugees in Burundi.

Indonesia experienced the loss of human rights defenders Sukardi and Jafar Siddiq Hamzah in the year 2000. Sukardi, a volunteer for the local environmental and human rights group based in Aceh, the Bamboo Thicket Institute (Yayasan Rumpun Bambu Indonesia), "disappeared" on January 31. Sukardi's body was found naked and bullet-riddled on February 1. Jafar Siddiq Hamzah, the founder and director of the New York-based rights group, the International Forum for Aceh, vanished on August 5, while on a visit to Medan, Indonesia. Jafar, one of Aceh's most accomplished human rights advocates, was found dead with his body showing signs of torture in an unmarked grave on September 3.

Some fifty miles outside Nairobi, Fr. John Kaiser, a well-known human rights activist in Kenya, was murdered during the night of August 24, 2000. Father Kaiser, a Catholic parish priest in the Rift Valley area and a U.S. citizen, worked in Kenya for thirty-six years and was an outspoken human rights activist. In 1999, the Law Society of Kenya had honored Father Kaiser with its annual human rights award.

In Colombia, four human rights defenders were killed and three "disappeared" in the year 2000. On July 11, Elizabeth Cañas, a member of the Association of Family Members of the Detained and Disappeared (Asociación de Familiares de Detenidos Desaparecidos-Colombia ASFADDES), was shot and killed in Barrancabermeja. Angel Quintero and Claudia Patricia Monsalve, also ASFADDES members, were "disappeared" in Medellín, Antioquia, on October 6. Indigenous activist Jairo Bedoya Hoyos, a member of the Antioquia Indigenous Organization (Organización Indígena de Antioquia, OIA) who worked on human rights issues, was "disappeared" on March 2. Demetrio Playonero, a displaced person and human rights leader was murdered apparently by paramilitaries on March 3. In May, Jesús Ramiro Zapata, the only remaining member of the Segovia Human Rights Committee, was killed near Segovia. Government prosecutor Margarita María Pulgarín Trujillo, part of a team investigating cases linking paramilitaries to the army and regional drug traffickers, was murdered in Medellín on April 3.

In Haiti, Jean Dominique, the director of Radio Haiti-Inter and one of Haiti's most prominent radio journalists, was shot to death the morning of April 3. Forced into exile in 1980 for his opposition to the Jean-Claude Duvalier regime, Dominique was a strong proponent of the free press and Haiti's struggle for democracy.

HUMAN RIGHTS WATCH WORLD REPORT 2001

HUMAN RIGHTS WATCH

AFRICA

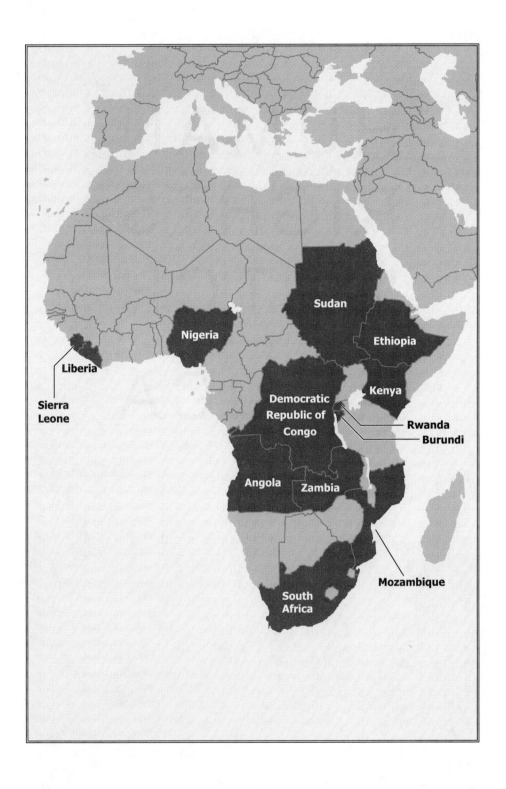

AFRICA
OVERVIEW

Reassuring Omens, Bold Visions

On May 13, 2000, the *Economist*, the venerable and influential magazine of the global English-speaking political classes, dubbed the continent "Hopeless Africa." Yet beyond the ubiquitous images of mayhem, positive, though less "newsworthy," changes were evolving at the societal level. Thanks to discernible changes in public attitudes and less willingness to accept the inevitability of authoritarian rule, it was at the grassroots that the most promising battles were being waged for a more humane Africa. Human rights groups, churches, academics, and other civil society activists demonstrated an uncommon resolve, courage and willingness to put their lives on the line to resist repression and lead the push among nongovernmental actors for transparency, participation, and accountability.

The indignant demand for more democracy came against a backdrop of deterioration and decay in the quality and performance of public institutions, in their ability to produce the results that people demanded and would respect. Demands for change resonated with the public at large, including sectors of society that were only tenuously tied to the system, with little access to employment, food, health care, education, or other benefits that government was supposed to bring. But their aspirations bumped up against governments that had been unable to provide political and social progress. As the pressure built up during the year, governments in a number of countries began to pay more attention as concepts of transparency and accountability took hold.

The phenomenal transition in Zimbabwe was the most dramatic illustration of a yearning for democracy and human rights, and of the dogged determination of civil society actors to engineer and orchestrate reform. Not so long ago the prospect of Zimbabwe's ruling party losing a referendum vote and coming close to losing control of parliament would have bordered on the surreal. But that was precisely what happened. First, the Zimbabwean electorate voted down a government-sponsored constitution at a referendum in April, and two months later the ruling party—that had been thought unassailable—came close to losing its parliamentary majority. The June elections came in the wake of a period of unprecedented violence in which supporters of the ruling party reportedly killed nineteen people, including white farmers and opposition politicians, beat up hundreds more, raped dozens of women, and occupied more than one thousand commercial farms. At the vanguard of pressure for change was a coalition of nongovernmental forces that confronted the powers that be, questioning not only their efficacy but also their legitimacy. This was an insurrection of courageous academics, high school teachers, priests, students, lawyers, judges, citizens, all seeking to move their country closer to the ideals of democracy and respect for human rights and the rule of law. They rose to that task very effectively and pulled off a people-power revolution that achieved astonishing gains in a short span of time.

The organizational effectiveness of the Zimbabwe groups was considerably helped by two factors: a popular backlash, especially among the urban electorate, against persistently high levels of unemployment, poverty, corruption; and an infusion of talent and organizing capabilities that rapidly professionalized the ranks of the civil society coalition and later the Movement for Democratic Change (MDC). Sophisticated and adroit, the opposition became highly effective media operators, ensuring a forceful projection of their message both at home and abroad. It did not lead to a change in government, but it marked a big step along the way.

As developments in Zimbabwe heralded bolder, increasingly courageous grassroots movements, the Ivory Coast too saw changes towards greater empowerment of nongovernmental forces, and renewed engagement of the Ivorian people. In massive demonstrations sparked by a controversial presidential election, thousands of Ivorians spilled onto the streets of Abidjan to force the Ivorian president General Guei from power. Moreover, in the general uprising, voters in the northern power base of opposition leader Alassane Ouattara largely boycotted the elections. Despite harsh repression under General Guei since his coup, and even in the face of intense gunfire, protesters demonstrated across Abidjan, storming state radio and television stations in what appeared to be a spontaneous popular revolution. This "people power revolution" was set off by mass dissatisfaction with Guei's attempts to rig and steal the elections, and also with an earlier court ruling that excluded two major political opposition figures from the presidential election.

Equally undaunted were civil society and human rights groups in the rebel-held eastern provinces of North and South Kivu in the Democratic Republic of Congo (DRC). Although the Congolese Rally for Democracy (RCD) authorities sought to limit the many and vigorous actors, civil society groups struggled to maintain their rights to free expression and association, serving as a channel for criticizing the RCD and its Rwandan allies. In addition to dozens of human rights associations, there were uncounted development and humanitarian nongovernmental groups, activist churches, and independent journalists. Although the rebel authorities and their Rwandan allies resorted to such tactics as physical assault, arbitrary arrest, and detention, activists courageously persevered to maintain the only line of defense against glaring human rights abuses by self-styled liberators.

In DRC's southern neighbor Zambia, a less dramatic but nonetheless crucial development took place during the country's World Bank Consultative Group (CG) meeting. For the first time in Africa, a transparent CG meeting where all deliberations were open to independent human rights and civil society activists was convened in Lusaka in July. Building upon the experience of a previous CG meeting in Malawi when a select number of NGOs were invited to a session on human rights and governance, the Bank and a number of bilateral donors used it as a precedent to persuade the Zambian authorities of the benefits of opening up the discussions. After strenuous objections to the participation of human rights and civil society activists, Zambia's Minister of Finance Katele Kalumba relented and agreed to have the entire meeting opened to civil society groups, both local and international, including traditionally tightly closed sessions. The human rights performance of the government was openly discussed during the meeting in the presence of NGOs. This was a significant opening given the strategic importance of a World Bank Consultative meeting to an aid-dependent government like Zambia. Seemingly, the success of the Lusaka meeting was due to good teamwork between Zambia's bilateral donors, and a new, more open team at the World Bank—reflecting a softening of the World Bank's compartmentalization of poverty reduction versus human rights, and some risk-taking by the Zambian government.

War-torn Angola also showed signs of pressure for change. With an eye to forthcoming elections, seventeen minor opposition parties met in May to fashion an alliance to foster opposition to the war, and advocate free and fair elections. Concurrently, Angola's churches—known to command the largest base of support in the country—formed a joint body to champion peace and national reconciliation. In Sudan too, in the face of overwhelming security obstacles, the New Sudan Council of Churches' "People-to-People" reconciliation process held a meeting in May in conflict-ridden southern Sudan, of people on the east bank of the Nile, despite overwhelming ethnic and military impediments. The May meeting sought to build upon the positive results of the west bank March 1999 meeting.

There were other interesting trends in Senegal, Eritrea, and Somalia. In Senegal, the electorate rejected President Abdou Diouf in his quest for a fourth consecutive term. Following a highly competitive March election, Diouf peacefully conceded defeat to veteran opposition leader Abdoulaye Wade who took almost 60 percent of the votes cast. Diouf, head of the party that had governed Senegal since independence from France in 1960, became only the third elected African head of government to leave office following an election. Prior to the elections, Senegal set another precedent in February 2000, when a Senegalese court indicted Chad's exiled former dictator, Hissein Habré, on torture charges and placed him under house arrest. It was the first time that an African had been charged with atrocities in his own country by the court of another African country and represented a major step toward promoting the rule of law and breaking the cycle of impunity in Africa. But Senegal somewhat tarnished its reputation when its judiciary dropped charges against Habré under what seemed to be questionable circumstances. An appeal by Chad's torture victims was still pending at this writing.

In Eritrea, although decision-making remained tightly controlled within the governing People's Front for Democracy and Justice (PFDJ), the sole party operating in the country since the country became formally independent in 1993, there were signs of possible openings. The constitution guaranteed freedom of expression and the press, but the government severely restricted those rights. The government owned all the broadcasting media, and the only printing press in the country. But following military setbacks in the war with Ethiopia during the first half of 2000, and the catastrophic displacement of almost a third of the Eritrean population as a result of that war, the pressure mounted for a genuine implementation of the constitution. An intense debate was reportedly taking place in Eritrean elite circles, behind closed doors, on how and why the country went to war in the first place. Questions were reportedly also being raised on the conduct of Eritrean diplomacy during several unsuccessful rounds of negotiations to end the

war. Probably in a concession to the mounting tide for change, the Eritrean National Assembly concluded its thirteenth session on October 2 by announcing that multiparty elections would be held in December 2001. The assembly formed a committee to draft regulations to govern political parties. Also in the aftermath of the war, about a dozen private newspapers and magazines started publication. The Eritrean government also softened the severe restrictions it had imposed in 1998 on foreign NGOs that had denied them any operational role, and limited their contribution to the health and education sectors, through government channels and approved programs. Facing a complex disaster resulting from war and drought, the government invited back several international NGOs that had left the country to protest the policy. The government even ended its decade-long feud with the International Committee of the Red Cross (ICRC) by inviting it to establish a delegation in Asmara soon after the war broke out. In midyear, the Eritrean government ratified the Geneva Conventions.

Even the sickest man of Africa, Somalia, showed prospects of renewal. After descending into a maelstrom of warring regions and factions since the 1991 ouster of the late ex-President Barre, Somalia had been without a national government. But following the Intergovernmental Authority (IGAD)-backed national reconciliation conference in August to discuss a peace plan put forward by Djibouti's President Ismael Omar Guelleh, a new transitional government was put in place. Shedding past fears, tens of thousands of Somalis staged demonstrations in the capital, Mogadishu, and other cities in support of President Guellah's peace proposals. President Salad Hassan subsequently reclaimed Somalia's U.N. seat and addressed the U.N. Millennium Conference in New York.

The most important question for Zimbabwe, Angola, Zambia, or Somalia—and by association, for Africa—was whether the changes would prove more than cyclical upturns. To the degree that developments mirrored a change in the public's state of mind, and a perception that they could influence the composition of a government and its policies, it appeared that the human rights advances would endure. These developments were driven by a combination of greater pressures on government and the gathering force of globalization, with Internet communications playing a growing role. As communications became close to instantaneous across international boundaries, African electorates, with nongovernmental forces at the vanguard as in Zimbabwe, became increasingly well informed and able to demand higher standards of governance. These developments would hardly change the face of Africa overnight. But they showed what could be done by ordinary people despite massive repression. The information revolution could in time accelerate political transformation and alter the political and human rights landscape in Africa and beyond.

Such challenges to the power base of President Robert Mugabe of Zimbabwe, a longtime and controversial strongman, the warlords in Somalia, or the rebel forces in the DRC, could help sway many who would otherwise have felt that the task was too daunting. But the durability of the courage and determination of civil society to bring change would remain in doubt in the absence of substantial financial and diplomatic support from abroad. Under the best of circumstances, civil society and other advocates of change would have a hard time challenging wrongs that had gone on for decades, presided over by entrenched regimes often with substantial foreign support. The lesson for the international donor community was that institutions and policy decisions that led to human rights abuses were not intractable and inevitable. Investments in civil society initiatives would help ensure that the momentum generated by the events of 2000 was sustained and would embolden those seeking to influence and change institutions and policies—though progress would quite likely be painfully slow. The international community should be generous.

Staying the Course in a Tempest-Tossed Climate

Other good news from Africa was that two sub-Saharan giants—Nigeria and South Africa—continued to make the transition to democracy, albeit on somewhat bumpy courses. Botswana, Ghana, Mali, Malawi, Mozambique, Tanzania, and Namibia also maintained steady growth. In particular, Mozambique's record was remarkable. Despite being pummeled by cyclone-driven floods, the worst in living memory, and severe tensions spawned by the 1999 December presidential and parliamentary elections, Mozambique was once again on its feet with the fastest growing economy in the world.

Still, the premier case for Africa remained decidedly focused on South Africa. The country continued to benefit from a holdover of political virtue derived from its political and constitutional transformation from apartheid to a constitutional democracy—despite the stormy political climate engendered by the crisis in Zimbabwe that threatened to engulf the entire sub-region. South Africa's rebound continued to be driven by responsible governmental actions in most areas of public policy. The constitutional framework was strengthened by passage of major legislation mandated under the 1996 constitution: the Promotion of Equality and Prevention of Unfair Discrimination Act, the Promotion of Access to Information Act, the Promotion of Administrative Justice Act, and Preferential Procurement Policy Framework Act. The National Assembly also passed legislation giving protection to "whistle blowers" disclosing information in the public interest. In a landmark September judgment on economic and social rights, the Constitutional Court found that the government had an obligation under the constitution to provide short-term housing for several hundred people evicted from their homes and in desperate need.

But though its achievements remained impressive, South Africa was not out of the woods. The growth, employment, and redistribution (GEAR) program implemented in previous years still failed to bring economic growth to some sectors of society, which had barely benefited or had even fallen further behind since 1994, leading to disagreement between the African National Congress (ANC) and its allies in the labor movement. In particular, joblessness remained intractably above 30 percent. There were other major problems: crime rates remained shockingly high; "taxi violence" between competing operators of minibus taxis remained a crime control riddle; violence against women, including sexual violence, remained alarmingly uncontrolled, with very high numbers of reported rapes; reports of police corruption and brutality were common during the year; and, despite over-congested prisons, the criminal justice system seemed unable to cope. Despite policies and laws designed to bring transformation to all sectors, implementation sometimes seemed a distant dream. The government's credibility and effective leadership also risked being undermined by conflict between health professionals and President Mbeki, who had controversially expressed doubt as to the link between HIV and AIDS, and the government's decision not to supply anti-retroviral drugs to HIV positive pregnant women to prevent transmission of the virus to their babies. Nonetheless, the ANC-led government continued to hold extraordinary political capital and the transformation program seemed broadly on course.

In Nigeria, Africa's most populous state and the economic heartland of the subregion, the military remained in the barracks. Viewed from the perspective of President Bill Clinton's two-day August visit, it seemed that Nigeria had much to celebrate. But after what some saw as a year of waffling by President Olusegun Obasanjo, a number of political worries tempered any optimism. Yes, things had changed, but the question was whether enough had changed. Little had been done to address serious and deep-rooted problems such as the unrest in the Niger Delta, secessionist demands from the southwest, high unemployment, the collapse of social services, and school closures. With worsening economic conditions and government failures to deliver any benefit from democracy, popular fatigue provided fuel for communal violence at flashpoints throughout the country. The declaration by several northern states that Islamic Sharia law would be extended to criminal law sparked deadly clashes between Muslims and Christians. The uncertainty caused by all these problems seriously damaged the country's prospects for desperately needed economic rejuvenation and for sustaining and deepening its democracy. Many ascribed much of the blame to Obasanjo—though the challenges he faced were more institutional than personal. He was accused of being reluctant and incapable of dealing firmly with important issues, including the bickering between the president and the legislature that seemed to have distracted attention from the need to make real progress.

Nonetheless, the good news was that none of those factors seemed likely to blunt the fundamental forces that had driven the switch from military rule to civilian government. The passage to democracy would be rough but would stay the course. A crucial element was that the major international actors kept their faith in Nigeria's democracy experiment. Would the armed forces risk making a bad situation worse by staging a coup? Given Nigeria's status as a bellwether for the region as a whole, the international response would be far from sanguine. The military would risk sharp international censure. The chances were that the military would probably not wish to turn the clock back. In the long term, nothing could do more to secure Nigeria's democracy than a decisive break with its past: constitutional reform to provide an agreed framework for the representation of Nigeria's disparate communities, the overhauling of a ramshackle legal and governmental structure, and human rights reforms to underpin the rule of law, accountability, and transparency.

Emblems of Bad Old Habits

While democracy was strengthened in select African countries, parts of the continent remained mired in authoritarianism, brutalized politics, and violent conflicts. At least thirteen nations in the region were engaged either in open conflict or heated disputes, some with internal groups and some with neighboring states, spawning large-scale forced migration and abuses of civilians either directly targeted or caught in crossfire. Ethnically inspired violence spread in Senegal's Casamance, the Great Lakes, the Horn of Africa, Guinea, Ivory Coast, and other regions, proving that self-serving political elites continued to play the ethnic or nationalist card in an effort to consolidate their power at the expense of civilian casualties. Even in countries such as Nigeria, where the government has worked to counter the negative use of ethnicity and religion by forces outside of the government, ethnic strife remained a concern. Several countries that had benefited from the wave of democratization with the promise of more participation, transparence, and accountability in the early 1990s saw tightening control and shrinking political space.

One electoral process after another stumbled into difficulty. Electoral manipulation, government spending to support its own candidates, and the pervasive pro-government bias of most local media left electoral landscapes badly tilted in favor of incumbents—despite the now ubiquitous presence of election observers and their ritualized post-election reports. Angola, Ethiopia, Eritrea, Guinea, Ivory Coast, Kenya, Liberia, Sierra Leone, Sudan, Uganda, and Zambia saw stagnation or regression.

In Ivory Coast, sub-Saharan Africa's third-largest economy, soldiers launched a coup that brought to power a strongman, General Robert Guei, on December 24, 1999, and clobbered Ivory Coast's standing as a stable financial and political power. The new military regime was expected to come under pressure to make good on its pledge to move quickly toward democracy and demonstrate more openness than the previously entrenched regime of ex-President Henri Konan Bedie. But such expectations were quickly dashed as General Guei deliberately

sought to disqualify his key rivals for the presidency in the October 22 elections. As widely expected, President of the Supreme Court Tia Kone announced on October 6 the disqualification of twelve presidential hopefuls—including Alassane Dramane Ouattara, leader of the Rassemblement des Republicains (RDR), the main opposition party—and the approval of only five—including Guei himself—ahead of the vote.

In another key country, the Kenyan state seemed to have run out of both money and ideas. The constitutional reform process which could have brought greater democratization remained unsettled. And yet the government of President Daniel arap Moi continued to block progress on promised reform. The political crisis was paralleled by a marked deterioration in the economic situation, caused by state fumbling and corruption. The standard of living for the average Kenyan continued to drop, and the year was typified by unprecedented electricity rationing and water shortages in the capital Nairobi and other cities. At the end of July, President Moi signed on to exceptionally exacting conditions in return for renewed International Monetary Fund and World Bank lending. Moi nominally committed himself to doing something desperately difficult: to change an immeasurably corrupt and authoritarian country.

Elsewhere in the sub-region, the ruling Ethiopian People's Revolutionary Democratic Front (EPRDF) won a victory in May's tightly controlled elections, two days after Ethiopia launched its largest military offensive against Eritrea. Allegations of fraud and violence marred these elections, particularly in rural areas. In Uganda, just four days after Zimbabwean voters defied massive intimidation to rebuke the de facto single party rule of President Mugabe, President Yoweri Museveni's de facto one-party system was extended in a referendum marked by poor voter turnout. The choice in the referendum was whether to return to a multiparty system or to continue Museveni's favored so-called no-party system. Having called for a boycott of the referendum poll, the traditional opposition parties declared a moral victory, saying that the turnout of roughly 40 percent was too low for a mandate on a key constitutional and human rights issue. In the long term, the outcome could be that the no-party system might undermine the efforts to develop what was needed to sustain several of the positive changes that Museveni's Movement system had introduced. Of greatest concern was that behind the illusion of inclusion under the no-party system was a concentration of power in the ruling elite, high-level corruption, and mismanagement of resources.

In Rwanda, General Paul Kagame was selected by the National Assembly as president following the sudden resignations of the speaker of the national assembly, the prime minister, and the president within the first three months of the year. Two of the those of who had resigned their posts left the country, saying they feared for their lives. As Kagame's party, the Rwandan Patriotic Front, consolidated its power, it announced communal-level elections for late 2000, in which political parties could play no role. Zambia's poor performance on the democratization front undermined President Chiluba's credibility as a broker for peace and democracy in the DRC. Political parties, NGOs and other civic interest groups were regularly denied permission to assemble by the government's political and security apparatus or had their meetings violently broken up by police on public security grounds.

After a year-long lull in fighting, Ethiopia and Eritrea went to war again. On May 12, Ethiopia launched a massive attack against Eritrea and successfully recaptured disputed territories that Eritrea had occupied. The two-year conflict was estimated to have killed and wounded tens of thousands of soldiers and civilians and uprooted nearly a million people. Displaced Eritreans fleeing the fighting credibly reported the involvement of the Ethiopian army in large-scale destruction and looting of civilian property, the harassment of civilians, particularly men of military age, and a high incidence of rape. On the home front, the Ethiopian government continued to face internal armed insurgencies in the Oromia and Somali regional states and other remote regions, and to hold without charge or trial thousands of people it suspected of sympathizing with the insurgents. By early 2000, Ethiopian authorities, citing broad threats to national security, had arbitrarily and harshly returned some seventy thousand Ethiopians of Eritrean parentage to Eritrea. For its part, the Eritrean government forced an estimated forty thousand Ethiopians back to Ethiopia in the months that followed the outbreak of hostilities. Eritrean authorities also interned thousands of Ethiopian residents under harsh conditions in the wake of Ethiopia's offensive in May, citing unspecified threats to national security.

Destructive wars persisted in Angola, DRC, Burundi, Sudan, Sierra Leone, and on the border between Liberia and Guinea. Noncombatants continued to bear the brunt of the interminable fighting. In the DRC it was 1999 redux: tangled webs of allies facing off in a devastating war with no end in sight. The conflict pitted the government of President Kabila, and allied troops from Zimbabwe, Angola and, Namibia, against the rebel Congolese Rally for Democracy (RCD), as a proxy for forces fielded by the governments of Rwanda, Uganda, and Burundi. The RCD had split into two competing groups in May 1999, with the mainstream faction supported by Rwanda, and the other backed by Uganda. In the northern province Equateur, the Movement for the Liberation of Congo (MLC) obtained military support from Uganda. Apparently fighting on the side of President Kabila's government were rural militia, known locally as the Mai-Mai; and predominantly Hutu fighters commonly known as Interahamwe. Human rights and humanitarian conditions continued to deteriorate throughout the country as both government and rebel forces and their backers were reported involved in patterns of civilian killings and widespread rape of women, while government forces carried out indiscriminate shelling in Equateur. There was no improvement between 1999 and 2000. And yet there was no tangible progress in efforts to stop the ruinous war and its associated senseless killings: peace talks aimed at reviving the moribund peace deal signed in Lusaka in 1999 crumbled without an agreement on peace enforcement mechanisms amid mutual accusations of cease-fire violations.

The war in the Congo was increasingly closely linked to the seven-year civil war in Burundi as Kabila reportedly supplied more and more weapons for the Burundian rebel movement, Forces for the Defense of Democracy (FDD), in return for its help in defending Lubumbashi. A Burundian peace agreement, promoted by former South African President Nelson Mandela and U.S. President Clinton, had no effect on the combat, which grew considerably in the months after its August signing. Although parties to the war increasingly fought a classic war, they also continued to target civilians, with more than a thousand killed by October. An estimated one hundred and fifty thousand persons have been killed since the start of the war. The FDD and a rival rebel movement talked of new peace negotiation in early November but set conditions which made an agreement appear unlikely.

In Angola, a series of major victories by the government that pushed the rebel National Union for the Total Independence of Angola (UNITA) out of its strongholds in the central highlands of Angola in late 1999 raised expectations that the war might be nearing a decisive phase. At this writing, fierce fighting was raging, particularly in the areas close to the Zambian border, resulting in significant refugee inflows into Zambia. Human rights violations, a hallmark of the Angolan war, remained widespread and systematic. Disoriented and smarting from setbacks suffered at the hands of government forces, UNITA resorted to guerrilla attacks and indiscriminate killings.

As the country's ravaging seventeen-year war raged on, Sudan remained a blatant human rights abuser, while rebel groups committed their share of violations. The Khartoum government intensified its bombing of civilian targets in the war in the south and its efforts to hamper relief food operations to needy civilians. For its part, the Sudan People's Liberation Movement/Army (SPLM/A), the principal rebel movement in the country, continued to foster glaring abuses including looting of food and other provisions from the population, sometimes with civilian casualties; recruitment of underage boys; and rape. In the meantime, the government's war machine was poised to benefit substantially from new oil revenue. According to a government announcement, 20 percent of its 2000 revenue would be spent on defense, including an arms factory near Khartoum. It was estimated that following the first export of oil in August 1998, defense spending in dollars had increased 96 percent in two years.

In Sierra Leone, despite the Lomé Peace Accord signed on July 7, 1999 that committed the rebels to lay down their arms in exchange for representation in a new government, the war and its associated abuses continued, though at a lower intensity and with a reduction in the rebels' signature abuses, the amputation of limbs, for the first few months of the year. The May collapse of the peace process after the capture of some five hundred United Nations peacekeepers, reversed this trend and ushered in an increase of all classes of human rights abuses by the rebel Revolutionary United Front (RUF) and other militias, including limb amputation, and a disturbing intensification of abuses by pro-government forces, against whom previous allegations had been few. Women were particularly targeted for sexual violence. In thousands of cases, rape and other forms of sexual violence were followed by the abduction of women and girls who were forced into bondage to male combatants in slavery-like conditions. If that was not enough, the war became increasingly regionalized, sucking Guinea and Liberia into a tangled web of cross-border attacks with devastating consequences for noncombatants and refugees living in border areas.

The Private Press: Beaten Back But Not Cowed

The rapid growth of independent media

endured, although the degree of media freedom differed widely. For the most part, levels of freedom corresponded with levels of democratic development. The Internet also dramatically enhanced the access and distribution capabilities of the independent press, fostering freer flows of information in general. Eroding governments' ability to control the press and manipulate facts, the Internet also relieved the financial stresses that many African news agencies faced. South Africa, Nigeria, Botswana, Mauritius, Mali, Senegal and some others generally continued to register high levels of media freedom. But in several countries, severe levels of intolerance persisted. Many a government seemed all too alert to the danger that a free flow of information in society could undermine their grip on power. During the year, there was a rampant use of intimidation, assaults and detention, banning and radio closures, prolonged prosecutions and libel suits, or economic coercion to silence independent media.

Despite an improved climate for freedom of expression in Angola, a campaign of harassment against journalists continued. The privately owned media was targeted, apparently because it had increased its investigative and critical posture. Since November 1999 at least six journalists had been convicted of libel or defamation by government officials. On December 10, the directors of *Folha 8*, and the privately owned weekly newspapers, *Agora* and *Actual*, were ordered by police to retract stories that concerned a report by the U.K.-based NGO Global Witness, saying the government had corruptly used oil revenues. For its part, the official media published detailed refutations of the Global Witness report. On July 27, the Angolan government signaled its intention to tighten further controls on the media when it published a draconian new draft media bill that guaranteed presidential immunity to criticism and would send journalists to prison for criticizing or questioning government officials. The bill would allow the government the right to decide on who could practice journalism, seize and ban publications, and

to detain journalists for thirty days before charges were filed.

The independent media also continued to come under legal pressure in Zambia, where the trial of six journalists from the *Post* who were detained in March 1999 for publishing a story that criticized Zambia's military capability and preparedness in the face of a possible military attack from Angola dragged on. All the reporters, including editor-in-chief Fred M'membe, were charged with "espionage." All twelve pleaded not guilty to the charge, and on August 18, after repeated trial adjournment, the state dropped its charges against all except M'membe. An unexplained fire on September 3 at the *Post* offices damaged some U.S.$500,000 worth of equipment.

In South Africa, eyebrows were raised when more than thirty editors and writers were subpoenaed to appear before the South African Human Rights Commission to answer charges of racism. They were ordered to produce documents related to their editorial decisions, and the commission had the power to search their offices. The journalists could face fines or up to six months in jail if they failed to comply. The journalists stood their ground but offered to give evidence voluntarily if the subpoenas were withdrawn. Following a public outcry, the commission relented and withdrew the subpoenas. The hearings followed the release of an interim report commissioned by the Human Rights Commission and much criticized on methodological grounds, which found that the South African media was riddled with racism and racial stereotyping. The final report, which included material from the hearings, received a much more favorable reception, and included constructive recommendations to address these problems.

In Liberia, the year witnessed numerous incidents of detention and ill-treatment of journalists, a community under heavy attack since President Taylor took power in 1997. In March, Suah Dede, head of the Liberian Press Union, was briefly detained without charge after giving a radio interview condemning the closure of two radio stations. In April, Isaac Redd, radio broadcaster on the state radio station, was detained and held without charge for several days by the police. He was later accused of speaking against the president and charged with "criminal malfeasance." In August, four members of a foreign news film team, in Liberia to film a documentary, were arrested, charged with espionage, and detained for a week. The team had been given official permission to film in Liberia, but were accused of filming in restricted areas and seeking to damage the country's image by falsely linking President Charles Taylor to diamond smuggling. They were released following international pressure.

For its part, the Ethiopian government continued to abuse freedom of speech and of the press. At least twenty-seven journalists lived in exile at this writing, having fled their homeland due to repeated arrests, ill-treatment in detention, and the threat of extraordinarily high bail amounts. Eight reporters remained behind bars. In mid-August, sudden increases in printing costs, by more than a third, put additional pressures on some thirty-six private publications as well as the government press in Ethiopia. The private newspapers went on strike in September, and warned that the high production costs could eventually force them out of business. They urged the government to reduce taxation on imported paper and other print inputs.

In April, several journalists were assaulted in Zimbabwe. On April 22, a bomb shook the premises of privately owned Zimbabwean *Daily News*. On 6 April, Nyasha Nyakunu and Tsvangirai Mukwazhi, respectively editor and a photographer with the *Daily News*, were held for two hours by youths from the ZANU-PF armed with iron bars. A week earlier a photographer and a journalist with Agence France-Presse, and a cameraman from the British news agency Reuters had been threatened by about fifty men armed with machetes and iron bars.

In the DRC, scores of journalists were imprisoned apparently without legal justification. President Kabila's government had detained over 110 journalists and harassed many others since it took power in 1997. Private newspapers and radio and television stations were often shut down or banned from coverage of news deemed sensitive by the government. A special military court in mid-September sentenced two journalists to two years in prison for defying such directives. There were also numerous accounts of torture and other inhumane treatment. In Bukavu, the capital of rebel-held south Kivu province, photographer Jean Pierre Tanganyika, also known as Dudjo, was arrested after a grenade explosion on August 26 for having taken pictures of the injured victims at the scene. He was detained without formal charge at the local army barracks, briefly released on September 16, and rearrested again on the same day. His whereabouts remained unknown.

Aware that a large proportion of the population relied on radio for news, governments sought to silence independent radio broadcasting. The government-owned radio station provided the only news broadcasts heard by most Liberians. Two independent radio stations came under attack in March 2000: Star Radio and Radio Veritas, the radio station of the Catholic Church. Star Radio was forcibly closed, and remained so at this writing. At the beginning of October, the Zimbabwe police shut down Capital Radio, an independent radio station, and seized its equipment. The station began broadcasting after the Supreme Court ruled that Zimbabwe's broadcast monopoly was inconsistent with the country's constitutional provisions regarding the fundamental right to freedom of expression. President Mugabe's government then promulgated a presidential order outlawing private broadcasting without state approval. According to the police, Capital Radio had breached that order. At this writing, the station's legal action disputing the legality of the government's actions was still pending. In Kenya, however, several independent television and FM radio stations began broadcasting in 2000, obtaining licences after applications made several years earlier, some as far back as 1992. The growth of the independent broadcast sector resulted in a notable expansion in the airing of differing opinions, particularly on radio. These licences were, however, restricted principally to urban areas.

More Human Fallout

The massive numbers of displaced persons in Africa remained a major human rights catastrophe. As of January 2000, there were 6.3 million Africans of concern to the U.N. High Commissioner for Refugees (UNHCR), from an estimated 22.3 million worldwide. Of the top twenty countries from which people fled from around the world, eight were in Africa. Eleven African states hosted refugee populations of 100,000 or more. The figures were equally striking in terms of internally displaced populations (IDPs): eight African countries were among the twenty countries with the largest internally displaced populations. Indeed, in several African countries, as in Sierra Leone, armed groups purposefully uprooted civilians, creating massive populations of refugees and IDPs in order to forward political or military objectives with little or no regard for human suffering.

Sudan alone had approximately four million IDPs—the largest IDP population in the world. Angola's growing IDP population stood at some 2.5 million. The war between Eritrea and Ethiopia resulted in massive internal displacement, particularly in Eritrea where 1.5 million people were uprooted, including 90,000 who sought refuge in neighboring Sudan. Hostilities in the Democratic Republic of the Congo resulted in the displacement of 1.6 million people, one million of whom had little or no access to humanitarian assistance with dire consequences. The U.N. reported that infant mortality among the displaced was the highest in the region, and that maternal mortality was the highest in the world. Some of the longest and most forgotten refugee crises were on the African continent, with recurring refugee movements caused by conflicts spilling over into neighboring countries. Refugee crises in Africa invariably affected a whole subregion—and sometimes beyond.

The Horn of Africa countries continued to be producers and receivers of refugees simultaneously. And in West Africa, the interlocking conflicts in Sierra Leone, Liberia, and Guinea affected populations in all three nations. Balancing national security concerns with the obligation to provide safe asylum and protection to refugees was one of the most challenging issues for host governments in Africa. Internal conflicts alarmingly spilled across borders into neighboring countries, resulting in greater militarization of refugee settlements by armed elements, weapons flows, cross-border attacks, forced recruitment of refugee children, and rape and other physical attacks on refugee women and children in camps. The security risk increasingly associated with hosting refugees from intractable regional conflicts resulted in a growing unwillingness by host governments to provide asylum and protection. Xenophobia and anti-refugee sentiment continued to grow, even in countries with a generous history of hosting those fleeing conflict. The failure by African governments and the international community to separate out combatants from refugees in the camps exacerbated the problem and made refugee camps more likely targets for attack.

For example, in September, tensions rose between Liberia, Guinea, and Sierra Leone, each accusing the other of supporting rebel activity. Guinea, one of the largest refugee hosts in Africa, intermittently closed its border with Sierra Leone, fearful of incursions by Sierra Leonean rebels. In September, an inflammatory public statement by the president of Guinea provoked widespread rapes and other attacks by Guinean police, soldiers, and civil militias against Sierra Leonean and Liberian refugees.

Defending Human Rights

The human rights movement continued to register significant strides across the continent, although there were variations in the environments in which they operated. Many countries continued to liken human rights advocacy by local NGOs to disloyal political opposition or collaboration with those fighting the government of the day.

In several countries, including DRC, Zimbabwe, Kenya, Liberia, and Ethiopia, individual activists faced intimidation, arrest, assault, and sometimes death for their advocacy of human rights. The risk that rights defenders faced was underscored on August 24 when Fr. John Kaiser, a well-known human rights activist in Kenya, was brutally murdered at night by unidentified persons some fifty miles outside Nairobi. A Catholic parish priest in the Rift Valley area and a U.S. citizen, Father Kaiser had worked in Kenya for thirty-six years and had been an outspoken human rights activist. In 1999, the Law Society of Kenya had honored Father Kaiser with its annual human rights award.

The DRC continued to be one of the most dangerous places for human rights activists. The government in late May detained for weeks Félicien Malanda Nsumbu and Georges Kazimbika, respectively the secretary and financial officer of the national umbrella group for developmental organizations, and accused them of contacting the rebels. In early June, the government prevented representatives of civil society and the political opposition from leaving the capital to attend preparatory talks for the inter-Congolese dialogue in Cotonou, Benin. On January 16, security forces of the RCD arrested at her home Immaculée Birhaheka, president of the women's group Promotion and Support of Women's Initiatives (PAIF), and her colleague Jeannine Mukanirwa, PAIF's vice president. The two, and other women held like them at the infamous "Bureau 2" detention center in Goma, were whipped with a piece of tire. On October 9, RCD soldiers broke up a meeting held by the umbrella group for human rights organizations in Bukavu. Congolese and Rwandan soldiers beat them with sticks and fists in front of a big crowd. The rights groups were planning to discuss follow-up activities to the previous week's visit to eastern DRC of

United Nations High Commissioner for Human Rights Mary Robinson.

President Charles Taylor of Liberia and other high-ranking government officials also continued to attack human rights groups for publicizing abuses and blamed the human rights community for the withholding of international aid. In December, 1999, James D. Torh, the executive director of a child-rights organization, Fore-Runners of Children's Universal Development, was detained and charged with sedition for a speech he made. Torh was denied bail for five days and upon release, he fled the country. In Namibia, a Zambian-born human rights activist and a founder member and executive of the Namibian Society for Human Rights who had lived in Namibia for sixteen years was on February 21 expelled by immigration officials because of his alleged support for Caprivi secessionists.

But in Nigeria, numerous and sophisticated human rights groups were able to operate freely throughout the year. The human rights movement, long recognized as the one of the most vibrant networks on the continent, strengthened its advocacy—to the extent that its legislative and reform program was vastly more ambitious than that of the government. In South Africa too, activists continued to operate in an environment of freedom. Occasional government hostility to NGO criticism was neutralized by strong collaboration in government-NGO partnerships elsewhere.

There was also some encouraging news from countries whose dedicated human rights networks operated in less than favorable circumstances. In Rwanda, the League for Promoting and Defending Human Rights (La Ligue Rwandaise pour la Promotion et la Défense des Droits de l'Homme, LIPRODHOR) monitored judicial proceedings related to the genocide and made plans to observe a new alternative justice process set to begin operating early in 2001. The Association for the Defense of Human Rights and Public Liberties (Association pour la Défense des Droits Humains et des Libértés Publiques, ADL) executed a useful study of villagization, a government policy of forced resettlement of the rural population. The League for the Defense of Human Rights of the Great Lakes (La Ligue des Associations de Défense des Droits de l'homme des Grands Lacs, LDGL) initiated a campaign among its member organizations to end impunity in the region and to extend the mandate of the International Criminal Tribunal for Rwanda, as did the Burundian Ligue Iteka. The Burundian Association for the Defense of Prisoners did the first nation-wide census of persons jailed in national prisons and secured the release of prisoners who had already served their terms and yet remained in jail.

In an environment which was not known for tolerance of independent monitoring, the Ethiopian Human Rights Council (EHRCO) continued to report on the human rights situation in the country. Several civic organizations, including EHRCO, the Ethiopian Economic Association, the Inter-Africa Group, and the Addis Ababa Chamber of Commerce convened panel discussions that allowed ruling party and opposition candidates to air their programs before urban voters, mainly in the capital. The Ethiopian Women Lawyers Association conducted training for women candidates. Progress was registered toward the establishment in Ethiopia of national institutions and an international presence for the protection and promotion of human rights. The outgoing parliament in July unanimously approved bills establishing the Ethiopian human rights commission and the office of the ombudsman. However, the government continued to deny recognition to the Human Rights League, which was founded in 1997 by members of the Oromo community. The government arrested eight board members of the league shortly after they applied for registration of the association, and confiscated its office records and equipment in 1998. Garuma Bekele, executive secretary of the league, and also editor of *Urji*, and Addisu Beyene, secretary of the Oromo Relief Association and prominent rights advocate, together with some fifty other prominent Oromo civic leaders, remained in jail since their arrest in October 1997. Their trial for conspiracy continued in camera. Mary Robinson, the U.N. high commissioner for human rights, said during a visit in October that her agency planned to open a regional office in Addis Ababa to work with the countries of the Horn of Africa and the OAU.

Organization of African Unity

As countries in Africa continued to erupt in violence, the Organization of African Unity (OAU) once again failed to rise to the challenge of effectively dealing with issues of stability and democracy throughout the continent. Through measures taken at several summits, the OAU attempted to become a more proactive, unified body; however, its efforts were undermined by decisions which called into question its commitment to democracy and stability. Working mostly in tardy reaction to crisis situations, the OAU found its actions largely futile in solving the civil strife in many countries. The one exception, the OAU's success story for the year, was the cessation of hostilities agreement which helped halt the two-year war between Ethiopia and Eritrea, with a June 18 agreement to end hostilities and work out a final settlement. The cease-fire, which was a product of OAU intervention, consisted of detailed plans to disengage the two armies and to allow a U.N. peacekeeping force to patrol parts of the established buffer zone. As part of its efforts to oversee the agreement's implementation, the OAU sent military observers in September to monitor the cessation of hostilities.

In countries like the DRC, Comoros, Sierra Leone, and the Ivory Coast, the OAU's presence was either not very visible or for the most part ignored. In April, leaders of European and African states met under the auspices of the European Union (E.U.) and the OAU in Cairo. In the first summit of its kind, participants discussed human rights, good governance, trade, illegal arms, debt relief, and other issues. A Civil Society Forum scheduled to take place prior to the summit was blocked at the last minute. Convened by the North-South Center, the gathering was moved to Libson, which diminished its potential impact on the summit. The OAU's apparent silencing of civil society groups weakened its credibility as an organization committed to the promotion of democracy. African nations had hoped to make economic issues a priority at the conference, particularly the issue of debt relief. The E.U. decided to remove trade barriers to Africa, but refused to establish new measures to address Africa's burgeoning debt. The summit resulted in the 110-point Cairo Declaration, which included an affirmation of the promotion of human rights, but no new initiatives for their protection.

The thirty-sixth annual OAU summit held in Lomé, Togo, in July symbolized the organization's desire to move toward greater unity despite deep divisions. During a summit in Syrte, Libya, the previous year, the OAU issued a declaration committing itself to the establishment of an African union. The aims of the union included the promotion of stability, political and economic integration, and solidarity between countries. Twenty-seven of the thirty-three member states that attended the Lomé summit signed a draft of the African Union Treaty, and it was expected that two-thirds of OAU member states would have ratified the treaty by the next year's summit. This step toward greater unity was however overshadowed by several countries' boycott of the summit. Angola's president, José Eduardo dos Santos, asked that the summit's venue be moved to Addis Ababa after Togolese President Gnassingbe Eyadema was implicated in diamond and arms trafficking with UNITA by a U.N. report. As host of the summit, Eyadema stood to inherit the chair of the OAU for the upcoming year. Ignoring both Angola's request and a recommendation by Robert Fowler, head of the Security Council sanctions committee, to avoid holding conferences in sanctions-busting states, the OAU decided to keep the summit in Togo. Namibia and the DRC expressed solidarity with Angola and also boycotted the summit. During the summit, OAU members extended support for the efforts of the Angolan government to restore peace, while condemning UNITA for its violent actions in Angola.

The summit sought to address current crises as well as those from the past. Initiatives were proposed to investigate the illegal trade of conflict diamonds and the resumption of fighting in Sierra Leone. A mini-summit was held among West African leaders, U.N. Secretary-General Kofi Annan, and the executive secretary of ECOWAS to discuss the continuing hostilities in Sierra Leone. The absence of Angola, the DRC, and Namibia prevented a mini-summit from being held to discuss the conflict in the DRC. The OAU members also voted to enact a maritime blockade on Anjouan to discourage its secession efforts from the Comoros. Perhaps grabbing the most international attention was a report released by the OAU's International Panel of Eminent Personalities demanding the payment of "significant reparations" by countries that failed to prevent the 1994 genocide in Rwanda. Belgium, France, and the United States were specifically mentioned as guilty of inaction, along with the U.N. Security Council. The report also called for attention to alleged war crimes by the Rwandan Patriotic Front during the genocide.

In many countries in Africa, the OAU's efforts to restore peace and stability had little or no result. In 1999, OAU Secretary General Salim Ahmed Salim had "morally guaranteed" the Lomé peace agreement for Sierra Leone, which included a blanket amnesty for all abuses committed prior to its conclusion. Since then, the agreement had been torn to shreds as fighting had resumed and human rights abuses were rampant. In June, the OAU named a special envoy to Sierra Leone in hopes of enhancing its efforts to end the conflict. A delegation in Freetown pressed for a cease-fire but President Kabbah stated he would not comply until the rebels had returned the areas seized since the signing of the Lomé Accord. Since many of these areas include diamond mines, the fighting continued with no signs of stopping. In August, OAU chair Gnassingbe Eyadema called for a change in the U.N. monitoring force's mandate from one of peace enforcement to peacekeeping. The African Commission on Human and Peoples' Rights sent a delegation led by the commission's chair, EVO Dankwa of Ghana, to Freetown in February 2000, after strong lobbying from NGOs attending the commission's October 1999 session in Kigali. The delegation, continuing a tradition of ineffective missions by the OAU organ, met with no victims and almost no local human rights groups, did not go outside of Freetown, and produced no written report of its findings or recommendations.

After leaving the construction and implementation of the Lusaka Accord for the DRC in the hands of Zambian President Chiluba, who was representing the Southern African Development Community (SADC), the OAU appointed Sir Ketumile Masire to be the facilitator of an internal dialogue on the future of the DRC. Throughout the year, the accord was repeatedly violated and an internal dialogue never materialized. President Laurent Kabila rejected Masire on the grounds he was biased toward rebel groups. Despite the OAU's repeated calls for a cease-fire, all parties continued to engage in fighting. After a regional leaders' summit sponsored by SADC was held in August, Kabila suspended the implementation of the peace accord and called for direct negotiations with Rwanda, Uganda, and Burundi, to be overseen by the U.N. and OAU. At this writing, no movement had been made in that direction.

The situation in the Comoros provided an excellent example of the OAU's efforts being largely ignored. The OAU had sought to defuse the Anjouan island secession crisis in the Indian Ocean republic for three years. In April 1999, Colonel Azali Assoumani staged a bloodless coup and established a military government. Assoumani refused to hold elections until the secession attempt was ended. The OAU repeatedly criticized the coup and Assoumani's unwillingness to hold democratic elections. Early in the year, the OAU increased pressure on Anjouan separatists by enacting a travel embargo and

freezing the financial assets of the leaders. Assoumani asserted that the OAU had failed to resolve the crisis and Comorans could find a solution themselves. In August, the military government and Anjouan separatists held talks, which resulted in an agreement ending the secession attempt. The OAU criticized the agreement because its formation did not include the input of a majority of the Comoran people, and failed to adhere to the framework established by the 1999 OAU brokered reunification accord. Despite OAU condemnation of the agreement for threatening the unity of the Comoros, the military regime and Anjouan separatists called for the OAU to lift its trade and travel embargo.

The OAU condemned General Robert Guei's coup in Côte d'Ivoire and called for elected president Henri Konan Bedie to be reinstated. Guei refused to step down, but declared that elections would be held in October. Staying true to its decision that military juntas would not be allowed to participate in the OAU, Guei was banned from this year's summit. At its summit in July, the OAU created the "Group of Ten" to ensure that the upcoming governmental transition in the Côte d'Ivoire was peaceful. The group consisted of Togo, South Africa, Algeria, Burkina Faso, Djibouti, Gabon, Ghana, Mali, Nigeria, and Senegal. At the end of September, the Group of Ten called upon Guei and the leaders of political parties to form a National Transitional Council to guide the country toward peaceful elections. The OAU also requested that presidential elections be postponed until legislative elections had taken place. There were mixed reactions to the group's proposal among the political leaders in Côte d'Ivoire. As of this writing, the OAU's requests remained ignored.

The International Response

Trapped in The Basement Of Global Priorities?

There was little new movement in international policy on African issues. As the international community seemed reconciled to the notion that Africa was locked in a permanent pattern of annihilation and turbulence, big powers seemed unprepared to elevate the plight of millions of Africans trapped by conflict and human rights abuse to a global priority. The year opened on a high note and witnessed a flurry of activity: hectic agendas and rounds of announcements; high-powered delegations traversing the continent; commissions galore examining and reexamining urgent issues; declarations and resolutions continued to be churned out; reports and documents adorned with the habitual exhortations and reaffirmations of lofty visions continued to be released. But real action that could curb cataclysmic trends if rhetoric was matched by commitment inched forward at a snail's pace. When it came to the pivotal issue of funding, major players resorted to fudging, making no commitments, only "options to consider." As a result, it became predictable that once again pledges would be unfulfilled.

The United Nations' Strategic Ghetto

The year 2000 was inauspicious for the United Nations in Africa, although it aimed much of its official rhetoric toward the continent and its current activities there. This increase in rhetoric was not matched with a comparable increase of financial support or other resources. The woes of the U.N. in Africa, especially its peacekeeping missions, seemed to represent system-wide failures of the U.N. Furthermore, the major powers were reluctant to intervene in Africa under U.N. supervision and the forces of the countries that took part in peacekeeping missions were often ill-trained and ill-equipped. While the U.N. and the Security Council no longer treated Africa with the indifference that it did during the early 1990s, it clearly failed to address African issues with the material resources they so desperately needed.

The U.N. engaged in a rare bout of self-criticism at the close of 1999. The Report on the Genocide in Rwanda severely condemned the lackadaisical manner in which the Security Council treated Rwanda, due to its and Africa's marginalized status within the international community. The report, released on December 16, 1999, declared that, "the Security Council, led unremittingly by the United States, simply did not care enough about Rwanda to intervene appropriately." The report went on to denounce the Security Council's tragic decision to reduce UNAMIR in the face of killings, rather than to try to muster political will to try and stop them. Ultimately, "[The Security Council's] refusal to sanction a serious mission made the genocide more likely." In response to the report, Secretary-General Kofi Annan called for more effective U.N. engagement in Africa and better coordination between the Security Council and regional organizations.

As if in response to these views, the United States representative to the U.N., Richard Holbrooke, used the U.S. stint as president of the Security Council to lead the U.N. to focus its attention on Africa during January 2000. Undertakings were made that the U.N. would lead from the front in addressing Africa's problems and make Africa safe for human rights and dignity. The Security Council held meetings on the effects of HIV and AIDS in Africa, the growing problems of refugees and internally displaced persons in the continent, and the conflicts in Angola, Burundi, and the Democratic Republic of the Congo, which U.S. Secretary of State Madeleine Albright called "Africa's First World War."

The issue of AIDS in Africa received additional attention during the month, as the United States declared it a national security threat, the first time a health issue had been linked to national security in the United States and within the Security Council. Annan declared that the impact of AIDS on Africa was no less destructive than that of warfare itself, and many speakers called for the conspiracy of silence about AIDS to end. Dr. Peter Piot, director of UNAIDS, noted that roughly U.S. $1-$3 billion was needed to sustain and expand these campaigns. What happened after the ringing speeches? Only a tiny fraction of that total sum had been raised at this writing. Moreover, the international community continued to be less and less responsive to Africa's refugee and IDP emergencies. Food deliveries were curtailed during the year and relief programs for Africa remained drastically underfunded. For example, UNHCR programs throughout West Africa faced a U.S.$27 million funding shortfall in an overall budget of U.S.$77 million. Similarly, in Tanzania, which hosted the largest number of refugees in Africa, refugee food rations were cut in September due to insufficient funding. The international community's lack of response to African crises continued to contrast sharply with its generous and relatively speedy response to alleviate the suffering of displaced persons in 1999 during the humanitarian crises in Kosovo and East Timor.

The Millennium Summit, held in New York September 6-8, 2000, gave world leaders another opportunity to convey their concern and interests in Africa affairs. Following closely after the release of the Brahimi report, which scrutinized U.N. peace and security operations, the Security Council in resolution 1318 decided unanimously to overhaul U.N. peacekeeping operations to create a more effective and better-financed force "by adopting clearly defined, credible, achievable and appropriate mandates." The Brahimi report, released on August 17, 2000, criticized the concept of impartiality, which had guided U.N. peacekeeping efforts in the past that had led to the failure to distinguish between the victim and the aggressor. In addition, the report demanded that peacekeeping missions should specify orders to use force to better serve as a credible deterrent, a veiled reference to the U.N. peacekeeping mission debacle in Sierra Leone. The report also noted that "spoilers" of peace accords tended to be those with access to funds to supply weapons, a reference to the illicit trade in diamonds that supported continued fighting in Angola, the DRC, and Sierra Leone. Resolution 1318 pledged to enhance the effectiveness of the U.N. in addressing all stages of the conflict, reaffirmed its determination to give special attention to the promotion of durable peace and sustainable development in Africa given the specific characteristics of African conflicts, and emphasized the importance of continued cooperation and effective coordination between the U.N., the OAU, and African sub-regional organizations in addressing conflicts in Africa.

As part of this trend, Secretary-General Annan's Millennium Report urged developed nations to make special provisions for the needs of Africa, to fully support Africans in their struggle to overcome the continent's problems, and to curb the illegal traffic in small arms by supporting regional disarmament measures. Despite the renewed focus on Africa, many African leaders felt that not enough was being done within the Security Council to address African issues, quickly or effectively. South Africa's President Thabo Mbeki stated, "Our collective rhetoric conveys promise. Our offense is that our actions convey the message that we do not care." Indeed very little had been accomplished by the peace and security operations in Africa between January and September. Overall, the U.N. remained as ill-prepared for the next big crisis as it was for the last.

Following two years of fighting between Ethiopia and Eritrea, the United Nations established UNMEE, the United Nations Mission in Ethiopia and Eritrea, when a new outbreak of hostilities erupted. A severe drought in the Horn of Africa had affected roughly ten million people in the region, which the fighting exacerbated, causing a severe humanitarian crisis, and the Security Council called on the OAU to immediately initiate peace talks between the countries. On June 18, 2000, the foreign ministers of both countries signed an Agreement on Cessation of Hostilities under the auspices of the OAU, with representatives from the United Kingdom and the United States present. The following month the Security Council passed Resolution 1312, which called for one hundred military observers to be sent to the region to verify the cessation of hostilities between the two countries in order to prepare for a larger peacekeeping mission. On September 15, Security Council Resolution 1320 authorized the deployment of up to 4,200 troops until March 1, 2001 to monitor the cease-fire agreement. Although the security conditions improved, as Annan noted in a report on September 18, the humanitarian issues caused by the drought were still a cause for serious concern.

Combat and tension continued to plague the DRC, despite the Lusaka peace agreement signed by the government of the DRC, five neighboring countries, and one of the two main rebel groups in July of 1999. The disengagement plan hammered out by the United Nations and a joint military commission drawn from the governments and the factions involved provided that the belligerents should start simultaneously withdrawing their forces forty kilometers (twenty-five miles) from the frontline within weeks. But there was little evidence to validate the optimistic messages by the U.N. that the ceasefire was holding. Although Security Council Resolution 1279 extended the mandate of MONUC in November 1999, authorizing five hundred U.N. military observers to the region, fighting continued between government troops and rebel groups in the eastern region of the country. Some members of the Security Council, specifically the United States and Great Britain, did not want U.N. troops in the region while fighting continued, further delaying the deployment of U.N. troops to the country. Security Council Resolution 1291 expanded MONUC to 5,537 soldiers in February 2000, to monitor the implementation of the cease-fire agreement and to supervise the disengagement and redeployment of troops. The whole concept of MONUC seemed to have been founded more on hope than experience. Many analysts doubted its viability, given the impossibility of protecting civilians in the huge country with such a small force. At this writing, U.N. optimism had waned considerably, though MONUC's mandate was extended by a further two months in October 2000. There seemed to be a real chance that MONUC would simply wither and die.

U.N. High Commissioner for Human Rights Mary Robinson visited eastern Congo for three days in early October to meet with the leadership of the Congolese Rally for Democracy (RCD), local human rights activists, and representatives of U.N. agencies working in the country. Upon her return, she pledged to make the humanitarian situation within the DRC a higher priority for the U.N.

The peacekeeping mission in Sierra Leone illustrated many of the structural flaws that hindered the effectiveness of the United Nations. Since the inception of UNAMSIL in October of 1999, officials in charge of the mission appeared unable to address the most basic security issues or cooperate among themselves. Besides the U.N.'s inability to protect its own staff, UNAMSIL's most egregious failure was its inability to protect civilians in the face of increasing human rights violations, a clear failure to fulfill its mandate. In May, the killing of at least ten and the capture of roughly five hundred U.N. peacekeepers forced the U.N. to reassess its role in Sierra Leone and the future of U.N. peacekeeping missions in Africa. Even the successful rescue of the U.N. hostages in July and the SLA capture of the notorious leader of the RUF, Foday Sankoh, in May did little to repair the public image of UNAMSIL. Contributing countries were reluctant to continue supporting a costly and seemingly doomed peacekeeping mission. At the end of September, the Indian government announced its intention to withdraw its troops from UNAMSIL; its 3,059 troops made up one quarter of the 12,477 troops and were the best equipped. The Indian commander, Major General Vijay Jetley, had engaged in a public row with leaders from Nigeria, the largest troop contributor to UNAMSIL, accusing them of undermining the operation and doing business with the RUF in diamond mining operations. He also upbraided the Jordanian troops for collaborating with dissident former government soldiers known as the West Side Boys, by giving them supplies. Jetley was criticized for his treatment of soldiers from other nations under his command and his lack of communication with other military and political leaders during the hostage crisis in May. Following India's decision, Jordan reportedly decided that it did not want its troops to remain in Sierra Leone unless a NATO country was persuaded to play a significant role in the U.N. force. Additionally, the U.N. was unwilling to stiffen its mandate from peacekeeping to peacemaking, although it continued to increase the troop size of the mission. On August 4, UNAMSIL's mandate was expanded and its authorized troop presence was increased in successive resolutions; from the original six thousand in October 1999 to thirteen thousand in May. In September, the secretary general recommended that the troop strength be further increased to 20,500.

The United Nations Security Council agreed on August 14 to set up a war crimes tribunal for Sierra Leone to try crimes against humanity, war crimes, and other serious violations of international humanitarian law, as well as crimes under relevant Sierra Leone law committed within its territory. But the measure stopped short of actually establishing the court or deciding its composition and functions. The sticking point seemed to be how the authority of the court should be shared between Sierra Leone's judicial system and neutral international experts. The Security Council asked the secretary-general to address these and other questions and produce a detailed blueprint for the court within thirty days. The blueprint—a draft statute for the special court—was published in October. The provisions regarding the court's jurisdiction, competence, fair trial guarantees, rules of procedure, and evidence all seemed to be satisfactory to assure that the court would receive a broad mandate to prosecute those responsible for the atrocities, that it would be backed by a strong international presence. The report that accompanied the draft statute emphasized the need for adequate funds.

Nevertheless, concerns remained as to whether the court would be free from political manipulation, and would try not only Sankoh and his comrades but also leaders of other fighting factions, including those supporting the government, who had committed heinous crimes against humanity. A struc-ture that failed to establish a broad-based justice would in the long run gravely undermine a strong and impartial rule of law that would be essential to sustainable recovery. In addition, the Statute would limit the temporal jurisdiction of the court to crimes committed since November 1996, yet unspeakable crimes were committed from the inception of the war in 1991.

One of the main causes of fighting in the DRC and Sierra Leone was the illegal diamonds-for-arms trades that rebel groups, as well as external allies, used to sustain continued fighting. Diamonds played a pivotal role in funding the fighting between the government and the RUF rebels in Sierra Leone. In recognition of this link, the Security Council passed Resolution 1306, which banned imports of rough diamonds from Sierra Leone for the next eighteen months, except those diamonds that were certified by the government. It also called for a five-person panel to examine sanctions violations and the link between trade in diamonds and small arms in Africa, with observations and recommendations to be presented by October 31, 2000.

In Resolution 1237, the Security Council decided to establish an independent inquiry into the breaking of sanctions against Angola's UNITA, which prohibited the sale or delivery of arms, military equipment, and petroleum products, and most importantly, the purchase of diamonds mined in areas controlled by UNITA. On March 10, the Report of the Panel of Experts on Violations of Security Council Sanctions Against UNITA was released; it was a ground breaking report in that it openly named sanction-breakers and established its own sources for information and investigation. The report cited two African presidents, Gnassingbe Eyadema of Togo and Blaise Compaore of Burkina Faso, who openly broke the sanctions to aid UNITA, while it said President Omar Bongo of Gabon supplied UNITA with large amounts of fuel.

The report explicitly linked UNITA with the diamond-for-arms trade, stating that, "Diamonds had a uniquely important role within UNITA's political and military economy. UNITA's ongoing ability to sell rough diamonds for cash and to exchange rough diamonds for weapons provide the means for it to sustain its political and military activities." The Security Council approved the report and called for tougher measurers to restrict UNITA access to diamonds, fuel and arms. By July, the Security Council declared that UNITA's conventional war capacity had been destroyed and no longer posed an immediate threat to the Angolan government, citing UNITA's increasing difficulty in selling diamonds on the international market as a dominant factor in addition to rebel territorial losses on the battlefield. The writing of the report signaled the Security Council's growing interest in the illegal trading activities of UNITA and its supporters and became a deterrent to those that would break the U.N. sanctions against UNITA.

The report made thirty-nine recommendations, including that the Security Council should apply sanctions to those governments, officials, and enterprises that break sanctions against UNITA, and that the diamond certificate of origin system should be reformed. Despite its strong stance against sanction-busters and innovative and reasonable recommendations, the Experts Panel suffered from the lack of a centralized office to coordinate its work, not involving Interpol in its efforts, and by the failure of member states to share intelligence with the panel.

Badgered by the controversy regarding "conflict diamonds," De Beers Consolidated Mines, the dominant force in the international diamond industry, in July announced a radical shift from its seventy-year marketing strategy of manipulating prices by stockpiling to a new one of selling diamonds as branded luxuries. Essentially, the new strategy seemed to be a defensive response to protect De Beers' product from being tainted by conflict. Also in July, the International Diamond Manufacturers' Association and the World Federation of Diamond Bourses, meeting at the World Diamond Congress in Antwerp, adopted a global certification scheme for rough diamonds in order to identify conflict diamonds. The congress also agreed that all rough diamonds would have to be shipped in sealed packages certified by the authorities in the exporting nations and verified by a new international diamond council, and that countries knowingly involved in illegal diamond trading should lose their export accreditation. Both De Beers and the congress pledged that they would cooperate with the United Nations to help curb illegal trade in diamonds. These were important announcements, but the fundamental issue remained verification. In the absence of an independent monitoring regime-nagging questions would persist.

European Union, Norway, and the Donor Community

As in previous years, the European Union (E.U.) and the international donor community in general remained almost exclusively concerned with corruption and economic reform issues at the expense of civil and political rights concerns—and in seeming indifference too to economic, social, and cultural rights. It was still evident that policies were driven by the "full belly" thesis that civil and political rights were luxuries that could be put aside until the economy reached a certain degree of success. As a result of the compartmentalization approach, little progress was made in tackling the core issues—authoritarianism, arbitrariness and brutalization of politics—at the heart of Africa's political and human rights crises. International donor policy also continued to be undermined by the recurrent problem of inconsistency and double standards in the application of aid and human rights policies. For example, during 2000, donors demonstrated far less enthusiasm and determination in championing human rights issues in Burkina Faso, Ethiopia, Guinea, Eritrea, Kenya, Rwanda, Swaziland, Uganda, or Zambia than in their approach regarding the issue of good governance and human rights in Zimbabwe, the Democratic Republic of Congo, or Liberia. This tended to reinforce the perception that human rights was a tool used by donors against their "enemies" and ignored in respect of their "friends."

The largest aid and trade agreement between developed and developing countries, the fourth Lomé Convention, expired in February 2000. A new, more ambitious twenty-year partnership agreement was signed in June in Cotonou, Benin, between the E.U. and seventy-seven countries from Africa, the Caribbean, and the Pacific (the ACP bloc). The Cotonou Convention, replacing Lomé, included a clause stipulating that individual countries that were seriously corrupt would face sanctions, including the withholding of aid. A new procedure was also foreseen for consultation and the adoption of measures where human rights, democratic principles, and the rule of law were violated, placing the primary responsibility with the state concerned to take measures to rectify the situation. A separate Trade, Development, and Cooperation Agreement between the E.U. and South Africa (which, as a middle-income country, did not qualify for full Lomé/Cotonou terms) was also agreed upon in February 2000, cutting tariffs and liberalizing trade, after years of negotiations.

The Portuguese presidency of the E.U. during the first six month of the year promised particular attention to deepening cooperation with the African continent. But apart from the African-European Summit in Cairo on April 3-4, 2000, little was delivered. The summit itself was fairly neutral on human rights concerns save for a formal declaration that the parties "recognize the need to provide for greater inclusion of civil society in all areas of our partnership. In this context, we emphasize the need for greater participation of the citizen in decision-making concerning the management and the allocation of resources, whilst respecting the diverse and complementary roles of the State, decentralized local authorities and the other society actors concerned."

Otherwise the priority issue for the African participants was debt relief, and they seemed to have given short shrift to human rights and related governance issues.

France took the E.U. presidency during the second half of 2000, promising a follow-up to the Cairo Conference and proposing that priority be given to developing dialogue with the sub-regional organizations. But the French E.U. presidency remained relatively muted on virtually all the major flashpoints in Africa, with the exception of Ivory Coast. France's reaction to the coup in that country was read as evidence that France would no longer unconditionally support loyal but corrupt incumbents in its former colonies. France did not intervene to save Ivory Coast's president, Henri Konan Bedie, whose party reportedly cheated in the 1995 presidential elections and had arbitrarily changed the constitution to thwart his main rival. Analysts observed that if France did not intervene in the Ivory Coast, their most important economic partner in Africa, it was unlikely that they would do so to support the likes of Omar Bongo of Gabon or President Gnassingbe Eyadema of Togo. France also lashed out at General Guei's government of the Ivory Coast, following the barring of Ouattara from the presidential polls.

Britain's involvement in Africa was most dramatically marked by its armed intervention in Sierra Leone, following the collapse of the Lomé peace process in May 2000. British paratroopers were deployed after hundreds of U.N. peacekeepers were taken hostage by the RUF. The troops evacuated British nationals and established a sense of stability in the country. Britain provided U.N. forces with intelligence and logistical support, along with training and equipment. In September, eleven British troops were taken hostage and a rescue team was deployed to free them. Hundreds of British forces remained stationed in Sierra Leone throughout the year, but under a bilateral agreement with the Sierra Leonean government, not under U.N. command. Their primary responsibility was to train a reconstituted Sierra Leonean army.

Following its high level of engagement in Sierra Leone, Britain took a leading role in the international community's response to the use of conflict diamonds in fueling wars in Africa. In June, the British government introduced a draft U.N. Security Council resolution banning the trade of diamonds from Sierra Leone which were not certified by the government. In June Peter Hain, minister of the Foreign and Commonwealth Office, hosted a meeting of officials from diamond importing and marketing countries.

Next to the war in Sierra Leone, Britain was most outspoken with regard to the violence associated with Zimbabwe's presidential election and land redistribution there. Throughout the year, Britain criticized President Robert Mugabe's government for failing to uphold rule of law in the country. In May, Britain placed a national arms embargo on Zimbabwe because of the possibility that imported weapons would be used in the conflict in the DRC. Zimbabwe demanded that Britain fund its land reform in accordance with the 1979 Lancaster House independence agreement. However, the British government stated it would only finance a land redistribution policy that adhered to the transparent principles agreed upon during an international land conference in 1998.

The Netherlands, Sweden, and Norway maintained their tradition of engagement with Africa. All three countries froze or suspended government-to-government aid to Zimbabwe on the basis of good governance concerns, and to Ethiopia and Eritrea, as a result of the ongoing hostilities between the duo. Assistance to NGOs continued, often focusing on human rights and democratization programs. Denmark, however, continued its development assistance to Zimbabwe and Eritrea on the grounds that there was a greater chance of promoting democracy and human rights through development partnership and dialogue. All four countries also maintained their high profile on human rights and governance issues in dialoguing with African governments. However, Uganda, Zambia, and Ethiopia seemed to get gentler treatment than Zimbabwe or Eritrea. Moreover, economic interests could trump human rights concerns. Once Norwegian oil firms obtained lucrative footholds in

Angola's ultradeep offshore fields, Norwegian comment on Luanda's human rights abuses became muted. The Netherlands government agreed to send some seven hundred peacekeepers to the Horn of Africa to take part in the United Nations mission to monitor the cease-fire agreement that ended the war between Ethiopia and Eritrea.

Making bold pledges about debt relief turned out to be easier than acting upon them. Despite the high sounding declarations at the 1999 June Cologne Group of Seven (G-7) summit to enhance coordinated efforts to "support deeper, broader and fast debt relief," by mid-2000 only nine African countries had experienced any reduction in their debt payments—way off the G-7 target of writing off U.S.$100 billion of debt by the end of 2000. To help breathe new life into international debt relief efforts, Britain in July announced a special plan to provide extra money to help countries that stopped fighting and instead used their resources to combat poverty. Ahead of the G-7 summit, the E.U. and the ACP group agreed a deal to allow the release of U.S.$1.04 billion for global debt relief for the world's poorest countries. In its communiqué at the Okinawa summit, the G-7 conceded that the dilemmas of debt, health, and education were inextricably linked, and the heart of the economic difficulties facing the poorest countries. The Okinawa communiqué also for the first time addressed the need to combat diseases. It set three global targets to be achieved by 2010: to reduce the number of HIV infected young people by 25 percent; to reduce tuberculosis deaths, and prevalence of the disease, by 50 percent; and to reduce malaria by 50 percent.

China

In October 2000, nearly eighty ministers of foreign and economic affairs from forty-four African countries assembled in Beijing for the first China-Africa cooperation forum. China, making a fresh bid to emerge as a leader of the developing world, and building on a six-nation African tour undertaken by President Jiang Zemin in 1996, promised debt relief and business deals to those attending. In a passage clearly aimed at human rights interventions of the sort undertaken by NATO in Kosovo, the communiqué declared that "no country or group of countries has the right to impose its will on others, to interfere, under whatever pretext, in other countries' internal affairs, or to impose unilateral coercive economic measures on others." While affirming the universality of human rights, the communiqué went on to state that "Each country has the right to choose, in its course of development, its own social system, development model and way of life in light of its national conditions. Countries, that vary from one another in social systems, stages of development, historical and cultural background and values, have the right to choose their own approaches and models in promoting and protecting human rights in their own countries. Moreover, the politicisation of human rights and the imposition of human rights conditionalities on economic assistance should be vigorously opposed to as they constitute a violation of human rights."

U.S. Policy Towards Africa

The United States dedicated its month as president of the Security Council, January 2000, to African crises. During this "Month of Africa," various issues were discussed, from the refugee situation to the crises in Burundi and the Democratic Republic of Congo. This emphasis on Africa was reinforced by President Clinton's trip to Nigeria and Tanzania at the end of August—an unprecendented second visit to the continent. But these interventions only obscured a lack of commitment to promoting human rights and accountability when dealing with crises in Africa. The Clinton administration did make strides in bringing African issues into more mainstream U.S. policy, as exhibited by the record number of U.S. government agencies engaged in Africa, although African issues rarely galvanized high-level attention. In crisis after crisis, the administration continually failed to integrate human rights into its policies on economic development and regional security. Although a

rhetoric of human rights concerns remained on the U.S. agenda, trade and economic concerns as well as international terrorism continued to take precedence over human rights. While administration officials rarely mentioned their prior emphasis on Africa's "new leaders" or their support for the Lomé Accord ending the Sierra Leone peace process despite its blanket amnesty, the effects of these short-sighted policies were seen in the diminished credibility of U.S. Africa policy.

During his 1999 trip to Africa, Clinton avoided Nigeria as a sign of disapproval of its military dictatorship. Yet as he praised Nigeria's transition to a democracy in August 2000, Clinton's rhetoric focused more heavily on economic growth than human rights. Rewarding Nigeria for its democratic accomplishments, the U.S. promised to quadruple aid to the country. The U.S. also promised funding to build partnerships between the U.S. government, Nigerian government, oil companies, and the residents of the oil-producing areas in the hopes of resolving the ongoing conflict affecting oil production. Central to his visit, however, was Clinton's appeal to the Nigerian government to increase oil production in order to drive down world oil prices, then at an all-time high. After leaving Nigeria, Clinton visited Tanzania to witness the signing of the Burundi Peace Agreement. Prior to his visit, Clinton had sent a special envoy to Burundi to support the mediation effort. However, the U.S. did not push for prompt, effective justice to punish serious crimes committed during the war as part of the peace process.

After the United Kingdom, the U.S. made the greatest efforts to engage with the crises in Sierra Leone. The U.S. condemned the taking of U.N. hostages by the RUF rebels and asked that they be released, but did not commit to any actions against the RUF. The U.S. also discussed with the U.N. the prospect of expanding the rapid reaction force to Sierra Leone, but remained reluctant to put its troops at risk, and would not commit personnel for peacekeeping operations. Instead, the U.S. undertook the task of training and equipping additional battalions of Nigerian peacekeepers. In the Security Council, the U.S. was a leading force behind efforts to establish a special tribunal for Sierra Leone. It also pledged support for a Truth and Reconciliation Commission, as well as creating a reintegration program to train and educate rebel soldiers.

The U.S. also took the initiative with efforts to eradicate the use of illicit diamonds to fuel civil wars in Africa, declaring support for tighter measures to control the diamond sectors in all affected countries and in the international diamond trade, but warned that those efforts should not damage the markets of stable, democratic, diamond-producing states. The U.S. provided technical and financial support in the establishment of the Sierra Leone Commission on the Management of Strategic Resources, which was supposedly responsible for the management of the country's diamond sector. In July, representatives from the United States, United Kingdom, Belgium and the Diamond High Council met with officials in Sierra Leone to establish a diamond certification scheme in hopes of limiting the amount of RUF-controlled diamonds that made their way into the market. At this writing, Congress was hearing testimony on a bill that would block the import of conflict diamonds into the United States. With regard to illicit diamonds in Angola, the U.S. supported a U.N. resolution strengthening the implementation of sanctions against UNITA in an effort to further limit the export of diamonds and import of military supplies. There was disapproval expressed during the year over the unsafe environment for the press in Angola. However, such efforts were greatly outweighed by much more forthright lobbying of U.S. economic interests, and official criticism of other Angolan government rights abuses was muted by its embassy in Luanda. In addition, the Clinton administration encouraged the government to find a peaceful solution to the country's civil war. Reacting to the continuing humanitarian disaster, the U.S. committed U.S.$38 million to support humanitarian relief efforts and an additional U.S.$2 million for UNHCR assistance programs in northern Angola.

The U.S. expressed repeated concern over the Sudanese government's bombings of civilian targets, especially in areas where relief efforts were being conducted. The United States' engagement increased with the appointment of a special U.S. envoy who traveled to Khartoum to discuss reducing human rights abuses, improving humanitarian response, and renewing regional peace efforts. The United States continued to assert that the IGAD peace initiative offered the best hope of ending the war.

In March, the U.S. sent a special envoy on a two-week mission to support the mediation efforts of the OAU in the Ethiopia-Eritrea conflict. However, brokering the peace agreement largely fell on the shoulders of the OAU, despite its recent history of close relations with both Ethiopia and Eritrea. The U.S. supported a U.N. resolution to establish a mission in Ethiopia and Eritrea consisting of one hundred military observers until January 31, 2001. The U.S. condemned the coup in Ivory Coast and the exclusion there of many of the candidates in the presidential elections slated for October. All bilateral assistance and arms transfers were suspended until democracy was restored.

The U.S. position regarding HIV/AIDS in Africa advanced appreciably this year. The U.S. signed a U.S. $10 million agreement with the Southern African Community to fund a variety of programs, one of them an assessment of the impact of HIV/AIDS on sexual development. The Clinton Administration promised to request U.S.$332 million over the next two years to combat HIV/AIDS in Africa and globally. The U.S. also announced an HIV/AIDS awareness and prevention program in Angola that would cost U.S. $3 million over three years. The U.S. introduced a resolution in the U.N. that would allow for voluntary testing and AIDS education for U.N. peacekeepers. However, in July, the U.S. announced that U.S. $1 billion in annual loans to finance the purchase of anti-AIDS drugs would be available to countries in sub-Saharan Africa. Many

African nations responded coolly to the proposal, expressing concern that the loans would just add to their debt burden.

The U.S. promoted a plan to the G-7, which was designed to provide up to U.S. $90 billion in additional debt relief to developing countries. The primary beneficiaries would be African countries. In addition, the U.S. pledged U.S. $500 million in debt relief and an additional U.S. $120 million toward the promotion of democracy. But for all the soaring speeches and high-blown sentiment, performance fell far short of the expectations generated. The House of Representatives approved funding for debt relief to meet the Clinton administration's request of U.S. $225 million, but the measure flopped as the U.S. Senate bill earmarked a paltry U.S. $75 million for debt.

Despite high expectations that the year 2000 would bring greater international attention and resources to Africa, the major international powers remained at the sidelines during the worst episodes of human rights abuses and violations. Starting in January, the United Nations and the United States pledged greater levels of interest and support in African affairs, and vowed to do more to help their African counterparts. Africa had never garnered this much attention from the international community and its prospects for growth and development seemed brighter. However, as little was done during the year to fulfill these bold pledges, it very quickly became evident that business would remain as usual for Africa in the international arena. Furthermore, E.U. and U.S. policies lacked the desired balance between economic rights on the one hand and political and civil rights on the other, while the United Nations was unable to ameliorate any of the devastating conflicts that continued to plague the continent. The slow pace of debt relief promised by the United States and the E.U. did little to alleviate the health and education issues that burdened many African countries, nor did it appear that the pace of debt relief would increase in the near future. Moreover, the international community failed not only on its pledges for African development and debt relief, but accomplished very little in stemming the spread of AIDS despite the havoc that the pandemic was wreaking across Africa. Ultimately, numerous statements to the contrary notwithstanding, it remained clear that Africa was a low priority for the United States, the E.U. and to some extent, the United Nations. Africa remained trapped in the basement of global priorities.

The Work of Human Rights Watch

Human Rights Watch continued to focus on identifying the root causes of deplorable human rights violations in Africa. Human Rights Watch also dedicated significant resources toward improving relationships with local human rights groups and exploring ways of working together.

Human Rights Watch stepped up a three-track approach to expanding cooperation with local African nongovernmental organizations, striving to develop relationships with them based on interdependence, long-term commitment, and solidarity. A key strategic goal was to increase local NGOs' influence throughout the human rights movement in Africa by facilitating their access to Human Rights Watch's wide range of expertise.

First, in the context of massive human rights violations in the Great Lakes area, Human Rights Watch implemented a Great Lakes NGO field initiative to strengthen the research, networking, and advocacy capacity of NGOs. Second, Human Rights Watch promoted an African Fellows program that trained experienced human rights activists. The program developed the skills of those activists by exposing them to international partners, advanced research methodologies, and the international advocacy arena. Last, Human Rights Watch remained committed to protesting abuses against human rights activists in Africa.

Human Rights Watch continued to cover all of sub-Saharan Africa and expanded monitoring of French-speaking countries, but focused intensively on a nucleus of countries: Angola, Burundi, Democratic Republic of Congo, Eritrea, Ethiopia, Guinea, Kenya, Liberia, Nigeria, Mozambique,

Rwanda, Sierra Leone, South Africa, Sudan, Uganda, and Zambia. Additionally, the Africa division undertook cross-country, thematic research on arms flows, resources and corporate responsibility, national human rights commissions, the rights of children and women, refugees and the internally displaced, and prisons. Human Rights Watch maintained field offices in Kigali and Freetown—in Rwanda and Sierra Leone respectively—and created a new field office in Bujumbura, Burundi.

The Africa division fielded investigative missions to Angola, DRC, Guinea, Kenya, Liberia, Mozambique, Sierra Leone, South Africa, Sudan, Uganda, and Zambia, and also collaborated with the Arms, Children's Rights and Women's Rights divisions in their work on Angola, DRC, Kenya, Liberia, Rwanda, and Tanzania.

Concerned that noncombatants, refugees, and internally displaced persons were under severe attack, the Africa division published numerous reports and briefing documents on Angola, Burundi, DRC, Guinea, Liberia, Sierra Leone to raise international awareness.

Moreover, given the sporadic nature of high-level international attention devoted to Africa, it was especially important to ensure that Human Rights Watch policy recommendations focus on political rights issues as well as security and economics. Human Rights Watch remained active in advocating for aid conditionality at the World Bank Consultative Group (CG) meetings for Zambia. In July, Human Rights Watch launched a report at the CG meeting in Lusaka to encourage donors to continue to make balance of payments support conditional upon improvements in human rights practices. Human Rights Watch's information formed the basis of policy recommendations to guide donors' aid programs to these countries, and made clear recommendations to the governments in question.

The Africa division devoted significant resources toward advocacy during the year, especially targeting the United States and British governments, the U.N., and the E.U..

The Africa division's advocacy efforts focused on Angola, Nigeria and the crises in the Great Lakes, particularly Burundi and DRC, where it played a major role in providing information and analysis about a range of human rights abuses.

Human Rights Watch was called to testify before U.S. congressional committees on four occasions, dealing with the situation in Sudan and the ongoing crisis in the Great Lakes. Human Rights Watch held numerous briefings for congressional staff about its research and implications of U.S. policy. These analyses were also presented to administration officials on numerous occasions in official roundtables and in a series of meetings held with officials of the Department of State, the National Security Council, and the Pentagon.

In regular meetings, briefings, and submissions at the U.N., Human Rights Watch advocated for human rights. The organization continuously expressed concerns to the Security Council and the secretary-general about events in Sierra Leone. Human Rights Watch underlined the need for the U.N. to establish a criminal process to bring gross abusers of human rights to justice, to strengthen the U.N. mandate and capacity to protect civilians in Sierra Leone, and to address violations of the U.N. arms embargo by Sierra Leonean rebels. Human Rights Watch remained active in pressing the E.U., the OAU and the Commonwealth to focus on human rights issues, especially those with a bearing on Angola, DRC, Eritrea, Ethiopia, Sierra Leone, and Sudan.

Human Rights Watch focus on the need for accountability for human rights abuses stressed the need for justice at the national and international level in order to stop the cycles of violence in Africa. The Africa division worked with intergovernmental organizations, governments, and local human rights activists to compel abusers to adhere to internationally recognized human rights standards.

ANGOLA

Human Rights Developments

Angola's civil war continued. There was little sign of greater respect for human rights as the violations of the laws of war for which this conflict has been notable continued. Both the government and the rebels, the National Union for the Total Independence of Angola (UNITA), have been responsible for these violations. The number of internally displaced persons grew to an estimated 2.5 million, approximately 20 percent of the total population of Angola. Road access remained restricted throughout the country; only coastal roads and routes within security perimeters of major provincial cities were usable by humanitarian agencies. More than 70 percent of all humanitarian assistance was delivered by air because of insecurity on the roads.

An Angolan army counteroffensive pushed UNITA out of its strongholds in the central highlands of Angola in late 1999. In late October 1999, the government showed film footage of its control of the important UNITA bases at Bailundo and Andulo. Throughout late 1999 and for the first four months of 2000, the government continued to enjoy a string of successes. On December 24, government forces captured UNITA's former headquarters at Jamba. The government claimed that it had captured 200 UNITA soldiers during the fighting. It said 400 had been captured during fighting for Calai, which was taken by the Angolan Armed Forces (FAA) on December 10. The government claimed to have destroyed more than 80 percent of its fighting capacity, while seizing 15,000 tons of weapons, munitions, twenty-seven tanks, seven artillery emplacements, thirty missiles, and other equipment from the rebels.

During the first quarter of 2000, the government appeared to be in the ascendance on the battlefield and UNITA appeared disoriented, its actions limited to sporadic guerrilla attacks. As the year progressed, this changed, with UNITA adapting back to guerrilla attacks and high-profile hit-and-run ambushes on main roads. On April 30, a U.N. World Food Program convoy was attacked 85 kilometers inland from Lobito, in an area supposedly cleared of UNITA forces. The identity of the attackers remained in doubt.

The level of UNITA violence against civilians increased significantly as UNITA's tactics changed during the year. In January, as the FAA approached Chinguar town, UNITA embarked upon a killing spree, aimed at ensuring that residents would not be captured by government forces. Some 140 soldiers and civilians were reportedly killed. UNITA was also reportedly responsible for extrajudicial executions in localities such as Camaxilo in Lunda Norte, Katchiungo in Huambo, and Quimbele in Uige.

Deliberate mutilations have not been commonplace in the Angolan conflict, but the number of incidents increased during the year, with UNITA forces reportedly cutting off ears and hands. The purpose appears to have been to send a warning to others not to betray UNITA, or to attempt to flee to areas controlled by government forces. It was a response to the rebels' greater isolation and battlefield losses. Accounts of torture were not commonplace but were sufficient to suggest that the rebels used torture to attempt to extract information, especially from individuals thought to have military knowledge about the government's intentions.

UNITA increased its forcible recruitment of children and adults in its war effort. In ambushes on main roads, UNITA forces killed and looted, but also captured civilians and forced them to work for them. This appeared intended to compensate for the continued flight of people out of UNITA's grip, but violence and forced recruitment were also said to have been in retaliation for "not following orders," when UNITA demanded that residents abandon villages. Similarly, UNITA retaliated against villages who continued to cultivate land near areas that the government had recently taken over. Conscription of children continued to be commonplace with boys and girls as young as ten seized and trained as soldiers by the rebels.

Freedom of movement continued to be denied in all areas controlled by UNITA. A permit for travel even to the next village was demanded by those in command. In the central highlands, UNITA was also responsible for forced displacement as it lost or captured territory, and its forces continued to loot and destroy private property. Government officials, traditional authorities and aid workers were especially targeted during UNITA's operations. On August 9, the U.N. strongly condemned an armed attack on Catete which resulted in the deaths of a humanitarian worker and three other civilians.

After many months of negotiations, five Russian pilots were released at the Zambian border in June. However, UNITA officials said a British and a South African diamond mine worker missing after a UNITA attack in November 1998 were dead. On August 18 De Beers announced it had suspended its diamond exploration at its site in Cambulo, Lunda Norte. The announcement followed an attack by UNITA on another diamond mine near Camafuca during which seven workers were abducted and a South African security consultant killed.

In September, an armed UNITA unit destroyed a Total/Elf/Fina oil well near Soyo, in the northwest of the country. Meanwhile, a faction of the Front for the Liberation of the Cabinda Enclave (FLEC) kidnapped three Portuguese and Angolan nationals working for a construction company in Cabinda province.

There were numerous allegations of continued abuses by government forces, although these were fewer than those regarding UNITA. The government's late 1999 and early 2000 offensives included a scorched earth policy, burning villages and killing civilians, particularly in Cuando Cubango and Lunda Sul provinces. Government forces reportedly executed villagers. In at least one location in Lunda Sul, a mass grave that the government claimed was holding victims of UNITA's excesses was in all probability the result of systematic extrajudicial killings by the government.

In the central highlands, allegations of rape by government soldiers increased. Soldiers broke into houses and raped women, or raped women they encountered working in the fields. These occurrences were widespread near military camps. Rape was especially commonplace during *batidas*, house-to-house searches, when units arrived in an area, and ordered local people to collect food and non-food items for them and to help transport looted goods. Those who refused to do so were often beaten and sometimes raped. These searches and foraging operations were especially common in areas recently occupied or reoccupied by government forces, such as large areas of Bie, Huambo and Uige provinces. The U.N. reported that in June some army and local police elements were accused by local NGOs of perpetrating human rights abuses, including the killing of suspected UNITA sympathizers in Lunda Norte, Lunda Sul, Malanje, and Mexico provinces.

The renewed conflict, and accompanying human rights abuses and violations of laws of war, were fueled by new flows of arms into the country, although arms purchases by the government significantly declined. Ukraine, Russia and Israel apparently remained the government's suppliers of choice. The Israel Aircraft Industries confirmed in May that it had exported weapons worth $86.5 million to Angola since 1997, including twenty-seven aircraft. The Slovak Republic delivered a number of military aircraft in early 2000 that were purchased through an oil-backed loan. In mid-September shipments of weapons from the Ukraine were unloaded at Luanda port.

A series of United Nations embargoes on UNITA remained in force, and the U.N.'s Security Council's Sanctions Committee on Angola produced a fifty-four-page report in March on UNITA sanctions-busting. (See Arms.) It was put together by an independent ten-person Panel of Experts, mandated in May 1999 to investigate sanctions violations. The report contained detailed new information, including evidence that President Gnassingbe Eyadema of Togo and President Blaise Compaore of Burkina Faso were playing an important role in supporting UNITA. The report also documented claims that Rwanda was an important location for gunrunning and diamond trading with UNITA, and that its government had full knowledge of this and was providing protection. Libreville in Gabon has been an important refueling location for sanctions-busting planes after they had been inside UNITA areas. It was found that most of the weapons imported by UNITA were from Bulgaria. UNITA's arms were believed to be funded largely by the illicit trade in diamonds. It also appeared that UNITA has had a general aversion for banks and normal banking channels, although its leaders had used credit cards. As already noted, the Sanctions Committee found that air transport has been the lifeline to UNITA.

Both Angolan government troops and UNITA rebel forces continued to use antipersonnel mines (See the Arms Division entry below). The number of mine victims was up sharply in 1999 (from 103 in 1998 to 185 in 1999 in Luena alone). There were worrying reports that Angolans trained in humanitarian de-mining had been employed to plant new mines.

In Luanda and along the coast, areas under government control, there was greater tolerance for discussions about rights, and a slight improvement in the observance of human rights by the police, but at the same time there was an ongoing campaign of harassment against independent journalists.

The privately owned media expanded its efforts throughout the year to inform Angolans about public affairs, criticize maladministration and corruption, and voice a variety of opinions. The government responded to these efforts by using powers under the law, and also by going beyond these powers, to stifle freedom of expression. In July, the government introduced a draft media bill that advocated harsh sentences for defamation.

At least six journalists were convicted of libel or defamation by government officials after November 1999 and faced possible imprisonment. At this writing, they were all awaiting the results of appeals. As in previous years, pretrial and trial procedures failed to conform to the requirements of international human rights law.

On December 10, the directors of *Folha 8* and the privately owned weekly newspapers *Agora* and *Actual*, were ordered by the head of the Department of Selective Crimes in the National Department for Criminal Investigation (DNIC) to withhold stories they were about to publish. These concerned a report by the British organization Global Witness, saying the government had used its oil wealth corruptly. *Folha 8* and *Actual* suppressed the text of the article, leaving blank pages, and *Agora* published an article approved by the DNIC, but was forbidden to mention the police action. In contrast, the government controlled media published detailed rejections of the Global Witness report.

The Luanda Provincial Court convicted journalists Rafael Marques and Aguiar dos Santos of defaming President dos Santos on March 31. Both were sentenced to six months' and three months' imprisonment respectively and asked to pay a large fine. Both were granted bail and have appealed their sentences.

Journalists outside Luanda suffered more. Isaias Soares in Malanje and Andre Mussamo and Isidoro Natalicio in Kwanza Norte province faced harassment. Mussamo was arrested in N'dalatando on December 2, held in incommunicado detention for two weeks, and detained for a further three months. He was put on trial on May 28 for obtaining "state secrets" and revealing them. He was acquitted on June 2.

On February 18, 2000, the opposition Angolan Party for Democratic Support and Progress (PADPA) led protests against a 1,600 percent rise in the price of fuel. The president and secretary general of PADPA were arrested and accused of not obtaining official permission to demonstrate although this is not required for a peaceful assembly under Angolan law. Despite the arrests, the demonstrators protested outside the Luanda

Provincial Government buildings on February 23 and were dispersed by police who beat some of them. Police armed with rifles surrounded a second demonstration on February 24 and arrested ten of those present, including the leaders of two opposition parties. Many of the demonstrators were beaten, three of them badly. On February 25, the police apologized for the arrests. On March 11, there was another demonstration against the fuel price and against the authorities' attacks on freedom of expression and assembly. This demonstration proceeded peacefully and there were no arrests.

On March 29, the Episcopal Conference of Catholic Bishops of Angola and São Tomé and Principe issued a pastoral letter appealing to the government not to dismiss dialogue and to grant a general amnesty in order to assist national reconciliation. The bishops also appealed for a greater respect for human rights. Angolan Church leaders have since continued to seek a negotiated peace. In June, they organized a march for peace that culminated in an open-air ecumenical service in Luanda with the participation of other members of civil society and of political parties, with the exception of the ruling party and government.

The churches' advocacy on this issue resulted in a slight shift in the government position on negotiations. On June 19, President dos Santos reaffirmed the validity of the Lusaka Protocol and indicated that UNITA leader Jonas Savimbi and his supporters could be "forgiven" if they renounced war.

Defending Human Rights

Open discussion about rights abuses became more acceptable in government areas, and a range of church groups and local and international NGOs were visibly promoting the respect of human rights. Although a local NGO was launched in June that attempted to document and expose appalling prison conditions in Luanda, there was little action of this kind by other local NGOs. In December 1999, Human Rights Watch launched its report, *Angola Explicada*, in Luanda, the first ever public release of a detailed report of government and UNITA's human rights abuses in Angola. Some two hundred people, including government officials, parliamentarians, including the speaker of the national assembly, as well as diplomats, members of church groups and NGOs attended. In September, the Committee to Protect Journalists visited Angola, heading a delegation that included Human Rights Watch, and discussed the draft media bill with senior government officials, journalists and NGOs. Meanwhile Amnesty International continued to be denied an official invitation to visit the country.

The Role of the International Community

On April 3, as part of a larger agreement between the International Monetary Fund (IMF) and the government of Angola to reform the economy, the IMF and government reached an agreement to monitor oil revenues that would be supervised by the World Bank. Overall, oil revenues comprise 92 percent of Angola's exports, between 70 and 90 percent of government revenues from 1994-1999, and over 50 percent of the country's Gross Domestic Product (GDP). This agreement was a positive first step that could help establish transparency and accountability within the government of Angola. (See Business and Human Rights.)

United Nations

The U.N.'s relationship with the government improved, mostly due to the efforts of Canada's ambassador to the U.N., Robert Fowler, to the efforts of the Angola Sanctions Committee he led, and to the release of a much publicized report on UNITA sanctions-busting in March. A second, smaller panel of experts was to have been appointed in May, but was finally formed only in late July following wrangling over nominations.

In February, the government officially approved the status of mission agreement for the United Nations Office in Angola (UNOA) and pledged to support the office. With the end of the U.N. peacekeeping mandate in Angola, the lead responsibility for UNOA within the U.N. Secretariat was transferred in January 2000 from the Department of Peacekeeping Operations to the Department of Political Affairs. U.N. Secretary-General Kofi Annan announced on July 31 that he had appointed Mozambican Mussagy Jeichande as the head of the up to thirty-strong UNOA. He arrived in Luanda to take up his post on October 1.

The U.N.'s ten-strong human rights division continued to support a number of institutional capacity-building efforts with the government and held a number of workshops. There were also efforts by the division to survey the role of multinational oil companies in the defense of human rights. The Human Rights Division was also measuring human rights awareness and understanding among the population in general. So far, research showed that Angolans knew their rights better than they knew the mechanisms for exercising them. Division chief Nicholas Howen resigned in March and had not been replaced at the time of writing.

European Union, Norway, and Canada

The European Union (E.U.) continued to be divided by sectoral and strategic interests. Commercial interests, particularly oil and trade, remained the prime issues of engagement and eroded the impact of periodic human rights demarches. A common E.U. policy document on human rights in Angola never reached the public domain after discord amongst the E.U. partners and a serious watering down of the draft. Portugal, the former colonial power and a member with Russia and the U.S. of the "Troika" monitors in the peace process, continued to be unable to voice human rights concerns because of the divisive nature of Angolan issues in its domestic politics. Canada continued to engage through its efforts on the U.N. sanctions committee, even after July when Robert Fowler moved to another diplomatic post.

United States

Angola remained the U.S.'s second largest destination for investment and third largest trading partner in sub-Saharan Africa in 2000. Petroleum was the defining issue, with projections that within ten years fifteeen percent of the U.S.'s oil consumption would be Angolan. This strategic relationship resulted in a warming of relations with a string of visits between Luanda and Washington D.C. of senior officials. U.S. policy shifted toward support of trade and commerce while issues such as human rights were downplayed. Although some U.S. interventions on freedom of expression abuses produced results, human rights issues were usually eclipsed by the higher priority given commercial interests. Underpinning the deepening of this relationship was the U.S.-Angola Bilateral Consultative Commission which met several times, focusing on trade and investment.

BURUNDI

Human Rights Developments

A peace agreement offered hope of ending a seven-year-long civil war, but combat between the largely Hutu rebel forces and the Tutsi-dominated government forces increased after its signing in August. Early in the year, fighting was worst in the south and east and, more sporadically, around Bujumbura, the capital. In August and September rebels continued pressure in the south and east, stepped up attacks near and in Bujumbura, and began combat in the central parts of the country. They targeted Tutsi civilians as well as Hutu who did not support their movements. Tutsi soldiers killed Hutu civilians, sometimes in reprisal for rebel attacks, sometimes because they suspected them of supporting the rebel movements. By October, more than a thousand civilians had been slain, thousands of others raped or otherwise injured, and hundreds of thousands displaced from their homes or deprived of their property. More than 120,000 persons had been slain since the war began in 1993.

Among the worst reprisal attacks by

soldiers was the December 1999 slaughter of at least forty civilians at Kabezi and the late September 2000 killing of more than twenty civilians in the Bujumbura neighborhood of Kamenge.

Soldiers and former soldiers also attacked civilians with no apparent provocation. Several checking identity papers shot an unarmed member of parliament, Gabriel Gisabwamana, in December 1999, and three soldiers and a former soldier shot and killed an Italian church worker at a roadblock in early October.

Rebels killed dozens of persons in ambushes on roads outside the capital. In one particularly serious ambush at Mageyo, they killed fifteen persons, including three children, and wounded twelve. In some incursions into the city, rebels seemed more intent on robbery than on killing, but in late September during their third attack at Mutakura, a poor, ethnically mixed neighborhood of the capital, they killed thirteen persons, including women and children.

Unidentified assailants killed and injured dozens of civilians in August and September through ambushes of vehicles, attacks on their homes, and a grenade thrown in the Buyenzi market in Bujumbura.

In January, former South African president Nelson Mandela assumed the role of mediator in the peace negotiations, replacing former Tanzanian president Julius Nyerere, who died in late 1999. From his first meeting with the nineteen delegations representing the Burundian government and various political parties, Mandela sounded the moral tone that would dominate his efforts. Throughout the year he condemned such government abuses as forcibly regrouping civilians in camps and jailing persons unjustifiably. In September, he condemned the rebels for ignoring a proffered cease-fire and for continuing attacks on civilians.

In late August, supported by the presence of President Bill Clinton and other international leaders, Mandela pushed most of the nineteen delegations into signing a peace accord. The rest signed a month later, but many reserved approval of one or more of the articles. Even more important, the two major armed movements making war on the government refused to sign because they had been excluded from early stages of negotiations by Nyerere. The two, the National Council for the Defense of Democracy-Forces for the Defense of Democracy (CNDD-FDD, usually called just FDD) and the Forces for National Liberation (FNL) of the Party for the Liberation of the Hutu People (PALIPEHUTU), later refused to join the talks, even at Mandela's urging.

The Burundian war became increasingly intermeshed with the war in the neighboring Democratic Republic of the Congo (DRC). Burundian rebels allied with Congolese opponents of the Rwandan-backed Congolese Rally for Democracy (RCD) and Burundian army soldiers cooperated with the RCD and Rwandan troops. Both Burundian rebels and Burundian soldiers attacked civilians in the DRC. (See Democratic Republic of the Congo.) Burundian rebels also attacked from Tanzania, leading to insecurity at the border and occasional skirmishes between Burundian and Tanzanian soldiers. During the course of the year, the rebels apparently grew in numbers and obtained new arms and other equipment, some of it said to have been furnished by Congolese authorities eager to support groups that challenged the RCD and Rwandans. Hundreds of Rwandan Hutu opponents of the Rwandan government, including former Rwandan army soldiers and militia members, also joined in the Burundian war. The Rwandans provided important support to the FNL until February 2000, when cooperation broke down and the FNL killed more than a hundred of the Rwandan allies.

The war began after soldiers of the minority Tutsi group killed Melchior Ndadaye, the first democratically elected president who was from the majority Hutu group. In the weeks immediately after, Hutu, sometimes under the direction of officials or party leaders, killed tens of thousands of Tutsi, and the Tutsi-led army slaughtered tens of thousands of Hutu, sometimes in reprisal, sometimes in places where there had been no attacks on Tutsi. The army permitted civilians to resume control, but the government was paralyzed by violence from extremist Tutsi militia and from Hutu opposition groups that took up arms. Major Pierre Buyoya, who had governed before the election of Ndadaye, took power in a coup in 1996, pledging to restore order. He established a "partnership" with elements of the opposition and began negotiations with the rebels, but he also oversaw first use of "regroupment camps," a practice extended in September 1999 to the region surrounding the capital.

The government claimed to be protecting civilians by regrouping them, but it aimed primarily to sever the links between rebels and their civilian supporters. By early January 2000, soldiers using force and threats had moved some 350,000 civilians into the camps around Bujumbura, where they lived in inhumane conditions. In the process, the soldiers shot and killed at least twenty civilians and injured scores of others. At first, they forbade humanitarian workers access to the camps, leaving the displaced with no food, water, or help in building shelters. Later they allowed humanitarian agencies to deliver assistance, but several sites were so difficult to reach that relief workers could provide residents with little or no aid.

Soldiers on a number of occasions selected camp residents whom they suspected of rebel sympathies and beat them to obtain information or to force them to join the government side. During such beatings, soldiers often tied suspects tightly with their arms behind their backs and sometimes suspended them in the air. In some cases, they beat the suspects to death. In other cases, persons arrested by soldiers were taken to military installations and have not been seen since.

Soldiers allowed camp residents to work their fields only irregularly, making it difficult for them to produce crops to supplement the meager food deliveries. They frequently exacted unpaid labor from residents and forced both adults and children to accompany them as guides or porters, including through areas where there was a high risk of rebel attack. Civilians, including children, were sometimes killed or injured on these work details. Soldiers supposedly protecting several camps raped women or coerced them into providing sexual services against their will. Soldiers and national policemen looted and destroyed the homes and other property of camp residents and sometimes stole goods from them within the camps, notably at Kavumu on May 7.

Soldiers were rarely held accountable for their abuses. In an exceptional case, one soldier was sentenced to death for having killed six and wounded seven civilians at Ruyaga camp. A commission of inquiry into the looting at Kavumu had not published a report months afterwards.

Rebels on several occasions launched attacks on Burundian soldiers from inside or near regroupment camps, exposing camp residents to crossfire. In attacks at Kavumu and Kabezi in February and Kinyankonge in May, at least six civilians were killed and twelve wounded. In March, rebels fired on a mixed group of soldiers accompanied by child porters and wounded three children. Rebels sometimes required camp residents to provide them with money, food, or other goods. On April 23, rebels raided Ruziba camp and killed one resident who balked at meeting their demands.

In January President Buyoya responded to heavy international criticism by announcing that the government would close the regroupment camps, but only after President Mandela exacted a similar promise from him in June did authorities move effectively to disband the camps. By October, most of the camps around Bujumbura were closed, but officials continued using "temporary" regroupment to make it easier for soldiers to "cleanse" areas of rebels. A substantial number of civilians were killed in many of these operations. In late July, soldiers allegedly killed fifty-three civilians, including eighteen women and sixteen children, in the eastern province of Ruyigi and in August they reportedly slaughtered several dozen more at Nyambuye near Bujumbura.

Political leaders and ordinary people insisted upon justice for past massacres. For many Tutsi, this meant justice for slaughter of Tutsi in late 1993, which was termed "acts of genocide" by a panel established by the U.N. Security Council, and for subsequent killings. For many Hutu, it meant justice for Hutu killed by Tutsi soldiers and civilians since 1993, but also for the massive slaughter of tens of thousands of Hutu in 1972. Into this debate President Mandela introduced the idea of freeing "political prisoners," including not only those jailed solely for their beliefs, but also those guilty of crimes of violence who had acted for political or ideological reasons.

The FDD adopted the closing of regroupment camps and the freeing of "political prisoners" as preconditions to beginning negotiations with the government. Although the first condition was largely met, the second was not and the FDD took this as a pretext for continuing combat.

The Arusha Agreement provided for both an international commission of inquiry into past killings and a national truth and reconciliation commission. It called for an international tribunal to prosecute war crimes, crimes against humanity, and genocide, but this institution would be established only after the international inquiry was done.

A new code of penal procedure went into effect in January 2000 that for the first time guaranteed the accused access to legal counsel before trial. It also strengthened restrictions on preventive detention and provided greater protection against physical abuse of detainees. Even as authorities introduced the new law, they recognized that implementing it required more resources than they had. In fact, the reforms were not widely implemented during the year, but judicial authorities did liberate some two hundred detainees against whom there was little proof or who had been detained for long periods of time. Some 9,000 remained in jail, the majority of them Hutu. Most were accused of crimes related to the 1993 massacres and had not yet been tried. Conditions of detention remained miserable due to overcrowding, poor nutrition, and lack of medical services. The International Committee of the Red Cross, absent from Burundi for several years after the killing of three of its delegates, returned in 1999 and immediately brought improvements in jail conditions.

Defending Human Rights

The Burundian human rights league, Iteka, continued its strong programs of monitoring abuses and education concerning human rights and undertook a campaign to establish an international criminal tribunal for Burundi. The Association for the Defense of Burundian Prisoners (ABDP) assisted prisoners both in preparing their cases for court and in improving the material conditions of life in the prison. It also drew public attention to an important case where a detainee was tortured and beaten to death and sought to bring the responsible officials to trial. To assist the backlog in the judicial system, Iteka provided transport to witnesses and complainants and ABDP transported judicial personnel to courts often many miles from their homes.

In general, human rights monitors worked without difficulty, but in a number of cases soldiers or officials excluded them from areas of alleged abuses, supposedly to protect them from harm. Following publication of information critical of the government, two human rights workers received a series of threatening phone calls, but there was no indication that these had been officially inspired.

The government established a National Human Rights Commission in April to monitor the situation of human rights generally and to ensure that governmental bodies observe human rights. The commission included representatives from the president, the vice-president, and the ministers of defense, justice, communications, and human rights.

The Role of the International Community

The international community focused on ending the war, in part because it understood how unstable the entire region was, in part because it was determined that Burundi not suffer a genocide like that which devastated neighboring Rwanda—with a population similarly divided on ethnic lines. President Clinton's brief stop to encourage signing of the Arusha Agreement underlined the importance the U.S. gave to ending combat in the region. The U.N. Security Council followed the diplomatic process closely, twice receiving direct reports by former President Mandela. The OAU, the E.U., and various individual governments, like the United States, all provided high-level diplomatic support to the peace process throughout the year and many donors helped pay its hefty expenses.

The U.S., like others, downplayed the need for justice as potentially impeding a settlement. At the same time they hoped to keep open the option of some form of international accountability for war crimes, crimes against humanity, and genocide. To improve judicial proceedings within Burundi, the U.S. provided some U.S. $3 million to support Burundian nongovernmental organizations under the Great Lakes Justice Initiative.

Donors gave humanitarian aid, but, except for France and Belgium, they did not resume the development aid that had been cut when an embargo was imposed after Buyoya's 1996 coup. President Mandela tried to push the immediate renewal of assistance, but donors refused at a September meeting because a cease-fire had not taken effect. The government faced bankruptcy early in the year, but the World Bank gave $35 million to stabilize the economy.

Most international actors, including the U.S., condemned the regroupment camps and demanded their closure. After several months, however, the Belgians implicitly accepted the camps and stressed merely the need to improve conditions for residents. When President Buyoya suggested that some regroupment camps might be transformed into "villages," the European Commission delegate immediately warned that no E.U. aid would be given without evidence that affected people favored this move.

The U.N. High Commissioner for Human Rights began the year with a strong statement condemning the human rights violations inherent in the regroupment policy, a position that was reiterated by the special rapporteur for Burundi, Marie-Therese A. Keita Boucoum, in her report to the commission in February. The special rapporteur, named in 1999, visited Burundi only briefly in late 1999, but spoke out clearly against killings and other abuses by both military and rebels.

The field office of the High Commissioner of Human Rights reduced its staff in late 1999 due to a security alert and did not substantially increase its personnel in 2000 after the security situation improved. Handicapped also by budget cuts, the office worked largely for improvements in the judicial system. It did not publicize any abuses that it documented, although it did address some of them with the authorities. Although the field office at one time circulated reports confidentially among the diplomatic community, it apparently stopped doing so in mid-1999.

Relevant Human Rights Watch Reports:
Emptying the Hills: Regroupment in Burundi, *7/00*
Neglecting Justice in Making Peace, 4/00

THE DEMOCRATIC REPUBLIC OF THE CONGO (DRC)

Human Rights Developments

Congo entered its third year of a devastating war in August, with no end in sight. The conflict pitted the government of President Laurent Kabila and allied troops from Zimbabwe, Angola, and Namibia against the rebel Congolese Rally for Democracy (RCD), fronting for forces sent by the governments of Rwanda, Uganda, and Burundi. In the northern Equateur province, the better organized Movement for the Liberation of Congo (MLC) also received significant military support from Uganda. Rwanda and Uganda invoked national security concerns for intervening in the Congo, citing the presence of exiled insurgent groups bent on destabilizing their respective countries. As the conflict settled into a protracted stalemate, it became increasingly clear that the two nations' economies were directly boosted by the exploitation of natural resources in areas of the DRC under their respective control. Myriad external actors, the ready availability of small arms, and ethnic mobilization by local warlords favored the resurgence of rural militias in eastern Congo. Locally known by the generic name of Mai-Mai, these autonomous militia groups fought primarily to repel what they perceived as foreign occupation of their homelands.

None of the actors fully respected their commitments under the Lusaka Cease-fire Agreement signed in July and August 1999. Rebel factions and their foreign backers and government troops showed little inclination to respect basic norms of international human rights and humanitarian law in their treatment of civilian populations. The fighting destroyed what was left of Congo's public services and infrastructure after decades of misgovernment under former President Joseph Mobutu, and brought the already moribund economy to a standstill.

Indiscriminate attacks, extrajudicial executions of civilians, rape, and large-scale destruction of civilian property characterized the conduct of the belligerents. Collective punishment for suspected loyalty to rival antagonists generated many of the civilian killings, as did localized interethnic strife fueled by the broader war. Perpetrators from all parties enjoyed total impunity.

By midyear, upward of 1.3 million Congolese were displaced, and another five million completely or partially separated from their traditional supply routes, mainly because of the generalized insecurity. Those uprooted by the war were deprived of access to humanitarian services by the same factors that caused their flight and isolation. From January to September, the number of Congolese refugees in neighboring countries, including Uganda, grew from some 130,000 to an approximate 220,000.

Using the war as a pretext, President Kabila's government continued to freeze its democratization agenda, and actively sought to derail the internal political dialogue with the rebels, opposition parties, and civil society groups provided for in the 1999 Lusaka Accord. Taking aim at these targets, on August 21 the government inaugurated a Constituent and Legislative Assembly/Transitional Parliament whose members it handpicked without consulting the opposition or civil society organizations.

Seeking to capitalize on the serious fallout between Rwanda and Uganda and the increasing unpopularity of the rebel RCD in eastern Congo, the government also gave contradictory signals about its readiness to cooperate with U.N. observers. During three days of government-orchestrated protests in early June, hundreds of demonstrators threw stones at the headquarters of the U.N. Mission to the Congo (MONUC).

The human rights situation throughout the country continued to deteriorate. On February 19, the government decreed a general amnesty for all Congolese prosecuted or condemned for crimes against the internal or external security of the state. More than two hundred people in detention were accordingly released in a matter of weeks. However, as Human Rights Watch pointed out in a letter to President Kabila in March, the government failed to free hundreds of eligible political and security detainees. Furthermore, the government continued to respond to challenges to its ongoing ban on political activities and free expression of opinion with arbitrary detention and stiff prison sentences, helping to fill detention centers and prisons that optimists had hoped the general amnesty would empty. Security agencies particularly targeted vocal opposition parties and groupings for repression. They arrested leaders and militants of the radical Innovative Forces for Unity and Solidarity, dispersed gatherings of the newly formed Collective for the Survival of Democracy, and detained for varying periods dozens of members of the main opposition parties, the Union for Democracy and Social Progress, and the Unified Lumumbist Party.

In January and February, the government violated its own pledge to the United Nations not to carry out the death penalty by executing nineteen people condemned to death by the special Court of Military Order. Established in 1997 by presidential decree, ostensibly to restore discipline in the army, the court increasingly became an effective tool for political repression, notably to punish outspoken civilian critics of the government. On September 12, the Court found four journalists guilty of "high treason" and "publication of articles hostile to the government." It sentenced two of them to two years in prison, and condemned the others to one year's imprisonment, with six months suspended.

Several competing security agencies zealously enforced the government's restrictions on political activities and free expression, constantly alternating roles in arresting, interrogating, and detaining suspects. This practice kept the door wide open for rampant abuses: compelling testimonies indicated the continual use of torture, in particular in police stations and in places of detention controlled by the military. Former detainees complained to Human Rights Watch about beatings, sexual abuse, humiliating treatment, and deprivation of food, sleep, or family visits. Victims of torture and ill treatment who protested to the government said that there was no follow-up to their complaints, indicating the prevalence of a culture of total impunity.

An investigation in March by Human Rights Watch in areas controlled by the mainstream RCD-Goma rebel faction, which is backed by Rwanda, documented a pattern of involvement of the rebels and their Rwandan Patriotic Army (RPA) backers in civilian killings and other extrajudicial executions. These were often conducted in retaliation for earlier raids by the Mai-Mai and Rwandan Hutu fighters, commonly called Interahamwe, operating in eastern Congo against the Tutsi-dominated RPA and its local allies. Human Rights Watch documented the killing of thirty people in a February 5 attack by the RCD and its RPA allies on the village of Kilambo in North Kivu. RCD rebels and Rwandan soldiers tied up men, raped their wives in front of them, and then killed them. In May, the RCD similarly killed at least thirty villagers in Katogota, south Kivu. Human Rights Watch also collected evidence that corroborated reports by a local rights group, Heritiers de la Justice, that RCD soldiers in late 1999 sexually tortured and buried several women alive in Mwenga, reports which the RCD vehemently denied. RCD soldiers also attacked civilians in towns, and routinely arrested and tortured RCD opponents and civil society leaders, often detaining them in secret places, including in Rwanda.

The Mai-Mai and Hutu fighters also committed atrocities against the civilian population, particularly communities identified with the Tutsis. The Mai-Mai reportedly killed dozens of fleeing civilians in late August in Shabunda territory. Hutu militiamen reportedly attacked civilians in Kahuzi-Biega national park in early September. Burundian Hutu and Mai-Mai fighters jointly attacked Congolese Tutsi communities in the Ruzuzu plain and the Haut Plateau areas of south Kivu.

Uganda hastily trained and equipped thousands of young Congolese, many of them children, to build armed wings for its local allies, the Liberation Movement for the Congo (MLC), which controlled Equateur province by mid-1999, and the Congolese Rally for Democracy-Liberation Movement (RCD-ML), which unconvincingly claimed to control northeastern areas in Congo along the Ugandan border. While the MLC enjoyed a measure of popularity among the estimated ten million inhabitants of Equateur, the RCD-ML and its newly trained armed wing had splintered into at least three factions by midyear, largely along ethnic lines. Frequent leadership dispute in the RCD-ML exacerbated ethnic tensions and re-ignited a deadly interethnic war in the region of Bunia between the the agriculturalist Lendu people and the pastoralist Hema, who are identified with the Tutsi and the Ugandan Hema. At least seven thousand people were killed, and another 200,000 were displaced in less than a year. Sparked in mid-1999 by individual disputes over land tenure between the two groups, the conflict flared up when Ugandan officials around the same time unilaterally decreed the creation of a province in the disputed area, and placed mostly Hema officials in control of its administration. Leaders of the RCD-ML told Human Rights Watch and the Kampala press on various occasions that commanders and soldiers of the Ugandan army frequently took part in that conflict on the side of the Hema, mainly to earn lucrative payments from Hema farm owners and businessmen. In August Human Rights Watch wrote to RCD President Ernest Wamba dia Wamba and to President Museveni of Uganda calling for an investigation into the role of the Ugandan army in recruiting children and manipulating ethnic tensions in the region.

Rwandan and Ugandan forces fought particularly destructive battles for the control of Kisangani in early May, and again in early June. Some seven hundred civilians were killed, and another one thousand were seriously wounded as the nominal allies indiscriminately clashed with heavy artillery and automatic weapons in the city. The fighting cut off the supply of electricity and water and caused widespread damage to civilian property.

Defending Human Rights

As Congo's vibrant human rights and civil society movement attempted to build a genuine grassroots movement for durable peace, it faced persistent persecution, both from the government and the rebels fighting to topple it. On January 16, security forces of the RCD-Goma arrested Immaculée Birhaheka, president of the women's group Promotion and Support of Women's Initiatives (PAIF), and her colleague Jeannine Mukanirwa, PAIF's vice president. The two, and other women held like them at the infamous "Bureau 2" detention center in Goma, were whipped with a piece of tire. The brief detention of the two activists was apparently linked to Mukanirwa's leading role in organizing a peace movement with a view to bringing together groups from government and rebel held areas. In late January, RCD-Goma authorities arrested three civil society leaders in Bukavu, in South Kivu and accused them of organizing for a planned general strike to protest the lack of payment of wages, taxation by the Rwandans, and the continuing presence in eastern Congo of Rwandan and Ugandan troops. Despite the arrests and threats by the RCD against several suspected protest leaders, the strike took place peacefully on January 31 in Bukavu. In late April, Rwandan security forces arrested Bruno Bahati, a leading member of the Coordination of Civil Society in South Kivu, on the Rwandan-Ugandan border after finding a Kinshasa newspaper in his possession. He was detained in Kigali for a while and was later transferred to Goma. Women's rights groups in north and south Kivu made of International Women's Day, March 8, an event to mark women's grieving for their husbands and relatives killed in the war. For their suspected role in organizing the event in Goma, RCD authorities summoned and threatened a women's activist, Zita Kavungirwa, and pressured the employer of another one, Marie-Jeanne Mbachu, into suspending her from her job.

RCD-Goma authorities often broadly accused dissenting church and civil society leaders of inciting ethnic hatred, but never prosecuted specific cases, preferring instead to use detention, repeated summons, and internal exile to silence opponents. In late August, the RCD authorities banished four leading civil society activists from Bukavu for three weeks after accusing them of having passed information to the international press. In September, the rebels allowed Mgr.

Emmanuel Kataliko, bishop of Bukavu, to return to the city after seven months of banishment to his hometown in north Kivu. They accused him of fomenting ethnic hatred after he criticized rebel authorities in his Christmas prayer. The bishop's sudden death of a heart attack in early October shocked the population and deepened its distrust of the RCD. In clamping down on the resulting unrest in Bukavu, RCD soldiers briefly detained thirteen human rights activists and publicly beat them.

In Kinshasa, the government similarly restricted the freedom of expression and movement of civil society groups. Alleging that they were in contact with the rebels, the government in late May detained for weeks Félicien Malanda Nsumbu and Georges Kazimbika, respectively the secretary and financial officer of the national umbrella group for developmental organizations. In early June, the government prevented representatives of civil society and the political opposition from leaving the capital to attend preparatory talks for the inter-Congolese dialogue in Cotonou, Benin.

The Role of the International Community

Southern African Development Community

The Southern African Development Community (SADC) tried to spearhead the regional peace efforts in a war that drew three of its member states to the side of its beleaguered member, the Congo. Zimbabwe, Angola, and Namibia proved ineffective in pressing the Congolese government to comply with the 1999 Lusaka cease-fire agreement at a SADC summit meeting on August 7, and again on August 14 at a summit of the parties to the agreement.

United Nations

The Security Council in an August 6, 1999 resolution authorized the deployment for three months of ninety U.N. military liaison personnel to the capitals of the belligerent states. Their mission was to establish contact with the Joint Military Commission formed by the belligerents to police the implementation of the truce. From January 24 to 26, the council held intensive deliberations on the Congolese crisis attended by seven African heads of state. This prepared the ground for Security Council resolution 1291, extending the mandate of the United Nations Observer Mission in the DRC (MONUC) to August 31, and authorizing its expansion to include a 500-strong military observer force plus another 5,537 troops for logistical and security backup. The council authorized the mission to take action to protect U.N. personnel and infrastructure, and civilians facing imminent threats of attack, and on October 13 extended its mandate to December 15.

While the ground was laid for a peacekeeping mission to the Congo soon after the parties agreed to disengage, the U.N. showed less resolve in moving to the deployment phase, principally blaming the parties to the conflict for failing to live up to their commitments. MONUC also encountered other crippling hurdles, as it was starved of resources, and member states were slow in pledging troops for it.

A Security Council mission to the region in early May pressed for the full cooperation and support of the belligerents for MONUC as a condition for its deployment, but at the time of writing these conditions had not been met. The council on June 16 demanded that Rwanda and Uganda "which have violated the sovereignty and territorial integrity" of the DRC, withdraw their forces from Congolese territory, and that the other parties to the conflict adhere to the timetable of the cease-fire agreement. The council also declared that Rwanda and Uganda should make reparations for the loss of life and property in Kisangani during their clashes there.

Roberto Garreton, the U.N. special rapporteur on human rights for the DRC, visited the country from August 13 to 26 at the invitation of the government. Leaders of the Liberation Movement for the Congo (MLC) and the mainstream RCD-Goma faction also received the special rapporteur in their respective headquarters of Gbadolite and Goma. In a powerful message to the RCD, the rapporteur inaugurated a workshop for the training of human rights monitors in which participants from several rebel-controlled cities were able to take part. The U.N. human rights high commissioner's field office in DRC, and its branch office in Goma, played active roles in monitoring the human rights situation in government and rebel areas. Solidarity with and support for the beleaguered Congolese human rights movement was an important aspect of the commission's interventions, in addition to its advocacy role with government and rebel authorities.

European Union

Provided that the signatories respected their own accord, the European Union remained committed to supporting the implementation of the Lusaka Agreement, promising assistance for the resettlement of the war displaced, fostering national reconciliation in the DRC, and supporting the country's rehabilitation plans. Indicative of this stance was the E.U.'s August boycott of the opening ceremony of the DRC's Constituent and Legislative Assembly on the grounds that the institution was not compatible with the national dialogue provided for by the Lusaka Agreement.

At a meeting with Ugandan government officials in mid-May, during which donors were due to confirm pledges they made during the Donor Consultative Group meeting in Kampala in March, the E.U. warned that the conflict between Uganda and Rwanda in Kisangani could jeopardize donors' budgetary support for both countries. In addition to the demand that the two countries end the situation they created in Kisangani, the E.U. appeared to make Uganda's compliance with the Lusaka Agreement a condition for the release of its budgetary support to the country.

A meeting of E.U. foreign ministers in Brussels in May decided to increase the E.U.'s economic assistance to the DRC and Burundi as an incentive for the peace processes there. However, the ministers failed to reach a consensus on the imposition of an arms embargo on the Great Lakes region, with some member states arguing that any such embargo would always be violated. This left member states with only the June 1999 E.U.'s presidential statement, which called on them to strictly adhere to the E.U.'s own Code of Conduct on Arms Exports and recalled that, under the E.U. code, countries agree not to authorize arms exports that might "aggravate existing tensions or armed conflicts in the country of final destination" or risk fueling human rights abuses. The Great Lakes and Central Africa region qualified for a strict imposition of an arms embargo under these guidelines.

Uganda's involvement in recruiting and training thousands of Congolese children, and in deploying them to battlefronts in their own country, completely escaped the attention of the European Parliament when it passed its strong July 6 resolution condemning the use of child soldiers by rebels in Uganda. The parliament strongly condemned the abduction and induction of children by the Lord's Resistance Army, and Sudan's role in supporting that rebel group, and called on the E.U. Commission to support rehabilitation efforts of demobilized children in Uganda.

United States

The U.S. repeatedly strongly supported the implementation of the Lusaka Agreement and the deployment of MONUC, as well as the convening of the Inter-Congolese Dialogue. In February, President Clinton lauded the Lusaka agreement, saying that "[i]t is more than a cease-fire; it is a blueprint for building peace. Best of all, it is a genuinely African solution to an African problem." The U.S. at the same time strove to reconcile its mediation effort with the preservation of its privileged relations with Rwanda and Uganda and its broader objective of containing President Kabila. An August 16 Department of State release exposed the inherent contradictions of the approach, asserting that "[e]xcept for the Congolese government, all parties to the conflict have affirmed their collective desire to put in place the conditions for the full implementation of the Lusaka Agreement." True, the Kabila government at the time publicly said it refused to abide by the agreement and obstructed the Inter-Congolese Dialogue. The government also denied MONUC permission to land at Mbandaka, and to deploy observers to Mbuji Mayi. However, the MLC and RCD rebels mirrored that refusal by blocking the mission's access to certain areas under their respective control. The highly publicized withdrawal of Ugandan troops from Kisangani in June was in turn followed by the airlifting of sizable Ugandan reinforcements to shore up the MLC against a punishing government offensive. The State Department statement only strengthened the perception in the region that U.S. policy was far from evenhanded.

The U.S. defined its interests in the DRC as the upholding of regional stability, and the prevention of the resurgence of genocide and mass killings in Central Africa. In testimony before the House Subcommittee on Africa of the International Relations Committee on February 15, Richard Holbrooke, the U.S. ambassador to the U.N., narrowly equated the prevention of genocide with the neutralization of the former Rwandan Army (ex-FAR) and Interahamwe militia, who were implicated in the 1994 Rwandan genocide and remained at large in eastern Congo. A more objective reading of the situation in the region, by Ambassador-at-Large for War Crimes Issues David Scheffer, later identified other actors involved in perpetrating war crimes there. Scheffer led a government team on an August 24-27 trip to Kinshasa, Kisangani, Goma, and Butembo in eastern Congo to investigate allegations of such crimes. According to an August 29 Department of State statement, Scheffer's team collected information that pointed to violations of international humanitarian law by armed groups supplied by the RCD government, Congolese rebel movements, and the armies of the Rwandan and Ugandan governments. Such strong findings put to a real test the U.S. rhetorical commitment to justice for victims of rampant violence in the Congo and its stated determination to take concrete steps to end the culture of impunity prevailing in the region. Secretary Albright gave an eloquent example of such pledges when she vowed before the Security Council during the "Month of Africa" on January 24 "[t]here is no rationale of past grievance, political allegiance or ethnic difference that excuses murder, torture, rape or other abuse. Here, today, together, we must vow to halt these crimes and to bring those who commit them to justice under due process of law." Months later, there was little progress to this end in the Congo.

The U.S. maintained a modest level of economic assistance to the DRC in FY 2000: U.S. $10 million in development aid through NGOs; $13 million in humanitarian assistance; $15 million in food aid; and $3 million under the Great Lakes Justice Initiative. The U.S. contributed an additional $1 million for the Joint Military Commission, and reserved an additional $1 million for the Inter-Congolese Dialogue. Although it would commit no troops to MONUC, the U.S. government made significant financial contributions to the mission, totaling an estimated 25 percent of the total U.N. cost of $164 million in FY 2000, and an estimated 25 percent of the mission's budget for FY 2001 which stood at $378 million at this writing.

Relevant Human Rights Watch Reports:

Eastern Congo Ravaged: Killing Civilians and Silencing Protest, 5/00

THE FEDERAL DEMOCRATIC REPUBLIC OF ETHIOPIA

Human Rights Developments

Prime Minister Meles Zenawi told the Ethiopian parliament in early July his government had successfully attained its three main objectives for the year: the recapturing of disputed territory in its war with Eritrea, holding general elections, and combatting drought. In pursuing these tasks, the government had more often than not ignored human rights and humanitarian standards despite its professed commitment to such standards.

Ethiopia on May 12 launched a massive attack against Eritrea and successfully retook disputed territories that Eritrea had occupied at the beginning of the war, while seriously weakening the military capacity of its former ally. The two countries on June 18 agreed to a cessation of hostilities agreement brokered by the Organization of African Unity (OAU). The two-year conflict was estimated to have killed and wounded tens of thousands of soldiers and civilians and uprooted nearly a million people. Displaced Eritreans fleeing the fighting credibly reported the involvement of the Ethiopian army in large-scale destruction and looting of civilian property, the harassment of civilians, particularly men of military age, and in a high incidence of rape.

By early 2000, Ethiopian authorities, citing broad threats to national security, had forcibly expelled some 70,000 Ethiopians of Eritrean parentage to Eritrea. The government arbitrarily seized those of Eritrean descent, held them in harsh detention conditions and allowed no challenge to their expulsion. By summarily denying the nationality rights of the overwhelming majority of those expelled, most of whom were lifelong Ethiopian citizens, the campaign in effect rendered them stateless. It divided families, forcibly separating many from spouses and children whose Ethiopian nationality was not challenged, and expropriated their properties.

An estimated forty thousand Ethiopian residents of Eritrea returned to Ethiopia under duress in the months that followed the outbreak of hostilities. Eritrean authorities interned thousands of Ethiopian residents under harsh conditions in the wake of Ethiopia's offensive in May, citing unspecified threats to national security, and the need to protect the internees from angry mobs. By the end of June, in addition to the tens of thousands who had fled at the onset of the war, some 4,600 Ethiopian residents left Eritrea after their release from weeks of internment. Their repatriation occurred under the auspices of the International Committee of the Red Cross (ICRC), acting as a mutually accepted neutral intermediary. Eritrea also repatriated several thousand Ethiopian residents without prior coordination with the ICRC and their government.

The war with Eritrea further fueled the ongoing low-level armed insurgencies in Ogaden region and in the state of Oromia. In these two and several other remote regions, the government continued to hold under harsh conditions, and without charge or trial, thousands of people it suspected of sympathizing with insurgents.

The Ogaden National Liberation Front (ONLF), the Oromo Liberation Front (OLF), and the southern Sidama Liberation Front (SLF) in a joint May 16 statement charged that famine affecting their eastern and southern states was the result of "deliberate negligence" from the central government. The three fronts complained that the government forcibly recruited thousands of young men from their regions to use them as "mine sweepers" and "cannon fodder" in its war with Eritrea. Independent journalists and NGO workers who interviewed Ethiopian prisoners of war in Eritrea said many were under the age of eighteen, and reported testimonies that tended to corroborate charges of coercive recruitment and poor training.

The OLF blamed the government for

ignoring a peace proposal it had tabled in February, and actively pursued in July and September the unification of several Oromo armed opposition groups under one umbrella to "increase the effectiveness of Oromo opposition to the government." There was no independent confirmation of claims by the OLF in August, and by the ONLF in September, that they had inflicted heavy casualties on government troops in separate clashes. The OLF claimed in early June that government soldiers arrested two hundred people in Malka Jabdu, a small village near the site at which a train ferrying military supplies from the port of Djibouti to the capital Addis Ababa was derailed in May by a landmine explosion for which the OLF claimed responsibility. Coming under government suspicion of active opposition to the war effort, many members of the Oromo community fled various forms of harassment and intimidation to seek asylum in neighboring Kenya and elsewhere.

Elections went ahead on May 14, two days after Ethiopia launched its largest military offensive against Eritrea since the beginning of the war. The government denied claims that the timing was meant to give an advantage to its ruling coalition, and said it needed no such assistance to win the elections. The government's assertion appeared well-founded in view of the level of control it exerted on the democratic transition to federalism. Independent opposition parties and coalitions of ethnically based groups opposed to the government continued to face severe government restrictions that limited their ability to freely compete in elections. The opposition to the EPRDF also suffered from internal organizational weaknesses and frequent divisions among its members, but several opposition parties and independent candidates competed in the May 2000 elections. Still, EPRDF affiliates were the sole contestants in over 50 percent of the constituencies in the contest for the lower house of parliament, eight of the nine regional councils, and the governments of the capital and the second largest city. The EPRDF scooped a predictable 85 percent of the seats in the federal legislature, and its members and satellite parties won control of the regional assemblies. On October 10, in its first sitting, the new parliament reelected Meles Zenawi prime minister for a five-year term.

Allegations of fraud and violence marred the May elections, particularly in rural areas. The independent monitoring group Ethiopian Human Rights Council (EHRCO) reported election related incidents of abuse of opposition candidates and supporters, including killings, the arbitrary detention of opposition candidates and their transfer or dismissal from employment, and incidents involving the wounding of opposition supporters by gunshots. EHRCO also reported in February that Ethiopians of Eritrean descent who remained in the country could not participate in the May elections because authorities questioned their citizenship. In early March, Beyene Petros, chairman of the opposition Southern Ethiopian Peoples' Democratic Coalition (SEPDC), accused the ruling EPRDF of subjecting members of his party to arbitrary arrest and imprisonment. After the polling started, Petros complained that police had killed seven SEPDC supporters who were protesting against electoral fraud outside two polling stations in the south. Responding to incidents of irregularities and violence, the election board nullified election results in sixteen districts in the southern region and organized fresh elections a month later.

The Ethiopian government continued to restrict the freedom of speech and the press. Twenty-seven Ethiopian journalists lived in exile at this writing, having fled their homeland due to repeated arrests and ill-treatment in detention. Among the latest to flee, in February, was Dawit Kebede, editor-in-chief of the Amharic weekly *Fiameta*, and member of the executive committee of the Ethiopian Free Press Journalists' Association (EFPJA). The government only recognized EFPJA in March, seven years after the independent association first submitted its application for registration.

Eight reporters remained behind bars. Four had been in custody for up to two years before being sentenced to one year imprisonment, and they remained in custody on new charges. Tamrat Gemeda, of the weekly *SeifNebelball*, and Tesfaye Deressa, Garuma Bekele, and Solomon Nemera, of *Urji*, were arrested in October 1997 for publishing "false information" for the prominence given by the two papers to Oromo issues and the conflict between the OLF and the government. The four faced new charges of membership in terrorist movements. The government held another thirty-one journalists on a short leash during 2000, having released them on very high bail pending court hearings.

In mid-August, sudden increases in printing costs, by more than a third, put additional pressures on some thirty-six private publications as well as the government press. The private newspapers went on strike from September 11-17, and warned that the high production costs could eventually force them out of print. They urged the government to reduce taxation on imported paper and other print inputs.

Defending Human Rights

The Ethiopian Human Rights Council (EHRCO) openly monitored and reported on the human rights situation in the country. Several civic organizations, including EHRCO, the Ethiopian Economic Association, the Inter-Africa Group, and the Addis Ababa Chamber of Commerce convened panel discussions that allowed EPRDF and opposition candidates to air their programs before urban voters, mainly in the capital. The Ethiopian Women Lawyers Association conducted training for women candidates. EHRCO critically analyzed the polling operations in its public statements and reports and denounced abuses when they occurred.

These freedoms continued to be denied to the Human Rights League, which was founded in 1997. Not only did the government refuse to register it, but it arrested eight of its board members shortly after they applied for registration and confiscated its office records and equipment in 1998. Garuma Bekele, executive secretary of the league, and also editor of *Urji*, and Addisu Beyene, secretary of the Oromo Relief Association and prominent rights advocate, together with some fifty other prominent Oromo civic leaders, remained in jail since their arrest in October 1997. Their trial for conspiracy with the OLF continued in camera. Family members were banned from attending the trial, although they could visit the prisoners. Fear of repression forced other groups, such as the Ogaden Human Rights Committee, to conduct their monitoring activities clandestinely, and to report their findings abroad.

There was some progress toward the establishment of national and international institutions for the protection and promotion of human rights. Days before the end of its five-year tenure, the outgoing parliament in July unanimously approved bills establishing the Ethiopian human rights commission and the office of the ombudsman. Mary Robinson, the U.N. high commissioner for human rights, said during a visit in October that her agency would open a regional office in Addis Ababa to work with the countries of the Horn of Africa and the OAU.

The Role of the International Community

Organization of African Unity

The Organization of African Unity (OAU) took the lead in mediating the conflict from the onset, with the backing of the United States and the European Union. In its attempts to prevent yet another round of deadly fighting, the OAU convened intensive talks from April 29 to May 5 aimed at bringing the two parties to agree on a document for the implementation of its peace plan, Ethiopia having rejected earlier technical arrangements to this end. Despite the mediators' efforts, the talks again failed to resolve the core disagreements between the two parties. Ethiopia's major offensive of May 2000 was clearly meant to break the impasse. Not only did the offensive lead to Eritrea's withdrawal from all disputed border territories, but it placed Ethiopian troops in firm control of undisputed territories inside Eritrea. Ethiopia gained considerable leverage as a result of this military advantage and the pressures resulting from the flight of at least a million Eritrean civilians ahead of the fighting. The terms of the cessation of hostilities accord signed on June 18 thus appeared to reflect Ethiopia's position of strength.

The accord provided for the deployment of a U.N. peacekeeping force in a temporary security zone, twenty-five kilometers inside Eritrea along the entire border, a time frame for the neutral demarcation of the bitterly disputed borders, and the conclusion of a permanent cease-fire. The accord reaffirmed the two parties' acceptance of the OAU Framework Agreement and the Modalities for its Implementation as endorsed by the OAU summit in July 1999. The framework agreement provided a basis for addressing the human rights and humanitarian problems that the conflict had created, committing the two parties to "put an end to measures directed against the civilian population and to refrain from any action which can cause further hardship and suffering to each other's nationals." They also agreed to "addressing the negative socio-economic impact of the crisis on the civilian population, particularly those persons who had been deported." The OAU in collaboration with the U.N. was to deploy human rights monitors "in order to contribute to the establishment of a climate of confidence between the two parties" under the terms of the Framework Agreement.

Unfortunately, the terms of the cessation of hostilities agreement and the relevant U.N. Security Council regarding its implementation appeared to focus primarily on technical considerations, namely the redeployment of the two parties and the demarcation of the border. In contrast to its active role in the mediation process, the OAU proved itself far less assertive when it came to the definition of formal mediation and arbitration mechanisms to address the human rights and humanitarian consequences of the conflict.

United States

The U.S. continued to give a high priority to the conflict between Ethiopia and Eritrea, two of its closest allies in the continent. It engaged the two parties in direct talks, while providing vital technical and logistical support to the OAU mediation effort. Susan Rice, the assistant secretary of state for african affairs, devoted significant portions of her time to the conflict. Anthony Lake, the U.S. lead mediator since October 1998, and a former national security advisor, shuttled between the two capitals several times during the year, coordinating his efforts closely with the OAU and the U.N.

The administration maintained an active behind-the-scenes role in its efforts to prevent the resumption of the fighting, while refraining from making public statements, including addressing the human rights situation. The Department of State issued statements in March and May calling on the two nations to remain "fully engaged" in the OAU peace process, and on June 10 the U.S. expressed strong support for what was then still a proposal for the cessation of hostilities. Once the accord was signed, the U.S. pursued this active involvement in the peace process by hosting indirect talks between Ethiopian and Eritrean "technical experts" in early July 2000 during which the two sides discussed the substantive issues of border demarcation and compensation for the damages resulting from the war. Quiet diplomacy remained the rule, even after the U.S. sent Ambassador Richard Bogosian, Special Assistant to the Greater Horn, to the region to raise human rights and humanitarian issues with both parties.

Because their intensive involvement had failed to prevent the latest round of deadly fighting, the role of the U.S. policy makers came under harsh scrutiny. Critics faulted the Clinton administration for failing to apply direct pressures on the two parties as reflected in its reluctance to press earlier on for a U.N. arms embargo, or to use its influence to slow the flow of bilateral and multilateral financial aid to the two countries at a time when they were spending hundreds of millions of dollars on arms purchases. Administration officials defended themselves by arguing that an arms embargo would have led the belligerents to discontinue their participation in the peace talks, and that cutting the meager U.S. aid going to vital sectors in their economies would have only punished the neediest people in both countries.

The U.S. used its leverage only sparingly and as a last resort in its efforts to press for restraint. Ethiopia continued to benefit from the International Military Education and Training program, at a cost of U.S. $385,000 in FY 2000, with the only limitation being that the training could not be conducted in Ethiopia. By contrast, the U.S. froze the training of Ethiopian troops within the U.S.-led peacekeeping training program under the African Crisis Response Initiative. The U.S. development assistance to Ethiopia remained largely unaffected, at $40.8 million in development aid and child survival funds. Ethiopia was also the recipient of $14.8 million in non-food donations, and $330.4 million for food aid.

European Union

The E.U.'s position remained one of repeated condemnations of the major outbreaks of fighting, and sustained expressions of support for the OAU peace process. The E.U. gave a hint of why it had limited its involvement to this support role at the occasion of its appointment, on the eve of 2000, of a special envoy to the Horn of Africa, Italian Deputy Foreign Minister Rino Serri. This step, the E.U. said, was meant "to bolster the OAU effort and help the E.U. countries to come up with a better understanding and interpretation of the situation."

The African, Caribbean and Pacific and E.U. Joint Assembly (A.C.P.-E.U.) sent a parliamentary delegation led by the assembly's vice-president John Alexander Corrie to the Ethiopian and Eritrean capitals in mid-December 1999 to advocate for a negotiated settlement of the conflict under the OAU process, obviously to no avail. The ban on arms sales that the European Council of Ministers had imposed on Ethiopia and

Eritrea in March 1999 remained effective.

The E.U. made substantial monetary and in-kind donations for the relief of civilians affected by drought and the conflict in both countries. These donations, together with aid provided bilaterally by E.U. member states, placed the E.U. as the top donor of food aid to Ethiopia, a position it has continually occupied in the past twenty-five years. However, the conflict led to significant reductions in the E.U.'s development cooperation with the two countries. The European Commission declared on May 19, 2000, that as a result of the tightening of conditions for the disbursement of credits of the Structural Adjustment Support Programs that it financed, the latter had not disbursed any budgetary support to Ethiopia since January 1999. An aide official told leaders of both nations during a trip to the region in early October that the E.U. was ready to reestablish cooperation with them if they consolidated their peace settlement. The E.U. had suspended its economic cooperation with them after they went to war.

United Nations

The U.N. Security Council fully backed the OAU peace process. Responding to a transient but ominous flare-up in the fighting, members of the Security Council on March 14 called on Eritrea and Ethiopia to cooperate "fully and urgently" with the OAU and to participate constructively in its efforts to settle the dispute between them. With clear signals in early May that fighting was about to resume, the Security Council extended the itinerary of its special mission to the Democratic Republic of the Congo to include Addis Ababa and Asmara. The mission found the differences between the two sides, "while real, were relatively small and manageable and could be resolved by intensive negotiations over time." Days after it left the region, fighting resumed with rare intensity over these differences. In reaction, the Security Council in its unanimous resolution 1298 of May 17, which the U.S. sponsored, finally imposed a formal embargo on arms sales to the two parties for a year. The belated U.N. embargo was destined to have little effect in the short and medium runs, coming as it did after both countries had amassed huge stocks of arms and munitions. A timid call by the council in February 1999 to member states to immediately end all arms sales to both sides obviously had failed to achieve the desired results.

In early July, the U.N. secretary-general dispatched an advance team to the region to pave the way for the deployment of U.N. peacekeeping mission. Based on the recommendations of the team, the Security Council on July 31 decided to establish a U.N. Mission in Ethiopia and Eritrea (UNMEE) of up to one hundred military observers and support staff in anticipation of a larger mission. The council authorized 4,200 troops for UNMEE in mid-September, and said member states were cooperating in offering troops and resources for the mission. By late September, some forty military observers were taking positions along both sides of the disputed border, and another group of military observers was to be dispatched to the mission area by mid-October.

In a remarkable omission, the advance team dispatched by the U.N. to prepare for UNMEE did not include a representative of the U.N. high commissioner for human rights, and the resulting mission structure had no human rights component, although a component was provided for in resolution 1320 (2000), which established the mission. The persistence of reports of wide-scale human rights abuses by both parties, even after the cessation of hostilities, appeared to have led the U.N. secretary-general to announce, on September 18, that he intended to establish a "small" component within UNMEE to follow human rights issues.

KENYA

Human Rights Developments

The promised constitutional reform process, which could have brought greater democratization in Kenya, remained stalled as the government of President Daniel arap Moi continued to block progress. This left in place a deeply flawed political system with power concentrated in the presidency, insufficient checks on the executive branch, a lack of accountability for government officials, and the barring of independent parliamentary candidates in a political party environment fraught with infighting and divisions. The political crisis was paralleled by a marked deterioration in the economic situation, caused in large part by state mismanagement and corruption. The standard of living for the average Kenyan continued to drop, and the year was characterized by electricity rationing and water shortages in the capital Nairobi and other cities.

The modalities of the constitutional reform process remained unresolved. In the face of an opposition boycott, the ruling party controlled parliament pushed through President Moi's plan to control the outcome. A parliamentary committee of twenty-seven was created, composed of fourteen ruling party parliamentarians with the remaining thirteen from the combined opposition, to draft the constitutional reforms. In opposition to this, a civil society initiative, the Ufungamano group, led by the religious sector including the Catholic Church, the Protestant National Council of Churches of Kenya (NCCK), the Muslim Supreme Council of Kenya, and the Hindu Council of Kenya, appointed a set of commissioners to carry out a more broad-based consultative process. As of October 2000, neither set of commissioners had embarked on the task of gathering citizens' views on the substance of a new constitution.

Although the Ufungamano initiative slowed down President Moi's attempts to push through a new constitution of his own choice, there was no resolution by year's end. All sides were aware that the stakes were high. The outcome of this issue, which promised to grow in urgency with the national election's approach by 2002, would serve as a critical juncture in Kenya's history. The existing constitutional provisions did not permit President Moi to seek another term in office and if unchanged would bring to an end his tenure of over two decades.

High-ranking government and ruling party officials continued to use the state machinery to obstruct freedom of association and assembly for the opposition. Though many more political opposition gatherings were able to take place, police officers continued to interfere with and violently disperse participants in violation of the laws relating to public meetings. The use of state-sponsored and protected gangs to break up meetings and rallies of government critics continued. In October, President Moi banned countrywide rallies called by Muungano wa Mageuzi (Peoples Movement for Change), a coalition group of opposition and civil society organizations.

Complaints of police harassment, use of excessive force, torture, and deaths in custody were frequent. In October, a 127-page internal police report titled, "Report of the Committee on the State of Crime in Kenya 1997 to 1998," was leaked to the press. The report, the result of a two-year study conducted by a five-person police team to study problems in the police force, concluded that the police force was unable to address crime due to poor management, corruption, a break down in discipline and a disregard for rules.

The situation was no better in the prisons. The impunity of state agents was highlighted in August with the brutal clubbing to death by prison warders of six prisoners who were apprehended as they attempted to escape. The public outcry forced the government to announce that it would carry out an investigation into "dereliction of duty" by the prison authorities. The legal community continued to complain of corruption and political control in the judiciary, which has always been used by the government for political ends.

A wide array of independent and outspoken newspapers were able to publish relatively freely. But the biggest gains for freedom of expression in Kenya were made by the coming on line of several newly licensed independent television and FM radio stations (some of which had pending applications dating as far back as 1992). The growth of the independent broadcast sector resulted in a notable expansion in the airing of differing opinions, particularly on radio. These licences were, however, restricted principally to broadcasting in urban areas and rural broadcasting remained as restricted as before. Nor was this free expression without danger. The minister of home affairs threatened retaliation against the hard-hitting political satire group *Reddykulus* which appeared on the Nation TV station.

Hundreds of thousands of internally displaced persons remained unable to return after being driven from their homes in state-sponsored attacks since 1991 directed against members of ethnic groups perceived to support the political opposition. The authorities continued during the year to fail to provide adequate security to those who sought to return to their homes under assurances of safety, nor were land titles restored to those who were wrongfully deprived. Nor had the government held those responsible for the violence accountable. In 1999, a presidential Commission on the Ethnic Clashes wound up after eleven months of hearing evidence, including from Human Rights Watch, about the violence between 1991 and 1998. As of October 2000, the commission's findings had still not been released, though the completed report had been submitted to the president over a year before.

Defending Human Rights

A wide array of local human rights organizations were engaged in monitoring human rights in Kenya. Although these organizations were able to function, they periodically came under attack from the government for their work. The risk that human rights defenders faced was highlighted on August 24 when Father John Kaiser, a well-known human rights activist, was found dead by the side of the road shot in the head. The brutal murder was carried out at night by unidentified persons on the Naivasha Road, some fifty miles outside Nairobi. A Catholic parish priest in the Rift Valley area and a U.S. citizen, Kaiser had worked in Kenya for thirty-six years and had been an outspoken critic of state-sponsored "ethnic" violence and other rights violations. Most recently, he had brought attention to a case in which two girls had allegedly been raped by a local politician, and had helped furnish the evidence that the Federation of Women Lawyers in Kenya (FIDA) used to institute a private prosecution against Julius Sunkuli, minister of state in the office of the president. Following the murder of Kaiser, FIDA officials reported anonymous death threats over the telephone. In November 1999, the immigration department had refused to renew Kaiser's work permit, normally routine for foreign priests working in Kenya, until pressure was brought by the church and human rights groups which accused the government of trying to silence the priest. In 1999, the Law Society of Kenya had honored Kaiser with its annual human rights award. Kaiser was the fifth priest to have been killed since 1994 either by police or by unidentified gunmen. In none of these cases have the perpetrators been held accountable.

There were some hopeful efforts in 2000 to strengthen the weak mandate and capacity of the government's Human Rights Standing Committee. The Standing Committee, a marginal and largely ineffective body, was founded by the president in 1996 in response to donor pressure. By law, its members were appointed by the president, it reported only to him, action was decided by him, and only the president could remove its members. In 2000, after two years, the attorney general finalized a proposed bill to provide greater powers to the committee, including subpoena powers, financial autonomy through the parliament instead of the attorney-general's office, and security of tenure. In March 2000, a consultative workshop, funded by the United Nations Development Programme (UNDP), was held to discuss the draft National Commission on Human Rights Draft Bill with relevant representatives from government and civil society groups as well as the Office of the U.N. High Commissioner for Human Rights. The proposed law had not been passed by parliament as of October 2000.

The Role of the International Community

The international donor community remained almost exclusively concerned with corruption and economic reform issues at the expense of human rights concerns. As a result, the government continued to make great efforts to give the appearance of economic reform, but did little toward improving human rights. The year was dominated by the government's wooing of the international financial institutions for the resumption of lending which had been suspended in 1997.

Increased concern on the part of donors and the international financial institutions about Kenya's precarious and worsening economic situation prompted the World Bank and International Monetary Fund (IMF) to restore funding that had remained suspended for three years due to concerns about corruption and "key governance criteria." In a momentous decision in July, the IMF pledged a U.S.$198 million three-year loan and the World Bank pledged a U.S.$150 million loan for budget support. The renewal of this assistance was strictly conditioned on stated reforms including audited public accounts, civil service retrenchment, strengthening of accountability institutions (namely the Kenya Anti-Corruption Authority and the Office of the Controller and Auditor-General), and the enactment of an Economic Crimes Bill and Code of Ethics for public servants. Notably absent were any conditions that would have required the government to address governance criteria such as respect for the rule of law and judicial independence. The government's lack of commitment to genuinely addressing rule of law issues was underscored in October when the draft Economic Crimes Bill (a requirement of the renewed funding) it issued contained provisions that allowed the government to selectively apply the law, allowing high-ranking government officials to evade prosecution on corruption charges.

As expected, the international financial institutions' decision cleared the way for aid from other countries and institutions that had been similarly withheld. One of the first to respond was the United Kingdom (U.K.), a traditional ally of President Moi, whose minister for international development Clare Short announced the immediate release of some U.S. $42 million (U.K. £30 million) in budget support for civil service reform. The European Union (E.U.) followed suit with U.S. $30 million for the power sector, and the African Development Bank pledged U.S. $50 million for infrastructure maintenance. It was also expected that the renewed IMF aid would allow Kenya to reschedule her debt payments and to push for a Consultative Group meeting for bilateral donors to make new pledges for project aid.

The approach of the international community—in considering corruption and economic reform measures as wholly distinct from good governance issues such as political accountability and other rights—fell short of addressing the key issue, absolute executive control, which was at the heart of Kenya's political crisis. The Dutch Government was the only government that remained firm about the link, reiterating that all bilateral development assistance to Kenya would end by 2002 due to "bad governance, human rights abuses, and impeded democratization."

United States

Although human rights concerns remained on the U.S. agenda, trade and economic concerns as well as international terrorism tended to take precedence over human rights. As did other donors, the U.S. focused its attention on criticizing corruption. In 2000, U.S. development aid to Kenya totaled U.S.$34.95 million, including $5.85 million for political reform and democratization, $10.7 million for environmental issues, and $18.4 million for women's reproductive health and HIV/AIDS programs. Approximately two-thirds of this aid was allocated to program assistance directed almost entirely to nongovernmental organizations. Following the murder of Father John Kaiser, Federal Bureau of Investigations agents were sent to help the Kenyan police to investigate the case and Secretary of State Madeleine Albright pledged that the U.S. would follow the case closely.

LIBERIA

Human Rights Developments

Given the background of a brutal seven-year civil war, Liberia's transition process was slow and shaky. Three years after a U.N.-supervised election brought former faction leader Charles Taylor to power, the situation remained insecure despite progress toward demilitarization, the reabsorption of many ex-combatants into society, and a decrease in the number of military checkpoints. In 1999, the government publicly destroyed a huge cache of arms and ammunition collected during the disarmament period. Additionally, thousands of refugees and internally displaced persons returned to their home areas, despite the severe economic hardship they encountered. State institutions, which had all but ceased to function, were being restarted, albeit with major problems. For some in Liberia, these signs, however small, indicated tangible progress in the right direction.

The consolidation of power in the presidency and the lack of respect for the rule of law threatened to undermine prospects for sustainable peace. Taylor government officials regularly operated with little or no accountability or transparency, further exacerbating the divisions and resentments fueled by the war. State institutions that could provide an independent check on the Taylor administration, such as the judiciary, the legislature, the human rights commission, and the commission on reconciliation remained weakened and cowed by the executive.

The volatility of the situation was underscored by five serious outbreaks of fighting since the 1997 elections. Barely a year after the war ended, there were two outbreaks of violence in Monrovia in 1998 in which state security forces battled with faction leader Roosevelt Johnson's officially disbanded United Liberation Movement for Democracy in Liberia (ULIMO-J) and his predominantly ethnic Krahn supporters. In April and August 1999, Liberian rebels operating from neighboring Guinea carried out attacks in Lofa County, northern Liberia. Although not confirmed, the rebel attacks were thought to be led by former fighters from the ULIMO-K faction who were largely ethnic Mandingos. The fighting resulted in civilian deaths and displacement, forcing thousands of Liberians and Sierra Leonean refugees to flee.

In July 2000, another invasion was launched by a group calling itself Liberians United for Reconciliation and Democracy (LURD) from the Guinea border into Liberia, resulting in fighting and displacement yet again in Lofa County. These periodic eruptions of violence contributed to the continuing destabilization of the subregion, and within Liberia assumed an ethnic dimension as the government indiscriminately blamed members of the Krahn and Mandingo communities for the attacks.

One of the major human rights problems in 2000 was the complete impunity with which the security and police forces operated. Following his inauguration, President Taylor rejected the peace accord provision that provided for a transparent restructuring of the security forces by the West African peacekeeping force. Instead, former Taylor faction fighters were placed in the security and police forces without serious efforts to provide training or to meet pledges to incorporate members from the other factions. Former Taylor fighters have also been permitted by the government to create security firms for hire by private sector companies.

There were regular reports of harassment, extortion, mistreatment, killings, "disappearances," and torture by members of the police and armed forces who acted with complete impunity. Since taking office, President Taylor created two extralegal elite security forces known as the Anti-Terrorist Unit (ATU) and the Special Security Services (SSS). These security units had no legal basis for their existence, were not under the command of the Ministry of Defense, and were only accountable to President Taylor. Headed by, and heavily stacked with, former Taylor-faction fighters, these security forces were regularly responsible for abuses against the population. Other new security forces included an armed border patrol force under the Ministry of Justice's Bureau of Immigration specifically to man the borders and the creation of an elite force within the National Police Force, the Special Operations Division (SOD).

Ethnic Krahn and Mandingo people, historically seen to be allied with the repression of the former Doe government and with anti-Taylor factions during the war, were particularly susceptible to harassment at the hands of the state security apparatus. Following the violence in Monrovia in 1998, Krahn were targeted for extrajudicial executions, harassment, and politically motivated criminal charges. In the aftermath of the Lofa County incursions in 1999, security forces killed, tortured, and mistreated civilians, particularly members of the Mandingo ethnic group. During the incursions and counter-attacks in Lofa County, hundreds were killed and thousands of citizens as well as Sierra Leonean refugees were forced to flee the area. Although some of the alleged abuses by the security forces were investigated by the government, in all cases security personnel were treated leniently or exonerated. Since the 1999 and 2000 rebel incursions in Lofa County, Mandingo residents remain afraid to return to their homes.

Independent voices were increasingly silenced by the government in a bid to stem publicity and criticism of human rights violations by the government. Journalists and human rights activists came under increasing attack by President Taylor and other high-ranking government officials, including through threats, physical assaults, and politicallymotivated criminal charges. In March, Suah Dede, head of the Liberian Press Union was briefly detained without charge after giving a radio interview condemning the closure of two radio stations. In April, Isaac Redd, radio broadcaster on the state radio station, was detained and held without charge for several days by the police. He was later accused of speaking against the president and charged with "criminal malfeasance." In August, a foreign news film team—David Barrie, Tim Lambon, Gugulakhe Radebe, and Sorious Samura—who were in Liberia to film a documentary, were arrested, charged with espionage, and detained for a week. The film team had been given official permission to film in Liberia, but were arrested and accused of filming in restricted areas and seeking to damage the country's image by falsely linking President Charles Taylor to diamond smuggling. They were released following international pressure.

Aware that a large proportion of the population relied on the radio for their news, the government silenced independent radio broadcasting. The government-owned radio station provided the only news broadcasts heard by most Liberians. Two independent radio stations came under attack in March 2000: Star Radio and Radio Veritas, the radio station of the Catholic Church. Star Radio was forcibly closed by government security, according to the police director, for "hosting of political talk shows, news, interviews and programs that have damaging political effects that tend to undermine the peace, security and stability of Liberia." Some fifteen police raided the offices, assaulted two journalists, and ransacked and sealed the offices without giving a reason. Star Radio had already been requested a few months earlier by the Ministry of Information to provide two copies of their daily broadcasts before they were aired and were accused of putting negative reports on the internet. Radio Veritas was closed down for several days by the government on the grounds that it was making "political" broadcasts rather than religious ones. At the time of publication, Star Radio remained closed.

The internal conflicts within Sierra Leone, Liberia, and Guinea continued to spill over the borders, further destabilizing the region. In 2000, the Liberian government was accused of fueling the war in neighboring Sierra Leone by helping the Sierra Leonean rebel group, the Revolutionary United Front (RUF), a charge it strenuously denied. President Taylor, in turn, accused Sierra Leone and Guinea of providing a safe haven to Liberian rebels intent on destabilizing his government. In September 2000, tensions rose between Liberia, Guinea, and Sierra Leone, each accusing the other of supporting rebel activity. A crisis in the region was prompted when Guinean President Lansana Conte publicly accused refugees of rebel activity against his government, resulting in round-ups, detentions, and violence against Sierra Leoneans and Liberians in Guinea.

Voluntary repatriation of Liberian refugees from neighboring countries continued. While many thousands of Liberian refugees were able to return to Liberia without fear of political persecution, some members of the Mandingo and Krahn communities continued to have valid fears. In 2000, there were still some 100,000 Liberian refugees in Guinea and over 85,000 in Ivory Coast. Of those, some 15,000 Krahn in Ivory Coast were deemed by UNHCR to have a well-founded fear of persecution and were being assisted to remain and integrate with local communities in Ivory Coast. The situation for Liberian refugees in Guinea remained difficult: July 2000 insurgent attack from the Guinea border into Liberia prevented refugee return and Liberian refugees in Guinea were subjected to violence in September 2000. UNHCR was planning to end its repatriation assistance to Liberian refugees by the end of 2000. After that, assistance would be provided only inside Liberia for rehabilitation of infrastructure in areas that people were likely to return to. UNHCR planned to close its Liberia operation by March 2001.

Defending Human Rights

President Taylor and other high-ranking government officials continued to attack human rights groups for publicizing abuses and blamed the human rights community for the withholding of international aid. Human rights lawyers who represented perceived government critics also came under attack. Human rights activists continued to flee the country fearing government reprisal for their work. In December 1999, James D. Torh, the executive director of a children's rights organization, Fore-Runners of Children's Universal Development, was detained and charged with sedition for a speech he made. According to the indictment, Torh was charged for allegedly telling students, among other things, that "[President Charles] Taylor is running this government from his pocket and that those who voted for this government must repent that it is failing" and "we are prepared to tell whoever that is in power that it is time of the Liberian people to stand up and tell you to step down." Torh was released on bail after five days and fled the country.

Despite these attacks, the nongovernmental human rights community continued to expand its activities. In contrast, the National Human Rights Commission created by the government in 1997 was virtually inactive. Only three of the five mandated members were appointed by the senate, and the commission's chair remained outside the country for much of the year.

The Role of the International Community

Diplomatic missions, although still few, began to reopen in Liberia. In 2000, there were a dozen or so missions or embassies in Monrovia, including those of Burkina Faso, Egypt, the European Union (E.U.), Ivory Coast, Libya, the Netherlands, Taiwan, and the United States (U.S). Most international donors were wary about giving direct assistance to the Taylor government, conditioning this on improvements in microeconomic reporting, fiscal discipline, and respect for human rights. Most foreign aid was given through international relief organizations or local civil society groups.

The international community remained concerned by evidence of Liberian support for Sierra Leonean rebels by a flow of diamonds-for-arms through Liberia. It focused on pressuring the Taylor government to withdraw its support to the Sierra Leonean Revolutionary United Front (RUF), which was subject to a U.N. embargo on trafficking in arms and diamonds, its primary source of wealth. The link between the Taylor government and the RUF dated back to the Liberian civil war when Taylor headed the National Patriotic Front of Liberia (NPFL). The NPFL and RUF provided military and other support to each other through the years in a relationship that continued after the election that brought Taylor into office. Charges were subsequently made that the Taylor government was facilitating arms transfers to the RUF in return for Sierra Leonean diamonds. Over the last two years, official annual diamond exports by Sierra Leone dropped to half, to U.S.$30 million. In the same period, diamond exports by Liberia—a country that possesses relatively few diamond fields—rose to U.S.$300 million.

In late July, U.S. Undersecretary of State for Political Affairs Thomas Pickering delivered a blunt warning to President Taylor that Liberia would be subjected to sanctions if it did not halt support to the RUF. Several days later, at U.N. Security Council hearings on Sierra Leone diamonds on July 31, the U.S. again threatened sanctions against Liberia and Burkina Faso for illegal diamond and arms trafficking which it said was fueling the war in Sierra Leone. The U.S. ambassador to the U.N., Richard Holbrooke, stated that the U.S. had evidence showing that President Taylor and senior RUF leaders had personally taken large commissions for facilitating illegal diamond and arms transfers. In October, the U.S. acted on its threats by imposing a visa ban on President Charles Taylor and senior members his government. U.S. President Bill Clinton noted: "[t]he absence of any positive response from the [Taylor] government leaves little choice but to impose these restrictions," and added that the policy would not be reviewed until Liberia ended its support for the RUF.

The E.U. also took a strong stance regarding the Taylor government. In July, following U.K. allegations that President Taylor was selling weapons to the RUF in return for diamonds, the E.U. suspended approximately U.S. $50 million in aid to Liberia as a signal to the Taylor government to cut its support to the rebels in Sierra Leone. The only government that generously gave direct aid to the Liberian government in 2000 was the government of Taiwan, in return for Liberia's diplomatic support at the U.N.

United Nations

The U.N. Department of Political Affairs retained a small U.N. Peace-Building Support Office (UNOL) following the withdrawal of the U.N. observer mission in July 1997, to serve as a focal point and coordinate post-conflict U.N. peace-building activities in Liberia as well as to provide advisory services to the government in defining post-conflict priorities, to raise international funds for Liberia, and to coordinate and liaise between the government and the international community. This unit remained under the leadership of Representative of the Secretary-General Felix Downs-Thomas and maintained a low profile. It was not prominent in raising human rights issues. A U.N. Security Council arms embargo against Liberia since 1992 remained in place, but there was little evidence of its effective enforcement.

MOZAMBIQUE

Human Rights Developments

Floods, caused by two cyclones and record rains in early 2000, were the worst in living memory. Over 200,000 people were displaced but international relief efforts avoided serious loss of life. Despite the floods, Mozambique was ranked as among the world's fastest-growing economies during the year. Improvements in the respect for human rights were not as dramatic.

The floods followed presidential and parliamentary elections on December 3-5, 1999, which were rated as free and mostly fair. President Joaquim Chissano was sworn in again on January 15, having won 53.3 percent of the presidential vote against 47.7 for his rival, Afonso Dhlakama; in the voting for the national assembly, Chissano's ruling Front for the Liberation of Mozambique (FRELIMO) scored 48 per cent and took 133 of the 250 seats, against 38.81 percent and 117 seats for Dhlakama's Mozambique National Resistance (RENAMO)-led opposition coalition. The parties' regional strength roughly matched that shown by the 1994 elections. FRELIMO made some gains in the north but RENAMO kept control over large areas there and in the center. In the south, where the RENAMO vote was insignificant in 1994, it did slightly better. The 5.3 million votes cast represented 74 percent of registered voters, down from the 88 percent turnout of 1994.

RENAMO at first rejected the declared results, then grudgingly accepted them when the Supreme Court declined its suit, then openly contravened the law governing party administration by declaring it had moved its headquarters to Beira, a party stronghold. Throughout the year, reports of intimidation by RENAMO and FRELIMO supporters increased.

Beira was particularly tense in February following the overnight distribution of leaflets by RENAMO saying Chissano was "a thief" and calling for a division of the country along the east-west line of the Save river. Riot police were deployed and a number of arrests of RENAMO supporters followed.

The most serious incident was on May 5, when a group of one hundred people led by senior RENAMO figures in the district, armed with clubs and bushknives, attacked a police station in the locality of Aube in Angoche district with the intention of stealing weapons. The police said they opened fire in self defense, killing four attackers (RENAMO puts the number of dead at eight and the Human Rights League a figure of six dead). The incident appeared to have been provoked by a dispute over paying tax in the local marketplace and the arrest of a RENAMO supporter by the police. A number of people were arrested, including RENAMO's political delegate in Angoche district, who was released on bail on May 18.

Police in the district of Sanga, in Niasa province, detained an opposition RENAMO supporter in July for reportedly conducting a campaign of intimidation, including arson, against government supporters. RENAMO in turn reported a rise of attacks against its supporters and provided Human Rights Watch with a list which could not be verified.

Police behavior remained the source of the majority of complaints Human Rights Watch received from Mozambique in 2000. Arbitrary detention and extortion were also common allegations, while prison conditions continued to be appalling. Despite publicity and debate on this issue, prisons such as the provincial facility in Nampula remained badly overcrowded. The Nampula civil provincial prison was built to house seventy-five prisoners, and at the time of this writing held 482, over half of them on remand awaiting trial. This prison lacked running water, food, or blankets, and the prisoners relied upon relatives to maintain them. Overcrowding was due to a lack of resources and space but also due to an overburdened criminal justice system.

Mozambique continued to play a leadership role in supporting the international ban on landmines and served as co-chair of the Standing Committee of Experts on Mine Clearance. Mozambique introduced U.N. General Assembly Resolution 54/45B, which was adopted in December 1999. In April 2000, work began on a national landmines survey. About five square kilometers of land were cleared of mines in 1999, bringing the overall total to 194 square kilometers. Despite fears that the February and March 2000 floods would result in an increase in mine

casualties, the number continued to decline, falling from 133 in 1998 to sixty casualties in 1999. Foreign Minister Leonardo Simão attended the whole of the Second Meeting of States Parties of the Ottawa Landmine Ban Treaty, in September, the most senior official present for the duration of the conference.

Weapons left over from the civil war remained a problem, too. The Mozambican Council of Churches reported in September that its "Weapons to Hoes" project had met with success, collecting more than 55,000 weapons for destruction, and that a second phase of the project had begun in May.

Defending Human Rights

The Mozambican Human Rights League continued its work to monitor and remedy poor prison conditions and bad policing. The league had expanded its work into the provinces and had been successful in drawing domestic attention to ongoing abuses.

The Role of the International Community

The international community's prime focus during the year was on humanitarian assistance at the time of the floods. For postflood, reconstruction emergency aid was quickly deployed and South Africa played an important role, including through helicopter rescue operations, while Western countries procrastinated during the early stages of the crisis. As with Hurricane Mitch in Central America fifteen months before, debt relief quickly became a central issue. Mozambique continued to be part of the Heavily Indebted Poor Countries (HIPC) initiative, which had reduced debt service payments by about U.S.$1 million weekly.

United States

United States-Mozambique relations deteriorated over the election period, especially after the U.S. issued a statement in December 1999 suggesting that the government had been responsible for electoral fraud. A subsequent *Washington Post* article, quoting an undisclosed senior State Department official saying the government probably won by fraud, resulted in an even frostier period. The U.S. response to the flooding crisis led to a rapid improvement of the relationship as U.S. Marines were sent to assist in the relief efforts. During 2000 the U.S. continued to be the largest bilateral donor in Mozambique.

NIGERIA

Human Rights Developments

Nigeria entered a second year of civilian rule under the presidency of (former general and military ruler) Olusegun Obasanjo. Yet the new government failed to fulfil the hopes raised by the elections of 1999. The National Assembly passed only five bills during the year, and was struck by repeated corruption scandals, even as it debated new anti-corruption legislation. Ethnic and communal tensions among and within Nigeria's thirty-six states were exacerbated by the lack of a democratically drafted constitution, as well as the heritage of military rule—in particular, ongoing security force abuses. More positively, the government affirmed its commitment to the international human rights regime by signing the treaty for the establishment of an International Criminal Court in June 2000.

The seven-member commission chaired by retired judge Chukwudifu Oputa, appointed by President Obasanjo on becoming head of state to investigate past human rights abuses, made little headway during the year. The commission's public activities and the training of its personnel were funded by donors working with civil society groups. However, in October, the commission announced a series of public hearings to be held in five cities by February 2001. The Nigerian government brought charges in October 1999 against a number of members of the regime of General Sani Abacha, including his son Mohammed Abacha, for offenses including murder, attempted murder and conspiracy in relation to "death squad" activity, and theft of public funds.

Despite commitments to respect the rule of law, government agencies refused in some cases to honor court orders. In one case in late 1999, the National Drug Law Enforcement Agency failed to release suspects granted bail by the Federal High Court for several months. Many laws continued to reflect their military origins and infringe on the rights of the Nigerian people, including the Public Order Act and the National Drug Law Enforcement Agency Decree.

The government continued a program of prison decongestion, but prison conditions remained life-threatening. In January 2000, the government announced that all prisoners awaiting execution for twenty years or more would be granted pardons, and that those awaiting execution between ten and twenty years would have their sentences commuted to life imprisonment. Minister of State for Internal Affairs Alhaji Danjuma Goje stated in July that pretrial detainees represented over 70 percent of the prison population, and that 32,000 were currently incarcerated awaiting trial.

The Nigerian government recruited more than 33,000 officers to the police, in an effort to fulfil plans to nearly double the size of the force from its June 1999 strength of 135,000. But the force was still regulated by a colonial law first promulgated in 1943. In July 2000, civil society groups established a network on police reform to which government officials were invited.

There was some media harassment during the year. On January 19, 2000, more than fifty police invaded the International Press Centre, Lagos, and arrested everyone present, including several journalists, following a press conference given by the Oodua Liberation Movement. Several individual journalists were detained for various periods throughout the year after reporting on alleged calls for a military coup, demands for ethnic self-determination, or protests at an increase in the price of fuel.

The rights of women in Nigeria were routinely violated. The Penal Code explicitly stated that assaults committed by a man on his wife were not an offense, if permitted by customary law and if "grievous hurt" was not inflicted. Marital rape was not a crime. Child marriages remained common, especially in northern Nigeria. Women were denied equal rights in the inheritance of property. It was estimated that about 60 percent of Nigerian women were subjected to female genital cutting. Cross Rivers and Edo States adopted legislation banning the practice and imposing criminal penalties; the governor of Rivers State announced that he would follow suit. Child labor, especially in domestic work, often completely unpaid, remained common. There were numerous reports of the organized trafficking of children between Nigeria and other West African countries, and of women within West Africa and between Nigeria and Europe. In February 2000, police announced the arrest of a Lagos-based businessman in connection with the sale of women and girls to Europe; in August, another man was arrested in Anambra State for trafficking children to other countries in West Africa.

Several states in northern Nigeria extended the application of Islamic Sharia law to criminal offenses or announced plans to do so. Sharia law punishments, including amputation and flogging, were imposed for offenses such as cattle theft and fornication, and local Islamic voluntary organizations worked with Sharia courts to enforce the Sharia laws.

Hundreds of people lost their lives in communal violence across Nigeria. In late 1999 and early 2000, there were riots in which the Oodua Peoples Congress (OPC), a Lagos-based ethnic militia demanding devolution of power or even independence for the Yoruba southwest of the country, clashed with Hausas living and working in Lagos. A committee of the Lagos State Senate investigated the violence, and found that at least nine policemen, seven OPC members and 163 bystanders had lost their lives, and twelve police stations were burned down. Reports of the planned introduction of Sharia law led to clashes between Muslims and Christians in Kaduna in February

2000 and fresh violence in May. At least 700 people were killed in these disturbances and reprisal killings that followed in southeastern Nigeria, and thousands were displaced. Protracted communal and ethnic violence continued between the Aguleri-Umuleri (Anambra State), Ife-Modakeke (Osun State), and Jukun-Kuteb (Taraba State) communities.

The government response to this violence was often itself abusive. Speaking on national television in November 1999, President Obasanjo announced that police would be given orders to shoot on sight members of the OPC who refused to give themselves up. Police raids for suspected members of the OPC resulted in the arbitrary detention of hundreds of people and summary execution of dozens. In October, the presidency banned the OPC and ordered the arrest of its leaders, following further riots in which more than one hundred Hausas were killed by members of the ethnic militia. During the February riots in Kaduna, dozens were arbitrarily arrested and others shot by police. In April 2000, Mobile Policemen went on a rampage in the town of Suleja in Niger State and killed at least twenty civilians in a shooting spree following an attack by unarmed civilians on their post during communal riots protesting the appointment of a traditional leader. In July 2000, the governor of Anambra State stated that the "Bakassi Boys," a vigilante group also involved in anti-Hausa violence, had been renamed the "Onitsha vigilante services" and endorsed their activities. Although Minister of Police Affairs David Jemibiwon spoke out against the Bakassi Boys and other militias following this statement, he later seemed to back down from his position.

Ralph Uwazuruike, leader of an Igbo group called the Movement for the Actualization of the Biafran State (MASSOB), was detained for several days in April after he announced that the organization intended declaring the launch of a "new Biafra" on May 27. Uwazuruike was arrested again in August in Lagos, as he prepared to stage a demonstration at the U.S. embassy; in the same month, fifty-four MASSOB members were arraigned for treason.

The Nigerian government continued to deploy large numbers of soldiers and paramilitary Mobile Police across the oil-producing regions of the Niger Delta. As elsewhere in Nigeria, security force action was often indiscriminate, or targeted those who had done nothing but exercise their rights to freedom of expression, assembly, and association. The federal task force charged with protecting oil pipelines carried out several extrajudicial executions in oil-producing communities in Delta State. The victims were persons accused of vandalizing pipelines or the theft of petroleum products. In late November 1999, Nigerian soldiers moved into Odi, a community of perhaps 15,000 people in Bayelsa State in the Niger Delta, and engaged in a brief exchange of fire with a handful of young men, after the killing of twelve policemen there. They then proceeded to raze the town. The troops demolished virtually every building and killed dozens of unarmed civilians. In September 2000, President Obasanjo again threatened to deploy the army across the delta.

In March and April 2000, repressive force was once again used in Ogoniland, Rivers State, home of the Movement for the Survival of the Ogoni People (MOSOP), of which Ken Saro-Wiwa was leader before his 1995 execution. Paramilitary Mobile Police were deployed following disturbances in objection to development projects to be funded by Shell, killed at least one civilian, razed a number of buildings, and arrested several Ogoni activists, including Ledum Mitee, a MOSOP leader. President Obasanjo visited Ogoniland in September 2000.

In response to local demands for greater resource ownership and benefits, President Obasanjo introduced a bill to establish a Niger Delta Development Commission (NDDC). Conflict among the two houses of the National Assembly and the presidency meant that the bill had still not become law by September.

Defending Human Rights

Nigeria's numerous and sophisticated human rights groups were able to operate freely throughout the year. Indeed, civil society groups had a more ambitious legislative and reform program than the government.

The government-appointed National Human Rights Commission (NHRC), created in 1996, held a number of meetings to discuss human rights issues, most of them co-sponsored by nongovernmental human rights groups. In June 2000, the government dissolved the board of the NHRC and appointed new members, amid controversy as to the legitimacy of the procedure.

The Role of the International Community

Bretton Woods Institutions

Several delegations from World Bank and International Monetary Fund (IMF) visited Nigeria during the year. The IMF established a monitoring program at the Central Bank and finance ministry and in July 2000 agreed to a U.S. $1 billion standby credit facility. In May, the World Bank approved three new projects totaling U.S. $75 million, the first since 1993, to assist in the provision of universal basic education and to strengthen management of the economy, including measures aimed at increasing its transparency.

European Union and its Member States

The British government gave significant assistance to the new Nigerian government, emphasizing the restructuring of the military, tackling corruption, and economic reform (leading to debt relief) in its bilateral relations. Secretary of State for International Development Clare Short visited Nigeria in March and committed £15 million (U.S.$21 million) on development assistance to Nigeria in 2000/2001 and £25 million for 2001/2002. British Foreign Office Minister Peter Hain visited Nigeria in January, and Deputy Prime Minister John Prescott in June. Both

Hain and High Commissioner Graham Burton (in a November 1999 speech) emphasized that democratic dialogue was the only way to resolve the Niger Delta crisis. President Obasanjo visited France in February and the U.K. in September 2000.

In September 1999, the French ambassador to Nigeria, speaking for the E.U., pledged a U.S.$40 million grant to Nigeria for 1999 and a further $30 million for 2000, a large part of which would be plowed into projects in the Niger Delta. Human rights-related assistance focused on strengthening civil society capacity, judicial and prison reform, rebuilding the trade union movement, and independent media.

United States

In August 2000, President Clinton became the second U.S. head of state to visit Nigeria. He pledged support for efforts to recover public funds looted during the Abacha era and for debt relief, and assistance to fight HIV/AIDS. He also called on the Nigerian government to increase oil production in an effort to lower world oil prices. Clinton did not publicly raise human rights concerns. The Export-Import Bank signed a deal for U.S.$1.2 billion in loan guarantees, and Clinton announced that Nigerian exports would be eligible for duty-free treatment under the GSP (generalized system of preferences) program.

Military Professional Resources Incorporated (MPRI), a Virginia-based private security company, advised the U.S. government on reprofessionalization of the Nigerian armed forces, and a U.S. military team was based in Nigeria for most of the year. Defense Secretary William Cohen visited Nigeria in April 2000, and announced a U.S.$10.6 million military aid package, including funds to refurbish aircraft and train pilots. Nigeria participated with five other African countries in the U.S. West Africa Training Cruise in November 1999, allowing Nigerian naval officers to take part in various training exercises. In August, several hundred U.S. special operations forces began training and equipping five Nigerian battalions for peacekeeping work in Sierra Leone.

Secretary of State Albright visited Nigeria in October 1999 and urged Nigeria to complete the political reforms necessary to underpin the restoration of civilian rule, including repeal of repressive laws, strengthening of the judiciary, and consolidation of civilian control over the military. She endorsed efforts to investigate and prosecute past abuses, and stressed the U.S. desire to see solutions to the crisis in the delta based on the rule of law, not the use of force. Albright also pledged to "work with Congress" to triple or quadruple U.S. aid to Nigeria. U.S. aid for the year increased from the previous U.S.$7 million channeled through NGOs to U.S.$170 million, involving twenty-four U.S. government agencies. In January, Albright singled out Nigeria's transition program as one of four critical U.S. foreign policy issues in the coming year. Several other high-level U.S. officials visited Nigeria during the year.

Although Nigeria in March was deemed not to be in compliance with requirements for counter-narcotics certification under Section 481 of the Foreign Assistance Act (FAA), the administration issued a national interest waiver for the second year, thus allowing the U.S. to support assistance to Nigeria in six multilateral development banks and to restore FAA and Arms Control Export Act assistance to Nigeria. A five-year ban on flights between Nigeria and the U.S. was lifted in December 1999, and direct flights to Nigeria were scheduled to resume in October 2000.

The U.S. also launched an initiative to promote democratic governance and economic development in the Niger Delta by promoting dialogue among the U.S. and Nigerian governments, residents of the delta, and U.S. oil companies.

RWANDA

Human Rights Developments

The speaker of the national assembly, the prime minister, and the president all quit their posts under pressure within the first three months of the year, leaving a shrinking circle of power holders in control of the Rwandan government. The former vice-president, General Paul Kagame, was elected president in April by the assembly, and for the first time openly presided over the government he had reputedly run from behind the scenes since 1994. Kagame, from the Tutsi minority, replaced a Hutu president, thus ending the practice of having a member of the majority ethnic group serve as titular head of the republic. A reshuffle of cabinet positions gave ten of eighteen seats to Kagame's party, the Rwandan Patriotic Front (RPF), violating the arrangements made in the Arusha Accords of 1994.

The government announced that communal officials, now appointed, would soon be elected. Political parties exist in Rwanda, guaranteed by the Arusha Accords, but the government limited their importance by such measures as prohibiting public meetings. In the proposed elections, political parties will not present candidates.

Two of the three top officials who left their posts in early 2000 also left the country, saying they feared for their lives. The former prime minister was the latest of several important Hutu political leaders to chose exile. The speaker of the national assembly, Joseph Kabuye Sebarenzi, however, was the first leading Tutsi politician to flee. His departure highlighted the rift between Tutsi survivors of the 1994 genocide and the RPF over such issues as jobs in the administration, military promotions, aid to genocide victims, and justice for the genocide.

Sebarenzi, reportedly accused by President Kagame of "inappropriate" political ideas, was said to favor the return of the former king, Kigeri Ndahindurwa, ousted in 1961 and now in exile in the U.S. Another genocide survivor accused of encouraging Tutsi soldiers to "desert to the king" spent nearly a year in jail without trial before being released. In February 2000, two soldiers and three civilians, all genocide survivors suspected of ties to the king, were kidnapped in Burundi and Tanzania where they had fled. Their Rwandan military captors forced them to return to the country, although those taken in Tanzania had been under the protection of the United Nations High Commissioner for Refugees (UNHCR). Some of them were reportedly tortured, but after months in jail without trial, all were released.

A presidential councilor linked to genocide survivors' associations was gunned down by men in military uniform in early March. No arrests had been made in the case by late in the year. When the brother of the deceased, vice-president of the survivors' association Ibuka, tried to leave Rwanda, police confiscated his ticket and passport and took him for questioning. After intervention by several foreign ambassadors, he was later permitted to leave the country. Other leading members of Ibuka also fled Rwanda, as did a number of Rwandan soldiers. Some forty university students, most or all of them Tutsi, left for Uganda in December 1999, denouncing the "dictatorial" nature of the government.

In the first part of the year, local authorities jailed dozens of persons in Ndusu and Bulinga communes on charges of supporting the king. Most were later released without trial.

Two leaders of the opposition Movement Democrat Republicain (MDR), the largest political party in Rwanda, were released from prison without trial: Bonaventure Ubalijoro, who had been detained since 1999, and Sylvestre Kamali, who was arrested in 1994. But a former member of the national assembly, Jean Mbanda, was jailed in June, shortly after publicly criticizing the RPF. He was accused of committing fraud six years before.

The Rwandan government fought armed opponents largely in the neighboring Democratic Republic of the Congo (DRC), where its troops committed numerous violations of international humanitarian law. (See section on Democratic Republic of Congo). Its soldiers suppressed an insurgency in northwestern Rwanda in 1998 and 1999, with enormous civilian casualties. But small groups of insurgents resurfaced in Gisenyi prefecture in December 1999 to massacre thirty-one Tutsi at Tamira and in May 2000 to kill nine persons at Rwerere. In May others killed three secondary school students and wounded three others in Kinigi and killed two Local Defense Force members in Ruhondo, both in Ruhengeri. Insurgents recruited adherents, supposedly including children, to serve as combatants.

Soldiers reportedly killed civilians suspected of being insurgents in Rubavu, Ruhondo, Giciye, and Karago communes and imprisoned many others, some of them in military facilities, like the Milpoc detention center in Gisenyi, where they suffered from harsh conditions and in some cases from torture.

In the southeast in midyear, several bodies were sighted floating down the Akagera River, and other persons were said to have "disappeared." Apparently reflecting fear of increased violence, more than three thousand mostly Hutu Rwandans from this region fled to Tanzania from April to July, twice the number for all of 1999.

Members of the Local Defense Forces—young people recruited, trained, and armed by the government supposedly to defend their communities—killed more than a dozen people and raped and robbed many others in different parts of the country. Nominally under the supervision of local authorities, they in many cases escaped punishment for their abuses.

The government reportedly forcibly recruited men and children for the army and the Local Defense Forces. Authorities freed some 300 military detainees and prisoners from Rilima and Kibungo prisons in midyear, supposedly because they agreed to go fight for Rwanda in the DRC.

In 1999 and 2000 the government tried more persons accused of participating in the 1994 genocide than in the two years since trials began. The total tried by March 2000 was some 3,000, but more than 125,000 still languished in prisons. As in previous years, courts varied considerably in the regularity and thoroughness of their proceedings. Of those found guilty, some 14 percent were sentenced to death, a decrease from earlier years. The percentage of persons acquitted rose slightly to nearly 20 percent. The government repeatedly extended deadlines permitting the detention of persons without any case files, a practice otherwise forbidden by Rwandan law. In December 1999, a new deadline was set for June 2001. An estimated 18,000 persons were held without files, some of them detained since 1994.

In a case which drew international attention, Bishop Augustin Misago was acquitted of genocide charges in June. Arrested immediately after the former president accused him at a mass meeting in April 1999, the bishop was jailed for more than a year as the prosecution presented a flimsy case against him. Several persons acquitted of charges of genocide were attacked after their release and at least one of them was killed. Others were re-arrested soon after their release.

Three judges were arrested and charged with "genocide"—one of them for the second time—and a fourth was suspended from his post in November 1999 after having been previously arrested and freed for lack of proof.

Conditions in prisons were miserable and in some cases inhumane and life-threatening. The food supply was irregular in some central prisons and the government called upon families to bring food to detainees, a practice previously usual only for communal lockups. Delivering food to detainees imposed a substantial burden on households where there was only one adult, particularly where the prison was distant.

Throughout the year, the government promised an alternative form of communal justice, called *gacaca*, but late in the year the necessary legislation had not been passed. Although the program offered some hope of trying the accused more rapidly, it raised concerns about the rights of the accused, particularly because it provided no right to counsel. Although no gacaca law existed, authorities implemented a kind of gacaca in many prisons at the direction of the Ministry of Justice. There was no public explanation of how these sessions were conducted or what use would be made of their conclusions.

The government continued a program of forced "villagization." Although enforced less harshly than in preceding years, as late as midyear, authorities still required people to move against their will to government-designated settlements. Some homeowners were forced to destroy their houses before moving. Lacking the necessary resources to build new houses, hundreds of thousands of people lived in temporary shelters made of tree limbs, leaves, and pieces of plastic. Some cultivators were forced to cede their fields to serve as settlement sites. Many village residents had to walk miles further each day to reach their fields or sources of water and firewood than when they lived in their previous homes. Difficulty in reaching fields and insecurity over land tenure resulting from villagization caused a decline in agricultural production, which was further cut by drought. Toward the end of the year, serious food shortages threatened regions where villagization was most advanced.

The government permitted considerable press criticism on certain questions, but balked at negative comment on others. Three journalists fled the country in 2000, saying their lives were at risk because of reports they had published. One foreign journalist was threatened with expulsion for having filed a dispatch that displeased authorities, and several Rwandan journalists were questioned by police after publishing information critical of the government.

Defending Human Rights

The Rwandan League for Promoting and Defending Human Rights (La Ligue Rwandaise pour la Promotion et la Défense des Droits de l'Homme, LIPRODHOR) effectively documented abuses, particularly outside the capital, and monitored judicial proceedings related to the genocide. It also conducted a poll showing that 93 percent of the respondents favored the proposed gacaca system. LIPRODHOR, as well as other local human rights organizations, prepared to assist the gacaca process, both through training programs and by monitoring the sessions. The Association for the Defense of Human Rights and Public Liberties (Association pour la Défense des Droits Humains et des Libértés Publiques, ADL) carried out a useful study of villagization. The regional umbrella group, League for the Defense of Human Rights of the Great Lakes (La Ligue des Associations de Défense des Droits de l'homme des Grands Lacs, LDGL), began a campaign among its member organizations to end impunity in the region and to extend the mandate of the International Criminal Tribunal for Rwanda into Burundi and the Democratic Republic of Congo.

The National Human Rights Commission, elected in mid-1999, organized widespread public education efforts and worked quietly to resolve several problems concerning property and, most notably, to protect and secure the release of jailed Tutsi genocide survivors.

The Rwandan government made a detailed response to reports published by Human Rights Watch and Amnesty International, an initiative that would have been more promising had the responses been cooler in tone and more factual in content.

The Role of the International Community

International Justice

At the end of 1999, a United Nations investigative commission reported how and why the United Nations and its member states failed to halt the 1994 genocide. Six months later, a commission of the Organization of African Unity (OAU) made the same critical conclusions and particularly condemned the United States for impeding action by the U.N. and France for supporting the genocidal government. The OAU report also examined alleged RPF crimes against humanity committed in 1994. President Kagame initially welcomed the OAU publication as "a good report," but two months later, Rwandan authorities attacked it as "biased."

The International Criminal Tribunal for Rwanda completed trials of a factory director and a leader of the Interahamwe militia and found them guilty of genocide. The court found a third person guilty after he confessed to his role in inciting to genocide over the radio. Still plagued by lengthy proceedings, the appeals and trial chambers adopted reforms meant to speed trials. An internal audit found that all branches of the tribunal needed to become more efficient, both in terms of time and money.

In November 1999, the appeals chamber ordered the release of Jean-Bosco Barayagwiza on the grounds of procedural errors by the prosecution. The Rwandan government immediately suspended cooperation with the court and for a brief period refused a visa to the chief prosecutor. In early 2000, the appeals chamber reheard the case. The prosecutor argued for reversal on legal grounds but also stated that prosecutions for genocide could not continue without cooperation from the Rwandan government. The appeals chamber reversed its decision, allowing Barayagwiza to be tried. In late 1999, the tribunal decided to receive an official and permanent representative of the Rwandan government, and in 2000, judges of the trial chamber visited Rwanda where they were received by President Kagame. These developments, together with the absence of any prosecutions of RPF members for alleged crimes, raised questions about the impartiality of the tribunal.

Such doubts were fueled by publication of a confidential U.N. memorandum suggesting that the previous prosecutor had halted an investigation into RPF involvement in downing the airplane of President Juvenal Habyarimana, the catalytic event which set off the genocide.

Another press account revealed, however, that the tribunal was investigating pos-sible RPF crimes. In August, a Belgian investigating magistrate opened a similar inquiry following a complaint filed by several Rwandans.

In judicial proceedings elsewhere related to the genocide, a Swiss appeals court reduced to fourteen years the life sentence of a Rwandan burgomaster condemned in 1999 for violations of the Geneva conventions. French judges investigated the downing of Habyarimana's airplane and a case of genocide against a Rwandan priest. In Canada, an appeals court deliberated on the motion of Leon Mugesera to avoid expulsion from the country for having incited to genocide in Rwanda in 1992. In Belgium, a trial began for two religious sisters and two others accused of genocide.

United Nations

The U.N. Security Council acknowledged human rights abuses committed by all sides in the war in the DRC. It asked both Rwanda and Uganda to make reparations for the loss of life and property damage inflicted on civilians when they fought each other in the Congolese city of Kisangani. In another resolution, the council deplored the deterioration of human rights in the eastern DRC, including attacks on civilians in which Rwandan troops presumably were involved.

The U.N. Human Rights Commission remarkably enough showed less concern than the Security Council for such combat-related abuses. Both the commission and the special representative of the high commissioner for human rights, Michel Moussalli, commended the Rwandan government for its progress, ignoring its abuses in the DRC and minimizing those inside Rwanda.

European Union

The European Union (E.U.) and its member states said little about Rwandan human rights abuses and contributed generously to government funds. Unlike 1999 when the E.U. expressed concern about abuses related to villagization, in September 2000 it adopted a common position that criticized nothing and encouraged "the ongoing processes...of protecting and promoting human rights." In March, the E.U. resumed development aid which had been interrupted in 1994.

The United Kingdom continued its ten-year program of assistance, with grants of some U.S. $70 million, with Cooperation Secretary Clare Short enthusiastically supporting the Rwandan government and initially denouncing critical human rights reports as "political propaganda." The Dutch, initially hesitant to list Rwanda among its privileged aid recipients, did so in 2000 in consideration of economic progress and promised implementation of the Lusaka Accords. Belgium proffered an official apology for its conduct at the time of the genocide and promised increased assistance, particularly in the area of health. Germany gave some U.S. $6 million for education and legal assistance. Even France, seen as hostile since 1994, sent its minister of cooperation to Rwanda.

While governments at home generally kept silent on human rights issues, diplomats from the Belgian, German, Swiss, and Dutch embassies intervened locally during the year to assist persons whose rights had been abused.

United States

Generally viewed as strongly supportive of the Rwandan government, the U.S. this year helped it acquire the only advanced radar in central Africa and cut the Rwandan debt to the U.S. by 67 percent. It also signed three grants totaling U.S. $15.1 million for assistance in establishing the rule of law, transparency in governance, and health and social services.

Like their European colleagues, U.S. embassy staff followed individual cases of human rights abuse and intervened several times.

Ambassador for War Crimes David Scheffer worked to end impunity in central Africa, a goal supported at least nominally by Secretary of State Madeleine Albright. As the year ended, administration officials were considering possible ways to bring violators of international humanitarian law to justice.

The U.S. supported the international tribunal for Rwanda, although in May 2000 it pointed out the need for better use of funds. Senator Russ Feingold sought to encourage the arrest of suspected perpetrators of genocide by asking the U.S. Senate to establish a rewards program similar to that set up for the international tribunal for ex-Yugoslavia.

Relevant Human Rights Watch Reports:
The Search for Security and Human Rights Abuses, 4/00

SIERRA LEONE

Human Rights Developments

The Lome Peace Accord signed on July 7, 1999 between the Revolutionary United Front (RUF) and the government of Sierra Leone committed the rebels to lay down their arms in exchange for representation in a new government. It also included a controversial general amnesty for all crimes committed during the war. Despite hopes that the peace process would bring an end to the atrocities that characterized this brutal nine-year war, abuses continued unabated.

The nine months following the signing of the agreement brought about a relative reduction in abuses and few cases of the RUF signature atrocity—limb amputation—were documented. However, sexual assault against women and girls continued unabated. The collapse of the peace process in May, after the capture of some five hundred United Nations peacekeepers serving with the United Nations Mission in Sierra Leone (UNAMSIL), reversed this trend. Renewed conflict ushered in increases in human rights abuses by the RUF and rebel militias, including limb amputation, and a disturbing intensification of abuses by pro-government forces.

The success of the peace process had been measured by enrollment in the cornerstone Disarmament, Demobilization, and Reintegration (DDR) program, with little respect for human rights and the establishment of the rule of law. The collapse of the peace process brought about a reassessment of the provision for a general amnesty in the Lome Accord and mobilized national and international support for a war crimes tribunal.

Rebel United Front (RUF) and Armed Forces Revolutionary Council/ex-Sierra Leonean Army (AFRC/ex-SLA)

In the months following the signing of the accord, the overwhelming majority of cease-fire violations registered by UNAMSIL were rebel attacks against civilians.

Rebel combatants filtering back into the capital, Freetown, committed extortion, car theft, robberies, and other acts of lawlessness. The authorities demonstrated a reluctance to investigate or to arrest rebels responsible for such crimes, in part for fear that such arrests might threaten rebel cooperation with the DDR program.

Following the resumption of hostilities in May, RUF forces intensified their attacks on civilians. There were frequent reports of RUF abuses including murder, widespread rape, limb amputation, forced labor, abduction, and looting. Most of these attacks occurred in the context of raids for food. There were several cases of limb amputation, even of women, elderly, and children as young as twelve. Within the areas under their control, the RUF continued to use intimidation to impose a "taxation" system, extorting food and money from civilians.

When indiscriminate attacks by a government helicopter gunship provoked a mass exodus of civilians from areas under RUF control, the RUF responded by becoming particularly brutal, setting off a further exodus of civilians from RUF areas. There were also many cases of forced labor within the diamond mining areas of Kono, and the RUF reportedly murdered civilians accused of mining without its approval. On May 8, armed men inside the home of RUF leader

Foday Sankoh opened fire on a crowd of civilian demonstrators, killing nineteen.

Starting in May, the RUF began conscripting many children and adolescents, including some girls, and scores of civilians had the letters RUF carved into them with knives or razors. In May, RUF commanders in Makeni forced some forty demobilized child soldiers living within an interim care center to rejoin the RUF's ranks. Fear of conscription contributed to the flight of thousands of civilians from rebel-held areas. The RUF frequently used "buying back" of conscripted youth by family members as another tactic for extorting money.

Members of the AFRC/ex-SLA based around the Occra Hills (forty miles from Freetown) also imposed a reign of terror on villagers within Port Loko and Masiaka districts. These soldiers carried out rape, murder, torture, abduction, massive looting, forced labor, and indiscriminate ambushes along a major highway. The AFRC/ex-SLA murdered numerous civilians for not having enough money, for being unable to carry looted items, or for refusing to have sexual relations with a combatant. This violence forced thousands of villagers into camps for the internally displaced. The Sierra Leonean Government, Economic Community Cease-fire Monitoring Group (ECOMOG), and UNAMSIL forces made very few efforts to actively pursue the rebels or to protect the civilian population. The attacks only ended in September after an operation by British paratroopers to free British and Sierra Leonean soldiers previously taken hostage by the AFRC/ex-SLA.

Thousands of abducted prisoners continued to be held in rebel areas. Before the collapse of the peace process, the AFRC/ex-SLA released several small groups of prisoners, but continued to abduct others. At this writing, some four thousand children registered by UNICEF as missing during the war had yet to be located. The vast majority were presumed to have been abducted by the RUF.

Government Forces

The collapse of the accord brought about a marked increase in human rights abuses by government forces. These included rape, extortion, the Sierra Leonean Army's indiscriminate use of a helicopter gunship, and the killing of RUF prisoners by members of the Civil Defense Force (CDF) militias, the largest and most powerful of which were the Kamajors.

The Sierra Leonean government caused massive civilian casualties and displacement through helicopter gunship attacks during May and June against rebel strongholds in Makeni, Magbaraka, and Kambia. The indiscriminate use of the gunship against market places caused at least thirty civilians deaths.

The tribally based CDF militia became considerably less disciplined. Extortion and brutality by CDF militiamen at checkpoints became routine. Violence against women had been very uncommon among CDF militias until recently, primarily because of the belief that a warrior's power was dependent upon sexual abstinence. However, numerous cases of sexual assault were documented this year, including gang rape by Kamajor militiamen and commanders. There were several cases of CDF militias ransacking villages and commandeering cars from civilians and aid agencies. There were numerous reports of CDF militias torturing and killing suspected RUF rebels. CDF militiamen routinely intimidated and threatened policemen attempting to enforce the rule of law. In Kenema in September the police chief was badly beaten by Kamajors protesting the arrest of one of their members on drug charges.

Following the May crisis, the government of Sierra Leone detained hundreds of suspected rebels and their collaborators under the 1991 State of Emergency Act. The names of only 121 of them were later made public by the government, as required under the act. Several hundred more were held illegally, including at least thirteen children. In August, 173 detainees were released as a gesture of good will toward the RUF, while ninety-two remained in custody. The government had yet to authorize the International Committee for the Red Cross to work within jails and detention facilities.

Women

While there was a relative reduction in most classes of gross human rights abuses in the months following the Lome Accord, sexual assault against women and girls, particularly by members of the RUF and AFRC/ex-SLA, continued unabated. There were numerous cases of rape of children as young as ten. Commanders from all government and rebel factions were involved in perpetrating and ordering sexual abuse, and the authorities made little effort to protect women.

Children

Children continue to be subjected to all forms of violence and be recruited as combatants by both rebel forces and to a lesser extent the CDF. Several children were murdered by the RUF and at least two suffered limb amputations. Numerous girls, as young as ten, were subjected to sexual abuse both in Sierra Leone and as refugees in Guinea. Children were abducted from villages and off of buses by rebel forces, and used as forced labor to carry looted goods, as sexual slaves for male combatants, and for work in the diamond mines. Over 1,700 child combatants were demobilized before the collapse of the peace process, but from the May collapse to this date, only 115 had been registered. While some eight hundred children were reunified with their families between January and August, some four thousand children were still registered as missing (most abducted by rebel forces).

Internally Displaced People and Refugees

Following the May crisis, both RUF abuses and the indiscriminate use of the government helicopter gunship caused a mass exodus of some 330,000 civilians from behind rebel lines. Of these, 15,000 fled across the border to Guinea. Once out of RUF territory, civilians were often captured and accused of being rebel sympathizers by government militias which sometimes beat them, extorted money, and murdered them. Following a government offensive in the Kono region in August, thousands of civilians attempting to flee into Guinea were denied entry. After pressure from UNHCR, some women, children and elderly refugees were allowed to enter into Guinea. In September, some five thousand Sierra Leonean refugees in Guinea were rounded up and detained in response to cross-border attacks into Guinea from Sierra Leone and Liberia. There were reports of several deaths, widespread rape, and massive looting during the attacks. Some 380,000 refugees in Guinea continued to be subject to frequent intimidation by the Guinean military and civilian militias.

Humanitarian Workers and Journalists

Aid workers and their beneficiaries came under frequent attack by the RUF and to a lesser extent by pro-government militias. Following the crisis in early May, aid workers were forced to withdraw from RUF-held areas and had access to less than half of the country. The RUF attacked and looted feeding centers, threatened local and expatriate doctors with death, abducted aid workers, and, in one case, raped malnourished beneficiaries.

Rebel forces killed one Sierra Leonean and two foreign reporters in May. The Sierra Leonean was shot on May 8 when RUF combatants inside the house of leader Foday Sankoh opened fire on a crowd of demonstrators, and two foreign reporters were killed on May 27 in a rebel ambush on their convoy near Rogberi Junction. It was not known if they were targeted for being journalists or because Sierra Leonean soldiers accompanied them. An editor from a local paper was detained in May after being accused of being an RUF collaborator. Several other journalists reported being beaten or detained.

The Truth and Reconciliation Commission and the Special Court

The Truth and Reconciliation Commission (TRC) mandated to be established within ninety days of the signing of the Lome Peace Accord had yet to be set up. Following the May crisis, activity toward establishing the TRC was officially frozen by the U.N. Office of Human Rights. U.N. and other organizations struggled to determine whether the TRC was still relevant following the resumption of hostilities, and if so, what its relationship would be with the proposed Special Court.

In July 1999, the special representative of the secretary-general added a reservation to the Lome Accord, stating that the U.N. did not recognize amnesty insofar as it applied to crimes of genocide, crimes against humanity, war crimes and other serious violations of human rights and international humanitarian law. Nevertheless, the U.N. made no effort to pursue justice for such crimes until the hostage crisis in May. The crisis and the apprehension of Foday Sankoh put justice squarely on the international agenda. In June, the Sierra Leonean government asked for U.N. assistance to establish a court in Sierra Leone with a mix of local and foreign prosecutors and judges. The RUF remained the target, and there were concerted efforts to retain the Lome amnesty for other parties to the conflict.

The U.S. eventually took the lead in the Security Council and drafted a proposal for a special court for Sierra Leone that would not be an organ of the Security Council, and would thus avoid time-consuming U.N. bureaucracy. On August 14, the Security Council adopted Resolution 1315, authorizing the secretary-general to enter into negotiations with the government to establish an independent, special court to bring perpetrators of the most serious violations of international humanitarian law to justice. On October 5, the secretary-general submitted a report with recommendations and proposals for the establishment of the special court, which was under consideration by the Security Council. The report proposed the court be a hybrid using both international and Sierra Leonean law, judges and prosecutors. It also included a controversial proposal to put child soldiers between fifteen and eighteen years of age on trial and proposed that the jurisdiction should extend back to November 30, 1996, the date of Sierra Leone's first peace agreement.

Treaties

This year, Sierra Leone ratified the Rome Statute to establish an International Criminal Court and enacted legislation to make the Convention Against Torture and the International Covenant on Civil and Political Rights and its Protocols a part of Sierra Leonean law.

Defending Human Rights

Most of the some twenty human rights organizations that operated in Sierra Leone worked exclusively in the capital Freetown and lacked proper funding, expertise, and institutional support. In the months following the signing of the Lome Peace Accord, these groups did very little monitoring of continuing human rights abuses and instead focused on human rights education for the public.

After the May crisis, these groups became somewhat more vocal and active in both monitoring and advocacy, and several groups called for the establishment of an international war crimes tribunal.

The formation of an autonomous, quasi-judicial national Human Rights Commission as provided for in the Lome Accord made only limited progress. The United Nations Office of the High Commissioner for Human Rights sent a consultant to assist the government in shaping and drafting the legislation for the commission, but Parliament had yet to consider a draft. UNAMSIL blamed the lack of progress on the breakdown in the peace process and lack of personnel within its own human rights section.

Meanwhile, the preexisting governmental body, the National Commission for Democracy and Human Rights (NCDHR), effectively did no monitoring, documentation of human rights violations, or advocacy, and neglected to take a public stand on the war crimes tribunal.

The Role of the International Community

The RUF's capture of U.N. peacekeepers and subsequent resumption of hostilities unleashed a wave of international condemnation against the RUF for having precipitated the collapse of the peace process. However, frequent violations that gave rise to the crisis had gone largely ignored for months by key members of the international community who did more to appease rebel leaders than confront them.

The moral guarantors of the Lome Accord: the U.N., OAU, the Economic Community of West African States (ECOWAS), the Commonwealth of Nations, and the Government of Togo, all failed to condemn or apply requisite pressure on the RUF and ex-SLA/AFRC for their repeated attempts to delay and frustrate the peace process, for their continued acts of lawlessness and human rights violations against civilians.

Following the resumption of hostilities, most international actors acknowledged the importance of using military force to disarm the RUF, which occupied over 60 percent of the country. However, members of the international community demonstrated little willingness to do so themselves. With the U.N. unwilling to stiffen its mandate from peacekeeping to peacemaking, and without any international body willing to commit troops, the task of pressuring the RUF back to the negotiating table was left to the under funded, under-trained, and poorly led Sierra Leonean Army.

The collapse of the peace process forced most key members of the international community to reassess their respective policies toward Sierra Leone, but military objectives remained clearer than political goals. The collapse of the peace process effectively rendered obsolete most key provisions of the Lome Accord, including disarmament, the amnesty, the transformation of the RUF into a political party, and the inclusion of the RUF and AFRC in the government. Despite this, the U.N., U.S. and U.K. insisted that the Lome Accord must form the basis for any future peace.

Attacks on Guinean villages by RUF and Liberian forces that began in September, highlighted fears that the war could spread beyond Sierra Leone's borders.

United Nations

In May, the killing of at least ten and capture of some five hundred United Nations peacekeepers precipitated a collapse of the Sierra Leonean peace process, and forced the United Nations to reassess the viability of the 1999 Lome Peace Accord, the efficacy of the United Nations Mission in Sierra Leone, and the future of U.N. peacekeeping operations in Africa.

Prior to May, the RUF and rebel factions repeatedly delayed and frustrated the implementation of the peace process, especially after UNAMSIL attempted to deploy into the diamond-producing areas.

Contributing countries demonstrated minimal political will to change the mandate from peacekeeping to peace-enforcing. Instead, the Security Council responded to UNAMSIL's weaknesses by mandating successive increases in troop strength: from the original 6,000 in October 1999, to 11,000 in February (Resolution. 1289), to 13,000 in May (Resolution 1299). The secretary-general's sixth report on UNAMSIL recommended a further increase in troop strength to 20,500.

Internal divisions within the military and political leadership of the mission worsened the crisis. In his July 5 report on UNAMSIL, Kofi Annan said there had been "a serious lack of cohesion within the Mission." In part due to these problems, contributing countries were divided on whether or not to support the mission, the largest and most expensive in the world, at a projected $782 million for 2000-2001.

In response to problems within UNAMSIL and growing insecurity within the region, an eleven-member Security Council delegation visited Sierra Leone and four other West African countries in October.

Their report reaffirmed the need to maintain military pressure on the RUF, yet failed to resolve differences over the need for a more aggressive mandate. On several occasions, UNAMSIL failed to aggressively interpret the part of their mandate that allowed for the protection of civilians "under threat of imminent physical violence." In June, Kenyan UNAMSIL troops abandoned the northern town of Kabala while under attack by the RUF. Jordanian UNAMSIL troops failed to adequately secure the strategic Freetown-to-Mile 91 highway from frequent attacks and ambushes on civilian vehicles by the AFRC/ex-SLA. Civilians described being robbed or abducted by the militias within view of the peacekeepers.

The human rights section under the UNAMSIL mission was mandated in January to have fourteen human rights monitors, but it never operated with more than nine and functioned without a permanent chief. They conducted regular and thorough monitoring missions but put out few press releases and lacked a regular channel for disseminating information.

On July 5, the U.N. Security Council adopted Resolution 1306, which imposed an eighteen-month ban on the trade in rough diamonds from Sierra Leone that did not have a government certificate, in a bid to prevent the RUF from funding its war. It also mandated setting up a five-person panel of experts to look into possible violations of sanctions and the link between the trade in diamonds and arms. The panel, which did several fact-finding missions to the region, was to present its findings by October 31.

ECOWAS and ECOMOG

In the first several months of 2000, ECOWAS, despite its position as one of the moral guarantors of the Lome Accord, did little to pressure the RUF to comply with its provisions. ECOWAS nations were openly dissatisfied with the lack of U.N. financial support for ECOMOG troops in Sierra Leone, and with the U.N. decision to deploy U.N. peacekeepers to facilitate the implementation of the accord instead of funding

ECOMOG troops.

Following the collapse of the peace process, ECOWAS heads of state directly blamed and condemned the RUF and, in an emergency summit in Nigeria on May 10, announced their decision to use every means possible to defend Sierra Leone's government. They followed this up on May 29 by endorsing a proposal made by ECOWAS defense ministers and chiefs of staff to send an additional three thousand troops to Sierra Leone, on the condition that the United Nations would pick up the cost. At this writing, ECOWAS troops, mostly from Nigeria, were being trained by the United States. ECOWAS also called for UNAMSIL's mandate to be changed from peacekeeping to peace enforcement and called for the force to be headed by a West African.

Organization of African Unity

In May, the secretary general of the Organization of African Unity strongly condemned the killing and abduction of U.N. peacekeepers and the resumption of hostilities and backed up an ECOWAS resolution to deploy three thousand ECOMOG troops. In June, OAU Secretary General Salim Ahmed Salim appointed South African Ambassador to Ethiopia Kingsley Mamabolo as his special envoy to Sierra Leone. In July, a mini-summit on Sierra Leone was held during the OAU summit in Lome, Togo, between the OAU, ECOWAS, and U.N. Secretary-General Kofi Annan. In August, OAU Secretary General Salim visited Sierra Leone and donated U.S. $250,000 to the Disarmament, Demobilization, and Rearmament program and other institutions.

The European Union, United States, and United Kingdom

European Union

In May, the European Union issued a declaration condemning the RUF for attacks on UNAMSIL personnel and the violation of the Lome Accord. A May 23 resolution by the European Parliament condemned the "assumed participation of Burkina Faso, Liberia and Togo," in support for the RUF and their involvement in illicit diamond smuggling. In June, the E.U. expressed its concern that continued violations of arms embargoes in Sierra Leone and Angola were contributing to the continuation of these conflicts. Also in June, E.U. foreign ministers suspended aid to Liberia because of its support for the RUF rebels. In September, the E.U. general affairs council reaffirmed its support for the Lome Accord as the basis for future peace in Sierra Leone, and expressed its willingness to help the United Nations and Sierra Leonean government set up a special tribunal.

Since 1995, the European Commission had given Sierra Leone more than 94 million euros (U.S. $80 million) for development and rehabilitation projects over five years. Since the beginning of the year, an additional 12 million euro (U.S. $10 million) was administered through the European Community Humanitarian Office (ECHO) for emergency humanitarian assistance in Sierra Leone, and for Sierra Leonean refugees in Guinea.

United Kingdom and United States

The United Kingdom and United States continued to play a pivotal role in political and military developments in Sierra Leone. The collapse of the peace process prompted both countries to intensify their military engagement with and on behalf of Sierra Leone, while political issues were effectively put on hold.

United Kingdom

When Freetown, the capital, was briefly threatened by the RUF in May, the U.K. deployed over five thousand military personnel, including six hundred ground troops, to secure key strategic areas, and to advise and support both UNAMSIL and the Sierra Leonean Army. Although the bulk of U.K. forces were withdrawn by mid-June, two hundred soldiers remained in the country in order to strengthen a training team already involved in restructuring the Sierra Leonean Army before the May crisis. A further sixty advisers (to increase to ninety) were mostly deployed within the Sierra Leonean Defense Headquarters, and played a key role in advising and directing military operations.

During a June 8 visit, Foreign Secretary Robin Cook acknowledged that Britain was making a long-term commitment to Sierra Leone, and on October 10, further military assistance, including a hundred additional trainers, equipment for the Sierra Leone Army, an offer to provide officers to fill staff appointments at UNAMSIL headquarters, and an offer to provide a rapid reaction force of up to five thousand troops was announced.

After the renegade "Westside Boys" rebel faction took eleven British soldiers hostage from the training team on August 25, British forces were deployed and mounted an operation to free them. During the September 10 operation, one British soldier and some twenty-five Westside Boys were killed.

U.K. assistance to Sierra Leone since March 1998 was over GBP 70 million, including the funding of demobilization camps and humanitarian assistance. In coordination with the commonwealth secretariat, the U.K. provided funds for training and administration of the Sierra Leonean police, including the provision of the inspector general.

United States

Until the hostage crisis in May, U.S. policy toward Sierra Leone failed to attract high-level attention within the administration. Most U.S. officials continued to defend the amnesty under Lome, despite the February report by David Scheffer, ambassador at large for war crimes issues, who reported the ongoing atrocities and abuses, and acknowledged the inadequacy of mechanisms for accountability.

U.S. policy subsequently became more active. The U.S. worked to get the United Nations behind a more robust peacekeeping response to the crisis, and played a key role in moving the Security Council and the Sierra Leonean government toward the creation of a special court for Sierra Leone. During a July visit by Deputy Secretary of State for Political Affairs Thomas Pickering to West Africa, and in the testimony of Ambassador Richard Holbrooke before the Security Council hearings on diamonds in Sierra Leone, the U.S. publicly accused Liberia and Burkina Faso of supporting the RUF, and threatened sanctions against them.

In August, the U.S. launched a substantial operation to train and equip up to seven West African battalions, largely Nigerian, for duty with UNAMSIL. The administration stated that all participating troops would be vetted in accordance with U.S. law, which prohibits assistance to military units that have been responsible for serious human rights abuses.

In October, the U.S. hardened its position towards Liberia for its continued support of the RUF by imposing a visa ban on Taylor and other Liberian officials, their families, and close supporters.

The U.S.'s total humanitarian and emergency contribution in 2000, including grants to NGOs and aid agencies, was U.S. $55 million. In July the U.S. announced a $20 million aid package for training Nigerian and Ghanaian troops to strengthen the U.N. effort in Sierra Leone.

SOUTH AFRICA

Human Rights Developments

President Thabo Mbeki completed his first year as president of South Africa, leading a government dominated by the African National Congress (ANC), though the Inkatha Freedom Party (IFP) remained a junior partner. In July, a new opposition political party was formed, the Democratic Alliance, which brought together the National Party, the old party of government, and the Democratic Party, its former parliamentary opposition. The ANC's partners in a longstanding "tripartite alliance," the Communist Party and the Congress of South African Trade Unions (COSATU), seriously challenged the government, not only on its neoliberal economic policies, but also on

President Mbeki's expressed doubts as to the link between HIV and AIDS. Local government elections on the basis of new municipal boundaries were scheduled for December 2000, after delays caused by opposition from traditional leaders, many of them IFP-aligned, to the new boundaries and the proposed role of chiefs in the new structures.

In January, the National Assembly passed four important acts required under the 1996 constitution: the Promotion of Equality and Prevention of Unfair Discrimination Act, the Promotion of Access to Information Act, the Promotion of Administrative Justice Act, and the Preferential Procurement Policy Framework Act. In May, the National Assembly passed legislation giving protection to "whistle blowers" disclosing information in the public interest. In a groundbreaking September judgment, the Constitutional Court found that the government had an obligation under the constitution to provide short-term housing for several hundred people evicted from their homes and in desperate need. In January 2000, South Africa ratified the OAU Charter on the Rights and Welfare of the Child. Respected former truth commissioner Faizal Randera was appointed "inspector general of intelligence" in April 2000, with responsibility for ensuring respect for the constitution by the intelligence services.

The Truth and Reconciliation Commission (TRC) continued hearing applications for amnesty. By the end of 1999, the amnesty committee had resolved 6,037 cases, or 91 percent of all applications received. It had granted amnesty in 568 cases and refused amnesty in 5,287 cases, while 815 matters remained outstanding. Victims' groups expressed concern at the delay in making payments of reparations, in accordance with the recommendations of the TRC's 1998 report. Although R.30 million (U.S. $4.2 million) had been paid out to 10,000 victims by June 2000, the total required to fulfil the recommendations was approximately R.3 billion (U.S. $420 million). The trial on charges ranging from drug trafficking to murder of Wouter Basson, a chemical weapons expert

with the old South African army, continued throughout 2000. Among the revelations of the trial was the apartheid government's involvement in the murder of hundreds of members of the Namibian liberation movement, the South West Africa People's Organization (SWAPO).

The Independent Complaints Directorate (ICD), set up in 1997 to investigate or oversee the investigation of complaints against the police, reported 681 deaths in custody or as a result of police action during the year to March 2000, a slight decrease on the previous year. The number of complaints lodged with the ICD increased by 50 percent. Velaphi Kwela, a senior investigator with the ICD, was shot dead by unknown gunmen in July, while on his way home from the ICD provincial office in Durban. In July, two police filmed by a BBC TV crew brutally assaulting suspected car thieves were convicted of assault with intent to do grievous bodily harm, fined the equivalent of U.S. $600 and $900, and given suspended sentences. According to a report of the auditor-general released in May 2000, payments to police members suspended on disciplinary charges amounted to more than R.21 million (U.S. $3 million) during the financial year ending March 31, 1999, only R.6 million less than the budget for the ICD over the same period. According to police statistics, 212 police were killed during 1999, eighty-one while on duty.

The first hundred police officers were appointed to the new "Scorpions" detective unit within the office of the National Director of Public Prosecutions in January; they were sent for training by Scotland Yard in the U.K. and by the FBI in the U.S. Legislation setting out the powers of this unit was debated in parliament in September.

Overcrowding in prisons continued to worsen: on April 30, 2000, the prison population was 172,271 (of whom 63,964 were awaiting trial), against approved accommodation for 100,384 inmates. More than five thousand of the prisoners awaiting trial had been held in prison for more than a year. At an estimated 416 inmates per 100,000 citizens, South Africa had one of the highest incarceration rates in the world. In September, the government announced that about 11,000 prisoners awaiting trial on lesser offenses would be released. Assaults on prisoners by warders and other prisoners remained serious problems, including widespread prisoner-on-prisoner rape. In March, the minister of correctional services signed a contract with a private company, the Ikwezi Consortium, to design, build, and operate a maximum security prison in Bloemfontein, the first such contract in South Africa. In April, President Mbeki appointed Judge Johannes Fagan to head the judicial inspectorate. In April, the director-general of the Public Service Commission told parliament in a management audit report that the government had lost control over the department, detailing incidents of corruption, intimidation, organized crime, sexual harassment, and rape.

Hundreds of children were held in prison, despite a formal government commitment that detention should be a last resort for juveniles: on May 31, there were 4,253 children in prison, of whom 2,519 were unsentenced and 1,734 sentenced. Conditions of overcrowding for children were particularly severe at Pollsmoor prison in Cape Town, where 300 children aged fourteen to seventeen were held awaiting trial in March. An interdepartmental task team was appointed to address this issue, but the number was only reduced to 208 by September. The Cape High Court ruled in July that the children should be immediately examined by a doctor and given medical and psychological care. The government stated that there was insufficient alternative accommodation to hold the children, many of them charged with serious offenses.

A report of the national prosecuting authority revealed a backlog of more than 180,000 court cases in July. The National Directorate of Public Prosecutions deployed "rescue teams" to clear case loads at problematic courts. In February, Minister of Justice Penuell Maduna released a ten point plan to bring fundamental changes to the justice system, including the creation of specialized courts and improved prosecution services.

Former Ethiopian president Col. Mengistu Haile Mariam visited South Africa from Zimbabwe, where he was living, in late 1999 for medical treatment. Despite appeals to arrest him and bring him to justice for human rights crimes committed while he was head of state, the government refused to do so. The government also did not accede to a request for Mengistu's extradition by the Ethiopian government. In September, the government deported a Rwandan to Kenya, despite being informed that he was indicted by the Arusha tribunal in connection with the 1994 genocide.

Violence against women, including sexual violence, remained a very serious problem. The Domestic Violence Act and the Maintenance Act came into force in December 1999, improving the system for the award and enforcement of court orders restraining perpetrators of violence in the home and the collection of maintenance payments from absent fathers. An interdepartmental steering committee led efforts to train magistrates, prosecutors, and police in the new laws. The justice ministry hosted a three-day workshop on sexual offenses in February.

"Taxi violence" between rival operators of minibus taxis continued; reports continued to implicate members of the police in this violence. Attacks focused on the Golden Arrow bus company operating in Khayelitsha, a Cape Town township, had led to the deaths of at least four bus drivers, a taxi driver, and two passengers by the end of July, as well as dozens of injuries. In an attempt to halt the killing, the Western Cape government cordoned off the entire township for twenty-four hours in August, and the police made several arrests. Continuing a two-year series, a number of bomb explosions occurred in Cape Town during the year, the most serious a blast at a bar on November 28, 1999, in which forty-eight people were injured. Police alleged that members of the vigilante group People

Against Gangsterism and Drugs (PAGAD) were responsible. In September, a Cape Town magistrate who had heard some cases involving PAGAD was shot dead in what appeared to be a planned assassination. Violence also continued to plague KwaZulu-Natal, and several ANC and IFP leaders were killed in what appeared to be political assassinations. One of the worst incidents occurred in November 1999, when eleven people were killed in a shoot-out at a taxi-rank in Empangeni. In July 2000, police shot dead ANC MP Bheki Mkhize at his home near Ulundi during an operation they claimed was a search for illegal weapons. The ICD immediately began an investigation; three public order policeman were arrested and charged with murder.

The government brought a new Refugee Act into force in April 2000, which addressed several concerns about defects in the existing system, while failing to provide asylum seekers with the right to a hearing before those who would adjudicate their case. The government also published a heavily criticized draft migration bill. A very high percentage of people arrested during a police "operation crackdown" in February and March were "suspected illegal immigrants," leading to severe overcrowding at the detention facility where foreigners without papers were held pending deportation. Many of those detained had asylum claims pending, had been granted refugee status, or were South African citizens. Several government officials made statements implying that all undocumented foreigners were involved in criminal activities. In December 1999, the Constitutional Court ruled that homosexual couples must be given the same rights to naturalization under immigration law as heterosexuals; in June 2000, the court ruled that a restrictive section of the Aliens Control Act relating to the grant of temporary residence permits to spouses of South African citizens was invalid, and that the government must grant such permits unless good cause existed to refuse.

Defending Human Rights

South Africa's vigorous human rights community continued to monitor adherence to national and international standards. Occasional government hostility to NGO criticism was counteracted by strong collaboration in government-NGO partnerships elsewhere. The constitutionally guaranteed South African Human Rights Commission (SAHRC) criticized the government in its annual report for often ignoring its recommendations. The Commission on Gender Equality faced substantial internal difficulties during the year, and several key staff resigned. The government reduced the size of the much-criticized Youth Commission in June.

In November 1999, the SAHRC released an interim report on racism in the media, based on two methodologically controversial research papers, and requested responses from the industry. When little response was forthcoming, the commission decided to subpoena editors and others to appear before it, provoking an outcry that this threatened freedom of expression. A compromise was agreed by which the subpoenas were withdrawn and editors voluntarily attended hearings on media racism in March and April 2000. The commission published a final report in August that was less critically received, and made recommendations to reduce racism in the media. In September, the commission hosted a high-profile conference on racism in preparation for the U.N. World Conference Against Racism, Racial Discrimination, Xenophobia, and Related Forms of Intolerance, to be held in South Africa in 2001.

The Role of the International Community

United Nations

In January 2000, the U.N. Committee on the Rights of the Child considered South Africa's first report to that body. The committee welcomed legal reforms and steps taken to implement them, but expressed concerns about a number of areas, including the juvenile justice system, especially the holding of children in adult detention facilities. South Africa chaired the tenth U.N. Congress on the Prevention of Crime and the Treatment of Offenders, held in Vienna in April 2000. U.N. Special Rapporteur on the Independence of Judges and Lawyers Dato Cumaraswamy visited South Africa in May, on a fact-finding mission during which U.N. technical aid to South Africa was also discussed.

The office of the U.N. high commissioner for human rights, under a project in operation since April 1998, offered technical assistance to South Africa. A manager for the project was based at the SAHRC's headquarters in Johannesburg. In addition, the Pretoria office of the U.N. High Commissioner for Refugees gave logistical and other support to the SAHRC's work on xenophobia.

South Africa continued to receive substantial international donor funding: an estimated R.760 million during the 1999/2000 financial year (U.S.$110 million) and R.800 million (U.S.$116 million) in 2000/2001.

United States

President Mbeki visited the U.S. in May, his first state visit. The U.S. Agency for International Development's Program for South Africa focused on six strategic areas, including democracy and governance, as well as law enforcement. In May, USAID pledged U.S.$250 million for social development programs over the next five years.

European Union

Under the terms of an "in principle" agreement in December 1999, the E.U. Foundation for Human Rights in South Africa pledged continued funding until September 2003 of human rights and development projects with funds from the European Commission's Programme for Reconstruction and Development in South Africa. Individual E.U. member states also made bilateral contributions to human rights initiatives. In June 2000, E.U. foreign ministers approved a 885 million euro (U.S. $840.7

million) program. Several European ministers traveled to South Africa during the year. A Trade, Development, and Cooperation Agreement between the E.U. and South Africa was finally agreed in February 2000, cutting tariffs and liberalizing trade, after years of negotiations. President Mbeki visited the U.K. in May, and attended the third annual meeting of the U.K.-South Africa forum.

The Commonwealth

In November 1999, South Africa hosted the Commonwealth Heads of Government Meeting in Durban; in August the Commonwealth Parliamentary Association met in Cape Town. A number of Commonwealth governments provided assistance for human rights projects, including the Australians and the Canadians.

Relevant Human Rights Watch Reports:

A Question of Principle: Arms Trade and Human Rights, 10/00

SUDAN

Human Rights Developments

The government of Sudan remained a gross human rights abuser, while rebel groups committed their share of violations. In the seemingly endless seventeen-year civil war, the government stepped up its brutal expulsions of southern villagers from the oil production areas and trumpeted its resolve to use the oil income for more weapons. Under the leadership of President (Lt. Gen.) Omar El Bashir, the government intensified its bombing of civilian targets in the war, denied relief food to needy civilians, and abused children's rights, particularly through its military and logistical support for the Ugandan rebel Lord's Resistance Army (LRA), which held an estimated 6,000 Ugandan children captive on government-controlled Sudanese territory. As for the Sudan People's Liberation Movement/Army (SPLM/A), the principal armed movement of the south and of all Sudan, its forces continued to loot food (including relief provisions) from the population, sometimes with civilian casualties, recruit child soldiers, and commit rape. On both sides, impunity was the rule.

Sudan's human rights record of gross abuses was one factor in the General Assembly vote in October that denied a Security Council to Sudan, nominated by the Organization of African Unity, and instead granted the African seat to Mauritius.

In Khartoum and other government-controlled areas, the Islamist government's repression of political opponents continued. While some openings in civil liberties occurred, and one major opposition party, the Umma Party, returned from exile, these openings did not appear to be uniformly applied. The Umma Party sought more human rights guarantees before it would participate in presidential and legislative elections that the government announced for December 2000.

The government's outreach to exiles appeared to grow out of the internal power struggle within the ruling Islamist party, the National Congress (previously the National Islamic Front or NIF), which the president controlled. Expulsion of the Hassan al Turabi faction led him to create a new political party, the Popular National Congress (PNC), which felt the heat of arrests and injuries in anti-government demonstrations.

Negotiations to end the war appeared fruitless, whatever the forum or venue. The parties remained stalled on the issues of the relation of religion to the state and self-determination. Sudan's Arab and African, Muslim and non-Muslim population is spread between nineteen major ethnic groups and 597 subgroups speaking Arabic and more than 115 indigenous languages.

Government Abuses

Torture and impunity remained a government policy. Security forces continued a campaign of harassment, intimidation, and persecution targeting political opponents and human rights defenders by means of arbitrary searches and arrests, followed by incommunicado and protracted arbitrary detention without judicial review. Security used "non-detention" as a ploy as in prior years: it ordered individuals to report to security headquarters early in the morning and sit there all day, doing nothing. They were released at night but ordered to return the next day.

Two Catholic priests and more than eighteen other defendants who had been tortured to confess to charges of sabotage and conspiracy in 1998 were pardoned in January 2000. Their credible allegations of torture were not investigated. Islamic student militias operating under the protection of the security forces abducted and tortured a number of student activists. Security agents enjoyed de jure and de facto immunity from prosecution. Despite formal complaints by families of torture victims and the U.N. special rapporteur for Sudan, the government did not seriously investigate any cases. A doctor at Atbara hospital demanded an investigation into the torture he suffered at security's hands, but government officials disavowed responsibility, downplaying torture as a personal act committed by security agents whom the state cannot control.

Some sixty or more PNC members were arrested by security and blamed for fomenting a series of September demonstrations where deaths and destruction of public property occurred, as in western Fashir, where one woman student was killed and fourteen injured (as were five police) in a street protest against utility shortages and nonpayment of teachers' salaries.

Press-gang military recruitment of young men and underage boys from buses and public places continued. Demonstrators in Khartoum and other cities participated in anti-conscription protests that damaged government property and banks. Authorities responded with what appeared to be excessive force, killing several students and unemployed.

Conditions in Omdurman Women's Prison remained shocking: chronic overcrowding, lack of sanitation, diseases, and death from epidemics among children who lived with their mothers. The government annually pardoned women, temporarily easing overcrowding before bringing in the next batch of prisoners; in 2000, the government pardoned more than 700 women. These included more than 500 mostly poverty-stricken, illiterate southerners convicted of brewing and selling alcohol to help their families survive.

Public Order Police frequently harassed women and monitored women's dress according to the government's stereotype of Islamic correctness. Public Order Courts remained the state's primary weapon against women striving for freedom and equality; women received summary justice in these courts, often followed immediately by flogging, without effective right to appeal.

In September 2000, the governor of Khartoum State decreed that women would be banned from some public service jobs such as gas station attendant and restaurant and hotel employee. Security forces tear-gassed and beat women demonstrating against the decree, arresting twenty-six of them for trial by Public Order Courts. Even the government-created unions protested and the court suspended the decree in September pending a judicial hearing.

The nongovernmental press exercised more freedom despite arrests of journalists. In March 2000, security authorities held five journalists and a poet for questioning over articles deemed "anti-government" and critical of the armed forces. In August, security forces arrested two journalists from private newspapers, both of which had been shut down several times in 1999 for accusing the government of corruption.

In an encouraging development, in July the government issued exit visas to some political party leaders, advocates, and activists to attend a convention in Kampala, Uganda, also attended by NDA and civil society members, on the future of Sudan and human rights in transition. Representatives of the Masaalit in western Sudan denounced new attacks on their people, and on the Dagu, Fur, and Zaghawa, by Arab militias armed, supported, and given immunity from prosecution for their acts by the government. In July, reported massacres of these Africans by Arab militias claimed nineteen, sixteen, and five victims in different incidents.

The government pursued its policy of harassment of Christian churches and believers. Apostasy, or conversion by Muslims to another faith, remained a capital crime. The accelerated top-level discourse of jihad to encourage enlistment for the war against the infidels in central, east and southern Sudan sustained a climate of intolerance.

About twenty security officers stormed and searched the Catholic Comboni College compound in July 2000. In early July, a Mexican clerical student was detained and suffered abuse at the hands of security. The Khartoum state government continued to destroy Christian structures such as chapels, schools, and clinics that served the southern population in the city's vast slums. Two of the four million Khartoum residents were people displaced from other parts of the country, most of whom struggled to survive in the informal economy.

War-Related Abuses

Government of Sudan

Fighting spread further into the southern area of Western Upper Nile, inhabited mainly by the African Nuer. The government continued its campaign of creating a cordon sanitaire around new oil fields by forcibly displacing the Nuer population. In addition to aerial bombardment and scorched-earth attacks by government troops, the government armed Nuer proxies to fight against anti-government Nuer. The government routinely banned U.N. relief aircraft from Western Upper Nile on security grounds, although its military campaigns produced tens of thousands of freshly displaced civilians, who were burned and looted out of their homes by pro-government Nuer militia and the government army.

The government's 1997 Khartoum Peace Agreement with former rebel forces, headed by Nuer ex-rebel leader Riek Machar, unraveled when Machar, claiming the government had materially breached the agreement, resigned in January 2000 from the government and returned to the bush. He formed a new rebel group. Many Nuer commanders, without Machar's presence, had reached a degree of unity at a conference at Waat, Upper Nile, where on November 4, 1999, they announced they were fighting against the government. That ended in July, when Machar's new rebel group fought in the oil fields against the Nuer troops of Peter Gatdet, who was by then allied with the SPLA. Machar's troops had apparently accepted government arms again.

The warlord syndrome, where human rights were rarely recognized by the local toughs, spread in Upper Nile wherever local commanders could secure direct government funding and arms, serving as government militias.

The Mine Ban Treaty, signed by Sudan in 1997, remained unratified and the government did not destroy antipersonnel landmines as required. It continued to use landmines in some areas, such as the eastern front. The government refused the International Committee of the Red Cross (ICRC) access to those detained in connection with the conflict; failure to acknowledge holding rebel soldiers prisoner pointed to a continuing government policy of secret summary executions.

The government announced that its new oil revenue, constituting 20 percent of its 2000 revenue, would be used for defense, including an arms factory near Khartoum. Defense spending in dollars increased 96 percent from 1998 to 2000. Not coincidentally, government use of air power and bombing increased.

When SPLA violations of the cease-fire in Bahr El Ghazal temporarily halted the movement of the government's military train, the government counterattacked by bombing not only the cease-fire area, but also the rest of the south, the Nuba Mountains, and the eastern front. In July, 250 bombs hit civilians and their infrastructure in the attacks, which set a new high, according to conservative calculations based on U.N. relief reports. In August, government forces stepped up targeting of relief, health, and school facilities, apparently aiming to deter or shut down the U.N.-led humanitarian operation in the south, Operation Lifeline Sudan (OLS). And despite promises to stop the bombing in September, more government bombs in October hit Catholic church facilities in different locations in Equatoria.

The government bombed a school in the Nuba Mountains in February, killing fourteen, mostly children and one teacher. Although the government gave permission for U.N. needs assessments in the rebel areas of the Nuba Mountains in 1999, only two were completed before the government put a halt to the activities, in the middle of a vaccination campaign.

The government also armed tribal militias of the Arabized Baggara tribes (the muraheleen of Western Sudan) for use as proxy fighting forces against the Dinka civilian base of the SPLA in Bahr El Ghazal. Although slave-taking became their trademark, the muraheleen conducted few successful slave raids in 2000 because the SPLA deployed forces in northern Bahr El Ghazal and armed the Dinka boys guarding the cattle camps. Even so, the government continued to use the muraheleen to guard the military train to Wau, from which they attacked villages and looted cattle and food.

Meanwhile, those captured in prior years remained in slavery-like conditions, forced to work hard for no pay: physical punishment and verbal and sexual abuse were common. The numbers of those still in captivity were estimated by different groups to be from 5,000 up. The government denied all slavery allegations, but in May 1999 set up the Committee for the Eradication of the Abduction of Women and Children (CEAWC) to address abduction and forced labor. Its members included James Agware, a Dinka nongovernmental activist experienced in locating and retrieving Dinka children from slavery. Although the committee retrieved slaves from their owners through local political/tribal intervention, its work was marred by the detention of Agware himself several times by local authorities. The government's deliberate decision to not record the identity of the abductors or forced labor owners, let alone prosecute anyone involved, was a serious setback in the fight against abuse of women and children. All the while, Western anti-slavery groups continued to redeem slaves by the thousands, notwithstanding UNICEF's denunciation of the buying of human beings for any purpose.

At an international conference on war-affected children in Canada in September, the Sudanese government was condemned in strong language by the former UNICEF Deputy Director Stephen Lewis, who claimed the government routinely lied to and manipulated the donors. He denounced Sudan's broken promises to facilitate the release of some 6,000 Ugandan children held in LRA camps inside Sudan. His remarks received a standing ovation. Sudan and Uganda agreed in October that the LRA would be disarmed and its camps moved 1,000 kilometers from the Ugandan border, and that the abducted Ugandan children would be returned. Uganda agreed to halt support for the SPLA.

SPLA and Other Rebel Groups

Despite church peacemaking efforts between the Didinga of Chukudum in Eastern Equatoria, and the Bor Dinka who dominated the SPLA garrison in Chukudum, hostilities continued. Sometime after the August 1999 cease-fire, the SPLA assigned commanders of local origin to the garrison, but the local population remained reluctant to return to their homes and fields because of the landmines that the SPLA promised to remove but did not.

Even though SPLA leaders promised to stop their troops' looting, the confiscation of relief food from civilians by SPLA soldiers and officers continued. In March 2000, an SPLA commander in Bahr El Ghazal took the entire contents of a relief warehouse, valued at $500,000, according to an investigation carried out by the SPLA's relief arm and international relief agencies. Several looting incidents, at or after relief food distributions, occurred in Eastern Equatoria. When angry civilians on one occasion tried to prevent the SPLA from taking the food, the soldiers fired into the crowd, killing several.

In 2000, negotiations on a memorandum of understanding (MoU) between the SPLA's Sudan Relief and Rehabilitation Association (SRRA) and the nongovernmental organizations (NGOs) operating in SPLA territory—in which the SPLA sought to impose new demands and operating conditions on relief organizations—foundered. Some eleven of forty NGOs operating in SPLA territory refused to sign for fear of compromising their neutrality and safety. They had to withdraw from that territory by the SPLA deadline of March 1, 2000. The SRRA's executive director claimed he did not care if 50,000 or 100,000 southerners died as a result of the NGO pullout. In later months, several nonsignatories signed the MoU or restarted operations in SPLA territory. Some NGOs did not return. Meanwhile the E.U. withheld funding from NGOs who signed the MoU.

Visitors to rebel areas continued to see armed youth who looked younger than eighteen. Cooperation with UNICEF's program for demobilization of child soldiers was uneven. One SPLA commander remobilized several hundred boys when UNICEF failed to provide promised school books and other supplies for the boys. On the eastern front, visitors received credible complaints from military and civilian victims that the Sudan Alliance Forces (SAF), an NDA member, committed abuses against its soldiers accused of spying or defecting to another rebel group, including summary executions, torture, and detention of prisoners in a pit in the ground. The allegations were denied by the SAF.

Defending Human Rights

While one organization, the National Alliance for the Restoration of Democracy, continued in outspoken defense of political detainees and others, no other independent human rights organization existed in government-controlled areas until a small group, operating with a commercial rather than nonprofit license, started up low profile in mid-2000. Independent attorneys defended those tried for sabotage, conspiracy, and related charges but the judicial system remained useless for security cases. Churches attempted to defend their parishioners' rights, and the Dinka committee retrieving enslaved Dinka children continued its work, under government CEAWC sponsorship. Women's groups, usually considered less threatening, were organized on a small scale and made their voices heard when the Khartoum governor attempted to ban some women's work.

Human rights monitors operated in the SPLA areas of the Nuba Mountains, but there were no human rights organizations in southern rebel-held areas. The Nairobi-based South Sudan Law Society and women's organizations such as Sudanese Women's Association in Nairobi (SWAN) raised human rights issues in various forums. The Sudan Human Rights Association, based in Kampala, monitored conditions at Sudanese refugee camps in Kenya and Uganda. The New Sudan Council of Churches in Nairobi (encompassing churches working in rebel areas of Sudan) conducted one other peace and reconciliation meeting, but was slow to reinforce the Wunlit agreement of 1999.

The Role of the International Community

United Nations

The U.N. continued its massive emergency assistance program for Sudan under the umbrella of Operation Lifeline Sudan. Several organizations withdrew from OLS in protest of its failure to take a lead in negotiating access on their behalf with the SPLA in the MoU controversy among other things. OLS remained severely underfunded due to donor fatigue. Several U.N. agencies on occasion protested in press statements or quietly the government's denial of humanitarian access and government bombing of relief and other civilian facilities.

In April 2000, the U.N. Commission on Human Rights expressed concern about human rights violations in Sudan by the government and SPLA. It renewed the mandate of the special rapporteur on human rights in Sudan. In October, the General Assembly voted against Sudanese membership on the Security Council and for the membership of an African country with a more credible human rights record, Mauritius.

European Union members continued to urge that greater engagement and a less confrontational approach on human rights would lead to improvements. E.U. countries rushed to do business in the petroleum sector, despite government of Sudan statements that oil development would be put to military use.

But in July, the European Parliament issued a declaration condemning the LRA and the government of Sudan for sponsoring it, and in August the E.U. Presidency issued a declaration expressing deep concern about the government bombing of civilian targets in the south. The ACP-E.U. Parliament also issued a resolution condemning Sudan and the SPLA for human rights violations.

United Kingdom

The United Kingdom continued to monitor human rights and raise human rights issues with the government. Domestically, it denied many Sudanese applicants political asylum and issued a visa application form for Sudanese that sought to curb their right to apply for political asylum once they reached the U.K. That form was withdrawn with an apology after being widely denounced. The U.K.'s international commerce agency touted Sudan as a country suitable for investment until the Foreign Office, under pressure, reminded the agency of Sudan's human rights problems.

United States

The United States government's policy of isolating the Sudan government diplomatically proved unworkable. The U.S. worked successfully for months, however, on a unilateral campaign to deny Sudan a seat on the U.N. Security Council.

Congressional conservatives sponsored one-year legislation that permitted the president, at his discretion, to provide food aid to the military members of the NDA, of which the SPLA constituted the largest force. In February 2000, President Clinton declined to authorize food aid to the NDA.

Harry Johnston was appointed U.S. Special Envoy for Sudan in 1998 with a mandate to focus on three areas: human rights, humanitarian issues, and peace negotiations. One of the benchmarks the U.S. administration proposed to the Khartoum government for improving relations was that it call a halt to bombing civilians. While Johnston was still in Khartoum with this message, the government bombed a hospital in the south sponsored by a U.S. nonprofit religious group.

A 1997 executive order imposing stiff sanctions on all financial transactions between U.S. and Sudanese persons and entities remained in effect. The State Department's annual human rights report accused both government and opposition forces of human rights abuses.

A divestment campaign against Talisman Energy Inc., a Canadian company engaged in production and development of oil in Western Upper Nile, was endorsed by Secretary of State Madeleine Albright. The U.S. government balked at another tactic, denial of the use of U.S. capital markets to Sudan and its business partners.

Canada

Canadian church groups and NGOs waged a struggle to force the government to impose sanctions on all Canadian companies doing business with Sudan. Canada's Foreign Minister, Lloyd Axworthy, announced in October 1999 that he would send a human rights team to investigate whether oil development, and specifically Talisman Energy Inc., had caused an increase in human rights abuses and exacerbated the conflict. If so, he threatened, the Canadian government would consider imposing sanctions on its companies operating in Sudan. In February 2000, the human rights team headed by John Harker responded affirmatively to both questions after visiting north and south Sudan and Canadian operations there. Sanctions, however, were never imposed.

ZAMBIA

Human Rights Developments

The situation in Zambia improved over the year. The government of President Frederick Chiluba implemented a number of promised economic reforms and promised to quicken the pace of greater democratization. As in past years, abuses of freedom of assembly and association, freedom of expression, and the government's lack of action against torture undermined the more meaningful economic reforms.

The government continued to promise its bilateral donors that it wanted to improve its rights record and there was some progress even while it showed indifference or hostility to public protests at home. Early in May 2000, Minister of Legal Affairs Vincent Malambo met donors to report on the implementation of the government's National Capacity Building Program for Good Governance. Malambo presented a slightly revised document and also discussed the findings of four consultative meetings. Many of the fundamental human rights challenges that Zambia faces were recognized. Minister Malambo met on June 19 with a number of local nongovernmental organizations to discuss their participation in the July 2000 consultative group meeting.

For the first time the consultative group meeting was held in Lusaka, on July 17 and 18, following a full day of consultation on human rights and governance issues on July 16. It was a watershed event. Minister of Finance Katele Kalumba invited civil society groups, including Human Rights Watch, to attend the full meeting, including closed sessions with bilateral donors.

Restrictions on the freedom of association remained in force outside the meeting, where police arrested an opposition United

Party for National Development (UPND) member of parliament and nine other constituency officials on July 16 for holding an "unlawful meeting" on June 14.

Opposition parties, NGOs, and other civic interest groups were regularly denied permission to assemble or had their meetings canceled on public security grounds. The ruling Movement for Multiparty Democracy (MMD), in contrast, continued to hold meetings, rallies, and pro-government demonstrations without permits.

Under Zambia's Public Order Act, any group of citizens wishing to hold a public demonstration must notify the police seven days before the demonstration. However, the police abused the law and arbitrarily determined when a gathering could or could not take place. Breaches of the law's provisions on lawful assembly carry a maximum sentence of seven years imprisonment. On May 7, 2000, Inspector-General Sailus Ngangula said the police would continue to arrest people holding processions without permits since disregarding the Public Order Act could "create anarchy" in Zambia.

Opposition parties, NGOs and other civic interest groups have regularly been denied permission to assemble or had their meetings canceled on public security grounds. The ruling Movement for Multiparty Democracy (MMD), in contrast, continued to hold meetings, rallies, and pro-government demonstrations without permits.

On January 13, 2000 a joint opposition UPND, United National Independence Party (UNIP), and Zambia Alliance for Progress (ZAP) demonstration in Ndola, to demand the reinstatement of striking doctors who were dismissed, was canceled after police at the last minute revoked its permit. The authorities deployed riot police at Ndola Central Hospital to ensure the rally did not go ahead. On January 16, 2000, police in Solwezi arrested and charged opposition UPND leader Anderson Mazoka, Solwezi mayor Logan Shemena, and twenty other senior UPND party officials on a charge of holding a public meeting without a permit. Mazoka was arrested at a fund-raising braai (barbe-cue) for addressing the meeting. According to the UPND, the arrest was doubly arbitrary in that police had granted UPND Northwestern province chairperson Webster Makondo permission to hold the braai from 5:00pm until late. According to a press report, police chief Hudson Beenzu maintained that while a permission to hold a braai was given, this did not authorize Mazoka to address the gathering. The opposition UPND claimed that the police refused it permission to hold rallies in Lusitu, Chirundu, Siavonga and Chibombo districts in June and in Shesheke in July.

Attacks on freedom of expression by the Zambian authorities have continued in 2000. Six journalists from the privately owned *Post* newspaper were detained in March 1999 for publishing a story headlined "Angola Worries Zambia Army." The story criticized Zambia's military capability and preparedness in the face of a possible military attack from Angola. All the reporters, including editor-in-chief Fred M'membe were later charged with "espionage." Two of the journalists, Lubasi Katundu and Amos Malupenga, were on leave at the time of arrest while Rueben Phiri and Mukalya Nampito were out of the country. Their case was taken before the High Court on April 16, 1999 and on November 1, 1999, twelve other *Post* journalists appeared before the High Court in Lusaka on a charge of espionage. All twelve pleaded not guilty to the charge and were at liberty on bail. On August 18, the state dropped charges against all the journalists except editor-in-chief Fred Mmembe. An unexplained fire on September 3 at the *Post* offices damaged some equipment worth U.S.$500,000.

On January 24, 2000, following pressure from the Ministry of Information, the privately-owned Radio Phoenix announced it was discontinuing a live phone-in program, "Let the People Speak: The Doctor's Strike." The program was sponsored by human rights NGO AFRONET to provide a forum for striking resident doctors to air their grievances. Following AFRONET's public complaints about this incident, the program was restarted a few days later, but it was prerecorded, edited, and the phone-in was discontinued.

On January 4, 2000, after fifty-four-years residence in Zambia, sixty-two-year-old Asian and a British national, Majid Ticklay, was deported with one hour's notice to Britain after his letter to the *Post* appealing to Zambians of Asian origin to play a more active role in politics was published. The Minister of Home Affairs, Peter Machumgwa, announced in a press statement that Ticklay had been deported for "sowing messages designed to promote ethnic divisions, hatred, racial discrimination, and anarchy among the people of the county." He was deported under the Immigration and Deportation Act, which gives the minister discretionary powers to deport persons whose presence is deemed "inimical to the public interest."

Teddy Nondo continued to serve as deputy director of the Drug Enforcement Commission despite accusations that he tortured suspects in 1997. The Human Rights Commission recommended, in its March 30, 1998 report on allegations of torture of detainees following the 1997 coup attempt, that officers accused of the offense of torture, including Nondo, be retired in the public interest, but advised against instituting criminal proceedings. Article 15 of the Zambia Constitution forbids torture. A commission of inquiry into the evidence of torture was headed by High Court Judge Japhet Banda, who had himself sentenced to death fifty-nine of those accused, on the basis of confessions allegedly rendered under torture. It began hearings in late 1999. All those named in the Human Rights Commission torture report denied the charge during hearings. The commission of inquiry presented its completed report to President Chiluba in late July, but the report's findings had not been made public.

Defending Human Rights

In early 2000, human rights NGOs came under increasing attack from the government. On January 31 MMD chairperson for information and publicity Vernon Mwaanga warned that AFRONET and the Zambia Independent Monitoring Team (ZIMT) were a "danger to democracy" and could face deregistration if they continued "their irresponsible conduct." On February 2, the minister of information and broadcasting services, Newstead Zimba, warned that the government would take "drastic action" against two NGOs if they did not end their "betrayal" of Zambia. The relationship with human rights NGOs improved later in the year following the consultative group meeting. AFRONET published its third detailed human rights report in 2000.

The Role of the International Community

The World Bank's first ever consultative group meeting in Zambia in July provided greater transparency, due to good teamwork between Zambia's bilateral donors, a new more open team at the World Bank, and some political risk taking by the minister of finance. Human rights issues were openly discussed as integral to the larger concept of "good governance" during the meeting, and NGO observers attended for the first time. Sweden, the United Kingdom, Denmark, and the U.S. delivered strong speeches pushing for a further improvement in the government's human rights record. Surprisingly, the Netherlands was muted in voicing its human rights concerns. Zambia's cooperating partners indicated that they had plans to make available slightly over U.S. $1 billion (with U.S. $355 million for balance of payments and in support of Zambia's economic reform and poverty reduction programs). A number of donor countries retained performance-related benchmarks for balance of payments release.

The U.S. was not a major donor to Zambia. Its main focus was on Zambia as a country with three unstable neighbors: Angola, Democratic Republic of Congo (DRC), and Zimbabwe. The U.S. also continued to support President Frederick Chiluba's mediation efforts in the war in the DRC.

HUMAN RIGHTS WATCH

AMERICAS

AMERICAS OVERVIEW

Human Rights Developments

Contrasts marked the year in the Americas. The already dire situation in Colombia deteriorated further, and the deep political and institutional crisis in Peru continued to make broad respect for human rights but a distant goal. On the other hand, in Mexico, where presidential elections in July heralded the first change of party in the presidential mansion in more than seventy years, hopes grew that the new president would undertake much-needed human rights reforms. A coup in Ecuador and a failed coup attempt in Paraguay reminded the region of the fragility of democracy. Meanwhile, Chile moved forward in its attempt to prosecute former dictator Augusto Pinochet, and an Argentine judge requested his extradition to face criminal charges for the 1974 Buenos Aires car-bombing of former Chilean army commander-in-chief general Carlos Prats and his wife. Distress signals from Haiti included electoral fraud and unchecked street violence, while in Argentina, nine people, including two members of the former military junta, remained under house arrest, under investigation for their role in the kidnapping of babies during the former military regime.

Through the year's ups and downs, though, one thing remained constant: the everyday violation of human rights—including police abuse, torture, and lack of access to effective justice systems—required far greater attention from policy makers than they were willing to recognize or give.

Colombia constituted the region's most urgent human rights crisis. As fighting intensified in the thirty-year conflict, human rights abuses proliferated. The victims were largely civilians caught between the parties to the conflict, all of which—the military and the paramilitaries with whom they maintained close ties, and the opposition guerrillas—committed atrocities with impunity. Despite claims to the contrary by the Colombian government, there was irrefutable evidence that the country's armed forces continued to be implicated in human rights violations as well as in support for the paramilitary groups responsible for the majority of serious abuses. Troops attacked indiscriminately and killed civilians, among them six elementary school children on a field trip near Pueblo Rico, Antioquia, on August 15. According to witnesses, soldiers fired on the group for forty minutes.

The character of the conflict changed with the entry of the United States as a major investor, providing an infusion of U.S. $1.3 billion of mostly military aid for the government. The package included seven rigorous human rights conditions, including the need for the Colombian armed forces to demonstrate a break with the paramilitaries. The U.S. secretary of state certified that Colombia had met only one of the conditions, related to ensuring civilian, not military, jurisdiction over crimes against humanity committed by soldiers; President Bill Clinton waived the other conditions on national security grounds, effectively sending the message that U.S. policy subordinated human rights to other interests.

A burgeoning crisis in Peru did nothing to alleviate the shadow that Colombia cast over the region. In April, after manipulating the constitution to allow him to run, President Alberto Fujimori won a third presidential victory in an electoral process roundly denounced as fraudulent by Peruvian and international observers. Then, in September, scandals involving his government's bribery of opposition politicians and his security chief's alleged undercover sale of arms to Colombia's leftist Revolutionary Armed Forces of Colombia (Fuerzas Armadas Revolucionarias de Colombia, FARC) led to an abrupt change of plans. Fujimori disolved the feared National Intelligence Service (Servicio de Inteligencia Nacional, SIN), and announced that he would call new elections but not stand again for the presidency. Nonetheless, ten years of

Fujimori's abusive leadership left the country's judicial and political systems in shambles, virtually assuring that efforts to rebuild democracy would be hobbled. At this writing, Fujimori remained in the presidency, and his former security chief, Vladimiro Montesinos, had returned to the country after unsuccessfully seeking asylum in Panama.

Mexico, too, experienced the promise of political change, but with a decidedly more upbeat forecast than in Peru. After more than seventy years in power, the Institutional Revolutionary Party (Partido Revolucionario Institucional, PRI) lost presidential elections in July. The victor, Vicente Fox of the National Action Party (Partido Acción Nacional, PAN), demonstrated an openness to human rights unprecedented among Mexico's leaders. Scheduled to take office on December 1, Fox quickly met with human rights groups in Mexico, Canada, the United States, and Germany. He announced a thorough and much-needed overhaul of the country's justice system and called for the establishment of a "transparency commission," to seek answers to long-standing questions about some human rights abuses and corruption under successive PRI governments.

With a few setbacks, efforts to obtain justice for past human rights violations in the region prospered. Cause for optimism in the fight against impunity surfaced in Chile, where Pinochet was stripped of his parliamentary immunity after returning home in March, following seventeen months of house arrest in the United Kingdom. Released for health reasons, Pinochet had been held for possible extradition to Spain to face human rights charges there. The former dictator faced more than sixty criminal complaints within Chile, lodged since January 1998 by relatives of victims of extrajudicial executions, "disappearances," and torture, and by political parties, trade unions, and professional groups. In August, the country's Supreme Court concurred with a lower court that there was enough evidence against Pinochet to warrant removing his immunity. Advances also took place in other cases against former military

officers and members of the intelligence services under Pinochet's former military government. In July, two former army majors and a cadet received life sentences for the 1982 murder of Juan Alegría Mandioca, the scapegoat for the murder of a union leader.

The same Spanish judge who had ordered Pinochet's arrest in London, Baltasár Garzón, also sought the detention of former Argentine military officer Ricardo Miguel Cavallo in August. Living in Mexico, Cavallo was accused of genocide, terrorism, and torture stemming from his alleged role as a torturer at Argentina's infamous Navy Mechanics School under military rule. At this writing, Cavallo fought extradition while waiting in a Mexican prison.

Argentine authorities also contributed to the fight against impunity in cases related to the kidnapping of children during the military dictatorship in the 1970s and 1980s. Nine people, including former presidents brigade general Reynaldo Bignone and general Jorge Videla, and former junta member admiral Emilio Massera, were under house arrest in relation to the alleged kidnapping of over 200 children.

The fight against impunity received a setback in Italy, though, in a case involving another accused Argentine human rights violator. Former army Maj. Jorge Olivera was detained in Rome in August, following an extradition request from a French judge, Roger Le Loire. Olivera stood accused of torture, kidnapping, and "disappearance" in the case of French citizen Marieann (or Marie Anne) Erize in 1976, but was released after an Italian court ruled that Erize was dead, not "disappeared," and that the statute of limitations had run out for the other crimes. The court made its finding on the basis of what later turned out to be a falsified death certificate.

The United States contributed to another serious setback to the otherwise positive worldwide trend toward the application of universal jurisdiction for crimes against humanity. In March, based on legislation obliging the United States to prosecute torturers, justice department officials detained Peruvian army intelligence agent Maj. Tomás

Ricardo Anderson Kohatsu, sparking hope that he might be prosecuted for serious human rights abuses that he allegedly committed in Peru. Anderson was implicated in numerous violations, including the torture of a former intelligence agent who was left paraplegic as a result. But in a regrettable decision, the Department of State obtained Anderson's release, claiming that he enjoyed immunity because he was brought to the U.S. to participate in a hearing before the Inter-American Commission on Human Rights.

Within the United States, two former military leaders in El Salvador faced wrongful death charges in a federal court in Florida. Former defense minister Gen. José Guillermo García and Gen. Carlos Eugenio Vides Casanova, who headed that country's notoriously brutal National Guard, stood accused of the wrongful death of four U.S. churchwomen who were raped and murdered in El Salvador in 1980. In 1984, lower-ranking members of the National Guard were convicted in the case in El Salvador. The civil case was brought in the United States by relatives of the victims.

The cause of truth, if not justice, also received a boost in Guatemala, after the January inauguration of President Alfonso Portillo. Just months after taking office, he declared a national day in honor of the estimated 200,000 victims of Guatemala's thirty-five-year civil conflict, ratified the Inter-American Convention on Forced Disappearances, and admitted state responsibility for past violations in many well-known cases, including the 1990 murder of anthropologist Myrna Mack and the December 1982 Dos Erres massacre of at least 162 people.

If cause for optimism was to be found in efforts to hold human rights violators to account, events in Ecuador and Paraguay underscored the fragility of democracy in the region. On January 22, the Ecuadoran military, allied with a coalition of indigenous groups, toppled elected President Jamil Mahuad, replacing him briefly with a three-man junta. Just days later, the military stepped aside for Vice-President Gustavo Noboa. In Paraguay in May, army officers failed in an attempt to oust President Luis González Macchi.

A host of other human rights violations also took place during the year. In countries including Argentina, Brazil, Guatemala, Haiti, Mexico, and Venezuela, abuses by security forces and impunity remained serious problems. A common denominator was the failure of these countries' justice systems to provide effective remedies for victims of human rights violations. The case of Teodoro Cabrera García and Rodolfo Montiel Flores in Mexico highlighted the problem. Environmental activists from Pizotla, Guerrero, they were accused by authorities of drug- and weapons-related offenses. Despite evidence that soldiers planted the evidence used against them, and that the defendants were forced to sign incriminating statements, they were found guilty, demonstrating the abysmal failure of Mexico's justice system. In Guatemala, where United Nations officials documented more than two dozen extrajudicial executions, the weak justice system led to a climate of insecurity and lynchings of alleged criminals by vigilantes.

The case of Sandro do Nascimento demonstrated the problem in Brazil. Nascimento's attempt at armed robbery in Rio de Janeiro ultimately led to kidnapping and murder. Deserving of a trial for his serious offenses, police strangled him to death instead, shortly after his arrest. In São Paulo state, police killings of civilians surged from 525 in 1998 to 664 in 1999, the highest total since 1992, when police killed 111 inmates in a massacre at Carandiru prison. This violent trend intensified over the first six months of 2000, as police in the nation's most populous state killed 489 civilians, an increase of 77.2 percent over the comparable 1999 figure. A study released in July by the police ombudsman shed light on these shockingly high figures. Analyzing the autopsy reports of 222 persons killed by police gunfire in 1999—one-third of the victims of fatal police actions—it reported that 51 percent had been shot in the back and 23 percent had been shot five or more times. The findings suggested that many had been summarily executed, and not killed as a result of legitimate use of lethal force in shootouts, as authorities routinely reported.

In Haiti, electoral fraud and unchecked politically motivated street violence raised serious concerns about the government's willingness and ability to apply the law. Much of the violence was carried out by supporters of Fanmi Lavalas, the party of former President Jean-Bertrand Aristide, in the context of parliamentary elections held in May.

Human rights violations in Venezuela also continued. Following flooding and mud slides in December 1999, the armed forces murdered suspected looters in Vargas state. Army paratroopers, police, and members of the National Guard were blamed for the execution-style killing of what the state ombudsman said were more than sixty people. The number of extrajudicial executions of criminal suspects elsewhere in the country also increased over the prior year; the nongovernmental Venezuelan Program for Education and Action on Human Rights (Programa Venezolano de Educación-Acción en Derechos Humanos, PROVEA) said it knew of seventy-six reports of violations of the right to life by police during the first six months of the year alone.

Press freedom also remained precarious in the region, most severely in Cuba, where authorities maintained almost total control over the flow of news within the island. In Haiti, Radio Haïti-Inter journalist Jean Dominique was ambushed and killed on April 3, along with station bodyguard Jean-Claude Loiussant. Dominique was an outspoken proponent of the rule of law. In Chile, too, journalists suffered restrictions. José Ale Aravena, court reporter for the daily *La Tercera*, was convicted in February of "insulting" former chief justice Servando Jordán in an article summarizing the judge's controversial career. The journalist's 541-day suspended sentence reminded the country of the authoritarian mentality of some Chilean judges and the weak free speech protections offered under the law. A new law to regulate the press was pending in Congress at this writing. If passed, as expected, the law would provide greater and much-needed protection in several important areas, including by removing jurisdiction from military courts over cases of journalists accused of sedition or espionage under military laws, and by repealing the crime of "contempt of authority" from the State Security Law.

Inhumane conditions of detention remained a common feature throughout the region, with particularly abusive situations found in Venezuela, Brazil, Haiti, Panama, and El Salvador. The continued growth of inmate populations exacerbated overcrowding, at the root of a host of other problems. Yet, all over the region, prisons and jails were not crammed with convicted prisoners, but instead with pretrial detainees, turning the presumption of innocence on its head.

Defending Human Rights

The burgeoning of the human rights movement, even in countries with environments hostile to activism, remained a regional highlight. In addition to groups focusing on the traditional array of civil and political rights, nongovernmental organizations (NGOs) emerged over the last decade in the defense of women's rights, children's rights, the rights of indigenous populations, refugee rights, and in some countries gay and lesbian rights. With increasingly sophisticated methods of documentation and advocacy, these groups played an indispensable role in monitoring and reporting on human rights developments in the region.

Yet, even in countries where human rights defenders could work with no apparent personal risk, they frequently faced an unsympathetic public, suspicious of their defense of criminal suspects and other despised groups. Worse, in a number of countries they were the subject of threats, harassment and physical violence.

Colombia remained the most dangerous country in which to monitor human rights, with four defenders killed and three "dissappeared" during the first ten months of 2000. Elizabeth Cañas, a member of the Association of Family Members of the Detained and Disappeared (Asociación de Familiares de Detenidos Desaparecidos-Colombia, ASFADDES), was shot and killed in July. Cañas lived in Barrancabermeja, where paramilitaries systematically intimidated human rights defenders, sending dozens of death threats over the course of the year. Also slain were Demetrio Playonero, an internally displaced person (IDP) and human rights leader; Jesús Ramiro Zapata, the only remaining member of the Segovia Human Rights Committee; and Margarita María Pulgarín Trujillo, a government prosecutor who was developing cases that linked paramilitaries to the army and drug traffickers.

Civilian groups, including human rights organizations, also faced attack from the FARC, which in October 2000 characterized them as "paid killers [for the Colombian military]." In a statement on why they failed to honor an invitation to an October 2000 peace meeting in San José, Costa Rica, sponsored by a broad coalition of human rights, peace, and community groups, the FARC dismissed the effort as organized by "the enemies of Colombia and its people." In this way, the guerrillas contributed to a general atmosphere of fear and intolerance that endangered human rights defenders.

The Colombian government's efforts to protect threatened defenders were slow and inadequate. Moreover, recklessly endangering defenders' lives, members of the Colombian military continued to make public statements accusing government investigators and human rights groups of guerrilla sympathies.

Failed assassination attempts were reported in Brazil. In September, a jeep carrying members of a commission that monitored rural violence and land reform issues was fired upon in the northeastern state of Paraíba, but its occupants survived. That same month, São Paulo representatives of Amnesty International and of a gay pride organization received bombs in the mail, but the police safely deactivated the devices.

In an alarming development, particularly when viewed in historical perspective, Guatemala witnessed a notable increase in threats, harassment, and targeted violence against human rights organizations and activists. In one disturbing incident in August, a representative of the Center for Legal Action in Human Rights (Centro para la acción legal en Derechos Humanos, CALDH) was detained, beaten and robbed by individuals posing as journalists but thought to have links with active and retired military officers.

Death threats, frequent in Colombia, were also reported in Guatemala, Chile, Brazil, Mexico, Argentina, and Peru. In Cuba, human rights monitors, whose legitimacy the government stubbornly refused to recognize, faced harassment and criminal prosecution for their activities.

In Venezuela, the Supreme Court determined in separate decisions in June and August that human rights organizations that received funding from abroad were not members of "civil society," thereby depriving them of the right to participate in the nomination of candidates for the Supreme Court, to be ombudsman, and for other important government posts.

Authorities continued to apply pressure to human rights monitors in Mexico, too, where they were sometimes blamed for some of the crime problems suffered in the country. Losing presidential candidate Francisco Labastida of the PRI, for example, noted during the campaign, "Let it be known that the law was made to protect the human rights of citizens, not criminals." This anti-human rights rhetoric contributed to a hostile environment for human rights defenders. According to the nongovernmental All Rights for All Network of Human Rights Organization (Red de Derechos Humanos Todos los Derechos para Todo, known as the Red), its offices in Mexico City were under surveillance by agents of the federal National Security System (Sistema Nacional de Seguridad, SISEN) in June.

The Role of the International Community

Organization of American States

The OAS's electoral observation capacities were severely tested this year in both Peru and Haiti, where election monitoring missions nevertheless successfully avoided the shortcomings of past such teams. In Peru, a mission led by former Guatemalan minister of foreign affairs Eduardo Stein conducted a forthright, transparent, and proactive observation of the electoral process. In Haiti, Barbadian Ambassador Orlando Marville led a team of observers that were the first to discover the fraudulent calculation method that tainted the results of senatorial elections. Both bodies ended up deciding to quit their host countries prior to the completion of the elections, after it had become clear that electoral abuses would not be remedied.

But the OAS showed less initiative in dealing with the results of its monitoring efforts. With regard to Peru, in particular, the OAS Permanent Council rejected a proposal by the United States and Costa Rica for an ad hoc meeting of foreign ministers under Resolution 1080—the provision appropriate to responding to interruptions of democracy—to discuss sanctions against Peru. By a substantial majority, member states showed themselves to be unwilling to take strong measures to respond to unfair elections. This consensus revealed the limits of the OAS's effectiveness in managing interruptions of the democratic process that fall short of a coup d'etat. The limits of Resolution 1080 were also on display in the case of the coup in Ecuador. Despite the ouster of the president, the OAS failed to take action.

Nor did the OAS take concrete actions with regard to Haiti. At this writing, OAS Deputy Secretary General Luigi Enaudi was engaged in negotiations with the Haitian authorities to try to alleviate the worst aspects of the summer's elections, but no reforms had yet been announced.

The Inter-American Commission on Human Rights sent multiple death penalty cases against Trinidad and Tobago to the Inter-American Court. In 1998, the country announced that it would withdraw from the American Convention on Human Rights so as to eliminate the inter-American human rights system as an avenue of appeal for death row inmates. The withdrawal became effective in 1999, but the cases referred by the commission to the court involved incidents that had occurred when Trinidad and Tobago was still bound by the convention.

In a contrary and positive direction in the Caribbean, Barbados recognized this year the jurisdiction of the court.

United Nations

The United Nations maintained a permanent human rights presence in Colombia and Guatemala, and to a lesser extent in Haiti. In other countries, visiting special rapporteurs and other mechanisms lent their expertise to efforts to address human rights problems. The August-September mission of the U.N. special rapporteur on torture to Brazil, for example, drew public attention to prison abuses and strengthened the credibility of local monitoring groups. Earlier in the year, at the April meeting of the U.N. Commission on Human Rights, a resolution censuring the Cuban government for its intolerance of peaceful dissent, among other problems, was instrumental in maintaining pressure for reform.

The Bogotá office of the U.N. High Commissioner for Human Rights continued its invaluable work in 2000, visiting regions shaken by war and pressing the Colombian authorities to implement needed reforms. The office's annual report was an accurate and compelling portrayal of the dire state of human rights in Colombia. In a wise decision, the Colombian government agreed to maintain the office until April 2002. Yet, disturbingly, U.N. staff noted a marked drop in cooperation from Colombian officials.

The United Nations Verification Mission in Guatemala (Misión de Verificación de las Naciones Unidas en Guatemala, MINUGUA), established after the 1996 peace accords, published reports on the peace process that included detailed analyses of human rights issues. Under the 1996 peace accords, the mandate of MINUGUA was due to expire at year's end. Although President Portillo had requested that MINUGUA extend its stay, at this writing the U.N. General Assembly had not yet decided on the extension.

In Haiti, the six-year-old U.N. human

rights monitoring mission departed the country in early 2000, together with the U.N. peacekeeping mission. A smaller human rights mission was subsequently installed: the United Nations International Civilian Support Mission in Haiti (Mission internationale civile d'appui en Haïti, MICAH).

High Commissioner for Human Rights Mary Robinson visited Mexico in November 1999, signing an agreement with the government to undertake a human rights technical cooperation program. At this writing, the U.N. and Mexican government had not agreed on the exact nature of the program. Following the high commissioner's visit, the special rapporteur on extrajudicial, summary, or arbitrary executions released a report on Mexico. Although it noted that the government had taken some positive steps, the report concluded: "Unfortunately, these positive undertakings have not been sufficient to correct the situation."

United States

The year 2000 marked the emergence of the United States as a major player in the armed conflict in Colombia, with the approval of the U.S. $1.3 billion aid plan. Debated heatedly yet passed overwhelmingly by the U.S. Congress, the Colombia aid package was the largest ever approved for a Latin American country. Although the aid was conditioned on Colombia's compliance with strict human rights conditions, President Clinton waived six of the seven conditions for reasons of U.S. national security on August 22.

Clinton's use of the waiver, made just prior to his visit to Colombia, allowed aid to go forward even as U.S. officials acknowledged that the forces they were funding maintained ties to paramilitary groups, had failed to suspend or prosecute implicated officers, engaged in human rights abuses, and refused to enforce civilian jurisdiction over human rights crimes. With brutal candor, a spokesperson for the office of White House adviser and drug czar retired Gen. Barry McCaffrey explained the president's decision: "You don't

hold up the major objective to achieve the minor."

In December 1999, the first U.S.-trained Colombian army battalion completed its training and was deployed. A second battalion began to train the following August. U.S. law mandated that fewer than 500 U.S. troops be in-country at any one time barring an emergency. But reflecting a global trend to "outsource" war, some analysts projected that as many as 1,000 U.S.-related personnel could be in Colombia on any given day, many of them working for private companies under contract to the U.S. military.

The southern Colombian department of Putumayo, home to 50 percent of Colombia's illegal coca crop, was to be the first target of the U.S. eradication strategy. Officials acknowledged that forced population displacement was a likely outcome of the eradication effort, and proposed to set up government-controlled "temporary" camps to distribute assistance. Groups working with the internally displaced protested, saying that the planned activities risked "fomenting the conflict, targeting innocent civilians, and substantially increasing internal displacement in Colombia."

The Clinton Administration, backed by Congress, initially took a strong line against the manipulation of the electoral process in Peru that led to Fujimori's third term. President Clinton directly suggested that the U.S. relationship with Peru would be damaged if democracy was not respected. Yet, when other OAS members states failed to rally to the U.S. call for an ad hoc meeting of ministers under Resolution 1080, the U.S. did not appear to push hard for the measure.

Behind-the-scenes negotiations of U.S. officials during the September video scandal were said to be critical in convincing Fujimori to agree to leave office and to dismantle his hated intelligence apparatus. Yet instead of promoting full accountability in Peru's return to democratic rule, the United States threw its weight behind a scheme by which intelligence chief Vladimiro Montesinos escaped to Panama to seek political asylum. In October, Montesinos returned to Peru after unsuccessfully seeking asylum in Panama.

On the positive side, important progress was made in the declassification of U.S. documents relating to human rights violations in Chile under military rule. By mid-year, in accordance with a 1999 declassification directive, thousands of documents from the State and Defense Departments and other U.S. agencies, including the Central Intelligence Agency (CIA), were released. Some files were held back on the order of the CIA's director, George Tenet, supposedly to conceal sensitive information about intelligence-gathering methods. At this writing, the CIA and other government agencies were preparing for another massive release of documents.

A breakthrough in understanding the role of the CIA in Chile came in September, in response to a 1999 amendment to the fiscal 2000 Intelligence Authorization Act authored by member of the House of Representatives Maurice Hinchey. It required the CIA to submit a report to Congress on its relations with Pinochet's military government, among other aspects of CIA involvement in Chile. In the report, the CIA revealed that it had maintained a liaison with Manuel Contreras, the infamous director of Chile's security agency from 1974 to 1977. The relationship lasted throughout the period in which human rights were grossly and systematically abused in Chile, and it ended a year after the car-bomb murder in Washington, D.C. of Allende's former foreign minister, Orlando Letelier, and his colleague Ronni Moffitt, for which Contreras had been indicted in the United States and convicted in Chile.

Small but symbolic steps were also taken toward easing the decades-old U.S. economic embargo on Cuba, an outmoded policy instrument that Human Rights Watch and many other observers believed to be counterproductive to the human rights cause. After months of debate in congressional committees, both houses of Congress passed legislation in October to allow limited food and medicine sales to Cuba. The measure signaled the first meaningful retreat in nearly four decades in the U.S. policy of economic sanctions against Cuba, but was unlikely to yield more than a small volume of actual business. Because of compromises with conservative lawmakers opposed to loosening the restrictions, no U.S. export credits or private financing would be allowed on food sales. And on the negative side of the balance, the legislation codified restrictions on the travel of U.S. citizens to Cuba.

The Work of Human Rights Watch

While responding to crises throughout the hemisphere, the Americas division of Human Rights Watch primarily focused attention on a core group of countries experiencing the most serious human rights problems. Human Rights Watch sought, in each country, to address the most pressing human rights issues: the Pinochet prosecution and freedom of expression in Chile; violations of international human rights and humanitarian law in Colombia; unfair election conditions, weakening of the rule of law, and impunity in Peru; deficiencies in the justice system in Mexico; political violence and electoral fraud in Haiti; accountability in Argentina; the protection of NGOs and human rights defenders in Guatemala; the use of excessive force by police and military in Bolivia; and overall human rights conditions and the U.S. embargo in Cuba.

In addition to documenting abuses through published reports, Human Rights Watch responded rapidly to breaking events by directly addressing high-level government officials and representatives of relevant regional and international bodies, and generally pressing our human rights concerns in a firm, concise, and timely way. Human Rights Watch also conveyed its views in meetings with senior government officials of Argentina, Brazil, Colombia, Chile, Haiti, Guatemala, Mexico, Panama, and Venezuela. In meetings and correspondence, we made specific recommendations for improving human rights conditions.

As the region's gravest human rights crisis, Colombia was the division's major focus during 2000. In February, just as the U.S. Congress was debating a massive military assistance package for Colombia, Human Rights Watch released its report, "The Ties That Bind: Colombia and Military-Paramilitary Links." This documented the continuing close relationship between Colombian military and paramilitary forces, directly rebutting the Colombian government's claim that the military was not responsible for paramilitary abuses. And to ensure that the message was heard, the division's executive director and Colombia researcher both testified before the U.S. Senate as to the report's findings, arguing that tough human rights conditionality be included in any proposed assistance to Colombia.

The report made front-page headlines in Colombia, where top military leaders tried to discredit its findings by suggesting, grotesquely, that Human Rights Watch was in the pay of drug traffickers. Not long after, Cuban government representatives facing censure at the U.N. Human Rights Commission mounted a similar attack, alleging that Human Rights Watch received substantial funding from U.S. "special services." But such politically motivated invective rightly carried no weight or credibility, the more so because neither source could refute the carefully documented facts that were the basis for Human Rights Watch's conclusions.

After President Clinton invoked the Colombia aid law's national security interest waiver—after the State Department found that Colombia had failed to meet six of the law's seven human rights-related conditions—Human Rights Watch vigorously protested the Administration's subjugation of human rights imperatives to counter-narcotics interests. Members of the European Union, skeptical of Plan Colombia, approved only a third of the funds requested, and dedicated all of their aid to nongovernmental organizations, as opposed to official entities.

Fujimori's crisis of legitimacy dominated Human Rights Watch's work on Peru. On the advocacy front, Human Rights Watch urged the OAS and others in the international community to adopt a firm posture on Peru's democratic deficit. In early May, Human Rights Watch wrote to OAS Secretary General Cesar Gaviria, comprehensively detailing deficiencies in Peru's electoral conditions. In June, after the election, the division's executive director attended the OAS General Assembly in Windsor, Canada, urging member states to press Fujimori to "restore the interrupted democratic process" in Peru. In September, as the political crisis unfolded in Peru, Human Rights Watch sought to ensure that the human rights abuses committed during Fujimori's decade in power were not left in impunity, including by directly challenging the efforts of Vladimiro Montesinos to secure immunity from potential prosecution by obtaining political asylum in Panama. In pursuit of this, Human Rights Watch wrote to the Panamanian president, setting out the reasons why any granting of asylum would be profoundly mistaken, and sent a delegation to Panama to discuss the question with relevant officials.

The historic prosecution of Pinochet was Human Rights Watch's primary focus in Chile. In late April, the division's executive director published an opinion piece in the Chilean daily *El Mercurio* that critically analyzed Pinochet's due process arguments against prosecution. This was published shortly before the Santiago Appeals Court began hearings on stripping Pinochet of his parliamentary immunity from prosecution. Human Rights Watch's Chile researcher attended the hearings, the only international observer permitted to do so, and closely monitored the legal developments that culminated in the lifting of Pinochet's immunity.

The Americas division made important strides toward the broad dissemination of its human rights information by entirely revamping Human Rights Watch's Spanish-language website. With materials arranged chronologically by country and by issue, the site presented a detailed picture of human rights conditions in the region. The goal was to be comprehensive—providing documents that ranged from letters to reports to opinion pieces on each country and issue—as well as timely—effecting the simultaneous release in electronic and traditional formats of all of the division's public materials.

ARGENTINA

Human Rights Developments

Fernando de la Rúa was inaugurated as Argentina's president on December 10, 1999, having been elected at the head of a coalition of opposition parties. His government faced its first major human rights test with the arrests in August of two former members of Argentina's armed forces. The two men, arrested separately in Mexico and Italy, faced prosecution in European courts for abuses committed under military rule. The De la Rúa administration did not attempt to obstruct the cases and provided no more than consular assistance to the detainees. Argentina's current human rights record was marred by serious violations, notably those committed by police forces. Torture and deaths in police stations were frequently reported, and while some cases of abuse were investigated and prosecuted, others were not.

Among the suspicious deaths reported in 2000 was that of twenty-two-year-old Ramón Rojas, found hanged in the Ninth Police Station in the provincial capital of Santiago del Estero on March 19. Another detainee in that city, construction worker Aldo Bravo, claimed that he had been kidnapped from his home by ten to fourteen hooded and armed men on July 7, and held for three days at the police station, during which time he was tortured. The police acknowledged having detained Bravo, but denied his claims of torture, despite corroborating medical evidence. In September, the head of the municipal office for children and adolescents, Father Mario Tenti, accused the Santiago del Estero provincial police of torturing three minors on September 2. The police denied the charges, saying that the boys' injuries were the result of their fighting amongst themselves. None of these cases had been prosecuted as of this writing.

In La Rioja, a police officer was detained for the hanging death of nineteen-year-old Cristian Ruiz in a police cell in March 1999, after it was confirmed that Ruiz had been tortured to death. The head of the La Rioja provincial police, Paulino Zenón Cobresí, admitted that the police beat detainees, although he denied that such treatment was systematic.

Another detainee who apparently died in police custody was twenty-five-year-old Juan Carlos Sánchez. Sánchez was detained by the Corrientes provincial police on January 10, and taken to the headquarters of the Special Crimes Division (formerly the Investigations Brigade) in the provincial capital, a building where at least fifteen people had reported being tortured in recent years. His parents were later told that he had been released, although witnesses said he had not left the building. Workers near the site later claimed to have heard screams from that location. Although the body was never found, eight police officers were indicted on charges of torturing Sánchez to death.

The Sánchez case was not the only suspicious death at the hands of this Corrientes police division: on February 9, twenty-six-year-old Germán Morales was shot dead in front of witnesses near his home by four police officers. No investigation into the events was conducted. In July, however, a commissioner and three police officers were detained and accused of torturing twenty-six-year-old Jorge Marcelo González, a prisoner on furlow, and then shooting him dead on June 30. The Corrientes provincial police chief resigned following the case, and seventy-three other officers were forced to retire.

In Jujuy province, the local delegation of the Federal Police was believed responsible for the shooting death of a storekeeper on July 2. Ten police officers, participating in an anti-drug raid, fired more than forty shots at Manuel Fernández, who was killed by a shot to the head fired at point-blank range. Police said that the shooting occurred because Fernández was carrying drugs and offered resistance, but relatives alleged that he was shot because he had witnessed an illegal act by the police who later shot him. The ten officers were in detention at this writing.

Buenos Aires provincial governor Carlos Ruckauf, who took office in December 1999, reestablished the post of a single police commissioner for the whole of the province, undoing reforms undertaken by the former governor. Ruckauf then appointed Eduardo Raúl Martínez, who had been prosecuted on charges of torturing a German citizen in 1978, although the case was later dismissed. Ruckauf, who during his electoral campaign had called for a harder line on criminals—urging that they be shot—named former rebel army officer Aldo Rico to the post of provincial minister of security. Rico was forced to resign a few months later and was replaced by retired police commissioner Ramón Oreste Verón, who claimed to be the officer with the largest number of killings to his name in provincial history.

On August 30, the president of the Buenos Aires provincial Supreme Court, Guillermo David San Martín, called on Security Minister Ramón Verón to take steps to stop the torture of minors in police stations. San Martín made the demand after reviewing allegations that five young people had been ill-treated in Buenos Aires provincial police stations in Virreyes, San Fernando, Villa Martelli and Escobar (all in Greater Buenos Aires). According to a report by the government adviser for minors in San Isidro, allegations of beatings of minors in police stations doubled in the first seven months of 2000, reaching a total of 159 cases in thirty-three police stations.

The director of security of the municipality of San Miguel (whose mayor was Aldo Rico), former army officer Hugo Vercellotti, asserted in July that the police do and should kill criminals, lamenting that the law represented "an obstacle in the fight against insecurity."

In Mendoza province, two alleged police informers, twenty-eight-year-old José Segundo Zambrano, and twenty-five-year-old Pablo Marcelo Rodríguez, "disappeared" on March 25, reportedly after meeting with a police corporal. Their bloodstained car was found several days later, but their bodies were not discovered until July 3, when they were found in an area used by the police for shooting practice. The police corporal was accused of the killings, which were said to be related to a police "mafia," and twenty officers were detained. On August 24, the trial began of seven former Mendoza police officers implicated in the killing of seventeen-year-old Sebastián Bordón, whose body was found on October 12, 1997, after he had been in police detention. The trial continued at this writing.

In Córdoba, a transvestite known as Vanesa Lorena Ledesma died in police custody on February 16, after being held incommunicado at the eighteenth precinct for five days. The cause of death was reported as "cardiac arrest" but the body reportedly showed signs of torture and beatings. As in previous years, there were frequent allegations of human rights violations against sexual minorities throughout Argentina, with police arbitrarily detaining gay men and transvestites for infractions such as "crimes against public decency" or scandalous conduct.

Fourteen members of the Federal Police were detained after violently suppressing an April 19 demonstration against the government's announced labor reform. The police beat demonstrators, who offered little resistance, attacked one with a knife and shot another man in the testicles. In all, thirty-five demonstrators were wounded by police, while fifty others were detained.

Attacks and threats against journalists continued to be reported. Two of the most serious cases involved the provincial newspapers *El Liberal* (Santiago del Estero) and *La Voz del Interior* (Córdoba). In early August, a fake bomb was placed under the car of *El Liberal* journalist Gregorio Layus. The newspaper, in a previous editorial, had accused the provincial government of Carlos Juárez (governor since 1949 virtually without interruption) of seeking to ruin it. Claiming to be the only independent voice in the province, the newspaper stated that it and its journalists had been the subject of persecution, espionage and legal harassment due to its investigation of corruption and irregularities in the provincial government. *La Voz del Interior* reported that its correspondent in Santiago del Estero had received telephone calls in July warning him that he could "suffer an accident" if he continued to write critical articles about the governor, and had later received explicit death threats.

Shattering the myth that international justice was a matter of northern countries imposing their will on the south, an Argnetine judge requested that former Chilean dictator Augusto Pinochet be extradited to face criminal charges for his responsibility for the assasination of Gen. Carlos Prat and his wife. They were killed by a car bomb in Buenos Aires on Spetember 30, 1974. The judge also sought the extradition of other Chileans in the case, including the former chief of Chile's secret police, Manuel Contreras Sepulveda, who was in prison in Chile for having carried out a 1974 car-bombing in Washington, D.C. that took the life of former foreign minister Orlando Letelier and his assistant Ronnie Moffitt.

Nearly a quarter century after the coup d'etat that brought to power the military government that ruled from 1976 until 1983, Argentina continued to grapple with its cruel legacy of killings, "disappearances," and other abuses. Federal judge Adolfo Bagnasco investigated the theft of babies during military rule, a case brought by the Grandmothers of Plaza de Mayo (Abuelas de Plaza de Mayo) in 1996 that was not excluded by the country's amnesty laws. The case involved the armed forces' practice of taking babies who were forcibly "disappeared" with their parents or who were born in captivity after the detention of their parents, and of handing them over to military families and others not considered subversive. Over 200 children are alleged to have been kidnapped in such circumstances. Nine defendants remained under house arrest, including former presidents brigades general Reynaldo Bignone and general Jorge Videla, former junta member admiral Emilio Massera, and former Buenos Aires security zone chief general Carlos Guillermo Suárez Mason. On August 10, another officer was placed under house arrest: retired Gen. Santiago Omar Riveros, the former commander of Military Institutions implicated in the theft of babies born in the Campo de Mayo military hospital. The previous week, the Supreme Court

had rejected a petition from the Supreme Council of the Armed Forces to hand jurisdiction over the case to the military courts.

Although the armed forces publicly accepted the prosecution of retired officers in connection with the kidnapping of children, they expressed concern over judicial efforts to collect information from officers still on active service. In July, army chief Lt. Gen. Ricardo Brinzoni sent his secretary general, Eduardo Alfonso, to visit Armando Barrera, a former officer detained in Bahia Blanca for refusing to testify before a federal court investigating those cases. The government also expressed support for a proposal by Brinzoni to establish a "reconciliation panel," involving the army, human rights groups and the Catholic Church, as a means to try to determine the fate of the "disappeared" without resorting to the courts, a proposal scrapped when human rights organizations rejected it outright.

Defending Human Rights

Although threats against human rights defenders were rare, a few activists faced serious abuses. On July 30, Elisabeth Ceballos was kidnapped, beaten and threatened by three masked men after her husband, journalist Miguel Hernández, participated in a demonstration at the house of Miguel Angel Pérez, a former army officer who had admitted to assassinating a political prisoner in 1976. Ceballos was finally left, bound and gagged, near the meeting place of a human rights group in the town of Cosquín, Córdoba. Hernández and other human rights activists in Cosquín also complained of a series of telephoned death threats, and on July 17 Hernández's house was stoned.

The Role of the International Community

European Union

On December 30, 1999, Spanish judge Baltazar Garzón issued an international arrest warrant for forty-eight former officers, previously indicted by him in November, with a view to making a formal extradition request. In August, Justice Minister Ricardo Gil Lavedra stated that the request involved "political questions" relating to national sovereignty, relevant to the executive not the courts, and indicated that the defendants would not be detained since their crimes had already been dealt with in Argentina.

The most encouraging development in Garzón's prosecution was the August 24 arrest of Ricardo Miguel Cavallo in Mexico. Cavallo, accused of being a former torturer in the Navy Mechanics School (ESMA), was allegedly implicated in the deaths of at least two people who "disappeared" under military rule. After the arrest, French judge Roger Le Loire also announced that he would seek Cavallo's extradition. Argentine Interior Minister Federico Storani indicated that the government would not intervene in the case and would take no steps to prevent extradition, although consular advice would be available to the detainee. On a September visit to Mexico, President De la Rúa said that he did not discuss the Cavallo case in his official meetings. When questioned by the press, he did, however, express support for the principle of territoriality, indicating that such crimes should be tried in Argentina.

Just a few weeks earlier, on August 6, former army Maj. Jorge Olivera was detained in Rome following an extradition request from French judge Le Loire. Olivera was accused of responsibility for the kidnapping, torture and "disappearance" of French citizen Marie Anne Erize in San Juan province on October 15, 1976. On September 18, however, an Italian court of appeal ordered Olivera's release on the basis of a purported death certificate indicating that Erize had died on November 11, 1976, although the certificate was later shown to have been falsified. Reasoning that Erize was not "disappeared" but dead, the court ruled that the statute of limitations under Italian law had run for the other crimes of which Olivera was accused.

The armed forces made no comment on the case while Olivera was in detention, but following Olivera's release army chief Brinzoni called the detention an offense against Argentine justice. He argued that Olivera had already been judged by the Argentine courts and released under the Due Obedience Law, noting, in addition, that the army was compiling information with a view to advising other military officers who might travel abroad and face prosecution for human rights violations.

In May, Le Loire requested authorization from the Argentine government to travel to the country in order to question some 140 military officers linked to the forced "disappearance" of French citizens. The petition was received by the Argentine Ministry of Justice days after the detention of Olivera, and was under consideration at this writing.

Suits against General Suárez Mason being pursued in the Italian courts since 1986, which involved the "disappearance" of eight people of Italian origin during the military government, were upheld by the First Penal Court of Rome in March. The court rejected the defense lawyers' argument that the cases were barred because of Argentina's Full Stop and Due Obedience Laws. In his ruling, judge Renato D'Andria also underscored the Argentine authorities' lack of cooperation with his investigations of these cases.

Israel

The Israeli Parliament announced in August that it had formed an inter-ministerial commission to investigate the fate of some 1,800 Jewish Argentines who "disappeared" in the period 1976 to 1983, in order to establish the whereabouts of their bodies and bury them with appropriate religious rites.

Organization of American States

The OAS special rapporteur on freedom of expression, Santiago Cantón, condemned the threats and attacks suffered by the newspapers *El Liberal* and *La Voz del Interior*, calling on provincial authorities to investigate the incidents and punish those found responsible. The Inter-American Commission on Human Rights (IACHR) received 123 complaints relating to Argentina during 1999, and, as of mid-2000, maintained fifty-eight open cases on the country.

In one important case, the IACHR requested the Argentine government to provide information on police powers of detention. The commission was examining a controversial November 1998 decision of the Argentine Supreme Court, in which the court upheld the power of the police to detain a person, without an arrest warrant, solely on the grounds that he or she was deemed to have been acting "suspiciously."

The IACHR also reiterated its call for the thirteen prisoners convicted of the 1989 attack on the La Tablada barracks to be granted a new trial, in light of the serious irregularities marring the first proceedings. Abundant evidence suggested that the prisoners had been tortured while in the custody of the army, while others had been killed. On September 6, it was announced that the remains of Iván Ruíz and Carlos Quito Burgos, two of the five persons who "disappeared" after attacking the barracks, had been identified. Both had apparently been shot by members of the army, probably after capture. In Congress, a bill was introduced to permit the conditional release of the prisoners while their conviction was being reviewed, but as of this writing it had not been debated.

By invitation of the Argentine government, the IACHR was also to send an observer to review investigations of the 1994 bombing of the Argentine-Israeli Mutual Association Association (Asociación Mutual Israelita-Argentina, AMIA), an attack in which eighty-six people died.

United States

On a brief visit to Buenos Aires in August, U.S. Secretary of State Madeleine Albright met with NGO representatives and Jewish community leaders, and promised U.S. government cooperation in investigating the AMIA bombing and the 1992 bombing of the Israeli embassy. Albright also vowed to cooperate in the investigation of abuses that occurred during the military government, stating that she would seek to ensure that the State Department opened its archives on the repression of that period.

BRAZIL

Human Rights Developments

On June 12, Sandro do Nascimento, a former street child and survivor of the 1993 Candelária massacre of eight youths by Rio de Janeiro police, boarded a Rio city bus intending to rob its passengers. Informed of the hold up, police blocked off a street and surrounded the bus while Nascimento held the passengers hostage for several hours, and television crews assembled and began broadcasting the siege on national television. After more than four hours, Nascimento exited the bus, pointing a gun at the head of the hostage, Geisa Gonçalves. Before negotiations could move forward, a police officer fired at Nascimento but struck the hostage. Nascimento then fired three shots, killing the hostage before police overpowered him and took him away. An hour later, they left Nascimento's lifeless body at a local hospital. During the ride there, autopsy reports later confirmed, the officers had strangled him to death.

The incident was an emblematic one, typifying the problems of urban violence and police abuse in Brazil. It involved a social outcast, abandoned by society, a brutal incident terrorizing not only those directly affected but also millions of observers appalled by the brazenness of the criminal attack, an incompetent police response and, in the end, two cold-blooded murders. Despite the gruesome and unjustified police response—a flagrant violation of basic rights—reaction to the event focused almost entirely on the initial crime and the police failure to protect the hostage, rather than the assailant's killing. However, the public prosecutor's office indicted the five officers involved on homicide charges after they had served thirty days in pretrial detention. Unsurprisingly, the massive public outcry that followed the incident led to the approval of a national public security package loaded with crime-fighting measures but conspicuously lacking in reforms to control police abuse or professionalize the security forces.

Throughout the year, Brazilian authorities, media and the public viewed a range of human rights abuses—including police killings, torture, and problems in prisons and juvenile detention centers—through the lens of public security. Urban residents felt themselves to be most vulnerable to crime, but even rural conflicts, particularly those involving the Landless Workers' Movement (Movimento dos Trabalhadores Rurais Sem Terra, MST), were seen as public security issues. Indeed, the federal government seized the opportunity presented by a series of high-profile MST building occupations to try to portray the issue of rural poverty and underdevelopment as one of law and order.

The most visible example of police violence in response to social protest came during celebrations of the arrival of the first Portuguese explorers to Brazil in 1500. During the ceremonies to mark the 500-year anniversary of this event, military police in Bahia state beat demonstrators and fired rubber bullets into crowds, injuring at least thirty demonstrators and arresting more than one hundred. The police decision to impede a march organized by 2,000 indigenous leaders from throughout Brazil, and the violence employed by shock troops against indigenous activists, led the president of the government's indigenous institute, FUNAI, to resign in protest.

This incident was the most widely publicized case of police violence against protesters, but it was not the most serious in outcome. At two other protests, military police shot and killed unarmed landless demonstrators. On May 2, police prevented buses carrying hundreds of landless workers from entering Curitiba, capital of Paraná state. Officers beat protesters, hurled tear gas canisters and fired rubber bullets into the crowd. Nearly 200 protesters were injured, and police shot Antônio Tavares Pereira, age thirty-eight, in the chest with a live bullet, killing him. On July 25, police fired into a group of landless demonstrators, killing José Marlúcio da Silva, age forty-seven, in Recife, capital of Pernambuco state.

Police violence continued to stand out as Brazil's major human rights problem in other contexts as well. In São Paulo state, police killings of civilians surged from 525 in 1998 to 664 in 1999, the highest total since 1992, when police killed 111 inmates in a massacre at Carandiru prison. This violent trend intensified over the first six months of 2000, as police in the nation's most populous state killed 489 civilians, an increase of 77.2 percent over the comparable 1999 figure. A study released in July by the police ombudsman shed light on these shockingly high figures. Analyzing the autopsy reports of 222 persons killed by police gunfire in 1999—one-third of the victims of fatal police actions—it reported that 51 percent had been shot in the back and 23 percent had been shot five or more times. The findings suggested that many had been summarily executed, and not killed as a result of legitimate use of lethal force in shootouts, as authorities routinely reported. More than half of the victims had no prior criminal record.

In Rio de Janeiro, efforts to improve the human rights record of the police suffered a serious setback when Gov. Anthony Garotinho drove noted reformer Luis Eduardo Soares, the assistant secretary of public security, from office in March. Governor Garotinho insisted that Soares' removal was legitimate, but the circumstances suggested that he was removed due to pressure from the Rio police, with whose corrupt and violent elements he had been coming increasingly into conflict. Several other reformers in the Garotinho government, including Police Ombudsperson Julita Lemgruber, resigned in protest at Soares' removal.

On June 28, a group of Rio de Janeiro police officers, acting without an arrest warrant or probable cause, seized Anderson Carlos Crispiniano from his home in the Morro do Adeus *favela* (shantytown) and took him to a local police station. According to press reports of the incident, and statements by Crispiniano's family to the Brazilian NGO Global Justice, the officers beat the young man severely, tore out his toenails on one foot, and threatened to plant narcotics on him and charge him with drug trafficking unless he convinced his family to pay a ransom in excess of U.S. $2,000. After more than twelve hours, the police, through an intermediary, released Crispiniano in exchange for the sum demanded. Three weeks later, Crispiniano died from his injuries. The Crispiniano case attracted significant attention in the local media, as well as the concern of the U.N. special rapporteur on torture, both before and during his August-September visit to Brazil. Nonetheless, at this writing, the internal police investigation into the case was at a standstill.

Accountability for police crimes remained elusive. After the August conviction of two low-ranking police officers—Daniel da Silva Furtado, sentenced to sixteen years in prison for two homicides, and Airton Ramos Morais, sentenced to eighteen years for three homicides—for the massacre of landless squatters in Corumbiara, Rondônia state, prosecutors overtly politicized the proceedings. The trial was based on events that occurred on August 9, 1995 when, in the early morning, heavily armed police entered the Santa Elina *fazenda* (large commercial farm) in Corumbiara to forcibly evict squatters, who resisted them. In the initial skirmish, two police and several of the squatters were killed. After the situation had been brought under control, the police tortured and humiliated the survivors, killing several more of them and arresting a landless worker whose corpse surfaced days later in a nearby river.

In the course of one of the trials, in which the prosecution itself requested the acquittal of two officers (permitted under Brazilian law) who oversaw the operation, state attorney Tarciso Leite de Mattos referred to the landless as "Nazis" and told the jury that "Either Brazil does away with the landless movement, or they will do away with Brazil." After three weeks of proceedings, the jury convicted two landless leaders for their role in the conflict, and the court sentenced Cícero Pereira Leite Neto to six years and two months in prison and Claudemir Gilberto Ramos to eight years and six months in prison. After the initial convictions of the two officers, the jury acquitted nine military police officers and convicted one ranking officer, Cpt. Vitório Régis Mena Mendes, who was sentenced to nineteen years in prison for three homicides.

In August, a Rio de Janeiro jury acquitted former police officers Hélio Vilário Guedes, Paulo Roberto Borges da Silva, William Moreno da Conceição and Hélio Gomes Lopes, who had been charged with homicide for their roles in the 1993 massacre of twenty-one residents of the Vigário Geral favela in Rio de Janeiro. The following month, the same jury convicted former military policeman José Fernandes Neto, and the court sentenced him to forty-five years in prison. In October, the court jury convicted Alexandre Bicego, another former military policeman, for the homicides; the court imposed a sentence of seventy-two years. The verdicts meant that more than seven years after the incident only six police officers had been convicted of the killings, significantly fewer than the thirty to fifty police involved in them. Nineteen police had been acquitted; six others awaited trial at this writing.

Led by the MST, the landless rural poor embarked on a national campaign of occupying farms and government buildings, part of a larger effort to force the authorities to accelerate the process of land reform. The federal government responded to these actions by creating a division within the federal police to investigate agrarian conflicts, and by expanding federal jurisdiction to cover occupations of municipal and state buildings, as well as federal institutions. These measures were criticized by rights groups, which contrasted the government's eagerness to expand federal competence to manage social movements with its continued failure to establish federal jurisdiction over human rights violations.

The MST's occupations frequently evoked a violent response. Although the Pastoral Land Commission (Comissão Pastoral da Terra, CPT) had not yet released data for the year 2000 at this writing, their figures showed that twenty-four people were killed in land disputes in 1999, down from 1998 figures but consistent with figures from recent years. Nonetheless, areas with high numbers of land occupations showed an increase in violence. Prominent among these was the southern state of Paraná. From 1997 to late June 2000, fifteen laborers were killed in Paraná and twenty more survived attempted homicides. Seven laborers were tortured by state police during 1999 and the first half of 2000. While eighteen were injured in police actions in 1999, this number soared to 232 in the first half of 2000. During the course of forced evictions in 1999, the police in Paraná arrested 173 people, mostly without probable cause, detaining them for extended periods in police lockups and jails; in the first six months of 2000, this figure rose to 141.

Detention conditions continued to violate international norms. The latest census figures—from August 1999—showed that while Brazilian prisons had capacity for just over 107,000 inmates, 194,074 were confined. According to research by the U.N. Latin American Institute for the Prevention of Crime and Treatment of Offenders (ILANUD), the prison population surpassed 200,000 in 2000. Official figures indicated that from 1995 to 1999 the number of prisoners increased by 30.5 percent. In São Paulo, where the government raised capacity by more than 12,000 over the past several years through new prison construction, the inmate population reached 90,000 in September. The state prison system, however, had capacity for only 44,872, forcing the authorities to maintain 34,232 prisoners in jails and police lockups that were themselves designed to accommodate at most 17,635 short-term detainees. Not surprisingly, the miserable conditions of such places—characterized by overcrowding, abysmal sanitary facilities, no job training or educational infrastructure, and constant physical violence—sparked numerous inmate riots over the course of the year. Contributing to the ongoing prison crisis was the failure of judges to sentence eligible convicts to non-prison terms, in accordance with the provisions of law no. 9.714/98, passed in November 1998. While São Paulo's prisons administration secretary had 1,942 slots for non-prison sentences, only 650 were being used in late 2000.

Prisoners in such facilities were also frequently subject to extreme forms of violence at the hands of special police forces and guards. On June 2, after a disturbance at the Americana City Jail in São Paulo state, the special police made more than one hundred detainees strip and then run a gauntlet. Police in two parallel lines beat the semi-naked prisoners with whips, bats, iron bars, bottles, and other objects; afterwards, they poured vinegar and saltwater over the prisoners' open wounds. A week later, at the Fiftieth Police District, twelve police officers entered the lockup, forced detainees to strip to their underwear, and engaged in an abuse session that included severe beatings with bats and metal bars, and electric shocks. Police repeatedly beat detainee Nilson Saldanha on the head, injuring him so severely that he died ten days later.

Conditions of detention for juveniles remained well below international standards as well as the minimum guarantees set out in Brazil's progressive Children's and Adolescents' Statute (Estatuto da Criança e do Adolescente). The tenth anniversary of the law was celebrated in the midst of a wave of flagrant abuses against youths held in the detention centers of the Foundation for the Well Being of Minors (Fundação pelo Bem Estar do Menor, FEBEM) in São Paulo. Over the course of 2000, rights groups documented numerous cases of mass beatings; on several occasions, public prosecutors entered FEBEM detention centers and also filmed the fresh wounds of dozens of detainees.

Defending Human Rights

Human rights organizations, neighborhood and community associations, religious groups and unions documented and denounced violations of human rights without formal legal impediment throughout the year. Nonetheless, several who demonstrated the courage to accuse officials responsible for abuses faced intimidation, including meritless law suits, harassment, threats, and even attempted murder. On September 5, a jeep carrying several members of the CPT in the northeastern state of Paraíba was struck by 12-gauge shotgun fire. Father João Maria Cauchí, the

CPT's state coordinator, and sister Maria Ferreira da Costa were both injured but survived the attempt on their lives.

On two consecutive days in September, representatives of Amnesty International and a gay pride organization, both in São Paulo, received packages containing bombs through the ordinary mail. Police deactivated the bombs without injury. At the same time, Renato Simões and Ítalo Cardoso, the presidents of the human rights commissions of the São Paulo State Legislative Assembly and the City Council, respectively, received letters containing threats directed at themselves and others who defend human rights. At this writing, neither the state nor federal police had succeeded in identifying those responsible for the bombs and threats.

Other human rights defenders faced threats and unwarranted criminal and civil lawsuits. In February, Darcy Frigo, an attorney with the CPT in Paraná state, received death threats by phone, as did another CPT employee, Dionísio Vandresen, in June. Frigo also faced charges of resisting a judicial order in connection with a mass eviction operation on November 27, 1999, in Curitiba, Paraná, in which he was badly beaten by police. The incident took place before members of the local and national media and hundreds of onlookers, including the local Catholic bishop, Dom Ladislau Biernaski, a defense witness in the proceedings against Frigo. Authorities in Natal, Rio Grande do Norte, indicted Human Rights Watch's former Brazil director James Cavallaro for the crime of defamation, initiating criminal proceedings against him. In previous court testimony and interviews with a local newspaper, Cavallaro had provided information regarding suspects in the 1996 murder of human rights lawyer Gilson Nogueira.

Human rights commissions of state, municipal, and federal legislative bodies, although governmental by definition, continued to demonstrate significant independence throughout the year, reviewing allegations of abuse, monitoring police, prisons and other state agents, and denouncing abuses to prosecutors and the media.

The Role of the International Community

United Nations

Visits by key human rights officials demonstrated the U.N.'s commitment to promoting respect for basic rights in Brazil. In May, U.N. High Commissioner for Human Rights Mary Robinson visited Brasília, São Paulo and Rio de Janeiro, reaching a working agreement with the government regarding technical assistance.

The second visit of a U.N. human rights official—a mission by the special rapporteur on torture in August and September—provided an important platform for groups investigating and denouncing this abuse to make themselves heard. In three weeks of intensive on-site research that took him to Brasília, São Paulo, Rio de Janeiro, Belo Horizonte, Recife, Belém, and Marabá, the special rapporteur, Sir Nigel Rodley, documented scores of cases of severe beatings and torture. At the end of his visit, he expressed deep concern over the state of the country's detention facilities, explaining that Brazilian prisoners were routinely subject to subhuman conditions and severe physical abuse. His full report—to be released during the 2001 session of the U.N. Human Rights Commission—was awaited with great anticipation.

Organization of American States

In June, for the second time in five years, the Inter-American Commission on Human Rights (IACHR) visited Brazil. The previous visit—in December 1995—led to a substantial report on the country's human rights situation. This visit, by several commission members, underscored the importance of the work of the OAS's primary human rights body on individual petitions. During its stay in São Paulo, the IACHR received dossiers from groups working on violations ranging from prison conditions and the situation in juvenile detention centers, to abuses in rural Brazil, racism, and women's rights.

In its annual report, released in June, the IACHR published its findings in three cases against Brazil, including one condemning the government's failure to prosecute the military police responsible for the massacre of 111 inmates in the Carandiru prison complex in October 1992. Brazilian rights groups made greater use of the petitions process during the year. Unfortunately, the Brazilian government failed to heed the IACHR's recommendations in cases already decided, failed to respect deadlines, and did not submit complete responses to some petitions.

United States

Over the year, the U.S. gave relatively little direct assistance to Brazil. For fiscal year 2000, Congress approved U.S. $1.5 million in counter-narcotics assistance; for fiscal year 2001, the administration requested $2 million for the same item. For fiscal year 2000, Congress approved $225,000 for Brazil through the International Military Education and Training (IMET) program. The administration requested $250,000 in IMET funding for fiscal year 2000.

The State Department's chapter on Brazil in its *Country Reports on Human Rights Practices for 1999* fairly portrayed the country's human rights situation.

CHILE

Human Rights Developments

On March 11, Ricardo Lagos Escobar, candidate of the center-left coalition that has governed since former dictator Gen. Augusto Pinochet left power in 1990, began a six-year presidential term, replacing President Eduardo Frei. His inauguration was overshadowed by Pinochet's return to Chile on March 3, after British Home Secretary Jack Straw ordered the former dictator's release on medical grounds from house arrest in England. Pinochet was detained in London on October 14, 1998, and had spent more than sixteen months in England under police guard in a secluded residence, after Spain and three other European countries requested his extradition to face trial for human rights violations. At the time of his return to Chile, Pinochet faced

more than sixty domestic criminal complaints lodged since January 1998 by relatives of victims of extrajudicial executions, "disappearances," and torture, and by political parties, trade unions, and professional groups.

While Pinochet was on his way home, human rights lawyers acting for the victims made a formal request to the appeals court judge investigating the complaints, Juan Guzmán Tapia, that Pinochet be stripped of his immunity as a senator (a process known as *desafuero*) so that he could face trial. Under the 1980 constitution, Pinochet had awarded himself the non-elected post of lifetime senator when he stepped down as president.

On May 23, the Santiago Appeals Court voted by thirteen to nine to remove his immunity, finding that there were sufficient grounds for Pinochet to be prosecuted. The Supreme Court confirmed the decision by an even larger majority—fourteen to six—on August 8. The verdict was greeted as a landmark victory for justice both in Chile and internationally. Although Pinochet's poor health made it unlikely that his trial would be concluded, his shield of immunity, which a few years earlier had seemed impenetrable, was in tatters. Moreover, the Chilean judiciary, which had been widely questioned for its failure to defend human rights during Pinochet's rule, had shown independence in resisting pressure, thereby consolidating the rule of law.

Then, in October, Argentine judge Juan Jose Galeano requested the extradition of Pinochet and other former military officials to face criminal charges in the 1974 Buenos Aires car-bombing that killed former army commander-in-chief general Carlos Prats and his wife, Sofía Cuthbert.

There were also important advances in other human rights cases involving former military officers and members of the intelligence services under the military government. On July 19, the Seventh Chamber of the Santiago Appeals Court sentenced two former army majors and a cadet to life imprisonment for the murder in 1982 of a carpenter, Juan Alegría Mandioca. Alegría's body had been found with a suicide note in which he "confessed" to the murder of another victim of extrajudicial execution, trade union leader Tucapel Jiménez. Approximately twenty former police and army agents were on trial for Jiménez's murder, one of the most notorious cases of the 1980s.

The dramatic developments in the courts, and in particular Pinochet's loss of immunity, led to some tense moments between President Lagos's government and the armed forces and their civilian supporters. President Lagos made it clear at every opportunity that his government would not intervene in court decisions, and that whatever political agreements were reached on the human rights legacy, justice must proceed regardless. He headed off military pressure in the days leading up to the Supreme Court verdict and replied to military protest afterward by firmly asserting his constitutional authority.

Pinochet returned to a country already accustomed to his absence. He had scarcely been mentioned by either candidate during the election campaign. The business-as-usual atmosphere changed, however, the moment the former dictator set foot on the tarmac at Santiago's airport. A contingent of top military brass, former ministers of his government, and their families was awaiting his arrival. Pinochet's unassisted walk to greet his supporters and his raised stick salute shocked many who were expecting to see the man whom the United Kingdom had released on humanitarian grounds carried from the plane on a stretcher. The army ferried him by helicopter to the roof of the Military Hospital, pointedly flying over the presidential palace, and escorting him from the aircraft behind a wall of heavily armed soldiers. In a public statement, President Frei said he had kept his promise to bring Pinochet home before the end of his mandate. But, he pointed out, "All our efforts to get Senator Pinochet home have had a sole objective: that it should be Chilean courts not those of another country that apply the law."

Congress approved a constitutional reform giving parliamentary immunity to former presidents that have served a full term, thus encouraging Pinochet to resign from the Senate without forfeiting his protection from prosecution. Human Rights Watch, which shared the concern of Chilean human rights lawyers that the reform could give Pinochet additional legal immunity as well as establish a worrying regional precedent, wrote to President Lagos urging him to veto the measure. The reform became law in April, but Pinochet had not resigned his Senate position at this writing.

Although there were more than seventy criminal suits open against him, the desafuero proceedings concerned one case in particular, the so-called Caravan of Death. One month after the military coup that brought Pinochet to power in 1973, a helicopter-borne army unit under the command of one of the coupmakers, Gen. Sergio Arellano Stark, had visited the towns of Cauquenes in the south, and La Serena, Copiapó, Antofagasta, and Calama in the north. They secretly executed seventy-two political prisoners removed from local prisons. General Arellano had acted as Pinochet's personal emissary, with written orders "to streamline the administration of justice for political prisoners."

In July 1999, the Supreme Court had unanimously confirmed the indictment of General Arellano and four other senior retired army officers for kidnapping nineteen of the victims, whose bodies had never been located. Arellano and the others were accused of aggravated kidnapping, a charge that allowed the prosecution to surmount an amnesty law decreed by the military government in 1978. Since the fact of death could not be established, the court held, it was impossible to know that the nineteen had been killed within the five-year period covered by the amnesty law, and the amnesty was therefore found to be inapplicable.

At the oral hearings in the Santiago Appeals Court, held during the last week of April 2000, Pinochet's counsel, Ricardo Rivadaneira, argued that Pinochet's health was too poor for him to instruct his defense, and that the proceedings violated his right to due process. However, on May 3 the court rejected ordering medical tests before ruling on Pinochet's immunity. While the court studied the dossier, the armed forces stretched their constitutional role to the limit in proclaiming their support for the former ruler. On several occasions, however, President Lagos firmly reminded them of their constitutional obligation to remain neutral. After the four commanders-in-chief met on May 15 for a widely publicized lunch in an elegant Santiago restaurant, Lagos stated pointedly that "it is not necessary to show to anyone the unity of the armed forces, because the armed forces are united behind the president of Chile."

The Supreme Court verdict confirming the desafuero not only held that Pinochet could be prosecuted on the kidnapping charge. It argued that, even if the crimes were eventually found to be homicides, he could still be stripped of his immunity, since it was up to the trial judge to establish whether or not the amnesty or a statute of limitations was applicable. The judges referred to the vertical chain-of-command in the armed forces as a *prima facie* indication of Pinochet's responsibility, quoting the general's own aphorism, "The most useless person in life is he who knows neither how to give orders nor to obey." The court also referred to a declaration by one of the caravan of death officers, Col. (Rtd.) Sergio Arredondo, who indicated that he had known the true, lethal purpose of the mission before it began.

The Council for the Defense of the State (Consejo de Defensa del Estado, CDE), an autonomous body that represents the interests of the state in criminal proceedings, announced on March 7 that it had decided unanimously to join the proceedings as a party against Pinochet. The previous June, the CDE had turned down a government request to make itself a party.

During the year, the armed forces participated in talks, known as the Roundtable Dialogue (Mesa de Diálogo), with human rights attorneys and representatives of churches and civil society, which had been convened under the government of President Eduardo Frei. Although the discussions were almost abandoned more than once due to deep disagreements between the parties, the participants signed an accord on June 13. Each

branch of the armed forces, including the uniformed police, the Carabineros, agreed to provide the fullest information possible on the whereabouts or fate of the "disappeared" at the end of six months. They also acknowledged "the responsibility of agents of organizations of the State" for grave human rights violations during the military regime, the first such admission since Pinochet relinquished power to an elected government a decade ago. On June 21, Congress, acting by an overwhelming majority, passed legislation enacting the agreement.

At this writing, Congress was expected to pass shortly a law to regulate the press, which it had been debating since 1993. The new law would strengthen freedom of expression guarantees in several important respects. Courts would no longer have powers to ban reporting of sensitive criminal cases, and would have to respect the confidentiality of journalists' sources. Military tribunals would no longer exercise jurisdiction over journalists charged with sedition or espionage under military laws. The bill would also remove the crime of contempt of authority from the State Security Law. Article 6(b) of that law punished those who insulted the president, cabinet ministers, senior judges, commanders-in-chief of the armed forces, or members of congress. At least thirty people had been charged and several convicted under this law since 1990, many for criticizing Pinochet or members of the Supreme Court he had appointed.

In December 1999, a new statute governing public administration and local government entered force, establishing for the first time that official documents were public, and providing a legal mechanism for redress if officials arbitrarily denied access to such public documents. Legislation to amend the constitution in order to end film and video censorship, and to restructure and revise the powers of the board of film censors, was also under parliamentary debate, but had not been approved at this writing. While President Lagos inherited these freedom of expression reforms from his predecessor, he had promised during the elections to give them high priority.

The conviction in February of journalist José Ale Aravena, court reporter for *La Tercera,* was a reminder of the authoritarian mentality of many of Chile's senior judges, and the meager protection they have given to freedom of expression through a decade of democratic rule. On February 15, the Second Chamber of the Supreme Court sentenced Ale to a 541-day suspended prison term for "insulting" former Chief Justice Servando Jordán in an article summarizing the judge's controversial career. Ale, who had referred in his article to comments that Jordán had been a member of a privileged clique in the judiciary, had been acquitted repeatedly by lower courts. The judge who drafted the sentence insulted and threatened the journalist at a public gathering two weeks before the verdict, calling him a "professional slanderer," thereby removing any semblance of impartiality from the verdict. President Lagos granted Ale a presidential pardon. The law regulating "insult" that led to his conviction was due to be removed from the statute books as part of the new press law.

Paula Afani Saud, also of *La Tercera,* was facing charges of breaching the secrecy of a criminal investigation under the Law on Abuses of Publicity and a similar charge under the Law against Illegal Drug-Trafficking brought by the CDE in April. In June 1998, Afani had written a series of articles in *La Tercera* and *La Hora* about a high-profile investigation being conducted by the CDE into a drug-trafficking and money-laundering conspiracy, which became known as "Operation Ocean." The articles included the testimony of former members of the criminal group who were interviewed in prison in the United States by Chilean police officials. Afani had refused to identify to the police her sources of information, and was consequently held solely responsible by the CDE for the leaked information, an offense that carried a five-year prison sentence under the drug-trafficking law. The case established a troubling precedent at a time when the government had committed itself to protecting the confidentiality of journalists' sources and the public's right of access to information in the public interest.

Defending Human Rights

The Supreme Court's decision stripping General Pinochet of his parliamentary immunity was a triumph for Chile's human rights movement, and especially for the victims of his rule who had campaigned for justice for twenty-five years. Often their work incurred personal risk. On December 15, 1999, Viviana Díaz Caro and Mireya García, president and secretary general, respectively, of the Association of Relatives of the "Disappeared" (Agrupación de Familiares de Detenidos Desaparecidos, AFDD) received a Christmas card with the inscription, "Lets hope that Father Christmas will give us the opportunity to meet face to face in the year 2000, so that we can blow your brains out. Enjoy your last Christmas... you will not be around for the next. Greetings to your family. . . . Merry Christmas to all. FNL— Villa Grimaldi Editions."

Villa Grimaldi is the name of a former torture center in Santiago, now converted into a "park for peace." A group calling itself the Nationalist Front for Fatherland and Freedom (Frente Nacionalista Patria y Libertad, FNL), believed to be made up of pro-Pinochet fanatics and former military personnel, had menaced other individuals and groups during the year. After Pinochet's return to Chile, however, no further threats were reported.

A group of young people known as the Funa, whose activities are dedicated to unmasking former torturers, was the object of a criminal complaint lodged in August by an opposition member of the Chamber of Deputies, who accused them of "criminal association." The group engaged in nonviolent vigils, accompanied by drums, whistles, and chanting, outside the homes or offices of individuals known from legal records to have participated in torture and killings. The evening newspaper *La Segunda* referred to them as "an ultra-left group that decided to exchange their molotov cocktails for a more sophisticated weapon: character assassination."

The Role of the International Community

United States

Following Pinochet's arrest in London, the White House ordered U.S. national security agencies to release confidential documents that shed light on human rights violations in Chile from 1968-1990. By mid-2000, some 7,500 documents had been released, but they did not include crucial Central Intelligence Agency (CIA) documents believed to reveal the details of U.S. covert action in Chile prior to and following the election of the Allende government that was overthrown by the military coup of 1973, and information on U.S. support for the military junta. Following pressure from freedom of information groups, the CIA carried out a search of its archives and gave written assurances to the National Security Council that its documents would be declassified in time to be released in September 2000. However, CIA Director George Tenet went back on this commitment in August, by deciding not to release hundreds of documents on grounds that they could compromise intelligence sources and operational methods. Of particular concern was the fact that the missing documents might contain information crucial to Pinochet's trial in Chile, such as the functioning of his secret police, the DINA, and the CIA's liaison with it.

During a visit to Santiago in August, however, U.S. Secretary of State Madeleine Albright pledged to push for the "fullest possible declassification." A breakthrough in understanding the role of the CIA in Chile came the following month, in response to a 1999 amendment to the fiscal 2000 Intelligence Authorization Act authored by member of the House of Representatives Maurice Hinchey. It required the agency to submit a report to Congress on its relations with Pinochet's military government, among other aspects of CIA involvement in Chile. In the report, the CIA revealed that it had maintained a liaison with Manuel Contreras, the DINA's infamous director, from 1974 to 1977. The relationship lasted throughout the period in which human rights were grossly and systematically abused in Chile, and it ended a year after the car-bomb murder in Washington, D.C. of former Allende foreign minister Orlando Letelier, and his colleague Ronni Moffitt, for which Contreras had been indicted in the United States and convicted in Chile. At this writing, the CIA and other agencies were preparing for a release of 16,000 declassified documents related to the U.S. role in Chile.

The U.S. continued to investigate Pinochet's role in the Letelier-Moffitt assassination. On March 22, U.S. law enforcement officials arrived in Santiago to question witnesses, after the Chilean Supreme Court agreed to subpoena forty-two people at the request of the U.S. government. Without the presence of the U.S. investigators, a Chilean judge asked the witnesses, including Contreras, questions provided by the U.S. authorities. The Chilean Supreme Court has requested the extradition of one of the DINA agents convicted in the U.S. for the Letelier crime, Armando Fernández Larios, to answer charges in the caravan of death case.

COLOMBIA

Human Rights Developments

During the year, Colombia saw little progress beyond rhetoric toward a negotiated end to prolonged conflict. Both the Revolutionary Armed Forces of Colombia (Fuerzas Armadas Revolucionarias de Colombia, FARC) and the Camilist Union-National Liberation Army (Unión Camilista-Ejército de Liberación Nacional, UC-ELN) sent delegations to Europe in government-approved efforts to further talks. Yet, in Colombia, individuals who spoke out in favor of peace and protection for civilians were eliminated ruthlessly by all sides. Continuing a disturbing trend from 1999, the average number of victims of political violence and deaths in combat rose in 2000 from twelve to fourteen per day according to the Colombian Commission of Jurists (Comisión Colombiana de Juristas, CCJ). All parties to the conflict routinely committed violations of international humanitarian law.

Colombia's armed forces continued to be implicated in serious human rights violations as well as support for the paramilitary groups considered responsible for at least 78 percent of the human rights violations recorded in the six months from October 1999. Troops attacked indiscriminately and killed civilians, among them six elementary school children on a field trip near Pueblo Rico, Antioquia, on August 15. According to witnesses, soldiers fired for forty minutes, ignoring the screams of the adult chaperones. Colombian army commander Gen. Jorge Mora seemed to justify the attack by telling journalists, "These are the risks of the war we are engaged in." Another case took place on June 18, when troops belonging to the Rebeiz Pizarro Battalion fired on a car carrying six adults and two children returning from a party, wounding all.

There continued to be abundant, detailed, and continuing evidence of direct collaboration between the military and paramilitary groups. Government investigators, for example, contended that active duty and reserve officers attached to the army's Third Brigade in Cali had set up and actively supported the Calima Front. In the twelve months since it began to operate in July 1999, the Calima Front was considered responsible for at least 200 killings and the displacement of over 10,000 people.

On February 18, some 300 armed men belonging to the paramilitary Peasant Self-Defense Force of Córdoba and Urabá (Autodefensas Campesinas de Córdoba y Urabá, ACCU) set up a kangaroo court in the village of El Salado, Bolívar. For the next two days, they tortured, garroted, stabbed, decapitated, and shot residents. Witnesses told investigators that they tied one six-year-old girl to a pole and suffocated her with a plastic bag. One woman was reportedly gang-raped. Authorities later confirmed thirty-six dead. Thirty other villagers were missing. "To them, it was like a big party," a survivor told the *New York Times*. "They drank and danced and cheered as they butchered us like hogs."

While these atrocities were being carried out, the Colombian navy's First Brigade maintained roadblocks around El Salado that prevented the International Committee of the Red Cross (ICRC) and others from entering. Thirty minutes after paramilitaries had withdrawn safely with looted goods and animals, navy troops entered the village.

Officers implicated in serious abuses remained on active duty, and only in exceptional cases were they suspended. Military judges generally continued to ignore a 1997 Constitutional Court decision requiring that cases involving soldiers accused of gross human rights violations be prosecuted in civilian courts. According to the Bogotá-based office of the U.N. High Commissioner for Human Rights, the Superior Judicial Council (Consejo Superior de la Judicatura, CSJ), charged with resolving jurisdictional disputes, also continued to flout the Constitutional Court and continued to transfer "cases of serious human rights and international humanitarian law violations to military courts."

Defense Minister Luis Fernando Ramírez declared in July that military tribunals had already transferred 533 police and military cases to civilian jurisdiction, demonstrating compliance with the 1997 decision. However, after a review of 103 cases that the army disclosed to Human Rights Watch, only thirty-nine were found to be cases that could be considered human rights violations. Most of these involved low-ranking soldiers; none were senior officers alleged to have ordered or orchestrated human rights violations. Many of the 103 were prosecuted for offenses such as drug trafficking, theft, lying, and brawling. Dozens of cases involving high ranking military officials that Human Rights Watch has followed since the 1980s should have been transferred to civilian jurisdiction, but remained shielded before military tribunals.

The government claimed major improvements in curtailing abuses by paramilitaries, but the facts did not bear this out. Paramilitary activity increased and paramilitary groups were considered responsible for ninety-three massacres in the first five months of 2000. Most arrest warrants issued by the attorney general against paramilitaries were not enforced due to inaction by the military, and paramilitary leaders remained at large and collected warrants like badges of honor. At this writing, there were twenty-two outstanding arrest warrants against Carlos Castaño, the main paramilitary leader, for massacres, killings, and the kidnapping of human rights defenders and a Colombian senator, among other crimes.

The government repeatedly claimed that it had set up special units to pursue paramilitaries, but these groups appeared little more than paper tigers. One, the "Coordination Center for the Fight against Self-Defense Groups," announced with fanfare on February 25, had not even met more than six months later.

Carlos Castaño often announced publicly and well in advance what his forces planned to do, yet military commanders commonly failed to deploy troops to protect civilians, even when local authorities informed them about threats. Since January, Human Rights Watch learned through publicly available sources of over twenty threatened attacks on villages that were later carried out. Only in exceptional cases were measures taken to protect civilians and pursue paramilitaries known to be in the area. Authorities also received reliable and detailed information about the location of permanent paramilitary bases, often within walking distance of military sites, yet failed to act against them, contributing to an atmosphere of terror.

Castaño, who claimed to command 11,200 armed and trained fighters, maintained many permanent bases and roadblocks, moved himself and his troops with apparent ease, and used computers, the Internet, radios, vehicles, and helicopters to prepare death lists and coordinate massacres. In an unprecedented hour-length television interview in March, Castaño described himself as the "fighting arm of the middle class."

Armed opposition guerrillas also committed abuses, and were considered responsible for 20 percent of the killings of civilians recorded in the six months from October 1999. The FARC received foreign dignitaries, U.N. officials, and Wall Street billionaires in the five southern municipalities ceded to them to promote peace talks, but continued to murder civilians, execute captured government soldiers and rival guerrilla combatants after surrender, threaten and kill civilians who refused to accede to their demands, take hostages, and force thousands of Colombians to flee and become displaced. The group maintained an estimated seventy battle fronts throughout Colombia thought to include at least 17,000 trained, uniformed, and armed members.

In dozens of attacks, the FARC employed methods that caused avoidable civilian casualties in violation of international humanitarian law, including the use of gas canisters packed with gunpowder and shrapnel and launched as bombs. In an attack on Vigía del Fuerte, Antioquia, in March, for example, FARC-launched canisters left the town a virtual ruin and caused numerous civilian casualties, including the town mayor. Witnesses told journalists that some of the twenty-one police agents who died were executed by the FARC, among them several who had sought medical attention in the local hospital.

After a visit to the FARC area in June, Human Rights Watch investigated evidence linking the group to at least twenty-six murders there. In addition, the office of the Public Advocate (Defensoría) reported sixteen cases of missing persons, either forcibly recruited, killed by the FARC, or forced to flee. Thousands more were believed to have fled the area as forcibly displaced. The FARC publicly acknowledged nineteen executions.

In an interview with Human Rights Watch in Los Pozos, Caquetá, FARC commander Simón Trinidad dismissed international humanitarian law as "a bourgeois concept."

The FARC rarely punished its members for committing abuses. To the contrary, the few cases they acknowledged showed that punishment amounted to little more than a slap on the hand and rarely extended to the commanders who ordered or covered up killings. For example, the two guerrillas who killed Americans Terence Freitas, Lahe'ena'e Gay, and Ingrid Washinawatok on March 5, 1999, were eventually sentenced to construct fifty meters of trench and clear land.

For their part, far from respecting dissent, UC-ELN guerrillas threatened groups that supported humanitarian accords meant to protect civilians, among them Children, Planters of Peace (Niños, Sembrando Semillas de Paz) and Conciudadanía, both based in Antioquia. The group continued attacks on oil pipelines and power pylons, and for prolonged periods prevented transit on vital roads, converting thousands of detained travelers into human shields against army counterattack.

In northeastern Colombia, where the UC-ELN attempted to win government support for a protected territory where they could operate openly and hold talks on social change and possible peace, violence was particularly acute. In the municipalities of San Pablo, Cantagallo, and Yondó, thousands of civilians protested the proposed government withdrawal, fearful of guerrilla abuses, paramilitary retaliation, and more war. At the same time, the area was increasingly controlled by advancing paramilitaries apparently tolerated by the Colombian military. A report by nongovernmental organizations found that over 3,700 people in the region had been forcibly displaced during the first three months of 2000 and dozens had been murdered.

The UC-ELN tried to generate talks similar to those between the government and the FARC, and even negotiated the temporary release of jailed leaders to take part in July discussions in Geneva, Switzerland, and an October meeting in San José, Costa Rica. However, talks appeared to bring little hope, and the group's estimated 1,500 fighters were increasingly pressed in the field by offensives launched by Colombian the armed forces, paramilitaries, and rival FARC units.

In areas where control was contested and around its camps, the UC-ELN continued to use landmines.

Both the FARC and UC-ELN continued to kidnap civilians for ransom or political concessions, a violation of international humanitarian law. Colombian police estimated that half of the over 3,000 kidnappings carried out each year were the work of guerrillas; the rest were attributed to common criminals. In April, FARC commander Jorge Briceño, known as "Mono Jojoy," announced that all Colombians with assests of over U.S. $1 million should pay the FARC what he cynically termed a "peace tax" or risk being taken hostage. Some hostages, including a three-year-old and a nine-year-old, were imprisoned in the area reserved for government talks. As of this writing, three passengers seized on an Avianca airlines flight on April 12, 1999, remained in UC-ELN custody, used as bargaining chips to compel the government to make concessions.

Forced displacement of civilians remained acute. In a report released in 2000, Francis Deng, the U.N. secretary-general's representative on internally displaced persons, described Colombia's situation as "among the gravest in the world. . . . [D]isplacement in Colombia is not merely incidental to the armed conflict but is also a deliberate strategy of war."

According to the U.S. Committee for Refugees, there were at least 1.8 million forcibly displaced people in Colombia and between 80,000 and 105,000 Colombian refugees in Venezuela, Ecuador, and Panama, although they were not recognized as such by the governments of these countries. In only the first six months of 2000, an estimated 134,000 Colombians were newly displaced, most by paramilitaries, followed by guerrillas and the armed forces.

Although law 387, passed in 1997, outlined a broad and comprehensive plan to assist the forcibly displaced, it had yet to be implemented and key elements, like a national network of information, remained unaddressed. Indeed, Colombia's Constitutional Court ruled in August that the state had failed to enforce the law and was in violation of its duties. However, it appeared unlikely that even this unusual decision would stimulate the political will necessary to address the problem.

In January, Panama granted temporary protection to 393 Colombians who had fled combat in Juradó, Chocó. Most later returned to Colombia. Church workers in Sucumbíos, Ecuador, estimated that in the first seven months of 2000, at least 5,000 Colombians had crossed into Ecuador. Nevertheless, only 120 had gained formal status as refugees and received assistance from the United Nations High Commission for Refugees (UNHCR). In 2000, the Canadian government provided resettlement to over 500 refugees from Colombia.

Journalists continued to be attacked and threatened for their work. In one particularly brutal incident, *El Espectador* reporter Jineth Bedoya was abducted on May 25 by paramilitaries while inside La Modelo, Bogotá's maximum security prison. Bedoya was taken from the lobby in full view of guards, drugged, bound, gagged, and driven to a city three hours away. There she was beaten, tortured, and raped by four men who accused her of being a guerrilla sympathizer. Before abandoning her at a local garbage dump, the men told her they had plans to kill more journalists.

In February, FARC commander Manuel Marulanda Vélez told journalists that they had been unfair to his group and would be made to pay. At the time, the FARC was holding seventy-three-year-old media businessman Guillermo "La Chiva" Cortés hostage. Cortés was later rescued. Other journalists who wrote frequently about the war, including Francisco Santos of *El Tiempo* and Ignacio Gómez of *El Espectador*, left the country because of threats.

The government made limited progress in establishing legal structures intended to protect human rights. On January 13, President Andrés Pastrana signed the Ottawa Convention on landmines and promised to rid the country of an estimated 50,000 devices. After languishing for twelve years, a bill criminalizing "disappearance," torture, and forced displacement was made law.

Political conflict extended to Colombia's 168 prisons. In December 1999, a paramilitary group broke through a wall at Bogotá's La Modelo prison, and killed eleven inmates. Four months later, paramilitaries attacked the La Modelo cellblock housing common criminals. After a day of fighting, authorities counted thirty-two dead, including one dismembered prisoner, and dozens wounded. Overcrowding remained a serious problem.

Defending Human Rights

Human rights defenders, community leaders, government investigators, and journalists continued to face threats, attacks, and death throughout the year. Four human rights defenders were killed and three "disappeared" during the first ten months of 2000.

Threats were particularly acute in the oil-refining city of Barrancabermeja, long the home of a vibrant and broad-based human rights movement. On July 11, Elizabeth Cañas—whose son and brother were seized by paramilitaries in 1998 and have yet to be found—was shot and killed in Barrancabermeja. Cañas was a member of the Association of Family Members of the Detained and Disappeared (Asociación de Familiares de Detenidos Desaparecidos-Colombia, ASFADDES). By September, dozens of human rights defenders and trade unionists had received death threats. Almost all appeared to be the work of paramilitary groups who vowed to "sip coffee" in guerrilla-controlled neighborhoods by year's end.

Angel Quintero and Claudia Patricia Monsalve, also ASFADDES members, were "disappeared" in Medellín, Antioquia, on October 6. Indigenous activist Jairo Bedoya Hoyos, a member of the Antioquia Indigenous Organization (Organización Indígena de Antioquia, OIA) who worked on human rights issues, was also "disappeared" on March 2.

The Regional Corporation for the Defense of Human Rights (Corporación Regional para la Defensa de los Derechos Humanos, CREDHOS) received over a dozen telephone death threats in August and September. Its members were featured on a death list circulated in Barrancabermeja in September; a trade unionist on a separate list was murdered in July, a lawyer remained in critical condition after an attack, and another lawyer had fled Colombia.

Demetrio Playonero, a displaced person and human rights leader, was murdered, apparently by paramilitaries, on March 31. After shooting him in the head in front of his wife at his farm outside Yondó, Antioquia, the gunmen breakfasted, then stole the farm's cattle. In May, Jesús Ramiro Zapata, the only remaining member of the Segovia Human Rights Committee, was killed near Segovia.

Government prosecutor Margarita María Pulgarín Trujillo, part of a team investigating cases linking paramilitaries to the army and regional drug traffickers, was murdered in Medellín on April 3, apparently because of her work. Several of her colleagues had already fled Colombia because of death threats from a gang of hired killers known as "La Terraza," close allies of Carlos Castaño. Although several members of "La Terraza" were either dead or under arrest by October 2000, the group remained active and able to instill terror in those it threatened.

Civilian groups, including human rights organizations, also faced attack from the FARC, which in October 2000 characterized them as "paid killers [for the Colombian military]." In a statement on why they failed to honor an invitation to an October 2000 peace meeting in San José, Costa Rica, sponsored by a broad coalition of human rights, peace, and community groups, the FARC dismissed the effort as organized by "the enemies of Colombia and its people." In such ways, the guerrillas contributed to a general atmosphere of fear and intolerance that endangered human rights defenders.

Government efforts to protect threatened defenders continued to be slow, inadequate, and often irrelevant. Even as government offices provided bullet-proof glass to threatened offices and distributed bullet-proof vests, defenders continued to be murdered by experienced killers who often benefitted from impunity. Cases involving the murder of human rights defenders—among them the 1996 killing of Josué Giraldo Cardona; the 1997 killings of Mario Calderón, Elsa Alvarado, and Carlos Alvarado; the 1998

killings of Jesús Valle Jaramillo and Eduardo Umaña Mendoza; and the 1999 killing of Julio González and Everardo de Jesús Puerta—remained either under investigation or with only the material authors of the crimes identified or under arrest. In all cases, the people who planned and paid for the killings remained at large.

Members of the Colombian military continued to accuse government investigators, agencies, and nongovernmental organizations of having been infiltrated by opposition guerrillas, and questioned the legitimacy of investigations. The Colombian Armed Forces General Command maintained on its official web site a text that directly accused Human Rights Watch and the U.S. embassy's human rights officer of forming part of a "strange and shameful alliance" with a criminal drug trafficking cartel. After the February 2000 release of Human Rights Watch's report, "The Ties That Bind: Colombia and Military-Paramilitary Links," Gen. Fernando Tapias, Colombia's commander-in-chief, and army General Mora, echoed this rhetoric by suggesting that Human Rights Watch was in the pay of drug traffickers.

The Role of the International Community

United Nations

The Bogotá office of the U.N. High Commissioner for Human Rights undertook invaluable work, visiting regions shaken by war and pressing Colombian government authorities on the dozens of recommendations made by U.N. rapporteurs and others that remained unaddressed. Presenting the office's blistering annual report, Mary Robinson noted that the situation "has deteriorated significantly. This is a sad and sobering comment to have to make, as I reflect back on my own visit to Bogotá in October 1998."

The report paid special attention to continuing evidence of ties between the military and paramilitary groups. The office noted that "disciplinary and judicial investigations reveal that direct links between some members of the Armed Forces and paramilitary groups persist" and described the government's efforts to break these links as virtually nonexistent.

However, a weaker message was sent in April, when the Commission on Human Rights issued an unusually mild chairperson's statement, drafted by the E.U. and adopted by consensus. The statement welcomed "the continued readiness of the Colombian Government to cooperate with the permanent office of the High Commissioner," ignoring the Bogotá office's reports to the contrary. Even as the Colombian government agreed to allow the office to remain until April 2002, U.N. staff noted a marked drop in cooperation by Colombian officials.

These concerns were echoed in July, when Secretary-General Kofi Annan expressed "deep concern" about human rights in Colombia, "particularly the high incidence of kidnapings and massacres of civilians."

The UNHCR continued to expand its presence in Colombia, and opened three field offices in 1999 and 2000, in Barrancabermeja, Apartadó, and Puerto Asís.

United States

The character of Colombia's conflict changed with the entry of the United States as a major investor. The $1.3 billion infusion of mostly military aid was meant to be only one part of Plan Colombia, a multinational proposal to assist the country; yet, as of this writing, there were few other contributions to what was meant to be support totaling $7.5 billion.

In response, the FARC announced rewards for the capture of combat pilots, increased attacks on military helicopters and airplanes, and reportedly began arming villagers in southern Colombia to resist the fumigation of drug-producing crops, meant to be a centerpiece of the U.S. effort. Guerrillas used mainly rifles and rocket-propelled grenades, and claimed to have downed at least one National Police helicopter in April. In September, a FARC spokesperson declared U.S. military personnel "legitimate targets" of guerrilla operations.

Debated heatedly yet passed over-whelmingly by the U.S. Congress, the Colombia package was the largest single military assistance program ever approved for a Latin American country. The plan included $519.2 million for the Colombian military, most designated for the purchase of UH-60 Black Hawk and UH-1H Huey helicopters, logistical support, intelligence, and training; $116 million for the Colombian National Police; $68.5 million for alternative development, crop substitution, and assistance for peasants who may be forced to abandon their farms; $58 million for law enforcement and judicial reform; $51 million for human rights programs; and $37.5 million for programs benefitting the forcibly displaced.

Among those actively supporting the aid were Occidental Petroleum, which has major drilling sites in Colombian war zones; Lockheed Martin, manufacturer of the P-3 "Orion" radar surveillance airplane used to track drug smuggling and included in the package; Texas-based Textron, which will make the UH-1H Huey helicopters included in the plan; and United Technologies, whose Connecticut-based subsidiary, Sikorsky, will make the UH-60 Black Hawk helicopters.

Although the package featured strict human rights conditions, President Clinton waived all but one for reasons of U.S. national security on August 22, allowing aid to go forward even as American officials acknowledged that the forces they were funding maintained ties to paramilitary groups, had failed to suspend or prosecute implicated officers, engaged in abuses, and refused to enforce civilian jurisdiction over human rights crimes. "You don' t hold up the major objective to achieve the minor," said a spokesperson for the office of White House adviser and U.S. drug czar retired Gen. Barry McCaffrey.

Human Rights Watch protested the waiver and single certification issued by the State Department, issued after President Pastrana signed a directive based on the entrance into law of a new military penal code. Along with Amnesty International and the Washington Office on Latin America, Human Rights Watch argued that the directive complied only partially with U.S. law, so should have resulted in a denial of certification.

The persistence of human rights abuses within the Colombian military was underscored in September, when the U.S. suspended aid and training to the army's Twelfth and Twenty-Fourth brigades. Both had previously passed the vetting process carried out by U.S. officials and mandated by the Leahy Amendment, which prohibits the United States from funding foreign security force units accused with credible evidence of having committed human rights violations.

Colombia's neighbors also expressed serious concern that the U.S. plan could push coca growing and drug trafficking across Colombia's borders, generate new refugee flows, and cause fighting to spread. During a visit to Colombia, Ecuadoran President Gustavo Noboa reportedly asked President Pastrana to notify his government of all military operations in southern Colombia so that the Ecuadoran army could prepare for repercussions. Brazilian leaders openly criticized the aid, and began to reinforce their border with Colombia.

In December 1999, the first U.S.-trained Colombian army battalion completed its training and was deployed. A second battalion began to train the following August. U.S. law mandated that fewer than 500 U.S. troops and 300 contractors be deployed in Colombia at any one time barring an emergency. But reflecting a global trend to "out-source" war, some analysts projected that as many as 1,000 U.S.-related personnel could be in Colombia on any given day, including retired U.S. special forces members employed by for civilian companies such as DynCorp Inc. and Military Professional Resources Inc. (MPRI), which were hired by the U.S. State and Defense Departments.

The department of Putumayo, along Colombia's southern border with Ecuador and home to 50 percent of Colombia's illegal coca crop, was to the be the first target in the U.S. strategy, which had as its centerpiece a "Push into Southern Colombia" to eradicate coca bushes, destroy cocaine laboratories, and disrupt supply and shipment routes. U.S. officials acknowledged that forced displacement was one likely outcome of the strategy, and proposed setting up government-controlled "temporary" camps to distribute assistance. However, groups working with the internally displaced protested, arguing that this strategy risked "fomenting the conflict, targeting innocent civilians, and substantially increasing internal displacement in Colombia."

The potential for new human rights abuses became clear as the U.S. strategy was implemented. Paramilitaries virtually took over Putumayo's urban centers, such as Puerto Asís, where armed fighters walked with guns in their belts, yet with no interference from either the army or the police. In September and October, an armed strike called by the FARC had left residents without food, gas, medicine, or telephone service, and combat between guerrillas and paramilitaries raged while government troops remained largely in their barracks.

Europe

European leaders proved deeply skeptical of the U.S. military build-up in Colombia even as the E.U. and member states supported negotiations with guerrillas and greater respect for human rights. Although President Pastrana asked the EU to contribute $1.5 billion to Plan Colombia, at a July donors' summit of twenty-six nations in Madrid, he came away with almost nothing. Of the E.U. member states, only Spain pledged $100 million. France's *Le Monde* termed the meeting a "crushing failure for Colombian diplomacy."

Prior to the meeting, 150 delegates representing Colombian and international nongovernmental organizations, academics, environmentalists, and human rights groups met in Madrid and called on the international community to fund peace initiatives, not the Colombian military. The E.U. found that argument persuasive, and in October announced that its $144 million contribution to Plan Colombia would go to nongovernmental, economic, and humanitarian aid programs focused on peace, human rights, and economic development.

The E.U. publicly denounced abuses by all sides and called on the Colombian government to address "persistent grave violations." After her September visit to Colombia, British cabinet minister Mo Mowlam, an architect of the Northern Ireland peace accords, said that the United Kingdom and most European countries would withhold individual donations to Plan Colombia unless the Colombian security forces reformed.

Five countries—France, Spain, Switzerland, Norway, and Cuba—pledged to help the Colombian government negotiate with the UC-ELN. Yet, even as some of these governments met with the UC-ELN leadership to discuss possible talks, the European Union exerted strong pressure to end kidnappings and release all hostages.

Relevant Human Rights Watch Reports:
The Ties That Bind: Colombia and Military-Paramilitary Links, 2/00

CUBA

Human Rights Developments

Despite a few positive developments over the course of the year, the Cuban government's human rights practices were generally arbitrary and repressive. Hundreds of peaceful opponents of the government remained behind bars, and many more were subject to short-term detentions, house arrest, surveillance, arbitrary searches, evictions, travel restrictions, politically-motivated dismissals from employment, threats, and other forms of harassment.

Although Cuba's human rights conditions improved little in 2000, U.S. policy toward Cuba did begin to change. The high-profile case of Elián González, the six-year-old Cuban shipwreck survivor who stayed seven months in the United States against the wishes of his father, brought increased public attention to the United States' policy of isolating Cuba. After the boy returned home in June, congressional efforts to relax some

aspects of the thirty-eight-year-old U.S. economic embargo against Cuba gained momentum.

Cuba's repressive human rights practices were undergirded by the country's legal and institutional structure. The rights to freedom of expression, association, assembly, movement, and of the press remained restricted under Cuban law. By criminalizing enemy propaganda, the spreading of "unauthorized news," and the insulting of patriotic symbols, the government effectively denied freedom of speech under the guise of protecting state security. The authorities also imprisoned or ordered the surveillance of individuals who had committed no illegal act, relying upon laws penalizing "dangerousness" (estado peligroso) and allowing for "official warning" (advertencia oficial). The government-controlled courts undermined the right to a fair trial by restricting the right to a defense, and frequently failed to observe the few due process rights available to defendants under the law.

Even Cubans' right to leave their country was severely restricted, as the government prosecuted persons for "illegal exit" if they attempted to leave the island without first obtaining official permission to do so. Such permission was sometimes denied arbitrarily, or made contingent on the purchase of an expensive exit permit.

Pro-democracy activists planned a series of protests to coincide with the ninth annual Ibero-American Summit, held in Havana in November 1999. Yet, the authorities cracked down hard on public dissent, arresting over 200 dissidents in the weeks before and after the summit. Many of them were placed under house arrest, while others were temporarily detained in police stations. This wave of repression continued through February 2000. The Cuban Commission of Human Rights and National Reconciliation (Comisión Cubana de Derechos Humanos y Reconciliación Nacional), a respected Havana-based nongovernmental group, announced in early March that 352 dissidents had been arrested over the preceding four months, while another 240 had their freedom of movement restricted, normally by being ordered to remain at their homes.

While the vast majority of those arrested were eventually released without any criminal charges being brought against them, a few were prosecuted. The most serious case was that of thirty-eight-year-old Dr. Oscar Elías Biscet González, who received a three-year prison sentence on February 25 for protests that included turning the Cuban flag upside-down and carrying anti-abortion placards. Biscet, the president of the Lawton Human Rights Foundation, was convicted of dishonoring patriotic symbols, public disorder, and instigating delinquency. It was reported in August that he had experienced severe weight loss in prison, suffered from health problems, including an untreated gum infection, and had been held in solitary confinement for months at a time.

Also on February 25, immediately after Biscet's trial, Eduardo Díaz Fleitas, vice-president of the Fifth of August Movement (Movimiento 5 de Agosto), and Fermín Scull Zulueta, were convicted of public disorder by the same court. Díaz Fleitas was sentenced to a year of incarceration, while Scull Zulueta received a year of house arrest. Like Biscet, they were anti-abortion protesters, and had carried signs at a November 10 demonstration.

The most encouraging development of the year came in May when three leaders of the Internal Dissidents Working Group (Grupo de Trabajo de la Disidencia Interna, GTDI) were freed prior to the expiration of their sentences. Economists Martha Beatriz Roque Cabello, engineering professor Félix Antonio Bonne Carcasses, and attorney René Gómez Manzano were granted provisional liberty within two weeks of each other, but Vladimiro Roca Antúnez, the fourth leader of the group, remained incarcerated at this writing. The four had been sentenced in March 1999 to several years of imprisonment for "acts against the security of the state," after having spent nearly nineteen months in pre-trial detention. They were first detained in July 1997, a month after the GTDI released "The Homeland Belongs to All" (La Patria es de Todos), an analytical paper on the Cuban economy, human rights, and democracy.

Whether detained for political or common crimes, inmates were subjected to abusive prison conditions. Prisoners frequently suffered malnourishment and languished in overcrowded cells without appropriate medical attention. Some endured physical and sexual abuse, typically by other inmates with the acquiescence of guards, or long periods in isolation cells. Prison authorities insisted that all detainees participate in politically oriented "re-education" sessions or face punishment. Political prisoners who denounced the poor conditions of imprisonment were punished with solitary confinement, restricted visits, or denial of medical treatment.

At least twenty-four prisoners faced the death penalty, according to a list circulated in August by the Cuban Commission of Human Rights and National Reconciliation, which also provided the names of twenty-one others who had been executed in 1999. Although the organization noted that all of the executions involved defendants convicted of homicide, Cuban law permitted the use of the death penalty for numerous other crimes, including international drug trafficking and the corruption of minors. Cuba's secrecy regarding the application of the death penalty—the government did not provide information on execution—made it difficult to ascertain the actual number of death sentences imposed and carried out. The Cuban legal system's serious procedural failings and lack of judicial independence, which violated the rights of all criminal defendants, were especially problematic with regard to capital offenses. Miscarriages of justice were also unlikely to be remedied upon review by a higher court, since Cuban law afforded convicts sentenced to death minimal opportunities to appeal their sentences.

The Cuban government maintained a firm stance against independent journalism, regularly detaining reporters and sometimes prosecuting them. On November 10, 1999 Angel Pablo Polanco, the director of Noticuba, was arrested and held for a week, allegedly to prevent him from reporting on protests surrounding the Ibero-American Summit. On January 20, 2000 José Orlando González Bridón, president of the Cuban Confederation of Democratic Workers (Confederación de Trabajadores Democráticos de Cuba) and writer for the Cuba Free Press, was detained for several hours. Police reportedly questioned him about his writings and threatened to prosecute him. Other journalists detained and questioned for brief periods over the course of the year included Ricardo González Alfonso, Jadir Hernández, Jesús Hernández, and Luis Alberto Rivera Leiva. Others were harassed or prevented from working by police.

Victor Rolando Arroyo Carmona, a long-time government opponent who wrote for the Union of Independent Cuban Journalists and Writers (Unión de Periodistas y Escritores Cubanos Independientes), was sentenced on January 25 to six months of imprisonment for "hoarding" toys. Police had confiscated toys that he had planned to give away to poor children in his area; they had been paid for by Cuban exiles in Miami. Just after Arroyo's trial, the Cuban authorities freed another independent journalist, Leonardo de Varona González, who had served a sixteen-month sentence for "insulting" President Fidel Castro. At least three other independent journalists remained incarcerated: Bernardo Arévalo Padrón and Manuel Antonio González Castellanos, serving sentences of six years and of two years and seven months, respectively, for "insulting" Castro; and Jesús Joel Díaz Hernández, serving four years for "dangerousness," who was reportedly held in solitary confinement until early August.

On October 16, after his release from prison, Arroyo was reportedly beaten and insulted by state security agents. He and another dissident were picked up from a friend's house, driven to the police station in Güines, beaten en route, and then driven dozens of miles away and released after being beaten again.

Foreign journalists too faced government harassment if they attempted to work with or assist their Cuban colleagues. Italian freelance journalist Carmen Butta was re-portedly detained by police on June 18 after meeting with independent journalists as part of her research for an article on the Cuban independent press. In August, three Swedish journalists were arrested in Havana by state security agents. They had traveled to Cuba on tourist visas but had held a seminar on press freedom for independent journalists. The three were deported after spending two days in detention. Earlier that same month, French journalist Martine Jacot was detained and interrogated at the Havana airport by six members of the Cuban security forces. She had spent a week in Cuba interviewing independent journalists and family members of incarcerated journalists. Jacot's equipment, including a video camera, was seized, as were some documents.

While the government permitted greater opportunities for religious expression than in past years and allowed several religious-run humanitarian groups to operate, it continued to maintain tight control over religious institutions, affiliated groups, and individual believers.

The government recognized only one labor union, the Worker's Central of Cuba (Central de Trabajadores de Cuba, CTC), and restricted labor rights by banning independent labor groups and harassing individuals attempting to form them. It tightly controlled workers employed in businesses backed by foreign investment. Under restrictive labor laws, the authorities had a prominent role in the selection, payment, and dismissal of workers, effectively denying workers the right to bargain directly with employers over benefits, promotions, and wages. Cuba also continued to use prison labor for agricultural camps and ran clothing assembly and other factories in its prisons. The authorities' insistence that political prisoners work without pay in poor conditions violated international labor standards.

Defending Human Rights

The Cuban government continued its systematic harassment and repression of human rights defenders. The authorities routinely used surveillance, phone tapping, and intimidation in its efforts to restrict independent monitoring of the government's human rights practices. In some instances, they employed arbitrary searches, evictions, travel restrictions, politically-motivated dismissals from employment, threats and other forms of harassment against local activists.

The Cuban government denied international human rights and humanitarian monitors access to the country. The International Committee of the Red Cross (ICRC) had not been allowed to conduct prison visits in Cuba since 1989, making Cuba the only country in the region to deny access to the ICRC. Human Rights Watch had not been allowed to send any representatives to monitor human rights conditions in Cuba since 1995.

The Role of the International Community

United Nations

At its April session, the United Nations Commission on Human Rights voted once again to censure Cuba for its human rights abuses. The resolution passed by a wider margin than in previous years, but did not make provision to appoint a special rapporteur to monitor human rights conditions. Sponsored by the Czech and Polish governments, the resolution criticized Cuba's treatment of political dissidents and urged the Cuban authorities to allow visits by U.N. human rights investigators. Cuba retaliated the vote by staging a mass demonstration outside the Czech embassy in Havana and temporarily recalling its ambassador from Argentina. (Argentina was among the twenty-one countries that supported the resolution.)

In February, just prior to the commission's session, U.N. Special Rapporteur Radhika Coomaraswamy released her report on violence against women in Cuba. The report, which was fair, objective, and comprehensive, was the fruit of an unprecedented mission to Cuba undertaken by the special rapporteur in June 1999. (The Cuban authorities had once allowed the U.N. high commissioner for human rights to visit the island, but had otherwise consistently denied

access to U.N. human right monitors, including thematic rapporteurs and mechanisms.) While criticizing the U.S. embargo for its adverse impact on Cuban women, the report urged the Cuban authorities to undertake legal reforms to deal more effectively with the problems of domestic violence, rape, and sexual harassment. It also denounced the arbitrary detention of women whose political views are unacceptable to the government.

The report evoked a stridently defensive response from the Cuban authorities, who sent a *note verbale* to the Office of the High Commissioner for Human Rights that complained that the special rapporteur's visit was "manipulated" by the U.S. government, and that challenged the applicability of the special rapporteur's "bourgeois democratic-liberal concept of human rights." The Cubans also vociferously attacked Human Rights Watch, whose 1999 book on Cuban human rights conditions was among the sources cited in the special rapporteur's report. It erroneously asserted that Human Rights Watch received substantial U.S. government funding, when, in fact, the organization accepts no funding from any government, either directly or indirectly.

Ibero-American Countries

The Ibero-American Summit brought the Spanish king to Cuba, in what was the first visit to the island by a reigning Spanish monarch, as well as high officials from twenty-one countries. Heads of state from all over Latin America were in attendance, although a few declined to participate because of Cuba's lack of progress on democracy and human rights. In a welcome break from the usual protocol, a number of officials, including Spain's Prime Minister José María Aznar and Portugal's President Jorge Sampaio, took advantage of their visit to meet with prominent dissidents such as veteran activist Elizardo Sánchez.

The summit culminated in the adoption of a series of documents, including the Havana Declaration, in which signatory states expressed a commitment to democracy and human rights and called for the U.S. to end its embargo against Cuba.

Organization of American States

Latin American political leaders had a further opportunity to collectively assess their engagement with Cuba during the thirtieth Organization of American States (OAS) General Assembly, held in Windsor, Canada, in June. While a number of Caribbean countries spoke up for Cuba's reintegration into the OAS—Cuba was suspended from the regional grouping in 1962—no concrete steps were taken toward this end.

European Union

The European Union's relationship with Cuba remained formally defined by its 1996 Common Position, which conditioned full economic cooperation on human rights reforms. But in 2000 there were indications that the E.U.'s approach to Cuba was changing. In February, Cuba formally requested integration into the multilateral grouping established under the Lomé Convention, a trade and aid agreement linking the European Union to African, Caribbean and Pacific states. The application sparked considerable debate regarding whether Cuba's association would be consistent with the agreement's criteria on democracy and human rights. In April, however, just after the adoption of the U.N. human rights resolution supported by many E.U. states, the debate was mooted by Cuba's decision to withdraw its application. The Cuban government also cancelled an ambitious visit planned for late April by senior E.U. officials. Yet, in August, once again, Cuba reportedly expressed interest in associating with the E.U.'s aid pact, now called the Cotonou Agreement.

Although Cuba remained the only Latin American country not to have entered into a formal development and cooperation agreement with the European Union, the regional bloc still provided the largest amount of international aid to Cuba. European trade and investment in Cuba also continued to flourish, with countries such as Spain, Italy and France being among Cuba's most significant partners in the areas of trade and finance.

With several bilateral agreements being signed in recent years, all E.U. member states had official bilateral economic relations with Cuba.

United States

The issue of the decades-old economic embargo on Cuba received renewed congressional attention in 2000, and steps, albeit small ones, were taken toward easing it. After months of debate in congressional committees, both houses of Congress passed legislation in October to allow limited food and medicine sales to Cuba. Farmers, agricultural interests and pharmaceutical companies had lobbied heavily for access to the Cuban market.

But the practical impact of the legislation was likely to be less than its symbolic importance. While it signaled the first significant rollback of U.S. sanctions against the island in nearly four decades, the package was unlikely to yield more than a small volume of actual business. Because of compromises with conservative lawmakers opposed to loosening trade restrictions, no U.S. export credits or private financing would be allowed on food sales. Indeed, as the bill reached a final vote in the House of Representatives and Senate, Havana denounced its conditions as "humiliating and unjust." An editorial published on the front pages of the Communist Party daily *Granma* promised that Cuba would "not buy a single cent of food or medicine from the United States."

And in a step backwards, the bill contained provisions codifying the rules that generally banned U.S. tourism to Cuba. To travel legally to Cuba, Americans had to obtain a license, available only to narrow categories of visitors, or be invited by a non-U.S. group that met the costs. By limiting travel to Cuba, these restrictions violated article 19 of the International Covenant on Civil and Political Rights, to which the United States is a party.

U.S. authorities continued to detain and repatriate Cuban asylum seekers aboard vessels intercepted at sea, giving them only onboard screening interviews to determine whether they had a "credible fear" of persecution in their homeland. As exemplified by the case of Elián González, whose mother died attempting the voyage, large numbers of Cubans continued to risk their lives at sea in the hope of reaching and obtaining asylum in the United States.

GUATEMALA

Human Rights Developments

Human rights issues received unprecedented official attention following the January 2000 inauguration of President Alfonso Portillo. Within two months, President Portillo declared a national day in honor of the estimated 200,000 victims of Guatemala's thirty-five-year civil conflict, ratified the Inter-American Convention on Forced Disappearances, and, before the Inter-American Commission on Human Rights (IACHR), admitted state responsibility for past violations, including the 1990 murder of anthropologist Myrna Mack and the December 1982 Dos Erres massacre of at least 162 people. President Portillo also called the brutal 1998 murder of Bishop Juan Gerardi and its botched investigation a "national embarrassment," publicly committing himself to bringing those responsible to justice.

Yet, serious human rights problems remained. The country's weak judicial system continued to allow perpetrators virtual impunity. The new government's record was also marred by increased threats against and harassment of human rights activists, killings of community leaders, and retrograde steps on capital punishment. Moreover, President Portillo's political alliance with Gen. Efraín Ríos Montt, Guatemala's former military ruler, who became president of the Congress in January 2000, was a worrisome reminder of the country's inability to surmount its legacy of repression.

The absence of effective law enforcement and the high incidence of common crime contributed to a climate of insecurity, and the continued use of lynching as a form of vigilante justice. The United Nations Verification Mission in Guatemala (Misión de Verificación de las Naciones Unidas en Guatemala, MINUGUA), established after the 1996 peace accords, reported twenty-two instances of lynching or attempted lynching in the first half of 2000, resulting in five deaths and thirty serious injuries to victims. In 1999, there were forty-eight deaths from lynching. In April, a Japanese tourist and his bus driver were killed by a mob in the village of Todos Santos apparently because of rumors that the tour group was planning to steal local children. Nine people were arrested in May for the lynching. In July, eight men apparently suspected of kidnapping and rape were doused with gasoline and burned by a mob of 200 villagers in Xalvaquiej. MINUGUA reported in August that military personnel were behind some of these apparently vigilante actions.

On- and off-duty officers of the National Civilian Police (Política Nacional Civil, PNC) were reportedly responsible for numerous human rights abuses, notably those involving excessive use of force. MINUGUA found that inadequate recruitment, selection, and training of police fostered abuses, which were further encouraged by ineffective internal disciplinary mechanisms. In February, a PNC officer in an Esquintla nightclub reportedly shot and killed a waiter. That same month, in a separate confrontation, PNC members shot and killed a marketplace vendor in Guatemala City. In May, plainclothes SIC agents were allegedly responsible for the "disappearance" of Mynor Pineda, a suspect previously in their custody, whose whereabouts remained unknown at the time of this writing. MINUGUA also found that the Criminal Investigation Service (Servicio de Investigación Criminal, SIC) of the PNC used torture to elicit confessions from suspects.

Under the 1996 peace accords, the military was to give up its role in internal security and devote itself to external defense. In June, however, Congress approved a decree allowing the military to assist the PNC in fighting common crime.

MINUGUA reported twenty-six extrajudicial killings and nineteen cases of torture from October 1999 through June 2000. In March, the body of Garifuna leader Giovanni Roberto Sanchez was found at the Livingston Hotel where he was employed; he had been hanged and his body showed evidence of beating. In May, community worker and mayoral candidate José Anacio Mendoza was murdered in Camotán, Chiquimula; his body was found in a well and also showed signs of torture. In July, Mayan leader José Quino and his colleague, María Mejía, were killed after being ambushed by unknown assailants near Lake Atitlan.

In May, Human Rights Ombudsman Julio Arango identified possible instances of "social cleansing," characterized by an apparently greater degree of premeditation than lynching, after four bodies were found with their hands and feet tied together and bearing signs of torture. MINUGUA established the possible involvement of the PNC and an ex-military commissioner in these murders.

Journalists and other representatives of the media were targeted for harassment and other abuses apparently to influence their reporting. In July, *Prensa Libre* columnist Eduardo Villatoro reported receiving threats demanding that he stop writing articles critical of the Mixco authorities. Earlier, in February, the television program "T-mas de Noche" was canceled apparently due to its critical stance toward the government. This sparked a national debate over the ownership of four of Guatemala's television stations by an individual with family connections in the Ministry of Communications. After an April visit to Guatemala, Organization of American States (OAS) Special Rapporteur on Freedom of Expression Santiago Cantón recommended the implementation of clear rules to avoid any conflict of interest between public authorities and the media. President Portillo expressed concern over the "T-mas de Noche" incident and proposed the establishment of a state-run, public television channel as a mechanism to address some of the problems highlighted by Cantón.

Despite President Portillo's self-imposed deadline to bring to justice those responsible for the 1998 killing of Bishop Juan Gerardi—which occurred shortly after the bishop released a church-sponsored report on human rights violations during the armed conflict—the six-month deadline passed without any resolution of the case. In April, Flor de María García Villatoro, the third judge to handle the case, ordered that Father Mario Orantes, a close colleague of Bishop Gerardi, and cook Margarita López, stand trial for the murder. In May, Judge García Villatoro ordered that charges also be brought against Obdulia Villanueva, former member of the Presidential General Staff (Estado Mayor Presidencial, EMP), Captain Byron Miguel Lima Oliva, and his father, retired Col. Byron Disrael Lima Estrada. The trials of the five suspects were scheduled to begin in October. Witnesses, prosecutors, judges and the Archbishop's Human Rights Office (Oficina de Derechos Humanos del Arzobispado, ODHA), which Gerardi had headed prior to his death, continued to receive threats related to the case. In August, Carmen Zanabria, after receiving a series of threats, became the fifth important witness to flee the country for security reasons.

Even though President Portillo accepted the principle of state responsibility for past human rights crimes, formidable barriers to justice existed in practice. U.N. Special Rapporteur on the Independence of Lawyers and Judges Param Cumaraswamy issued a report on Guatemala in March. This described how the justice system continued to suffer from the deficiencies that it had exhibited during the armed conflict, including corruption, influence peddling, lack of resources, and threats and intimidation of lawyers and judges. Cumaraswamy found that only 10 percent of all homicide cases went to trial, and that very few of these ever resulted in convictions. He also found that the country's indigenous majority continued to face discrimination in seeking access to justice, particularly because of the absence of translation services in judicial proceedings.

In November 1999, an appeals court extended the sentences, commutable by payment, of ten of the twenty-five soldiers convicted for the 1995 killing of eleven people in the community of Xamán, to include twelve-year prison terms. However, it absolved the other fifteen defendants. In April, the Supreme Court of Justice (Corte Suprema de Justicia, CSJ) overturned these decisions, stating that the case was fraught with irregularities; it ordered the ten convicted men to remain in prison and the other fifteen to be rearrested. In July, Judge Josué Villatoro ordered the arrest and detention of ten ex-military officials accused of the murder of 162 people in the Dos Erres massacre in 1982. At this writing, the Constitutional Court had yet to rule whether the Dos Erres massacre constituted an act of genocide, which would exempt it from the application of the 1996 amnesty law and clear the way for prosecutions to proceed.

After a second acquittal in April 1999, former military commissioner Cándido Noriega—accused of 155 counts of torture, rape, murder, and kidnapping—was sentenced in November 1999 to 220 years in prison for eight murders and two homicides. In September, a judge ruled that the case against Gen. Juan Guillermo Oliva and two former colonels for the 1990 murder of anthropologist Myrna Mack should remain in the civilian courts, rejecting the defense's call for the case to be placed under military jurisdiction. At this writing, no date had been set for the trial.

On May 12, Congress rescinded the law allowing the president to grant pardons in capital cases, bringing Guatemala into violation of both the American Convention on Human Rights and the International Covenant on Civil and Political Rights. Earlier in the year, President Portillo had reviewed four pending cases and, in a welcome decision, commuted the death sentence of Pedro Rax Cucul to thirty years' imprisonment. Rax Cucul, a member of Guatemala's indigenous community who was believed to be mentally disturbed at the time of the crime, reportedly had lacked an interpreter when making his deposition and been assisted only by a mental patient. In the other three cases, President Portillo denied clemency to the sentenced men. On June 29, Amilcar Cetino Pérez and Tomás Cerrate Hernández, both convicted of kidnapping and murder, were given lethal injections; their executions were broadcast live on national television.

As of late October, some thirty people remained on death row. In February, an appeals court commuted the death sentences of three former Civil Patrol members convicted of murdering two of the 143 persons killed in the 1982 Rio Negro massacre, reducing their sentences to fifty-year prison terms.

A U.N.-sponsored report released in April found that conditions in half of Guatemala's detention centers failed to meet minimum international standards.

In December 1999, Nobel peace prize laureate Rigoberta Menchú Tum filed suit in Spain against six military officers and two civilians for genocide and torture. In March, the Spanish High Court agreed to hear the case and in April it began calling witnesses. Judge Guillermo Ruiz Polanco allowed additional plaintiffs to join the case, including the family of a Spanish priest who was murdered in Guatemala in February 1981, and Guatemala's human rights ombudsman. In April, lawyer Julio Cintrón Galvez filed suit against Menchú for treason for filing the case in Spain, a charge that carries a ten to twenty year prison term.

General Ríos Montt, current president of the Congress, was among those named in Menchú's suit as being responsible for genocide and torture during the period when he ruled the country from March 1982 until August 1983. In August, his position as congressional president was threatened when a scandal erupted over his alleged participation in improperly lowering an alcohol tax, but the case had not been resolved at this writing.

On October 13, 1999, armed men detained the five-member executive committee of the Union of Banana Workers of Izabal (Sindicato de Trabajadores Bananeros de Izabal, SITRABI) and held them hostage for several hours. SITRABI represented some 2,500 workers employed by the local subsidiary of Del Monte. The gunmen forced two of the union's leaders to make a radio announcement calling off a work stoppage, planned for the next day to protest the company's failure to reinstate 918 workers who had been fired the previous month in violation of a collective bargaining agreement. In March 2000, Del Monte and the International Union of Foodworkers (IUF), representing SITRABI, signed an agreement to reinstate the fired workers and prosecute those responsible for the attack on the union leaders. In June, a court ruled that twenty-five people should be tried for coercion, illegal search, and illegal detention, but at this writing, no date had been set for the trial, nor had any of the workers been reinstated.

The Minors' Code, which the Guatemalan legislature passed in 1996 but postponed implementing until the year 2000, was again postponed indefinitely in February. The legislation would extend procedural protections—such as the right to a lawyer—to children accused of crimes, and introduce other changes to bring domestic law into conformity with the U.N. Convention on the Rights of the Child, which Guatemala ratified in 1990. In September, Guatemala signed a newly-adopted optional protocol to the children's convention prohibiting the involvement of children in armed conflict. In August, the ODHA released a report on the forced "disappearance" of children during the civil war, attributing 92 percent of the eighty-six documented abductions to the military.

In proceedings before the IACHR in March, President Portillo accepted state responsibility for the events leading to the 1995 murder of Marco Quistinay, a thirteen-year-old streetchild whom two officers handed a bag he believed was food, but which contained a grenade that exploded and killed him. In December 1999, the Inter-American Court of Human Rights ruled that two police officers were responsible for the 1990 deaths of five street youths and that the Guatemalan government had failed to protect the rights of the victims. The decision called for the investigation and prosecution of those responsible for the crime.

Defending Human Rights

In 2000, there was an alarming increase in threats, harassment, and targeted violence against human rights organizations and activists. In the first half of the year, MINUGUA registered fifty-six threats to human rights activists, witnesses and judicial authorities in human rights cases. Rigoberta Menchú and several colleagues at her foundation received death threats.

Organizations and individuals making human rights claims in the courts were particularly targeted. In September, gunmen entered the offices of the Families of the Detained and Disappeared of Guatemala (FAMDEGUA), a group that had initiated proceedings against General Ríos Montt for the Dos Erres massacre, forcing three staff members to the floor at gunpoint. The gunmen repeatedly threatened to kill the three and stole computers, money, and a vehicle. In August, Celso Balan, a representative of the Center for Legal Action in Human Rights (Centro para la acción legal en Derechos Humanos, CALDH) was detained, beaten, and robbed by individuals posing as journalists but thought to have links with active and retired military officers. MINUGUA noted that such threats were not adequately investigated by the authorities.

The Role of the International Community

United Nations

Under the 1996 peace accords, the mandate of MINUGUA was due to expire at year's end. In March, President Portillo asked MINUGUA to extend its stay, but at this writing the U.N. General Assembly had yet to decide on an extension. Significant aspects of the accords have yet to be implemented, so indicating a need for continued international verification.

MINUGUA's reports on aspects of the peace process contained detailed human rights analyses. In September, MINUGUA issued a human rights report for the period October 1999 to June 2000, and at other times it issued communiques on specific human rights abuses.

European Union

The European Parliament passed a resolution in May offering support for Guatemala's prosecution of crimes against humanity, for witness protection and for other protection measures for judges and lawyers. In March, cooperation between the PNC and Spain's Civil Guard (Guardia Civil), who had been providing technical assistance to the Guatemalan police since 1998, was suspended. The European Union was to provide funding to the police in the amount of some 34 million ECUS (approximately U.S. $40 million) between 1998 and 2003.

Organization of American States

The IACHR praised President Portillo's March admission of state responsibility in three pending cases as an "example for the entire Hemisphere." In August, President Portillo followed up on his March statements by agreeing to settle ten additional cases involving two massacres and sixteen executions and "disappearances," a step that obliged his government to provide compensation to the victims or their relatives, and to oversee the investigation and prosecution of each case. At the time of this writing, dozens of Guatemalan cases remained pending before the IACHR.

United States

In March, the U.S. Central Intelligence Agency (CIA) awarded one of its highest honors, the Distinguished Career Intelligence Medal, to former official Terry Ward, who was dismissed from the agency in 1995 for failing to report CIA ties to a Guatemalan colonel implicated in the murders of Efraín Bamaca Velásquez and U.S. citizen Michael Devine. After fierce political debate, Guatemala in April approved the deployment of U.S. military forces to the country to combat illicit drug trafficking. In June, the National Security Archive, a Washington, D.C.-based NGO, released a report entitled "The Guatemalan Military: What the U.S. Files Reveal." This named 232 Guatemalan officers and contained information on their activities and command responsibilities, so assisting NGOs and victims in their efforts to identify and bring to justice those responsible for gross abuses during Guatemala's civil war.

HAITI

Human Rights Developments

Police and government passivity in the face of intimidation and violence by supporters of the Fanmi Lavalas party raised serious human rights concerns. Fanmi Lavalas, the party of former president Jean-Bertrand Aristide, employed fraud to boost its electoral gains and win near total control over the parliament that was sworn in on August 28.

The year 2000 was dominated by elections: local and parliamentary polls on May 21, second-round and rescheduled voting through August, and presidential and partial senatorial contests planned for November and December 2000. Haiti had been without a functioning parliament since President René Préval dissolved it in January 1999, following eighteen months without a prime minister. By 2000, this political impasse had led to the suspension of some U.S. $500 million in multilateral assistance, creating enormous international pressure for the Préval government to hold legislative elections. The country's dire economic circumstances, characterized by the lowest average incomes in the Western Hemisphere, magnified the impact of the aid suspension.

The most glaringly fraudulent aspect of the deeply flawed May elections was the method used to calculate the results of the first-round Senate races. Bypassing the country's constitution and electoral law, which required first-round winners to have an absolute majority of votes cast, the Provisional Electoral Council (Conseil Electorale Provisoire, CEP) dramatically shrunk the pool of votes counted, eliminating all but those accruing to the four or six leading candidates in each province. As a result, all nineteen Senate seats at issue in the elections were won in the first round, eighteen of them by Fanmi Lavalas. When Léon Manus, the seventy-eight-year-old president of the council, objected to the calculation method, Préval and Aristide pressured him to accept it, making veiled threats that led Manus to flee the country. The government's refusal to reconsider the skewed results led the Electoral Monitoring Mission of the Organization of American States (OAS-EOM) to quit Haiti before the second-round balloting, labeling the elections "fundamentally flawed." Fanmi Lavalas then cemented control of local and national government, ending up with seventy-two of eighty-three seats in the Chamber of Deputies, and two-thirds of some 7,500 local posts.

The runup to the elections was marred by political violence, with the OAS recording at least seventy violent incidents from January to May 21, the day of local and first-round parliamentary elections. The violence included several killings, including that of Haiti's most renowned journalist, Jean Dominique, the sixty-nine-year-old director of Radio Haïti-Inter. Gunmen ambushed and shot both him and Jean-Claude Louissant, a station security guard, on the morning of April 3. Dominique was a controversial and outspoken figure, and a firm defender of the rule of law. His radio station bore the marks of numerous bullet holes from earlier attacks. Police arrested several men said to have taken part in the assassination, but there was no official word by October on who was responsible for it, fuelling widespread rumor and speculation.

Members of "popular organizations" supporting Fanmi Lavalas were responsible for violent street demonstrations and other mob actions that went largely unchallenged by the Haitian National Police (Police Nationale d'Haïti, PNH). At the October 24, 1999 launching of the CEP's civic education campaign in Port-au-Prince, a score of Aristide supporters shouted slogans, threw trash and plastic soft drink bottles filled with urine, and tried to attack opposition leader Evans Paul. In late March, during a dispute between Préval and the CEP over the date of elections, mobs set up barricades of burning tires and lobbed rocks at passing cars, calling for the

CEP's dismissal. Charging through the big Croix des Bossales market, they burned hundreds of storage depots, stores, and nearby homes. Five people were reported killed in the days of violence, with fighting among criminal gangs nearly indistinguishable from political violence.

The most dramatic pre-election incident of mob violence occurred on April 8, when some one hundred protesters burned down the headquarters of the opposition coalition, Space for Dialogue (Espace de Concertation). Earlier in the day, at funeral services for Jean Dominique, members of the mob had publicly announced their plans to burn the building and kill Space for Dialogue spokesman Evans Paul (whom they were unable to find). Police, who were on the scene, did not interfere, nor did they make any arrests.

The May 21 elections were largely peaceful, if disorganized, and well over 50 percent of registered voters turned out. But as night fell and polls closed, armed men stole or burned electoral materials in some districts. In others, because a lack of electricity deprived polling precincts of light, electoral workers tallied ballots in places such as police stations, sometimes barring party poll watchers from observing the count. The morning after the vote, the press photographed Port-au-Prince streets littered with ballots and ballot boxes deposited during the night. The OAS-EOM concluded that serious irregularities had compromised the elections' credibility but that, in local balloting, "since one political party won most of the elections by a substantial margin, it is probably unlikely that the majority of the final outcomes in local elections have been affected." Opposition parties alleged massive fraud and intimidation, although most could not document their charges. Contrary to the electoral law, most complaints of irregularities received no serious investigation.

Post-election incidents again demonstrated the problem of selective enforcement of the law. On May 22, Fanmi Lavalas supporters attacked the downtown Port-au-Prince headquarters of a small party, the Rally of Patriotic Citizens (Rassemblement des Citoyens Patriotes, RCP), nearly killing one man and badly injuring another. Although the attack took place a few blocks from a police station during a period of supposed "zero tolerance" for violence, police did not intervene or make arrests.

In the wake of the elections, police arrested some thirty-five opposition candidates and activists, many of whom had been involved in protests against electoral fraud. Those held included former senator and candidate for re-election Paul Denis of the Organization of People in Struggle (Organisation du Peuple en Lutte, OPL) and four others arrested in Les Cayes on May 23. Special police units searched Denis' house without a valid warrant and arrested him after claiming to have found several firearms. The five were released after three days in appalling detention conditions. Others arrested post-election included Limongy Jean, candidate for deputy; fifteen Space for Dialogue supporters in Petit Goâve; a mayoral candidate and two other members of the Open the Gates Party (Pati Louvrye Barye, PLB) in Thomazeau; and ten OPL candidates and activists in Thiotte. But no Fanmi Lavalas supporters were arrested. In July, in Maïssade in the Central Plateau, police who intervened in a conflict between Fanmi Lavalas and Space for Dialogue allowed Fanmi Lavalas supporters to accompany them in house searches and to beat Space for Dialogue members who were arrested.

Nor did police respond effectively to the dramatic mid-June shut-down of Port-au-Prince. On June 19, in a show of force intended to intimidate the CEP into confirming erroneous first-round election results, several hundred members of pro-Fanmi Lavalas popular organizations erected barricades of burning tires, logs, and other debris on the city's roads. The roadblocks halted nearly all traffic, effectively confining most inhabitants to their homes for the day, but the police took no action against those responsible. Similar but smaller protests occurred in other cities.

Fanmi Lavalas members also fell victim to post-election violence. Supporters of an independent candidate for mayor killed two Fanmi Lavalas supporters on July 2 on the Ile-à-Vache, claiming that the Fanmi Lavalas mayoral candidate had stolen the election. Police arrested and charged a former mayor with organizing the attacks. In Ansed'Hainault, supporters of a mayoral candidate who narrowly lost to the Fanmi Lavalas candidate set houses on fire and ransacked a community radio station, reportedly wounding twelve people.

While figures for 2000 were unavailable as of this writing, 1999 saw a rise in police killings. The U.N./OAS International Civilian Mission (MICIVIH) reported sixty-six suspicious killings by the police in 1999, including several possible extrajudicial executions, an increase over the thirty-one reported in 1998. Fifty of the 1999 killings occurred in the second quarter of the year and led to the arrest of some officers. Allegations of police beatings and torture of criminal suspects also continued. Carmel Moise, a Florida resident and publisher of *Caribbean Magazine*, said that uniformed police entered her suburban Port-au-Prince house on July 6, demanding money and drugs, then beat her and burned her with a hot iron, leaving wounds that showed clearly in subsequent photographs.

According to the police inspector general, 673 police officers were dismissed from the PNH between its creation in 1995 and October 1999, 407 of them on the basis of his office's investigations, and the rest by decision of the leadership of the police. Probable human rights violations were committed in at least 130 cases, according to the MICIVIH.

Haiti's prisons continued to be filled far beyond capacity, with an estimated 80 percent of inmates in pretrial detention, roughly one-third of them for more than a year. A local NGO network continued to monitor conditions in many of the country's nineteen prison facilities.

In December 1999, responding to a hunger strike, a Port-au-Prince prosecutor freed on humanitarian grounds twenty-one long-term pretrial detainees, many of whom had never been formally charged. The men included Evans François, brother of military government police chief Michel François, charged with subversion in April 1996, and nine former military officers who had been held for fifteen months on charges of endangering state security after protesting non-payment of their pensions. Former Duvalier-era army general Claude Raymond, detained since 1996 on charges of plotting against state security, died in detention in February after several release orders issued by the judge in his case were ignored by the authorities.

Impunity for past abuses remained a serious concern, but there were encouraging steps toward justice. Two important trials took place. The first, that of six police officers accused of the 1999 murder of eleven people in the capitol's Carrefour Feuilles district, was held in August. During three weeks of proceedings, the prosecution presented physical evidence as well as twenty-seven witnesses, including PNH General Director Pierre Denizé. The defendants, who included former Port-au-Prince police chief Jean Colls Rameau, were assisted by qualified legal counsel. Most defendants received three-year sentences for manslaughter, a penalty criticized as inappropriately lenient by local human rights groups.

The second key trial—that of former army officers and paramilitaries implicated in an April 1994 massacre in Raboteau, Gonaïves—opened on September 29. This long-awaited prosecution was based on several years of preparation by a mixed Haitian and international prosecutorial team. Of the fifty-eight defendants in the case, twenty-two were in custody, while others such as Raoul Cedras and Michelle François, leaders of the 1991 coup, and Emmanuel "Toto" Constant, the leader of the paramilitary organization FRAPH, were in exile.

A French court in November 1999 dismissed a lawsuit filed by several Haitians against former dictator Jean-Claude Duvalier, resident in France since 1986. The suit accused him of crimes against humanity, but the court ruled that French law does not cover such crimes committed prior to 1994, except those that occurred during World War II.

Defending Human Rights

The Haitian government did not systematically target human rights monitors, but the polarized political environment complicated the task of defending human rights. At an April 7 demonstration to protest Jean Dominique's assassination, for example, some 300 women belonging to a coalition of seven leading women's organizations were harassed by male supporters of Fanmi Lavalas, apparently because they did not accuse opposition political leaders of responsibility for the journalist's death.

No progress was made in the investigation into the March 1999 shooting of Pierre Espérance, Haiti director of the National Coalition for Haitian Rights.

In a welcome development that attested to the maturity of the Haitian human rights movement, a number of groups participated in well-organized election monitoring efforts, producing credible reports documenting fraud and other irregularities.

The Role of the International Community

By 2000, the three-year political impasse in Haiti had led to the suspension of some U.S. $500 million in multilateral assistance, with donor countries pressing the government of René Préval to restore a working parliament ahead of presidential elections scheduled for the end of 2000. But the initially positive reaction to the May 21 elections began to shift with news of the arrests of opposition candidates and supporters, and turned into a tide of criticism when Haitian officials refused to acknowledge that the Senate calculation method was incorrect. Focusing on the calculation issue, the United States, Canada, France, and the U.N. Security Council called on the Haitian government to revise the election results. The Caribbean Community (CARICOM) sent a high-level mediator to Haiti in early July, but to no effect.

With the fraudulent election results firmly entrenched, Haiti's main bilateral donors began to signal aid cutbacks. France, in its role as president of the European Union, initiated a review of provisions of the Lomé Convention, to which Haiti is a party, which could lead to the suspension of a nearly $200 million aid package. Canada also announced a reevaluation of its aid programs.

Relations between Haiti and the international community were further strained in July and August by several grenade or Molotov cocktail attacks on foreign missions and foreigners in Port-au-Prince, which, however, did not result in injuries.

United Nations

The six-year-old human rights monitoring mission, MICIVIH, and the U.N. peacekeeping mission departed Haiti in early 2000 and were replaced by the smaller United Nations International Civilian Support Mission in Haiti (Mission internationale civile d'appui en Haïti, MICAH).

In January, U.N. Special Rapporteur for Violence against Women Radhika Coomaraswamy released a report based on her June 1999 visit to Haiti. Among the problems she noted were the country's "dysfunctional judiciary" and the fact that most women prisoners share living quarters with male prisoners, exposing them to violence and sexual abuse. At its April session, the U.N. Commission on Human Rights passed a resolution on Haiti expressing its concern over delays in the electoral process and calling upon Haiti to hold "free, fair and prompt elections." It also extended the mandate of its independent expert on Haiti another year.

Organization of American States

The OAS-EOM, staffed by twenty-two international observers and assisted by about eighty delegates provided by national governments, arrived in Haiti in late February to monitor the elections and provide technical assistance to Haitian election officials. When Haiti went ahead with the second-round elections on July 9, the OAS-EOM declined to monitor the balloting, withdrawing its observers from the country.

The OAS held a special session on Haiti on July 13, followed by a mission to Haiti headed by Secretary General Cesar Gaviria on August 17-19. Reporting on the mission, Gaviria voiced the international community's "skepticism and worries" about democracy in Haiti. At this writing, mediation efforts continued. The Inter-American Commission on Human Rights visited Haiti in August 2000, identifying as the most worrisome aspect a "deterioration of the political climate to the point where there seems to be no political consensus on how to consolidate the country's nascent democracy."

United States

In September, the U.S. announced it would provide no aid to the Haitian government and no support for the presidential elections. "We will pursue policies that distinguish between helping the people of Haiti and assisting the government of Haiti," said the U.S. ambassador to the OAS. Earlier, the United States had shut down its five-year-old program of support for Haitian police training.

The Clinton Administration continued to block efforts toward truth and justice in Haiti by retaining some 160,000 pages of documents seized from the Haitian military and FRAPH in September 1994. U.S. officials stated they would only hand the materials over to the Haitian government after excising the names of U.S. citizens, a condition the Préval government continued to reject. FRAPH leader Constant, previously an informer for the Central Intelligence Agency (CIA), remained in Queens, New York, having been extended protection from deportation. Fifteen high-ranking Haitian officers, including most of the coup-era high command, were also resident in the United States, having emigrated from Haiti after Aristide's return.

MEXICO

Human Rights Developments

Serious human rights violations, including torture and arbitrary detention, continued in Mexico during 2000. Faced with abuses by police and soldiers, prosecutors and courts largely failed to take a stand for human rights. The July electoral victory of opposition presidential candidate Vicente Fox raised hopes that deep-seated human rights problems would be addressed head-on by the new government, scheduled to assume power on December 1. Little doubt remained after the presidential elections that reforms that increased the independence of the federal elections-monitoring agency had greatly facilitated the exercise of political rights in the country. Yet, overcoming the country's long history of human rights abuse, and the legal and other deficiencies contributing to it, would not be easy. That history constituted the legacy of the Institutional Revolutionary Party (Partido Revolucionario Institucional, PRI), ousted after more than seventy years in power, and posed a formidable challenge to the new government.

After winning the election, Fox appeared much more open to human rights reform than previous Mexican leaders. Signalling that, in August, he met first with local human rights organizations and then with U.S., Canadian, and European human rights and environmental groups. His foreign policy advisors suggested that his government, when it took office, would be more responsive to international human rights mechanisms than previous administrations. Fox also promised to establish a "transparency commission" to examine PRI excesses, including human rights issues.

During his election campaign, Fox proposed to abolish the Office of the Federal Attorney General (Procuraduría General de la República, PGR) and submit prosecutors to much stricter control by judges to overcome deficits in the administration of justice. He also suggested creating an investigative police separate from prosecutors and moving a host of thematic tribunals, including those dealing with labor issues, from the executive to the judicial branch of government.

Deficiencies in the administration of justice indeed were of major concern. Prosecutors frequently ignored abuses by police and also directly fabricated evidence, and

judicial oversight of their work was seriously inadequate. Police carried out arbitrary arrests and they and prosecutors often falsified evidence. Courts accepted evidence obtained through human rights violations, including illegal searches, and judges cited legal precedents that vitiated human rights guarantees.

Teodoro Cabrera García and Rodolfo Montiel Flores were two victims of such abuse. Environmental activists from Pizotla, Guerrero, they worked with the Organization of Peasant Environmentalists of the Mountains of Petatlán and Coyuca de Catalán (Organización de Campesinos Ecologists de la Sierra de Petatlán y Coyuca de Catalán). Soldiers detained the two in May 1999, killing another man, Salomé Sánchez Ortiz, at the time. Soldiers held them illegally for two days, and tortured them before turning them over to prosecutors. On August 28, a district judge sentenced them to ten and seven years in prison, respectively, for drug- and weapons-related offenses. Defense lawyers for the accused argued that the military planted the weapons and drugs that formed the basis of the charges against the two, an accusation confirmed in a report issued by the government National Human Rights Commission (Comisión Nacional de Derechos Humanos, CNDH) in July 2000. Soldiers forced the activists to sign incriminating confessions, which were used against them in court. A decision on their appeal was pending at this writing.

Deficiencies in the judicial system were evident in urban as well as rural areas. In February, the respected Human Rights Commission of Mexico City, an agency of the city government, reported that the main suspect in the high-profile murder case of television personality Francisco "Paco" Stanley, gunned down in 1999, had been framed by prosecutors. Prosecutors refused to accept the commission's recommendation that charges be dropped against the suspect. Instead, they began a campaign of intimidation against the commission. This, in turn, led the commission in May to issue a stinging report accusing the Office of the Attorney General of Mexico

City (Procuraduría General de Justicia del Distrito Federal, PGJDF) of playing politics with judicial investigations. The office had opened four "notoriously unfounded" investigations against a judge who had ruled against the attorney general in Mexico City, according to the commission.

In Chiapas, there was continued violence between pro-government civilians and real or alleged opponents of the PRI. On August 3, members of the Peace and Justice group, which local human rights defenders described as "paramilitary," attacked the community of El Paraíso, in Yajalón municipality, expelling sixty families, burning houses, and beating inhabitants. But, according to press reports, supporters of the leftist Zapatista Army of National Liberation (Ejército Zapatista de Liberación Nacional, EZLN), which had launched an armed rebellion in January 1994, also committed forcible expulsions, driving PRI supporters from the community of Nuevo Pavo, Ocosingo municipality, on August 11. The victims were reported to be supporters of the PRI; EZLN supporters denied the accusation.

Police in Chiapas also came under attack. Seven members of the state Public Security Police (Policía de Seguridad Pública) were killed in a June 12 ambush on the border between El Bosque and Simojovel municipalities. The attack took place on the second anniversary of a government raid on a breakaway pro-EZLN municipality formed in El Bosque, but at this writing it was unclear who carried out the attack. In July, authorities detained two men and accused them of possession of marijuana, participating in the ambush, and being EZLN supporters. However, according to the Chiapas-based Fray Bartolomé de las Casas Human Rights Center (Centro de Derechos Humanos Fray Bartolomé de las Casas), the men were illegally detained and police planted evidence on them. At this writing, one of the detainees had been released for lack of evidence.

Following the opposition victory in Mexico's presidential elections, voting in Chiapas in August also resulted in the election of an opposition candidate, Pablo Salazar, as state governor. This raised hopes that long-standing problems, including misuse of power by police, prosecutors, and courts for partisan gain, might be resolved, and that stalled peace talks with the EZLN might be reactivated. Both Fox and Salazar said that if the EZLN returned in good faith to the bargaining table they would support a peace agreement at which the prior federal government had balked, and would also consent to a military rollback.

Foreigners continued to face restrictions in obtaining visas for human rights work in Mexico. Applicants were required to describe their plans to consular officers in copious detail, including all destinations to be visited. In an encouraging development, advisors to President-elect Fox indicated that the visa requirements would be relaxed after he took office.

Authorities still used expulsion or the threat of removal from the country against foreigners. Ted Lewis, director of the Mexico program at Global Exchange, was expelled from the country before the presidential elections, allegedly for entering the country under false pretexts; the official justification, however, was full of contradictions. Kerry Appel, one of a group of foreigners detained in Chiapas at the beginning of the year, was told to leave the country for having violated the terms of his visa; authorities accused him of participating in a party celebrating the six-year anniversary of the EZLN uprising. Appel won an appeal of the expulsion order in June, with the judge ruling that the immigration authorities had failed to justify the reasons for his expulsion, and calling on them to properly document the order. Instead, according to the Fray Bartolomé Center, immigration officials simply repeated the same claims against Appel and, in September, again ordered that he leave the country. In a contrary move, however, immigration authorities permitted Tom Hansen, the director of the Mexico Solidarity Network, who had been expelled in 1998, to return to Mexico.

The government maintained legal restrictions on workers' freedom of association and the right to strike, and labor tribunals responsible for hearing unfair dismissal and other cases were not impartial. In its year 2000 report by the Committee of Experts on the Application of Conventions and Recommendations, the International Labor Organization (ILO) again criticized legal restrictions on freedom of association and the right to strike in Mexico. The report also condemned the ongoing practice of requiring female job applicants to submit to pregnancy tests as a condition of employment, which it described as a violation of the ILO's convention on employment discrimination. (For further information on pregnancy testing, see the Women's Rights section.) The labor side agreement of the North American Free Trade Agreement (NAFTA) continued to generate meager results in the promotion of labor rights in Mexico.

Journalists also suffered continued threats, and at least two reporters were killed during the year, according to the New York-based Committee to Protect Journalists (CPJ). José Ramírez Puente, a radio journalist, was stabbed to death in April in Ciudad Juárez, Chihuahua state, and Pablo Pineda, of the Matamoros daily La Opinión was also killed that month. In both cases, the motives and identity of the perpetrators were unclear. On June 22, gunmen fired on T.V. Azteca news anchor Lilly Téllez as she travelled by car in Mexico City; she escaped unharmed, but the driver and bodyguards accompanying her because of threats made in retaliation for her reporting on drug trafficking, were wounded. Several journalists also faced legal harassment for their reporting. For example, prosecutors charged Melitón García of the Monterrey daily El Norte with falsifying documents, after he published a two-part story in May describing how easy it was for him to obtain a false voter credential. For a crime to have taken place, according to CPJ, the reporter would have had to have acted with malicious intent, something that was clearly lacking in this case.

The government took several positive human rights initiatives. In June, it ratified the 1951 Convention relating to the Status of Refugees and the 1954 Convention relating to the Status of Stateless Persons. It signed the statute of the International Criminal Court in September. The government's lack of commitment to the obligations it undertook by ratifying the refugee convention became clear in October 2000, however, when authorities summarily deported Cuban national Pedro Riera Escalante, a government official who had sought political asylum. Riera Escalante faced grave danger in Cuba, given his opposition to the policies of the Cuban government, but Mexico sent him back, in violation of the convention's prohibition on returning refugees if they would face a threat to life or liberty at home.

In August, the Mexico City authorities passed legislation establishing the crime of "disappearance," a step that human rights organizations, including Human Rights Watch, had long urged the central government to take, but there were no moves to create analogous federal legislation.

At the request of Spanish judge Baltasár Garzón, the authorities arrested former Argentine military officer Ricardo Miguel Cavallo in August. Garzón, who had sought the extradition of Chile's Gen. Augusto Pinochet from the United Kingdom in 1998, sought to prosecute Cavallo on genocide and torture charges stemming from his alleged role as a torturer at Argentina's infamous Navy School of Mechanics under military rule. Judge Garzón requested that Carvallo be extradited to Spain, but, at this writing, extradition proceedings within Mexico were still in process. French authorities were also investigating Cavallo's possible involvement in the torture and murder of French citizens in Argentina.

In August, Mexican officials announced the arrests of Mexican generals Arturo Acosta Chaparro and Humberto Quierós Hermosillo, whom they accused of links to drug traffickers. Human rights groups immediately called on the government to take steps to broaden the charges against Acosta Chaparro, who had been linked to "disappearances" and torture in Mexico's southern state of Guerrero in the 1970s.

Defending Human Rights

Human rights defenders continued their detailed reporting and energetic advocacy but faced renewed pressure from politicians who sought to blame them for some of the country's crime problems, particularly during the presidential election campaign. At one campaign stop, for instance, the PRI's presidential candidate courted the get-tough-on-crime vote by announcing: "Let it be known that the law was made to protect the human rights of citizens, not criminals." A similar slogan had worked for a successful PRI gubernatorial candidate in 1999.

The pressure created was more than simply theoretical; it helped create a hostile environment for human rights defenders. In June, authorities appeared to act on this distrust of human rights groups as the All Rights for All Mexican Human Rights Network (Red de Organismos Civiles de Derechos Humanos Todos Derechos para Todos, known as the Red) reported that their Mexico City office was under surveillance. According to the Red, the city prosecutor's office later revealed that agents of the federal National Security System (Sistema Nacional de Seguridad, SISEN) had been filming the office, although the motive of the surveillance was not made known to the group. The same month, Digna Ochoa of PRODH received telephoned death threats. She was the lead defense lawyer representing the detained environmentalists in Guerrero.

Arturo Solís, director of the Center for Border Studies and Promotion of Human Rights (Centro de Estudios Fronterizos y de Promoción de los Derechos Humanos, CEFPRODAC), also came under attack during the year. An immigration official and private citizen in Tamaulipas state, home of the center, accused Solís of defamation in July, after CEFPRODAC provided federal prosecutors with information in June on corruption within the National Immigration Institute (Instituto Nacional de Migración, INM). Authorities failed to investigate Solís' claims in depth, but moved the defamation case forward, according to the center. In August, the center received telephoned death threats, and unidentified individuals kept Solis' house under surveillance. Some witnesses who supported Solís retracted their statements after receiving threats.

The Role of the International Community

United Nations and Organization of American States

The full scope of Mexico's human rights violations was brought into focus in November 1999, when United Nations High Commissioner for Human Rights Mary Robinson visited the country. The Mexican government did not consent to an advance research team, limiting the high commissioner to gathering information during her visits to Mexico City, Chiapas state, and Baja California state. Nonetheless, more than one hundred nongovernmental organizations (NGOs) prepared a human rights report for the high commissioner, listing their most pressing concerns. In addition to problems with the administration of justice, the report strongly criticized the involvement of the military in matters of internal security, inadequate protection of indigenous people's rights, weaknesses in economic and political rights, and attacks on human rights defenders.

The high commissioner spoke out strongly against human rights violations in Mexico. After meeting survivors of the December 1997 massacre in Acteal, Chiapas, for example, she pointed to "the failure in too many cases to punish rights violators."

In July, the Office of the High Commissioner planned to move forward with a two-part technical cooperation program to be implemented with Mexico. Its first segment, scheduled to begin before Fox assumed the presidency, was to include limited training programs for the judicial police, enhancing the federal government's National Human Rights Commission (Comisión Nacional de Derechos Humanos, CNDH), and working to strengthen the ability of indigenous rights groups to work with the United Nations. The office hoped to implement a more ambitious program under the new administration. At this writing, the first segment of the technical cooperation program had yet to begin.

After the high commissioner's visit, Special Rapporteur on Extrajudicial, Summary or Arbitrary Executions Asma Jahangir released a report based on her July 1999 mission to Mexico. "The Government has taken some initial steps to guarantee the right to life of all persons," the report found, but it concluded: "Unfortunately, these positive undertakings have not been sufficient to correct the situation, as extrajudicial killings and the impunity enjoyed by the perpetrators continue."

The Inter-American Commission on Human Rights issued two case reports on Mexico and accepted two new cases for review. In its report on the 1986 murder by non-state actors of Pedro Peredo Valderrama, the commission blasted the Mexican government for precisely the type of irregularities that continued to plague the justice system: arrest warrants for the accused were not carried out until 1996, nine years after they were issued; one of the accused had escaped arrest in 1988 with the aid of police; and a judge acquitted two of the accused after committing a series of irregularities, including relying on information never entered as evidence and wrongly attributing exculpatory statements to defendants.

Another case handled by the commission—involving Brig. Gen. Francisco Gallardo—remained unresolved. Incarcerated since 1993 in retaliation for his call for improved respect for human rights in the military, the general faced a prison sentence of more than fourteen years. In 1996, the commission called for his release.

European Union

The Global Agreement between Mexico and the European Union entered into force in July, replacing an interim accord in place since 1999. The agreement included a standard democracy clause, which was nevertheless a subject of contention during negotiations. In addition, the Global Agreement included a chapter on political dialogue and cooperation programs—including issues related to human

rights. Article 39 of the agreement, for example, noted that cooperation would focus mainly on the development of civil society, the implementation of training and information measures to help institutions function better, including in the human rights field, and the promotion of human rights and democratic principles. The agreement did not expressly exclude the development of such programs with nongovernmental organizations (NGOs), but neither did it specify that NGOs would take part in such activities.

United States

As in the recent past, the U.S. Department of State issued a strong report on the situation of human rights in Mexico, noting: "Continued serious abuses include extrajudicial killings; disappearances; torture and other abuse; police corruption and alleged involvement in narcotics-related abuses; poor prison conditions; arbitrary arrest and detention; lengthy pretrial detention; lack of due process; judicial inefficiency and corruption; illegal searches; attacks and threats against journalists; some self-censorship; assaults, harassment, and threats against human rights monitors; violence and discrimination against women; child prostitution and abuse; discrimination against indigenous people; violence and discrimination against religious minorities; violence against homosexuals; limits on worker rights; extensive child labor in agriculture and in the informal economy; and trafficking in persons."

Despite these criticisms, strong bilateral action to promote human rights appeared again to take a back seat to higher priority issues such as economic relations, immigration control, and narcotics. During a meeting in August, President Bill Clinton told President-elect Fox that the United States wished to see his government make progress on human rights.

PERU

Human Rights Developments

Peru experienced its most turbulent year since 1992, when President Alberto Fujimori dissolved Congress and assumed dictatorial powers. The circumstances in which Fujimori was sworn in for his third consecutive term on July 28 were symptomatic of the deep crisis of legitimacy facing his government after a decade in power. Police cordoned off the Congress building and employed water cannon and teargas against thousands of demonstrators. As the president handed over his sash and received it back again from his loyal congressional leader, Martha Hildebrandt, all but six representatives of the opposition staged a noisy walk-out. Flawed from the outset because the president's candidacy was evidently unconstitutional, the April 9 presidential and congressional elections were among the most widely questioned the region had seen in years.

The National Intelligence Service (Servicio de Inteligencia Nacional, SIN), headed by Fujimori's shadowy advisor Vladimiro Montesinos, was widely blamed for harassing opposition candidates, and manipulating the press, the courts, and the electoral bodies to secure Fujimori's re-election. On September 16, to public astonishment, Fujimori announced that he would dismantle the SIN and hold new elections in which he would not be a candidate. The announcement followed the broadcasting on television of a video apparently showing Montesinos bribing an opposition congressman to defect to the government party. A week later, Montesinos left for Panama, where he unsuccessfully sought asylum. He returned to Peru in October, just after the government proposed to extend a 1995 amnesty law to cover human rights crimes committed since 1995, and to write the law into the constitution. At this writing the amnesty had not been extended. Although Fujimori took some measures to distance himself from Montesinos, he nonetheless replaced the chief of the armed forces in October with a general

widely considered to be a close ally of Montesinos.

The Fujimori re-election campaign was plagued by scandals and irregularities, and only concerted international pressure applied at the eleventh hour seems to have convinced Fujimori to concede a second round, after inexplicable delays in the announcement of the first round result. He then had fifty days to make reforms detailed by the electoral observation mission of the OAS before the presidential run-off scheduled for May 28. As that date approached, opposition candidate Alejandro Toledo withdrew his candidacy, considering the conditions still to be unfair. The OAS mission, present in Lima since early March, asked the electoral board to postpone the date so that its minimum conditions could be met, but the electoral board refused. Fujimori was then elected as the sole candidate.

During the inauguration, the Lima police used excessive force against protesters. They fired tear gas cartridges from moving vehicles and roof-tops as well as from positions in the street, sometimes at body height and directly at protesters, and also used teargas in enclosed spaces. Several people were seriously injured when struck by cartridges, including Aldo Gil Crisóstomo, who lost an eye, artist and human rights activist Victor Delfín, and U.S. journalist Paul Vanotti. During the morning, unidentified individuals set fire to several public buildings in the city center, including the National Bank, in which six security guards perished. Armed gangs then attacked firemen and destroyed fire-fighting equipment, harassed journalists, and threatened human rights observers, who were prevented from gaining access to the scene. Suspicions of government complicity in the violence were aroused by the failure of the police to protect the buildings or to arrest any of those responsible. On July 29, a pro-Fujimori congresswoman laid charges of "intellectual authorship" of the previous day's violence against opposition leader Alejandro Toledo, and Congress members Anel Townsend and Jorge del Castillo.

Fujimori and Montesinos subjected their

actual or potential critics to legal harassment and character assassination. Through his influence over the courts and the taxation office, Fujimori had secured the support of several television channels and radio stations previously critical of him. Bogus criminal accusations were launched against independent media, such as Peru's most respected daily newspaper, *El Comercio*. The hand of the government in these maneuvers was disguised by their appearance as boardroom disputes between shareholders. In the provinces, journalists suffered physical attacks for their opposition opinions. Popular tabloids widely believed to be sourced by the SIN engaged in a campaign of scandalous allegations against and lampooning of opposition candidates and the media supporting them. Many believed the constant barrage of malicious rumors to have destroyed the presidential chances of former Lima mayor Alberto Andrade. Government supporters shrugged off these attacks claiming they were a legitimate exercise of freedom of expression.

On February 29, *El Comercio* revealed that a pro-Fujimori councilor had arranged the forgery of more than one million signatures to ensure the registration of the Peru 2000 Front (Frente Peru 2000), a member of the pro-Fujimori electoral alliance, using names from the 1998 municipal election register. The scandal obliged the National Electoral Board (Jurado Nacional de Elecciones, JNE) to cancel the registration of the party. In addition, two candidates implicated in the fraud were forced to resign, and two officials of the National Office of Electoral Procedures (Oficina de Procesos Electorales, ONPE), which is responsible for the vote-tally and the computation of the results, were dismissed. However, the electoral authorities failed to carry out a thorough and transparent investigation. Instead, the JNE handed responsibility to special prosecutor Mirtha Trabucco Cerna, whose investigation was inordinately delayed, and finally accused only one low-level official, as well as some of those who participated in the fraud and later denounced it. On June 28, four months after the scandal broke, a parliamentary investigative commis-

sion produced conclusions that amounted, in effect, to a whitewash. The forgery scandal reinforced the lack of credibility of both the JNE and the ONPE.

Peru's ombudsman, Jorge Santistevan, and the nongovernmental monitoring group Transparencia documented other serious irregularities in the campaign. These included the refusal of open-access television channels to sell air-time to opposition candidates (until the very end of the campaign, when a slight improvement was noted); the meager, biased and distorted news coverage of the opposition campaign; physical attacks on, and disruption of, opposition rallies; and the misuse of state resources and personnel in support of the campaign conducted by Fujimori's electoral alliance, Peru 2000. The use of food-aid and other programs of assistance to the poor to garner support for, and deter votes against, Fujimori's election was among the abuses documented.

A quick assessment carried out by Transparencia on the evening of the elections, April 9, indicated that neither candidate had come close to the 51 percent needed for a first round victory. The ONPE, however, delayed twelve hours before giving out its first partial results, which then put Fujimori ahead of Toledo and close to victory with 49.88 percent. It's Lima computing centers remained closed until the afternoon of April 10, preventing the OAS observers from monitoring the vote count. The computing system produced extraordinary anomalies, such as the apparent registration of more than one million votes in excess of the number of registered voters. After firm pressure from the United States, the OAS, and some European countries, the JNE finally announced on April 12 that a second round to the election would be held. Much longer delays affected the calculation of the results of the congressional elections.

The government employed various means to harass and intimidate opposition media. On February 2, 2000, the 30th First Instance Court confiscated the transmitters of Radio 1160, owned by Genaro Delgado Parker, implementing an embargo on behalf of a creditor. The confiscation silenced broadcasts by a popular opposition political commentator, César Hildebrandt. The program went back on the air with a replacement transmitter, but this too was embargoed and removed on the orders of a provisional judge without tenure and consequently vulnerable to political pressure.

Opposition print media that suffered judicial harassment included *El Comercio* and *Liberación,* an outspoken opposition paper of which Hildebrandt was director. *Liberación* narrowly escaped closure when a provisional judge ordered the embargo and seizure of its printing press. Almost simultaneously a Lima judge ordered the seizure of bank accounts and printing presses belonging to the Editora Correo publishing house, which publishes *El Correo de Piura,* following a U.S. $600,000 defamation suit brought by a pro-Fujimori congressman against the paper. In August, the director of the company that publishes *Expreso,* a pro-Fujimori tabloid, launched a U.S. $1 million defamation suit against Hildebrandt and two other *Liberación* journalists.

Opposition journalists also received anonymous death threats. On June 8, Monica Vecco, an investigative reporter for *La República,* Peru's leading opposition tabloid, received a threatening e-mail message from a group calling itself the April 5 Group (a reference to the date that Fujimori assumed dictatorial power in 1992). *La República* had published a report that day by Vecco linking officials of Peru 2000 to the SIN. Four journalists from Lima's Santa Rosa radio station were physically attacked or threatened in separate incidents in May. They had reported on attempts by Peru 2000 to pressure attendants at soup kitchens in poor neighborhoods to vote for Fujimori's reelection. Physical attacks and death threats against radio journalists were also common in rural areas.

Despite a law outlawing torture promulgated in 1998, the practice remained widespread and perpetrators were rarely convicted. In one incident, police belonging to the Division of Special Operations (División de Operaciones Especiales, DIVOES) detained Alejandro Damián Trujillo Llontop on the evening of March 1, 2000 in Lima while he was in the company of some friends, and took him away in a personnel carrier. On March 14, his father denounced his "disappearance" to the district attorney, but DIVOES denied having arrested anyone on March 1. On May 8, Trujillo's relatives were informed that the body of a twenty-five-year-old man had been found on the beach in Callao on March 2. Fingerprint and other tests confirmed that it was Trujillo's body. An autopsy indicated that his death occurred within four hours of his arrest on March 1, and that the body bore injuries consistent with torture.

The mandate of the commission set up by President Fujimori in 1996 to recommend presidential pardons for hundreds of innocent prisoners wrongly charged or convicted under the draconian anti-terrorist laws was not renewed when it expired at the end of 1999. Although the commission had secured the release of 481 prisoners, more than fifty applications approved for release by the commission awaited decision by the president, while four or five times that number had been presented by nongovernmental human rights groups. Those released received no compensation for the serious abuses they had suffered. At the end of August, the Supreme Council of Military Justice accepted an appeal by U.S. citizen Lori Berenson, convicted by a "faceless" military court to life imprisonment for treason. In what was widely interpreted as a gesture to U.S. opinion, Berenson was to be retried in a civilian court on a charge of terrorism.

Defending Human Rights

Human rights ombudsman Jorge Santistevan de Noriega was attacked in the pro-Fujimori media in early March when he transmitted allegations about the forgery of signatures to the JNE and the ONPE and asked them to investigate. Cabinet ministers and pro-Fujimori congressmen claimed that Santistevan had sought to discredit the elections by leaking information to *El Comercio,* and hinted that they might press for his impeachment. However, as President Fujimori later acknowledged, the constitution empowers the ombudsman to monitor the actions of public entities, including those of the electoral authorities. Santistevan's office, together with Transparencia, played a key role in monitoring irregularities during the election campaign. His comment that the elections had a "factory defect"—a reference to Fujimori's unconstitutional candidacy—irritated the government, but after the firm intervention of the OAS, the U.S. State Department and several European ambassadors, the sniping at Santistevan ceased.

On June 12, the wife of Jesús Agreda Paredes, president of the Tacna Association for the Defense of Human Rights, received a telephone call from an unidentified man who said, "Tell your husband not to meddle in the Pachia case, because if he does we'll kill him." Agreda was acting on behalf of the widow of Nelson Díaz Marcos, a detainee who had died in custody allegedly as a result of torture.

During the second week of August, members of the Legal Defense Institute (Instituto de Defensa Legal, IDL), a well-respected human rights NGO, received anonymous death threats by e-mail. One of the messages, also received by political commentator Carlos Ivan Degregori, said, "Die, bastard!" According to Degregori, friends of his had received a warning that "you are being watched and we know all your movements. We know who your friends are and what they are doing.....you keep away. You are in time.... First warning." The message came form a group calling itself Colina 2000 (The Colina group was a notorious army death squad that operated in the 1990s).

The Role of the International Community

The Organization of American States, the European Community, the European Parliament, and individual states, including the United States, Canada, Japan, and several European countries, issued statements expressing concern about irregularities in Peru's elections.

Organization of American States

The OAS electoral observation mission led by former Guatemalan foreign affairs minister Eduardo Stein conducted a forthright, transparent, and proactive observation of the electoral process. Unlike earlier OAS missions, whose shortcomings had been widely criticized, Stein's team covered pre-electoral conditions for a full month before the April 9 vote, met continuously with the electoral bodies in an effort to obtain fairer conditions, and reported publicly on progress in periodic bulletins. The mission served as a model for future regional election observation.

An extraordinary session of the Permanent Council, held in Washington, D.C. on May 31, rejected a proposal by the United States and Costa Rica for an ad hoc meeting of foreign ministers under Resolution 1080—regarding the OAS's response to the interruption of democracy in member countries—to discuss sanctions against Peru. The vote against the motion showed that most member states opposed taking punitive measures against another member state because of an unfair election, so revealing the limits of the OAS's effectiveness in responding to interruptions of the democratic process that fall short of a coup d'etat.

The political situation in Peru was discussed intensely at the annual General Assembly of the OAS. On June 5, the General Assembly agreed unanimously to send immediately a high-level mission to Peru, consisting of OAS Secretary General César Gaviria and Canadian Foreign Minister Lloyd Axworthy, to explore options for reforming the electoral process, restoring the independence of the judiciary, and strengthening freedom of the press. Reflecting the reluctance of the General Assembly to confront the illegitimacy of the election, both delegates made clear on their arrival in Lima on June 27 that they did not intend to propose a timetable for new elections. The mission left two days later, having agreed with the government and opposition a list of twenty-nine reforms to be implemented. The OAS established a permanent mission in Lima, headed by

Eduardo Latorre, former foreign minister of the Dominican Republic, to broker the reforms and assist in their implementation. The September bribery scandal, however, abruptly changed the picture. Following President Fujimori's surprise announcement of new presidential and congressional elections, OAS-sponsored talks between the government and the opposition led to an agreement at the end of October to hold the elections by April 8, 2001.

The Inter-American Commission on Human Rights's Second Report on Human Rights in Peru, published in June, noted that "the electoral process in Peru clearly constitutes an irregular interruption of the democratic process," and called for new elections.

United Nations

In November 1999, the United Nations Committee against Torture published its concluding observations on the report submitted by Peru under article 19 of the Convention against Torture. It expressed concern about continuing allegations of torture, the authorities' failure to investigate and prosecute those responsible, and the lack of independence of members of the judiciary who lacked security of tenure. In January 2000, the Committee on the Rights of the Child published its conclusions on Peru's report under the Convention on the Rights of the Child. It regarded laws enacted to protect children from domestic and sexual violence as positive steps. However, it criticized decree laws passed in 1998 that lower the age of criminal responsibility for children to below the limits permitted in the convention.

United States

The Clinton Administration played a key behind-the-scenes role in the negotiations at the meeting of the OAS General Assembly that resulted in the Gaviria-Axworthy mission. But the decision to send a mission was a weaker response than expected, given the strong nature of the first White House and State Department reactions to the May 28 election result. "Free, fair, and open elections are the foundations of a democratic society. Without them, our relationship with Peru will inevitably be affected," President Clinton warned, while a State Department spokeswoman stated, "we do not see the election as being valid. The manner in which the Fujimori regime handled these problems is a serious threat to the Inter-American system and its commitment to democracy." In Congress, both Democrats and Republicans backed firm action if Fujimori continued to defy international opinion. On April 7, Congress passed Joint Resolution 43, which warned that if the international community judged the elections not to be free and fair, "the United States will review and modify as appropriate its political, economic, and military relations with Peru and will work with other democracies in this hemisphere and elsewhere toward a restoration of democracy in Peru." After the unwillingness of other OAS members to support the U.S. proposal to apply Resolution 1080, however, the Clinton Administration did not persist.

On March 9, U.S. officials detained Maj. Tomás Ricardo Anderson Kohatsu, a Peruvian army intelligence agent implicated in gross human rights violations. After a lightning operation by U.S.-based human rights groups to gather evidence, immigration officials arrested Anderson at Houston airport before he could board a flight back to Lima. Overwhelming evidence implicated Anderson in the torture in 1997 of Leonor La Rosa Bustamante, a former intelligence agent who was left paraplegic as a result of the torture. The Department of Justice was preparing to prosecute Anderson under the Torture Act 18 USC 2340A, that allows for the extraterritorial prosecution of individuals implicated in torture. However, in a regrettable decision, the Department of State blocked the arrest, claiming that Anderson enjoyed immunity because he had been brought to the U.S. by the government of Peru to participate in a hearing before the OAS Inter-American Commission on Human Rights. Anderson was released and allowed to leave the U.S. after being held for questioning for twelve hours.

European Union

The European Union (E.U.) withdrew its election observers from Peru after the JNE announced that it would not accept recommendations for a postponement. The E.U. stated that the elections would not be credible or satisfy international standards, and that acceptance of democratic principles was a pre-condition for the development of its political and economic ties with Peru.

VENEZUELA

Human Rights Developments

The government of former paratrooper Hugo Chávez Frías, comfortably endorsed by 59 percent of the vote in general elections held on July 30, failed to mount an effective response to Venezuela's deep-seated human rights problems, in particular the ingrained abusiveness of its police forces and appalling prison conditions. The government introduced ambitious plans for prison reform, but attention to overcrowding in Venezuela's prisons did not result in a significant decline in inmate violence. Police killings of criminal suspects increased from 1999, and some measures authorities proposed to combat violent crime raised serious human rights concerns.

Introduced in December 1999, the constitution included forty-two articles protecting human rights, including some of the most advanced in the hemisphere. However, it also greatly expanded the power of the presidency and enhances the political role of the armed forces. The wholesale dismissal of judges, Chávez's revolutionary rhetoric and his verbal jousts with press critics raised questions about his government's respect for the rule of law and tolerance of criticism. For the first time in many years, freedom of expression emerged as a human rights issue in Venezuela.

Human rights groups and trade unions also came under pressure during the year. In separate decisions in June and August, the Supreme Court determined that nongovernmental organizations that received funding from abroad were not members of "civil society," thereby depriving them of the right to participate in the nomination of candidates for the Supreme Court, to be ombudsman, and for other important government posts. Trade union independence was called into question in early September, when President Chávez harshly criticized the leadership of the Venezuelan Workers' Confederation (Central de Trabajadores Venezolanos, CTV) and announced plans to create a parallel workers' movement dominated by the ruling party.

In the aftermath of disastrous flooding and mud slides on the Caribbean coast in December 1999, in which at least 20,000 people died, the armed forces went on a murderous rampage against suspected looters in the state of Vargas. The respected nongovernmental human rights group, Venezuelan Program for Education and Action on Human Rights (Programa Venezolano de Educación-Acción en Derechos Humanos, PROVEA), reported that army paratroopers, the political police known as the Directorate of Police Intelligence Services (Dirección de Servicios de Inteligencia Policial, DISIP), and members of the National Guard were responsible for execution-style killings.

The story became the first major human rights test of the Chávez government. At first, Chávez dismissed the reports as "suspicious" and "superficial," but the evidence soon obliged the president and other top government officials to acknowledge the seriousness of the situation. In January, the ombudsman of Vargas state announced that more than sixty people had been executed. Their bodies were apparently buried along with those of flood victims.

In January, PROVEA lodged habeas corpus writs on behalf of four victims who had "disappeared" after being detained in Vargas state: Roberto Javier Hernández Paz, Marco Antonio Monasterio Pérez, José Francisco Rivas, and Oscar José Blanco Romero. Roberto Hernández "disappeared" on December 23, after being arrested in his home by DISIP agents, who showed no warrant. According to testimonies collected by PROVEA and other human rights groups, his uncle heard a shot and Hernández's shouts begging the agents not to kill him. He was taken away wounded in a truck. A local judge ruled that since DISIP's director had denied his arrest, the court had no evidence on which to proceed. The courts did, however, confirm the arrests of Monasterio and Blanco, who were detained on December 21 by a paratroop battalion and handed over the same day to the DISIP. The DISIP, however, said it had no record of having received them. The body of another victim, Luis Rafael Bastardo, was exhumed in March from a cemetery. He had been shot several times.

Extrajudicial executions of criminal suspects by police and military forces continued to be a major problem in other parts of Venezuela. The Ministry of the Interior stated in July that more than 500 suspected criminals had died in armed clashes with the police during the first six months of the year. However, according to human rights groups, police frequently staged violent crime scenes to conceal the execution of a suspect who was unarmed or in police custody. Based in part on press sources, PROVEA said it knew of seventy-six reports of violations of the right to life during the same period. The number represented an increase of nearly 50 percent over 1999.

Pressure from the ombudsman and human rights defenders averted proposals by politicians to introduce "fast track" justice for criminal offenders. In February, the then-governor of the Federal District, Hernán Grüber Odreman, proposed to reactivate the infamous "loitering statute," known as the Law on Vagrants and Delinquents, which had been declared unconstitutional in 1997. That law gave the police the power to detain people in the street caught committing crimes or merely suspected of vagrancy, and send them to prison without trial for up to five years. In early March, Dávila said he planned to set up control points in four sectors of Caracas where a team of judges, prosecutors, defense lawyers, and representatives of the ombudsman would be on duty around the clock to dispatch justice to offenders in ten minute trials. Chief Court Inspector René Molina

warned that judges who followed the procedure would be in breach of the law.

In July, the temporary legislature approved amendments to the Code of Criminal Procedure that would restore the police's powers to make arrests on their own authority if they had reasonable grounds to suspect a person's involvement in a crime. Under the code's existing provisions, police were authorized to make arrests only on the orders of a judge or if the suspect was caught in the act. The amendments gave judges the power to hold suspects detained on suspicion for six days before deciding whether to charge or release them. In the past, such provisions allowed police ample opportunity to force suspects to confess.

Prison conditions remained inhumane, and prisons continued to be extremely violent. Between October 1999 and March 2000, for instance, the press reported 169 deaths in prison. Earlier prison violence had prompted the creation of an inter-institutional commission that included nongovernmental, congressional, and ministerial representatives. The commission found El Rodeo and Yare prisons to be completely under the control of the inmates, who even had the keys to their own cells. In El Rodeo, in which forty-one prisoners were killed between October 1999 and March 2000, only four officials were guarding 1,800 prisoners.

The work of the commission and the new Code of Criminal Procedure led to the release of thousands of prisoners. In October 1999, a Ministry of Justice official said that 2,526 prisoners had benefited. According to figures compiled by PROVEA, by the end of 1999 the total prison population had fallen to 15,227, compared to 24,833 in September 1998, while the percentage of prisoners awaiting trial fell from sixty-four to fifty-two. However, according to PROVEA, the measures lacked clear selection criteria and institutional coordination. Justice officials admitted that many errors had been made in granting releases. As a result, politicians blamed the rising violent crime rate on the country's progressive new code of criminal procedure. Leading criminologists, however, asserted that the fault lay not in the code itself, but in its implementation.

In March, President Chávez announced a national public security plan that earmarked the equivalent approximately U.S. $9 million for prison reconstruction and re-equipment. The European Union signed a cooperation agreement for prison improvements with the Ministry of Justice.

Freedom of expression became a precarious right during the year. The Inter-American Press Association (IAPA) complained in March to President Chávez about a "climate of hostility toward the press," after the president persistently engaged in belligerent attacks on his press critics. "If they attack me, let them watch out, they'll get as good as they give" and "what there is behind the supposed freedom of expression is a freedom of manipulation," were typical remarks made by the president. The IAPA expressed concern about article 58 of the 1999 constitution, which establishes the right to "timely, truthful, and impartial information." It could allow the courts or the government to judge what information should be disseminated and serve as the basis for prior censorship, according to the group.

Under current laws, journalists convicted of defamation could be sent to prison and prevented from exercising their profession forever. Tobías Carrero, a prominent businessman with close ties to the Chávez government, used criminal defamation suits in an effort to silence press criticism. In August, a judge ordered Pablo López Ulacio placed under house arrest for refusing to attend a court hearing in a defamation suit filed in October 1999 by Carrero, owner of the Multinacional de Seguros insurance company. Articles published in September 1999 in *La Razón,* of which López is editor-in-chief, accused Carrero of benefiting from favoritism in the award of government contracts and the auctioning of state-owned ratio stations. In June 2000, the judge prohibited López from publishing any further information on Multinacional de Seguros, and placed him under house arrest. Another judge lifted the order then reimposed it when López failed

to appear in court in August. The publishing ban remained in force at this writing.

In April, the Inter-American Commission on Human Rights issued precautionary measures in favor of Ben Amí Fihman and Faitha Marina Nahmens, director and reporter, respectively, of the magazine *Exceso.* A defamation suit against them for the publication of an article about the murder of a businessman had been in the courts since 1997. In February, a judge ordered their arrest to make them appear in court despite the expiry of the statute of limitations under the new Code of Criminal Procedure.

Defending Human Rights

Venezuela's Defender of the People, or Ombudsman, which position was created under the new constitution as an official human rights watchdog body, was established in December under the leadership of Dilia Parra Guillén, an attorney and former member of the human rights department of the Attorney General's Office. Some of its senior officials, including its director general, Juan Navarrete Monasterio, had been members of the nongovernmental human rights community. Other officials were appointed to ombudsman posts in each of Venezuela's states. The ombudsman expressed forthright critical opinions on several government-backed crime-fighting initiatives that would have violated due process principles, and was influential in pressing for a full investigation of atrocities in Vargas state.

In April, Hoover Quintero and Suilvida Rausseo, members of the human rights office of the dioceses of Ciudad Guyana, received repeated threatening phone calls. They had denounced abuses by members of the Technical Judicial Police in Ciudad Guyana.

The Role of the International Community

United Nations

In November 1999, the United Nations Committee on the Rights of the Child published its concluding observation on Venezuela's report on implementation of the

Convention on the Rights of the Child. The committee expressed its concern about "alleged cases of killings of children during anti-crime operations." It also expressed concern about "the persistent allegations about children being detained in conditions which amount to cruel, inhuman or degrading treatment, and about children being physically ill-treated by members of the police or the armed forces."

Organization of American States

The Inter-American Commission on Human Rights brokered a friendly settlement between relatives of the victims of a 1992 massacre in the prison of Catia and the Venezuelan government. It included a promise by the government to carry out several important prison reforms.

United States

The Clinton administration continued to treat Chávez and his "peaceful revolution" with caution, and did not comment on human rights, except in the annual State Department Country Reports on Human Rights Practices for 1999. The report concluded that "although there were improvements in some areas, serious problems remain." In a letter to U.S. Ambassador John Maisto, Venezuelan Foreign Minister José Vicente Rangel criticized the report for being out-of-date and unilateral, and said that it did not fairly reflect the political changes occurring in the country.

The United States objected to President Chávez's visit with Iraqi President Saddam Hussein in August. Chávez was the first head of state to visit Baghdad since the Gulf War. Chávez claimed that the visit was related only to Venezuela's role as a member of the Organization of Petroleum Exporting Countries (OPEC).

HUMAN RIGHTS WATCH

ARMS

ARMS

Human Rights Developments

In 2000 the intractability of violent conflicts demonstrated the role of weapons transfers in fueling brutal wars—and their tragic humanitarian consequences. The continuation of armed conflicts across the globe was marked by the terrible toll of high civilian casualties, mass displacement, and the widespread destruction of civilian infrastructure. In many cases, armed groups, including both government and rebel forces, routinely targeted civilians in clear violation of human rights and international humanitarian law. In Africa in particular, wars resisted resolution, and associated human rights abuses continued unabated. As the international community increasingly came to realize, unimpeded arms flows were an important part of the problem.

Arms shipments to the Horn of Africa fed an internecine border war between Ethiopia and Eritrea, where fighting had already caused massive displacement of civilians and tens of thousands of mostly military casualties before an arms embargo was imposed and a cease-fire was agreed. In the Democratic Republic of the Congo (DRC) the continuous flow of arms to the war's many participants helped to undermine a 1999 peace agreement and prolong a highly abusive war. Former allies Rwanda and Uganda turned their foreign-supplied guns on each other in DRC, leading to hundreds of civilian deaths and injuries. In Burundi, the lack of so much as a pledge to halt weapons purchases, together with other factors, raised concerns that a shaky, hard-won peace deal would not last, and that as a result civilians would continue to fall victim to abusive armed forces.

In Angola a peace process intended to end a longstanding, brutal war instead brought only disillusionment. Poorly enforced sanctions, including embargoes on arms and diamonds, did little to curb the Angolan rebels' ability to terrorize innocent civilians. In Sierra Leone, a 1999 peace accord crumbled when rebels who were supposed to have disarmed instead captured hundreds of U.N. peacekeepers, seizing their weapons and holding them hostage for weeks. After May 2000, the rebels who had long targeted civilians also turned their weapons against peacekeepers and pro-government forces. As in Angola, a neglected arms embargo in Sierra Leone (as well as neighboring Liberia) allowed rebels to use diamond revenue to amass weapons and ammunition with which to commit horrific atrocities.

As arms flows fed conflict in Africa and elsewhere, the search for solutions to this grave problem took many forms. Governments, often acting through multilateral organizations, focused on imposing new sanctions or cracking down on illicit arms trafficking by tightening controls on arms brokers. They also acted against the illicit trade in diamonds that, in some cases, facilitated illicit arms sales. Civil society groups, many of them joined in a global campaign to tackle the proliferation of small arms, supported such measures, but also argued for concerted action to further regulate the legal trade in weapons and specifically prevent weapons transfers to areas of violent conflict.

Antipersonnel Landmines

Overall, global progress toward the complete elimination of antipersonnel landmines continued at an impressive pace. Extensive use of mines in the conflicts in Chechnya and Kosovo were disturbing reminders of how far there was to go. Between November 1999 and October 2000, the number of nations ratifying the 1997 Convention on the Prohibition of the Use, Stockpiling, Production and Transfer of Antipersonnel Mines and On Their Destruction (Mine Ban Treaty) grew from eighty-seven to 107. At the time of this writing, a total of 139 countries had signed, ratified, or acceded to the treaty.

The treaty's intersessional work program, established in May 1999, was proven highly successful. The five Standing Committees of Experts met regularly to identify areas of concern and develop plans to ensure swift and effective implementation of the treaty. Their work served to facilitate better coordination and to spur progress globally on the range of mine issues. In September 2000, the Second Meeting of States Parties to the Mine Ban Treaty was held in Geneva. States Parties, in close cooperation with the International Campaign to Ban Landmines (ICBL), developed an extensive action program for the coming year. Human Rights Watch headed the official delegation of the ICBL to this diplomatic conference.

Parties to Amended Protocol II on landmines of the 1980 Convention on Conventional Weapons (CCW), which only restricted certain types of use of some antipersonnel mines, held their first annual conference in December 1999. The United States made a number of proposals, primarily related to antivehicle mines. A formal review conference of the CCW was scheduled for late 2001. For the fourth straight year, governments were unsuccessful in placing antipersonnel mines on the agenda of the Conference on Disarmament.

The International Campaign to Ban Landmines, the Nobel Peace Prize-winning coalition of more than 1,400 nongovernmental organizations (NGO)s in more than ninety countries, continued to play its lead role in promoting a comprehensive ban on antipersonnel mines and more resources for mine clearance and victim assistance programs. The ICBL was extensively involved in the intersessional work program, and Human Rights Watch was the primary liaison to the key Standing Committee dealing with General Status and Operation of the treaty, as well as the Standing Committee on Stockpile Destruction. The ICBL continued to develop its Landmine Monitor system—the unprecedented initiative marking the first time that civil society groups monitored a disarmament or humanitarian law treaty in a systematic and coordinated way. The Landmine Monitor network grew to 115 researchers in ninety-five countries. Human Rights Watch was the lead organization in developing, coordinating, and implement-ing the Landmine Monitor system.

In September 2000, the ICBL released the 1,100-page *Landmine Monitor Report 2000*, with information on every country of the world with respect to mine use, production, stockpiling, trade, mine clearance, and victim assistance. Human Rights Watch served as the coordinator, editor, and publisher of the report. The report found that since the Mine Ban Treaty entered into force in March 1999, virtually every indicator of progress was positive: decreasing use and production, a near complete halt to trade, more than 22 million stockpiled mines destroyed by at least fifty nations, increased funding for mine clearance, more land returned to communities, and decreasing numbers of mine victims in heavily affected nations. However, Landmine Monitor identified eleven governments that had apparently used antipersonnel mines in this period, including treaty signatories Angola, Burundi, and Sudan (none of which had ratified the treaty), as well as at least thirty rebel groups.

As part of its efforts to get all governments to ratify or accede to the Mine Ban Treaty, and to promote effective implementation of the treaty, the ICBL hosted or co-hosted with governments a number of regional conferences (in Azerbaijan, Belarus, Egypt, Georgia, Malaysia, and Slovenia), as well as national seminars and workshops (in India, Iran, Japan, Nepal, Nigeria, and the U.S.). ICBL members also undertook advocacy missions to Kosovo, South Korea, and the United Arab Emirates, in addition to meetings at the United Nations in Geneva and New York.

Conventional Weapons

In 1999 global military spending rose, marking an end to the sharp decline in spending from Cold War-era peak levels. According to the Stockholm International Peace Research Institute (SIPRI), worldwide defense spending grew to approximately U.S. $780 billion in 1999 ($719 billion in constant 1995 U.S. dollars), the most recent year for which figures were available in October

2000. SIPRI attributed this increase of about 2 percent from 1998 to resurgent spending by a handful of the world's largest military spenders and higher military expenditures by African countries engaged in armed conflicts.

Competition for weapons contracts remained intense, with many arms suppliers vying for clients and a few countries dominating the market for expensive weapons systems. The United States Congressional Research Service (CRS) reported the delivery of arms worth $18.4 billion by the U.S., more than half the total value of arms deliveries worldwide. The United Kingdom ranked second, delivering $4.5 billion in weapons, and Russia third, delivering $2.7 billion. These top three arms exporters together accounted for 75 percent of global arms deliveries, which declined from $36.4 billion in 1998 to about $34 billion in 1999.

In addition to completed arms deliveries, another $30.3 billion in arms sales were negotiated worldwide in 1999, a sharp increase over the previous year's figure of $22.98 billion. The United States once again dominated the field, negotiating almost $11.8 billion in agreements, followed by Russia, whose efforts to boost arms exports resulted in $4.8 billion in agreements, a sizable jump from $2.6 billion the previous year. The value of third-ranked Germany's arms transfers agreements slipped to $4 billion from $5.1 billion in 1998.

Chemical Weapons

At this writing 140 states had ratified or acceded to the 1993 Convention on the Prohibition of the Development, Production, Stockpiling, and Use of Chemical Weapons and on their Destruction (Chemical Weapons Convention, CWC). The most notable addition in 2000 was the Federal Republic of Yugoslavia, which acceded in April. Thirty-four states had signed the treaty but not yet ratified it. While many states parties failed to comply with all aspects of the CWC's timetables, as of May 2000 all had submitted their initial declarations to the Secretariat of the Organization for the Prohibition of Chemical Weapons (OPCW), the body overseeing the implementation of the CWC. However, well under a half of the states parties had enacted national legislation required by the CWC. In addition, Russia had to ask the Fifth Conference of States Parties to extend the April 2000 intermediate destruction deadline (for the destruction of 1 percent of its chemical warfare munitions stockpile) mandated in the CWC. The OPCW had conducted 739 inspections of 352 sites in thirty-five states parties by May 2000. By the third year after entry into force of the CWC on April 29, 2000, non-states parties to the CWC could no longer import, or were severely restricted in importing, certain chemicals that could be used to synthesize chemical warfare agents.

In an exception to this progress, the Iraqi government continued to reject cooperation with the United Nations Monitoring, Verification and Inspection Commission (UNMOVIC), the successor of the U.N. Special Commission (UNSCOM). UNMOVIC, charged with inspecting Iraq's weapons of mass destruction (WMD), was again denied access in August, amplifying concerns that Iraq was seeking to revive its WMD programs. An examination of available information and materials (primarily soil samples) by British, U.N., and other officials in response to claims that the government of Sudan had used chemical weapons in southern Sudan in 1999 found no concrete evidence to support the allegations.

Biological Weapons

As of October 2000, 144 states had ratified the 1972 Convention on the Prohibition of the Development, Stockpiling, and Use of Bacteriological (Biological) and Toxin Weapons and on their Destruction (Biological Weapons Convention, BWC), while eighteen states had signed but not yet ratified. Negotiations continued on a legally binding protocol to improve implementation of the treaty. An ad hoc group charged with developing verification mechanisms, which began negotiating a draft compliance protocol in 1997, found broad agreement on many key issues. However, several issues remained unresolved after the group's July/August meeting, including definitions of which facilities should be required to submit declarations, the scope and purpose of visits, and procedures for launching and conducting investigations. The ad hoc group hoped to finalize the text of the protocol before the fifth review conference of the BWC in 2001.

Mechanisms of Arms Control

United Nations

The member states of the United Nations, as well as the U.N. Secretariat, focused greater attention on international transfers of small arms and light weapons in 2000. These weapons were a particular source of concern because of the enormous humanitarian impact of their widespread availability and misuse. In areas of violent conflict in particular, well-armed, unaccountable actors often used small arms to carry out attacks on civilians.

Following the recommendation of U.N. experts, the U.N. General Assembly agreed in December 1999 to hold in mid-2001 the United Nations Conference on the Illicit Trade in Small Arms and Light Weapons in All its Aspects. As of October 2000, planning for the event had proceeded slowly. An initial meeting of the preparatory committee for the conference, held in February/March 2000, yielded few results. The venue and date remained undecided, and decisions on the scope of the conference, the desired outcome, and the participation of NGOs likewise remained unclear. Further preparatory meetings were scheduled for January and March 2001. In the interim, several regional conferences and initiatives on small arms allowed governments to develop and refine policy positions and build momentum for the 2001 U.N. conference. For example, the Organization for Security and Cooperation in Europe (OSCE) convened a small arms seminar in April 2000 and worked to negotiate an OSCE text on small arms to be adopted later in the year.

At U.N. headquarters, Secretary-General Kofi Annan continued broadbased consultations with governments and some NGOs to identify the magnitude and scope of illicit trafficking in small arms, measures to combat such trafficking, and possible U.N. contributions to information-sharing on small arms. He released reports on these consultations in September 1999 and August 2000, for review in advance of the 2001 conference. The U.N. group of experts on small arms also worked throughout the year to prepare a background study and recommendations for consideration at the conference, with special attention to the feasibility of limiting the manufacture and trade in small arms. Only a handful of states had responded to a request by the secretary-general request for comments on the recommendations provided in earlier expert reports on small arms. These replies were included in a July report to which future responses could be added. The goal of curbing the small arms trade was noted repeatedly in different U.N. fora, including at the Millennium Summit of world leaders in September.

In 2000 the United Nations compiled information on weapons transfers for the eighth year. The U.N. Register of Conventional Arms was established in 1992 as a transparency and confidence-building mechanism relying on data submitted voluntarily by states. In 1999 eighty states supplied information to the register, a marked decline from ninety-seven responses the previous year. As in the past, many states furnished incomplete information or supplied it late, while others declined to participate. The 2000 register, which contained composite information regarding 1999 transfers, was issued in August and included information from eight-four states at that time. Responding to a request by the General Assembly, a U.N. group of experts met in 2000 to consider the further development of the register, as well as mechanisms to increase transparency related to weapons of mass destruction, and their conclusions were described in a separate August report. Government comments regarding the proposed expansion of the U.N. register were appended to the register itself.

In December 1999 the General Assembly requested states to furnish information about their military expenditures annually. The first composite report with the resulting thirty-two responses was issued in July 2000. The secretary-general also responded, in an August report, to a General Assembly request for information on international assistance to curb illicit arms trafficking and provide assistance with weapons collection programs.

Under U.N. auspices, negotiations continued on an International Convention Against Transnational Crime, to be supplemented by three protocols. The General Assembly requested an ad hoc committee to prepare a draft Protocol against the Illicit Manufacturing of and Trafficking in Firearms, Their Parts and Components and Ammunition, as well as two protocols on other topics, for approval by the General Assembly before the end of 2000. The ad hoc committee approved a draft of the convention itself in July, but had not finalized the draft firearms proposal as of October 2000, when another negotiating session was scheduled to take place.

European Union

The European Union Code of Conduct on Arms Exports entered its second year in 2000. Under the non-binding code, states agreed, among other provisions, not to authorize arms exports to human rights abusers, areas of violent conflict, or countries that might retransfer the weapons to unauthorized third parties. The E.U. member states claimed the code was a success, but the lack of transparency about its implementation made it impossible to verify that the code had led to a convergence of arms export practices. The first report on the implementation of the code was published under pressure from the European Parliament, NGOs, and others. It was disappointingly short on information. It was not clear at this writing whether the E.U. Council of Ministers would publish the second report, due before the end of the year. There were few indications that it would include information on the weapons sold or identify arms recipients, as urged by NGOs.

The E.U. Code, already subscribed to by more than a dozen non-E.U. countries, further extended its reach when the United States endorsed the code in December 1999. The E.U. hesitated to use this commitment to influence arms export policies of the countries in question, in particular the candidate countries for E.U. membership. E.U. member states also were reluctant to strengthen the code by making it legally binding, improving end-user control, and introducing rules for brokering and licensed production. The E.U. achieved agreement in 2000 on control lists for military goods and dual-use goods under the code.

At the national level, the German cabinet in January 2000 adopted guidelines to bring its arms export controls in line with the E.U. Code, and Germany joined France in issuing its first national report on arms exports in 2000. This brought the number of member states that publish annual arms exports reports to eight (Belgium, Italy, Netherlands, Spain, Sweden and U.K. being the others). In the U.K., the ruling Labor Party announced in September that it would introduce a system of licensing for arms brokering and trafficking, as strongly advocated by NGOs.

North Atlantic Treaty Organization

The North Atlantic Treaty Organization (NATO), which had been slow to recognize the dangers small arms proliferation posed to human rights and the security interests of the alliance, made strides in 2000 to begin work in this area. In February 2000 NATO's Euro-Atlantic Partnership Council (EAPC), which brings together NATO allies and former Warsaw Pact countries, incorporated a chapter on small arms into the work program of NATO's Partnership for Peace. This move created new training and assistance programs to destroy surplus small arms and improve the management and security of weapons stockpiles in partner countries. As of October 2000, few countries had taken up the offer of help. Under an initiative sponsored by the U.S., Germany, and Norway and announced in September 2000, Albania was to destroy 130,000 small arms by the end of 2000. A small arms destruction team traveled to Bulgaria in October for an assessment visit, but it was unclear at this writing whether the discussions would result in agreement to undertake a small arms destruction program.

The EAPC's working group on small arms, which spurred creation of the new programs, as well as a series of seminars on various small arms topics, could not agree to take up concrete action on more politically sensitive topics, such as transparency in the arms trade and arms export controls. A planned November seminar was expected to identify practical assistance needs related to export controls that could be met through partnership-sponsored assistance programs, such as the provision of software and equipment. There was little expectation that a consensus would emerge to move forward on harmonization of such controls.

For the first time NATO aspirants were required in 2000 to report on participation in major arms control agreements in an appendix to their annual Membership Action Plans. NATO, however, did not ask aspirant countries to report on compliance with key policy commitments, such as the E.U. Code of Conduct, that explicitly addressed the human rights implications of conventional arms transfers.

At a Euro-Atlantic Partnership Council ministerial meeting in May 2000, Canadian foreign minister Lloyd Axworthy linked NATO membership to responsible arms trading practices. He stated that national parliaments would be unlikely to approve NATO enlargement unless candidates did their best to halt irresponsible flows of surplus weapons, echoing a warning that NATO officials said was communicated privately to aspirant countries. Human Rights Watch had repeatedly called on the alliance and individual member states to use such leverage to press for reform of aspirant countries' arms trade behavior.

Military modernization efforts in Central and Eastern Europe, linked to NATO enlargement, continued to result in vast quantities of surplus small arms, as well as heavy weapons, being offered for sale. NATO member states made assistance available to partners to destroy surplus small arms, as noted, but did not adopt a broader approach. Human Rights Watch called for NATO states to provide incentives for the disposal of excess weapons, including heavy military equipment, that otherwise risked being sold to human rights abusers. To stem the dumping of Soviet-standard weapons into the marketplace, Human Rights Watch further called for the provision of newer, NATO-standard equipment to candidate countries and new allies to be made contingent on their responsible disposal of quantities of surplus arms.

Other Regional Mechanisms

The Wassenaar Arrangement on Export Controls entered its fifth year of operation and the thirty-five participating states concluded the first overall assessment of its functioning in 2000. Participants agreed to improve the efficiency and effectiveness of the General Information Exchange on non-participating states, and to improve transparency in the exchange of information on arms deliveries. States also affirmed that: "there should be strong, effective, transparent and national law-based enforcement of export controls. The elements of export control enforcement include a preventive programme, an investigatory process, penalties for violations, and international cooperation." Members also discussed for the first time including small arms and light weapons in the regime, as well as the possibility of also developing common export guidelines for man-portable surface-to-air missiles, a proposal heavily favored by the U.S. The U.S. also proposed expanding the list of seven reporting categories for weapons to seventeen, and that member countries report all arms transfers to areas of armed conflict. In addition, the U.S. publicly encouraged Wassenaar states to enhance the transparency of arms exports through the publication of annual reports.

In November 1999, members of NATO and the former Warsaw Pact agreed to update the 1990 Conventional Forces in Europe (CFE) Treaty to impose national, rather than bloc-to-bloc, ceilings on holdings of certain heavy weapons. The adapted treaty will take effect once thirty states ratify it.

Also in November 1999, on the occasion of an OSCE summit in Turkey, the participants in the Stability Pact for South Eastern Europe issued a declaration on small arms and light weapons. They agreed to combat illicit arms trafficking and to destroy surplus and seized weapons.

Within the Organization of American States (OAS), at this writing the United States Senate had not acted to provide its advice and consent for ratification of either the 1997 Inter-American Convention Against the Illicit Manufacturing of and Trafficking in Firearms, Ammunition, Explosives and Other Related Material or the 1999 Inter-American Convention on Transparency in Conventional Weapons Acquisitions. Only one state, Canada, had ratified the Transparency in Conventional Weapons Acquisitions convention, which seeks to increase transparency and build confidence and security among American states. At this writing, there were ten states party to the OAS illicit arms trafficking convention.

At the December 1999 summit in Togo of the Economic Community of West African States (ECOWAS) the sixteen member states adopted an action plan to complement the three-year moratorium on the import, export, and manufacture of light weapons announced in 1998. The action plan included a code of conduct outlining the procedures and requirements for obtaining a waiver, and the creation of a prototype arms register and weapons database for the West Africa region promoted as a forerunner for an Africa-wide register. Although the small arms moratorium had great symbolic value, ECOWAS lacked the financial resources to provide for substantial monitoring and enforcement mechanisms to prevent highly abusive forces, including rebels in Sierra Leone, from receiving further weapons. The moratorium therefore achieved little success in curbing the flow of small arms in West Africa, as arms continued to flow to member states such as Liberia and Sierra Leone and make their way into the hands of human rights abusers. ECOWAS received some international assistance, including a grant from the United States to assess individual states' ability to control the flow of small arms, as well as the support of NGOs who sought to strengthen the moratorium.

In Southern Africa, the states of the Southern African Development Community negotiated a draft of a Firearms Protocol to combat the illicit manufacturing, trafficking, possession, or use of firearms. At this writing, the text had not been finalized and adopted.

Arms Embargoes

There were important developments with regard to mandatory U.N. arms embargoes in 2000, including a groundbreaking U.N. report released in March detailing how a highly abusive rebel group in Angola breached a 1993 arms embargo. The report was prepared by an expert panel overseen by the chair of the Security Council Angola sanctions committee, then Canadian ambassador to the U.N. Robert Fowler. The "Fowler report" was remarkable for naming the individuals (including heads of state), companies, and countries implicated in sanctions-busting and also for calling for their punishment. That call went unanswered, with the Security Council deferring action until a further investigation could be completed, anticipated for October 2000. The government of Bulgaria and the presidents of Burkina Faso and Togo, for example, rejected charges that they helped Angola's UNITA rebels breach international sanctions.

As was the case with a previous ad hoc U.N. arms inquiry on Rwanda, Human Rights Watch's efforts to document violations of embargoes imposed on human rights abusers helped pave the way for the U.N.'s investigation. In addition, Human Rights Watch offered a sympathetic critique of the Angola panel's work, highlighting lessons that would later inform the creation of a dual arms/diamonds inquiry for Sierra Leone. The Security Council mandated the Sierra Leone inquiry in July 2000, two months after Revolutionary United Front (RUF) rebels overran U.N. peacekeepers and NGOs, including Human Rights Watch, proposed this and other measures to prevent the RUF from rearming to continue an unspeakably brutal war. At the same time, to cut off the RUF's source of financing, the Security Council imposed an embargo on all diamond sales that were not authorized by the government of Sierra Leone. In line with the Fowler report's "naming and shaming" approach, several governments, particularly the U.S. and U.K., publicly chastised Liberia and its president for supporting Sierra Leone's rebels, including by trading arms for diamonds, and named Burkina Faso as a transit point for illegal arms shipments. These statements were repeated at a U.N. Sierra Leone sanctions committee hearing on the diamond and arms trades in Sierra Leone, at which Security Council members and others, including a Human Rights Watch representative, made statements. The U.N.'s Sierra Leone investigative panel was due to prepare a report by the end of October. At this writing, the Security Council had not taken needed steps to ensure effective enforcement of the neglected arms embargoes on Sierra Leone and Liberia, for example the deployment of well-equipped U.N. forces to monitor borders (especially with Liberia), roads, and airstrips bordering on rebel-controlled areas and halt any weapons shipments they detect.

As of October 2000, embargoes remained in place against grossly abusive non-state groups in Angola, Rwanda, and Sierra Leone, as well as against Iraq, Liberia, Somalia, and the Federal Republic of Yugoslavia. The 1992 embargo on Libya was suspended in 1999. A new mandatory arms embargo was imposed on Ethiopia and Eritrea in May 2000 in response to derailed peace talks and continued fighting, but was limited to a twelve-month time frame. This move reflected an ongoing debate about reform of U.N. sanctions regimes. The Security Council convened a special debate on sanctions in April 2000, and a Security Council working group subsequently began studying sanctions in order to propose measures to enhance their effectiveness. This debate was informed by several initiatives both within and outside the U.N. to analyze weaknesses in U.N. sanctions regimes and develop recommendations for action. A proposal, advanced by Human Right Watch and other nongovernmental organizations, to create a permanent U.N. embargoes unit appeared to gain support in 2000.

Tackling Small Arms Proliferation

Small arms and light weapons continued to be the weapons of choice in wars around the world. Plentiful, highly portable, easy to maintain, and relatively inexpensive, these weapons were often turned against civilians. A 1999 study by the International Committee of the Red Cross (ICRC) noted that even by very conservative estimates drawing on the ICRC's database of treated weapons injuries, more than a third of all victims of armed attacks were civilians. The ICRC argued for legal restraints on the trade in small arms based on respect for international humanitarian law.

With the U.N. conference on small arms planned for 2001, NGOs geared up for the event. The International Action Network on Small Arms (IANSA), which counted well over two hundred participants, including Human Rights Watch, pressed for the conference to address the legal trade in arms, as well as illicit trafficking; to result in concrete actions rather than mere rhetoric; and to be inclusive of the views of civil society. The formation of an Eminent Persons Group on Small Arms brought several high-profile figures to the global campaign.

Although IANSA participants recognized that supply-side measures alone could not fully address the impact of arms flows on civilians, reining in weapons exporters and arms brokers continued to be an important element of the small arms campaign. For example, tons of surplus arms sold cheaply by former Warsaw Pact countries that were new or aspiring members of NATO contributed to the widespread availability of small arms and their low price. These countries, as well as several former Soviet republics and China, had much greater need for hard currency than for large stockpiles of aging Soviet-standard military equipment. As with small arms originating in countries with lax controls, surplus heavy weapons were often sold without consideration for the dangers posed by arms sales to areas of conflict marked by gross human rights abuses.

Bulgaria in particular was scrutinized for its record of arms transfers, with several governments and organizations joining Human Rights Watch in criticizing the country's poor controls. U.S. President Bill Clinton raised arms trade concerns with the Bulgarian prime minister during a November 1999 visit, and NATO officials also stated that the topic had been discussed at high levels with Bulgarian officials. These efforts were reinforced by the U.N.'s Angola panel, which named Bulgaria as the UNITA rebels' main arms supplier in March 2000 and called for NATO to weigh Bulgaria's membership bid with this behavior in mind. The head of the panel also explicitly linked Bulgaria's pending accession to the European Union with efforts to clean up its arms export practices.

These efforts began to bear modest fruit as the Bulgarian government, feeling the pressure, promised to tighten controls. It undertook to restrict the use of falsified arms trade documents by working with other southeast European countries to develop standardized and hard-to-forge alternatives, moved to create an independent oversight agency for the arms trade, asked for help destroying surplus small arms stocks, and promised to push for adoption of reforms to the national arms trade law. Still, much remained to be done. Proposed legal changes were insufficient to close important loopholes, and neglected to incorporate into law human rights criteria for arms exports. Bulgaria also repeatedly reneged on its pledge to adhere to the non-binding E.U. Code of Conduct on Arms Exports, while implementation and enforcement of the country's existing arms trade law remained a serious problem.

South Africa, another arms exporter, has disappointed human rights and arms control advocates with some of its sales. While its arms control policy was in principle quite strong, Pretoria had furnished weapons to clients such as Algeria which did not meet South Africa's code of conduct criteria on human rights and conflict. Further, a long-awaited bill intended to formalize the remarkable arms control reforms made since 1994 (the end of the apartheid era) fell seriously short of expectations. Among other shortcomings, the bill presented to parliament in July 2000 left out the human rights criteria at the core of South Africa's ethical arms export policy. After strong protest from NGOs, the bill was withdrawn for redrafting.

Weapons and the Conduct of War

Targeting in Warfare and Civilian Casualties

In a report released in February 2000, based on an investigative mission in August 1999, Human Rights Watch estimated that the seventy-eight-day bombing campaign against Yugoslavia resulted in about 500 civilian deaths in ninety separate incidents. Human Rights Watch concluded that NATO violated international humanitarian law, but did not commit war crimes. One-third of the incidents and one-half of the deaths were the result of attacks on illegitimate or questionable targets, including Serb Radio and Television, heating plants, and bridges. Human Rights Watch criticized the use of cluster bombs in populated areas, insufficient precautions in warning civilians of attacks, and insufficient precautions in identifying the presence of civilians when attacking convoys and mobile targets. Human Rights Watch called for changes in targeting and bombing doctrine to ensure compliance with international humanitarian law.

Cluster Bombs

The use of cluster bombs by NATO in the Kosovo conflict generated extensive attention to the negative humanitarian impact of these weapons. U.S. and U.K. aircraft dropped about 1,600 cluster bombs on Yugoslavia, containing about 300,000 individual bomblets. According to a Human Rights Watch investigation, at least ninety and as many as 150 civilians died in incidents involving NATO use of cluster bombs—15 to 25 percent of all civilian deaths in the conflict. The large number of civilian casualties reflected both the difficulty of accurately targeting cluster bombs, and the decision to use them in populated, urban areas.

Cluster bombs not only posed a special danger to civilians during conflict, but like landmines, continued to take civilian victims even after the war ended. Cluster bomblets that did not explode on impact as designed became de facto antipersonnel mines that would then explode from the contact of a person. Using a very conservative estimated failure rate of 5 percent, the air war resulted in some 15,000 unexploded bomblets littering the country. Those bomblets had caused several hundred civilian casualties since the end of the bombing campaign in June 1999; more children had been killed or injured by cluster bomblets than landmines.

In December 1999, in a memorandum to delegates to the Convention on Conventional Weapons, Human Rights Watch called for a moratorium on the use of cluster bombs by all nations until humanitarian concerns can be adequately addressed. Subsequently the International Committee of the Red Cross and other organizations also called for a use moratorium. In September 2000 the ICRC called for a new "remnants of war" protocol to the CCW that would require users to be responsible for post-conflict clean-up and require self-destruct mechanisms on munitions such as cluster bombs.

United States Policy

Antipersonnel Landmines

There was no change in the Clinton administration policy announced in May 1998 that the U.S. would join the Mine Ban Treaty in 2006 if the Pentagon was successful in identifying and fielding alternatives by that time. After several years of inaction, Pentagon spending and activities related to the search for alternatives expanded, but it also became increasingly clear that the 2006 date was unlikely to be met. While the U.S. deserved credit for continuing to increase the amount of money it devoted to mine clearance programs around the world, it had not taken adequate steps to move closer to a comprehensive ban on the weapon.

There were several disturbing developments in 2000. For the second year in a row, the Pentagon asked for $48 million for a new mine system called RADAM that would contain not only antitank mines, but also antipersonnel mines banned under the Mine Ban Treaty. Congress cut funding to $8 million in 1999 and appropriated $28 million in 2000. Moreover it came to light that the "alternative" that was farthest along in the developmental stages, the so-called man-in-the-loop system, still contained a feature that when activated would return the munition to traditional antipersonnel mine status, and therefore be prohibited by the ban treaty. Human Rights Watch also discovered U.S. Air Force plans to stockpile antipersonnel mines in Qatar, a party to the Mine Ban Treaty.

Conventional Weapons and Military Transfers or Training

U.S. efforts in 2000 to control the flow of conventional weapons focused on illicit trafficking in small arms and light weapons. In February 2000, the Department of State released a fact sheet outlining U.S. priorities in this area, which included increasing domestic and international transparency of arms transfers, helping other countries destroy surplus weapons stocks, and enforcing U.N. arms embargoes. These priorities reflected input from U.S.-based NGOs, often acting in concert as members of the Small Arms Working Group and the Arms Transfers Working Group.

In November 1999 the International Arms Sales Code of Conduct Act of 1999 was signed into law as an amendment to the Consolidated Appropriations Act for Fiscal Year 2000. The amendment, the result of a compromise between Representatives Cynthia McKinney (Democrat, Georgia) and Sam Gejdenson (Democrat, Connecticut), required the Clinton administration to support efforts to negotiate an international code of conduct for arms transfers. The following month, the U.S. endorsed the 1998 E.U. Code of Conduct on arms exports. At this writing, the U.S. government had not incorporated into national regulations E.U. Code criteria that went beyond those already followed by the U.S., so it was unclear how the U.S. intended to adhere to the criteria. Also in the Consolidated Appropriations Act, Congress required the Secretary of State to submit by May 2000 reports on small arms proliferation and the arms export licensing process. At this writing, both reports to Congress were pending.

At a NATO meeting in May 2000, Secretary of State Madeleine Albright announced arms export reforms to facilitate U.S. arms exports to close allies. Under the Defense Trade Security Initiative, the U.S. introduced seventeen changes to its domestic arms regulations, most aimed at expediting the export licensing process. NGOs expressed concern that the exemptions would undermine efforts to monitor U.S. weapons exports and ensure that they are not illegally diverted to unauthorized end users.

The Leahy Amendment, which prohibited the U.S. from giving security assistance to abusive forces, continued to have a beneficial impact on U.S. policy. In August, U.S. Special Forces arrived in Nigeria to help train and equip battalions of Nigerians to serve as peacekeepers in Sierra Leone. In order to comply with the Leahy law, the U.S. pledged to screen all potential trainees and exclude those suspected of having committed human rights abuses. It did not, however, take the further step of promoting prosecution of human rights abusers as a condition for such assistance.

In March 2000 the Departments of Defense and State released a three-part report outlining foreign military training programs in fiscal years 1999 and 2000, of which two parts were classified. The declassified portion of the report was a disappointing setback for efforts to increase transparency in foreign military assistance. It no longer identified the foreign military units trained, for example, and thus made more difficult the monitoring of U.S. compliance with the Leahy law.

In July 2000, the U.S. General Accounting Office released a report summarizing U.S. efforts to stem the proliferation of small arms. It stated that between 1996 and 1998, the U.S. authorized transfers or delivered $3.7 billion in small arms, primarily to close allies (Turkey was one top recipient), and acknowledged that some of these weapons had ended up on the black market. The GAO also noted U.S. contributions to international efforts to control the trade in small arms and its role in helping other states destroy excess weapons. In a second report, released in August, the GAO examined the U.S.'s end-use monitoring efforts. The GAO concluded that the Department of Defense was failing in three areas: requiring field personnel to conduct and report on end-user checks; requiring field personnel to conduct such checks in response to specific circumstances or for certain weapons systems; and complying with the reporting requirements of the Arms Export Control Act of 1996. The report attributed these failures to inadequate training and guidance provided to field personnel on end-use monitoring requirements.

In September 2000 the Defense Department released its portion of the annual "Section 655" report, detailing arms sales for fiscal year 1999. As of October 2000, the State Department had not yet released its complementary portion.

Chemical and Biological Weapons

The United States was in "technical non-compliance" with the 1993 Chemical Weapons Convention until May 2000, when, three years late, it began submitting its initial declarations under the treaty with respect to possession or production of chemical weapons. Although U.S. declarations included almost 600 chemical manufacturing facilities, it was unclear if all facilities that should be declared were included. Inspections of U.S. industry facilities also began in May. According to the U.S. General Accounting Office, the United States would most likely not meet the 2007 deadline for the complete destruction of its chemical weapons stockpiles.

There was concern in 2000 that the U.S. was not providing needed leadership in the negotiations for a compliance protocol to the 1972 Biological Weapons Convention (BWC). The ad hoc group charged with negotiating the protocol hoped to complete its work before the fifth review conference of the BWC, scheduled for late 2001, but absence of U.S. support for this effort undermined its prospects for success.

Relevant Human Rights Watch Reports:

Angola Unravels: The Rise and Fall of the Lusaka Peace Process, 9/99
Landmine Monitor Report 2000: Toward a Mine-Free World and the Executive Summary: Landmine Monitor Report 2000, 9/00
NATO: Civilian Deaths in the NATO Air Campaign, 2/00
South Africa: A Question of Principle: Arms Trade and Human Rights, 10/00
United States: Clinton's Landmine Legacy, 7/00

HUMAN
RIGHTS
WATCH

ASIA

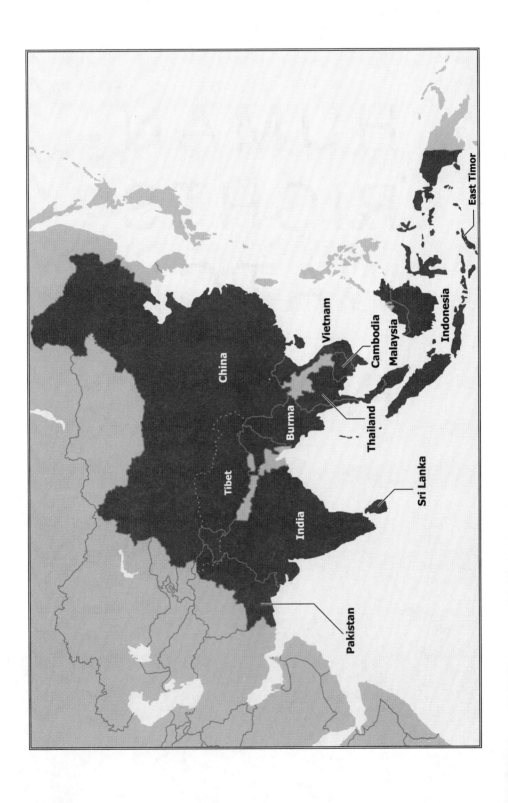

ASIA
OVERVIEW

In East and Southeast Asia, governments relied on Asian initiatives during the year to address economic, political, and human rights issues. Gone was the rhetoric of "Asian values" with its pre-financial crisis premise that economic development and protection of individuals rights were incompatible. In its place was simply a determination, from democratic and authoritarian governments alike, to show that solutions to Asian problems were to be found within the region, despite the diversity of cultures and political interests involved. South Asia, as always, was a region apart, so divided by rivalries and security concerns that regional cooperation was all but impossible.

On the economic side, one example of East Asian regionalism was the movement toward developing the equivalent of an Asian Monetary Fund involving China, Japan, South Korea and the ten countries of the Association of Southeast Asian Nations (ASEAN). It had a political parallel with the all-Asian resistance in late 1999 to an international tribunal for East Timor, balanced by the prominent Asian participation in the U.N. Transitional Administration for East Timor (UNTAET) in which peacekeeping forces were headed first by a Filipino and then a Thai. In October 2000, South Korean President Kim Dae-Jung received the Nobel Peace Prize for his efforts to ease tensions with North Korea, a wholly homegrown initiative. At the governmental level, the "We'll do it our way" stance was partly a case of resistance to solutions imposed from outside but also one of perceived common interest in building regional strength across a variety of fields—including human rights.

Asian regionalism was helped by the fact that the influence of the international donor community was near an all-time low, although aid levels were never higher: witness the helpless outrage of donor countries during the year over the treatment of women in Afghanistan; the attacks on minorities in India; the aftermath of the October 1999 coup in Pakistan; the continuing restrictions on Aung San Suu Kyi in Burma; Indonesia's failure to stop militia violence in West Timor; the obstructions placed by Cambodia in the way of a tribunal to try the Khmer Rouge; the arrests of political and religious activists in China; or the coup and hostage crisis in Fiji in May. In all these countries, domestic political imperatives far outweighed any fear of international reaction, and as it turned out, there was not much to fear from donors worried that pressure would inflict more damage on themselves than on the offending country.

Unlike the years immediately prior to the financial crisis when East and Southeast Asian governments steadfastly refrained from criticizing each other (South Asian governments felt no such hesitation), Asian regionalism in 2000 was more accommodating of different viewpoints. This may have reflected the impact of democratization in important countries in the region such as Thailand, whose foreign minister broke ranks with other ASEAN countries and openly criticized Burma's suppression of opposition political activities. It also reflected distrust between the big regional powers, China, India, and Japan, and suspicion within the less powerful countries about the long-term political and economic agendas of the big three.

The phenomenon of finding strength as a region without necessarily constituting a solid political bloc may also have reflected the many internal conflicts that strained bilateral relations. Kashmir remained a constant source of tension between India and Pakistan. Indonesia's inability to control the conflict in Aceh worried Malaysia, just across the Straits of Malacca. The raid into eastern Malaysia by guerrillas of the Abu Sayaf wing in the southern Philippines led to the deportation of thousands of Filipinos from Malaysia and strained that relationship. The ongoing ethnic insurgencies in Burma affected relations with India, Bangladesh, and Thailand, all of which had to shelter thousands of refugees from those conflicts.

Both governments and regional and local nongovernmental organizations (NGOs) were committed, where possible, to regional approaches to resolving regional human rights problems such as exploitation of migrant labor, human trafficking, and child prostitution. There was less support among governments for the international system for protecting human rights. Not only did China work harder than ever to escape censure at the U.N. Commission on Human Rights in Geneva, weakening that body as a result, but the Australian government in September bitterly rejected the actions of several U.N. bodies that had questioned its treatment of aboriginals and refugees.

Asian NGOs as a group, however, remained an important voice for the expansion of the international system, pushing—as their governments, with few exceptions, did not— for ratification of the Rome Statute of the International Criminal Court, an end to the use of child soldiers, and implementation of human rights commitments made at the Beijing Women's Conference in 1995.

Human Rights Developments

In general, a rising concern with justice for past abuses did not translate into effective measures to prevent new ones. Serious problems remained in terms of protecting civilians in areas of conflict; ensuring basic civil rights under authoritarian governments; and providing protection to refugees, migrants, and trafficking victims.

The Pinochet precedent was very much on the minds of governments and NGOs in the region during the year, as accountability for past abuses was an issue as never before. In South Korea, efforts were underway to hold the U.S. accountable for the No Gun Ri massacre in July 1950, during the Korean war, in which some 400 civilians may have died. Throughout the countries occupied by Japan during World War II, women forced into sexual slavery as "comfort women" were still campaigning for individual compensation from the Japanese government. Relatives of fami-

lies of those killed or unaccounted for in the Thai army's May 1992 firing on unarmed demonstrators demanded and got release of classified government documents about the incident and continued to demand the prosecution of those responsible. Relatives of Tiananmen Square victims filed a civil complaint in a U.S. court in September against Li Peng, then Chinese premier, now head of the National People's Congress in Beijing. In Cambodia, international pressure forced the Hun Sen government to agree reluctantly to a tribunal over which it would not have complete control to try former Khmer Rouge leaders for crimes against humanity committed from 1975 to 1979. The final establishment of the tribunal, which would be based in Phnom Penh and have a majority of Cambodian over non-Cambodian judges, was still awaiting action by the Cambodian parliament by late October. A special panel of the Dili district court in East Timor was set up in June to try those responsible for crimes against humanity and serious crimes committed during the period January to October 1999.

In part because of a rising interest in accountability, the International Criminal Court attracted more attention in the region. By the end of the year, New Zealand and Fiji had ratified the Rome Statute while South Korea, Thailand, Bangladesh, Australia, the Solomon Islands, and the Marshall Islands had all signed. A conference of Asian NGOs, held in Bangkok in June, decided to make ratification of the statute a key priority for regional advocacy.

Even as moves to punish past abuses were gathering strength, serious human rights problems continued to plague the region. Some were linked to separatist or nationalist movements and governments' abuse of security laws to detain, torture, "disappear," or kill suspected opponents. Some were classic examples of the refusal of authoritarian governments to tolerate peaceful political opposition. Others were linked to communal violence, still others to the failure of governments in the region to protect refugees and migrants.

In all countries where armed rebellion

against the central government was underway, all parties to the conflict were responsible for abuse. In Sri Lanka, civilians in the northeast of the country were caught in the middle between the Liberation Tigers of Tamil Eelam (LTTE) and government forces. In Kashmir, Indian security forces used draconian counterinsurgency measures, including arbitrary arrest, torture, and staged "encounter killings", against Muslim citizens who were suspected of supporting guerrilla activity, while armed Islamists were believed responsible for mass killings of Hindu civilians. In Nepal, an ongoing Maoist insurgency continued to spread from four midwestern hill districts to encompass nearly the entire nation. In Aceh, in Indonesia, the Gerakan Aceh Merdeka (GAM, Free Aceh Movement) was reported to have killed suspected informers; government security forces were responsible for the torture and killing of suspected GAM supporters. Separatist conflicts were also underway in West Papua, Indonesia; northeast India; Xinjiang, in western China; and around all of Burma's borders. In Laos, armed insurgency from ethnic Hmong in the highlands and ethnic Lao rebels based in Thailand and Laos increased during the year, and in June, the government initiated a national security alert after a series of unclaimed bomb blasts were attributed to those Lao insurgents. Governments tended to deal harshly with any rebels arrested, sometimes judicially, sometimes extrajudicially, but their prosecutions of their own agents for human rights violations were rare. Several South Asian governments responded to internal armed conflicts by introducing or enhancing existing anti-terrorism legislation or emergency powers.

Fundamental rights to freedom of association, expression, and assembly were tightly restricted in North Korea, Burma, Vietnam, and Afghanistan. China, despite some liberalization, still banned any group or publication that it considered a threat to the Communist Party's hold on power.

But even in more open societies, like Malaysia, Singapore, Pakistan, and Cambodia, politics could be a risky occupation, as the trials of Anwar Ibrahim and Nawaz Sharif made clear. The use of draconian internal security legislation remained an issue in many of the region's democratic or democratizing countries. In Bangladesh, for example, the government signed the Public Security Act into law in January, affording sweeping powers to the police and circumventing guarantees of due process.

Where public advocacy was possible, human rights defenders were working toward legislative change. In South Korea, for example, President Kim Dae-Jung announced in August his willingness to repeal the harsh National Security Law, as recommended by the United Nations Human Rights Committee and demanded by a coalition of more than 200 local rights organizations; as of October, it was still on the books, but former prisoners who had been unfairly detained under it by previous administrations became legally eligible for rehabilitation and compensation. (In fact, a 1999 law made anyone who had suffered detention, job loss, or expulsion from universities as a result of involvement in prodemocracy activities eligible for "restoration of honor" and compensation.) In India, NGOs campaigned against the introduction of the Prevention of Terrorism Bill into parliament.

In much of the region, communal, ethnic, or caste tensions were caused or exacerbated by government actions. In India, Hindu nationalist policies of the ruling party encouraged attacks on Dalits ("untouchables"), Muslims, and Christians. In China, perception of organized meditation groups as a potential political threat led to widespread persecution of Falun Gong practitioners and members of other *qi gong* groups. Ethnic tensions rooted in longstanding social and economic grievances and a perception on the part of indigenous elites of dispossession by "migrants," led to the coup in Fiji in May and the attempted coup in the Solomon Islands in June. In Fiji, many of the "migrants" were in fact third- and fourth-generation Fijians. In the Moluccas, in Indonesia, a bitter communal conflict with similar socioeconomic roots was fueled by the participation of security forces in the conflict, with the army largely siding with Muslims and the police with Christians. There was not a single ethnic or communal conflict in the region that was reducible to "ancient hatreds," and impartial government policies, had they been in effect, could have gone a long way to reducing the potential for violence.

Protecting refugees, migrants, and victims of trafficking was a huge issue across the region, made more complicated by the fact that it was, by definition, transnational. To combat trafficking of Thai women to Japan, for example, both the Thai and Japanese governments needed to reform legislation and crack down on corruption of police and immigration officials. To protect foreign migrant workers against abuse in Malaysia or South Korea, countries exporting labor needed to prosecute illegal labor recruiters while the receiving countries needed to step up investigations and prosecutions of abusive employers.

The Japanese Ministry of Foreign Affairs hosted the January 20 Asia-Pacific Symposium on the Trafficking in Persons, but the conference did not generate any concrete preventive measures. The governments of the United States and the Philippines organized a conference of the Asian Regional Initiative on Trafficking of Women and Children (ARIAT) from March 29-31 in Manila. That conference did produce an action plan for tackling human trafficking in the region.

Throughout the region, huge numbers of refugees and internally displaced people continued to need protection. On the eve of the fiftieth anniversary of the Office of the U.N. High Commissioner for Refugees (UNHCR) only five Asian countries were parties to the 1951 Convention relating to the Status of Refugees or to its 1967 Protocol. Serious issues of refugee protection arose even in some of those five during the year. In Australia, for example, a riot in August at an immigration detention center in Woomera, South Australia, drew international attention to the government's harsh treatment of undocumented migrants. In China, reports of forcible return of North Korean refugees were almost impossible to verify because UNHCR was allowed no access to the area concerned. In some countries, protection in the host country was the problem. Many refugees from East Timor were virtual hostages of militia leaders in Indonesian West Timor, for example. In others, the country from which refugees fled obstructed their efforts to return. Despite international pressure to secure the right to return for approximately 100,000 Bhutanese refugees living in camps in Nepal since late 1990 and 1991, Bhutan continued to resist proposals for their repatriation. The UNHCR pledged to continue its voluntary yearly repatriation of thousands of Afghan refugees from Pakistan and Iran; the refugees returned to face ongoing civil war and severe violations of human rights.

In many countries that offered little or no protection for refugees, desperate asylum-seekers tried to enter the workforce of the host country, blurring the line between refugees and migrants, and making deportation of undocumented migrants tantamount in many cases to refoulement. This was the case with three groups of Burmese refugees: ethnic Shan refugees in Thailand, ethnic Chin in India; and ethnic Rohingya in Malaysia.

Protection of the internally displaced remained weak in some countries and non-existent in others. Many of the estimated one million internally displaced in Sri Lanka faced restrictions on fundamental freedoms and discrimination at the hands of Sri Lankan security forces; there were even allegations that army and police used displaced villagers as forced labor north of Batticaloa in eastern Sri Lanka. The Indonesian government for much of the year obstructed efforts of international agencies to assist the more than 300,000 Indonesians displaced by the communal conflict in the Moluccas. By October, some aid was getting through. In Afghanistan, aid agencies faced an ethical dilemma of whether to continue to provide assistance in light of the ruling Taliban's policies on women when to halt all assistance could have a disastrous impact on the displaced population. A Taliban offensive in northeastern Afghanistan resulted in a massive exodus from Takhar province into neighboring

Badakshan. Up to 90,000 were believed to be homeless, and a humanitarian crisis loomed as winter approached.

Defending Human Rights

Human rights work continued to be a dangerous occupation in some parts of Asia. Human rights activists across the region condemned the murder of Acehnese human rights defender Jafar Siddiq Hamzah, whose body was found outside Medan, Indonesia, three weeks after he "disappeared" on August 5. He was believed to have been killed by military forces, although as of October, Indonesian police investigators reported no leads to the identity of his killers. In other countries, local defenders took risks in reporting government abuses. Several Cambodian human rights defenders came under attack in August for reporting on alleged extrajudicial executions in Kratie province; afterwards, the defense ministry threatened to sue the main Cambodian human rights coalition. Chinese activists who campaigned to organize a new association to uphold the rights outlined in the two international rights covenants that China had signed were detained, tried, and imprisoned.

In some countries, human rights defenders moved into new and unaccustomed roles. In Malaysia, several leading activists stood for parliament in the November 1999 elections as an expression of opposition to the government's treatment of former Deputy Prime Minister Anwar Ibrahim. In Indonesia, by contrast, some human rights organizations found themselves in the position of advising the democratically elected government of Abdurrahman Wahid on policy. ELSAM, a rights advocacy organization, drafted legislation for a proposed truth commission.

Increasingly, governments were finding it in their interests to establish national human rights institutions. Malaysia established a commission, known by the acronym Suhakam, in April, and began receiving complaints shortly thereafter, primarily of police abuse. Nepal established a national commission in May. The Thai parliament passed legislation setting up a human rights commission in 1999 but only began appointing members in October 2000. In September, South Korea's Ministry of Justice submitted a bill establishing a national human rights commission to Congress; NGOs had opposed it because they wanted the commission to be more than an advisory body and to be more independent of the government than the bill envisaged. Cambodia has three semi-official human rights commissions, which are largely seen as partisan and ineffective: the Senate Human Rights Commission, the National Assembly Human Rights Commission, and the government's Human Rights Committee. In July, NGO leaders and government representatives established an informal working group to discuss establishing an independent national human rights commission. The Cambodian working group is a member of a regional working group based in the Philippines that is working to set up an ASEAN Human Rights Commission. National human rights institutions were already operating in India, Indonesia, the Philippines, Sri Lanka, Australia, and New Zealand.

The Role of the International Community

United Nations

The U.N. had a high profile on human rights during the year, most prominently with respect to Afghanistan, Burma, East Timor and Cambodia. In the latter two countries, prosecutions of past abuses were high on the agenda. In East Timor, the Office of the High Commissioner for Human Rights (OHCHR) and the special rapporteurs on torture; extrajudicial, summary or arbitrary executions; and violence against women conducted inquiries into grave abuses associated with the 1999 scorched earth campaign; UNTAET was responsible for further investigations and prosecutions. In Cambodia, negotiations over an international tribunal were conducted by the U.N's Office of Legal Affairs.

The OHCHR maintained field offices in Phnom Penh and Jakarta. While staff in the former included human rights monitoring in their brief, the Jakarta office was restricted to technical advisory services. High Commissioner Mary Robinson visited China, Indonesia, East Timor, and South Korea during the year; she was scheduled to return to China in November to work on a plan to give China technical assistance to bring its laws into conformity with international standards.

At the fifty-sixth session of the Commission on Human Rights in March, U.N. Special Rapporteur on Afghanistan Kamal Hossain and Special Rapporteur on Violence against Women Radhika Coomraswamy submitted their reports based on research conducted in Afghanistan and Pakistan in 1999. Hossain found widespread violations of international humanitarian and human rights law by Taliban forces and commanders against ethnic Hazaras and Tajiks in central and northern Afghanistan. Eyewitness testimony included accounts of forced displacement of civilians, deliberate burning of houses and crops, summary executions of non-combatants, arbitrary detention and forced labor. In newly occupied areas of central and northern Afghanistan, the special rapporteur found that women and children were frequently separated from their families and transported by truck to other regions of the country or to Pakistan. There were also many accounts of young girls in these areas being forcibly married to Taliban commanders. Coomaraswamy's report drew attention to a rise in violence against Afghan women, including domestic violence, honor killings, and trafficking of Afghan refugee women in Pakistan.

Burma reacted in a similar fashion to the report in October of the special rapporteur on Myanmar, Rajsoomer Allah, who for the fifth consecutive year was not permitted to visit the country on which he was tasked to report.

Most of the regional reporting to the U.N. treaty bodies was fairly routine, but the highly critical conclusions by the Committee on the Elimination of Racial Discrimination to a report submitted by Australia helped provoke the Australian government's angry statement in September that it would not necessarily allow further visits by treaty bodies.

United States

The Clinton Administration took a selective interest in Asia. Securing normal trading relations with China was a priority; so was preventing any escalation of the conflict in Kashmir. By the end of the year, developing a dialogue with North Korea, building on Kim Dae-Jung's "sunshine policy," was also a high priority. A state visit to India drew Indo-U.S. relations closer than ever before; a state visit to Vietnam in November was expected to put relations on an important new, trade-focused footing. Indonesia was very much a center of attention, but it was clear that neither the U.S., nor any other major international actor, knew exactly how to respond to a democratically chosen government that was so manifestly weak in terms of strategic vision and capacity to govern. The U.S. took an active role in supporting the UNTAET in East Timor and in pressing Indonesia to take action against militias in West Timor.

In general, trade and economic relations and strategic interests in the region took precedence over human rights, yet many Asian governments believed that the U.S. continued to give far too much attention to rights. Without any other international support, for example, the U.S. tried and failed to get a resolution critical of China adopted at the U.N. Commission on Human Rights. The U.S. was the only donor at the World Bank-chaired Consultative Group on Indonesia meeting in October that suggested loans might be conditioned on Indonesia's progress toward resolving the refugee situation in West Timor.

The U.S. government's promotion of religious freedom—largely due to congressional pressure—drew a mixed response in Asia, appreciated by victims of persecution, seen by governments as meddling. The U.S. Commission on International Religious Freedom held hearings on abuses in China, India and Pakistan, and religious freedom was expected to be a priority of Clinton's trip to Vietnam in November. In general, the impact of U.S. appeals or interventions was marginal.

The office of the U.S. Ambassador-at-Large for War Crimes took a strong interest in justice issues relating to possible crimes against humanity in East Timor and Cambodia.

Japan

Japanese diplomacy was at a post-Cold War peak this year, and human rights received attention as an important, if limited, component of Japanese policy in Asia. Japan hosted the G-8 summit in Okinawa (July 21-23), and continued to emphasize building economic and political relations with its neighbors in Southeast and South Asia; the prime minister toured South Asia for the first time in a decade. A pre-summit gathering of G-8 foreign ministers issued a statement endorsing "fundamental principles of democracy, the rule of law, human rights and an open economy" as "indispensable" in an era of globalization. But at the summit itself, the G-8 leaders side-stepped some of the most controversial issues.

Promoting reform and stability in Indonesia was a top priority for Japan, which hosted the annual donor meeting for Indonesia in October. It also provided major assistance for East Timor's reconstruction and urged a resolution of the crisis in West Timor. Japan maintained good relations with Burma, trying to nudge the military towards democratization but also helped to deflect criticism of Burma internationally. Japan continued its campaign to give full economic and political support to the Hun Sen government in Cambodia, while also urging its cooperation with the U.N. on a Khmer Rouge tribunal. Relations with China, despite a visit to Tokyo by Jiang Zemin late in the year, remained rocky, largely because of mutual wariness on security issues; human rights concerns were marginal to Japan's bilateral agenda with Beijing.

European Union

The European Union was active in promoting peaceful resolution of the conflicts in Sri Lanka (backing Norway's mediation offer) and Kashmir. The first ever E.U.-India summit took place in June. Following the October 12, 1999 coup in Pakistan, the E.U. quickly distanced itself from the military government, and only restored political dialogue with Islamabad in September 2000.

Otherwise, the E.U. was concerned with expanding economic relations across the region, capped by the third Asia-Europe Meeting (ASME) summit in Seoul in October, which brought together heads of state from fifteen European countries and ten Asian governments to discuss expanded economic cooperation.

The E.U. put a high priority on finalizing a trade agreement with China in the context of the WTO negotiations, while including human rights in its political dialogues and summit meetings. But the E.U.-China human rights dialogue received increased scrutiny during the year as it failed to deliver tangible results, and by year's end was under internal review.

During the year, the E.U. used its influence as a leading donor to support human rights and democratization in Vietnam, Cambodia, and Indonesia and East Timor. In the case of Burma, however, splits within the E.U. made it difficult to develop a stronger common position towards the ruling State Peace and Development Council (SPDC) following the SPDC's September crackdown. An E.U.-ASEAN meeting in Laos remained on the calendar for December.

World Bank

Two of the World Bank's top five loan recipients this year were in Asia (India, U.S. $1.8 billion and China, $1.67 billion). The social and economic consequences of the Asian financial crisis were key factors in sparking further reforms within the World Bank. Those reforms included more engagement with civil society, strong attention to combating corruption, and an interest in examining the bank's potential role in supporting basic judicial reforms.

World Bank President James Wolfensohn's extraordinary appeal to Indonesian President Abdurrahman Wahid urging an end the violence in West Timor had a major impact in Jakarta and helped frame an overall international agenda for dealing with the crisis.

The bank's emphasis on participation as an element of good governance led to consultations with civil society in advance of bank-convened donor meetings, with NGOs actually participating in some of the donor conferences, for example, on Indonesia and Cambodia. But in countries where NGOs were non-existent or tightly controlled, such as China and Vietnam, the bank effectively let the governments set the terms of any "consultation" with people likely to be affected by bank projects.

In East Timor, the bank was a key promoter of democratization efforts through a community empowerment project involving election of local councils to decide on development priorities.

A new World Bank report on Burma, leaked late in 1999, explicitly linked deteriorating economic and social conditions in Burma to the lack of progress on political reform and human rights. This set a useful precedent and example for the ongoing debate in Asia on the linkages between rights concerns and governance and development issues.

BURMA

The Burmese government took no steps to improve its dire human rights record. The ruling State Peace and Development Council (SPDC) continued to pursue a strategy of marginalizing the democratic opposition through detention, intimidation, and restrictions on basic civil liberties. Despite international condemnation, the system of forced labor remained intact.

In the war-affected areas of eastern Burma, gross violations of international human rights and humanitarian law continued. There, the Shan State Army-South (SSA-S), Karenni National Progressive Party (KNPP), and Karen National Union (KNU), as well as some other smaller groups, continued their refusal to agree to a cease-fire with the government, as other insurgent forces had done, but they were no longer able to hold significant territory. Tens of thousands of villagers in the contested zones remained in forced relocation sites or internally displaced within the region.

Human Rights Developments

The SPDC continued to deny its citizens freedom of expression, association, assembly, and movement. It intimidated members of the democratic opposition National League for Democracy (NLD) into resigning from the party and encouraged crowds to denounce NLD members elected to parliament in the May 1990 election but not permitted to take their seats. The SPDC rhetoric against the NLD and its leader, Aung San Suu Kyi, became increasingly extreme. On March 27, Senior Gen. Than Shwe, in his Armed Forces Day address, called for forces undermining stability to be eliminated. It was a thinly veiled threat against the NLD. On May 2, a commentary in the state-run *Kyemon* (Mirror) newspaper claimed there was evidence of contact between the NLD and dissident and insurgent groups, an offense punishable by death or life imprisonment. In a May 18 press conference, several Burmese officials pointed to what they said were linkages between the NLD and insurgents based along the Thai-Burma border, and on September 4 the official Myanmar Information Committee repeated this charge in a press release after Burmese security forces raided the NLD headquarters in Rangoon.

The SPDC released several high-profile political prisoners during the year, but continued to arrest individuals engaged in peaceful political activities. It extended clemency on medical grounds to NLD Youth member Tun Zaw Zaw, also known as Tun Tint Wai, on December 19 after his mother appealed for him to be released to seek treatment for an eye disease. He had served two years of a seven year prison term imposed on politically-motivated charges of forgery and cheating. Moe Thu (Sein Myint), former editor of the economics magazine *Danna*, was released on January 3, 2000, following the death of his wife. He had been in prison since June 1996. On May 22, the government released Cho Nwe Oo, who had been in prison since 1995 for a protest at the funeral of the former prime minister, U Nu. The thirty-two-year old doctor had two years of his sentence still to serve at the time of release. The government released six elderly men, five of them reportedly NLD members, shortly after a request for the release of the men and other prisoners made by the U.N. Secretary-General's special envoy for Burma, Razali Ismail, during his October 2000 visit to Burma. On October 20, the government released British activist James Mawdsley following strong protests earlier in the month by the British foreign ministry over reports that Mawdsley had been beaten in detention and a statement by the U.N. Working Group on Arbitrary Detention that he was being held unlawfully. He had served one year of a seventeen-year sentence for distributing pro-democracy leaflets in Burma.

There were also new arrests. On April 24, the SPDC detained a member of the Committee Representing the People's Parliament (CRPP), the shadow legislature established by the NLD. Aye Tha Aung, chairperson of the CRPP's Committee on Ethnic Nationalities Affairs, was reportedly sentenced to twenty-one years of imprisonment in June to be served at Insein prison, where conditions were particularly harsh. In May, the authorities arrested Tint Wae, Kyaw Myo Min, and Ma Htay Htay for allegedly distributing the dissident newspaper *MoJo*, and sentenced them to seven years in prison. Later the same month, the government arrested over one hundred NLD members in an apparent attempt to suppress political protests to mark the tenth anniversary of the 1990 election.

The International Committee of the Red Cross (ICRC) continued to monitor the conditions of thousands of prisoners, and was able to establish offices in Kengtung in Shan state, Pa-an in Karen state, and Moulmein in Mon state to begin to monitor the condition of civilians in eastern Burma.

On August 24, Burmese officials took action to prevent the freedom of movement of NLD General Secretary Aung San Suu Kyi, Deputy Chairman Tin Oo, and a dozen other party members, forcing their two vehicles off the main road in the town of Dala, on the outskirts of Rangoon. Government forces refused to allow the party to proceed to the NLD branch office at Kunyangon, thirty miles from the capital, and urged them to return to Rangoon because of "security concerns." The NLD officials refused to do so and, instead, camped in their cars, but on September 3, police forcibly returned them to Rangoon. Officials reportedly handcuffed Aung San Suu Kyi and Tin Oo. The day before, security forces had raided the NLD headquarters in Rangoon and confiscated numerous documents. The government claimed that the raid had uncovered damning evidence that NLD members were helping insurgent groups to smuggle explosives into Burma and confined nine NLD executive committee members to their homes pending completion of an investigation. The government's move sparked international condemnation. Foreign diplomats were permitted to visit the nine detainees on September 14 and the NLD members were then permitted to move about Rangoon.

On September 21, however, the government blocked a bid by Suu Kyi and other NLD members to travel by train to Mandalay. Suu Kyi and eight other NLD executive members were placed under effective house arrest. Deputy Chairman Tin Oo was held at an unknown location. The nine executive members were still being held as of October 2000.

The SPDC failed to put a stop to its use of forced labor for infrastructure development, the construction of Buddhist structures, maintenance of military camps, and portering for army patrols. A delegation from the International Labour Organization (ILO), visited Rangoon and other areas at the SPDC's invitation from May 23-27, shortly before the June annual conference of the ILO. In its report on the visit, the ILO again called for the SPDC to cease the use of forced labor, repeal or amend legal provisions for forced labor in the Village and Towns acts, monitor compliance, and penalize those who employed forced labor. Burmese Minister for Labour Maj. Gen. Tin Ngwe wrote a letter dated May 27 to the ILO's director-general, stating that the SPDC leaders "have taken and are taking the necessary measures to ensure that there are not instances of forced labor in Myanmar." The ILO conference, however, concluded that the SPDC had failed to end the practice and gave the SPDC until November 2000 to institute reforms or suffer possible sanctions. On October 19, an ILO delegation traveled to Rangoon to assess whether forced labor was still in use.

Tens of thousands of villagers in the conflict areas of central Shan state, Karenni state, Karen state, Mon state, and eastern Tenasserim division remained in forced relocation sites and faced curfews, looting, and restrictions on movement at the hands of the Burmese army. Shan refugees escaping to Thailand reported that strict curfews had been implemented in Burmese government relocation sites forbidding Shan villagers from leaving their homes between dusk and dawn and, in some instances, prohibiting speaking and imposing a strict lights-out policy. Tens of thousands of other villagers in eastern and southeastern Burma remained displaced in the forests or in areas contested by the army and insurgent groups.

In the west, the SPDC continued to deprive ethnic minority Muslim Rohingya of full citizenship rights. The Rohingya were subject to restrictions on their freedom of movement, arbitrary taxation, and extortion by local officials. Forced labor was also common. A direct consequence of ongoing abuses was the gradual movement of Rohingya refugees into the Bangladeshi labor market. Some 20,000 refugees remained in Nayapara and Kutapalong refugee camps in Bangladesh as of October 2000, but the camps remained officially closed to new arrivals.

On July 27, the SPDC reopened many of the country's universities, which had been closed since 1996. Many campuses, however, had been relocated to rural areas since the mid-90s and the doors of the University of Rangoon, a former hotbed of political activity, remained shut for all but final year students.

Defending Human Rights

No human rights organizations were allowed to operate in Burma.

The Role of the International Community

The international community was still far from developing a common approach to continued human rights abuses in Burma. In March, fourteen governments were represented at a meeting in South Korea convened by the United Nations to discuss how to advance Burma's political development. They included the U.S., Australia, Canada, and several E.U. and Southeast Asian states, as well as the U.N. secretariat and the World Bank, but no new and coherent strategy emerged.

United Nations

In April, U.N. Secretary-General Kofi Annan appointed Malaysian diplomat Razali Ismail as his new special envoy for Myanmar, replacing Alvaro de Soto. Razali made his first visit to Rangoon from June 30 to July 3 when he met with SPDC officials, NLD leaders, and foreign diplomats. During his second visit on October 9-12, he met with Aung San Suu Kyi and Senior Gen. Than Shwe, the first time any special envoy had been able to do so.

The U.N. General Assembly and U.N. Commission on Human Rights passed consensus resolutions in November 1999 and April 2000, respectively, expressing concern over human rights abuses in Burma and the ongoing political stalemate. In reports in January and August, U.N. Special Rapporteur Rajsoomer Lallah focused on the lack of respect for civil and political rights, obstacles in Burma to the realization of economic, social, and cultural rights, and abuses faced by vulnerable groups. The SPDC refused to admit Lallah to Burma for the fifth year in a row.

United States

The U.S. government position on Burma did not change. On May 19, President Clinton renewed sanctions on new private investment in Burma. On June 19, the U.S. Supreme Court unanimously rejected a Massachusetts state law, which would have penalized companies investing in Burma, ruling that Congress had preempted it by establishing a sanctions policy. In another case brought by fifteen Burmese villagers, a U.S. federal court ruled on September 1 that Unocal corporation and its partners knew of and benefited from forced labor on the Yadana natural gas pipeline between Burma and Thailand, but that there was insufficient evidence that Unocal could control the abuses, and that the court therefore lacked jurisdiction over the case. The plaintiffs planned to appeal to the federal appeals court in San Francisco.

Two U.S. government reports sharply criticized the SPDC. In February, a Labor Department report concluded that forced labor, denial of the right to organize, and forced relocation remained pervasive, while abusive child labor was not uncommon. In September, the State Department announced that Burma was one of a number of countries that maintained serious restrictions on religious freedom.

On August 31, both Vice-President Al Gore and Secretary of State Madeline Albright publicly condemned the SPDC for its treatment of Aung San Suu Kyi and other NLD members and called for the SPDC to guarantee their freedom of movement and other fundamental human rights. In his September 6 address to the U.N. Millennium Summit, President Clinton denounced the SPDC for confining Aung San Suu Kyi to her home. On September 11, the State Department released a joint statement signed by Albright and ten other women foreign ministers condemning the SPDC's violation of the basic human rights of NLD members.

European Union

The European Union (E.U.) tightened sanctions against Burma's leaders while renewing engagement with the Association of Southeast Asian Nations (ASEAN), of which Burma is a member. On April 10, the E.U. strengthened its common position by prohibiting the sale, supply, and export to Burma of equipment which could be used for internal repression or terrorism, and by freezing the funds of important government functionaries and publishing their names. On September 21, the E.U. issued a statement of concern about the treatment of Aung San Suu Kyi and called for the SPDC to lift all restrictions on her freedom of movement. The E.U. went ahead, however, with plans for the first meeting of E.U. and ASEAN foreign ministers since Burma joined ASEAN in 1997, scheduled at this writing to be held in December in Vientiane, Laos. Switzerland and Liechtenstein in October placed sanctions on Burma in line with the E.U. common position. On October 6, the E.U. presidency issued a declaration in support of the U.N. special envoy's mission.

Japan

Japan continued its two-track policy towards Burma, urging democratization and respect for human rights and suspending any new aid until there were "visible signs" of progress, while also maintaining political ties with Rangoon. On November 28, 1999, Prime Minister Keizo Obuchi met with Senior Gen. Than Shwe at the Manila summit of leaders from ASEAN, China, South Korea, and Japan. His meeting was followed a few days later by a "personal" visit to Burma by former Japanese premier Ryutaro Hashimoto. Both leaders told the SPDC that Japan would not resume official development assistance absent visible political and economic reform. Hashimoto also recommended that the SPDC re-open all Burmese universities. In late June, Japan sponsored a two-day workshop on economic reform in Rangoon, originally scheduled when Obuchi and Senior Gen. Than Shwe met in Manila in November 1999. No new Official Development Assistance (ODA) loans or grants were announced during the workshop, though it was widely viewed as a possible step towards resuming bilateral aid. Some Japanese companies—including a fertilizer manufacturer and Toyota car dealer—pulled out of Burma during the year due to the difficulties they encountered operating there. In September, the Japanese government protested the virtual house arrest of the NLD executive committee.

In multilateral forums, Japan sought to dilute or deflect actions critical of the SPDC. It voted against the resolution on forced labor at the ILO and did not cosponsor the Burma resolution adopted by the U.N. Commission on Human Rights.

Australia

Australia sought to cultivate greater respect for human rights through a long-term strategy of engagement with Burmese authorities on human rights. Urging the creation of a Burmese national human rights commission, the Australian government financed two human rights workshops in July for mid-level Burmese civil servants and a third in October. On August 10, at meetings of the Asia Pacific Forum of National Human Rights Institutions, the SPDC reiterated its intent to establish a commission. Not everyone within the Australian government had confidence in the SPDC's rhetorical commitment to change, however. In a July 21 cable to Prime Minister John Howard and Foreign Affairs Minister Alexander Downer, Ambassador Trevor Wilson wrote that the SPDC was "determined to remain in power at all cost, allowing only marginal reforms in the economy and society." The Australian government criticized Rangoon over the treatment of the NLD but did not reassess its existing policy.

Association of South East Asian Nations

Thailand broke with the ASEAN position of non-interference in the internal affairs of member nations by abstaining from the vote on the ILO resolution criticizing Burma (all other ASEAN members voted against), and, in August, by criticizing the SPDC's treatment of Suu Kyi and the NLD. Foreign Minister Surin Pitsuwan said Burma's actions could scuttle the planned December meeting of ASEAN and E.U. foreign ministers. In September, the Thai government called for the ASEAN troika—the association's present and immediate past and future chairpersons—to address the situation in Burma. Vietnam, the current chair, refused to activate the troika, claiming the issue was a Burmese internal affair.

World Bank

The World Bank in a report in late 1999 linked Burma's poor economic performance to poor governance. The bank continued to deny loans to Burma and refused to consider sending a high level delegation to Rangoon unless the SPDC affirmed in writing its commitment to carrying out significant economic reforms.

Relevant Human Rights Watch Reports:
Living in Limbo: Burmese Refugees in Malaysia, 8/00
Burmese Refugees in Bangladesh: Still No Durable Solution, 5/00

CAMBODIA

After more than two years of negotiations, Cambodia and the United Nations tentatively reached agreement in July to establish a national tribunal with international participation to bring former Khmer Rouge leaders to justice for genocide, crimes against humanity, and war crimes committed between April 1975 and January 1979. As of October, however, the government had yet to submit revised legislation establishing the tribunal to the National Assembly, casting doubt on the government's resolve. Although the high level of political strife that had plagued Cambodia in recent years receded, serious human rights violations continued, including political killings and torture, attacks on opposition leaders, human trafficking, substandard prison conditions, and violations associated with labor and land conflicts.

Human Rights Developments

Cambodia and the U.N. reached agreement on the Khmer Rouge tribunal in July, after a series of negotiating sessions in Phnom Penh, New York, and Havana. As a compromise to a fully international tribunal, the U.N. agreed that the tribunal would be located in Cambodia, as a three-tiered special chamber within the Cambodian court system, consisting of a majority of Cambodian judges and a minority of foreign judges. All judges were to be appointed by the Cambodian Supreme Council of Magistracy (SCM), which is dominated by the ruling Cambodian People's Party (CPP), although the U.N. secretary-general was to put forward a list of foreign jurists as nominees for consideration by the SCM.

Previous stumbling blocks, such as who would control prosecutions, were resolved through a concession brokered by the United States, in which co-prosecutors— one Cambodian and one nominated by the U.N.— would issue indictments. Any differences between co-prosecutors would be resolved through a pretrial chamber composed of Cambodian and foreign judges, with decisions to block indictments requiring the consent of a majority of the judges plus at least one foreign judge. The plan was criticized by Cambodian and international human rights organizations. They said it set an international precedent by watering down standards of judicial independence and creating a politically charged indictment process.

Official impunity remained a major problem. Virtually none of the perpetrators of hundreds of politically-motivated extrajudicial killings, incidents of torture, and other abuses committed before and after the 1997 coup and 1998 elections were brought to justice during the year. According to the U.N. special representative for human rights in Cambodia, as of April 2000 the government had investigated only nine of these cases, leading to the trial and imprisonment of three culprits. An emerging trend was for victims of rape or physical assault committed by government agents to be pressured to settle cases out of court, with the encouragement of local officials, police and/or court staff.

Commune-level elections, which had been repeatedly postponed since the 1993 national elections, were not expected to be held until mid-2001 at the earliest. In order to reduce political violence, Cambodia's independent nongovernmental election monitoring coalitions advocated passage of a Commune Election law requiring candidates to run on an individual basis and not as political party members. They also called for the dismantling of commune militia, which were reportedly used during previous elections to carry out violence and intimidation of opposition supporters.

Numerous incidents of violence took place against local commune leaders, mostly directed at members of the opposition Sam Rainsy Party (SRP). These included the February 10 slaying of SRP member Chim Chhuon in Kompong Cham, for which a commune militiaman was later arrested; the June 3 killing of Prak Chhien, commune candidate for the royalist Funcinpec party in Kampot, for which the incumbent commune chief was later arrested; and the August 17 murder of Khhim Nhak, a SRP commune council member in Kompong Cham, for which the commune's deputy police chief was subsequently arrested. Other SRP commune candidates in Kompong Cham, Kampot, and Prey Veng were also threatened or attacked during the year. While rights workers concluded that most of these incidents were motivated at least in part by local political rivalries or the victims' role in publicizing local abuses of power, government officials insisted that the violence reflected nothing more than personal disputes. The effect, however, was clear: the attacks conveyed the message that involvement in politics could be life threatening.

Further harassment of the SRP occurred in May, when mobs attacked the SRP headquarters in Phnom Penh and destroyed a memorial erected by the party in front of the National Assembly. In March, two SRP members, Mong Davuth and Kong Bun Heang, who had been arrested in September 1999 for an alleged 1998 assassination attempt against Prime Minister Hun Sen, were released from prison for lack of evidence. The judge said that both men remained suspects in the case and could be re-arrested at any time. In December 1999, another SRP member, Sok Yoeun, who had fled the country after also being named as a suspect in the alleged assassination attempt, was arrested in Thailand. He was charged with illegal entry and sentenced to six months in prison there. Cambodia sought his extradition to face criminal charges but at this writing Sok Yoeun, having completed his sentence, was still in a Thai prison pending an extradition hearing.

In October, a uniformed soldier threatened to shoot SRP parliamentarian Cheam Channy during a standoff on a Phnom Penh street that lasted more than an hour. Police at the scene did not intervene, despite requests from U.N. human rights workers, who were eventually able to get the parliamentarian to safety.

Non-partisan organizations carrying out voter education were also harassed. In August, provincial authorities in Kampot threatened to arrest members of the Committee for Free and Fair Elections (Comfrel), an election monitoring group, for allegedly inciting civil unrest by advocating that candidates run as independents rather than as party members. After intervention by Comfrel's Phnom Penh office and the Ministry of Interior, the charges were dropped. In September, a district chief in Kampot ordered police officers to close a Comfrel meeting being held in a pagoda, allegedly because the organization lacked written permission from the governor to convene the meeting.

In August, rights workers received reports that alleged members of the Khmer Serey (Free Khmer Movement, or FKM), a group accused of plotting to overthrow the government, had been extrajudicially executed or "disappeared" by government forces. As many as thirty men were reportedly taken to a military base in Kratie province in April after having supposedly defected to the Royal Cambodian Armed Forces (RCAF). It was unclear how many of them were members of the FKM; some, apparently, were tricked into claiming to be members by promises that they would receive U.S. $150 a month if they defected. Three of the leaders of the group were later executed. When their bodies were found, they were blindfolded and had their arms tied behind their backs. Others were reported missing and were believed "disappeared." RCAF Deputy Commander Meas Sophea stated that at least seven men were killed in a gun battle with government forces in Kratie in May but alleged that they were all bandits. On August 29, the Department of Defense announced that it would file a defamation suit against the Cambodian Human Rights Action Committee (CHRAC), which had publicly condemned the killings and "disappearances" and called for an official investigation.

Civilian mobs committed vigilante-style killings of suspected thieves, in some cases, with the apparent collusion of the police. On at least six occasions, suspects held in police custody were seized by, or handed over to, angry mobs and beaten to death. Between January and May, there were at least fourteen reported cases of mob violence against alleged criminals, in which ten people were killed. Law enforcement officers also made use of lethal force against criminal suspects. In one incident on August 3, police shot and killed a suspected motorcycle thief. The police said he was killed while trying to escape, but witnesses said he had been handcuffed and led down railway tracks by two men in plain clothes before he was shot.

Little progress was made in reforming Cambodia's judicial system, plagued by corruption and low-paid and poorly trained personnel. A council for judicial reform, established in 1999 at the urging of Cambodia's international donors, was completely inactive during the year. A legal reform unit established by the Council of Ministers in 2000 with World Bank funding accomplished little apart from hiring consultants to conduct a number of studies. The Supreme Council of Magistracy (SCM)— responsible for overseeing and disciplining judges and commenting on draft laws—began to meet more regularly. During the second half of the year the SCM Disciplinary Council investigated a number of complaints against court officials and took disciplinary action against five judges and one prosecutor.

In December 1999, ostensibly in an effort to curb rampant corruption in the judiciary, Hun Sen issued a directive to suspend several judges in Phnom Penh and rearrest more than sixty individuals who allegedly had bribed their way out of prison. No warrants were produced for the arrests, however, nor were established legal mechanisms employed. As of October, at least thirty-four of those rearrested remained in jail, beyond legal pre-trial detention limits.

The acquittal of former Khmer Rouge commander Chhouk Rin in July underscored the weakness of the judicial system. Rin was tried on July 18 for armed robbery, terrorism, and destruction of public property in conjunction with the murder of three Western hostages in 1994. Rin, who defected to the RCAF in 1994, was acquitted on the basis of a 1994 law that granted an amnesty to Khmer Rouge who defected within six months of the law's promulgation, despite the fact that the kidnaping took place after the law was passed.

Prisoners continued to be subjected to excessive pre-trial detention, food and water shortages, lack of medical care, and shackling. 25 percent of prison inmates interviewed over a three-year period by the Cambodian League for the Promotion and Defense of Human Rights (Licadho), a local human rights group, stated that they had been tortured, threatened, or otherwise intimidated while in police custody after their arrests. As of August 2000, 369 inmates, some 25 percent of Phnom Penh's prison population, had been held awaiting trial longer than allowed by law. At this writing, the government had not taken any steps to punish the execution-style killing of two escaped prisoners upon their recapture by guards at the Sihanoukville prison in June 1999.

The government and the CPP continued to dominate the airwaves, but more than twenty privately-owned newspapers, some affiliated with opposition parties, were able to publish regularly. The Ministry of Information ordered the suspension of several newspapers, however, for allegedly defaming national leaders and endangering national security. In April, the ministry ordered the thirty-day suspension of *Pratebath Poramean Kampuchea* (Cambodian News Bulletin) for allegedly insulting government officials. The bulletin was suspended again in July for reprinting a *South China Morning Post* article that allegedly defamed the king. In February, two opposition newspapers, *Samleng Yuvachun Khmer* (Voice of Khmer Youth) and *Moneaksekar Khmer* (Khmer Conscience), were threatened with closure by the Ministry but then given a reprieve after they published letters of apology for allegedly inciting racial violence and insulting the king.

Ethnic Vietnamese minorities continued to face repression. In November 1999, Phnom Penh municipal authorities evicted approximately 600 ethnic Vietnamese residents from a floating village on the Bassac River, charging that they were illegal immigrants. A number of those evicted told rights workers that they were long-time Cambodian citizens and that local authorities confiscated their identity documents before the eviction. The villagers were forced to float downstream to a location near the Vietnamese border, where they remained as of this writing. Harassment and arrests of suspected "free Vietnam" members in Cambodia opposed to the government of Vietnam increased. As the twenty-fifth anniversary of the reunification of Vietnam on April 30 neared, Cambodian and Vietnamese authorities announced that they were conducting joint actions to thwart suspected terrorist attacks. In February, Truong Tan Hoang and Vinh Anh Tung, both alleged "free Vietnam" members, were arrested in different cities. In March, police in Phnom Penh surrounded and entered the homes of several other suspected members, who eluded arrest by going into hiding. Since 1996, more than twenty people suspected of belonging to anti-Hanoi organizations have been arrested in Cambodia. They have then either "disappeared" or been deported to Vietnam, where some have been tortured and imprisoned. Vietnamese asylum seekers in Cambodia appeared to be at higher risk of forcible return than asylum seekers from other countries because of inconsistent application of protection policies by the Phnom Penh office of the U.N. High Commissioner for Refugees.

Evictions and forcible confiscation of land by military and civilian authorities continued to rank as one of Cambodia's most pervasive human rights problems. One NGO, Legal Aid of Cambodia, estimated its land-related caseload at around 6,000 families, with the vast majority of the conflicts involving military commanders or provincial and local officials. Particularly vulnerable to land confiscation were Cambodia's indigenous ethnic minorities in the northeast, whose lands were threatened by logging concessions and industrial plantations. With assistance from NGOs and consultants from the Asian Development Bank, a revised land law was drafted and submitted to the Council of Ministers in July. In June, both King Sihanouk and Prime Minister Hun Sen expressed strong support for the revised law to provide communal land ownership rights for indigenous minorities.

Labor violations included arbitrary dismissal, unsafe working conditions, failure to pay the minimum wage, and discrimination and intimidation of union and worker activists. A labor code passed in 1997 met international standards, but enforcement was poor and procedures for registering unions remained cumbersome. In March, the Ministry of Labor issued a circular banning strikes that did not take place within the premise of a factory, enterprise or establishment and requiring at least seven days prior notice to the employer and the ministry in advance of a strike. Nevertheless, Cambodia's labor movement remained strong through the year. In June, thousands of garment workers went on strike in Phnom Penh to press for better working conditions and an increase in monthly wages.

Cambodia continued to be plagued by trafficking of people from rural areas and other countries for sexual exploitation or to work in substandard conditions in Phnom Penh sweatshops. Powerful figures running trafficking networks, and their accomplices —many of them government officials, sol-

diers, or police—were usually immune from prosecution. In twenty cases of human trafficking recorded by Licadho from late 1999 to early 2000, for example, only three perpetrators had been arrested and detained as of May 2000.

In one incident in February, fifty-one trafficked workers from Vietnam and China were detained and forced to work at the GT garment factory in Phnom Penh. Workers stated that they had been lured to Cambodia with promises that they would be paid U.S. $100 a month for eight hours of work a day. Instead, during their first three months at work they were paid around $50 a month and prohibited from leaving the factory. Police raided the factory and released the workers, but afterwards repeatedly threatened to arrest the workers for lacking proper documentation to work in Cambodia. No punitive action was taken against those who were responsible for smuggling the workers into Cambodia and detaining and exploiting them in the factory.

In another case in August, police raided the Best Western hotel in Phnom Penh, where seven women recruited from Romania and Moldova had been promised jobs as dancers. Instead, they had been kept against their will in the hotel or its affiliate, where they were forced to work as prostitutes. Many of their clients were reportedly government officials. The hotel owner, a Chinese-Canadian who had taken the women's passports from them when they arrived in Phnom Penh, was released by police after questioning, reportedly for lack of evidence. No arrests were made of those who recruited the women in Europe and facilitated their entry to Cambodia.

In September, the Ministry of Women's Affairs announced that it was establishing a blacklist system to banish suspected foreign sex offenders from Cambodia, whether or not they had been convicted. When some human rights workers criticized the blacklist system for circumventing due process and the presumption of innocence, the ministry defended the move by acknowledging that Cambodian courts could not be depended upon to uphold the law.

Defending Human Rights

Some forty Cambodian nongovernmental human rights organizations were active nationally in human rights education and investigating abuses. Rights groups that engaged in high-profile advocacy and investigations, however, were subject to government-sponsored attacks in the Cambodian press as well as threats of prosecution or physical harm. In August, rights workers investigating extrajudicial executions in Kratie were followed by soldiers, who then made a late-night visit to the offices of one rights group. . Local and national authorities, including the prime minister, made threatening statements against the Cambodian Human Rights Action Committee (CHRAC), a coalition of human rights organizations, after it publicly condemned the executions and "disappearances." He accused the CHRAC of "protecting criminals who have killed people." On August 29, in what appeared likely to become the strongest move against rights organizations in eight years, the Ministry of Defense announced that it would file defamation charges against the CHRAC because of its public statement. As of October, no charges had actually been filed.

In March, Phnom Penh authorities threatened to arrest Licadho staff members after the group provided humanitarian assistance to ethnic Vietnamese lacking proper work authorization. The same month, authorities in Koh Kong province threatened to arrest workers from the Cambodian Human Rights and Development Association (known by its acronym, ADHOC) in connection with a trafficking case, when a woman who had sold her daughter brought charges of physical assault against ADHOC's provincial coordinator. The woman later withdrew her complaint and admitted that she had been pressured by police to file the complaint. In October 1999, three suspects were arrested in conjunction with the December 1998 killing of Pourng Tong, an activist member of ADHOC. In March 2000, however, the suspects were released. In October, a soldier threatened to shoot not only SRP parliamentarian Cheam Channy but also U.N. human rights workers who had intervened on Channy's behalf.

The Role of the International Community

In October 1999, U.N. Special Representative for Human Rights in Cambodia Thomas Hammarberg negotiated a two-year extension for the Cambodia office of the U.N. High Commissioner for Human Rights (COHCHR). In August 2000, Peter Leuprecht, former deputy secretary general of the Council of Europe, was named as replacement for Hammarberg, who had left the post in January.

In April, the U.N. Commission on Human Rights agreed to a resolution on Cambodia that welcomed the government's investigations into some cases of politically-motivated violence, its efforts to reduce the numbers of police and military, and the development of a five-year plan by the Ministry of Women's Affairs to improve the status of women. The resolution also expressed concerns, however, about continued political violence and intimidation, impunity, torture, extrajudicial killings, excessive pre-trial detention, illegal land confiscations, and the inadequacy of the courts. In May, the U.N. Committee on the Rights of the Child considered Cambodia's initial report on its implementation of the Convention on the Rights of the Child, which it ratified in 1992. Among the committee's recommendations were that Cambodia establish a juvenile justice system, expand education and child health services, and demobilize child soldiers.

Major Donors

At the Consultative Group (C.G.) meeting of Cambodia's international donors, held in May in Paris, donors committed U.S. $548 million in aid to Cambodia. Donors expressed concern about continued human rights abuses and impunity, and agreed on the need to establish a formal working group on governance to address judicial reform and corruption. In July, a good governance working group chaired by the World Bank was established. Its members included the United States,

Japan, Australia, France, the European Union (E.U.), Germany, the United Kingdom, the U.N. Development Program, Asian Development Bank, and COHCHR.

Several countries contributed towards judicial reform programs; for example, part of a U.S. $5.2 million grant from the E.U. was earmarked for judicial and administrative reform. In March, Japan committed up to U.S. $20 million in aid to Cambodia, continuing its role as the country's largest donor. It also planned to send police experts to provide technical assistance, including education on human rights.

Other than the United States, the E.U., Japan, and Australia, donor interest in pushing for international standards for Khmer Rouge trials was low. During a visit to Cambodia in January, Japanese Prime Minister Obuchi urged Hun Sen to fully cooperate with the U.N. in establishing a tribunal and stated that Japan would not support any tribunal that was not endorsed by the U.N. Japanese officials raised the issue again when Hun Sen went to Tokyo in June for Obuchi's funeral. In February, the European Parliament adopted a resolution supporting the U.N.'s reservations about the Cambodian government's first draft tribunal law. On April 10, just before a meeting between Hun Sen and U.N. Secretary-General Kofi Annan, the E.U. issued a statement endorsing continued dialogue between Cambodia and the U.N. regarding the tribunal and called for the tribunal to conform to international standards. During a visit to Cambodia in May, Australian Foreign Minister Alexander Downer called for Cambodia to make progress on the tribunal and announced that a two-year $A28 million aid package would include funding for a criminal justice assistance project.

Advocacy in support of neutral and timely commune elections was largely conducted by domestic NGOs. At the CG meeting, the Dutch ambassador stated that the Netherlands would consider support for the commune elections only if the commune militia were dismantled, a more neutral National Election Commission was created, and election monitoring NGOs were allowed to be actively engaged in the process.

On labor rights, the United States sent customs investigators to Phnom Penh in March to check into reports that a garment factory was using forced labor and trafficked workers. In May, Cambodia and the E.U. signed a textile trade agreement in which Cambodian textiles could formally access the E.U. internal market quota-and duty-free. During a signing ceremony, European Commission official Michel Caillouet noted Cambodia's efforts to improve labor conditions in the textile industry.

CHINA AND TIBET

Chinese authorities showed no signs of easing stringent curbs on basic freedoms. Their preoccupation with social stability, fueled by a rise in worker and farmer protests, severe urban unemployment, and separatist movements in Tibet and Xinjiang, led to tight political control. The leadership continued to see unauthorized religious practices as potentially subversive.

China reacted to perceived threats with repression, control of information, and ideological campaigns. It released a few dissidents before their prison terms expired, but it imprisoned many more for acting in support of their political or religious beliefs. The government attempted to cut off the free flow of information within China and between China and other countries. The Internet and its potential for free exchange of ideas generated particular alarm in official circles, but academics, journalists, publishers, and film makers all faced censorship. On the ideological side, President and Party Secretary Jiang Zemin initiated two campaigns, the "three stresses" and the "three represents," to reinforce unity within the Chinese Communist Party (CCP) and convince China's citizens of benefits of the CCP's role.

On the positive side, Chinese authorities continued to reform the legal system, seeking international expertise to help design new legal structures, train judicial and legal personnel, and help disseminate information on the reforms to the public, the courts, and the police.

Human Rights Developments

The government systematically suppressed independent political activities. From October 25, 1999 through July 2000, courts in four cities sentenced ten leaders of the dissident-led China Democracy Party (CDP) to heavy prison terms, primarily on subversion charges. Wu Yilong, who helped set up CDP provincial preparatory committees, received eleven years; Tong Shidong, who put together the only on-campus CDP branch, and Zhu Zhengming, who took part in drafting the CDP's founding documents, received ten-year terms. Other members received sentences ranging from five and a half to eight years.

In December 1999, Wang Yingzheng received a three-year sentence for advocating political reform to combat corruption. In February 2000, the Hangzhou Intermediate Court sentenced Wang Ce, chairman of the exile organization Alliance for a Democratic China, to a four-year term for "entering China illegally and endangering state security." An Jun, founder of the nongovernmental organization Corruption Watch, was sentenced to four years in prison on April 5 on charges of inciting the overthrow of the government.

Chinese authorities struggled to gain control of the Internet, with its estimated 16 million users. By the end of 1999, regulations had already banned web operators from linking to foreign news sites, and companies operating websites from hiring their own reporters. New regulations issued in March 2000 forbade China-based websites from reporting news from "independent news organizations," thus limiting them to state-controlled sources. In January 2000, the Ministry of State Security announced the closure of web sites, chat rooms, and Internet news groups posting undefined "state secrets," and expressly banned the use of e-mail in that context. The government also announced regulations limiting the use of encryption programs.

Starting in March, some twenty provinces set up special Internet police to expand the *sao huang* ("sweep away the pulp") campaign, ostensibly aimed at removing pornography from the Internet. In practice it was used to ban postings the government considered objectionable.

In May, authorities shut down the private-sector China Finance Information Network after it published a report on corruption. On September 19, a Hebei court sentenced Qi Yanchen, a founding member of the quasi-independent China Development Union, to a four-year prison term, in part for posting parts of his book, *The Collapse of China*, on the Internet. Huang Qi, who ran a website out of Sichuan province, was charged with subversion after he posted letters criticizing the 1989 massacre. Officials in Sichuan accused Jiang Shihua, a high school teacher and Internet cafe manager, with subversion for posting articles critical of communist authorities. In August, state security police in Shandong province shut down New Cultural Forum, a website set up by pro-democracy activists.

Stringent new regulations came into force on September 26, 2000 banning any materials judged subversive, supportive of so-called cults, damaging to reunification efforts with Taiwan, or harmful to China's reputation. Content and service providers were required to keep records of all users and content for 60 days and to hand over the information to police on demand.

Chinese authorities continued to target the print media and publishing industry. In April, after removing the publisher of two popular newspapers, *China Business* and *Jingping Consumer's Guide,* the CCP reissued stern warnings that the media must "lead the ideology of the people through news propaganda." In June, the warnings were backed up the announcement that a new internal directive required all media to uphold the CCP line. In July, editors in about a dozen publishing houses were replaced, demoted, or transferred for flouting the directive. In September, authorities in Taiyuan, Shanxi province, confiscated over 60,000 copies of nine "illegal" newspapers and arrested an "illegal" editor-in-chief for setting up and distributing a newspaper without permission.

On August 12, the political unit of a local Public Affairs Bureau detained U.S.-based poet Bei Ling after his journal, *Qingxiang* (Tendency), was published for the first time in Beijing. The 400-page issue, all copies of which were confiscated, contained articles by well-known dissidents and a photograph of exiled student leader Wang Dan. After enormous international pressure, Bei Ling was deported on August 26, and his brother, Huang Feng, also detained, was released, but not until the family had paid part of a 200,000 *renminbi* (approximately U.S. $25,000) fine.

In January 2000, several weeks after the Chinese Cultural Renaissance Movement published the first and only issue of its *Bulletin*, police took four members into custody. All were released except Wang Yiliang in Shanghai, who was serving a two-year administrative sentence on the trumped-up charge of disseminating pornography. In June, Beijing Publishing House canceled the release of *Waiting*, the award-winning novel by expatriate Ha Jin, after it was attacked by a Beijing University professor as a plot to show "China's backwardness." In August, customs officials impounded and held for a month some 16,000 copies of *The Clinton Years* by a former White House photographer. The book, published in the U.S., printed in Hong Kong, and shipped to China for binding, included a picture of U.S. President Clinton and the Dalai Lama.

Chinese authorities refused permission to include works by a Hong Kong writer in an international book fair in Beijing because of his views on Taiwan. Officials also banned actor-director Jiang Wen from film-making in China after his film that won the Grand Prix at the Cannes Film Festival, *Guizi Laile* (Devils on the Doorstep), was judged unpatriotic.

Social scientists also came under increased pressure. Song Yongyi, a librarian at Dickinson College in the U.S., was detained in China in August 1999 in connection with his research on the Cultural Revolution. He was released in January 2000. In June, a *Guangming Daily* editorial criticized four prominent academics, Fan Gang, Mao Yushi, Liu Junning, and Li Shenzhi, for teaching Western theoretical perspectives. Liu was fired from his professorship at the Political Science Research Institute of the Chinese Academy of Social Sciences. He Qinglian, an economist and author of the highly critical *Pitfalls of Modernization*, was dismissed as editor of the *Shenzhen Legal Daily* in July. Shenzhen media and publishing houses were warned not to publish her writings.

The government continued to be suspicious of unauthorized contacts with foreigners. It intensified efforts to prevent Bao Tong, former aide to deposed Chinese Communist Party secretary Zhao Ziyang, from meeting with other intellectuals or with the foreign press. Authorities prevented Ding Zilin, whose son was killed on June 4, 1989 and who has rallied relatives of the Tiananmen Square victims, from meeting Lois Snow, widow of renowned journalist Edgar Snow.

The government's campaign to crush the Falun Gong continued unabated and was extended to include other *qi gong*, or organized meditation groups, that authorities accused of spreading superstition. In October 1999, the government formally deemed Falun Gong a cult, banned under the Chinese Criminal Code, enabling authorities to impose harsh sentences on its members. Trials of at least eight Falun Gong leaders in November and December 1999 resulted in prison sentences ranging between two and eighteen years, and trials of other members continued well into 2000. In August, the director of the Religious Affairs Bureau admitted that 151 Falun Gong members had been convicted of leaking state secrets, creating chaos, or other crimes. Many detentions came as a result of silent, peaceful protests. On National Day, October 1, and the days following, security forces beat and detained scores of protestors in Tiananmen Square in Beijing. By late October, Falun Gong practitioners were claiming that more than fifty members had died in detention or as a result of mistreatment.

Zhong Gong, a *qi gong* group claiming 38 million adherents, and several smaller groups were also targeted. Authorities closed down much of Zhong Gong's extensive business network, including its training centers, trading companies, clinics, and health spas, seized its assets, and detained several members. In September, the U.S. refused China's request to extradite Zhang Hongbao, the leader of Zhong Gong, whom Chinese authorities accused of rape. The Chinese government planned an appeal.

Despite the assertion by a Chinese delegation attending the August 2000 Millennium World Peace Summit in New York that "there is no religious persecution in China," Protestant house church members and Catholic "underground" believers came under increased pressure. A decree promulgated in late September by the State Administration of Religious Affairs imposed stringent new controls over the religious activities of foreigners. Also in September, a Communist Party official asserted that religious theology must be made compatible with the socialist system.

In Anhui province, new regulations that came into force in January led to an increase in detentions, particularly of Protestants; forty-seven members of the Full Circle Church were among those detained. The group's leader, Xu Yongzi, was released in May after serving a three-year sentence. Detentions and church closings occurred in other provinces as well, including an extensive crackdown in Guangdong in May. On August 23, police in Henan province detained some 130 members of the Fangcheng church, among them three U.S. missionaries who were released and deported within forty-eight hours. Eighty-five of the 130 were "reeducated," according to Chinese authorities, and returned home.

State interference in Catholic affairs was evident in January when the officially-sanctioned Chinese Catholic church, rather than the Pope, ordained five new bishops. As of October, at least seven Catholic bishops remained in detention in China, many of whom had been held for years. On September 14, sixty police officers took eighty-one-year-old Bishop Zeng Jingmu into custody, together with two priests.

Social unrest appeared to be growing. Local governments faced widespread demonstrations, riots, sit-ins, and other forms of protest. In November 1999, a court in Shaanxi province sentenced Ma Wenlin to a five-year prison term on charges of "disturbing the social order" for having brought farmers' complaints to the State Council in Beijing.

Legal reform moved forward, but judicial abuses were still common. In Hebei province, a high court on three occasions overturned murder convictions against four peasants, citing doctored evidence, torture, and threats. Local officials, however, decided to try the men again. In Guangzhou, in July 1999, a migrant woman who appeared upset and who failed to present identification to police, was gang raped after police took her to a psychiatric ward. Her decision to press for an investigation led to destruction of evidence and allegations that she had fabricated the case. Only after the case had been publicized in November 1999 was one of the perpetrators charged with rape and eventually convicted, and three police reportedly dismissed.

Chinese courts continued to impose the death penalty for a wide variety of offenses, a list that grew as authorities stepped up their anti-corruption campaign. In October, China's highest court issued a judicial interpretation calling for more aggressive use of the death penalty against smugglers of arms, counterfeit currency, and endangered species, and against government officials who aided them. The executions of two high CCP officials were extensively publicized as warnings to other officials involved in bribe-taking: Cheng Kejie, former vice-chairman of the Standing Committee of the National People's Congress (China's legislature), executed on September 14, was the highest ranking official executed since the founding of the PRC in 1949; Hu Changqing, former governor of Jiangxi province and former deputy director of the Religious Affairs Bureau, was sentenced in February and executed March 8.

South Korean NGOs reported the forcible repatriation of North Korean refugees by Chinese authorities, but independent confirmation was not possible.

Tibet

Chinese authorities continued to suppress suspected "splittist" activities in Tibet and exert control over religious institutions. Officials embarked simultaneously on campaigns to vilify the Dalai Lama and to convince the international community that Chinese policies in Tibet had ensured economic well-being and respect for human rights.

In December 1999, one of the most senior religious figures in Tibetan Buddhism, the then fourteen-year-old 17th Karmapa, fled Tibet for India. In the wake of his escape, authorities moved his parents out of Lhasa, capital of the Tibet Autonomous Region (TAR); detained several people at Tsurphu, the Karmapa's monastery; and replaced some monks. The same week as the escape, Chinese authorities announced their recognition of another high-ranking figure, the two-year-old 7th Reting Rinpoche, thereby once again asserting a government role in the selection and installation of Tibetan religious figures. In May, authorities detained eight Reting monks who protested the choice.

Between April, when officials of the TAR met in Chengdu, Sichuan province, and July, government controls over monasteries and religious rituals increased. A government circular severely curtailed celebrations of the Dalai Lama's birthday in July. Officials searched the homes of nongovernmental workers and non-CCP members for materials on the Dalai Lama or other evidence of religious activity. Vacationing students were warned to stay away from monasteries and temples on pain of expulsion, and, on July 4, the official *Tibet Daily* instructed parents and schools to enhance atheistic education to "help rid [the children] of the bad influence of religion." Later the same month, officials intensified their drive to reduce the numbers of monks and nuns.

Detentions of monks and nuns for their peaceful pro-independence activities continued. In March, authorities in Sog county detained eight Tibetans, five of them monks. Resistance to "patriotic reeducation" and involvement in independence activities resulted in one death and five arrests in Chamdo in May.

Starting in January, authorities again blocked broadcasts by the Oslo-based Voice of Tibet.

Xinjiang

Political and religious repression was evident in Xinjiang, but the Chinese government also faced a genuine security threat from armed groups. Premier Zhu Rongji visited in September and called for an "iron fist" stance against splittists, religious fundamentalists, and terrorists. At least twenty-four alleged terrorists, most of them ethnic Uighur Muslims, were executed during the year.

Chinese authorities initiated a propaganda campaign in Xinjiang in May 2000. In villages surrounding Kashgar, close to the Pakistan border, thousands of cadres, making use of film clips, exhibitions, and a drama based on local alleged terrorist activities, went house to house warning residents against the separatist danger and reiterating China's claim to Xinjiang. In September, a banner stretched across the marketplace in Hotan read, "Severely smash the separatist backbone elements, the violent terrorist criminals and the religious extremists who lead them."

In December 1999, the Regional Press and Publications Bureau, the Urumqi City Bureau for Industry and Commerce, and the Public Security Bureau closed a facility for printing "illegal religious propaganda."

In March, Uighur businesswoman Rebiya Kadeer was sentenced to eight years in prison for "illegally passing intelligence outside China." The information in question consisted of underlined newspaper articles sent to her husband, a U.S.-based political refugee. She had been detained in August 1999 just before a meeting with several U.S. congressional staff. Her eldest son and her secretary were administratively sentenced to two- and three-year terms in November 1999.

Over one hundred Muslims were reportedly detained in Urumqi for advocating the implementation of Islamic law.

Hong Kong

Human rights in the Special Administrative Region (S.A.R) of Hong Kong were generally respected but there were ominous signs of censorship and threats to academic freedom and judicial independence. On December 3, 1999, the Court of Final Appeal capitulated to Chinese government pressure and agreed to interpret more narrowly the right of residency in Hong Kong. (In May 1999, following an earlier Court of Final Appeal ruling which set wide eligibility parameters, Chief Executive Tung Chee-hwa had invited Beijing to review the decision. The U.N. Human Rights Committee's observations on the SAR's compliance with the International Covenant on Civil and Political Rights in November 1999 strongly criticized Tung's move.) In February 2000, Hong Kong officials agreed to consult Beijing before they began drafting laws on sedition, subversion, and treason.

In April, a senior official of the central government's Liaison Office warned Hong Kong journalists against advocating Taiwanese independence, saying they should report only what was in the interests of Beijing. The warning came after Taiwan's vice-president said on local television that Taiwan should be "a remote relative and close neighbor" of China. In June, an official representative of Beijing in Hong Kong told a meeting of SAR businessmen that choosing pro-independence Taiwanese partners could jeopardize their mainland business dealings. The Liaison Office also warned Hong Kong Catholics to keep celebrations "low key" over the canonization of 120 victims of the 1900 Boxer Rebellion in China. In September, the Chinese government warned Anson Chan, the head of the civil service in Hong Kong, that she and her entire staff must step up their support of the SAR's chief executive.

Controversy broke out in July when Dr. Chung Ting-yiu, director of the Public Opinion Program of the University of Hong Kong, made public his suspicions that Tung Chee-hwa might be behind pressure to stop the university from conducting polls on Tung's declining popularity. On August 29, an independent panel decided that messages from university administrators to Dr. Chung were "calculated to inhibit his right to academic freedom." In September, the administrators in question resigned.

A 1997 Public Order Ordinance came under attack in September after police used it to arrest five university student leaders who had led protests against a projected increase in tuition. The charges were dropped after three colleges urged leniency. The ordinance gave police effective veto power over proposed demonstrations

In September 2000, elections for the Legislative Council (Legco) were held for the second time since 1997. The pro-China Alliance for the Betterment of Hong Kong won eleven seats, while the liberal Democratic Party did only slightly better, winning twelve. Turnout was low. Earlier in the year, leaders of all democratic parties had called for direct election of all Legco seats by 2008 in place of the existing partly elected, partly appointed system.

Defending Human Rights

No human rights groups were allowed to function openly in mainland China or Tibet, although Hong Kong continued to have a dynamic group of activists working on the full spectrum of rights without obvious interference from the government.

The Role of the International Community

China escaped virtually all pressure on human rights as governments focused on its prospective entry into the World Trade Organization (WTO). In September, the U.S. Congress voted to grant China permanent normal trade relations (PNTR) without any human rights conditions, thereby doing away with the annual review of its trade status.

The European Union (E.U.), Australia, Japan, Canada, and others carried out bilateral "dialogues" on human rights, although officials acknowledged a lack of tangible progress. The dialogue with the U.S., cut off by China after the NATO bombing of its embassy in Belgrade, remained suspended.

Cooperation with the U.N. was minimal. U.N. High Commissioner for Human Rights Mary Robinson held a regional workshop in Beijing in March and was expected to sign a technical cooperation agreement with China later in the year. But the failure of the U.N. Commission on Human Rights to even debate a resolution on China at its annual meeting in Geneva in April gave China little incentive to ratify two key U.N. human rights treaties that it had already signed.

High level visits by Chinese leaders to Europe, Japan, and the U.S., and an E.U.-China summit in Beijing in October included only routine references to human rights, which China easily dismissed.

Foreign Internet companies ignored or turned down appeals to intervene privately with Chinese officials on behalf of those in China arrested for using the Internet to protest rights abuses.

United Nations

Once again, the U.N. Commission on Human Rights failed to hold China accountable. A "no action" motion by China, to keep the U.S.-sponsored resolution off the commission's agenda, was adopted on April 18 by a vote of 22 to 18, with twelve abstentions and one delegation (Romania) absent.

During a March visit to Beijing for an Asia-Pacific regional workshop on human rights, U.N. High Commissioner for Human Rights Mary Robinson held a press conference and strongly condemned the deterioration of human rights in China. She held talks with senior officials on a technical cooperation agreement aimed at helping China to bring its laws into conformity with treaty standards.

In May, the U.N.'s Committee Against Torture reviewed China's compliance with its obligations under the treaty. The committee acknowledged greater transparency in publishing information about claims of torture against Chinese police and security officials and limited efforts at prosecution. It emphasized, however, that early access to detainees and other safeguards were urgently needed to curb the widespread practice of torture.

The U.N.'s special rapporteur on torture continued to negotiate with the government on the terms of a mission to China, without success. Similarly, the International Committee of the Red Cross made no headway in its long-standing effort to gain access to Chinese prisons and detention facilities.

The International Labor Organization's Committee on Freedom of Association ruled in June that provisions of China's Trade Union Act were in violation of ILO principles of free association, called for the release of several detained trade union leaders, and urged China to accept an ILO "direct contact" mission. There was no response from Beijing.

The U.N. capitulated to Chinese pressure in August when it barred the Dalai Lama from attending the World Millennium Peace Summit.

European Union

The E.U.'s relations with China, the E.U.'s third largest trading partner, focused heavily on expanding commercial relations, including completion of an agreement on China's entry into the WTO. Formal but unsubstantial discussions of human rights took place during the E.U.-China summit, held under the Portuguese E.U. Presidency's leadership on December 21, 1999 in Beijing. Another summit, led by French President Jacques Chirac, was scheduled for late October 2000, also in Beijing.

Despite pressure from the European Parliament and admissions by E.U. officials that its human rights dialogue with China since 1998 had failed to produce substantive results, the E.U. refused to cosponsor a resolution at the U.N. Commission on Human Rights in March. Its members opposed China's "no action" motion at the Commission, however, but failed to convince all E.U. association countries to do the same, and Romania was absent during the vote.

In late September, an EU-China human rights dialogue was held in Beijing, following much the same model as an earlier one in Lisbon.

In July, Premier Zhu Rongji paid the

first visit ever by a Chinese leader to E.U. headquarters. He praised the E.U.'s decision not to take action in Geneva, and urged that differences on human rights be dealt with "through dialogue instead of confrontation." Human rights concerns were prominent on the agenda of talks in July between E.U. External Relations Commissioner Chris Patten and China's foreign minister.

The E.U. took the lead in strongly criticizing China's frequent use of the death penalty and calling for its abolition, and for a moratorium on executions to be established in one or more provinces as a first step.

United States

U.S.-China relations were dominated by the issue of China's WTO entry and a promise by President Bill Clinton to give China PNTR.

In late March, the White House's top national security adviser, Sandy Berger, went to Beijing to explain to Chinese officials the U.S. decision to sponsor a resolution on China in the U.N. Commission on Human Rights. After the Geneva vote, the foreign ministry urged the U.S. to end the "anti-China farce," linking restoration of a bilateral human rights dialogue to a U.S. pledge of no future action in Geneva.

Also in late March, the Clinton administration indicated to Congress that, while it rejected any attempts to condition PNTR on human rights improvements, it would accept the creation of a bilateral commission to monitor and promote human rights and labor rights. The commission would be a joint congressional-executive branch body that would report annually to Congress. The commission was included in the PNTR package enacted by the House of Representatives on May 24 by a larger-than-expected vote of 237 to 197. But the commission had no teeth, and attempts in the Senate to strengthen it by requiring an annual debate and vote on its findings were defeated. On September 19, the Senate voted 83 to 15 in favor of PNTR. Under the PNTR bill, Congress for the first time would also fund rule of law and labor law reform programs in China.

The State Department was outspoken in condemning the crackdown on Falun Gong, restrictions on religious freedom, and repression in Tibet. Reports issued by the government-created Commission on International Religious Freedom in May and by the State Department in September were sharply critical of abuses of religious freedom.

The U.S. successfully appealed for the release of Bei Ling, a Chinese poet and resident of the U.S., and his brother, both detained in early August. The detentions occurred just prior to a visit to the U.N. by President Jiang Zemin. Administration and congressional appeals for the release of the academic researcher Song Yongi were also successful, while repeated appeals for the release of Rebiya Kadeer, an imprisoned businesswoman in Xinjiang, were not.

Admiral Joseph Prueher, who was posted to China as the U.S. ambassador in November 1999, made his first visit to Tibet in August. He pressed for access to the Panchen Lama and the release of Tibetan prisoners, including Nwagang Choepel. China refused to allow either the State Department's special coordinator on Tibet, Julia Taft, or members of the Commission on International Religious Freedom, to visit China.

Pacific Rim Countries

Canada again refused appeals from Canadian NGOs to cosponsor the Geneva resolution, concentrating instead on Canada's bilateral dialogue process. Dialogue meetings took place in Beijing in November 1999 and in Ottawa from October 10-13.

Australia also declined to take action in Geneva and held the fourth session in its dialogue talks with China in Australia from August 14-17. Its officials raised the repression of Falun Gong, Tibet, and political dissidents, and China in turn protested Australia's treatment of aboriginals. No concrete results from the dialogue were announced; an expanded joint program of human rights "cooperation" was unveiled that included plans for officials of China's Ministry of Public Security to visit Australia to design a training project for Chinese police.

Japan vigorously supported China's admission to the WTO and in its bilateral relations with Beijing focused on China's increased military spending. There was no linkage between aid and China's worsening human rights record. A third Sino-Japanese human rights dialogue took place in Tokyo on January 13 with another session was set for December in Beijing. The meetings had no concrete results. Japan refused to cosponsor the Geneva resolution.

In April, the Dalai Lama was given a visa to travel to Japan despite protests from Beijing. China was also angered by Japan's decision to oppose World Bank funding for the Qinghai poverty reduction project in Tibet. As of mid-October 2000, the South Korean government continued to indicate it would not permit a visit by the Dalai Lama in November because the timing was too close to a planned visit by the Chinese premier.

World Bank

In fiscal year 2000, China received $1.67 billion in loans from the World Bank, bringing cumulative lending to China to almost $35 billion as of June 30, 2000. Intense debate continued through much of the year over a controversial $160 million poverty reduction project in Qinghai. A part of the project, set to receive $40 million in World Bank funds, involved the resettlement of some 58,000 predominantly non-Tibetan farmers into a traditionally Tibetan area. Though the project had been approved by the bank's board in 1999, a final decision was delayed pending receipt of an independent panel's report that proved highly critical. Attempts by World Bank managers to hold open the project for further reassessment and redesign failed in early July when key board members, including European governments, the U.S., and Japan, opposed China's request to go ahead with the loan. Beijing said it would implement the Qinghai project without World Bank funding.

The World Bank put a priority on fighting corruption but declined to intervene in the case of An Jun, head of an anti-corruption group convicted of subversion.

Relevant Human Rights Watch Reports:

Nipped in the Bud: The Suppression of the China Democracy Movement, 9/00
Tibet Since 1950: Silence Prison or Exile, 5/00

EAST TIMOR

East Timor's first year of freedom from Indonesia was largely devoted to recovery and reconstruction from the September 1999 violence that left the entire country a charred ruin. As they rebuilt, East Timorese and the U.N. Transitional Administration in East Timor (UNTAET) had to decide on how to handle past abuses, how to prevent new ones, and how to build basic institutions to ensure the protection of human rights. Progress was slow, particularly in bringing the perpetrators of the 1999 crimes to justice. By October, however, a new court system and police force were in place, two daily newspapers were circulating, NGOs were flourishing, and intense discussions on the country's future constitution were taking place.

The new East Timor was not free of human rights violations. Many East Timorese returning from West Timor were abused for alleged militia links by local officials of the National Council of East Timorese Resistance (CNRT), UNTAET's governing partner, and by members of the former guerrilla army, Falintil; several returnees were killed. U.N. police lacked the capacity and often the will to prevent such abuse. Members of the country's Muslim, Protestant, and ethnic Chinese minorities found themselves persecuted because of suspected ties to the Indonesian power structure. CNRT leaders were not always tolerant of political organizations with viewpoints different from their own.

Human Rights Developments

On October 19, the Indonesian People's Consultative Assembly voted to accept the results of the August 30 referendum in which close to 80 percent of East Timor's population had voted to separate from Indonesia. On October 22, Xanana Gusmao, for seven years a political prisoner in Jakarta, returned to Dili as president of the CNRT. UNTAET came into being through Security Council Resolution 1272 of October 25, 1999. East Timor became, for all intents and purposes, a U.N. protectorate governed by a special representative of the secretary-general with close to absolute powers. The first regulation adopted by the new administration noted that anyone holding public office or engaged in public duties in East Timor would be obliged to observe human rights standards embodied in a list of international treaties. (At its inception in 1998, the CNRT committed itself to upholding the same standards in its "Magna Carta of Freedoms, Rights and Duties for the People of East Timor.")

UNTAET had to create basic institutions from scratch. The first East Timorese judges, prosecutors, and public defenders were installed on January 7, 2000 but the court building, destroyed by the militias, was not ready until March. At one point, UNTAET's own police stopped making any arrests of suspected criminals, including those involved in the 1999 violence, because it had no place to put them; the one detention center in the entire country, a former Ministry of Tourism building, had long since exceeded capacity, and the main prison in the capital, Dili, was only rehabilitated in May. The police academy started training its first East Timorese recruits in late March.

As in many other peacekeeping missions, UNTAET's civilian police (civpol) were a major problem. Recruitment was agonizingly slow, and the overall quality of those recruited was low. Most civpols were recruited for three-month tours of duty, hardly enough time to understand the place or the people. Almost none spoke a language intelligible to the East Timorese, and interpreters were scarce, leading to a reliance on informal security forces set up by the CNRT, whose activities civpol had almost no capacity to monitor or control.

Because almost all of East Timor's law-yers had been trained in Indonesian universities, UNTAET decided in November 1999 that Indonesian law would be the applicable law except where it conflicted with international standards. It took until September, however, to come up with an acceptable provisional criminal procedure code. UNTAET police from close to fifty countries had little guidance in criminal procedure in the intervening months and often operated according to the procedures they knew from home.

The process of investigating crimes against humanity in East Timor was slowed by some of the same problems of lack of institutional infrastructure, untrained civpols, and bureaucratic divisions within UNTAET. As early as December 1999, UNTAET decided that an international panel of the Dili district court would be set up to investigate international crimes, such as crimes against humanity, and all serious offenses, such as murder and rape, that occurred from January 1, 1999 through October 25, 1999.

None of the civpol who were legally empowered to investigate the 1999 crimes, however, received any training in investigating crimes against humanity until late June. Most civpol treated each case as a routine homicide investigation, with no attention to the role of the Indonesian state or to the links among the different crimes. The short tours of duty meant that every new investigator coming in tended to start the questioning of witnesses from scratch.

Authority for investigations changed repeatedly. In late November 1999, a special five-member commission appointed by U.N. High Commissioner for Human Rights Mary Robinson arrived in Dili to hear testimony from over one hundred eyewitnesses to murder, rape, and arson. Known as the International Commission of Inquiry on East Timor (ICIET), the group issued a report on January 31, 2000, recommending, among other things, that an international tribunal be set up to prosecute those responsible for the abuses. In his letter forwarding the report to the Security Council, Secretary-General Kofi Annan did not endorse the recommendation for a separate tribunal, stressing that full cooperation should be given to Indonesian efforts to investigate the crimes, but recommended that UNTAET capacity for coordinating investigations be strengthened.

From November to late March, civpol alone had full authority for investigations. Its investigation unit, however, was responsible not just for investigating the 1999 violence but for all ongoing crimes as well. As law and order concerns in East Timor increased, attention to the 1999 crimes was often diverted. On March 22, a war crimes/human rights investigations unit was set up within civpol to be headed by an investigator from the Office of Human Rights Affairs. The change was only on paper; the new unit had no investigators other than civpol. In early June, a prosecution service was set up under UNTAET's judicial affairs department, separate both from civpol and from the Office of Human Rights Affairs (OHRA). On July 20, 2000, UNTAET formally shifted from its original peacekeeping structure to a coalition government with the CNRT. Among the eight "ministries" created was a Ministry of Judicial Affairs to which the investigation unit was formally moved in August.

In the meantime, six different agencies concerned with accountability for the 1999 crimes—judicial affairs, human rights, political affairs, legal affairs, civpol, and the East Timorese courts—went ahead with their efforts, sometimes tripping over each other in the process. East Timorese witnesses to these crimes grew resentful over repeated questioning without any obvious progress in bringing the perpetrators to justice.

If investigations into killings were slow, they were close to non-existent in rape cases. Serious investigations into rape as an element of crimes against humanity only began in July; before then only two rape cases from 1999 were under active investigation. One factor was the lack of women investigators. Less than 4 percent of the civpol force overall was female, and of the handful of women investigators, only one had special training in investigating sexual crimes.

Throughout the year, the relationship with the Indonesian investigation into crimes in East Timor remained delicate. The Indonesian Commission of Inquiry into Human Rights Violations in East Timor (KPP-HAM) visited Dili in December and January; the defense team for Indonesian army officers considered possible suspects in the violence came to East Timor on January 20. On January 31, KPP-HAM issued a thorough and professional report timed to coincide with release of the ICIET report.

The quality of the KPP-HAM report served to give the Indonesian effort more credibility than it otherwise might have had, but it also put pressure on the Indonesian Attorney General's Office to come up with indictments. To get those indictments, the attorney general needed UNTAET's help; his office had almost no evidence that would stand up in court. UNTAET, for its part, recognized that those most responsible for the 1999 violence were all in Indonesia. If UNTAET was fully cooperative with the Indonesian process, not only might the interests of justice be better served, but the Attorney General's Office also would have no excuse for not proceeding with prosecutions.

Accordingly, on April 6, UNTAET and the Indonesian government signed a Memorandum of Understanding that would facilitate the exchange of evidentiary materials and enable one country to request the other to question witnesses, make arrests, or "transfer" suspects as necessary. Indonesia made its first formal request under the M.O.U. on May 15 for assistance in five cases; it sent a team of seventeen investigators to pursue that request in July. As of August, UNTAET had made no requests of its own.

In mid-May, Xanana Gusmao, president of the CNRT, announced the establishment of a National Return and Reconciliation Commission. Plans for the commission were further developed in June, and by August, a coordinating committee led by UNTAET was considering a plan that would allow perpetrators of lesser offenses, such as arson or looting, to make a full confession of their misdeeds before the commission. Traditional justice mechanisms at the local level would then assign the perpetrator to some form of community service, but the misdeeds, the confession, and the "sentence" would be registered with the formal court system.

The focus on the 1999 violence tended to obscure ongoing violations. Violence against East Timorese returning from West Timor was a serious problem, although the vast majority of the more than 170,000 who had returned by September 2000 did so safely. Those linked, or suspected of having links, to militia groups or to the Indonesian army sometimes faced mob violence, particularly in late 1999 and early 2000 when the two major agencies involved in facilitating returns, the U.N. High Commissioner for Refugees (UNHCR) and the International Office on Migration (IOM), gave local communities little warning of planned returns.

In some cases, civpols working outside the capital ceded authority to CNRT or to the former guerrilla army, Falintil, to screen returnees and question them about past militia affiliations. In early February, a returning militia member was beaten and stabbed by members of an "investigation unit" of the CNRT in Liquica, a town near Dili. In the town of Tibar, even nearer to Dili, a suspected militia member was kicked to death in April after having been held for five days in an illegal detention facility. In the latter two cases, UNTAET civpols took the suspected perpetrators into custody, but the screening process was allowed to continue. In Aileu, the town in the interior chosen as the country's future capital by Xanana Gusmao, where Falintil guerrillas were stationed, Falintil ran detention and "reeducation" centers without serious interference from UNTAET.

Local CNRT leaders were also responsible for intimidation and harassment of minorities. Some 265 Indonesian Muslims remained virtually under siege in the Dili mosque to which they had fled in September 1999. Most had been long-term residents of Dili. Congregations of the Assembly of God Protestant church in the districts of Ermera and Aileu came under attack, most seriously on June 9 when three churches were burned. The pastors were accused of having links in 1999 to an Aileu-based militia. Indonesian businesspeople of ethnic Chinese background faced threats and extortion from gangs apparently under the control of CNRT leaders. The threats became particularly pronounced after a riot in the Dili sports stadium on April 30 in which two businessmen were accused of financially backing a group seen as opposed to the CNRT. No evidence to that effect was ever produced. East Timorese ethnic Chinese were also forced to pay protection money to gangs linked to local leaders.

Defending Human Rights

East Timor's beleaguered human rights community expanded in size and influence during the year. Organizations such as Yayasan HAK, a legal aid and human rights organization; the Sahe Institute, an independent think tank; Fokupers, a women's rights organization; and the Student Solidarity Council led the way in human rights training, discussions on constitutional development, and advocacy of greater participation in UNTAET decision-making. New professional associations like the East Timorese Jurists Association and the East Timorese Journalists Association helped generate discussion on how to protect and promote human rights.

On July 25, a workshop on human rights sponsored by UNTAET's Office of Human Rights Affairs together with the East Timorese Jurists Association secured a commitment from different political organizations to uphold political and economic rights in East Timor as the country moved toward independence. U.N. High Commissioner on Human Rights Mary Robinson gave the keynote address at the workshop.

The Role of the International Community

The international community wholeheartedly supported the reconstruction of East Timor, with U.S. $522 million pledged at a December 1999 donor conference in Tokyo, jointly chaired by UNTAET and the World Bank. Japan, the E.U., Australia, Portugal, and the U.S. all made significant contributions. At a follow-up conference in Lisbon in June 2000, donors agreed to cover the U.S. $16 million shortfall between expenses and revenue in East Timor's first-ever national budget. East Timorese leaders saw the aid less as overwhelming generosity than as an appropriate response from the countries that had long supported the former Soeharto government in Indonesia. Many bilateral and multilateral donors saw the reconstruction effort as an opportunity to help lay the foundations for a democratic society; they funded NGOs and local professional associations as well as UNTAET. Some donors earmarked funds specifically for human rights and justice projects: Britain helped with forensic equipment, Canada with forensic investigators, the U.S. with initial efforts toward a truth and reconciliation commission, Norway with criminal investigations, and so on. Australia played a particularly important role as the new state's nearest and largest neighbor.

The killings of two UNTAET soldiers in August and of three UNHCR workers in West Timor on September 6 sparked international outrage and demands for disarming and prosecuting the militias.

United Nations

U.N. Secretary-General Kofi Annan and the U.N. Security Council were supportive of UNTAET throughout the year. Annan was warmly received during his visit to East Timor in February, and he underscored his commitment to seeking justice for the 1999 violence. Security Council Resolution 1319, adopted on September 8, called the killings of aid workers in West Timor "outrageous and contemptible," demanded that Indonesia disarm and disband the militias, stressed that those responsible should be brought to justice, and called on UNTAET to "respond robustly" to the militia threat.

In early November 1999, the special rapporteurs on violence against women; torture; and extrajudicial, summary or arbitrary executions visited East Timor. Their report, released in December, linked grave human rights abuses, including murder and rape, to the Indonesian army and the militias it created. In November, the Office of the High Commissioner for Human Rights coordinated the visit of the five ICIET commissioners.

The UNICEF office in Dili took a lead role in addressing children's rights issues. Its main concern in this regard was the problem of children separated from their parents during the conflict; reports of hundreds of East Timorese children taken to Java in late 1999 were still being investigated as this report went to press. UNICEF also took a strong interest in juvenile detention and worked for regulations on adoptions by foreigners of East Timorese children.

UNHCR had a large office in Dili and together with the IOM had supervised the return of more than 170,000 East Timorese by September 2000. While heavily criticized in the first few months for failing to take adequate precautions to protect returnees who might be accused of militia connections, UNHCR's preparations improved as the year progressed.

International Financial Institutions

From its Joint Assessment Mission of October 1999 onward, the World Bank played a critical and positive role in East Timor. The bank was instrumental in securing commitments from donors at the Tokyo and Lisbon conferences and worked intensively with CRNT leaders to hammer out a budget that reflected CNRT priorities. The World Bank became the unlikely champion of village-level democracy through its Community Empowerment Project in which local councils, each composed equally of men and women, were elected to decide on distribution of development funds at the village, district, and subdistrict levels.

Australia

Australia played a decisive role in assisting East Timor. Australia assumed a critical leadership position in September 1999 in assembling the International Forces for East Timor (Interfet) under General Peter Cosgrove, and continued to play a leading part within UNTAET peacekeeping operations. Darwin, Australia was part of the mission area for UNTAET, and for many months was the only direct air link between East Timor and the rest of the world. It was from Darwin that most supplies were brought into East Timor, and Darwin provided training facilities for civilian police and other parts of UNTAET. The Australian government seconded hundreds of personnel to work in virtually every field of development, including democratization, and arranged for the design and construction of East Timor's first parliament building.

The government took a strong interest in the investigations into the 1999 violence. In mid-2000, it quietly turned over to the Indonesian Attorney General's Office all files on investigations conducted by Interfet into militia crimes, with witnesses names removed.

United States

The key contributors for the U.S. on East Timor were the State Department, including ambassadors to the U.N. and Jakarta, Congress, and President Clinton. In November, U.N. Secretary Richard Holbrooke and Stanley Roth, Assistant Secretary of State for East Asian and Pacific Affairs, made a highly publicized visit to the refugee camps in West Timor and pressed for an agreement between UNTAET and Indonesia on the repatriation of refugees. Holbrooke throughout the year raised the need to disarm and control the militias and end cross-border incursions. He was a major force behind Security Council Resolution 1319.

The State Department's Bureau of Democracy, Human Rights, and Labor, and Ambassador Robert Gelbard in Jakarta, provided strong support for investigations in Jakarta and Dili into the East Timor violence, securing funds from Congress to support the prosecution efforts in both capitals and to help with training of East Timorese police and the establishment of a criminal justice system.

In May, some members of Congress introduced language into the foreign aid bill for fiscal year 2001 forbidding direct U.S. military sales to or training programs for the Indonesian military until East Timorese were repatriated from West Timor and militia attacks against East Timor had ended. The bill was still pending in October. In September, a bill was introduced that would enable the U.S. to increase support for activities in East Timor as the country moved toward independence, including support for human rights, the rule of law, and reconciliation processes. Congress had not acted on it before adjourning in October.

European Union

At the December 1999 international donors' meeting, the European Commission pledged 60 million euros over a three-year period for East Timor's reconstruction. Also in December, the European Parliament voted to extend the arms embargo against Indonesia imposed on September 16, 1999 after the post-referendum violence. On January 17, 2000, the embargo expired without debate. The United Kingdom quickly resumed sales of Hawk jet fighters to Indonesia. All member states, however, remained individually bound by the European Union's (E.U.) Code of Conduct regarding arms exports. The E.U., with Portugal holding the Presidency from January 1 through June 30, 2000, followed closely the investigations into the 1999 violence and the situation of East Timorese refugees in West Timor. The E.U. repeatedly expressed concern about Indonesia's failure to disarm the militias, including in a Presidency statement on September 7, following the killing of humanitarian workers in West Timor.

Southeast Asia

The Philippines and Thailand supplied successive commanders of the UNTAET peacekeeping forces, and Southeast Asian countries were well represented both in those forces and in the civilian police.

Indonesian President Abdurrahman Wahid was given an enthusiastic reception by a crowd of thousands when he visited Dili on February 29. He appeared generally committed to normalization of relations with East Timor, but many members of his administration, particularly Foreign Ministry officials who had served in previous administrations, were willing to make few concessions to the normalization process.

The Association of Southeast Asian Nations, ASEAN, invited Xanana Gusmao and Jose Ramos Horta to attend its annual summit meeting in Bangkok in July.

Relevant Human Rights Watch Reports:
Forced Expulsions to West Timor and the Refugee Crisis, 11/99

INDIA

The Hindu nationalist policies espoused by India's governing Bharatiya Janata Party (BJP) and its affiliate organizations undermined the country's historical commitment to secular democracy. Violence against Christian, Muslim, and Dalit, or "untouchable," populations was one result. Areas of separatist violence such as Kashmir and northeast India were marked by grave human rights abuses on the part of Indian security forces and armed rebel groups. Violence against women continued, from infanticide to dowry-related deaths to attacks on women whose male relatives were sought by the police. A major campaign on Dalit rights gathered strength, but some human rights defenders were targets of a state-sponsored backlash against their activism.

Human Rights Developments
Abuses by all parties to the conflict were a critical factor behind the fighting in Kashmir. Emboldened by the successful hijacking of an Indian Airlines plane in December 1999 that secured the release of three jailed associates, pro-independence guerrillas or "militants" in the region stepped up their attacks on civilians, as well as on camps and barracks of government forces. The Indian army, operating under the Jammu and Kashmir Disturbed Areas Act and the Armed Forces (Jammu and Kashmir) Special Powers Act, continued to conduct cordon-and-search operations in Muslim neighborhoods and villages, detaining young men, assaulting other family members, and summarily executing suspected militants. Many Kashmiri civilians were killed or injured as a result of being caught in a crossfire between soldiers and militants, or in skirmishes and shelling between Indian and Pakistani troops across their countries' common border, known as the Line of Control.

In January, the Indian army, after its own investigation, announced that fifty-six of its personnel in Kashmir would be punished for committing human rights violations. The punishments ranged from discharge to denial of promotion. National and state human rights commissions, however, were barred from investigating army and paramilitary personnel.

On March 20, just before U.S. President Clinton's visit to South Asia, thirty-six Sikh men were shot dead in Chithisinghpora, Anantnag district, by unidentified gunmen reportedly dressed in army uniforms. In the weeks that followed, Sikh residents took to the streets demanding protection, while hundreds of Muslim villagers staged protests against Indian security forces. They alleged that in the aftermath of the Sikh massacre, blamed by the army on militants, many Muslim civilians had been "disappeared" or killed.

In early April, at least seven people were killed when police opened fire on Muslim protestors demanding the exhumation of the bodies of five men killed by members of the Indian army's Special Operations Group in Anantnag district. The protestors claimed that the men had been detained in the aftermath of the Chithisinghpora massacre and killed in a "staged" encounter. On April 6, the charred and disfigured bodies were exhumed. DNA tests were performed to confirm their identities, but as of this writing, the government had not released the results.

On June 26, the Jammu-Kashmir state assembly approved a controversial autonomy plan that was subsequently rejected by the Indian federal cabinet. On July 24, the Hizb-ul-Mujahideen, Kashmir's largest armed guerilla group, declared a unilateral ceasefire and announced its willingness to enter into negotiations with Indian authorities. On July 29, India suspended its offensive against the group, but hopes of a peaceful resolution to the conflict were dashed by a series of massacres on August 1 and 2 that left ninety Hindu pilgrims dead in Pahalgam, in the Kashmir valley. The massacres were believed to have been carried out by militant factions opposed to the ceasefire, but reports suggested that some of the victims were killed by fire from Indian security forces. On August 8, Hizb-ul-Mujahideen called off the ceasefire, citing the Indian government's refusal to include Pakistan in three-way peace talks. Indian Home Minister L.K. Advani on August 22 rejected calls for an immediate judicial inquiry into the Pahalgam massacre.

Militants were believed responsible for several attacks against Hindus, who form a minority in the state. On August 19, a group of men carrying assault rifles entered two houses in the village of Ind, Udhampur district, and opened fire on the occupants, killing four. Two nights earlier, another group of gunmen had raided several Hindu homes in the village of Kot Dara, killing six. Some of those killed in the Kot Dara attack were reported to have been members of the local Village Defense Committee (VDC), established by the state government in the hill districts ostensibly to protect all of the region's inhabitants. The VDCs recruited their members almost exclusively from local Hindu communities, however, and were seen by militants as adjuncts of the Indian security forces.

Caste violence continued to divide the impoverished state of Bihar. There, the Ranvir Sena, a banned private militia of upper-caste landlords that had been operating with impunity since 1994, waged war on various Maoist guerrilla factions, such as the People's War Group (PWG). These guerrilla groups advocated higher wages and more equitable land distribution for lower-caste laborers. The cycle of retaliatory attacks claimed many civilian lives.

On April 25, upper-caste Rajputs shot and killed four Dalits and seriously injured three in Rohtas district, Bihar. Rajputs subsequently burned down the entire Dalit hamlet, leaving all twenty-five families homeless. The attack was reportedly in retaliation for the killing of two Rajputs a few days earlier by members of the outlawed PWG. On June 16, in Miapur village in Bihar's Aurangabad district, the Ranvir Sena slaughtered thirty-four lower-caste men, women, and children. Survivors reported that police left the scene when the attacking mob entered the village. The massacre was reportedly to avenge the killings by Maoist guerrillas of twelve upper-caste Bhumihars the week before, and thirty-four Bhumihars in March 1999. Some Ranvir Sena members were arrested in the weeks that followed, but there was no precedent for successful prosecutions in such cases.

Police blamed the July 13 killings of four upper-caste Hindus in Garwah district on the PWG. On September 13 the Maoist Communist Centre, another armed group, slit nine people's throats in Ranchi district. The victims included Muslims and tribespeople.

Bihar was not the only state affected by caste violence. On March 12, seven members of a Dalit family were burned alive in their homes by an upper-caste mob in Kolar district, Karnataka state. The attack was preceded by the stabbing of an upper-caste man in a nearby village. Although police were aware of escalating tensions in the area, they failed to take preventive action.

Attacks against Christians, which have increased significantly since the BJP came to power in March 1998, continued. By midyear over thirty-five anti-Christian attacks had been reported throughout the country, with the states of Gujarat and Uttar Pradesh—both BJP-led—particularly hard hit.

Activists belonging to militant Hindu extremist groups such as the Bajrang Dal and the Vishwa Hindu Parishad (World Hindu Council, VHP) were often blamed for the violence. Both groups are members of the *sangh parivar*, an umbrella Hindu organization that boasts the ruling BJP as its political wing. These Hindu groups blamed the violence on popular anger over Christian efforts to convert Hindus. While government officials at the state and central level condemned the attacks, they did little to prosecute those responsible.

On January 31 a year-long manhunt came to an end with the arrest in Orissa of Bajrang Dal activist Dara Singh. Singh was wanted in connection with several murders, including those of Australian missionary Graham Stuart Staines and his two sons in 1999. Christian relief at the arrest was tempered, however, by a state government order, believed to be aimed at limiting the activities of Christian missionaries, requiring a police inquiry before anyone adopted a new faith.

The state governments of Gujarat and Uttar Pradesh lifted a ban against civil servants joining the Rashtriya Swayamsevak Sangh (National Volunteer Corps, RSS), a sangh parivar member. In Gujarat, Delhi, and Orissa, district administrations conducted surveys to assess the activities and whereabouts of minority community members and leaders. Meanwhile, the BJP and its allies continued to implement their agenda for the "Hinduization" of education, mandating Hindu prayers in certain state-sponsored schools and revising history books to include what amounted to propaganda against Islamic and Christian communities.

On April 11, three Christian missionary schools were ransacked and six people beaten in related attacks by the Bajrang Dal in Mathura, in BJP-led Uttar Pradesh. The group sought to justify its actions by calling the schools "machines for conversion." On April 21, a group of Christians was attacked near the city of Agra. These attacks followed the beating to death of two tribal Christians in Hazaribagh, and an attack on two nuns and a priest in Mathura.

On June 7, a Catholic priest was battered to death while sleeping outside his school in Uttar Pradesh. Government officials were quick to rule out any religious motive, attributing it to burglary. Within days the sole witness to the attack, Vijay Ekka, died in police custody. Ekka had told parishioners who visited him in detention that he was being tortured by the police and that he feared for his life. Two policemen were arrested and a

magisterial probe was ordered after a Christian organization filed a complaint.

In May, the National Commission for Minorities (NCM), a government agency, issued a report stating that attacks against Christians were either accidental or the unrelated actions of petty criminals. Outraged Christian activists said the report showed that the government condoned attacks on Christians. Earlier reports by the NCM, issued before it was overhauled by the central government in January, had recommended prosecutions for such attacks and accused the government of willful neglect at all levels.

In June, a series of blasts damaged Christian churches in Karnataka, Andhra Pradesh, and Goa. A month later, crude bombs were set off in two more churches in Karnataka. In August, police charged members of a Muslim sect, allegedly based in Pakistan, with masterminding the attacks. Human rights activists maintained that the arrests were meant to deflect attention from Hindu hardliners' campaign of anti-Christian violence.

On July 14, the Maharashtra state government announced its intention to prosecute Bal Thackeray, leader of the right-wing Hindu organization Shiv Sena, for his role in inciting Bombay's 1992-1993 riots in which over 700 people, the vast majority of them Muslims, were killed. The decision to prosecute came two years after a government-appointed judicial commission had named Thackeray as one of those responsible for the violence. On July 25, amid rioting by Shiv Sena supporters, Thackeray was arrested only to be released a few hours later after a judge ordered the case closed on the grounds that the statute of limitations relating to the incitement charges had expired.

Violence in the northeastern states, particularly Assam, continued throughout the year, claiming many civilian casualties. Members of the United Liberation Front of Assam (ULFA), a militant group seeking Assam's independence from India, repeatedly clashed with the police and with surrendered ULFA members working with the government, known as "SULFA." The Bodo Liberation Tigers (BLT) fighting for a separate homeland for the Bodo tribal people extended their ceasefire by one year beginning September 15.

In April, the Law Commission of India recommended the introduction of the Prevention of Terrorism Bill into parliament. If enacted, the bill would reinstate a modified version of the notorious Terrorist and Disruptive Activities (Prevention) Act (TADA), repealed in 1995. TADA had facilitated tens of thousands of unjustified arrests, torture, and other violations against political opponents, social activists, and human rights defenders. Human rights organizations protested against the bill arguing that, if enacted, it would have similar effects.

In a positive move, the law commission also called for sweeping changes to the country's rape laws following an increase in the incidence of sexual violence. Women's rights activists welcomed this recommendation. Female infanticide persisted as the female to male ratio continued to drop—a reflection of the lower status of women and girls, who were more likely to be deprived of food, education, or health services, or to be seen as an economic liability under the dowry system.

Women whose relatives were sought by the police continued to be detained. In February, in Tamil Nadu, twelve women were illegally detained and tortured and repeatedly sexually assaulted in custody because of their ties to a suspected robber who had himself died in police custody. The National Human Rights Commission, a government-appointed body, also took particular note of alarming numbers of deaths in police custody.

Police brutality against Muslim students of the Jamia Millia Islamia, an institution of higher education in Delhi, made national headlines. On April 9, while searching for two criminal suspects, hundreds of police broke into one of the institution's dormitories and physically assaulted Muslim students, destroyed their property, and vandalized the campus mosque.

Two days earlier, members of the State Reserve Police beat and arrested up to forty-six demonstrators following a protest against the proposed Maroli-Umbergaon Port Project in Gujarat. While all were released on bail within forty-eight hours, six of the protesters were beaten in custody by police. One, Col. (retired) Pratap Save, suffered a brain hemorrhage, went into a coma, and died from his injuries on April 20.

In June, the Indian navy alerted Sri Lankan authorities to the presence of forty-seven Sri Lankan refugees who had become stranded on an island between the two countries while fleeing to India. A Sri Lankan naval vessel then picked them up and took them back to Sri Lanka. In August, Indian authorities in Mizoram state forcibly repatriated over one hundred ethnic minority Chin refugees who had fled from Burma.

Defending Human Rights

Many human rights defenders were physically attacked, while others were labeled threats to national security. On December 9, 1999, six armed men entered the office of the Save the Narmada River Movement (Narmada Bachao Andolan, NBA) in Baroda, Gujarat, assaulted an activist, and vandalized the office. They warned the activist that the NBA, which had been campaigning against big dam projects along the Narmada river, would face dire consequences if it did not leave the state. When the NBA organized a march in Khargone district, Madhya Pradesh, in January, over 500 protestors were arrested for demonstrating in defiance of the local authorities' orders. Among them was prominent author and activist Arundhati Roy. All were released the following day. On October 18, in a major setback to the fifteen-year old anti-dam campaign, the Supreme Court ruled that construction on the controversial Sardar Sarovar dam along the Narmada river could continue. Large-scale protests followed the decision which activists criticized as sanctioning the continued displacement of hundreds of thousands of villagers.

On April 20, a mob of local residents and politicians raided the Almora and Jageswar offices of SAHAYOG, a NGO working primarily on women's health and empowerment in Uttar Pradesh. The attack was in response to a pamphlet SAHAYOG had published in September 1999 on HIV transmission, which made reference to a specific sexual practice of the area. By day's end eleven staff members and trainees had been arrested; some were physically assaulted by the police and protestors. Six were charged with the "production and distribution of obscene literature to under-age persons," and "inciting Army/Airforce to violence/mutiny." The remaining five were charged with disturbing the public peace. Five of the eleven were released within days and on April 24, after their offices had been closed and bank accounts frozen by order of the district magistrate, SAHAYOG was made to issue an unconditional public apology for hurting public sentiments with their study. On May 10, the National Security Act was invoked against four staff members, but later revoked after much public protest. On May 29, the remaining six detainees were released on bail after spending forty days in jail. As of this writing, the charges against SAHAYOG were still pending.

In July, the national convenor of the United Christian Forum for Human Rights, John Dayal, asked for and ultimately received armed protection through the National Human Rights Commission after numerous threats to his life. He was publicly accused by a member of India's National Commission on Minorities of engaging in "anti-national activities," and threatened with treason charges by a spokesperson for the BJP.

On the eve of Human Rights Day 1999, the National Campaign for Dalit Human Rights presented Prime Minister A.B. Vajpayee with a petition bearing 2.5 million signatures. Collected from across the country, the petition demanded the abolition of untouchability and full implementation of national legislation criminalizing abuses against Dalits. On April 18 and 19, the campaign held a "national public hearing" in Chennai to "try" fifty-eight cases of atrocities against Dalits, selected from over a dozen states. A jury of three former high court judges and several senior lawyers issued a statement condemning India's caste system as "hidden apartheid."

The Role of the International Community

Once again the conflict in Kashmir featured prominently in India's dealings with the international community. While many governments pushed for a peaceful resolution to the crisis, India maintained that no talks would be possible until Pakistan ended its support of militant groups in the region.

United Nations

In January, during its review of India's initial report under the Convention on the Rights of the Child, the Committee on the Rights of the Child concluded that the caste system was an obstacle to children's human rights. The Committee also expressed concern about India's juvenile justice system, prison conditions, and the use of the death penalty against juvenile offenders.

The Committee on the Elimination of Discrimination against Women also raised concerns about the caste system during its February review of India's initial report under the Convention on the Elimination of All Forms of Discrimination against Women. The Committee expressed concern over extreme forms of physical and sexual violence against women belonging to particular castes or ethnic or religious groups, and over customary practices such as dowry, *sati*, and the *devadasi* system, all of which contribute to a higher incidence of gender-based violence in the country.

In March, Secretary-General Kofi Annan expressed his outrage over the Chithisinghpora massacre and urged both Pakistan and India to find an immediate "political solution to this long-standing dispute." On August 2, he reiterated this plea after the killings of over ninety Hindu pilgrims. In August, in response to a NGO briefing organized by the International Dalit Solidarity Network—of which Human Rights Watch is a member—the U.N. Sub-Commission on the Promotion and Protection of Human Rights passed without a vote a resolution on "discrimination on the basis of work and descent." The resolution was aimed at addressing the plight of Dalits. The Committee on the Elimination of Racial Discrimination considered the term "descent" to encompass caste.

United States

Buoyed by President Clinton's visit to India in March, the first of a U.S. president in over twenty years, Indo-U.S. relations improved markedly. While the massacre of Sikhs on the eve of Clinton's visit forced Kashmir to the forefront of discussions, the trip was notable for its lack of attention to rights issues.

In September the U.S. Department of State released its second annual report under the 1998 International Religious Freedom Act detailing attacks on religious minorities throughout India and many other countries. The State Department indicated that India was close to earning the dubious distinction of "Country of Particular Concern" because of the many attacks on religious freedom during the year. Later that month, the U.S. Commission on International Religious Freedom held public hearings on religious persecution in India and Pakistan. The hearings were followed by a visit to India in November by members of the commission.

Japan

During his South Asia tour in late August, Japanese Prime Minister Yoshiro Mori urged a resumption of talks on Kashmir and condemned violent attacks on civilians caught in the conflict. Despite Japan's suspension of all new grants and loans to both India and Pakistan following their successive nuclear tests in May 1998, Mori announced that U.S. $176 million would be provided for two existing projects in India.

European Union

The European Union (E.U.) condemned the violence in Kashmir and in various public statements called upon both India and Pakistan to resolve the conflict quickly and peacefully. A joint declaration resulting from the first ever E.U.-India summit in June emphasized the importance of coordinating efforts to promote and protect human rights. Both sides pledged to work towards the universal ratification and implementation of all major international human rights instruments. Echoing last year's initiatives, the European Parliament also pressed India to foster tolerance and protect freedom of religion; ratify the torture convention; and impose a moratorium on executions and step up efforts to abolish the death penalty.

INDONESIA

Indonesia lurched further toward democracy during the year, but serious regional conflicts, a weak legal system, and delicate civil-military relations posed ongoing obstacles to the protection of human rights. While most of the country continued to benefit from increased civil and political liberties, three areas wracked by conflict—Papua, Aceh, and the Moluccas—continued to experience widespread violations. The government failed adequately to protect the hundreds of thousands of people displaced in Aceh and the Moluccas as well as East Timorese refugees in West Timor. Efforts of human rights defenders and some government officials to hold perpetrators of past serious abuses to account produced some results, but huge obstacles remained to bringing senior culpable leaders to justice.

Human Rights Developments

For the first time in more than four decades, Indonesians had both a freely elected parliament and a democratically chosen president. On October 20, 1999, the People's Consultative Assembly (*Majelis Permusyawaratan Rakyat*, MPR) chose Abdurrahman Wahid as the country's fourth president in a cliffhanger vote. Megawati Soekarnoputri, head of the Indonesian Democratic Struggle Party (Partai Demokrasi Indonesia - Perjuangang, PDIP) became vice-president. The jockeying for power among the most influential parties characterized domestic politics for much of the year, with Wahid struggling to outmaneuver the opposition. In

August, unhappy parliamentarians forced him to issue Presidential Decree 121, turning over some of his administrative tasks to Megawati, but a cabinet reshuffle later the same month showed he was very much in charge. Throughout the year, Wahid proved strong on the symbolism of human rights and weaker on the implementation of safeguards.

From the outset, although he retained several senior military officers as ministers, Wahid began to assert civilian control over the military. He appointed a civilian as defense minister and, in February 2000, removed General Wiranto from his Cabinet pending the outcome of investigations into Wiranto's role in the 1999 East Timor violence. On March 11, President Wahid formally disbanded the hated internal security organization, Bakorstanas. In April, commander-in-chief Admiral Widodo endorsed the concept of civilian supremacy and announced that the military no longer claimed a social and political role. In a number of highly publicized cases, generals who had previously enjoyed absolute impunity were questioned by investigators in connection with past military atrocities. Through its nationwide network of territorial commands, however, the military's dominant role in local government continued and, in August, the MPR approved a decree allowing the armed forces (*Tentara Nasional Indonesia*, TNI) to retain a bloc of appointed seats in that body through 2009.

Regional armed conflicts continued to pose a challenge to the democratic transition and undermine human rights. In Aceh, disaffection with the central government showed itself both in the form of a strong civil society-based movement for a referendum on Aceh's political status and in an armed rebel group, the Free Aceh Movement (*Gerakan Aceh Merdeka*, GAM). Indonesian security forces made little distinction between the two. While army, police, and GAM were all responsible for abuses, including extrajudicial executions of civilians, the violations were disproportionately on the government side. A special government-appointed commission of inquiry into past violations in Aceh produced five priority cases for trial, but not one of them

from the worst period of abuses, 1989 to 1992. On May 17, 2000, twenty-four soldiers and one civilian were sentenced to between eight and a half and ten years in prison for the 1999 massacre of a Muslim teacher, Teungku Bantaqiah, and fifty-six of his followers, but the commander who gave the orders went into hiding as investigations were underway and was not apprehended.

On May 12, the Wahid government, through the intervention of the Henri Dunant Institute in Geneva, signed a Memorandum of Understanding with GAM, agreeing to a three-month "humanitarian pause" in the conflict. The agreement was controversial inside Indonesia, as some saw it as the first step toward legitimizing the rebels. Abuses diminished with the agreement but did not stop. In September, it was extended until January 2001.

On August 5, one of Aceh's most prominent human rights defenders, Jafar Siddiq Hamzah, founder and director of the New York-based rights group International Forum for Aceh, vanished while on a visit to Indonesia's third largest city, Medan. His body, showing signs of torture, was found with four other corpses in an unmarked grave on September 3. Jafar was the third well-known Acehnese activist to have "disappeared" in Medan. On January 24, an Acehnese parliamentarian went missing from his home; his body was found several days later. On June 3, a former student activist and spokesman for GAM, Ismail Syahputra, vanished. No information about his whereabouts had emerged by mid-September. On September 16, Safwan Idris, a prominent university rector in Banda Aceh who had supported a referendum, was shot and killed at his home. While the army was widely blamed in all of the above cases, there was no hard evidence as of October to indicate who was responsible.

A civilian pro-independence movement gathered strength during the year in Papua, formerly Irian Jaya. President Wahid offered the name change on January 1, 2000 to signal a change in policy toward the rebellious province. (The name change had not been approved by parliament by the end of the year.) A month earlier, tens of thousands of Papuans had celebrated the thirty-eighth anniversary of "West Papuan independence" in ceremonies throughout the province, the first time that such coordinated pro-independence demonstrations were permitted. In a compromise with authorities, both the Indonesian and West Papuan flags were raised in the December 1 ceremonies. When demonstrators in Timika, on Papua's south coast, refused to take down a West Papuan flag flying in a church courtyard the day after the ceremonies, however, security forces fired into an angry crowd, wounding sixteen. Tension and conflict over flag raisings continued throughout 2000. Major clashes between civilians and security forces claimed the lives of three pro-independence youths in Nabire in late February and early March. Three more independence supporters were killed by government forces in Sorong on August 22.

On June 3, in Jayapura, the Papuan capital, a National Congress of leaders from throughout the province declared the desire of the Papuan people to separate from Indonesia. Papuan leaders repeatedly expressed their commitment to pursuing independence through peaceful means, but civilian defense "task forces" (*satuan tugas* or *satgas*) grew in size and importance throughout the year. Some such groups received Indonesian military support, leading many to draw parallels with the army-backed militias in East Timor in 1999; other groups were set up by pro-independence Papuans.

The conflict that produced the most civilian casualties, however, was not a rebellion against the center but rather a civil war in the Moluccan islands between Christians and Muslims. Exact figures on casualties were difficult to obtain, let alone verify, but estimates put the toll from October 1999 to September 2000 at over 5,000 dead. The conflict had erupted in 1999 in Ambon, the product of elite rivalries, a delicate communal balance upset by in-migration from other islands, and a changing socioeconomic structure. By 2000, the conflict had spread to the North Moluccan islands of Ternate, Tidore,

and Halmehera, and continued to engulf Ambon, Ceram, Buru, Saparua and other islands of the central Moluccan archipelago.

In May, thousands of volunteers for "holy war forces," or *laskar jihad*, arrived in Ambon from elsewhere in Indonesia, primarily Java, to strengthen the Muslim side, and attacks on Christian villages increased. On June 27, President Wahid ordered a state of civil emergency imposed in the two provinces of Maluku (Ambon and surrounding islands) and Maluku Utara (the North Moluccas). By mid-September, the latter was fairly calm, but there was no end in sight to fighting around Ambon. Civilian and military authorities in Indonesia, sensitive to the loss of East Timor and the nationalist backlash it engendered from a wide range of politically powerful groups, rejected any notion of outside assistance in resolving the conflict. While it appealed for humanitarian aid for the hundreds of thousands of displaced people, it also obstructed delivery of that aid. Groups inside and outside Indonesia also faulted the government for failing to ensure the neutrality of troops sent to stop the fighting and for failing to stop the dispatch of laskar jihad forces, although the police argued that as they were not armed when they boarded passenger ships for Ambon, the government had no legal means of stopping them. Critics also pointed to the ineffective interdiction of weapons bound for Ambon and a failure to protect the rights of the displaced.

Treatment of internally displaced persons (IDPs) was a major issue during the year, with close to 400,000 displaced by the Moluccan conflict alone. The eruption in April of a separate Christian-Muslim conflict in Poso, Central Sulawesi, which had first emerged in a 1998 fight over a local political appointment, left at least 200 dead and an estimated 60,000 people temporarily displaced. In Aceh, the number of persons displaced by the conflict ebbed and flowed, but tens of thousands fled their homes over the course of the year, many in the face of violent police and military "sweeps" for suspected rebels. Thousands of non-Acehnese immigrants fled the province, many after having been threatened by rebels.

More than 170,000 East Timorese returned home from West Timor during the year, but more than 100,000 remained, many having been forcibly expelled during the post-referendum violence in East Timor in September 1999. Many remained under the control of militia leaders whom Indonesian authorities chose not to disarm or in any way challenge. Militia control over the refugee camps of Tuabukan and Noelbaki, outside Kupang, was particularly strong; these camps also housed East Timorese members of the police and army and their families. On August 13, after a series of militia incursions from West Timor into East Timor, the Indonesian government bowed to international pressure and announced that it would close the camps, offering the East Timorese there a choice between resettlement in Indonesia or return to East Timor. The decision was cautiously welcomed by the international community, but nothing happened. The level of militia intimidation in these and other camps was high, directed not just against refugees wishing to return but also against the staff of agencies such as the United Nations High Commissioner for Refugees (UNHCR).

From August 22 to 29, UNHCR temporarily closed down operations in West Timor after three of its staff were injured in an attack. Despite renewed promises from the Indonesian military that it would provide protection, three UNHCR workers were killed on September 6 in an attack by a mob that had gathered for the funeral of a notorious pro-Indonesia militia commander, Olivio Mendonca Moruk. International outrage prompted efforts at disarmament. Military and police organized searches in major camps and confiscated a few dozen firearms and hundreds of homemade guns. Even militia leaders acknowledged that they were retaining weapons, however, and, at this writing, there had been no new arrests on weapons charges or any evidence of a serious effort to identify the source of the large quantities of ammunition used by militias making incursions into East Timor.

Efforts to revamp Indonesia's corrupt and discredited judiciary made slow headway with the selection of sixteen new Supreme Court justices in September, but the administration failed to put forward a plan for systematic overhaul of the courts. Corruption proceedings against former President Soeharto held the spotlight for much of the year until the case was dismissed on September 28 on the grounds that Soeharto was unfit to stand trial. Public demands for justice for past army abuses in Aceh, Papua, Lampung, Tanjung Priok, and East Timor remained strong, but the government dithered in taking the necessary measures for prosecution. To get around the dysfunctional court system, plans were made for new human rights courts to hear cases involving gross abuses, but the enabling legislation was bogged down in parliament for much of the year and had not been passed as of October. In August, the MPR enacted a constitutional amendment, after heavy lobbying by generals, barring "retroactive" laws. As a result, many Indonesian legal scholars concluded that individuals responsible for orchestrating past atrocities could only be charged with ordinary criminal offenses and not with international crimes such as war crimes and crimes against humanity.

On September 1, Indonesian prosecutors formally named nineteen individuals, fifteen of them army and police officers, as suspects in the 1999 East Timor crimes. Although this was a long-overdue first step, advisors to the attorney general said that investigators had not even begun to unearth the kind of evidence needed for chain-of-command convictions. General Wiranto, commander-in-chief of the Indonesian armed forces at the time, was not on the list.

On a morning television show on March 14, President Wahid asked for forgiveness for the 1965-67 massacre of suspected members of the banned Indonesian Communist Party (Partai Komunis Indonesia, PKI), and for the role of his own organization, Nahdlatul Ulama, in the killings. He also called for repeal of a 1966 decree, TAP MPRS No.XXV, that instituted a pattern of discrimination against families of suspected PKI followers down to the third generation. The President's call, however, was greeted with noisy street protests from some Muslim groups and, in August, the MPR set aside the proposal, leaving the 1966 decree in effect.

Defending Human Rights

Human rights groups continued to be at the center of legal reform and justice efforts. Independent human rights lawyers, including Munir of the Commission for Disappeared Persons and Victims of Violence, played a key role in strengthening and professionalizing the work of the investigative team for East Timor put together by the Indonesian National Human Rights Commission (Komnas). On January 31, the Komnas team issued a hard-hitting report on the 1999 violence. Other human rights lawyers, including Ifdhal Kasim of the Institute for Research on Public Adovcacy (Elsam), were actively involved in drafting legislation on human rights courts and the first draft of a bill for a proposed "Truth and Reconciliation Commission." Still others were appointed to a team of experts advising the attorney general on the East Timor prosecutions.

Komnas also monitored the efforts of the attorney general and military courts on other leading human rights cases throughout the year. In June, Komnas was widely criticized for a weak report on 1984 army violence in Tanjung Priok, Jakarta, and for doing little to document ongoing abuses in Aceh and Papua. In October, Komnas issued new report on the Tanjung Priok case, naming twenty-three suspects, reportedly including high-ranking generals.

In Aceh, Papua, and the Moluccas, human rights defenders operated at great risk. The worst conditions were in Aceh, where assassinations were commonplace and perpetrators seldom identified. On January 31, Sukardi, a volunteer with the Bamboo Thicket Institute (Yayasan Rumpun Bambu Indonesia), a local environmental and human rights group based in Aceh, "disappeared"; his naked and bullet-riddled corpse was found on February 1. Dozens of other activists and local humanitarian aid workers were beaten and threatened, apparently because security forces suspected them of supporting the rebels.

The murder of Jafar Siddiq Hamzah, described above, again put a spotlight on the dangers faced by human rights defenders.

The Role of the International Community

In general, the international community was strongly supportive of the Wahid administration but deeply concerned about the regional conflicts, both in terms of the human cost as well as the impact on Indonesia's democratization policies and long-term political stability.

United Nations

Important U.N. concerns in 2000 also included protection of refugees in West Timor, justice for the 1999 scorched earth destruction of East Timor, and efforts to mitigate the impact of continuing economic crisis on Indonesia's poor.

On January 31, 2000, a U.N. commission of inquiry issued a report concluding that the systematic and large-scale nature of the East Timor crimes warranted the establishment of an international criminal tribunal. The U.N. Security Council, however, declined to establish such a court, deferring instead to the Indonesian government's stated intention to bring those responsible to justice. In a cover letter accompanying release of the international commission's report, Secretary-General Kofi Annan announced that he would "closely monitor progress" of the Indonesian effort to ensure that it was a "credible response in accordance with international human rights principles." In early August, U.N. High Commissioner for Human Rights Mary Robinson met with victims of the violence in East Timor as well as with Indonesian Attorney General Marzuki Darusman, reiterating that the U.N. would call for an international war crimes tribunal if Jakarta failed to bring the perpetrators of the Timor violence to trial.

The Security Council and Secretary-General also denounced continuing violence in West Timor. In a February visit to Indonesia, Annan complained to President Wahid about continuing harassment by militias in the refugee camps. After a Nepalese soldier serving with U.N. peacekeepers was shot and killed on August 11 by militias who had crossed the border into East Timor, the second peacekeeper killed in as many months, Annan issued a statement calling on Indonesia to take effective measures to control the militias and stop the incursions. In a unanimous resolution on September 8, the Security Council condemned the murder of the three U.N. refugee workers in West Timor and insisted that the Indonesian government take immediate steps to disarm and disband the militias believed to be responsible.

Asia-Pacific Region

Relations between Indonesia and China warmed following President Wahid's December 1999 visit to Beijing. Despite prior visits to other countries, Wahid called the December trip his first "formal" state visit to highlight the importance of the relationship. Wahid sought and obtained Chinese statements in support of the territorial integrity of Indonesia and against separatist movements in Aceh and Papua. In July, Indonesia lifted onerous visa requirements to make it easier and cheaper for Chinese citizens to visit Indonesia. Also in July, the two countries signed a bilateral agreement promising mutual legal assistance in fighting transnational crime.

Indonesia lobbied successfully to keep any reference to the continued bloodshed in the Moluccas out of the joint communique issued at the end of the annual Association of Southeast Asian Nations (ASEAN) Ministerial Meeting held in Bangkok in July, although instability in Indonesia was discussed by the ministers. Under the leadership of President Wahid, who had requested a meeting with Aung San Suu Kyi during a visit to Myanmar in 1999, Indonesia had been expected to move a step closer toward an ASEAN foreign policy of "flexible engagement," as recommended by Thailand and the Philippines. Instead, its actions hardened ASEAN's existing "non-intervention" policy.

Japan

In its bilateral relations with Indonesia, which received U.S. $1.6 billion in loans and grants in 1999 (latest figures published by the foreign ministry), Japan emphasized support for President Wahid's democratization efforts and for preserving the country's territorial integrity as it addressed regional violence. In April, Japan said it would reschedule $5.8 billion in Indonesian debt. Prime Minister Yoshiro Mori met with Wahid when he came to Tokyo in April and again in early June at the time of former Prime Minister Obuchi's funeral, and urged a constructive solution to regional conflicts. Japan was also considering providing police training to Indonesia. But the foreign ministry was reluctant to raise specific human rights concerns with Jakarta, or to send observers to trials in Aceh, though it did provide assistance for people displaced by the Aceh conflict. On October 18-19, Japan was scheduled to co-host with the World Bank the annual donor consultative conference for Indonesia.

Australia

Relations with Australia continued to be strained by Indonesian anger over Australia's role in East Timor and perceived slights to Jakarta in 1999, notwithstanding strong economic ties. Australia organized and commanded the International Force for East Timor (Interfet) that entered East Timor on September 20, 1999 to put an end to the militia violence. Australian troops were vilified in much of the Indonesian press. Although there were improvements in relations during the year, including increased ministerial contacts initiated by a January 24 meeting in Jakarta of Australian Foreign Minister Alexander Downer and President Wahid, each setback in West Timor reopened the diplomatic rift. A long awaited visit by President Wahid to Canberra was postponed in October when leading Indonesian legislators spoke out against the trip.

European Union

On January 17, the E.U., noting with approval the democratic developments in

Indonesia and the election of President Wahid, decided not to renew the sanctions imposed in September 1999 in the wake of the violence in East Timor, including a ban on arms shipments. The United Kingdom quickly resumed sales of Hawk jet fighters. The E.U. insisted, however, that its policy regarding arms exports would be governed by "strict implementation of the E.U. Code of Conduct" and that the E.U. would continue to monitor closely developments in Indonesia.

On February 2, the European Commission issued an important policy paper, "Developing Closer Relations between Indonesia and the European Union." It signaled the importance of human rights in those relations, calling promotion of those rights a prerequisite for democracy and sustainable development. The paper called for better delivery of justice, support for the Attorney-General's legal reform efforts, regular contacts with human rights organizations, and close cooperation with Indonesia's National Commission on Human Rights. It noted the "slow progress" of refugee repatriation from West Timor and of Indonesia's own investigation into human rights violations in East Timor. The "enhanced" partnership was officially launched on June 14 in a meeting between Indonesian Foreign Minister Alwi Shihab and E.U. foreign ministers. Chris Patten, External Affairs Commissioner, visited Indonesia at the end of May, raising concerns about obstacles to democratization and civilian supremacy; earlier in April, a delegation of members of the European Parliament went to East Timor and Indonesia. The European Parliament adopted a strong resolution on the Moluccas, urging Jakarta to permit international observers and allow NGOs free access. In September, the E.U. presidency issued a statement strongly condemning the deaths of UNHCR workers and continued insecurity in West Timor.

The E.U. consistently declared its support for Indonesian national integrity but urged dialogue as a means of resolving regional conflicts. It formally welcomed the May 12 M.O.U. ceasefire between the Indonesian government and the Free Aceh Movement, but distanced itself from the June 3 call of Papuan leaders for independence. On August 17, ECHO, the humanitarian aid office of the E.U., granted EUR \$2 million to be spent, among other things, aiding displaced persons in the Moluccas and West Timor.

The third biannual Asia-Europe Meeting (ASEM), held in Seoul October 20-21, was dominated by the issue of North Korea, with the United Kingdom and Germany announcing they would establish diplomatic ties with Pyongyang, while France said that progress on human rights and security issues must take place as a precondition for diplomatic relations. The final communique said ASEM III participants would "promote and protect all human rights...and fundamental freedoms," language that was adopted over China's objections.

Five ambassadors representing the E.U. visited Ambon and the north Moluccas in Indonesia from October 12-14 to assess the human rights and humanitarian situation.

United States

U.S. officials repeatedly and publicly expressed support for President Wahid but also spoke out strongly against the failure of the Indonesian military to rein in militias in West Timor and resolve the refugee crisis.

Early in the year, Secretary of State Madeleine Albright identified Indonesia as one of four priority emerging democracies for U.S. foreign policy. President Clinton welcomed Indonesian President Wahid to the White House shortly after Wahid assumed the Presidency, and numerous U.S. officials—including secretaries of treasury, defense, and state, as well as U.N. Ambassador Holbrooke—made high profile visits to the country. U.S. bilateral assistance to Indonesia was increased to U.S. \$125 million. Priorities included judicial reform and justice for past gross abuses, improving civil-military relations, police training, and professionalizing national and local parliaments. Even as the U.S. stepped up its efforts to assist democratization, leading officials spoke out forcefully on the need to disarm and disband militias in West Timor, and for accountability for past military atrocities, including the 1999 violence in East Timor.

The Clinton Administration in late August lifted an eleven-month ban on commercial military sales to Indonesia, approving the sale of spare parts for C-130 transport planes just one week before three U.N. refugee aid workers were killed in West Timor. The ban originally had been imposed in response to the 1999 East Timor violence. Congressional restrictions remained in place on military training and direct U.S. military sales. U.S. Defense Secretary Cohen visited Jakarta in mid-September. Prior to his visit, he confirmed that the Pentagon had decided to "re-engage" with the Indonesian military, inviting officers to conferences and participating in joint humanitarian exercise, but that the U.S. would stop short of directly selling arms. The State Department strongly condemned the abduction and murder of Jafar Siddiq Hamzah, urging at the highest levels a full investigation and prosecution, and supported the humanitarian pause in Aceh. Members of Congress expressed concern about the violence in the Moluccas; several House of Representatives members wrote to President Wahid in July urging him to invite international observers and humanitarian aid groups to the region and to prosecute members of the *laskar jihad* responsible for instigating new violence.

International Financial Institutions

In advance of the World Bank-convened annual consultative group conference in Tokyo in October, the president of the World Bank took the extraordinary step of sending a personal letter to Wahid urging his intervention in West Timor and warning that donor commitments could be affected. The donors pledged a total of $4.8 billion to support the Indonesian government's budget, plus an additional $530 million for Indonesian NGOs. Several donors addressed the government's response to crises in West Timor, Maluku, Aceh, and West Papua. The U.S. said it would condition its aid on Indonesia's full compliance with the UN Security Council's resolution on West Timor.

In 2000, the World Bank had outstanding commitments of $5.5 billion to Indonesia; of those funds, $2.8 billion had yet to be disbursed as of mid-September. In fiscal year 1999, the World Bank had said it would provide another $2.7 billion in future loans. Meanwhile, a new letter of intent was signed by the government with the International Monetary Fund (IMF) in September, opening the way for a package of U.S. $400 million in loans. In June, the IMF had approved a $372 million loan after it reviewed Indonesia's compliance with fiscal and structural reforms mandated by the IMF. Overall the IMF had offered $5 billion in assistance to Indonesia, contingent on progress in its reform efforts.

Relevant Human Rights Watch Reports:

Forced Expulsions to West Timor and the Refugee Crisis, 11/99

Human Rights and Pro-Independence Actions in Papua, 1999-2000, 5/00

MALAYSIA

The trial of former Deputy Prime Minister Anwar Ibrahim, culminating in his conviction for sodomy in August, provided the backdrop for the Malaysian government's ongoing repression of perceived political opponents. While continuing to target liberal activists, the government stepped up its attacks on the fundamentalist Islamic party PAS (Parti Islam Se-Malaysia), following elections in November 1999. Human rights activists, lawyers, politicians, and publishers affiliated with the opposition were prosecuted under expansively-worded laws restricting freedom of expression. Police broke up peaceful rallies, arrested protestors, and beat some detainees in custody. Anwar's conviction cast further doubt on the independence of Malaysia's judicial system. Refugees and migrants faced harsh conditions in immigration detention camps, and Malaysia continued to return refugees to countries where they faced persecution. The appointment of a Human Rights Commission held out the promise of greater government attention to human rights, but the extent of its power and effectiveness remained in question.

Human Rights Developments

The second trial of Anwar Ibrahim concluded in August. He was sentenced to nine years in prison on sodomy charges, to run consecutively with the six-year sentence for corruption imposed on him in 1999, which was confirmed by the Court of Appeal in April 2000. Anwar's adopted brother, Sukma Dermawan, was also convicted and sentenced to six years in prison and to receive four lashes with a rattan cane.

Anwar's prosecution was widely viewed inside and outside Malaysia as a case of political revenge by Prime Minister Mahathir Mohamad against his most prominent critic. His two trials were marred by heavy-handed tactics and irregularities. Key witnesses recanted their confessions and alleged that they were extracted through police coercion and physical abuse. The judge admitted into evidence a contested confession that interrogators had obtained from co-defendant Sukma Dermawan while he was in incommunicado detention without access to counsel, and that he subsequently retracted. Prime Minister Mahathir repeatedly stated publicly that Anwar was guilty before the court delivered its verdict. Defense attorneys Zainur Zakaria and Karpal Singh were prosecuted for statements made in court in the course of Anwar's defense. Finally, the court permitted the prosecution to twice change the dates of the alleged crime.

In March, former Inspector-General of Police Abdul Rahim Noor was convicted of "causing hurt" to Anwar for beating him in custody after his arrest. The charge was much reduced from the original, and Noor was sentenced to a fine and two months in prison. At this writing, he remained free on bail pending the outcome of his appeal.

Following November 1999 elections, the government retaliated against its opponents by charging them under broadly worded laws. Although Malaysia's ruling coalition, dominated by the United Malay National Organization (UMNO), maintained its two-thirds majority in parliament, it lost significant ethnic Malay support as a result of Anwar's controversial prosecutions. PAS won control of the state governments of Kelantan and Terengganu, giving it leadership of two of Malaysia's fourteen states.

Anwar's principal counsel, Karpal Singh, was one of four individuals charged in January with violating the Sedition Act, a colonial-era law that criminalizes any speech deemed to have a "seditious tendency," regardless of the speaker's intent and the statement's veracity. Singh, the deputy chairman of the Democratic Action Party (DAP), was arrested on January 12, 2000 for telling the trial court in September 1999 that Anwar might have been poisoned in custody and that he suspected that "people in high places" were responsible. As of October, his trial had not begun. The charge against Singh ran counter to international standards and Malaysian common law, which grants lawyers absolute privilege for all statements made during legal proceedings. Marina Yusoff, former vice president of the National Justice Party (Parti Keadilan Nasional or Keadilan), also faced sedition charges for allegedly "provoking racial discord." In a speech on September 29, 1999, Yusoff allegedly told a mostly ethnic Chinese Malaysian audience not to vote for UMNO because it had started the massacres of ethnic Chinese during the race riots of May 13, 1969. Her trial was ongoing in October. Zulkifli Sulong, editor of the popular PAS newspaper *Harakah*, and Chia Lim Thye, who held the permit for the newspaper's printing company, were charged with sedition for publishing an article allegedly written by Chandra Muzaffar, Keadilan's deputy president. The article alleged a government conspiracy against Anwar. Chia pleaded guilty and received a fine in May. Zulkifli pleaded not guilty, and his trial was ongoing at the time of this writing.

The Home Ministry used the Printing Presses and Publications Act to intimidate the press and restrict media associated with the opposition. On December 24, 1999, the ministry accused *Harakah* of breaching the conditions of its license by selling the paper to non-PAS members. On March 1, it restricted *Harakah* to two issues per month, down from twice weekly, and banned it from newsstands. The minister for energy, communications, and multimedia also stated that *Harakah*'s online edition would be limited to two issues per month, although the ministry had repeatedly said that the government would not interfere with the Internet.

On March 27, the Home Ministry refused to renew the publishing permit of *Detik* magazine, a privately financed publication on domestic politics which criticized the government. Among other things, the government alleged that the magazine had failed to print the publisher's address and had not obtained the ministry's consent to the editor's appointment. The ministry also banned *Al Wasilah*, a monthly youth magazine affiliated with *Detik*, in August. In September, it suspended the weekly tabloid, *Ekslusif*, for "imbalanced [sic] reporting and non-compliance with publication rules and regulations.

Police continued to use force to break up peaceful opposition demonstrations. On March 11, around 200 people gathered at the National Mosque to protest the government's decision to reduce the frequency of *Harakah*'s publication. Seven people, including prominent human rights lawyer Sivarasa Rasiah, opposition supporters, and journalists, were arrested for illegal assembly. On March 25, the government banned public rallies in the capital for an indefinite period. The ban applied to all outdoor gatherings in Kuala Lumpur of more than four people. On April 9, police shut down Keadilan's first anniversary celebration on the grounds that it had no permit and called in Dr. Wan Azizah Wan Ismail, Anwar's wife and head of Keadilan, for questioning.

In advance of protests planned to mark the anniversary of Anwar's corruption conviction on April 14, police arrested three opposition leaders and ordered four others to turn themselves in. Despite the arrests, as well as police roadblocks around Kuala Lumpur and a heavy police presence, several hundred people gathered at the National Mosque and were met by tear gas, water cannons, and police in riot gear using batons, bamboo canes, and dogs. Forty-eight people were arrested for illegal assembly. A judge ordered forty-six to be held for over a week without charges. Several detainees reported being beaten in custody by police. Police also arrested Cheah Kah Peng, lawyer for Keadilan vice-president Tian Chua, one of those charged with illegal assembly, when he tried to gain access to his client at a local police station.

On August 4, the day originally scheduled for Anwar's sodomy trial verdict, several hundred people gathered outside the courthouse; seven were arrested for illegal assembly. When the verdict was finally announced on August 8, around 700 people demonstrated peacefully; approximately twelve, including Tian Chua, were arrested. Several reported being punched, kicked, and partially choked by police officers during arrest and at the police station. Since September 1998, police had consistently refused to grant opposition parties permits for public rallies.

Opposition supporters also faced retaliation from the ruling party at the state level. In March, the Malacca state government blacklisted doctors, lawyers, architects, contractors, and other professionals who were opposition party members. The government transferred civil servants supportive of the opposition out of the state or to other agencies, forbade its employees from visiting the two states controlled by PAS, and withdrew some state funds from two banks with employees who had campaigned for the opposition. The banks responded by promising to take action against those employees. One, Bank Islam, gave the government a list of employees who openly supported the opposition, promised disciplinary action against them, and dismissed those who had stood as opposition candidates in the November elections. Chief Minister Mohamed Ali Rustam explained that the measures were intended "to serve as a warning to opposition party supporters that they have no place in Malacca."

Thirteen members were appointed to a

national Human Rights Commission (Suhakam) in April, with former Deputy Prime Minister Musa Hitam named as chair. The commission began receiving complaints in April, primarily of police abuse. It met with representatives of nongovernmental organizations (NGOs) in May and with members of the police in June. In late July, Musa Hitam acknowledged the public's right to peaceful assembly and stated that persons should be allowed to gather at the Kuala Lumpur High Court to hear the Anwar verdict. The Malaysian Home Ministry and the UMNO Youth deputy chief disagreed publicly with this statement. Wearing armbands, commission members observed the public gathering on August 8, the day of the Anwar verdict. Malaysian NGOs criticized the limited scope of rights falling under the commission's jurisdiction and its lack of powers.

In July the Malaysian High Court dismissed one of the four defamation suits brought by corporations against Param Cumaraswamy, the United Nations Special Rapporteur on the Independence of Judges and Lawyers. It ordered Cumaraswamy to bear the litigation costs, however, which were US $110,000 at the time and rising. The three other cases were still pending at the time of this writing. The corporations were seeking over US $100 million in damages for statements in Cumaraswamy's 1995 interview with *International Commercial Litigation* magazine in which he referred to allegations of corporate interference in the Malaysian judiciary. Malaysian courts have long refused to recognize the immunity granted him in his capacity as U.N. Special Rapporteur. In April, the Malaysian government attempted unsuccessfully to block Cumaraswamy's reappointment at the annual meeting of the U.N. Human Rights Commission.

The trial of Irene Fernandez, head of the Kuala Lumpur-based advocacy organization Tenaganita (Women's Force), entered its fifth year, making it the longest trial in Malaysian history. Fernandez faces the possibility of three years in prison on charges of malicious publishing for her July 1995 memorandum on abuses in immigration detention camps. The government maintained that the report was inaccurate. Beginning in January, former detainees from Bangladesh, after initially being denied visas by the Malaysian government, testified in court that they had been severely beaten, subjected to gross sexual abuse, and kept in crowded, mosquito-infested rooms with foul toilets.

Malaysia continued its policy of detaining and expelling persons recognized as refugees by the United Nations High Commissioner for Refugees (UNHCR), and continued to deny UNHCR permission to visit immigration detention camps where refugees were detained. In October 1999, Mohammed Sayed, a refugee from Burma, was arrested after he led a demonstration in front of the Burmese embassy in Kuala Lumpur. Scheduled for expulsion to Thailand several times, he was held in an immigration detention camp until June when, following domestic and international protest, he was resettled in Australia.

Defending Human Rights

Malaysia's human rights groups continued to operate despite government pressure. In April, Anwar's daughter, Nurul Izzah, met with United Nations High Commissioner for Human Rights Mary Robinson about her father's imprisonment and addressed the 56th Session of the United Nations Human Rights Commission in Geneva. Three Malaysian human rights organizations, Voice of the Malaysian People (Suara Rakyat Malaysia, SUARAM), Aliran, and the National Human Rights Society (Hakam) met in May with the new Human Rights Commission and delivered a memorandum signed by thirty-one NGOs. On August 1, SUARAM organized a gathering of NGOs to protest the fortieth anniversary of the Internal Security Act (ISA).

The Malaysian Bar Council in March adopted a motion urging Malaysia's chief prosecutor to withdraw the charges against Karpal Singh and to respect the rights of an independent bar. In June, the High Court enjoined the Bar Council from convening a special meeting to discuss allegations of impropriety against the chief justice. In July, the Court of Appeal affirmed a November 1999 decision that if the Bar Council held a special meeting on the independence of the judiciary, it would contravene the Sedition Act, erode public confidence in the judiciary, and be in contempt of court. In both instances, the court ordered that the Bar Council meet the litigation costs.

The Role of the International Community

Anwar's sodomy conviction evoked widespread condemnation.

Asia and the Pacific

Singapore Senior Minister Lee Kuan Yew called Mahathir's handling of the Anwar case "an unmitigated disaster," referring to the use of the ISA to detain Anwar and Mahathir's weak response to Anwar's being beaten in custody. (Lee later denied that he intended to criticize Mahathir.) Australian Prime Minister John Howard questioned the independence of Malaysia's judiciary and stated that the sodomy conviction was politically motivated. New Zealand's Foreign Affairs and Trade Minister Phil Goff expressed concern about the fairness of the trial, including questionable evidentiary rulings, restrictions on the defense, and the judiciary's independence from the executive.

United States and Canada

The U.S. in April criticized Malaysia's crackdown on freedom of speech and peaceful assembly and called on the government to respect its citizen's civil and political rights. In May, the U.S. expressed concern about the rejection of Anwar's appeal of his corruption convictions and urged the judicial system to address due process concerns. In August, the U.S. State Department stated that the U.S. was "outraged" by Anwar's conviction and that the cooperative relationship between the U.S. and Malaysia had been impeded by the latter's poor human rights record. Canada also strongly condemned the trial and the sentence, stating that they reflected poorly on

the impartiality of Malaysia's judicial system.

Europe

The European Parliament sent a five-member delegation to Malaysia in May. The delegation praised the creation of the national Human Rights Commission but expressed concern about the fairness of Anwar's trials and the independence of the judiciary and the press. Following Anwar's conviction in August, the European Union issued a statement of concern about the verdict and expressed serious doubts about the fairness of the trial.

United Nations and the World Bank

On April 10, United Nations High Commissioner for Human Rights Mary Robinson voiced concern about a possible crackdown against opposition leaders in the run-up to the anniversary of Anwar's conviction on April 14, stated that her office would actively monitor the situation, and called on all parties to respect the right to peaceful expression. In August World Bank President James Wolfensohn expressed concern about Anwar's conviction.

Relevant Human Rights Watch Reports:

Living in Limbo: Burmese Refugees in Malaysia, 8/00

PAKISTAN

Respect for civil and political rights deteriorated significantly in the year following the bloodless military coup, on October 12, 1999, that deposed Prime Minister Nawaz Sharif in Pakistan. General Pervez Musharraf's administration began to address some longstanding justice issues—notably, through the adoption of Pakistan's first federal juvenile justice law and the establishment of a commission on the status of women—but it also greatly augmented executive powers and curtailed the independence of the judiciary. It moved to neutralize political parties through the application of broadly defined laws governing terrorism, sedition, and public order, and through the establishment of a powerful extra-constitutional "accountability" bureau. Opposition party members were subjected to prolonged detention without charge; some were tortured in custody. Sectarian violence and attacks on religious minorities continued and, despite renewed attention to the issue, the government failed to provide meaningful recourse for women victims of domestic abuse and sexual violence.

Human Rights Developments

Early in the year, the military government moved to strip the judiciary of much of its power. On January 26, General Musharraf issued an order requiring all Supreme and High Court judges to take an oath binding them to uphold his proclamation of a national emergency and to adhere to the Provisional Constitution Order (PCO). Many, including the chief justice of the Supreme Court, refused to take the oath. A total of fifteen judges were removed. The PCO, which remained in effect at this writing, had been announced by Musharraf just days after the October coup. It suspended the constitution and legislative bodies and prohibited the Supreme and High Courts from making any decision against the chief executive.

On May 12, a reconstituted Supreme Court issued a verdict rejecting petitions challenging the coup's legality. The court set a deadline of three years for the holding of national and provincial elections, but reserved authority to review the continuation of the Proclamation of Emergency, leaving the door open to future extensions of military rule.

Top officials of the deposed government were detained on the day of the coup; two of them, former Information Minister Mushahid Hussain and former Petroleum Minister Chaudhry Nisar Ali Khan continued to be held without charge as of this writing. Nawaz Sharif himself was tried and convicted of hijacking and terrorism—for refusing to allow General Musharraf's plane to land in the hours leading up to the coup—under the Anti-Terrorism Act, and sentenced to life imprisonment on April 6 following a trial marred by procedural abuses.

In December 1999 the military government amended the Anti-Terrorism Act to add hijacking and conspiracy to the list of offenses falling within the Anti-Terrorism Court's jurisdiction. These offenses were then applied retroactively to Nawaz Sharif. Another amendment allowed the government to replace the judge originally assigned to hear the case, a Sharif appointee. In January, the new judge stepped down, publicly complaining of the presence of intelligence agents in his courtroom. In March, only days before the final arguments were to be presented in the trial, Sharif's lawyer, Iqbal Raad, and two of his colleagues were assassinated in their office. Other members of the defense team charged that the government had failed to provide them protection despite repeated warnings that they were being threatened. A month after Sharif's conviction by the Anti-Terrorism Court, he was shifted to Attock Fort—an army-occupied sixteenth century fortress west of Islamabad—to face trial on charges of concealing assets and evading taxes in connection with his acquisition of a helicopter. He was convicted on July 22, and sentenced to fourteen years in prison, with a fine of Rs. 20 million (U.S. $380,000).

The new government's principal vehicle for detaining former officials and party leaders, however, was the National Accountability Ordinance, a law ostensibly created to bring corrupt officials to account. The ordinance confers sweeping powers of arrest, investigation, and prosecution in a single institution, the National Accountability Bureau (NAB), and permits detainees to be held for up to ninety days without being brought before a court. The law was later amended to facilitate conviction by shifting the burden of proof during trial from the prosecution to the defense.

There were persistent reports of ill treatment in NAB custody, particularly in the case of high profile detainees who were held early in the year in Attock Fort. Persons convicted under the ordinance were prohibited from holding public office for a period of twenty-one years. An amendment to the Political Parties Act in August also barred anyone with a court conviction from holding party office. The combined effect of these acts, as they were applied, was to eliminate the existing leadership of the major political parties. While administration officials said that parties would be allowed to participate in future elections to the Senate and national and provincial assemblies, local government elections, scheduled to be held in December, were to be conducted on a non-party basis.

The Musharraf government also suppressed political activity by conducting raids on party offices, preventing political rallies from being held, and lodging criminal cases against rally organizers under laws governing sedition and the Maintenance of Public Order (MPO) Ordinance. The sedition law, Section 124-A of the Pakistan Penal Code, criminalizes speech that "brings or attempts to bring into hatred or contempt, or excites or attempts to excite disaffection towards, the Central or Provincial Government established by law." Section 16 of the Maintenance of Public Order Ordinance prohibits speech that "causes or is likely to cause fear or alarm to the public" or any section thereof, or which "furthers or is likely to further any activity prejudicial to public safety or the maintenance of public order."

Rana Sanaullah Khan, a member of the suspended Punjab provincial assembly from Sharif's Pakistan Muslim League (PML), was arrested in Faisalabad on November 28, 1999. The arrest came after he criticized the army at a meeting of former legislators and urged his colleagues to launch a protest movement against the military government. He was tortured while in custody, and criminal charges were registered against him under the sedition law and MPO .

On March 15, the government formally curtailed freedom of association and assembly with an order banning public rallies, demonstrations, and strikes. The order's enforcement against a procession from Lahore to Peshawar that Nawaz Sharif's wife, Kulsoom

Nawaz, had planned to lead, resulted in the arrests of at least 165 PML leaders and activists. On September 21 the ban was also invoked against 250 members of the hardline Sunni Muslim group, Sipah-e-Sahaba, who had planned a march to celebrate a religious anniversary.

Other police and army operations targeted the two leading ethnically-based parties in Sindh, the Jeay Sindh Qaumi Mahaz (JSQM) and Muttahida Qaumi Movement (MQM). Paramilitary rangers and police in Sindh province launched a crackdown against activists and leaders of the JSQM and the MQM on February 19, 2000 after the two parties jointly called for a strike against the government's dismissal of 400 Pakistan Steel Mills workers. Paramilitary troops and rangers responded with search and siege operations in the cities and a search for JSQM activists in rural areas of Sindh, resulting in the arrest of about forty activists.

The JSQM and MQM called for further protests to be held on February 22 against the police violence of February 19, but withdrew their call after setting a deadline for the government to accept two demands: the release of jailed MQM leader Farooq Sattar and the reinstatement of laid-off Pakistan Steel Mills employees. On the night of February 21, police and paramilitary rangers rounded up and detained fifty-four JSQM and MQM activists. They were released the following day.

Many local observers maintained that a major consequence of curbs on political parties and activism was that the relative influence of mainstream religious parties—whose authority General Musharraf largely refrained from challenging—would grow. Indeed, that influence was apparent from the government's abrupt withdrawal—in the face of planned protests by religious groups—of plans to restrict application of Pakistan's much criticized blasphemy laws and to repeal laws providing for separate elections for members of religious minorities. These laws are seen by many minority group advocates as having contributed to their communities' political marginalization. In the absence of legal reform, the blasphemy laws, which set forth stringent penalties, including capital punishment, for offenses against Islam, continued to be used against Muslims and non-Muslims alike.

Following up on promises made during a government-sponsored national human rights convention in April, President Rafiq Tarar announced the promulgation of a juvenile justice ordinance in July that incorporated a number of recommendations made by local and international nongovernmental organizations and the official Pakistan Law Commission. The ordinance included a ban on the death penalty on persons for crimes committed while they were under the age of eighteen, provision of state-funded legal assistance for juveniles, the creation of juvenile courts with exclusive jurisdiction over juvenile cases, a prohibition on joint trials of adults and children, and a requirement that probation officers prepare reports on a child's circumstances prior to adjudication of his or her case.

On September 1, the government announced the establishment of the National Commission on the Status of Women, with a mandate to safeguard and promote women's interests but few powers to implement it. The first issue that the commission was directed to examine was violence against women. The government—empowered by the Supreme Court to amend the constitution and enforce new laws without parliament's approval—also reserved one third of the seats for women in local government elections that were scheduled to commence in December.

Thousands of women fell victim to domestic violence, so-called honor killings, and sexual assault, with virtually no access to the country's justice system. Women who attempted to register a police complaint of spousal or familial physical abuse were invariably turned away and sometimes pressured by the police to reconcile with their abusers. Women who reported rape or sexual assault by strangers fared marginally better, but they too faced harassment by officials at all levels and risked being prosecuted for illicit sex if they failed to "prove" rape under the 1979 Hudood Ordinances, which criminalize adultery and fornication.

According to a report released by the Human Rights Commission of Pakistan in March, a nongovernmental body, more than 1,000 women died in Pakistan in 1999 as victims of honor killings—the practice of punishing women said to have brought dishonor to their families. Most of the killings, the report added, were carried out by the victims' brothers or husbands. The same report concluded that at least 1,000 people had been killed in religious or ethnic violence each year since 1990. Sectarian violence between rival Sunni and Shi'a Muslim groups continued in 2000, reaching its peak during the holy month of Moharram. On April 12, gunmen attacked a Shi'a prayer meeting in Rawalpindi, killing nineteen.

Religious intolerance continued to generate new abuses. In December 1999, several hundred persons looted and burned property belonging to a local Ahmadi leader, Mohammad Nawaz, in Okara district, Punjab. Nawaz was accused of planning to build an Ahmadi house of worship. Police personnel did nothing to stop the crowd and instead registered a case of blasphemy against Nawaz and his two sons. In May 2000, a lower court in Sialkot district, Punjab, sentenced two Christian brothers to thirty-five years' imprisonment and Rs. 75,000 (US$1,500) fine. They were convicted of desecrating the Koran and blaspheming against the Prophet Mohammed. Both cases were reportedly registered by an ice cream vendor who had fought with the brothers after insisting that his dishes were reserved for Muslim customers.

Though the government repeatedly stated that the Pakistani press enjoyed unconditional freedom, local human rights activists reported that self-censorship on political issues was increasingly common in the vernacular press, and there were indications that the English-language press was coming under official pressure as well. On September 27, an army monitoring team conducted an unannounced, four-hour inspection of the headquarters of Karachi's respected English-language daily *Dawn*. Although the ostensible purpose of the inspection was to check metering equipment for electricity billing fraud, the team demanded access to all floors of the publishing house, including the offices of the publishers, editors, and journalists. According to *Dawn*, the inspection was preceded by legal notices to the newspaper from the Information Ministry to restrict its coverage of a draft Freedom of Information Act, and by complaints from government officials about an article in *Dawn* stating that the administration was preparing new curbs on press freedom.

The UNHCR pledged to continued its yearly repatriation of 100,000 Afghan refugees from Pakistan, which is currently home to over two million refugees. Though the repatriation was voluntary, the refugees returned to face ongoing civil war and severe violations of women's human rights.

Defending Human Rights

Despite numerous crackdowns on political activism, human rights organizations, for the most part, were permitted to function freely. Groups such as the Human Rights Commission of Pakistan openly condemned the military government's treatment of detained political figures, and its curtailing of judicial independence. According to a report in *Dawn*, following the shutdown of nearly 2,000 NGOs and the imposition of new registration requirements for NGOs by the Punjab provincial government last year—a move that was initiated under the Sharif administration—NGOs in the province continued to require clearance from the Intelligence Bureau in order to register with the government. While NGOs in Sindh province did not require such clearance, the Sindh Social Welfare Department began scrutinizing the workings of all NGOs functioning in the province, including their financial records and sources of funding.

The Role of the International Community

In a bid to build international support, General Musharraf and other senior officials of the military government attempted to bolster diplomatic ties overseas. But the international community remained steadfast in its demands for a return to democratic governance and peaceful resolution of the conflict in Kashmir.

United Nations

In a December 1999 report, the U.N. Working Group on Enforced or Involuntary Disappearances stated that it continued to receive reports that Pakistani authorities failed to adequately investigate and prosecute "disappearance" cases. In March, the U.N. Special Rapporteur on violence against women submitted a written report on her September 1999 visit to Pakistan and Afghanistan. Among her findings were a rise in violence against Afghan women, including domestic violence, honor killings, and trafficking of Afghan refugee women in Pakistan. She also found that individuals working on the plight of Afghans, including members of Afghan nongovernmental organizations, the majority of which had moved to Pakistan, continued to receive death threats, were subject to harassment, and often lacked protection from local authorities. The rapporteur also noted local NGO concern over what they termed the "Talibanization" of Pakistan, and its impact on Pakistani women.

United States

During a brief stopover in Islamabad at the end of his South Asia tour in March, U.S. President Bill Clinton urged the military government to restore democracy, seek a peaceful resolution to the conflict in Kashmir, and pressure the Taliban in Afghanistan to both improve their treatment of women and cease sponsoring terrorist groups. Clinton took pains not to legitimize the military government by making a state visit.

In its second annual report on international religious freedom released in September, the U.S. Department of State noted that there was a "slight improvement" in the Pakistani government's treatment of religious minorities between July 1, 1999 and June 30, 2000. It cited General Musharraf's abandoning of his predecessor's proposal to impose Shari'a law through a constitutional amendment as a positive move, but asserted more generally that discriminatory legislation continued to fuel religious intolerance. Later that month, the U.S. Commission on International Religious Freedom held public hearings on religious persecution in India and Pakistan. At this writing, members of the commission were preparing for a visit to Pakistan in November following the government's invitation.

European Union

Almost a year after its forceful condemnation of the coup in Pakistan, the E.U. initiated political contact with the military government in an effort to formalize a timetable for national elections. Following the April verdict in the trial of former Prime Minister Nawaz Sharif, the E.U. also voiced concerns over the oath of loyalty to the PCO required of judges, retroactive application of amendments to the Anti-Terrorism Act, and the broader question of judicial independence, stating that the E.U. would closely follow Sharif's appeal.

The Commonwealth of Nations

Commonwealth Secretary-General Don McKinnon visited Pakistan in August to convey the Commonwealth's concerns regarding the restoration of constitutional and democratic rule. Pakistan was suspended from the councils of the Commonwealth following the military coup. The visit was followed by a warning by Commonwealth foreign ministers—who met with Pakistani Foreign Minister Abdul Sattar during the U.N. Millennium Summit in September—that Pakistan would face full suspension from the Commonwealth if it did not provide a firm timetable for a return to democracy.

Japan

As part of a South Asia tour in August, Japanese Prime Minister Yoshiro Mori used Japan's leverage as a top donor to call for a resumption of talks on Kashmir and condemned violent attacks on civilians. Mori urged Musharraf to restore civilian rule by 2002, and indicated that while most Japanese grants and loans would remain suspended following Pakistan's nuclear tests in May 1998, some funds might be released for development work in response to Pakistan's pledge to continue its freeze on nuclear tests. The Japanese government maintained, however, that Pakistan's refusal to sign the Comprehensive Test Ban Treaty was the main obstacle in the resumption of Japanese aid. Earlier in the year, Japan also provided small grants to NGOs carrying out Afghan refugee assistance in camps in Pakistan and inside Afghanistan.

International Financial Institutions

At this writing, the World Bank had yet to schedule the donor conference on Pakistan that had been put on hold since the coup. Proposed loans that were in the pipeline, but not yet approved, amounted to more than U.S. $800 million. In late September, the IMF and Pakistan were reported to have reached a preliminary agreement on a $3.5 billion loan program, to be spread out over three years. IMF cash credits during the first year would be limited to $700 million from the fund's Poverty Relief and Growth Facility (PRGF).

Relevant Human Rights Watch Reports:

Prison Bound, The Denial of Juvenile Justice in Pakistan, 10/99
Reform or Repression?: Post-Coup Abuses in Pakistan, 10/00

SRI LANKA

Renewed fighting between Sri Lankan government forces and the separatist Liberation Tigers of Tamil Eelam (LTTE) overshadowed other developments and generated serious abuses. Intensified battles for control of key territory in the northern part of the island claimed scores of civilian lives and displaced some 250,000 people, bringing the estimated number of internally displaced persons (IDPs) nationwide to more than one million. Emergency government powers, in place almost continuously since 1983 and enhanced from May to September by additional regulations, granted broad powers to security personnel to arrest and detain suspects, restricted freedom of association, and authorized media censorship. The LTTE was implicated in a series of suicide bombings that killed and injured hundreds of civilians. It continued to recruit and deploy child soldiers and to physically attack and intimidate critics in the Tamil community.

Although the government continued to press for constitutional changes aimed at a political resolution to the conflict, it failed to secure necessary parliamentary support. Political violence outside the war-zones increased in the run-up to parliamentary elections in October.

Human Rights Developments

On November 2, 1999, the LTTE launched operation "Unceasing Waves" to reclaim northern territory lost to government forces over the preceding four years. On November 22, artillery shells hit a Catholic shrine in the northern Vanni region that had long sheltered IDPs, killing forty-two and injuring sixty more. Each side blamed the other for the attack.

Intensified fighting in April 2000 near Jaffna town trapped thousands of civilians in conflict zones for several tense weeks. The LTTE called on the civilians to move south into the Vanni or into other parts of the Jaffna peninsula that they controlled. The army said civilians should stay in government-controlled territory closer to the town, moving north if necessary. By the end of July, a lull in fighting allowed many civilians to move to safer areas, and permitted the delivery of badly-needed medical supplies into the Vanni. On July 22, the two sides allowed International Committee of the Red Cross (ICRC) workers to evacuate residents of the Kaithady Elders' Home near Jaffna, where they had been trapped since May. Some thirty residents reportedly died during the two-month period, many as a result of shelling.

Civilian deaths and injuries on the Jaffna peninsula were reported in the hundreds, but casualty figures could not be confirmed because relief agencies and journalists were barred from the hardest hit areas. There and in eastern Sri Lanka, many conflict-related deaths were the result of errant shells and gunshots. On May 24, four adults and two children were killed in a village near Batticaloa when a shell fell on their house during a LTTE offensive against a nearby Sri Lankan army base. On August 10, army shelling injured three civilians, including a ten-year-old girl, near Muttur, in Trincomalee district. On September 12, mortar fire aimed at the LTTE damaged houses and injured four civilians in Kalkudah village, north of Batticaloa. Land mines and unexploded ordinance also continued to take a civilian toll. Four such injuries were treated by doctors in Mallavi in May; one victim was a ten-year-old child who lost both hands and eyes in the blast. Sri Lanka had still not signed the international treaty banning land mines due, the government said, to security concerns arising from the conflict with the LTTE.

Before the escalation in fighting in April, government-run welfare camps housed some 170,000 IDPs island-wide; some 600,000 other IDPs relied on friends or relatives for shelter. Although most received some government assistance, about 100,000 people in Sri Lanka's north and east were thought to be struggling for survival unassisted. By mid-September, another 250,000 people, almost all of them residents of Jaffna district, had reportedly been displaced.

Displaced persons and other Tamil civilians in the north and east also faced discrimination, restrictions on their freedom of movement, arbitrary arrest, and custodial abuse at the hands of government forces. Due to government restrictions, Tamil civilians were often unable to reach work sites to earn a living, attend schools, or seek urgent medical care. In eastern Sri Lanka, army and police units continued to impose forced labor, demanding that IDPs and other civilians work without pay building sentry posts, cutting wood, and cleaning military camps. In mid-

July, villagers north of Batticaloa were reportedly forced to construct a sand bulwark around an army camp; some were beaten for refusing to comply.

Mass arrests of Tamils occurred after violent incidents attributed to the LTTE and were often accompanied by reports of "disappearances" and torture in custody. In one two-week period in January, more than five thousand people were detained for questioning in search operations in Colombo neighborhoods. The Sri Lankan Human Rights Commission, a government-appointed agency, said in July that it had been unable to trace seventeen people detained by security forces in Vavuniya since the beginning of the year, while Amnesty International reported a rash of "disappearances" in Vavuniya in August. A Vavuniya district judge in September criticized local doctors for failing to report torture-related injuries, and threatened legal action against practitioners who submitted false reports denying custodial abuse by the army or police.

On October 25, a mob in Bandarawela stormed a government-run rehabilitation camp housing, among others, suspected LTTE supporters and former LTTE child soldiers, killing over twenty-five. According to initial reports, those killed ranged in age from fourteen to twenty-five. After the attack, police briefly detained more than 250 suspects from the majority Sinhalese community. At this writing, President Kumaratunga had called for two "high-level probes" into the incident, while Tamil community leaders alleged police complicity.

The LTTE committed numerous and gross abuses. Bombings of public places in the north and east, and suicide bombings in Colombo on December 18, 1999, January 5, 2000, March 10, June 7, September 15, and October 19 killed more than one hundred civilians and injured many more. Beginning in April, the LTTE engaged in increasingly aggressive recruitment drives in the Vanni, including recruitment of children as young as ten years old for combat. Schools and IDP camps were common targets for such drives. A July report by the Colombo-based University Teachers for Human Rights (Jaffna) provided information on fifteen children recruited since April 1999, nine of whom had been killed in the fighting within a year of their recruitment. The LTTE imposed restrictions on civilians wishing to leave areas it controlled and forced all villagers in some areas to join its civilian defense units. LTTE attacks and intimidation against what it referred to as "quislings" within the Tamil community had a chilling effect on dissent. Particularly at risk were members of Tamil political parties holding positions in local government. Between January and May, three members of local administrative councils in Jaffna were killed by unidentified gunmen. The LTTE held a number of political prisoners and prisoners of war, but access to detainees and details of confinement were unavailable. On February 28, the LTTE released four soldiers they had captured more than six years earlier.

Freedom of the press was also under attack by the government. Intensified press censorship and denial of independent access to conflict areas frustrated accurate war reporting and civilian access to vital security information. On May 3, as the LTTE pushed towards Jaffna, the government issued new emergency regulations banning live television and radio coverage of the war, requiring government approval before such news could be transmitted outside the country, and empowering the authorities to detain journalists, block the distribution of newspapers, seize property, and shut down printing presses. On June 5, the government relaxed restrictions on the foreign media, but those relating to the local press remained in place.

From May 13 to July 4, government censors closed Jaffna's only local Tamil daily newspaper, Uthayan, after it reported that five civilians had died in a May 12 air force raid and that President Kumaratunga had wept during a meeting with the head of the Indian air force. On May 22, police seized the Leader Publications printing plant, blocking the publication of the independent Sunday Leader and its Sinhala-language counterpart, Irida Peramuna, for publishing reports on the war that the chief censor said "would have benefitted the enemy." At the end of June, the Supreme Court struck down the ban on Leader Publications on procedural grounds. Days later, the president invoked new emergency regulations intended to correct those procedural problems. The move reimposed restrictions on all reporting deemed by the government to be detrimental to national security, preservation of public order, or the maintenance of essential services.

In September, the government suspended key emergency regulations banning public meetings and some of the broader censorship provisions, but restrictions on military-related news remained in place. At this writing, a ban remained in effect covering "any matter pertaining to military operations in the Northern and Eastern Province . . . [and] any statement pertaining to the official conduct, morale, or the performance of the Head or of any member of the Armed Forces or the police force."

Individual journalists also came under fire. In April, Nellai Nadesan, a senior columnist for the Tamil language newspaper Veerakersari, narrowly escaped a grenade explosion at his home in Batticaloa. In June, journalists attending a media workshop in eastern Batticaloa received threats after the government-owned media accused them of links to the LTTE. In September, Sunday Leader editor Lasantha Wickrematunga received a two-year suspended sentence for an article he published in 1995 criticizing President Kumaratunga's performance during her first year in office. Jaffna-based journalist Maylwaganam Nimalarajan was shot and killed by a group of unidentified attackers on the night of October 19. The attack occurred at his home during curfew hours in a high security area of Jaffna, and may have been linked to his reporting on vote-rigging and intimidation during the October parliamentary elections.

With renewed fighting taking center stage, there was little progress in obtaining justice for past human rights abuses although the identities of many perpetrators were known. Examples included the stalled "Bolgoda Lake" case, in which Special Task Force commandos were believed responsible for the 1995 murder of twenty-three Tamil youths; an army massacre of more than 180 villagers near Batticaloa in September 1990; and the 1980s crackdown on members of the left-wing insurgent group Janatha Vimukthi Peramuna (JVP) which resulted in tens of thousands of people being extrajudicially executed or "disappeared" by the authorities. On July 18, 2000, however, a court ordered retired Major General Ananda Weerasekera and two subordinates to stand trial on charges of murder and abduction. This was the first time that a high-ranking military officer had been ordered to stand trial in connection with the JVP "disappearances."

The government continued to press for constitutional revisions that would devolve more power to regional councils, thus increasing the autonomy of the Tamil-dominated north and east. The proposed revisions also would have granted citizenship to some 86,000 Tamils of Indian origin and their children, officially categorized as "Indian Tamils," who had been stateless for some forty years. The proposal was rejected both by the LTTE, as insufficient to satisfy its separatist demands, and by Sinhala hardliners, as a dilution of the unitary state and too accommodating of Tamil interests. On August 8, further consideration of the amendments was indefinitely postponed when it became clear that other political parties, including the main opposition United National Party, would not support the bill.

Political violence escalated in the weeks leading up to parliamentary elections in October. By October 10, the nongovernmental Centre For Monitoring Election Violence (CMEV) had recorded seventy-one election-related murders, at least twenty-six attempted murders, and over one thousand injuries, assaults, acts of intimidation, and other abuses.

Prominent social critics faced particular dangers from non-state actors. On January 5, Tamil lawyer and politician G.G. Ponnambalam was killed in Colombo. An outspoken supporter of Tamil separatism, Ponnambalam had acted as legal council in many important Tamil human rights cases. A group calling itself the National Front Against Tigers claimed responsibility for his murder, warning that it should be seen as a lesson by all those who supported the LTTE.

Defending Human Rights

Nongovernmental rights activists continued to play a critical role, sometimes in difficult and dangerous circumstances. In the lead-up to parliamentary elections, human rights defenders campaigned against political violence. Trade unions and media freedom groups joined them in opposing censorship and other emergency measures.

At the end of January, two hundred participants from around the world commemorated the life and work of Neelan Tiruchelvam, a renowned Tamil human rights activist who was killed in a LTTE suicide bombing in 1999. The gathering launched the Neelan Tiruchelvam Memorial Fund, dedicated to the promotion of human rights, minority rights, and the resolution of ethnic conflict. In late March, Sri Lankan human rights defenders welcomed the appointment of new commissioners to Sri Lanka's National Human Rights Commission, which had been criticized in its first three years of operation as lacking in leadership and resources.

Early on the morning of June 27, a grenade was thrown into the compound of the Save the Children Fund office in Colombo. A car parked at the premises was damaged but no one was injured in the attack.

In June, the Sri Lankan Press Council rejected a complaint filed by Sherman de Rose, founder of Companions on a Journey, a gay rights organization, against the *Island* newspaper for printing a letter that called for convicted rapists to be sent to attack lesbians. The council ruled that the letter was published in the "interest of the community," and that De Rose had no standing because he was male. The Council maintained that "lesbianism itself is an act of sadism," and noted that homosexuality was an offense under Sri Lanka's penal code. De Rose was ordered to pay the newspaper 2,100 rupees (U.S. $28) in costs.

In September, the Alliance for Democracy in Sri Lanka, composed of nearly seventy civic groups, trade unions, religious institutions of different faiths, and NGOs, launched a nationwide "yellow ribbon" campaign to support free and fair elections. The alliance sought to persuade one million Sri Lankans to wear yellow ribbons each day until the conclusion of the parliamentary elections in October to symbolize their support.

The Role of the International Community

International attention to Sri Lanka focused on support for a political settlement to the conflict and humanitarian efforts to mitigate the worst effects of the war. Sri Lanka sought and received increased military assistance from key donors and cultivated relations with potential arms suppliers, including Israel, with which it renewed diplomatic ties in May after a break of thirty years. Norway, India, and the United States played major roles in as yet unsuccessful efforts to bring about negotiations between the warring parties. Intensification of fighting in April caused a postponement of the annual meeting of the Sri Lanka Aid Consortium, but as the war raged on many of Sri Lanka's donors released statements encouraging Norway's efforts as a facilitator for peace between the warring parties.

Norway

In January, the Norwegian government announced that it would play an intermediary role in efforts to bring about an end to the seventeen-year war in Sri Lanka. Norwegian delegates met with government and LTTE representatives in separate meetings outside the country. Norway also sent senior officials to Colombo several times during the year for discussions on the escalation of fighting.

India

On May 8, the Indian government indicated for the first time that it would be willing to mediate in the crisis if asked by both sides. On May 23, Indian officials rejected suggestions in the press that the government of India was considering military intervention in Sri Lanka, amidst reports of an increased Indian naval presence off the Kerala coast. Meanwhile, India continued to play host to more than 100,000 Sri Lankan refugees, including about 65,000 in government-run camps in Tamil Nadu. Small numbers of refugees continued to arrive in India by boat during the year, but the Indian navy intercepted many vessels, preventing would-be refugees from landing on Indian soil and seized Indian fishing boats used to transport refugees. India offered to increase humanitarian assistance.

United States

The United States encouraged efforts by Norway and India to promote a negotiated settlement to the Sri Lankan conflict but continued to label the LTTE a "foreign terrorist organization," and increased anti-terrorism aid to the Sri Lankan government. On May 29, U.S. Undersecretary of State Thomas Pickering met with President Kumaratunga in Colombo. He expressed concern over the humanitarian crisis in northern Sri Lanka, urged the parties to press ahead with efforts to negotiate a political settlement short of secession, and encouraged the Sri Lankan government to lift press censorship and other restrictions on civil liberties. In June, President Clinton forwarded to the Senate for ratification a treaty signed in September 1999 that would facilitate extradition of LTTE members to Sri Lanka. Sri Lanka sought the treaty to prevent the LTTE from fund-raising or organizing political support in the U.S.

Other Major Donors

The E.U. joined Japan and most of Sri Lanka's other major donors in urging the LTTE and the government to cooperate with the Norwegian government's efforts to facilitate talks. Many donors also criticized the emergency measures imposed in May. On May 15, the E.U. emphasized the need to reestablish civil liberties, noting the responsibility of both sides to ensure the safety of the civilian population in conflict zones, and

calling for negotiations. The Japanese government issued a similar appeal and warned that the emergency measures and continued censorship of the media could violate Japan's Official Development Assistance human rights guidelines.

In July, following a fact-finding visit to Sri Lanka, two British members of the European Parliament criticized the government's human rights record stating that it had not done enough to protect civilians caught in the conflict and was using press censorship to cover-up abuses. They also urged the lifting of a military policy that banned even essential supplies, including food and medicine, from reaching areas controlled by the LTTE.

United Nations

In October 1999, the U.N. Working Group on Enforced or Involuntary Disappearances visited Sri Lanka to follow-up on more than 12,000 cases. Its December 1999 report stated that Sri Lanka was still second only to Iraq in numbers of unresolved cases, and noted that there had been few prosecutions of alleged perpetrators within the security forces, some of whom remained on active duty or had even been promoted.

In mid-March, U.N. Special Rapporteur on Violence against Women Radhika Coomaraswamy, who is herself Sri Lankan, emphasized the lack of government response to allegations of sexual violence by security personnel in Sri Lanka. She noted too, that, despite a presidential directive, little effort had been made to investigate the December 1999 gang-rape and murder by naval personnel of twenty-nine-year-old Sarathambal Saravanbavananthatkurukal near Jaffna.

UNHCR played an important role in assisting many of Sri Lanka's internally displaced in northern Sri Lanka, though its efforts to assist some of the newest IDPs were hampered by conflict-related restrictions. The agency had no presence in most of eastern Sri Lanka, and only a limited mandate for protection. In the past, the Sri Lankan government's rejection of a protection role for the agency had forced it to focus largely on humanitarian relief. In 2000, a core component of UNHCR's

SRI LANKA/THAILAND || 223

Sri Lanka program was seeking "access to national protection" for IDPs.

Representatives of the United Nations Children's Fund (UNICEF) made several statements expressing concern for child victims of war and denouncing the LTTE's use of child soldiers. In July, UNICEF representatives in Colombo accused the LTTE of breaking its promise not to recruit children for combat.

Nongovernmental Efforts

On May 6, the International Working Group on Sri Lanka, a coalition of aid agencies and human rights organizations, called on the international community to avert an impending humanitarian crisis in Sri Lanka. In mid-May, government and NGO delegates from thirty countries attending an Asia-Pacific conference on child soldiers appealed for a global ban on child soldiers. The delegates' "Kathmandu Declaration" noted that a growing number of children were being used in armed conflicts, particularly where insurgent groups were active, and said that Sri Lanka was among the worst offenders in the region.

THAILAND

While the government began to look into serious abuses of the past, it made little progress in addressing police abuse, human trafficking, and protection of refugees, particularly those from Burma. Thailand took major steps, however, toward instituting a more accountable and transparent political system and became the first country in Southeast Asia to sign the Rome treaty establishing the International Criminal Court.

Human Rights Developments

The Thai parliament took steps to increase the accountability of government officials and protect rights codified in the 1997 constitution by establishing three new institutions: a National Counter-Corruption Commission, a Parliamentary Ombudsman, and a Supreme Administrative Court. The govern-

ment also moved forward in establishing a National Human Rights Commission, with Senate selection in October of nine of eleven slated commissioners. The remaining two members were to be chosen at the next Senate session in early 2001. On October 3, Thailand signed the Rome treaty.

In June, after pressure from democracy advocates, the media, and victims' families, the government released a 605-page Defense Ministry report on the army's May 1992 shooting of pro-democracy demonstrators in Bangkok. A summary had been made public in June 1999. The government censored about 10 percent of the report, however, and the May 92 Relatives Committee, an organization of families of thirty-eight people whose fate has still not been clarified, demanded that the remaining material be revealed. The committee also called for the release of two other official reports on the incident.

Abuses against refugees remained a serious problem. Two incidents had a major impact on Thai refugee policy. On October 1, 1999, five Burmese gunmen calling themselves the Vigorous Burmese Student Warriors (VBSW) seized the Burmese embassy in Bangkok and held it for a day. Thailand's deputy foreign minister negotiated the release of hostages and accompanied the gunmen to the Burmese border aboard a military helicopter. On January 24, the VBSW and armed Burmese from the ethnic minority Karen insurgent group called God's Army seized the Ratchaburi provincial hospital, holding over 500 people hostage. The men demanded that civilians from a God's Army base be allowed to cross the border into Thailand and that the Thai army immediately cease shelling the area. Early in the morning of January 25, Thai commandos stormed the hospital and freed the hostages. Witnesses reported to the press that some of the attackers surrendered and were led away to a separate section of the hospital compound. Shortly thereafter, the corpses of ten men were displayed on the sidewalk. Human Rights Watch joined numerous Thai and international human rights organizations in calling for an impartial, public investigation into the incident. The Thai government claimed to have initiated an internal investigation, but as of October, no findings had been released.

Following these two incidents, the Thai government instituted measures that increasingly placed Burmese refugees at risk. In November 1999, the government announced that by the end of 2000 it planned to close the Maneeloy Student Center, a refugee camp primarily housing Burmese dissident refugees, and pressed other countries to accept its residents for resettlement. Thai authorities said all Burmese refugees in Bangkok and other urban areas should move to the border; those who stayed would be considered illegal immigrants and be deported. On February 28, five Burmese, four of whom had applied for refugee status to the Office of the United Nations High Commissioner for Refugees (UNHCR), were deported to the Burmese town of Myawaddy, where they were detained by Burmese authorities. Several reportedly received seven-year sentences, and Burma's state-run Radio Myanmar reported on May 19 that one of the men, Saw Tin Oo, had been sentenced to death for treason. He had been arrested by Thai authorities in front of the Burmese Embassy in Bangkok on the day of the embassy siege.

The transfer of urban refugees to the border was slow. The first refugees scheduled to be transferred in August were reluctant to move, and the community surrounding the refugee camp in Umphiem Mai, near the border town of Mae Sot, did not wish them to be moved there.

Throughout much of the first half of the year, senior Thai officials stated that the government wished to see the more than 100,000 refugees living in camps along the Thai border return to Burma within three years. In February, a district officer from Mae Hong Son province passed around a list for refugees in Mae Khong Kha camp to sign up for voluntary repatriation. No one volunteered.

Burmese newly arriving at Thailand's refugee camps had difficulty making asylum claims. At the end of 1999, the Thai government instituted a group status determination procedure, which initially recognized as refugees only those persons fleeing from immediate fighting. Throughout the first half of 2000, the new provincial admission boards rejected thousands of applicants, declaring them illegal immigrants. On June 12, Thai authorities expelled 116 refugees from Don Yang refugee camp in Kanchanaburi province. Of the 116, less than half came from the original group rejected by the provincial board. The others had been rounded up by Thai officials and had not yet appeared before a board. On August 17, approximately 100 persons were returned from Nu Pho refugee camp in Tak province. In August, the Mae Hong Son provincial board reversed an earlier decision to reject thousands of asylum seekers and agreed to admit some 3,400 refugees to camps in Mae Hong Son province.

Ethnic minority Shan refugees continued to flee to Thailand from Burma, but the majority of Shan asylum seekers did not have access to international protection and the refugee camps.

Other human rights problems persisted, including killings of suspected criminals in police custody. In October 1999, a Thai provincial court ruled that three police officers in Suphanburi province had killed three suspected drug dealers in their custody on November 27, 1996, but did not address the circumstances surrounding the killings. The attorney general was to determine whether to proceed with murder charges, but had not done so as of October 2000.

Several attacks on the press took place during the year. Amnat Khunyosingh, owner and editor of the northern Thai newspaper, *Phak Nua Daily*, was shot and wounded by three gunmen as he was returning home from work on April 18. Police arrested three army officers and said that the attack was probably related to the paper's coverage of Senate elections in Chiang Mai province. Early on August 24, a bomb exploded just outside the home of Suriwong Uapatiphan, news editor of *Khao Sod*, a leading Thai language daily, but there were no casualties. Suriwong had reported on police corruption and just before the attack had been sued by a police general for defamation. *Khao Sod's* offices had been bombed in 1999, but the perpetrator was not identified.

The Thai government instituted several measures to reduce statelessness. On May 3, the Local Administration Department decided to shift decision-making on the citizenship of hilltribe children born in Thailand from the provincial governor's office to that of the district chiefs. Decentralization of the procedures was intended to make access to citizenship easier. On August 29, the Thai cabinet granted citizenship to the descendants of three groups of displaced persons: Burmese who entered the country prior to March 1976, Nepalese migrants, and Chinese migrants who had migrated to Thailand since the 1960s. Members of other groups, however, remained without a nationality or full citizenship rights, including a number of Thailand's ethnic minority hilltribes. Around 300,000 such people registered with the government were permitted to reside and work in the country but faced restrictions on their movement, could not participate in elections, and could not own land. Hundreds of thousands of other hilltribe villagers remained unregistered and were officially considered as illegal immigrants.

Thailand continued to be a hub of human trafficking within the region. Enforcement of Thai laws on trafficking remained weak. In one exception, police and an activist from the Centre for Protection of Children on April 18 rescued two Lao girls, aged thirteen and sixteen, from a house where the girls were reportedly being prepared to work in the commercial sex industry. Police arrested the owners of the house. On March 20-21, the Thai government hosted a seminar for justice ministers from twenty Asian countries on combating transnational crime, including human trafficking.

The government's treatment of migrant workers from neighboring countries was unsatisfactory. During a November 1999 crackdown on undocumented foreign labor, overcrowding in a number of immigration detention centers reached dangerous levels. Many migrants still did not have an effective opportunity to challenge charges of illegal entry.

Defending Human Rights

Thai human rights organizations and other advocacy groups generally operated without restrictions. Some nongovernmental organizations providing assistance to Burmese dissidents and others monitoring the human rights situation in Burma were investigated by Thai authorities after the Burmese embassy siege in October 1999 and the Ratchaburi hospital incident in February 2000. These agencies remained under scrutiny in October 2000.

The Role of the International Community

The principal concerns of the international community continued to be the regional trade in narcotics and Thailand's recovery from the Asian financial crisis, but some governments remained engaged on refugee and human trafficking issues. Britain's foreign minister, Robin Cook, visited Tham Hin refugee camp on April 20, where he called for changes in Burma which would allow the refugees to return. Australia, Canada, the United States, and a number of European Union states agreed to resettle over 1,500 refugees from the Maneeloy Student Center. UNHCR continued to urge Thailand's provincial admission boards to apply a broad definition of refugee when screening asylum seekers. On October 17-18, U.N. High Commissioner for Refugees Sadako Ogata visited Thailand. Ogata urged the Thai government to sign the 1951 U.N. Convention relating to the Status of Refugees and requested a UNHCR presence in the refugee camps and a greater role in determining who would be admitted into the camps as refugees. Prime Minister Chuan Leekpai reportedly assured Ogata that the Thai government would not seek to repatriate Burmese refugees until UNHCR secured a presence on the Burmese side of the border and the U.N. agency was confident that returnees would not face persecution in Burma.

The trafficking of women and children to and from Thailand received attention in regional meetings. Delegates to the September 5-7 Asia-Pacific preparatory meeting of the U.N. World Conference against Racism, held in Bangkok, drew attention to the problem of human trafficking to and from Thailand.

The United States maintained a close relationship with Thai security forces. In May 2000, US, Thai, and Singaporean troops drilled for two weeks during "Cobra Gold"— the largest joint military exercise organized by the United States in Asia. The U.S. government sought funds for fiscal year 2001 in excess of U.S. $5.8 million for State Department training and assistance programs to Thailand ranging from de-mining to counter-narcotics operations. An additional U.S. $27.287 million was requested to underwrite commercial military exports to Thailand.

Relevant Human Rights Watch Reports:

Owed Justice: Thai Women Trafficked into Debt Bondage in Japan, 9/00

VIETNAM

The twenty-fifth anniversary of Vietnam's reunification saw the government maintaining tight control over freedom of expression and other basic rights. Highly publicized steps to liberalize the economy, including the signing of a landmark trade agreement with the United States and the establishment of the country's first stock exchange, were not accompanied by rights improvements. Authorities continued to take strong action against those who criticized the ruling Communist Party of Vietnam (CPV) or spoke out in favor of democratic change. Disaffected former CPV leaders, long-time academic critics, independent religious leaders, and the press were common targets. A wide range of political subjects remained off-limits to the media. In a show of reconciliation, the government granted amnesties to more than 20,000 prisoners during the year, but only a handful were people held for their political or religious views. The government restricted access to areas affected by social unrest.

Human Rights Developments

Twenty-fifth anniversary celebrations in April highlighted recent social and economic openings and the government's success in reintegrating returning refugees and bringing recovery after decades of war. Peaceful critics of the government, however, continued to have few outlets for independent expression. Communication among dissidents, and between them and the outside world, was hampered by official interception of mail, blockage of telephone lines, and denial of publishing rights. When dissidents or former political prisoners criticized the CPV or called for reforms they were subject to heightened surveillance or interrogation by officials. The 1997 Administrative Detention Decree 31/CP remained in force. It allowed officials to detain individuals suspected of posing a threat to national security without a warrant or prior judicial approval.

Early in the year, the CPV's ideological commission accused Nguyen Thanh Giang, a leading geologist and outspoken intellectual who had been detained for two months in 1999, of writing documents which showed "close collusion with reactionary forces abroad to disrupt the social order." Giang remained under surveillance throughout the year.

On May 12, police in Dalat put dissident intellectual Ha Si Phu (Nguyen Xuan Tu) under house arrest and threatened to charge him with treason under Article 72 of the Criminal Code. Authorities apparently linked him to dissident intellectuals who were drafting an open appeal for greater democracy. On April 28, police searched his house and confiscated his computer and diskettes. As of October, Ha Si Phu remained under investigation and confined to his home, although he had not yet been officially charged.

The government announced several times during the year that it was taking steps against terrorist plots allegedly supported by overseas Vietnamese and "imperialist countries." On August 16, *Nhan Dan* (The People) newspaper stated that more than forty people had been arrested since March 1999 for "directly participat[ing] in the reactionaries' sabotage plan," but it was unclear whether those arrested were indeed saboteurs or peaceful critics.

Several religious leaders and former political prisoners were denied exit visas to attend conferences abroad, including prominent dissident Nguyen Dan Que, Thich Tue Sy of the banned Unified Buddhist Church of Vietnam (UBCV), and Thich Thai Hoa, a leader of the Buddhist order in Hue.

Despite government repression, several dissidents issued critical public statements though, typically, they were able to do so only on the Internet and primarily reached an overseas audience. On May 19, five prominent dissidents issued a public appeal to the National Assembly for greater democracy, the withdrawal of charges against fellow dissident Ha Si Phu, and the repeal of Administrative Detention Decree 31/CP. In April, Thich Huyen Quang, supreme patriarch of the UBCV, who remained under pagoda arrest in Quang Ngai province throughout the year, issued a letter to the party leadership calling for greater religious freedom.

The domestic media remained under strict state control and published scarcely any criticism of the government. One exception, however, was criticism published in *Nhan Dan* by Vietnam's most prominent war hero, General Vo Nguyen Giap, who stated that the CPV should be more democratic and accused it of "ideological stagnancy." Requests by dissidents such as Tran Do and Thich Quang Do for publishing licenses were either denied or ignored by the authorities.

Provisions in the 1999 Press Law, which allowed media outlets to be sued for defamation whether the information they publish is accurate or not, were applied for the first time in September 2000. The Haiphong Agriculture Materials and Transport Company sued *Tuoi Tre Hanoi* (Youth News) for damaging the company's prestige because of its critical reporting on the company's operations. As of October, the case had not yet gone to trial.

The potential for press censorship increased in August when the Ministry of Culture proposed new regulations that would more than triple the number of activities, from 200 to 650, defined as offensive to Vietnamese culture. The regulations, which had not been officially adopted as law as of October, would impose fines for the production or possession of "culturally inappropriate" materials, including those which "distorted Vietnam's history or defamed its national heroes."

Foreign journalists based in Vietnam received strong warnings from government officials after trying to contact and interview dissidents. On December 26, 1999, Pham The Hung, a French journalist for Radio France International, was expelled from Vietnam after meeting with Catholics whose names were not on a list of interviewees he had submitted with his journalist visa request. In April, French reporter Arnaud Dubus, traveling on a tourist visa, was interrogated and had his notes confiscated by police after he met with several dissidents. On April 12, security police in Ho Chi Minh City arrested Sylvaine Pasquier, a reporter for the French weekly *L'Express*, after she tried to meet dissident Nguyen Dan Que. Pasquier was deported on April 14.

Vietnamese listeners had access to most international radio stations, but the government jammed access to Radio Free Asia and Hmong-language Christian broadcasts from the Far East Broadcasting Company. In June, the Foreign Ministry confirmed that the British Broadcasting Corporation (BBC), which had an application pending since 1993, would be authorized to open a Vietnam bureau.

While foreign language newspapers and magazines could be purchased in the major cities, an internal Customs Department bulletin in December 1999 announced a crackdown on illegally imported foreign publications because of their "poisonous" content. Singled out were the *South China Morning Post*, *Asian Wall Street Journal*, Singapore's *Straits Times*, and Thailand's *Nation*. Foreign publications were occasionally censored. In May, government censors blacked out an *International Herald Tribune* editorial that criticized Vietnam's human rights record. In

March, the Ministry of Culture and Information ordered the confiscation and withdrawal from circulation of a book by Hanoi author Bui Ngoc Tan. The only book to be banned during the year, *Chuyen Ke Nam 2000* (An Account of the Year 2000) described the author's experiences in North Vietnamese prisons between 1968 and 1973.

Internet access remained tightly controlled for Vietnam's approximately 85,000 subscribers (0.1 percent of the country's population). The government maintained control over Vietnam's only Internet access provider, Vietnam Data Communications (VDC), as well as over five Internet service providers operated by state organizations, including one owned by the army. VDC was authorized to monitor subscribers' access to sites and to use firewalls to block connections to sites operated by groups critical of the government. In January, the Foreign Ministry stated that all information relayed through the Internet in Vietnam must comply with broadly worded national security provisions in Vietnam's press laws and could not damage the reputations of organizations or citizens. These measures had been selectively applied in the past to keep critical voices out of public media. In September, the government launched a new domestic Internet service, which, unlike other services did not require users to register with the government. The new service, however, restricted subscribers to Vietnamese websites only. Several protests over alleged abuses by local officials reported during the year, although coverage was limited by strict controls on media access to the affected areas. In April, several dozen people from southern Dong Thap province assembled for several days in front of the CPV headquarters in Hanoi to protest corruption and lack of democracy in their province. That same month, villagers in Nam Dinh province denounced alleged interference by local Communist Party officials in commune-level People's Council elections. In June, citizens in Nam Dinh held two district party members hostage for a week. After promises that the hostage takers would not be punished, the officials were released. In August, a group of 150 ethnic Ede

highlanders in Dak Lak province stormed a lowland Vietnamese settlement in protest over encroachment on their land, part of which was being developed for coffee plantations and gem mining. In September, more than one hundred protesters from provinces in the south as well as the central highlands camped outside government offices in Ho Chi Minh City for several weeks, protesting graft and land confiscation.

As the Ninth Party Congress, scheduled for March 2001, neared, party officials appeared increasingly apprehensive about the potential for rural unrest to boil over, as it had in Thai Binh and Dong Nai provinces in 1997. Party Secretary Le Kha Phieu announced in September that cabinet-led inspection teams would be dispatched to fifteen cities and provinces to look into citizen's complaints about corruption and abuses by officials. In October, *Nhan Dan* reported that more than 2,000 government and party officials had been disciplined in Thai Binh as a result of peasant demonstrations in 1997 against graft and unfair taxation.

Religious freedom also remained sharply curtailed. The government's ban on independent religious associations continued, with all religious groups required to register with and seek the approval of the state. In March, a year-long controversy escalated over whether the party had the right to appoint, not simply to approve, abbots at the historic One-Pillar Pagoda in Hanoi. Congregation members contacted UBCV members abroad and prepared a petition protesting the replacement of their abbots with party appointees. In March, the Hanoi People's Committee ordered head abbot Thich Thanh Khanh to leave the pagoda by April 30; however, as of October, he remained in place.

Members of the Hoa Hao sect of Buddhism came under increased pressure, with at least twelve in detention or prison as of mid-2000. Sect elder Le Quang Liem's telephone line was disconnected in December 1999 and he was interrogated several times by police after he signed a joint appeal calling for greater religious freedom. Surveillance of Liem increased in February 2000, when he announced the restoration of the Central Hoa Hao Buddhist Association, separate from a government-dominated Hoa Hao committee established in 1999. Hoa Hao members in An Giang province clashed several times with police, who reportedly blocked a pilgrimage to their prophet's birthplace, and detained and beat some adherents in December 1999. Police arrested at least eight Hoa Hao members in March 2000 as tensions increased in the approach to a religious anniversary. On March 30, police detained ten Hoa Hao members and blocked thousands of other followers from observing the religious anniversary. Additional clashes with security forces broke out in An Giang in September, when Hoa Hao followers protested the trial and conviction of five members arrested in March.

Conflict continued between the government and the UBCV. In April, police made late-night visits to the pagodas of church leaders Thich Quang Do and Thich Tue Sy, ostensibly to conduct identity checks. On April 24, police took leaders Thich Khong Tanh and Thich Quang Hue to a Ho Chi Minh City police station for questioning. In July, Quang Ngai provincial officials and police interrogated UBCV Patriarch Thich Huyen Quang about a statement critical of the government that he had issued in April. In late September and early October, UBCV monks attempting to conduct independent flood relief missions in the Mekong Delta and distribute aid packages marked with UBCV labels clashed with local authorities. Government regulations limited flood relief operations to state-sanctioned organizations. On September 21, authorities halted a UBCV flood relief mission in An Giang province, led by Thich Nguyen Ly. In early October, a contingent of UBCV monks, including Thich Quang Do and Thich Khong Tanh, travelled to An Giang, where security police blocked their flood relief plans. Police reportedly detained the monks for twelve hours on October 7 before ordering them to leave the province and return to their pagodas in Ho Chi Minh City. The Foreign Ministry later denied that the monks had been detained.

The government also continued its attempts to suppress the growth of Protestant evangelical churches which had gained converts among Vietnam's ethnic minorities. While two dozen ethnic Hmong Protestants reportedly were released from detention at the end of 1999, at least eight other Hmong and Hre remained in prison or police custody as of October 2000. The government, however, began to recognize more "Tin Lanh" (Good News) churches, mostly in the North, and hundreds of Protestants were able regularly to attend un-recognized Tin Lanh churches in southern and central Vietnam.

Catholics, too, were not immune from state meddling, with the government continuing to restrict the number of parishes, screen candidates for the priesthood and for appointments as bishops, and to reject requests for a papal visit. One member of the Catholic Congregation of the Mother Co-Redemptrix was released in April, but at least three other Catholics remained in prison.

Unregistered sects and religious activities officially labeled "superstitious," prohibited by a 1999 decree on religion, came under increasing pressure. In November 1999, the state press reported that Vietnam had more than thirty illegal cults. That same month, officials fined members of an unregistered religious sect in Hanoi known as Long Hoa Di Lac (Chinese Dragon Buddha Sect) for unlawful assembly and use of religion for propaganda purposes. In June, the state press reported that police in Thai Binh were "cracking down on heresy." The target was the Thanh Hai Vo Thuong Su sect, originally established in Taiwan but led by a Vietnamese woman. In August, police in Quang Binh reportedly confiscated religious texts from the Tam Giao Tuyen Duong sect, forcing members to destroy altars and pledge to abandon the sect, and fined the group's leader for allegedly providing illegal medical treatment.

Prison conditions remained poor, with prisoners reporting the use of shackles, dark cells, and torture. Dozens of death sentences were issued during the year, with twenty-nine crimes considered capital offenses, including drug trafficking, many economic crimes, some sex offenses, murder, and armed robbery. In April, Canadian citizen Nguyen Thi Hiep was convicted of heroin smuggling and executed.

While the government insisted it had no political prisoners, in March the Public Security Ministry stated that more than one hundred people were then imprisoned for crimes against national security.

In its largest ever prisoner amnesty, Vietnam released 12,264 prisoners on April 30 to commemorate the reunification of the country, and a further 10,693 on National Day on September 2. The government did not publicly release the names of those freed, but political and religious prisoners known to have been released in the two amnesties included Catholic Brother John Euder Mai Duc Chuong, Hmong Protestant Vu Gian Thao, political dissident Nguyen Ngoc Tan (alias Pham Thai), Protestant Nguyen Thi Thuy, and Cao Daist Le Kim Bien.

Defending Human Rights

No domestic human rights organizations were allowed to operate in Vietnam, nor were international human rights organizations allowed to monitor conditions or conduct research there.

The Role of the International Community

In December 1999, Vietnam's donors pledged U.S. $2.8 million in aid to Vietnam, with $700 million conditioned on accelerated economic reforms. For the most part donors were publicly silent about human rights violations, aside from the international outcry after the execution of Canadian citizen Nguyen Thi Hiep. Convicted of drug trafficking, she was executed by firing squad in April, despite the fact that Vietnam had pledged to review her case on the basis of additional information provided by the Canadian government. Afterwards Canada temporarily withdrew its ambassador and its support for Vietnam's entry to the World Trade Organization. Talks on restoring full diplomatic ties resumed in September, when Hiep's mother, Tran Thi Cam, was granted an early release from prison.

In April, the U.N. Commission on Human Rights stated that it would be examining complaints against Vietnam for human rights violations under the "1503 Procedure," a confidential procedure whereby complaints are investigated and sent to the full U.N. Commission on Human Rights. In May, Vietnam was elected to the U.N. Commission on Human Rights for a three-year term. The U.N. Development Program's Growth in Governance program focused on legislative, judicial, and procedural reforms, including revision of the labor code.

United States

U.S. policy towards Vietnam centered on using trade and investment as a means to press for gradual political and economic reforms. Human rights concerns were addressed through a bilateral "dialogue" meeting that failed to include concrete incentives for progress and had minimal effect on overall U.S.-Vietnam relations. The State Department's annual report on religious freedom provoked an angry response from the Vietnamese government, which rejected being labeled one of several "totalitarian or authoritarian regimes" along with China, Myanmar, Laos, and North Korea. In July, after four years of negotiations, Vietnam signed a bilateral trade agreement with the United States. As of this writing the agreement had not received U.S. Congressional approval. In November, President Clinton was scheduled to become the first U.S. president to visit Vietnam since Richard Nixon in 1969.

Japan

Japan, which was Vietnam's largest donor, announced in June that it had extended Official Development Assistance (ODA) to Vietnam for another five years. The foreign ministry was considering including human rights and legal reform in a bilateral dialogue with Vietnam at the vice-foreign ministers' level beginning late in 2000. In 1999 (the latest year for which figures were available), Japan gave $680 million in loans and grants to Vietnam.

European Union

The E.U., Vietnam's third largest donor and its biggest trade partner, has provided approximately U.S. $2 billion in ODA since 1993. Most of the bilateral assistance to Vietnam came from France, Germany, Denmark and Sweden. During a visit to Vietnam in May, the Swedish Minister of Culture called for more openness in the media and greater democracy when she announced a grant of U.S. $4 million to support media training and live broadcasting programs. During a December 1999 visit to Hanoi, Czech Prime Minister Milos Zeman raised issues of democratization and political prisoners.

Relevant Human Rights Watch Reports:

The Silencing of Dissent, 5/00

HUMAN RIGHTS WATCH

CHILDREN'S RIGHTS

Human Rights Developments

New international protections pledged in 2000 held out hope for the many children who were exploited as laborers or abused as soldiers around the world. A new optional protocol to the Convention on the Rights of the Child prohibiting the use of children in armed conflict was adopted in May, and quickly garnered signatures from seventy countries. The protocol, achieved after six years of negotiations, raised the minimum age for compulsory recruitment and participation in armed conflict from fifteen to eighteen. A new Worst Forms of Child Labor Convention (International Labour Organization (ILO) Convention 182) went into force and achieved the fastest rate of ratification in ILO history. The convention, adopted by the 1999 International Labor Conference, targeted such practices as child slavery, sexual exploitation, debt bondage, and trafficking.

Despite these new promises and the nearly universal ratification of the Convention on the Rights of the Child, children's rights were widely disregarded and many countries failed to muster the political will to fulfill their legal obligations towards children.

Violence against children—frequently carried out at the hands of the state—remained an issue that governments were loath to address. Countless children continued to suffer violence resulting in physical injury, psychological trauma, and even death. Street children were subject to arbitrary detention and abuse by police; children in correctional or other institutions were beaten or tortured by staff; children in schools were subjected to severe beatings by their teachers; others were victims of summary and arbitrary executions. In many cases, the failure of law enforcement bodies to promptly and effectively investigate and prosecute cases of abuses allowed the abuse to continue.

As in past years, street children continued to suffer serious abuses at the hands of authorities. An egregious example was Honduras, where Casa Alianza reported that over 165 street children under the age of eighteen were killed between January 1998 and September 2000; a total of 320 street youth between the ages of nine and twenty-four were killed during this period. Police and security forces were found to be responsible for the deaths in thirty-six of the 320 cases. Nearly three-quarters of the cases remained unsolved.

In a welcome development, the Committee on the Rights of the Child agreed to focus on state violence against children for its annual day of discussion in September 2000. The committee invited written submissions and participation in two areas: state violence suffered by children in conflict with the law and by children living in the care of the state, including orphanages and other institutions. Based on the discussion in two working groups, the committee recommended that the U.N. General Assembly request the U.N. secretary-general to conduct an in-depth international study on the issue of violence against children. The committee recommended that such a study be as thorough and influential as the landmark 1996 Graça Machel study on the Impact of Armed Conflict on Children and include recommendations of effective actions to address violence against children.

During the year, governments began to prepare for the U.N. General Assembly's Special Session on Children in 2001, scheduled to follow up the 1990 World Summit on Children. At the 1990 Summit, an unprecedented number of world leaders adopted a declaration and plan of action devoted primarily to improving the health and education of children. The 2001 Special Session will review progress towards the goals set in 1990 and identify new commitments that must be made to address current threats and challenges facing children.

From May 30 to June 2, governments met for the first preparatory committee meeting in advance of the Special Session. Representatives admitted that many of the 1990 goals had not been met, that insufficient resources had been allocated to children, and that the continued prevalence of poverty, armed conflict, and the HIV/AIDS pandemic in particular posed continuing and even increased threats to the well-being and rights of children. However, it was unclear whether governments would be willing to make new commitments to implementing the full range of children's rights and move beyond the survival and development agenda that dominated the 1990 Summit.

Nongovernmental organizations struggled in particular to place exploitation and pervasive violence against children on governments' agendas and to insist that governments use the Special Session to commit to full implementation of the Convention on the Rights of the Child. A broad Child Rights Caucus formed to demand that issues such as violence, child labor and contemporary forms of slavery, sexual exploitation, trafficking, juvenile justice, and protection during armed conflicts be addressed in any new commitments resulting from the 2001 Special Session.

The United Nations Children's Fund (UNICEF), charged with producing a draft "outcome" document for the Special Session, was reluctant to address adequately the protection needs for children at risk of violence and exploitation. Despite a stated commitment to uphold the Convention on the Rights of the Child and the full range of children's rights, early drafts reflected a traditional agenda, focused on health, nutrition, basic education, and opportunities for adolescents to participate in and contribute to their societies, but largely ignoring the right of children to protection from exploitation, violence, and abuse.

Child Soldiers

A new international consensus to end the use of child soldiers was reached in January, when governments from around the world agreed on a new optional protocol to the Convention on the Rights of the Child, establishing eighteen as the minimum age for direct participation in armed conflict, for forced or compulsory recruitment, and for any recruitment or use by nongovernmental armed groups. The Coalition to Stop the Use of Child Soldiers estimated that approximately 300,000 children under the age of eighteen fought in armed conflicts worldwide.

The new child soldiers protocol was adopted by the U.N. General Assembly on May 25. By late September, it had garnered seventy signatures and three ratifications and seemed on course to enter into force in early 2001.

The new protocol represented a great advance over previous international standards, which allowed children as young as fifteen to be recruited and sent into combat. It was also a significant triumph for the global campaign led by the Coalition to Stop the Use of Child Soldiers (see Campaigns).

At a national level, positive developments were seen in Colombia and the Democratic Republic of Congo (DRC). In Colombia, legislation was signed on December 23, 1999, raising the minimum age for recruitment into governmental armed forces to age eighteen. The same month, the Colombian Army announced that it had discharged its final contingent of 980 soldiers under the age of eighteen. In the Democratic Republic of Congo, President Kabila signed a decree on June 9, establishing a national commission and an inter-ministerial committee to oversee the disarmament, demobilization, and reintegration into society of child soldiers.

However, such advances were overshadowed by the continuing recruitment and use of children in approximately thirty conflicts around the world. In Colombia, opposition guerrilla armies and paramilitary forces often linked to the armed forces continued to maintain at least 5,000 children in their ranks and used them as soldiers and spies, according to UNICEF. In January 2000, Revolutionary Armed Forces of Colombia (Fuerzas Armadas Revolucionarias de Colombia, FARC) Commander Manuel Marulanda told reporters that the FARC would not stop recruiting soldiers fifteen and older. "They are going to stay in the ranks," he emphasized. The Colombian army also reportedly continued to use captured guerrillas who were children as informants and spies instead of turning them over promptly to child welfare authorities. Facilities to rehabilitate former child soldiers exist in Colombia, but are severely underfunded.

In Sierra Leone, both the Revolutionary United Front (RUF) and pro-government forces continued to forcibly recruit children, including demobilized child soldiers, into their ranks. The RUF forced children to carry military equipment and to loot goods and engage in fighting. Rape of abducted girls was routine. Some forty demobilized child soldiers from a demobilization camp in Makeni were pressured by the RUF to rejoin through the use of threats, false promises, and false rumors. The civil defense militias also remobilized scores of child soldiers. Children continued to be subjected to all forms of violence, primarily by the RUF, including amputation, rape, and abduction.

In Ethiopia, credible sources reported that thousands of teenage boys were forcibly recruited into the Ethiopian army, particularly during the buildup to the major offensive launched against Eritrea in May. Children (primarily from Oromos and Somali ethnic groups) were targeted in schools and also press-ganged from marketplaces and villages. Once recruited, children were reportedly sent to camps for military training and indoctrination and then sent to fight.

Ethiopia also accused Eritrea of using child soldiers and circulated lists of Eritrean children whom Ethiopia had taken as prisoners of war.

In Burundi, children as young as twelve joined armed forces and served as spies, lookouts, scouts, and porters and helped loot property. Known as "doriya," the children wore cast-off military uniforms and received food and portions of loot from older soldiers. Burundian soldiers also forced children to supply firewood and transport supplies, and used girls to bring water from springs or rivers to the soldiers' camps. In March, three boys were wounded when soldiers forced them to carry food, water, and medicines through an area known for rebel attacks. The rebel National Liberation Forces (FNL) in Burundi also recruited and used "doriya" as soldiers and helpers. Often used initially as cooks and general helpers, some children later took up weapons and became regular fighters.

In the DRC, the civil conflicts in recent years had been marked by widespread recruitment of child soldiers by the Congolese government's forces and rebel groups, as well as by semi-autonomous militias. UNICEF estimated the total number of child soldiers to be about 12,000. Despite President Kabila's June 9 demobilization decree, the extent to which children were actually demobilized was unclear, and early in the year Human Rights Watch received reports that many child soldiers were detained in prison camps for deserting Kabila's forces.

Rebel groups in the DRC also continued to recruit and use child soldiers with the full support of their foreign backers. Of particular concern was the conduct of the Ugandan People's Defence Forces (UPDF), which had admittedly trained thousands of troops, many of them children, for the Movement for the Liberation of Congo (MLC), the main rebel faction supported by Uganda in northwestern Congo. In areas of north Kivu that were nominally controlled by another Ugandan-backed rebel faction, the Congolese Rally for Democracy-Liberation Movement (RCD-ML), the UPDF trained several battalions of young soldiers in the towns of Beni, Lubero, and Bunia in the first half of 2000. In each of these towns, recruitment was largely done along ethnic lines by local warlords loyal to Uganda. In August and September, the RCD-ML's armed wing splintered as a result of leadership disputes within the movement. Among one group of three hundred mutineers that later surrendered to the UPDF, nearly half were reportedly below the age of fifteen.

Although Africa continued to experience the most widespread use of child soldiers, children were also used in other parts of the world. In Nepal, evidence mounted that children as young as fourteen, including girls, were recruited by members of the armed opposition group, the Communist Party of Nepal (CPN) (Maoist). Between June and August, at least thirty children were reported abducted by the group, including several fourteen-year-olds. In Sri Lanka, the University Teachers for Human Rights reported in July that the Liberation Tigers of Tamil Eelam (LTTE) had initiated a strong new recruitment drive for child soldiers, despite the commitments they made in 1998 to U.N. Special Representative to the Secretary-General Olara Otunnu not to recruit anyone under seventeen years old. Much of the recruitment was forced, with only 5 percent of recruits estimated to be willing volunteers. In one instance, fourteen- and fifteen-year-old girls who resisted were isolated, taken to a room, stripped, and assaulted.

Regional and other intergovernmental bodies paid increasing attention to the issue of child soldiers. Resolutions or declarations urging support for the new optional protocol were adopted in April by member states of the Economic Community of West African States (ECOWAS) and in July by the Organization of American States (OAS), European Parliament, and the G-8 meeting of foreign ministers in Okinawa.

The Organization for Security and Co-operation in Europe (OSCE) identified children and armed conflict as a priority issue during its November 1999 Summit in Istanbul, followed up with a special inter-governmental/NGO seminar in Warsaw in May, and began considering an OSCE ministerial decision on the issue.

In another welcome regional development, the African Charter on the Rights and Welfare of the Child entered into force on November 29, 1999, after receiving fifteen ratifications by OAU member states. The African Charter is the only regional treaty that prohibits the recruitment or use of children in armed conflict. The charter sets a higher standard than the new optional protocol, as it sets eighteen as the minimum age for any form of recruitment (whether forced or "voluntary") and for any participation in armed conflict. At this writing, twenty-one member states had ratified the charter.

In July, the Security Council held a special debate on children in armed conflict, in follow-up to Security Council resolution 1261, adopted in 1999. The council received its first report on children and armed conflict from the U.N. secretary-general. Key recommendations of the report included ratification and implementation of the new optional protocol (with governments urged to declare a minimum age of at least eighteen years for voluntary recruitment), increased commitment of resources for the demobilization and rehabilitation of child soldiers, and targeted political and economic sanctions against parties to conflict which target and abuse children.

Security Council members held an informal briefing with NGOs on children and armed conflict, inviting representatives of the Coalition to Stop the Use of Child Soldiers, the small arms campaign, humanitarian organizations, and other networks to participate. Following its formal debate, the council adopted Resolution 1314, which condemned the targeting of children, and urged member states to sign and ratify the new protocol, and take other steps to better protect children in armed conflict situations.

In September, representatives from 132 governments, youth, nongovernmental and international organizations, and other experts participated in the first international conference on war-affected children, hosted by the government of Canada. Forty-five foreign ministers took part in the conference, which resulted in the adoption of an "Agenda for War-Affected Children," which called for increased efforts to protect children in conflict situations, end impunity for those who violate international human rights and humanitarian law, and strengthen humanitarian assistance for children affected by war.

Refugee, Immigrant, and Stateless Children

The rights and special protection needs of refugee, immigrant, and stateless children were frequently neglected. Among the world's most vulnerable, these children were often subjected to hazardous or exploitative labor conditions, sexual violence and other physical abuse, denial of education and health care, and other violations of their basic human rights.

In Malaysia's immigration detention centers, Human Rights Watch found young unaccompanied boys detained with unrelated adult men in camps where detainees were robbed, beaten, inadequately fed, and denied medical care. Girls in immigration detention camps were sometimes sexually solicited and touched by male guards. Girls as young as thirteen were separated from their parents and detained for extended periods with little or no contact. Children were also deported separately from their parents to the Thai-Malaysia border.

Children made up 65 percent of the 300,000 Sierra Leonean refugees in Guinea. Those who had become separated from their parents during flight often took refuge with foster families, where some were neglected, physically abused, denied food, deprived of an education, or exploited for their labor. At times, refugee girls as young as twelve worked as child prostitutes to support themselves. Compounding the risks to refugee children, some of the camps were located dangerously close to the border, with the result that many refugee children were vulnerable to armed raids and forced recruitment for service as child soldiers.

The United States Immigration and Naturalization Service (INS) continued to detain unaccompanied children for lengthy periods of time before deporting them or releasing them to family members or appropriate guardians. Human Rights Watch was particularly concerned that more than a third of the children in INS custody—nearly 2,000 children during the year ending in September 1999—were held in juvenile detention centers and county jails. Of the nearly 1,300 children held in secure confinement for more than three days, 58 percent were waiting to be transferred to a shelter care or similar facility or were there simply because the INS lacked any alternative for them. By failing to place children in the least restrictive setting appropriate to their circumstances, the INS violated international standards, its own regulations, and the terms of a court order.

International law guarantees all children the right to have their births registered and the right to a nationality. Children in many parts of the world were denied these basic rights, often affecting their access to an education, health services, or other benefits of citizenship.

Children born to Rohingya refugees in Malaysia were frequently turned out of primary schools when they could not prove legal residency. Not recognized as nationals of Burma, these children were not able to gain legal residency of any country. Although Malaysia's constitution provided citizenship to children born on its territory who would otherwise be stateless, it did not extend this provision to Rohingya children. Many could not obtain birth certificates; even those who could were often denied basic education and health services. Older children and adults were subjected to extortion by police and were not protected as refugees by the Malaysian government (see Malaysia chapter).

Children of longtime Bidun residents of Kuwait faced similar discrimination because their parents were considered stateless or otherwise unable to pass on their nationality under Kuwaiti law. Termed "illegal residents" despite their families' residence in Kuwait for decades, even generations, Bidun children were frequently denied birth certificates and other official documents needed to attend public and private schools or receive medical treatment (see Kuwait chapter).

Children in Conflict with the Law

Governments around the world abused youth during arrest and interrogation and held them in overcrowded, unsafe conditions in disregard of international standards. Juvenile detention facilities often failed to provide youth with adequate educational, medical, mental health, or rehabilitative services. In many cases, children were commingled with adults, in violation of international law.

The United States' treatment of children in conflict with the law presented particular concerns. It continued to detain and incarcerate large numbers of youth—over 100,000, by one estimate—even though juvenile arrests fell for the sixth year running. With four juvenile offenders executed in the first half of the year, it continued to defy the international standard forbidding the imposition of the death penalty for crimes committed below the age of eighteen.

Abuse in Policy Custody

Children in conflict with the law were often subjected to human rights violations during arrest and detention, including arbitrary arrest, physical abuse during interrogation, and other denials of due process. In particular, street children throughout the world were subjected to routine harassment and physical abuse by police and by private security guards who often acted with the acquiescence of the government.

According to the Russian Committee for Civil Rights, one third of all youth facing criminal proceedings in Russia are subject to violence during detention and interrogation. One in four youth was subjected to police violence on the street before the age of fifteen.

When Human Rights Watch interviewed a fourteen-year-old boy who had been frequently detained by Russian police, he reported that during one arrest, the police beat him and his friends, spraying tear gas in their eyes. His mother told us that when she picked him up the following day, he had bruises on his head, back, and legs. The bruising on his legs was "mostly on the hips, not round ones but stretched ones, as if they were beating with sticks." She also stated that his eyes were red and that he vomited shortly after he was released.

Human Rights Watch and other human rights organizations heard reports of similar abuses from children across the world. In Pakistan, a fifteen-year-old boy detained for the theft of a motorcycle told Human Rights Watch in 1998, "I was whipped with a rubber strap or lash used to rotate a motor, like a fan belt." In Jamaica, Human Rights Watch researchers heard numerous accounts of beatings with batons, sticks, and electrical cords during and shortly after arrest. In Bolivia, in one case documented by Amnesty International in April 2000, police detained a sixteen-year-old boy in Cochabamba, beat him with hoses and chains, and broke his nose.

The Israeli military reinstituted Military Order No. 132 in 1999, permitting its forces to arrest Palestinian children as young as twelve. Originally issued during the Intifada, the order had been suspended in 1993. Following the renewed implementation of the order, groups of Palestinian children reported that they were beaten or threatened with physical abuse during interrogation.

A sixteen-year-old girl continued to be held pending trial in Israel's Ramle prison after being arrested in December 1998. According to her parents, she was placed in solitary confinement and denied family visits for seventeen days after her arrest.

Palestinian security forces carried out sweeping arrests of secondary school and university students in the West Bank in response to violent demonstrations there, detaining many who reportedly took no part in the demonstrations or in acts of violence. Several of the students reported that they were kicked and beaten in Palestinian General Intelligence and Preventive Security Service detention centers (see Israel, the Occupied West Bank and Gaza Strip, and Palestinian Authority chapter).

In November 1999, the Inter-American Court of Human Rights found Guatemala responsible for the 1990 deaths of five street youth ranging in age from fifteen to twenty. Police officers shot four of the youth in the head and the fifth in the back; the officers then abandoned the bodies in Guatemala City's Bosque de San Nicolás. The court noted that the officers' actions in the case were consistent with a pattern of illegal acts against street children that included threats, arbitrary arrest, cruel, inhuman, and degrading treatment, and extrajudicial execution. The decision was the first by a regional human rights tribunal to address violations of the rights of street children.

Following the Inter-American Court's decision, Guatemala showed increased willingness to acknowledge abuses committed by its security forces against street children. At a hearing before the Inter-American Commission on Human Rights in March 2000, Guatemala accepted full responsibility for the death of Marcos Fidel Quisquinay, a thirteen-year-old killed in 1994 when two individuals handed him a bag of food containing explosives. In July 2000, Guatemalan authorities arrested a private security guard for the 1994 murder of a seventeen-year-old street youth. Also in July, the Guatemalan Human Rights Ombudsman found members of the National Civil Police's former Special Forces unit responsible for sexually assaulting a fifteen-year-old girl in front of another fifteen-year-old street child.

Conditions of Confinement

Children throughout the world continued to be confined in conditions that violated international law and standards. In many cases, children in confinement were subjected to violence at the hands of guards and other detainees, commingled with adults, denied access to education, medical, or mental health services, deprived of family visits, religious services, and other important contacts with their communities, and even denied adequate food or basic sanitary facilities.

Palestinian youth held in Israel's Telmond Prison said they were held in overcrowded conditions and experienced difficulties in receiving family visits and medical treatment. In addition, in November 1997, a Tel Aviv court ordered the prison authority to provide detained Palestinian children with an education equivalent to that offered to detained Jewish children, with the exception of instruction in subjects defined only as those that "threaten the security of Israel." According to Defence for Children International/Palestinian Section, the prison authority failed to implement the decision fully.

Children in Russia's investigation and pretrial detention centers were also subjected to cramped, filthy, and dangerous conditions. In December 1999, a representative of a local NGO observed twenty-eight boys in a cell with eighteen beds, only twelve of which had mattresses; the boys slept in rotations. The representative told Human Rights Watch that one boy was severely beaten by other youth: at the instigation of guards, another boy stood in the center of the cell, blindfolded and swinging a plastic bottle full of water; the others repeatedly pushed the first boy within range of the swinging bottle. The representative described the boy who had been beaten as "covered in bruises of every shape and color."

Human Rights Watch received reliable reports that children under eighteen were regularly held in adult detention facilities in Bahrain. Local NGOs in Cambodia, the Dominican Republic, Kenya, Mali, Nicaragua, Pakistan, Russia, South Africa, and Zambia also reported that children and adults were at times commingled, in violation of the Convention on the Rights of the Child and the International Covenant on Civil and Political Rights (ICCPR). Each of these countries was a state party to the Convention on the Rights of the Child; all except for Bahrain and Pakistan were states party to the ICCPR.

In March 1999, the Inter-American Commission on Human Rights ordered Honduras to compensate children detained in adult prisons between 1993 and 1997 to remedy Honduras' violations of the American Convention on Human Rights. By September 2000, however, only a few of the youth had received payment.

In the United States, abuses in South Dakota's juvenile detention facilities came to light after Gina Score, fourteen, collapsed and died during a forced run at the state's boot camp for girls in July 1999. Following her death, other youth and their parents charged that guards routinely shackled youth in spread-eagled fashion after cutting their clothes off (a practice known as "four-point-ing"), chained youth inside their cells ("bumpering"), and placed children in isolation twenty-three hours a day for extended periods of time. Girls held in the State Training School reported that they were strip-searched by male guards, sprayed with pepper spray while naked, and handcuffed spread-eagled to their beds. Human Rights Watch wrote to South Dakota Governor William Janklow in March 2000 to urge him to revamp policies and practices at all state juvenile detention facilities. The governor did not respond to our letter.

Prompted by Human Rights Watch's 1999 report on children in adult jails in the U.S. state of Maryland, community pressure, federal inquiries, and in some cases the prospect of litigation, detention officials in Maryland took some steps to address deficiencies in education. The Baltimore City Detention Center's school added additional teachers to its staff and began to offer a full school day to youth in the general population and protective custody sections, but youth in other sections, including segregation, continued to be deprived of regular classroom instruction. The Frederick County Detention Center entered into an agreement with the U.S. Department of Education to provide appropriate special education to all detainees under twenty-one years of age, as required by federal law. In Prince George's County—where youth were receiving no education at the time of our visit—the Department of Corrections and the county board of education agreed to provide educational services in September 2000, several months after the American Civil Liberties Union Fund of the National Capital Area notified the department that it intended to initiate a lawsuit.

In a welcome development, the Civil Rights Division of the U.S. Department of Justice notified Maryland Gov. Parris N. Glendening on October 16 that it would investigate conditions for all 3,000 detainees at the Baltimore City Detention Center, including an examination of whether youth were "subjected to excessive use of isola-tion." The division also planned to examine whether detainees, including youth, received appropriate medical and mental health care and adequate protection from harm.

In September 2000, the U.S. state of Louisiana agreed to implement significant changes in its juvenile detention system to protect youth from physical, sexual, and mental abuse and provide them with rehabilitative services and medical, dental, and mental health care. Under the settlement, health care services will be provided by the Louisiana State University School of Medicine; independent monitors chosen by the U.S. Department of Justice and lawyers for youth in detention will conduct regular compliance inspections. Educational services were addressed in an earlier settlement, reached in November 1999. The settlement brought an end to some twenty-seven years of litigation over juvenile detention conditions in the state. The Department of Justice had intervened in the lawsuits following a 1995 Human Rights Watch investigation and report.

Trial and Sentencing Practices

The trend in the United States of trying more children in the adult criminal system continued in 2000, depriving youth of the variety of rehabilitative dispositions that are available in juvenile proceedings. In California, voters approved a measure in March that made transfer to the adult system mandatory in some cases and gave prosecutors the final word in many others; before the measure's passage, youth were transferred to the adult system only after a judicial hearing. Even with the procedural safeguards of judicial transfers, minority youth in California and elsewhere in the United States were significantly more likely to be sent to adult courts than their white counterparts. A Justice Policy Institute study found that compared with white youth, children of color in California were 2.8 times more likely to be charged with violent crimes, 6.2 times more likely to be tried in adult court, and seven times more likely to be sentenced to prison when they were tried as adults.

In Pakistan, President Rafiq Tarar announced the promulgation in July of the Juvenile Justice System Ordinance, the country's first federal juvenile justice law. Incorporating the recommendations of Human Rights Watch, local NGOs, and the Pakistan Law Commission, the ordinance prohibited the imposition of the death penalty on children under the age of eighteen, provided a right to legal assistance at he state's expense, authorized the creation of juvenile courts with exclusive jurisdiction over juvenile cases, prohibited joint trials of adults and children, and required probation officers to prepare a report on the child's circumstances prior to adjudication. In addition, Punjab began to apply its provincial juvenile justice legislation, the Youthful Offenders Ordinance, throughout the province; it had previously been in force only in the district of Sahiwal.

The Death Penalty

Five individuals were executed between January and October 2000 for crimes committed when they were under the age of eighteen. Four of these executions took place in the United States; the Democratic Republic of Congo (DRC) carried out the fifth. The International Covenant on Civil and Political Rights and the Convention on the Rights of the Child forbid the imposition of the death penalty on juvenile offenders.

Douglas Christopher Thomas and Steven Roach were put to death in the U.S. state of Virginia in January 2000. The state of Texas executed Glenn McGinnis in January 2000 and Shaka Sankofa (Gary Graham) in June 2000. Texas and Virginia together accounted for over 70 percent of juvenile executions and nearly half of all death sentences carried out nationwide between 1976, when the death penalty was reinstated, and October 2000 (see section on United States).

The highest court of the U.S. state of Georgia postponed Alexander Williams' execution one day before his death sentence was scheduled to be carried out in August 2000; at this writing, the court had not reached a decision on his appeal. Williams would have been the fifth juvenile offender put to death in the United States during the year. The last time five or more juvenile offenders were executed in a single year in the United States was in 1954, when six people were put to death for crimes they committed as children.

Of the thirty-eight U.S. states that retained the death penalty, twenty-three permitted its imposition for crimes committed under the age of eighteen. Eighteen states allowed executions for crimes committed by sixteen-year-olds. Including Williams, seventy-one juvenile offenders were on death row in the United States as of July 1, 2000.

In Congo, a fourteen-year-old child soldier was executed in January 2000 shortly after being sentenced to death by the country's Court of Military Order. Established in 1997 by a presidential decree that was itself of questionable legality, the military court did not safeguard the due process rights of those brought before it. In particular, those convicted by the court had no right to appeal; the second president of the military court told Human Rights Watch in late 1998 that those condemned to death could legally be executed immediately following judgment. The sole power to commute death sentences lay with President Kabila, who was known to have granted only two pardons, including one for a thirteen-year-old soldier who had been sentenced to death in March 1998 (see Congo chapter).

Iran and Nigeria were the only other countries that were known to continue to permit the death penalty to be imposed on juvenile offenders. Iran executed a seventeen-year-old in October 1999; Nigeria carried out a death sentence against a seventeen-year-old in July 1997 for a crime committed at the age of fifteen.

Pakistan's July 2000 juvenile justice ordinance raised the minimum age at the time of the offense to eighteen for capital punishment to be imposed, three years after its last reported execution of an adolescent offender. China and Yemen banned the execution of juvenile offenders in 1997 and 1994, respectively.

Child Labor

After its unanimous adoption by 174 nations in June 1999, the new Convention on the Worst Forms of Child Labor (ILO Convention 182) had by mid-2000 achieved the fastest pace of ratification in ILO history. By late September, thirty-seven countries had ratified the convention, which entered into force on November 19, 2000. The new convention represented a global consensus to end the most abhorrent forms of child labor, and required states to take immediate measures to abolish such practices as child slavery, trafficking, debt bondage, child prostitution and pornography, and forced labor, including the forced recruitment of children for use in armed conflict.

A growing international commitment to address child labor was also seen through new and innovative programs for at-risk children and their families. In Latin America, programs in Brazil and Mexico provided monthly stipends for low-income families who kept children in school. The programs, which sometimes also provided after-school activities and income generating projects for families, served over 2.5 million children, and were designed to provide incentives for education and offset the poverty that most often drives poor children into the workplace. Similar initiatives were planned for Ecuador, Honduras, and Nicaragua.

Some ninety countries were engaged in the ILO's International Programme on the Elimination of Child Labour (IPEC). From just one donor country and six participating states in 1992, IPEC in 2000 had nearly twenty-five donors and more than sixty-five participating countries. In partnership with UNICEF, trade unions, the private sector, and nongovernmental organizations, IPEC initiated dozens of programs to prevent child labor, remove children from child labor and provide them with rehabilitation and relevant education, and provide their parents with improved livelihoods, jobs, or income.

The United States increased its contributions to IPEC from U.S. $3 million per year to $30 million per year over the last four years—a ten-fold increase that doubled IPEC's budget. In May, the U.S. Congress also adopted a landmark trade bill, which for the first time conditions U.S. trade benefits on a country's progress in eliminating the worst forms of child labor. The Trade and Development Act of 2000 denies U.S. trade preferences to countries in sub-Saharan Africa, the Caribbean, and Central America that have not implemented their commitments to eliminate the worst forms of child labor as established by ILO Convention 182.

However, despite increased donor support, programs and legal commitments, abusive child labor remained a serious problem around the world. The ILO estimated that 250 million children between five and fourteen worked for a living, and that over 50 million children under age twelve worked in hazardous circumstances. Child laborers hauled wagons underground in coal mines, drew molten glass in stifling temperatures, worked with glues and solvents in the shoe and leather industry, bent over carpet looms, picked garbage from dump sites, and toiled long hours as domestic workers.

One of the most common forms of child labor in both industrialized and developing countries was the use of children in agriculture. In the United States, over 300,000 children worked as hired laborers on commercial farms, frequently under dangerous and grueling conditions. Human Rights Watch found that child farmworkers in the United States worked long hours for little pay and risked pesticide poisoning, heat illnesses, injuries, and life-long disabilities. They accounted for 8 percent of working children in the United States but suffered 40 percent of work-related fatalities.

Children working on U.S. farms often worked twelve-hour days, sometimes beginning at 3:00 or 4:00 a.m. They reported routine exposure to dangerous pesticides that cause cancer and brain damage, with short-term symptoms including rashes, headaches, dizziness, nausea, and vomiting. Young farmworkers became dizzy from laboring in 100°F temperatures without adequate access to drinking water, and were forced to work without access to toilets or hand washing facilities.

Agriculture was the most dangerous occupation open to children in the United States and caused high rates of injury from work with knives, other sharp tools, and heavy equipment. An estimated 100,000 children suffered agriculture-related injuries during the year.

Long hours of work also interfered with the education of children working in the fields, making them miss school and leaving them too exhausted to study or stay awake in class. Only 55 percent of farmworker children in the United States finished high school.

The plight of child farmworkers in the United States was rooted in poverty-level wages that left adult farmworkers unable to support their children, weak enforcement of child labor laws, and inadequate legal protections that allowed children in agriculture to work at younger ages, for longer hours and under more hazardous conditions than minors in other jobs. Federal laws dating back to 1938 permitted children as young as twelve to work unlimited hours in agriculture, and allowed children of sixteen to work under hazardous conditions. In contrast, children in other occupations could not work before age fourteen, could only work three hours on a school day until age sixteen, and were not allowed to perform hazardous work until age eighteen. Because 85 percent of U.S. farmworkers were racial minorities—the vast majority Latino—the law's double standard amounted to de facto race-based discrimination.

Even to the limited extent that U.S. laws did protect farmworker children, they were not adequately enforced. The U.S. Department of Labor, charged with enforcement of the child labor, wage and hour provisions of federal labor law, cited only 104 cases of child labor violations in fiscal year 1998, even though an estimated one million child labor violations occur in U.S. agriculture every year. Compounding the problem, penalties were typically too weak to discourage employers from using illegal child labor.

On September 25, 2000, Senator Tom Harkin introduced legislation to amend U.S. labor laws to protect all working children equally. The bill was pending before the Senate Committee on Health, Education, Labor, and Pensions at this writing.

In Egypt, an estimated 1.2 million children took part in controlling cotton leafworm infestations during the summer months, by manually removing damaged portions of leaves. In October 1999, Human Rights Watch conducted an investigation into the use of child labor in Egyptian cotton pest management and found that the children were typically hired well below the minimum age for seasonal agricultural employment in Egypt, labored far in excess of the hours and days permitted under Egypt's Child Law, and were routinely beaten by their foremen. They also faced serious health risks posed by exposure to heat and, in some cases, pesticides.

The children were employed by the agricultural cooperative societies in their respective villages, acting under the authority of the agriculture ministry. According to an agricultural engineer with one of the cooperatives, children were exclusively recruited for the work because they could be paid less than adults, were more obedient, and had the appropriate height for removing damaged leaves. Although the Child Law set the minimum age for seasonal agricultural employment at twelve years, a majority of children engaged in leafworm control operations were below the age of twelve, with a significant proportion employed from the age of seven or eight.

Cooperatives appeared to have little difficulty in recruiting children. Growing rural poverty, coupled with a steady decline in the percentage of farm land allocated to cotton, gave rise to an ample supply of child wage labor in much of rural Egypt. Children typically earned an average of E£3 (about U.S. $1) per day and worked from 7:00 a.m. to 6:00 p.m. daily, with a one to two hour midday break, seven days a week. Supervising groups of fifteen to thirty, foremen routinely beat children with wooden switches whenever they perceived a child to be slow-ing down or overlooking leaves.

Measures to protect working children from heat-related illnesses were inconsistent and often inadequate. For example, children in some villages had to bear the cost of purchasing protective caps as well as a pail for storing water. Requests for water were often granted only at the discretion of their foremen.

In some cases, children may have been exposed to toxic organophosphate and carbamate pesticides. Such exposure can lead to pesticide poisoning that is both acute— with effects such as dizziness, vomiting, or diarrhea—and chronic, including disruption of the nervous, endocrine, or reproductive systems. In the villages Human Rights Watch visited, children either resumed work immediately after the fields were sprayed or following a twenty-four to forty-eight hour hiatus, which may still have been inadequate given the heightened susceptibility of children to pesticide intoxication. Although the agriculture ministry adopted an integrated pest management program to reduce pesticide use, farmers addressed a perceived shortfall in pesticide application with additional spraying of their own, often with readily available pesticides identified as highly hazardous by the World Health Organization.

Violence and Discrimination Against Students

Many children around the world experienced violence and discrimination as a regular part of their school experience. In some cases, school officials participated in acts of intolerance, ostracization, and violence directed at particular youth because of their gender, race, ethnicity, religion, nationality, sexual orientation, social group, or other status. In others, authorities failed to intervene to protect students from harassment and attacks by their classmates.

In many parts of the world, minority children did not have access to an education on equal terms with their peers from majority families. In some cases, minority children were placed in separate, inferior schools, or restricted to vocational curricula; in other instances, they were denied access to schools altogether.

In one case brought in July, a Jerusalem city counselor submitted a petition to the Israeli Supreme Court on behalf of 117 school children who were refused enrollment in Jerusalem public schools, in violation of Israeli law. The petitioner alleged that up to 2,000 children had been turned away in 1999 and thousands more had never applied because they did not know they had a right to public education.

Human Rights Watch also received reports of discrimination against Greek children in Turkey, Turkish children in Greece, Roma children in Bulgaria, Albanian children in Macedonia, Rohingya children in Malaysia, Bidun children in Kuwait, the children of Haitians in the Dominican Republic, and elsewhere.

Girls in many countries endured sexual harassment and abuse in educational settings at the hands of teachers and other students. In South Africa, for example, a 1998 study by CIETafrica, an NGO researching sexual violence, found that one in every three Johannesburg girls experienced sexual violence at school; two thirds of those subjected to sexual violence did not report the abuse to anyone. Human Rights Watch interviews in March and April confirmed that sexual abuse and harassment of girls by teachers and other students is widespread.

Lesbian, gay, bisexual, and transgender students in the United States and elsewhere were frequently targeted for harassment by their peers. Lesbian, gay, and bisexual youth were nearly three times as likely as their peers to have been involved in at least one physical fight in school, three times as likely to have been threatened or injured with a weapon at school, and nearly four times as likely to skip school because they felt unsafe, according to the 1999 Massachusetts Youth Risk Behavior Survey. Most alarmingly, the survey found that those who identified as lesbian, gay, or bisexual were more than twice as likely to consider suicide and more than four times as likely to attempt suicide than their peers.

Efforts to provide a safe, supportive environment for lesbian, gay, bisexual, and transgender students in the United States were hampered by discriminatory legislation in several states. For example, a South Carolina statute provided that health education in public school "may not include a discussion of alternate sexual lifestyles from heterosexual relationships including, but not limited to, homosexual relationships except in the context of instruction concerning sexually transmitted diseases." Similarly, a measure on the November ballot in Oregon would provide that "the instruction of behaviors relating to homosexuality and bisexuality shall not be presented in a public school in a manner which encourages, promotes, or sanctions such behaviors."

In addition to these challenges, many students also faced hostile school administrations. In two particularly prolonged disputes, school districts in Utah and California attempted to deny students the right to form clubs known as gay-straight alliances, in violation of the federal Equal Access Act. California's Orange Unified School District settled a lawsuit with El Modena High School students in September 2000, permitting their group to meet on school grounds and use the school's public address system to announce club meetings. The same month, Utah's Salt Lake City School Board voted to permit student noncurricular clubs to meet on school grounds, reversing a 1995 decision that had abolished all noncurricular clubs in an effort to bar East High School's gay-straight alliance.

Several states had legislation or programs in place to address harassment and violence of lesbian, gay, bisexual, and transgender youth. California, Connecticut, Massachusetts, and Wisconsin explicitly prohibited harassment and discrimination against teachers or students on the basis of sexual orientation. Massachusetts and Vermont, the only states to include questions relating to sexual orientation on statewide youth risk behavior surveys, had state programs to provide support to gay, lesbian, and bisexual youth. Challenges remained in implementing these programs and statutory protections and in preventing their erosion; in Vermont, for example, a backlash against "civil union" legislation enacted in April, which provided same-sex couples with recognition and benefits similar to those of marriage, threatened funding for the state's youth program.

In a welcome development, Kenyan Education Minister Kalonzo Musyoka announced in June that the government would ban corporal punishment in schools. This positive step followed a 1999 Human Rights Watch report that found that teachers routinely ignored nominal restraints on corporal punishment, caning children for minor offenses such as tardiness, talking in class, wearing torn or dirty uniforms, being unable to answer a question, or failing to achieve target marks set on exams. Students subjected to corporal punishment suffered physical injuries, psychological scars, and, in extreme cases, death.

In Thailand, the Ministry of Education announced in September that corporal punishment would be banned in schools beginning on November 1. South Africa's Constitutional Court upheld a prohibition on corporal punishment in August. In Tanzania, in contrast, the Ministry of Education rejected efforts to abolish corporal punishment in the country's schools.

Relevant Human Rights Watch Reports:

Burundi: Emptying the Hills: Regroupment Camps in Burundi, 7/00

Japan: Owed Justice: Thai Women Trafficked into Debt Bondage in Japan, 9/00

Kuwait: Promises Betrayed: Denial of Rights of Bidun, Women, and Freedom of Expression, 10/00

Malaysia/Burma: Living in Limbo: Burmese Rohingyas in Malaysia, 8/00

Tanzania: Seeking Protection: Addressing Sexual and Domestic Violence in Tanzania's Refugee Camps, 9/00

Turkey: Human Rights and the European Union Accession Partnership, 9/00

United States: Fingers to the Bone: United States Failure to Protect Child Farmworkers, 6/00

HUMAN RIGHTS WATCH

EUROPE & CENTRAL ASIA

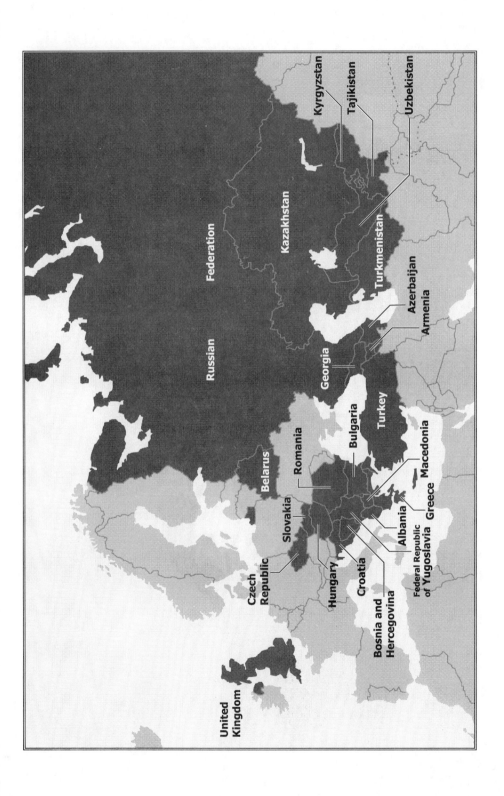

EUROPE AND CENTRAL ASIA OVERVIEW

Human Rights Developments

The civilian carnage in Chechnya and the further entrenchment of authoritarian governments in Central Asia dominated human rights concerns in 2000. The democratic defeat of Slobodan Milosevic, who had laid waste to democracy in Serbia and instigated the deadly Balkan wars, held out hope of a new hope for peace and rule of law in the Balkans. But the international community's selectivity in using leverage hindered efforts for positive change in human rights in the region, especially in the crises in Chechnya and Central Asia. While the victory of Vojislav Kostunica over Milosevic was strongly supported by the lifting of international sanctions, governments were reluctant to take a strong position on the need to bring Milosevic, an indicted war criminal, before the International Criminal Tribunal on the Former Yugoslavia (ICTY), as well as the broader issue of cooperation with ICTY.

The international community lacked the political will to exercise leverage with Russia to press for a halt to the massive abuses perpetrated by Russian forces in Chechnya. This stood in stunning contrast to international engagement in other crises in the world, notably East Timor, but was regrettably consistent with the international community's response to the 1994-1996 war in Chechnya. The pattern of impunity for abuse that so easily prevailed in that war persisted in the current war, as Russia clearly sensed it had nothing to lose by prosecuting the war without thought to civilian costs or to the consequences of wanton brutality.

Russian forces' violations of humanitarian law in the current war, which began in late 1999, caused some thousands of civilian casualties, the result of indiscriminate bombing. The capital of Chechnya, Grozny, was razed to the ground. At least 125 civilians were summarily executed in three massacres. Thousands of Chechens were detained arbitrarily on suspicion of rebel collaboration, and once

in Russian custody guards and riot police tortured many of them systematically.

The international community often lamented that it had no significant influence over Russia, but squandered real opportunities for leverage or sanctions in favor of political expediency. During one of the war's bleakest moments the World Bank refused to withhold credit payments to the Russian general budget. The U.S. government and other member states refused even to entertain the notion of conditionality. A U.N. Commission on Human Rights resolution might have had a positive impact, but the member states who so commendably sponsored it stood idle as Russia ignored the resolution's requirements. Chief among them was that Russia establish a national commission of inquiry that would lead to prosecutions for abuse. In a more principled move, the Council of Europe's Parliamentary Assembly voted to suspend Russia's delegation.

The blatant impunity for war crimes in Chechnya cried out for accountability, but there was none. This failure quickly became obvious, but governments were unwilling to take up a more robust commitment to international justice as they had in other parts of the world. No member state of the Commission on Human Rights had the courage to insist, for example, on an international commission of inquiry, which would have necessarily invoked higher standards of rigor and impartiality than the wan Russian effort. Council of Europe member states declined to lodge an interstate complaint at the European Court of Human Rights. Unlike the Kosovo conflict, where the international community responded quickly to the needs of ethnic Albanian refugees, security concerns and a lack of international interest meant that many of the needs of displaced Chechens went unmet. Food, safe water, medical care, gas, wood supplies, and electricity were provided haphazardly and often ran out. Most children had their education disrupted, and during the early days of the war, disease and exposure claimed the lives of some displaced persons.

As corruption and grinding poverty worsened in Central Asia, fighting terrorism and "religious extremism" was an overwhelming concern both to national governments otherwise intent on maintaining their grip on power, and to the international community. This came at the expense of human rights and a long-term vision for the rule of law in the region. Uzbekistan's unrelenting crackdown against political and religious dissenters continued unabated, and authoritarianism deepened in Kyrgyzstan, Kazakhstan, and Tajikistan.

For the second time in two years, violence erupted in Kyrgyzstan and Uzbekistan. In August pitched battles erupted between armed insurgents and government troops in southeastern Uzbekistan and neighboring Kyrgyzstan. Thousands were displaced from their homes by the clashes. The group responsible, the so-called Islamic Movement of Uzbekistan, demanded that the Uzbek government release what the group claimed were an estimated 100,000 wrongfully jailed Muslim prisoners and allow for the observance of Islamic law precepts, including permission for Muslim women to wear the veil.

Some observers viewed the August violence as the self-fulfilling prophesy of the government's multi-year campaign against "religious extremism," the product of fierce and violent repression of thousands of Uzbek citizens. This year the government's campaign to stop the spread of "religious extremism" expanded and caused pervasive fear. Hundreds more independent Muslims who chose to study Islam or worship outside government-controlled religious institutions joined thousands imprisoned in previous years. Many were sentenced to long prison terms, for alleged membership in illegal religious organizations, or distributing religious leaflets not approved by the state. They were often arrested on trumped-up charges of illegal possession of narcotics, weapons, or religious literature, held incommunicado and denied legal counsel, and convicted in grossly unfair trials at which judges routinely ignored credible evidence of torture.

Symbolic of the Uzbek government's confidence that concern about terrorism trumped its human rights obligations was its decision in October not to appear to defend its initial report to the U.N. Human Rights Committee on the day it convened. The government's explanation was that officials needed to prepare for a conference on terrorism.

Governments in other parts of Central Asia continued the drift toward worsening authoritarianism by manipulating elections, harassing the media, and jailing political rivals on trumped-up charges. The government of Kyrgyzstan employed these with a vengeance this year, which sobered those who still considered that country to be Central Asia's "island of democracy." The Kyrgyz government jailed prominent opposition candidates before the October presidential elections, persistently harassed the opposition media, and drove some nongovernment organization activists into exile. The government of Kazakhstan, firmly entrenched after last year's deeply flawed elections, continued to harass opposition media and political figures. The Tajik government flagrantly manipulated the February ballot to guarantee the election of a parliament dominated by the ruling party. In November 1999, Turkmenistan, one of the most repressive countries in the world, held utterly hollow parliamentary elections, followed by an indefinite extension of the president's term in office.

Once again, the international community chose not to use available policy tools to effect change or take a principled stand. This was particularly true of the United States government, which was concerned about losing its influence in Central Asia to Russia by putting too much emphasis on human rights. Yet the U.S. and its European allies were in unique positions to deliver the economic assistance that Central Asian countries badly want, whereas Russian influence served to weaken these countries' independence. The U.S. government declined to interpret the crackdown in Uzbekistan as one targeting people for their religious convictions, and for this reason did not name Uzbekistan as a country of particular concern in the area of religious freedom under the 1998 International Religious Freedom Act. By contrast, Serbia was considered a country of particular concern. The U.S. Department of State certified Uzbekistan as eligible for U.S. security assistance, available under U.S. law only to countries committed to upholding international human rights standards.

The European Union (E.U.), for its part, resisted using its lucrative trade agreements with Central Asian countries to press for human rights improvements. And the Organization for Security and Cooperation in Europe (OSCE), the chief regional organization with a mandate to strengthen human rights, emphasized economic and security cooperation instead, an approach that failed to yield any progress on human rights. OSCE missions in Central Asia did not engage in regular, frank, public reporting on the human rights situation in the region; this was a glaring failure, particularly when juxtaposed against the massive and laudable public documentation and reporting effort undertaken in Kosovo.

Authoritarianism deepened in other parts of the former Soviet Union as well. Under President Alexander Lukashenka, the Belarus government continued to jail opposition figures, drive the opposition media to bankruptcy, and intimidate human rights organizations with abandon. Its October parliamentary election process was deeply biased to favor pro-government parties, which prevailed on election day thanks to falsified election results. In Azerbaijan as well, prior to the November parliamentary elections, the government attempted to exclude major opposition parties and many individual candidates from participating.

In December 1999, Russian President Boris Yeltsin unexpectedly resigned. Vladmir Putin was elected president in March, riding a tide of domestic popularity with carefully-controlled information about the war in Chechnya and promises to get tough on crime and corruption. Putin was a career KGB agent who became head of the Federal Security Service, the KBG's successor. Despite numerous public assurances of support for democratic values, Putin's conduct of the war in Chechnya and his impulse to stifle critical media coverage fuelled fears of growing authoritarianism in Russia.

Political developments in Serbia and Croatia toward the rule of law were contrasted sharply, and positively, with those in the former Soviet Union. Perhaps the most dramatic event of the year was the deposing of Yugoslav president Slobodan Milosevic and the election of Vojislav Kostunica as president. Milosevic had attempted to remain in power by staging early presidential elections on September 24. The stakes were high, as Milosevic no doubt wanted to avoid facing trial by the ICTY. For the first time facing a united opposition, the government had engaged in an unparalleled effort to ensure victory by intimidating, at times violently, opposition members and movements, and brazenly rigging the electoral process. Despite these obstacles, the opposition prevailed in the vote. When Milosevic tried to force a run-off, citizens took the streets, seizing the parliament and television station and ultimately forced Milosevic to acknowledge his defeat.

Milosevic's departure from power meant new hope for the rule of law and human rights protections in Serbia. At year's end, top concerns were Serbia's cooperation with the ICTY, including the transferal of Milosevic and other indicted war criminals hiding in Serbia to The Hague, the release of hundreds of Kosovo Albanian political prisoners, restoring the independence of the judiciary, and bringing to justice police and security forces responsible for serious abuses under Milosevic.

Following the death of Croatian president Franjo Tudjman, the opposition came to power in the presidency and parliament in early 2000. Important progress in human rights quickly followed. The new government began a policy of full cooperation with the ICTY by transferring an indictee to the Hague and allowing the ICTY access to investigate the sites of alleged 1991 war crimes against Serbs. There were positive changes in governance and minority rights as well. The government made a dramatic commitment to the right of Serb refugees to return to Croatia and backed this up with a financial commitment, legislative reform that promised equal treatment for all returnees, and the creation of a new government structure to facilitate returns.

The international community had insisted on cooperation with The Hague as a condition for loans and other important benefits to Croatia. After the fall of Milosevic, however, the international community wavered in its commitment to press for cooperation with the ICTY. While legitimately acknowledging the difficulties for the new authorities if Kostunica attempted to arrest and transfer Slobodan Milosevic to the ICTY, the international community also appeared to postpone indefinitely the whole issue of cooperation with ICTY from its agenda with Serbia, rather than insisting on deliverable interim measures such as the start of negotiations between the ICTY and the new authorities on access for ICTY investigators, discussions on the opening of an ICTY office in Belgrade, and the transfer of official documents necessary for the ICTY's investigations. The international community's apparent willingness to compromise cooperation with ICTY as a condition of upgraded relations with Belgrade made it appear as though Serbia was receiving special treatment as compared to Croatia and Bosnia.

Between October 1999 and October 2000, eight indicted war criminals were arrested by NATO forces in Bosnia and transferred to The Hague. Another indicted war criminal killed himself in the course of an October 2000 NATO arrest operation. Croatia also transferred one indictee to the tribunal in 2000. Nonetheless, at this writing, wartime Bosnian Serb leader Radovan Karadzic and Bosnian Serb General Ratko Mladic remained at large. Although most North Atlantic Treaty Organization (NATO) member government officials continued to insist that they would eventually see their day in court, some continued to resist their arrest. No longer able to argue that Karadzic and Mladic were so prominent in Bosnia that their arrest would ignite popular protest and retaliation against the international community, opponents of the arrests shifted to arguing that these figures had become so sidelined in Bosnia that their detention was no longer necessary to the peace process.

International agencies bore responsibility for guaranteeing human rights in several of the region's major postconflict zones they oversaw in Kosovo, Bosnia, and Tajikistan. In Kosovo and Tajikistan, these agencies displayed a disturbing tendency to rush the holding of elections in order to satisfy a predetermined political schedule, even where the conditions for elections to be free, fair, and meaningful were absent, overlooking the harmful way in which serious, ongoing human rights problems undermine the prospects for long-term peace and democracy.

In Kosovo, a de facto protectorate of the international community after the 1999 war between NATO and Serbia, steady violence imperiled the lives of non-Albanians, who were for the most part confined to monoethnic enclaves and were unable to travel without KFOR peacekeepers as escorts. Kidappings, drive-by shootings, fire-bombing of homes, and grenade explosions were combined with threats and harassment by Albanians to force ethnic minorities to leave the province. NATO-led KFOR forces and United Nations Civil Police, which together had full responsibility for policing and security respectively, were either unable or unwilling to confront the armed elements of the former Kosovo Liberation Army and others implicated in the violence. U.N. police often lacked the resources and cooperation adequately to investigate and arrest those responsible. While the United Nations' peace implementation mission in Kosovo (UNMIK) oversaw the administration of justice, the courts were staffed primarily by local judges whose rulings raised serious questions about the impartiality of justice.

The 1996 Bosnian example demonstrated that rushed elections in a postconflict situation could serve to legitimize further some parties and leaders which had been responsible for gross abuses, but the international community chose to overlook this important lesson. Kosovo's first postwar elections, scheduled for October 28, were by all measures premature, driven more by the desire to meet a predetermined deadline set by the Rambouillet agreement than the need to create the minimum conditions and set the framework for long-term democracy. All but a handful of Serbs and many other minorities boycotted registration, rendering them ineligible to vote. Political violence resulted in the deaths of at least nine people affiliated with the Democratic League of Kosovo or parties linked to the former KLA, and there were politically motivated attacks on journalists.

Whereas in Kosovo the international community accepted premature elections in order to speed along the province's political development, in Tajikistan the United Nations (U.N.) presided over parliamentary elections in utterly inhospitable conditions as part of its strategy to hasten the end of its own peacekeeping operation. The result for human rights was disastrous. A 1997 U.N.-brokered peace agreement ending that country's civil war envisioned the elections, held in February 2000, as the last step in the implementation of the agreement. But opposition parties were excluded from the vote, there was widespread fraud, the media was clearly biased, and the overall rights situation was extremely poor. The vote served to legitimate the current president rather than to serve U.N. goals of democratization.

In Bosnia, members of minority groups returned in significant numbers for the first time since the end of the war. In the first six months of 2000, the United Nations High Commisioner for Refugees (UNHCR) registered nearly 20,000 minority returns in Bosnia, nearly three times the number recorded for the same period in 1999, thanks in part to focused international effort. With the success, however, has come a drop in funds from donor nations, even though a sustained, longer-term level of funding is necessary for the return of Bosnia's remaining refugees.

Croatia's new commitment to returns was effective in encouraging the return of ethnic Serbs: more than 10,000 returned during 2000, the highest number since the mass exodus of more than 200,000 in 1995.

In Serbia and Montenegro, about 230,000 persons were displaced from the Kosovo conflict and the postconflict persecution of minorities, and 500,000 were refugees from Croatia and Bosnia. This burden continued to strain the resources of Serbia and Montenegro.

Minority rights violations accompanied returns in Croatia and Bosnia, and were a problem elsewhere in the region. Bosniak returnees to Republica Srpska were the victims of violent attacks in March and July. Serb returnees to Croatia continued to face discrimination at the hands of local authorities, despite a raft of new antidiscrimination measures adopted by the new government in Zagreb, and Serb and Croat communities remained deeply mistrustful of one another.

Roma continued to suffer shocking levels of harassment, violent attacks, and malicious discrimination in Croatia, Hungary, Romania, the Czech Republic, Bulgaria, Serbia, Macedonia, and Slovakia, marring much of the region's record of progress on other human rights issues. Law enforcement authorities in all of these countries typically did not investigate violent attacks on Roma. Roma children often lacked access to education in Croatia, and in the Czech republic they were disproportionally channeled into classes for the mentally disabled. Municipalities in Serbia, Croatia, Hungary, and Greece forced Roma to abandon their homes, usually citing spurious zoning laws. Roma were evicted from their homes in Athens to clear land for facilities for the 2004 Olympics. In July, a municipal bulldozer, accompanied by the mayor and police, demolished numerous Roma huts in the Athens Aspropyrgos suburb. Greek and Albanian Roma families in the settlement situated on a garbage dump were ordered to leave within three days. In Bulgaria, villagers refused to allow Roma in public places and threatened them with expulsion after an unresolved murder. Roma homes in Macedonia were burned down in suspicious circumstances in the village of Stip. Roma homes in the village were the target of earlier arson attacks in 1992. And in a Serbian town, Roma were banned from a public pool.

Torture of detainees reached crisis proportions in government arrest campaigns in Uzbekistan and Russia (Chechnya). These crises were not aberrations, however, since torture had been part and parcel of the criminal justice systems of both countries for years. Torture of detainees held in Russian custody in Chechnya followed the same methods and patterns as torture perpetrated against common suspects in Moscow or Irkutsk. Similarly, torture to coerce testimony from people arrested in the crackdown against independent Islam in Uzbekistan was systematic.

Torture remained common in Turkey and was used to coerce testimony and confessions in both common criminal cases and security-related cases. In a positive development that suggested heightened government acknowledgment of the problem, the Turkish parliament's Human Rights Commission published nine detailed reports documenting the persistence of torture. The commission was able to find and photograph torture implements and a "torture room" described to it by victims. This was chilling testimony to the credibility of torture victims, whom governments often dismiss as unreliable or biased.

Several factors accounted for the persistence of torture, among them impunity and poor due process protections, especially in countries of the former Soviet Union. Some countries began to make progress toward reforming due process to prevent torture, but backtracking also occurred. Azerbaijan, where torture was widespread, adopted legislation that for the first time required detainees to be brought before a judge within forty-eight hours. Last year Georgia repealed important due process reforms, and took no steps this year to restore them.

The governments of nearly all Central Asia states took steps to restrict or control the Internet. In a positive move, Croatia decriminalized most aspects of libel, but criminal libel statutes were enforced in Greece and Romania. The governments of Azerbaijan, Kazakhstan, and Kyrgyzstan made liberal use of prohibitive libel suits to bankrupt critical media. In September a Turkish court acquitted Nadire Mater who had been charged with "insulting the armed forces" for writing *Mehmet's Book: Soldiers Who Have Fought in the Southeast Tell Their Stories*. Unfortunately, this was not part of a broader pattern of improvements in freedom of expression. Turkish media and politicians furiously debated many issues and openly criticized the government, but those who contradicted the official line on the role of ethnicity, religion, or the military in politics continued to risk prosecution and imprisonment.

Governments made little progress this year protecting women from violence in armed conflict, domestic violence, trafficking, and discrimination. Credible information surfaced about rape of the Chechen women by Russian forces, both in detention centers and during community sweep operations. Even in postwar periods, women's human rights were not protected. Kosovar women confronted discrimination, domestic violence, rape, trafficking, and abductions following the war. Particularly in the former Soviet Union, those who trafficked women for work in the sex industry continued to operate with impunity, while governments offered thoroughly inadequate protection to women willing to come forward as witnesses to this crime. Police made no visible progress in promoting among their ranks a better response to domestic violence. In Uzbekistan, local governments compounded the problem by pressuring women to stay in abusive marriages in order to keep the divorce rate low.

Defending Human Rights

The treatment of human rights defenders varied widely in the region. In some places they were able to initiate groundbreaking work, review national legislation, and seek remedies for abuse in domestic courts and at the European Court of Human Rights. In others, governments went to great lengths to curtail their activities and undermine their credibility.

On October 16, Antonio Russo, a journalist who had documented humanitarian law violations in Chechnya, was killed near his home in Georgia.

Some human rights defenders in the region have had to operate in exceedingly hostile circumstances. The record was extremely poor in Uzbekistan, where the government had a history of jailing human rights activists and denying registration to human rights nongovernmental organizations (NGOs). This year the government failed to release two activists and continued to harass those who brought their cases to human rights defenders. It frequently denied defenders access to public trials.

In Serbia, activists, braving constant and baseless accusations of being NATO spies, defended ethnic Albanian political prisoners' right to due process. One Serbian defender, Bojan Aleksov, was tortured by police.

In Kyrgyzstan the environment for defenders dramatically deteriorated, even as local defenders gained broader exposure to the international community. The government accused some activists of "destabilizing the social order" and threatened one of the country's most active defenders with arrest, driving him into exile. Turkmenistan refused to allow human rights monitoring of any sort.

Governments employed a range of tactics to impede the work of human rights organizations. The government in Serbia subjected several human rights organizations to groundless tax inspections. The Azerbaijani government banned prominent NGOs from monitoring elections. The Belarus government evicted a legal defense group from its office and was believed to be behind the unresolved series of break-ins and raids of other groups' offices. In Kazakhstan an unexplained fire damaged the office of one of the country's most prominent groups. In Georgia, the Ministry of Internal Affairs simply shut down an NGO program that would have provided round-the-clock pro bono legal services to detainees.

Defenders faced difficulties in conflict and postconflict zones. The Russian government carefully controlled access to Chechnya, making human rights reporting directly from the conflict zone extremely difficult. Human Rights Watch was repeatedly denied access to Chechnya, and Memorial, a leading Russian group, faced many problems with its work there. A coalition of Russian NGOs urged Council of Europe member states to file an interstate complaint against Russia with the European Court of Human Rights. In Kosovo, the compounding effects of years of repression, armed conflict, and the resulting inter-ethnic animosity made local human rights reporting extremely difficult.

In Europe, defenders actively took up discrimination and violence against Roma, often among the most marginalized groups in the region. Defenders in Romania and the Czech Republic lodged cases of discrimination against Roma with the European Court of Human Rights. In Greece, human rights defenders were able in one case to halt temporarily the eviction of Roma. Hungarian Roma families from Zamoly fled to France, applied for asylum, and lodged a complaint against Hungary for failing to protect them from discrimination and violence with the European Court of Human Rights.

The Role of the International Community

United Nations

Throughout the year, various U.N. actors voiced concern about violations of human rights and humanitarian law in Chechnya, but lacking political support from key member states' U.N. representatives failed to follow through in any meaningful way on these statements.

In early 2000, U.N. High Commissioner for Human Rights Mary Robinson took the lead on Chechnya. The Russian government responded to her repeated condemnations by refusing her February request to visit Chechnya. When she was finally permitted to visit the region in late March, she acknowledged evidence of summary executions, torture, and rape committed by Russian forces, but she refused to heed calls for an international commission of inquiry, opting instead to leave the accountability effort to the Russian authorities.

The European Union-sponsored resolution adopted in April at the U.N. Commission on Human Rights followed Robinson's approach. The resolution, the first ever adopted by the commission concerning the conduct of a permanent member of the Security Council, called upon the Russian government to establish a national commission of inquiry to investigate alleged abuses in Chechnya and to permit visits to the region by a number of U.N. human rights monitoring bodies.

Other than periodic calls for implementation of this resolution, no U.N. member state or representative showed an active interest in ensuring Russian compliance with these demands, despite the high commissioner's efforts. As of this writing, the Russian government had taken no meaningful steps to investigate or prosecute cases relating to abuses in Chechnya, and it had utterly refused to establish a commission of inquiry or invite most U.N. human rights representatives who requested to visit the region. Although the conflict occasionally spilled over Russia's border with Georgia and resulted in substantial cross-border refugee flows, the Security Council failed even to discuss the issue.

The U.N. continued to struggle with its peace implementation mission in Kosovo (UNMIK), as international attention shifted to flashpoints in other parts of the world. UNMIK made some progress in convincing ethnic Albanian and Serb leaders to participate in transitional power-sharing structures, but peace efforts were marred by political and ethnic violence. Progress was also made in establishing a local police force, but international civilian police lacked personnel to police in the interim, despite repeated requests to U.N. member states. Efforts to build an independent judiciary were undermined by UNMIK's reluctance adequately to supervise the courts, although it belatedly began to appoint international judges and prosecutors to local courts to counter concerns about bias, intimidation, and bribery among local judges and court officials. UNMIK established a special U.N. police unit for the protection of Serbs and began appointing international judges and prosecutors to local judicial systems to counter evident bias and to promote the rule of law.

The International Criminal Tribunal for the Former Yugoslavia continued its important contribution to peace in the Balkans by trying alleged war criminals, including the first-ever war crimes trial based solely on allegations of rape and sexual violence. Its efforts were undermined, however, by the continued failure of the international community to apprehend the indicted masterminds of ethnic cleansing in Bosnia, wartime Bosnian Serb leader Radovan Karadzic and Bosnian Serb general Ratko Mladic. Moreover, the failure of the international community to insist that deposed Yugoslav leader Slobodan Milosevic stand trial before the tribunal reinforced the perception that the worst offenders enjoy the most lenient treatment.

Organization for Security and Cooperation in Europe (OSCE)

After the Istanbul summit of its fifty-four heads of state in November 1999, with grand pronouncements about the organization's role in upholding human rights, the OSCE's contribution to human rights protection in the region depended on its willingness to withstand pressure and interference from member states. The result, for the most part, was singularly disappointing. The dogged efforts of the high commissioner on national minorities, the representative on freedom of the media, and the Office of Democratic Institutions and Human Rights (ODIHR) to condemn abuses, provide training, and convene seminars, were completely overshadowed by the failure of the OSCE to uphold its mandate to deploy a mission to Chechnya and by the organization's role in organizing and monitoring deeply flawed elections throughout the region.

The members of the OSCE Assistance Group to Chechnya sat in a Moscow office, prevented by the Russian government from redeploying to Chechnya or neighboring provinces where their monitoring and reporting could have provided protection for thousands of civilian victims of the conflict. The OSCE and its member states were unable to convince the Russian government to allow the group to operate in and around Chechnya, even though its right to do so had been clearly stipulated in its 1995 mandate and reaffirmed at the Istanbul summit by all member states, including Russia, and again by Russian Foreign Minister Igor Ivanov during April meetings with OSCE Chair-In-Office Austrian Foreign Minister Benita Ferrero-Waldner.

The OSCE's continued engagement in Central Asia, this year emphasizing economic and security cooperation, yielded no progress on human rights. For the third straight year, the government of Turkmenistan would not sign a Memorandum of Understanding with ODIHR regarding democratization activities in the country, which seriously called into question the utility of continued OSCE engagement there.

Perhaps because the OSCE did not have to contend with pressure from member states regarding its work on Kosovo, it engaged in active public human rights reporting there, which included thoughtful criticism of international institutions. This served as a positive model for what could be accomplished when political will is mustered.

In 2000, the OSCE monitored elections in Croatia, Tajikistan, Russia, Kyrgyzstan, Georgia, Albania, Macedonia, the Yugoslav Republic of Montenegro, Belarus, and Azerbaijan. Although OSCE election reports were generally accurate in identifying flaws, the decisions to send full assessment missions to Kyrgyzstan and Azerbaijan, and even the limited assessment mission it sent to Belarus, risked according legitimacy to electoral processes that were deeply, structurally flawed. OSCE officials argued that their presence during these elections was necessary to document electoral abuses and develop recommendations for improved processes. Unfortunately, 2000 saw little progress made in implementing OSCE recommendations de-veloped in the course of monitoring past flawed votes in, for example, Kazakhstan and Uzbekistan. The OSCE also organized the October municipal elections in Kosovo, pushing ahead under international pressure to demonstrate progress in peace implementation, although political and ethnic violence and attacks on journalists indicated at the time of writing that the elections would not likely meet OSCE standards.

Having failed to use the opportunity of the 1999 Istanbul summit to obtain any lasting human rights improvements in Turkey, the OSCE and its "human dimension" mechanisms remained underutilized in that country, where, had there been the political will, they might have made a significant contribution to the Turkish government's efforts to comply with E.U. accession criteria relating to democratization, rule of law, and minority rights.

The year saw continued OSCE efforts to address women's human rights issues, with the adoption of a Gender Action Plan in June and a special "human dimension" seminar to identify measures to combat trafficking. The apparent downgrading of the position of the gender advisor in the Vienna secretariat did not, however, bode well for efforts to implement these plans.

Council of Europe

The Council of Europe's profile expanded significantly in 2000, as the organization engaged in new and unprecedented field activities, technical assistance missions, and election monitoring activities with mixed results for human rights conditions.

Among international organizations, the Council of Europe enjoyed the most extensive dialogue with the Russian government regarding its conduct in Chechnya. The council's commissioner for human rights, the council-based European Committee for the Prevention of Torture, and several delegations from the its Parliamentary Assembly visited Moscow and the North Caucasus, condemned violations committed by both sides to the conflict, and urged steps to curb abuses and bring about an end to the conflict.

The secretary general invoked for the first time article 52 of the European Convention on Human Rights to request information from the Russian government regarding implementation of the convention in Chechnya and in April the Parliamentary Assembly suspended the voting rights of the Russian parliamentary delegation.

In response, the Russian government accepted deployment in Chechnya of a three-person Council of Europe team of experts to assist the office of Russian President Putin's Special Representative for Human Rights in Chechnya, Vladimir Kalamanov. This team, the only international personnel with a human rights mandate permitted to operate in Chechnya, surely made a positive contribution to the work of Kalamanov's office. At the same time, its deployment raised serious concerns that the Russian government was "forum shopping," essentially looking for the weakest institution that it could engage in order to avoid a stronger international reaction.

Indeed, the Council of Europe deployment was used by representatives of the U.S., the E.U., and other governments and institutions as an argument against creating an international commission of inquiry, even though Kalamanov and the Council of Europe staff working with him had no authority to investigate or prosecute alleged atrocities. Council member states also used the deployment as an excuse to forego more robust action, such as a lawsuit against the Russian Federation before the European Court of Human Rights, or a Committee of Ministers' action to monitor Russia's conduct in Chechnya or to expel Russia from the council. The deployment also weakened the case for an OSCE presence and gave the Russian authorities an argument against compliance with the U.N. Commission on Human Rights resolution. Council of Europe officials argued that it was better for them to be in Chechnya than not. This claim ignored the impact of their presence on the overall international response to the Chechnya crisis and the danger that the much-touted "complementarity" among international institutions in the field of human rights had, at least in Chechnya, become a race to the bottom.

Similar concerns arose over Council of Europe election assistance in Azerbaijan. Although the OSCE was already engaged in a dialogue with the Azerbaijani authorities regarding conditions for their November elections, the Council of Europe accepted an April request from the Azerbaijani government that it advise them too. Necessarily complicated by political considerations relating to Azerbaijan's pending Council membership application, the team's assessment of pre-election conditions sometimes conflicted with that of the OSCE.

A more productive division of labor occurred in Kosovo, where the OSCE had the task of organizing the October municipal elections and the Council of Europe ran the independent international monitoring mission.

Concerns persisted that the Council of Europe was admitting states before they were ready to live up to its human rights standards. In June, the Parliamentary Assembly voted to recommend admission for Armenia and Azerbaijan, and in a September report, the parliamentary rapporteur for Bosnia and Hercegovina's application seemed to set aside all but one of the eight conditions previously set for that country's admission. The prospect of premature admission of these countries heightened concern over the European Court of Human Rights' ever-expanding caseload. The court also faced an increased unwillingness among states to abide by its judgments; offending states included long-term members.

The year saw further progress in the emerging practice of member states electing to publish reports of the Committee for the Prevention of Torture, although a number of states continued to publish the reports selectively. As of August 15, 2000, the following states continued to refuse to publish at least one committee report: Albania, Austria, Bulgaria, Croatia, Estonia, Greece, Hungary, Italy, Latvia, Liechtenstein, Lithuania, Moldova, Portugal, Romania, Russia, San Marino, Macedonia, Ukraine, and the United

Kingdom. In the case of Turkey, no fewer than seven reports were outstanding.

North Atlantic Treaty Organization

The North Atlantic Treaty Organization continued its leadership role in the peacekeeping operations in the Balkans. In Kosovo, shortages of U.N. civilian police left the NATO-led KFOR with substantial policing responsibilities. KFOR troops conducted between 500 and 750 patrols every day, guarded more than 550 sites, and manned more than 200 vehicle checkpoints. KFOR's policing responsibilities challenged NATO troops trained for military operations, who despite some efforts to seize illegal weapons remained reluctant to detain or sanction members of the Kosovo Protection Corps or of the officially disbanded Kosovo Liberation Army implicated in political violence and attacks on Serbs, Roma, and other ethnic minorities. Although NATO claimed that half of all KFOR personnel were engaged in the protection of Serbs and other minorities, their response to violence against minorities, particularly Roma, remained inadequate. An October OSCE report on Kosovo's justice system also criticized KFOR and UNMIK for arbitrary and prolonged detentions of suspects without charge.

Most prominent among NATO arrests of indicted war criminals in Bosnia was the April detention of Momcilo Krajisnik, the wartime president of the Bosnian Serb Assembly and a postwar member of the Bosnian presidency. Krajisnik's arrest belied prior assertions by military and political leaders that arrests of high-ranking figures would result in protest and retaliatory attacks.

European Union

The European Union introduced the resolution on Chechnya at the U.N. Commission on Human Rights. Once the resolution went to a vote and passed, the E.U. was conspicuously absent from efforts to implement it. To the contrary, the late spring and summer saw European heads of government and state highly eager to meet with the new Russian President Vladimir Putin; criticism over Chechnya barely figured in these dialogues.

In the Federal Republic of Yugoslavia, the E.U. broke ranks with the U.S. to offer economic assistance to Serbia's opposition-controlled towns, and when the opposition took power in early October, the E.U. quickly lifted most country-wide sanctions. While the E.U. kept in place certain restrictions imposed on those indicted for war crimes and their allies, it failed to make a clear link between enhanced relations with the new authorities and their commitment to the international rule of law, including cooperation with the ICTY.

The year saw continued E.U. dialogue on human rights with the newly independent states in the context of Cooperation Council meetings held pursuant to the E.U.'s Partnership and Cooperation Agreements (PCAs). In a welcome development, official statements emerging from these meetings made explicit reference to the need for implementation of OSCE and Council of Europe human rights standards and recommendations.

Turkey's first year as an official candidate for membership in the E.U. produced little progress on its compliance with the human rights criteria for membership. Indeed the first few months of the year saw backtracking on positive steps taken in the run-up to the E.U.'s December decision to accord Turkey candidate status. As this report went to press, observers were awaiting publication of the E.U.'s Accession Partnership document, outlining the steps Turkey had to take to prepare itself for E.U. membership. Rights groups feared that the Accession Partnership would lack depth and specificity regarding needed reforms particularly in such areas as minority rights, which were controversial in Turkey, or the restrictions on the headscarf, which were controversial in Europe. They urged strict application of the Copenhagen criteria for Turkey's E.U. admission, in a manner consistent with the approach for other applicant states.

In October 1999, the European Commission proposed that updated agreements for candidate countries seeking to join the

European Union, including Hungary and the Czech Republic, make the improvement of the situation of Roma a short and medium term priority.

United States

U.S. officials repeatedly expressed concern over alleged atrocities in Chechnya and claimed that other aspects of U.S.-Russian relations would not compromise their response to these abuses. The U.S. government's lack of action on Chechnya belied this assertion.

At the U.N. Commission on Human Rights, when negotiations over a consensus chairman's statement acceptable to the Russian government broke down, the U.S. became a late cosponsor of the resolution on Chechnya.

President Clinton's June, July, and September meetings with Russian President Vladimir Putin yielded no progress on accountability for abuses in Chechnya nor on compliance with the demands of the U.N. Commission on Human Rights and the OSCE Assistance Group.

A travel ban imposed by the U.S. embassy in Moscow kept U.S. government officials from traveling to the North Caucasus to monitor and document the atrocities first-hand. This represented a stark contrast to U.S. and E.U. practice in Kosovo, where beginning in mid-1998, military attaches in Belgrade conducted regular, coordinated missions to Kosovo to monitor the conduct of Serb security forces. U.S. government personnel apparently made no concerted effort to monitor the status of Russian investigations of the abuses, although regular communication with responsible prosecutors would certainly have sent an important signal regarding U.S. expectations for the accountability process.

In the Federal Republic of Yugoslavia, the U.S., like the E.U., welcomed the opposition's rise to power by lifting most sanctions. U.S. officials continued to promise that former Yugoslav president Slobodan Milosevic would eventually be tried by the ICTY, but they refused to make any clear link between the extent of their support for new Yugoslav leader Vojislav Kostunica and his cooperation with the tribunal.

Close political and military ties between the U.S. and Turkey continued to dominate human rights concerns in that country. When the Turkish military announced in mid-year that it had chosen a U.S. manufacturer to supply U.S. $4 billion in attack helicopters, the U.S. government appeared to waver in its promise to condition the sale on human rights improvements to which President Clinton and then-President Mesut Yilmaz agreed in late 1997. A decision on the export license for the helicopters was not expected before early 2001.

Russian Federation

While the conduct of Russian government forces in Chechnya was among top human rights concerns in the region, the Russian government also stood to have a significant impact on human rights elsewhere. In September Russia became the 112th state to sign the Statute of the International Criminal Court, further isolating the U.S. and China as the sole remaining opponents to the court among Security Council permanent members. The extent of Russian commitment to the principles of international humanitarian law were, however, seriously called into question by its continued failure to rein in its troops in Chechnya and to prosecute soldiers responsible for abuses. The Russian government's disregard for international rule of law was also illustrated in May when it played host in Moscow to Yugoslav Minister of Defense Dragolub Ojdanic, an indicted war criminal, in what it later claimed was the result of an administrative error (the government had an obligation under Security Council resolutions to arrest Ojdanic).

International Financial Institutions

International financial institutions made some progress toward addressing human rights issues related to prospects for economic development in the region. A welcome development came in the form of decisions by the World Bank and the European Bank for

Reconstruction and Development (EBRD) to suspend financing in Turkmenistan due to the autocratic regime's corruption and utter resistance to reform. Unfortunately, these decisions did not dissuade the Asian Development bank from allowing Turkmenistan to become a member in August.

The World Bank's continued disbursement of structural adjustment loan payments to the Russian government without reference to abuses committed in Chechnya was a disappointment, standing in stark contrast to the bank's approach on abuses in West Timor. While refusing to make the link to Chechnya, both the World Bank and the EBRD demonstrated a growing appreciation of the need for institutional reform and improved governance in Russia.

Representatives of the international financial institutions repeatedly acknowledged the impact of corrupt and abusive law enforcement agencies on efforts to combat corruption and ensure the rule of law in the region, but they remained largely resistant to the idea of addressing needed criminal law reform through their own conditionality and technical assistance.

The Work of Human Rights Watch

Based on the model of the organization's work last year on Kosovo, Human Rights Watch launched an emergency response to the massive abuses in Chechnya, which together with Central Asia and postwar Kosovo, remained top priorities throughout the year.

When the war in Chechnya entered its deadly stage in late autumn 1999, Human Rights Watch deployed a rotating team of researchers to Ingushetia, where the majority of people displaced by the conflict had fled. We used this six-month research presence to document humanitarian law violations by both Russian and Chechen rebel forces, to press the international media to cover what had been an underreported conflict, and to use research results in timely advocacy with the Russian government and the international community.

Researchers interviewed more than 750 displaced people and immediately exposed abuses they experienced in a series of press releases. Three reports published in February, April, and June documented massacres of civilians by Russian forces in sweep operations: *Civilian Killings in Staropromyslovski District of Grozny, "No Happiness Remains": Civilian Killings, Pillage, and Rape in Alkhan-Yurt, Chechnya,* and *February 5: A Day of Slaughter in Novye Aldi.* In October, a fourth report, *"Welcome to Hell": Arbitrary Detention, Torture, and Extortion in Chechnya,* documented torture in Russian detention centers in the region. Researchers in the region worked with the international community and Russian agencies to ensure better protection to displaced persons as Russian forces attempted to pressure them to return prematurely to their homes.

Throughout the year we urged international institutions and governments to send representatives to the region to bear witness to the abuse, and to press the Russian government to stop abuses and to launch a credible accountability process. We engaged the World Bank, in letters and meetings, to withhold installments of structural adjustment loans and to link disbursements to the Russian government with compliance with its international humanitarian law obligations.

Since the Russian authorities did not conduct credible inquiries or institute criminal proceedings in response to abuses in Chechnya, we urged the international community to do so. To this end we formed a coalition of Russian and international human rights organizations to urge Council of Europe member states to file an interstate complaint against Russia at the European Court of Human Rights. We conducted advocacy at three sessions of the Council of Europe's Parliamentary Assembly to ensure that it would appropriately censure Russia, and urged the assembly to adopt resolutions calling for a rigorous domestic accountability process and calling on member states to file an interstate complaint. In a series of exchanges with the office of the secretary general and the departments for political affairs and human rights, we also cautioned the council about the potential pitfalls of sending its staff to work in the office of President Vladimir Putin's special representative on human rights in Chechnya.

Human Rights Watch also sought to have an international commission of inquiry established by the U.N. Commission on Human Rights. The organization urged the high commissioner for human rights to call for such a commission, and engaged member states to adopt a resolution to this effect at its fifty-sixth session. After the commission adopted a resolution calling for a national commission of inquiry and the deployment of thematic mechanisms, Human Rights Watch published a memorandum outlining Russia's failure to comply with the resolution and urged member states, particularly the U.S. and E.U., to call Russia to account. It was with this aim that we engaged U.S. president Bill Clinton in advance of his summit meeting with President Putin, and the E.U. in advance of its summit with the Russian government. In other advocacy, the organization testified twice before the U.S. Congress to emphasize that many of the abuses in Chechnya were effectively war crimes and twice before the Council of Europe's Parliamentary Assembly. The goals with respect to Chechnya at the OSCE focused on the redeployment of the Assistance Group to Chechnya. Recommendations on Chechnya were reinforced in opinion articles in the U.S. and European media.

Through field offices in Tashkent and Dushanbe, the organization continued to document the worsening human rights crisis in Central Asia, particularly in Uzbekistan. Researchers undertook fact-finding missions in seven regions of the country to document and publicize the arbitrary arrests and torture of hundreds of people accused of "religious extremism" and to monitor dozens of trials. The Human Rights Watch Tashkent office regularly urged the international community to monitor trials, briefed the diplomatic community about human rights developments, and brought victims of abuse together with visiting high-level officials from the U.S. and E.U. A mission to three regions of the country documented how government agencies at all levels compounded the problem of domestic violence by pressuring women to remain in abusive marriages.

The organization's Dushanbe office gathered information on civil and political rights violations relevant to the November 1999 presidential elections and the February 2000 parliamentary vote. In November 1999, a report was presented, *Freedom of Expression Still Threatened*, which documented the dramatic increase in harassment of and restrictions on the media, to the Tajik government in a series of high-level meetings. The organization launched an advocacy initiative in advance of both elections, publishing backgrounders detailing flagrant violations and addressing letters to the government urging redress. The Dushanbe office also regularly briefed members of the international community on human rights developments in the country.

The Europe and Central Asia Division strove to make the human rights crisis in Central Asia a priority issue among international actors, particularly the United Nations and the OSCE. This was also raised with U.N. High Commissioner for Human Rights Mary Robinson in February 2000 and in meetings with staff members for the U.N. special rapporteur on torture, the Working Group on Arbitrary Arrests and Disappearances, and the Committee against Torture, urging them to request visits to Uzbekistan.

Human Rights Watch focused special attention on Central Asia at the U.N. Commission on Human Rights in March 2000, urging the appointment of a special rapporteur on Uzbekistan. This forum was also used to release Leaving No Witnesses: Uzbekistan's Campaign Against Rights Defenders, in order to strengthen the call for a commission resolution on defenders. When Uzbek officials used U.N. Human Rights Committee complaint forms as evidence against a defendant in a religious extremism case, this was reported to relevant U.N. agencies in detailed letters.

U.N.-targeted advocacy on Tajikistan aimed to ensure a strong human rights component to the U.N.'s presence following the May 15 withdrawal of the U.N. Mission of

Observers to Tajikistan (UNMOT). A memorandum, based on ongoing research, was issued on April 21, concerning the government's poor human rights practices in the post-civil war period, and the implications that UNMOT's limited human rights mandate had for a long-term peace in Tajikistan. The organization formulated recommendations for the follow-on mission, urging a strong human rights component to its work. Letters outlining concerns were sent to members of the Security Council, and we conducted meetings with senior U.N. representatives from the Department of Political Affairs, the Office of the Secretary- General, and with representatives from the missions of major member states.

Human Rights Watch sought to keep human rights at the top of the agenda of U.S.-Uzbekistan relations, and urged the U.S. government to use explicit conditionality under the International Religious Freedom Act and the Cooperative Threat Reduction program. This was done in meetings with the secretary of state and other top officials and in many letters and memoranda. In congressional testimony we rebutted the Clinton Administration's argument that the crackdown in Uzbekistan qualified as political, not religious persecution.

With respect to Turkmenistan, Human Rights Watch strove to have international lending related to that countries linked strictly to human rights improvements. It urged the Department of State to declare Turkmenistan ineligible on human rights grounds for Export-Import Bank credits and urged the European Bank for Reconstruction and Development to end all lending to the country. In January, Human Rights Watch also published a press release condemning the arrest of Nurberdi Nurmamedov, perhaps the last remaining dissident in the country who publicly criticized the decision to extend indefinitely President Saparmurad Niazov's term in office.

Torture and due process violations remained a chief concern in the former Soviet Union. In November 1999, Human Right released *Confessions at Any Cost: Police Torture in Russia*, the result of a two-year,

multiregion research project on torture, at a press conference in Moscow. The organization held high-level advocacy meetings with Russian government officials and urged the international community to support the creation of a torture rehabilitation center.

These same issues were of top concern in the Caucasus. Through the Human Rights Watch field office in Tbilisi, Georgia, research was conducted on torture and on the setback in legal reforms that could have helped prevent torture and other due process violations. In September, the organization released *Backtracking on Reform: Amendments Undermine Access to Justice*, at a press conference in Tbilisi. The report documented the repeal of reforms in Georgia's criminal procedure code that would have granted criminal suspects and defendants the right to complain about due process violations directly to a court, prior to trial. Since the repeal of these reforms ran counter to Georgia's commitments upon admission to the Council of Europe, this featured prominently in our meetings with the Council of Europe's Monitoring Committee during its May visit to Tbilisi, and in advocacy with the Parliamentary Assembly.

Human Rights Watch advocated for the expansion of the World Bank's work in the area of legal and judicial reforms specifically to address reform of certain aspects of criminal law and procedure. In meetings in November 1999 and in February and July 2000 we argued that Georgia's setback in legal reform served to undermine public trust in the judiciary and hence bank programs that promote it. The organization urged the bank to adopt criminal procedure reform throughout the region as a policy trigger for future structural adjustment lending in its country assistance strategy; to expand its capacity to conduct analysis of judicial systems and criminal procedure, to enable it to identify provisions in legislation that are not in compliance with international human rights law and standards; and to assist in the formulation of lending targets in these areas.

In the run-up to Azerbaijan's November 5 parliamentary elections, Human Rights

Watch launched a month-long fact-finding mission to research civil and political rights abuses affecting the election. Researchers interviewed journalists for media outlets that were closed or fined arbitrarily, parliamentary candidates whose registration was arbitrarily denied, and opposition activists harassed by local governments.

Human Rights Watch priorities in the wake of the war in Kosovo were twofold. The organization responded to the compelling need for an independent record of the humanitarian law violations during the war. It also examined postwar human rights issues especially minority rights, due process, and freedom of movement that would have a lasting impact on efforts to build a sustainable peace in the province.

Throughout the year we assembled information on humanitarian law violations in the 1999 conflict with NATO. In March, the organization published a report documenting rape as a weapon of "ethnic cleansing" in Kosovo. The report included ninety-six cases of rape of Albanian women by Serbian and Yugoslav forces immediately before and during the 1999 NATO bombing campaign. An April Human Rights Watch report found that NATO forces had violated international humanitarian law in its bombing campaign, which resulted in the deaths of more than 500 civilians.

The organization's strategy on postwar Kosovo was to remind the international community of the lesson learned from Bosnia: that rushed elections in postwar situations, especially in the wake of massive violence and inter-ethnic hatred, undermined longer-term prospects for the rule of law. This message was presented in a March meeting with the OSCE chair-in-office, in follow-up correspondence, and in a June memorandum to diplomats and international organizations, and in an October backgrounder for the media and other observers of the elections. In June, we investigated access to protection and justice for minorities in Kosovo, focusing on the work of UNMIK police and KFOR. December 1999 and January 2000 meetings with the E.U. and the U.S. government raised fair-trial concerns regarding war crimes trials of Serbs before Albanian-dominated local courts in Kosovo.

Before the ouster of Slobodan Milosevic, Human Rights Watch aimed to call international attention to victims of his government's intensified harassment and to ensure maximum international assistance to civil society. The significance of elections mandated for 2000 was anticipated, and throughout the year the organization detailed the repression of the government's critics. A May report focused on measures the government took against civil society institutions which it perceived as a threat, including opposition parties, the independent media, student organizations, independent trade unions, nongovernmental organizations (NGOs), and civic activists in Serbia. Just prior to the elections, the organization published a backgrounder detailing how the authorities set about rigging the elections.

When Milosevic left office, Human Rights Watch deployed a researcher to Belgrade to identify a new human rights agenda for Yugoslavia: release of Kosovo Albanian political prisoners, cooperation with the ICTY as part of the general restoration of the rule of law, restoring the independence of the judiciary, and justice for past abuses by security forces. In a series of letters and press releases, Human Rights Watch called for the international community to adopt a policy on cooperation vis a vis Serbia consistent with that practiced throughout the Balkans.

In Croatia, the organization focused on minority rights and other basic civic freedoms in the transition from Tudjman period. A report published in December 1999, in anticipation of elections in early 2000, outlined violations of the rights to freedom of expression and assembly. After the election of President Stjepan Mesi and formation of a new government under Prime Minister Ivica Racan, Human Rights Watch wrote to both leaders, recommending legislative and administrative measures to ensure equal treatment for all Croatian citizens, including minorities, to promote the return of Serb refugees and the reform the country's state broadcaster. In

Croatia, we focused on minority rights and other basic civic freedoms in the transition from Tudjman period. A report published in December 1999, in anticipation of elections in early 2000, outlined violations of the rights to freedom of expression and assembly.

Research and advocacy on Bosnia focused on two aspects of refugee return: keeping the donor community engaged, identifying minority returns as an essential element for a lasting peace and the rule of law, and ensuring that progress on returns remained a condition for Council of Europe accession. In May Human Rights Watch published *Unfinished Business: Return of Displaced Persons and Other Human Rights Issues in Bijeljina*, which documented how authorities in that city obstructed the implementation of the Dayton Peace Agreement by providing neither protection nor equal rights to the Bosniak community there, and by actively deterring the return of Bosniaks who were driven from the city during the war. We continued with research in 2000 to investigate impediments to minority returns, including decrease in donor assistance, persistent failure by local authorities to enforce housing regulations, security concerns, and lack of long-term prospects for employment and education.

In Turkey research and advocacy focused on the opportunity for reform that emerged when Turkey became a candidate for membership in the European Union in December 1999. A September 2000 report outlined specific short-term steps the Turkish government should take to begin to demonstrate its willingness to meet the E.U.'s membership criteria. Recommended steps addressed torture, restrictions on freedom of expression and religious freedom, violations of minority rights, continued instability in the southeastern part of the country, and the death penalty. Human Rights Watch pressed this agenda throughout the year with governmental interlocutors in both Brussels and Ankara.

In May, Human Rights Watch staff traveled to Ankara to meet with Ministry of Justice officials and released a report outlining our concern that their proposed prison reform measures would subject detainees to an impermissible isolation regime. A November Human Rights Watch memorandum welcomed some improvements in the planned reforms and urged additional steps be taken to ensure that it would comport with international prison standards. Research also continued on the headscarf ban and followed closely developments relating to the pending sale of U.S. $4 billion worth of U.S.-manufactured attack helicopters to Turkey.

In 2000 the organization took on migrant worker' rights as its strategic focus in Western Europe. The multicountry project would document and expose the serious abuses committed against migrant workers in Western Europe, who were among the most vulnerable groups in that region, and the failure of states to protect their basic rights. Of particular concern were those migrant workers who worked in forced labor conditions, either in conditions of near-captivity for little or no wages or in debt bondage, where wages were immediately absorbed into repaying a "debt" owed to the employer. A fact-finding mission in October investigated these issues with respect to Greece.

Migrants and refugees were primary targets of the upsurge in xenophobia and racist violence in Western Europe in 2000. Focusing specifically on the relationship between xenophobia and many European governments' increasingly restrictive immigration policies and practices, we promoted migrants' rights and refugee protection in fora related to the U.N. World Conference Against Racism. Together with the European Council on Refugees and Exiles (ECRE), the organization released a memorandum at the Strasbourg regional preparatory conference critiquing the Draft General Conclusions of the European Conference Against Racism. The memorandum highlighted measures taken by Western European governments that undermined protections for asylum seekers and migrants, giving the media, public, and state agencies an apparent rational for discriminating against them. We recommended full compliance with the 1951 refugee convention and the promotion and protection of fundamental human and labor rights for all migrants as a way to stem the growing tide of anti-foreigner sentiment and violence in Europe.

Throughout the year, Human Rights Watch highlighted the need for greater coordination on human rights protection among international institutions active in the region. The organization emphasized the need for institutional and policy linkages between political institutions engaged in monitoring and promoting human rights and an international donor community that was increasingly cognizant of the role of governance and rule of law in fostering effective development. A welcome development in this regard was the emerging E.U. practice of citing Council of Europe and OSCE recommendations and commitments in statements regarding its Cooperation Council meetings with countries in the region.

In September, the organization's Europe and Central Asia Division participated in NGO meetings with World Bank and IMF officials organized in conjunction with those institutions' annual meetings in Prague. Human Rights Watch joined other nongovernmental organizations in pressing the World Bank in particular to operationalize its stated commitment to human rights. In a joint statement with the Federation Internationale des Ligues des Droits de l'Homme, the organization recommended that the bank incorporate reference to human rights law in its policies, consider appropriate human rights-related conditionality on its lending, expand the bank's internal staff capacity to assess human rights conditions relevant to development, and coordinate closely with and support the work of international human rights bodies.

ALBANIA

Human Rights Developments

With the rapid repatriation of over 450,000 Kosovar refugees from northern Albania to Kosovo by 2000, Albania was once again able to turn inward and focus on internal reforms. Problems remained with regard to corruption, excessive force used by the police, trafficking of women, and controls on the media. The two main political rivals in Albania—Sali Berisha, president of the opposition Democratic Party (DP), and Fatos Nano, president of the ruling Socialist Party (SP)—revived the bitter political feuding that had polarized Albanian society over the past decade and forestalled the emergence of younger, less divisive political leaders in Albania.

The bitter rivalry became notably evident in the preparations for the October local elections. Berisha had waged a relentless campaign of accusations against the SP since losing power in 1997 and accused the Central Electoral Commission (CEC) of bias. He called for the reinstatement of a bipartisan commission—rather than the intended nonpolitical body—and boycotted the CEC. In August, Berisha accused Organization for Security and Cooperation in Europe (OSCE) election observers of being partial toward the government and the SP and said he would refuse to cooperate with them during the election.

In June the Council of Europe expressed concern over the lack of progress in investigating the 1998 assassination of senior DP member Azem Hajdari. The authorities blamed key DP witnesses, who refused to cooperate with what they saw as a biased investigation. Another investigation, conducted by PricewaterhouseCoopers into the pyramid schemes that collapsed in early 1997 during Berisha's leadership, concluded in January 2000 that only U.S. $50 million of the public's lost money was recoverable. The lack of a conviction in the Hajdari case and inability of the accounting firm to locate and repatriate the bulk of the money lost in the pyramid schemes exacerbated the deep divisions in Albanian politics.

Despite the highly partisan political atmosphere, the Albanian government made some sincere efforts to confront official corruption and to establish public order in the country. After passing the Law on the State Police in December 1999, the Ministry of

Public Order began restructuring the police force, improving recruitment procedures, and training new police chiefs. The police also cracked down on armed gangs, and their number was reported to be decreasing.

Senior police officers supported by high-level politicians were still suspected of involvement in the escalation of drug trafficking in Albania, which was said to have increased corruption in the country. The police also at times utilized excessive force against suspects during arrests and in the initial period of detention. In September both government and parliamentary officials requested that the Western European Union extend its assistance program (of training, counseling, and logistical support) to the Albanian police for an additional year.

Violations of women's human rights continued unabated in Albania, as trafficking and domestic violence plagued women and girls throughout the country. Many women, lured with deceptive offers of lucrative work abroad, migrated to Western Europe only to find themselves sold as virtual slaves for approximately U.S. $1,000 each. Traffickers also abducted women and girls, stripping them of their passports and forcing them to work in brothels in Italy and other E.U. countries. Women trapped in forced prostitution and other types of forced labor feared turning to law enforcement for assistance, terrified that their "employers" would carry out threats of harm against them and their families. Domestic violence also devastated women's lives in Albania; nongovernmental organizations compensated for a lack of state response to the abuse by opening a shelter for battered women in Tirana with Italian funding. Girls suffered from a lack of educational opportunities, as fearful parents refused to allow thousands of school-aged females to attend school amid concerns about the girls' safety and "honor."

Smuggling of human beings expanded as a highly profitable business. Foreign nationals (increasingly Turkish Kurds) and asylum seekers transiting en route to the E.U., Albanian men seeking work in the E.U., and Albanian women and girls paid exorbitant amounts of money to be smuggled across the Adriatic Sea on speed boats. Low police morale and a faltering judicial system limited Albania's ability to combat organized crime.

Following the adoption of the Law on the People's Advocate in February 1999, the Albanian parliament named the country's first ombudsman, Emir Objani, in February 2000. Objani's office struggled throughout 2000 to acquire premises and become operational.

The October 1 municipal elections were seen as a major test of Albania's fragile democracy. There were some violent incidents prior to the electoral campaign, as when four DP activists from the Lezhe region were pulled over and beaten by masked special police forces on a road north of Tirana in March. But the fact that the DP's Sali Berisha was able to hold a peaceful political rally in May in the southern city of Vlora—traditionally a SP stronghold—was a sign of some growing stability. Only a few violent incidents were reported, a tribute to the government's efforts, as well as to the restraint of the political parties themselves.

Despite some irregularities, including errors and omissions in the new voter register, the municipal electoral commissions generally administered the voting procedures correctly. Police conduct was deemed appropriate by international monitors, who saw "significant progress" in the elections toward meeting international standards. The SP made significant gains in the first round, and an October 15 runoff led to an overwhelming SP victory. The ruling SP won in 262 out of 398 towns and municipalities in two rounds of the local elections. International monitors considered the second round "less transparent and inclusive" due to the failure to address inaccuracies in the voter lists, invalid ballots, and election complaints. In the southern coastal town of Himara, where a Greek minority resides, serious irregularities occurred, including intimidation of election commission members, the destruction of one ballot box in a violent incident, and fraud in three other voting centers. Nationalist rhetoric during the campaign, both at the local and national level, had heightened tension in the town over a possible victory by the local ethnic Greek Human Rights Union Party.

Albania's state television was criticized by the OSCE in the first week of the campaign period in early September for strongly favoring the SP in its coverage, particularly when it violated the electoral code by transmitting a full interview with SP chairman Fatos Nano. The OSCE simultaneously criticized the DP-controlled ATN-1 station in Tirana for covering DP electoral activities for twenty-four hours. Throughout this period the smaller parties received scant attention from the media. During the October 15 runoff vote candidates received limited coverage as the media focused on the threat of a DP boycott and developments in Himara. TVSH, the public television broadcaster, was reported to have provided the SP with a disproportionate amount of coverage, though the tone of the information provided was, overall, considered to be balanced.

Private media owners were often seen as being affiliated with or supporters of the SP or the DP, and many journalist were often induced or bribed to investigate the "other" party. Journalists also continued to face security risks while conducting their work. For example, in March police forces in the town of Korca physically abused a journalist from local radio ABC. In April, two journalists from TV KLAN, filming near the Foreign Ministry in Tirana, were allegedly attacked by five members of the Republican Guard. In May, two journalists from TV ATN 1 were illegally detained by police officers and beaten while in detention. Numerous private radio and television stations had also been broadcasting throughout the country since 1997 without any legal status, and Albania's National Radio and Television Commission planned to issue licenses for them in October, after the municipal election.

Defending Human Rights

The two major nongovernmental human rights organizations functioned, largely, without interference. The Albanian Human Rights Group (AHRG) reported that when it published a report in April on police misconduct in the city of Elbasan, the director of the organization as well as the authors of the report received anonymous phone calls threatening retribution for its publication. The AHRG continued receiving complaints from citizens regarding abuses, and the Albanian Helsinki Committee (AHC) continued its long-term project of monitoring pretrial detention centers administered by the police and prisons administered by the General Directorate of Prisons through visits to places of detention in numerous municipalities throughout Albania. The AHC initiated a project in May establishing a telephone hotline to be operational twelve hours a week where citizens—including those imprisoned or detained—could call in to report human rights violations and receive pro bono legal assistance. After the Albanian parliament enacted the Law on the People's Advocate in February, the AHC entered into a contract with the new ombudsman's office establishing a joint project to support the ombudsman's activities.

The Role of the International Community

Organization for Security and Cooperation in Europe (OSCE)

The OSCE focused much of its efforts on preparations for the October 1 local elections throughout Albania. Ambassador Geert Ahrens, the head of the OSCE Mission to Albania, chaired an election working group which met with Albanian officials and political party members almost daily—starting in March—to address specific concerns regarding the electoral code and voter registration procedures. The OSCE's Warsaw-based Office of Democratic Initiatives and Human Rights, which usually is not involved in municipal elections, sent eighteen long-term observers and 239 short-term observers to monitor the vote.

Council of Europe

Albania made substantial progress in meeting its legal reform obligations to the

Council of Europe. In September 1999 the government ratified the Council of Europe Framework Convention on the Protection of National Minorities, a step that could provide Albania's ethnic Greek minority (who constitute 3 percent of the population) with greater linguistic freedom, autonomy in education, recourse against discrimination, and increased access to the media. Following threats of expulsion from the Council of Europe if Albania did not end capital punishment, the Constitutional Court ruled in December 1999 that the death penalty was incompatible with the Albanian constitution. Confirming the decision in April 2000, Prime Minister Ilir Meta signed Protocol No. 6 to the European Convention on Human Rights, and the document was ratified by the Albanian government in September 2000. The Council of Europe appointed a special representative in Albania in May 2000 to increase contacts with the Albanian government and civil society.

North Atlantic Treaty Organization

Following the refugee crisis in 1999, 1,300 NATO troops remained in Albania in 2000 to provide support to NATO's neighboring Kosovo Force and to show NATO's commitment to supporting stability in Albania, a member of the alliance's Partnership for Peace program.

European Union

The E.U. provided 35 million euro (U.S. $31.5 million) in financial assistance to support Albanian reform efforts in 2000, but remained skeptical about initiating the integration of the country into E.U. institutions due to insufficient "institutional and political reform." Relations with most E.U. member states continued to improve in light of Albania's pro-Western stance during the Kosovo crisis. Based on a series of agreements, Italy and Albania increased cooperation in fighting organized crime and cross-Adriatic smuggling and trafficking in humans.

United States

The U.S. government continued to maintain close ties with Albania in 2000, allocating an estimated U.S. $32 million in aid to support the country's reform efforts and strongly supporting the government's participation in the Balkan Stability Pact. The U.S. also strengthened economic relations with Albania when the Senate voted in November 1999 to grant Albania Normal Trade Relations status with the U.S.

International Financial Institutions

Citing the Albanian government's steadfast pursuit of sound macroeconomic policies and a Gross Domestic Product (GDP) growing at around 7 percent, the International Monetary Fund (IMF) gave Albania a positive economic assessment in June 2000 and continued providing financial assistance for poverty reduction and the facilitation of economic growth. The World Bank also continued to provide Albania with loans to support water supply rehabilitation, a microcredit project, as well as reform in the fields of education, the judiciary, public administration, and the banking and insurance industries. Albania also joined the World Trade Organization in September 2000.

ARMENIA

Human Rights Developments

The investigation of the 1999 murder of the prime minister, Vasken Sarkisyan, and seven others in the Armenian parliament dominated the political scene in 2000, with fierce accusations of bias. Infighting among government officials over the investigation sapped efforts to address the country's stagnating economy and poor human rights record.

The military procuracy led the investigation of the October 27, 1999, shootings in the parliament. The arrest of a member of President Robert Kochariyan's staff, Aleksan Harutunyan, prompted accusations that the military procuracy investigators, allied with associates of the former prime minister, were attempting to use the investigation to implicate and oust the president. Charges against Harutunyan were later dropped.

President Kochariyan struggled to maintain his grip on power, coopting some senior government officials who had been linked to the slain prime minister, while reshuffling others. In May, the minister of defense was replaced with a close Kochariyan associate, Serge Sarkisyan.

Some of the suspects detained during the investigation said they were ill-treated in custody. Detainees were also reportedly denied access to lawyers and family members. Nairi Hunaniyan, the chief suspect in the shootings, retracted testimony he said he was coerced into signing after being physically abused, and on July 25 denounced his state-appointed lawyer. Armenian National Television Deputy Director Harutiun Harutunyan also stated that he was subjected to physical abuse while in detention. Harutunyan was arrested in January after being accused of participation in the crime, but later released.

On March 22 several gunmen attempted to assassinate Arkady Ghukasian, who held the title of president of the ethnic Armenian separatist Nagorno Karkbakh region in Azerbaijan. After the attempt, a number of individuals were arrested, including the enclave's former defense minister, Samvel Babayan, his brother Karen Babayan, and several of Babayan's bodyguards. Babayan and other defendants reported that they were physically abused in custody and deprived of access to lawyers. On March 28, Nagorno Karabakh authorities ordered journalist Vaghram Aghauaniyan to serve one year of imprisonment for libel after dubious proceedings in which Aghauaniyan alleged he was denied the right to call witnesses.

Although newspapers in Yerevan reprinted Aghauaniyan's article alleging misconduct on the part of the Nagorno Karabakh prime minister, Armenia lacked a vigorous independent press. A record of physical assaults on journalists for which the government had failed to bring perpetrators to account, as well as spurious libel suits, had fostered a climate of self-censorship among journalists. On June 6, journalist Vaghan Gukasiyan said that he was summoned to the Ministry of Interior and severely beaten by Hrach Harutunyan, head of the criminal investigation department, in retaliation for a paper he wrote that was critical of Harutunyan and the investigation into the October 1999 parliamentary shootings. On July 8, local authorities reportedly removed copies of *Azg* newspaper from newsstands because it contained an article critical of them.

Defending Human Rights

Human rights monitoring groups functioned, but there was a lack of vigorous and open public debate about important human rights issues.

The Role of the International Community

United Nations

The U.N. Committee on the Rights of the Child said in January that there were significant gaps in the preparation of Armenia's initial report to the committee. The committee noted that cooperation with nongovernmental organizations in preparation of the report had been limited and recommended that civil society be included in all stages of implementation of the Convention of the Rights of the Child. The committee also expressed concern over a broad range of issues, including children living and working on the streets and about allegations that young children had been conscripted into the armed forces. The committee reiterated concerns previously expressed by the U.N. Human Rights Committee and the U.N. Committee on the Elimination of Discrimination against Women that the government has failed to acknowledge and address the issue of domestic violence.

The committee also expressed serious concern regarding the absence of a system of juvenile justice in Armenia, and in particular the length and conditions of pretrial detention, limited access to visitors for children detained prior to trial, the often disproportionate length of sentences in relation to the seriousness of offences, the frequent detentions of juveniles with adults, and the absence of facilities for the physical and psychological rehabilitation and social reintegration of juvenile offenders.

In May, the U.N. Committee against Torture had been set to examine Armenia's second periodic report about implementation of the Convention against Torture and Other Cruel, Inhuman or Degrading Treatment or Punishment, but one month prior to the meeting, the Armenian government canceled its appearance.

Organization for Security and Cooperation in Europe (OSCE)

In July, the OSCE chairperson-in-office, Benita Ferrero-Waldner, traveled to Yerevan officially to open an OSCE office. The office had actually begun activities in February. Ferrero-Waldner stated that economic development in Armenia could only be enhanced if there was significant progress toward a political settlement of the Nagorno-Karabakh conflict. Negotiations to resolve the conflict had been ongoing, with no tangible results, for the past several years under the auspices of the OSCE Minsk Group.

The new OSCE office engaged in a number of projects, including review of legislation and administration of the electoral framework in line with recommendations made by OSCE election observers, training of prison staff, public awareness of human rights, and a round table on tolerance for ethnic and religious groups.

Council of Europe

On June 28, the Parliamentary Assembly of the Council of Europe voted favorably on Armenia's accession to the organization, but full membership as of this writing still required a favorable Committee of Ministers decision. Although the Parliamentary Assembly maintained that progress had been made, the long list of conditions that Armenia would be required to meet after accession served only to highlight just how far the country was from establishing the legal frame-work necessary to guarantee the rule of law and respect for human rights.

The Parliamentary Assembly's conditions included adoption of a number of new laws, including on the media, on political parties, on nongovernmental organizations, on the establishment of an ombudsman office, on the civil service, and on alternative military service. The assembly required that amendments to the current law on local authorities be made to give them greater independence. With regard to the court system, it required that independence of the judiciary be fully guaranteed, that the Judicial Council be reformed to ensure its independence, and that access to the Constitutional Court be granted to individuals in certain instances. It also stipulated as a condition the transfer of certain detention facilities from the responsibility of the Ministries of Internal Affairs and National Security to the Ministry of Justice.

European Union

The Second Annual E.U.-Armenia Cooperation brought E.U. praise for human rights improvements and promises of continued E.U. assistance aimed at facilitating resolution of the Nagorno-Karabakh conflict and further improvement in democratization and human rights.

United States

In May a U.S.-Armenia Task Force on Economic Reform held its first meeting. At its initial meeting, the task force said that it would concentrate its efforts on private sector development, combating corruption, and Armenia's energy needs. The administration requested renewed foreign assistance, stated that the U.S. supported assistance to help transform Armenia into a democracy based on the rule of law with an active civil society and free markets, at peace with its neighbors and integrated in the world economy. Officials argued that Armenia would thus be less likely to engage in armed conflict with Azerbaijan or to disrupt the export of hydrocarbons from the Caspian Basin. Secure routes for oil and gas transit from the region, and through Turkey, were a key U.S. policy concern in the region.

International Financial Institutions

In September, the World Bank approved the equivalent of U.S. $11.4 million for judicial reform in Armenia. The project, with the aim of assisting in the development of an independent, accessible, and efficient judiciary, was a welcome attempt at improving legal institutions that were woefully incapable of addressing the country's abysmal human rights practices. It included assistance in the area of court administration, infrastructure rehabilitation, training of judges and court personnel, improved enforcement of court decisions, and increased access to legal information.

AZERBAIJAN

Human Rights Developments

The succession to Azerbaijan's ailing president, Heydar Aliyev, dominated political debate in 2000. Since the speaker of parliament was next in the line of succession, obstacles to a free and fair vote for the November 5 parliamentary elections gained greater prominence. The Parliamentary Assembly of the Council of Europe (PACE) voted on June 28 to recommend Azerbaijan's accession and asked Azerbaijan "to ensure that its planned elections be free and impartial, liberate or re-try prisoners held on 'political grounds' and guarantee freedom of expression and the independence of the media." While the government in 2000 adopted several laws that aimed to strengthen civic freedoms, its human rights record remained poor, and the PACE recommendation of accession was premature.

The government tried to manipulate parliamentary elections by adopting an unfair election law, wilfully delaying the registration of opposition parties and candidates, cracking down on critical journalists and media outlets, and banning most domestic, nonpartisan nongovernmental organizations (NGOs) from monitoring the vote. Parliament enacted Azerbaijan's election law on July 5 and then amended it on July 21. As a result of these amendments, and in the words of the Organization for Security and Cooperation's Office for Democratic Institutions and Human Rights (OSCE/ODIHR), which had been providing assistance with election legislation since 1998, the "current legislation does not provide for the full participation of all main political interests in the election administration's decision-making process and is therefore a step back compared to the legislation initially adopted." Moreover, no provisions were made for domestic observers in that law.

Opposition groups protested the law on April 29. According to domestic sources, more than fifty people were injured when police armed with clubs beat demonstrators, scores of protesters were sentenced to three to fifteen days of imprisonment on misdemeanor charges, and others were fined and later released. Criminal cases were brought against eleven of the detained, including Vagif Hajibeyli, chairman of the Ahrar party, and members of the prominent opposition parties Popular Front and Musavat. Authorities subsequently rejected numerous permit applications for public demonstrations—especially those that envisaged more than fifty participants (anything larger than a picket). On June 13, President Aliyev signed into law the controversial Law on NGOs, which barred domestic NGOs from monitoring elections if they received certain levels of foreign funding. As a result, this law prevented For the Sake of Civil Society, which had observed the 1999 and 1995 elections, from monitoring the November vote.

In September, the Central Election Commission (CEC) rejected the registration of most parties, including Musavat, and the Azerbaijani Democratic Party, among others, by declaring signature lists invalid. Individual candidates faced similar problems. Spurious reasons for disqualifications were abundant. Dubious "experts" rejected numerous signatures on opposition signature lists as false, even though many of these signatures were shown by the opposition candidates to be legitimate. By contrast, the signature lists of pro-government candidates and parties were abundant despite opposition allegations of fraud. In a controversial decision, in response to international pressure, on October 6 President Aliyev requested that the CEC reverse its rulings barring all but five of the thirteen parties that applied to contest the elections under the party list system. On October 8, the supposedly independent CEC complied by registering all parties for the proportional ballot.

As the pre-election cycle heated up, the authorities used arbitrary licensing laws, fines, and trumped-up tax charges to intimidate the opposition media. On May 8, Elmar Husseinov found the office of his weekly journal, *Monitor Weekly* (formerly *Monitor*), sealed by the Baku tax inspectorate, allegedly for printing articles critical of Aliyev. The independent newspaper, *Uch Nokta,* had battled the courts from November 1999, and faced large fines as well as closure for months prior to the elections. The editor-in-chief and founder, Khoshgadam Bakhshaliyeva, claimed that state pressure was meant to serve as a warning to editors who might consider criticizing the government in the run-up to the elections. A large fine was imposed on the newspaper *Avropa* for publishing reports that Hussein Husseinov, a high-ranking government employee, was the subject of a corruption investigation in Uzbekistan. The Azerbaijan Broadcasting Agency (ABA), an independent station that does not broadcast political material, was suddenly closed from October 3 until October 13. The closure appeared related to a visit paid to the station by two opposition parties who expressed an interest in purchasing air time but were rejected. The president, Faiq Zulfugarov, believed that the closure was a threat from the government not to get involved in politics. He worried that his station would be closed again following the elections.

Yeni Musavat (New Musavat), an opposition newspaper, was a particular target. In February, their Nakhichevan offices were ransacked. On August 22, police arrested Rauf Arifoglu, editor of *Yeni Musavat* and Musavat party candidate for the parliamentary elections, interrogated him for several hours without a lawyer, and searched his apartment. Authorities charged Arifoglu with serious crimes, including conspiracy to commit a terrorist act, an airplane hijacking, calling for a coup d'etat, and illegal possession of a firearm (allegedly planted on him by the police). Arifoglu was released on October 5, but charges against him remained and he was required to submit a written assurance that he would not flee the city before the trial.

According to Radio Free Europe/Radio Liberty, electricity to the independent channel, ANS, was cut for fifteen minutes on July 14 in order to censor an interview with Chechen field commander Shamil Basaev that was being aired at the time because the government felt that the interview contained terrorist propaganda. Electricity cuts by regional authorities during opposition candidates' broadcasts were a common complaint of opposition parties in the final weeks before the parliamentary vote.

Advances in religious freedom came only upon intervention of the president's office, indicating that religious tolerance was not institutionalized in Azerbaijan. After a spate of attacks, primarily on evangelical Christians toward the end of 1999, in November 1999 President Aliyev made a statement committing the country to greater religious freedom. In December 1999 the authorities registered the Jehovah's Witnesses, after intervention from the president's office. However, according to Keston News Service, at the end of 1999 the authorities deported the German pastor of a Lutheran church congregation.

In June, President Aliyev issued a decree providing amnesty to many political prisoners, and in October, dozens were released by presidential pardon. Casting serious doubt on official statements that these were the last political prisoners in Azerbaijan, however, human rights groups claimed hundreds remained in custody, chiefly those convicted on charges related to terrorism, alleged coup attempts, and abuse of office. At the end of September, prison authorities reportedly charged many of these prisoners with disciplinary offenses in what prisoners said were trumped up accusations intended to justify arbitrary confinement in punishment cells or transfers to harsher prison regimes. Significantly, under a new penal code that entered into force in September, many prisoners with good records would have been eligible for early release.

Breaking an impasse between the International Committee of the Red Cross (ICRC) and the government, an agreement was reached on June 1 allowing ICRC staff members to visit detainees. The accord granted ICRC representatives access to all places of detention and to all detainees—both sentenced and unsentenced. On June 23, ICRC staff, including a medical delegate, visited Gobustan prison—a facility administered by the Ministry of Justice and with a history of problems.

Defending Human Rights

Domestic nongovernmental organizations remained active throughout 2000, as demonstrated by their regular criminal reporting, especially with regard to the elections, and their dissemination of information. Eldar Ismailov, head of the domestic monitoring organization, For the Sake of Civil Society, protested the Law on NGOs that was adopted in July, for it barred his organization from monitoring the November 5 elections as it had in past elections.

The authorities responded by putting economic pressure on the protesting NGOs. Local utility charges were doubled, and organizations were required to pay these bills in a timely manner or be shut down—at a time when other organizations were not under the same constraints.

The Role of the International Community

United Nations

In November 1999, the U.N. Committee against Torture reviewed Azerbaijan's initial report. The committee expressed concern that torture was not expressly criminalized and about reports of torture and the lack of accountability for it. Upon the committee's recommendation, Sir Nigel Rodley, the U.N. special rapporteur on torture, conducted a fact-finding mission to Azerbaijan in May.

Organization for Security and Cooperation in Europe (OSCE)

The OSCE officially opened an office in Baku in July designed, according to its mandate, to "promote the implementation of OSCE principles and commitments as well as the co-operation between the OSCE and the Republic of Azerbaijan in all the OSCE dimensions, including human, political, economic and environmental aspects of security and stability." Under the auspices of the Minsk Group, the OSCE made several efforts to resolve the Nagorno Karabakh conflict. Concerning electoral progress, it issued several statements, among others noting that the July 5 election law contained "serious shortcomings" and that it was "extremely concerned that seven political parties were denied registration by the [CEC]...." After Aliyev intervened, the remaining parties were registered.

Council of Europe

The Parliamentary Assembly voted on June 28 to recommend to the Committee of Ministers that Azerbaijan be admitted to the Council of Europe (COE). This move severely undermined the council's leverage with the government to foster the implementation of legal and institutional reform (including reformed courts, police, and procuracy) desperately needed to improve Azerbaijan's human rights record. At the time of this writing, the committee had yet to act on that PACE resolution.

The PACE recommendation favoring Azerbaijan's membership found that Azerbaijan is "moving towards a democratic, pluralist society in which human rights and the rule of law are respected...." However, the document's lengthy list of conditions which the country was required to meet after its accession indicated just the opposite: that the government has made very little progress. The wide-ranging post-accession requirements included ratification of a number of significant treaties, an overhaul of domestic election laws, strengthening of parliament—currently little more than a rubber stamp—relative to the executive, reform of procedures on appointment of judges, opening individual's access to the constitutional court, and registration of nongovernmental associations. The PACE also proposed adoption of a law allowing the right to an alternative to military service, a law on the media, a law on ethnic minorities, and a law on lawyers' associations. Other measures required included the release of political prisoners, prosecution of law enforcement officials responsible for torture, and improved access of humanitarian organizations to prisons. At the request of the government, the Council of Europe also deployed an election assistance group to provide advice regarding the organization of elections.

European Union

In October, the E.U. and Azerbaijan conducted their second annual Cooperation Council meeting under the Partnership and Cooperation Agreement. The council addressed human rights issues in the bilateral relationship, including Azerbaijan's obligation to implement OSCE and COE commitments. Reflecting the lack of progress over the past year, public statements following the meeting were more guarded about the relationship than after the 1999 council meeting.

United States

The U.S. State Department monitored events surrounding the parliamentary elections and issued many statements criticizing the government's campaign conduct. It condemned the Azerbaijani parliament's decision to allow the Central Election Commission to function without opposition party members present. It chastised Azerbaijan for continuing its distorted registration policy preventing certain political parties from participating. And it described the election law as "seriously flawed." Nevertheless, it supported Azerbaijan's accession to the Council of Europe.

REPUBLIC OF BELARUS

Human Rights Developments

Respect for human rights deteriorated as Belarusian president Lukashenka maintained his grip on power and the government staged deeply flawed parliamentary elections. Another well-known opposition figure "disappeared" in July, while the year witnessed a spate of political show trials. In the run-up to parliamentary elections the government intensified its crackdown on the opposition, which struggled to remain unified in calling for a boycott. Due to extensive election violations, no intergovernmental organization recognized the election results.

On July 7, Russian Public Television (ORT) cameraman Dmitri Zavadsky traveled to Minsk-2 airport where he was to have picked up a colleague, but Zavadsky never arrived. Police found his car, reportedly wiped clean of fingerprints, in the airport parking lot. Not active in politics, Zavadsky rose to prominence in 1997, when he spent three months in jail following arrest while filming at the border in a controversial incident. Zavadsky's nonappearance was widely attributed to the government's campaign to intimidate the media prior to the parliamentary elections.

In December 1999, Tamara Vinnikova, thought to have been detained in April 1999, reappeared in Western Europe. Vinnikova told the media she had fled the country because she feared for her life. There was no news as to the welfare or whereabouts of three others—former interior minister Yury Zakharenka, opposition activist Victor Gonchar, and publisher Anatoly Krasovsky—who were also last seen in 1999.

At a March 25 demonstration police detained over 200 persons, including thirty journalists, three Polish parliamentary officials, and a U.S. employee of the local OSCE office. Although the journalists and officials were released after a few hours, police confiscated video and audio recordings. At other demonstrations police arbitrarily and sometimes violently arrested participants.

In the first of a series of politically motivated trials of opposition activists in 2000, the Belarusian Supreme Court on January 14 sentenced former minister of agriculture Vasily Leonov to a four-year prison term for "bribery" and "abuse of power." On March 17, a Minsk court sentenced Andrei Klimov, entrepreneur, leading government critic, and member of the disbanded Thirteenth Supreme Soviet, to six years of imprisonment for "embezzlement" in a decision considered politically motivated. Klimov was arrested one day after he distributed a letter detailing constitutional violations committed by the Lukashenka administration. Klimov was severely beaten by prison guards on December 13, 1999, and appeared barefoot in court in torn clothes. He was later hospitalized and diagnosed as suffering from concussion.

On May 19, a Minsk court sentenced ex-prime minister Mikhail Chygir to three years of imprisonment for "abuse of power," suspended for two years. Chygir had been arrested shortly after his announcement that he would run in the "alternative" presidential elections held in May 1999 and spent over six months in pretrial detention. In September, authorities launched a fresh criminal investigation against him, this time for tax evasion while Chygir worked for a German company in Moscow in 1996.

On June 19, a Minsk court sentenced veteran opposition activist and Thirteenth Supreme Soviet deputy Valery Shchukin and the chair of the Belarusian Social Democratic Party (BSDP), Nikolai Statkevich, to suspended jail terms for "organizing and participating in mass actions that violated public order" during the October 17, 1999, Freedom March that turned violent. Both men were also barred from participating in the October 2000 parliamentary and June 2001 presidential elections.

Independent trade unions came under increasing pressure from the government. Members of the Independent Trade Union of Belarus faced continual pressure at their workplace to join state unions or lose their jobs. Members typically smuggled copies of the Independent Trade Union newspaper *Rabochi* (The Worker) into their place of work under their clothing. On December 16, police detained seven members of the Independent Trade Union of Steel Workers and confiscated 3,000 copies of *Rabochi* outside the entrance to the Minsk Automobile Plant.

Months of OSCE-mediated negotiations between the opposition and the government failed to ensure free or fair parliamentary elections on October 15 or broader media access. Central to the dispute was a deeply flawed electoral code, adopted on January 31, that ignored all of the OSCE-recommended amendments. The code failed to address the imbalance of power between the president and parliament or to include opposition representatives on the various local election commissions. While media access for the opposition was guaranteed on paper, in practice this was not observed. The opposition, grouped under the Congress of Democratic Forces, announced a boycott of the elections. Open calls to boycott elections are outlawed under article 167(3) of the administrative code. The police detained over one hundred people under this article; others were harassed and fined.

At a September 16 rally marking one year since the disappearance of Viktor Gonchar and Anatoly Krasovsky, unidentified men tried to seize three opposition leaders whose parties are boycotting the October elections. On September 21, four masked individuals broke into and raided the headquarters of the BSDP. On September 22, the Election Commission released a list of the 574 candidates registered to run in the elections; most of the opposition candidates were refused registration. Belarusian authorities declared the elections a success, with overall turnout 60.6 percent, but the opposition claimed widespread election violations and an actual turnout of 45 percent, and thus a successful opposition boycott.

On December 17, 1999, authorities passed a law amending the already restrictive law on the press, forbidding the publication of information on unregistered nongovernmental organizations, political parties, and trade unions. A December 7, 1999, decree amended the law on public associations, banning NGOs and political parties from using the words "Belarus," "Republic of Belarus," "national," and "popular" in their titles.

Authorities continued to threaten to close independent newspapers. On May 29, the State Press Committee issued warnings to the *Belaruskaia Delovaia Gazeta* (Belarusian Business Paper) and *Narodnaia Volya* (The People's Will) for "abusing" freedom of information.

On September 13, authorities seized the entire print run of *Rabochi*—12,000 copies—and detained editor-in-chief Viktor Ivashkevich and three others, including the director of the offending printing press, for publishing articles detailing the opposition's plans to boycott the parliamentary elections. On September 21, two individuals were detained in Homel for distributing the same issue of *Rabochi*, and 16,500 copies were confiscated.

Defending Human Rights

The government continued to harass human rights activists and NGOs. A series of unsolved burglaries of NGO offices, in which unknown raiders stole computer equipment, raised suspicion of state involvement.

On December 17, 1999, unknown persons raided the Minsk offices of the Belarusian Helsinki Committee, removing three computers that stored the organization's database. Police reportedly reacted with lethargy to the raid, while a previous break-in and robbery four months earlier remained unsolved.

Belarusian authorities continued to harass independent human rights lawyer Vera Stremkovskaia, threatening her with disbarment from the Minsk bar association and interrogating her clients. On May 31, unidentified raiders broke in to the newly established Center for Human Rights, of which she is president, removing computer equipment and a photocopier.

On March 7, Oleg Volchek, head of the Minsk-based Public Legal Aid organization, informed a press conference that his organization was being evicted from its premises for the fourth time in the past eighteen months. He said that the Ministry of Justice had a month earlier revoked his organization's license to provide legal aid to individuals, allowing assistance only to legal entities. The organization had initiated an independent investigation into the fate of Yury Zakharenka and the 1999 Nemiga metro stampede tragedy. On May 20, raiders broke into the Public Legal Aid organization's offices, stealing computer and office equipment.

On September 5, the Belarusian Association of Journalists was forced to abandon an independent press festival in Vitebsk when authorities rescinded permission to use a local community center.

The Role of the International Community

United Nations

On January 31, the Committee on the Elimination of Discrimination against Women met in New York to consider the third periodic report on Belarus. While the report focused largely on gender inequality, especially in political life, one committee expert expressed concern about the lack of freedom of expression in general.

On June 12, the U.N. special rapporteur on the independence of the judiciary visited Belarus, meeting with relevant government officials, judges, and lawyers, along with law professors and human rights groups. The Sub-Commission on the Promotion and Protection of Human Rights met at its fifty-second session in August and, soft-peddling its criticism, stated that Belarus' human rights record was "mixed."

Organization for Security and Cooperation in Europe (OSCE)

The OSCE's Advisory and Monitoring Group (AMG) in Minsk spent much of the year in fruitless negotiations between the government and the opposition to resolve the political impasse over parliamentary elections. The OSCE issued several protests about the arrest and trial of leading opposition figures and the arbitrary detention of peaceful demonstrators. The OSCE technical assessment mission said of the October parliamentary elections, "The minimum requirements were not met for the holding of free, fair, equal, accountable and open elections." The European parliamentary troika—the OSCE Parliamentary Assembly, the European Parliament, and the Parliamentary Assembly of the Council of Europe—concurred with that statement.

Council of Europe

Though Belarus' special guest status in the Council of Europe remained suspended, on July 31 a Parliamentary Assembly delegation paid an official visit to Belarus to assess whether conditions existed for free and fair elections. The delegation concluded that the Council of Europe should not send observers to the parliamentary elections, citing "disappointment" with Belarus' lack of progress, although surprisingly, the assembly later agreed to send a limited mission.

European Union

The European Union voiced concern over the arbitrary and violent arrest of demonstrators, along with the trials of opposition activists. It cosponsored negotiations between the opposition and the government over the parliamentary elections. In November 1999, the Belarusian government gave formal approval, following slight amendments, to a 5 million euro program aimed at developing civil society.

United States

The U.S. government continued its policy of selective engagement, funding independent media outlets, supporting pro-democracy initiatives, and providing no direct aid to the government. On July 3, in recognition of labor rights violations, the U.S. stripped Belarus of its trade status, known as the Generalized System of Preferences, worth U.S.$26.7 million in 1999 to Belarus. The State Department regularly condemned the prosecution of opposition activists and called for charges against Mikhail Chygir, among others, to be dropped. The State Department called the parliamentary elections "not free, fair, or transparent" in an October 16 statement.

BOSNIA AND HERCEGOVINA

Human Rights Developments

A breakthrough occurred in one of the most serious of Bosnia and Hercegovina human rights issues: the return of refugees and displaced persons. For the first time since the signing of the Dayton Peace Accords (DPA) refugees and displaced persons returned in relatively large numbers to areas where they would be part of an ethnic minority. In other progress in human rights, nine persons were detained who had been indicted by the International Criminal Tribunal for the Former Yugoslavia (ICTY) and the death penalty was formally abolished in Republika Srpska (R.S.).

The progress was still not self-sustained: it required the strong involvement of the international community to ensure that Bosnia stayed its course to become a democratic state with the full protection of human rights.

The April municipal elections brought significant gains for the moderate Social Democratic Party in Bosniack areas of the federation, at the expense of the nationalist Bosniak Party of Democratic Action (SDA). However, in the Croat areas of the federation, the nationalist Croat Democratic Union (HDZ) managed to maintain its position, while the Serb Democratic Party founded by Radovan Karadzic remained in control of the vast majority of municipalities in the Republika Srpska. Parliamentary elections were scheduled for November 2000.

In July, President Alija Izetbegovic announced that he would resign from the three-person Bosnian presidency in October 2000. Because the Bosnian constitution did not specify the succession procedure, the parliamentary assembly adopted a controversial law to do so. The law gave control over appointment to the appointed members of the House of Peoples, excluding the directly elected members of the House of Representatives from the process. The international community's high representative in Bosnia, Wolfgang Petritsch, imposed an amendment to rectify this.

War Criminals

Several more indictees were transferred to the ICTY's detention unit in The Hague after being detained by the NATO-led Stabilization Force (SFOR). Among them was Momcilo Krajisnik, the wartime president of the Bosnian Serb assembly and a postwar member of the Bosnian presidency, who was the highest ranking politician arrested so far. The Krajisnik detention showed that even high-ranking figures can be detained without widespread retaliation by the civilian population. Others arrested in 2000 included Mitar Vasiljevic, Dragoljub Prcac, Dusko Sikirica, and Dragan Nikolic, the first person indicted by the ICTY. Moreover, the Croatian authorities in March transferred Mladen Naletilic after delaying this for months for medical reasons. In January, indictee and notorious paramilitary leader Zeljko Raznjatovic, also known as "Arkan," was shot and killed in the lobby of a hotel in Belgrade.

Despite the increased willingness of the SFOR to detain indictees, twenty-six publicly indicted persons, including Bosnian Serb wartime leaders Radovan Karadzic and Ratko Mladic, remained at large, while an unknown number of others were the subject of sealed indictments. The Bosnian Serb authorities, despite improved cooperation with the ICTY, still had not arrested a single indictee. Therefore, the role of the international SFOR troops remained essential to the accountability process.

Return of Refugees

Members of minority groups returned in significant numbers for the first time since the end of the war. In the first six months of 2000, the U.N. high commissioner for refugees (UNHCR) registered 19,751 minority returns, as compared to 7,709 during the same period in 1999. The increased return movement, which started in late 1999, was caused by several factors. The international community had focused much more attention on return; the legislation facilitating return was finally in place, and implementation started; and displaced persons started to realize that if they did not return soon, they might not return at all. This resulted in many spontaneous returns: rather than waiting for organized return, small groups of displaced persons returned and started to clean or rebuild their homes. Returns, albeit in small numbers, also took place to areas in eastern R.S. that were previously completely closed to returnees.

The increased return was accompanied by an increasing number of return-related abuses throughout Bosnia. One of the worst abuses took place in Bratunac, where a large group of protesters attacked four buses carrying Bosniak returnees, and Janja, where a series of incidents took place in March and again in July.

Despite the increased number of returns, over one million Bosnians remain displaced, the majority of them within Bosnia and Hercegovina. A survey conducted by the UNHCR showed that 61 percent of the displaced still wish to return to their homes. However, the returns process continues to face serious problems. The implementation of the legislation enabling return was extremely slow. There was a lack of political will to enable return, in particular among the Bosnian Croat and the Bosnian Serb authorities.

Just when the returns process was finally picking up speed, many donors were decreasing their funding for reconstruction and return, or pulling out altogether. Rights groups and other observers urged the international community to remain committed to return, arguing that continued assistance could produce speedy, substantial, and sustainable results, while withdrawal could mean that hard-fought gains would be squandered and the nationalists' policy of ethnic cleansing would have succeeded.

Human Rights Institutions

A provision in the R.S. constitution described the R.S. as the "state of the Serb people," whereas the federation constitution had a provision stating that Bosniaks and Croats were the "constituent peoples" in the federation. In July, the Constitutional Court decided that these provisions were discriminatory and contradicted the Bosnian constitution. This decision was strongly criticized by Bosnian Serb and Bosnian Croat politicians, but Constitutional Court decisions are binding and cannot be appealed. The decision may have an enormous impact, because many Bosnian laws based on the same ethnic principles may have to be revised.

In February, the R.S. National Assembly passed a law establishing an ombudsmen for the R.S. The establishment and composition of this institution had been the subject of protracted negiotiations between the Office of the High Representative in Bosnia and Hercegovina (OHR), the Organization for Security and Cooperation in Europe (OSCE), and the R.S. government. Ultimately, it was decided to create a three-person, multi-ethnic institution, which was expected to be able to receive claims by the end of 2000. In July, the federation parliament passed a law harmonizing the laws on the ombudsmen institutions in the federation with that in the R.S., and allowing the federation parliament to appoint new ombudsmen in 2001.

The Human Rights Chamber, which together with the Office of the Ombudsperson for Bosnia and Hercegovina forms the Human Rights Commission, continued to issue decisions on numerous issues including employment discrimination, property rights, and fair trial.

Although the human rights institutions noticed increased compliance by the authorities with its decisions and recommendations, funding for the institutions was still inadequate, and several important decisions remained unimplemented. For instance, the Human Rights Chamber's June 1999 decision ordering the municipality of Banja Luka to

issue permits for the reconstruction of seven mosques was still not implemented. R.S. Prime Minister Dodik said that reconstruction might begin after the November elections but that any activities without permits would be stopped immediately.

An important step was made toward the independence of the judiciary by the adoption of laws governing the selection and dismissal of judges and prosecutors. These laws, imposed by the high representative in the federation and adopted but later amended in the R.S., provided for appointment and dismissal based on merit alone. The OHR, in cooperation with the United Nations Mission in Bosnia-Hercegovina (UNMIBH), in July started a comprehensive review program to evaluate all judges and prosecutors.

Media

Harassment of the media was a growing problem, and numerous abuses were recorded throughout the year. The OSCE's Free Media Helpline received more than one hundred complaints in a period of less than ten months. Zeljko Kopanja, the editor-in-chief of *Nezavisne Novine* who lost both legs in a car bomb explosion in October 1999, was again threatened several times. The driver of federation Prime Minister Edhem Bicakcic attacked a journalist of the daily *Dnevni Avaz*. In June, the SDA used a tax audit to harass *Dnevni Avaz*, a daily that used to be aligned with the SDA but recently had taken a more critical approach.

R.S. Minister of Information Rajko Vasic called for criminal prosecution of a journalist for alleged false reporting, but resigned from his post after being criticized severely by journalists' associations, the OHR, and the OSCE. In August, Marko Asanin, a former Bosnian minister and current director of the R.S.-owned electricity company, beat and kicked journalist Ljubisa Lazic. Many other journalists and media outlets were attacked or received threats.

The federation authorities in December 1999 presented a draft Law on Compensation for Damage Caused by Defamation and Libel, which was severely criticized for the excessive fines it sanctioned. As of this writing, the law had not yet been adopted. The OSCE and the OHR together presented a draft Freedom of Information Act that established the right of access to information held by government and other public bodies. The law, which would significantly enhance media freedom, had not yet been passed by parliament.

Defending Human Rights

Local and international human rights organizations were generally able to monitor and report on the human rights situation, although some organizations and monitors occasionally experienced harassment. The Human Rights Commission and the federation ombudsmen continued their important work to ensure respect for human rights, and the office of the R.S. ombudsmen is expected to be operational by the end of 2000.

The Role of the International Community

The international community's close involvement continued to be necessary to move the peace process along, as witnessed by the many decisions and amendments imposed by the high representative. However, many in the international community were losing patience with the slow progress in Bosnia, and international attention was shifting to other areas.

Office of the High Representative

The OHR continued to take the lead role in coordinating the civilian aspects of the Dayton Peace Agreement. High Representative Wolfgang Petritsch maintained three objectives: strengthening Bosnian institutions and ensuring the rule of law, transforming the economy and stimulating investment, and enhancing the return of displaced persons and refugees. Although Petritsch made the idea that the responsibility for the future of Bosnia lies with the Bosnians and their leadership the basis of his tenure as high representative, he did not shy away from taking decisive action to further these objectives. Numerous political and government figures, including ministers and governors, were dismissed for failing

to implement the DPA, and Petritsch imposed many decisions on issues as diverse as the R.S. Law on the Prosecutors Office, the Privatization Law, and the Law on Presidential Succession. Bosnian politicians continued to lack the political will to take these decisions themselves, and sustained international involvement remained necessary to continue the peace process and avoid a return to the brutal nationalist policies of the recent past.

Stabilization Force

The NATO-led Stabilization Force in Bosnia and Hercegovina (SFOR) continued to play a significant role in Bosnia in, among other areas, the return process. SFOR also detained more persons indicted by the ICTY than ever before, including Momcilo Krajisnik, the highest ranking politician apprehended so far. Despite fears that high-level arrests might create civil unrest, the situation remained relatively calm throughout Bosnia.

The strength of SFOR was reduced to some 20,000 troops, down from 30,000 the previous year, although its presence in Bosnia and Hercegovina appeared necessary for years to come: the peace remained fragile, and many feared that violence would break out again if SFOR withdrew. Moreover, as the local authorities continued to refuse to arrest ICTY indictees, it remained SFOR's duty to bring those indicted for war crimes to face justice.

United Nations

The largest section of the United Nations Mission in Bosnia and Hercegovina (UNMIBH) was the International Police Task Force (IPTF), charged with overseeing and restructuring the local police forces. Lacking exact information on who is engaged in law enforcement activities, the IPTF initiated a program to register, screen, and certify all police officers by the end of 2001, while working with the respective Ministries of the Interior to recruit minority police officers. These efforts met with limited success: according to the U.N. secretary-general's report of June 2, the federation had around 600 minority officers of a total of about 11,500 officers; the R.S. only had fifty-seven minority officers of a total of 8,500 officers.

The Human Rights Office (HRO) continued its work in monitoring human rights abuses at the hands of the police, and other measures to improve the human rights record of the police forces, such as an audit of arrest and custody procedures and instruction on the role of police at evictions. The U.N.'s Judicial System Assessment Program continued to monitor the functioning of the judiciary and published reports about problems related to implementation of amnesty legislation, delays and detention, and trials in absentia.

The United Nation's High Commissioner for Refugees (UNHCR), together with the OHR, played a leading role in stimulating return in Bosnia, both by guiding the policy and through its own programs. Unfortunately, decreases in UNHCR's budget hampered its ability to operate effectively.

During its fifty-sixth session, the U.N. Commission on Human Rights adopted a resolution on Yugoslavia, Croatia, and Bosnia in which it called upon the authorities to work on human rights issues such as the return of refugees, independence of the judiciary, the role of the police, and freedom of expression. Moreover, the commission renewed the mandate of Special Rapporteur Jiri Dienstbier, whose December 1999 report once again drew attention to those and other human rights issues in Bosnia.

On November 15, 1999, U.N. Secretary-General Kofi Annan published a report on the events in Srebrenica from the establishment of the Safe Area in 1993 through the fall of Srebrenica in July 1995, after which over 7,000 Bosniaks disappeared and were most probably killed. The report, which was surprisingly critical of the U.N.'s own role, was well received by many Bosnians, who considered it to be a recognition of what had actually happened and of the mistakes made by the international community.

International Criminal Tribunal for the Former Yugoslavia

In March, Tihomir Blaskic, a Bosnian Croat general, was found guilty of crimes against humanity committed in the Lasva Valley and sentenced to forty-five years in prison. The Appeals Chamber in July dismissed Anto Furundzija's appeal and confirmed his ten-year sentence. After a trial marred first by prosecutorial misconduct in withholding evidence from the accused and then by disclosures that failed to respect victim amd witness privacy rights, Furundzija was convicted for aiding and abetting rape, among other charges. Zlatko Aleksovski saw his sentence on appeal increased to seven years, while Dusko Tadic's sentence was lowered to a maximum of twenty years. Goran Jelisic was convicted on all but one count and sentenced to forty years of imprisonment. In the Ahmici case, five Bosnian Croats were convicted and sentenced to prison terms of six to twenty-five years, while one indictee was acquitted.

In 2000, the ICTY commenced trials in the Keraterm and Omarska case, the Srebrenica case, and the Foca case. Miroslav Tadic, Simo Zaric, and Milan Simic were provisionally released in May 2000, because two years after their voluntary surrender a trial date had still not been set.

The R.S. slowly improved its cooperation with the tribunal. R.S. authorities reportedly released files to the ICTY, and several high-ranking R.S. officials visited the tribunal, including Prime Minister Dodik, who promised that the R.S. would soon pass the Law on Cooperation with the ICTY.

Organization for Security and Cooperation in Europe (OSCE)

The conditions for the municipal elections organized by the OSCE were better than in the past, although candidates continued to face harassment and press freedom was limited. Despite OSCE's campaign encouraging Bosnians to "vote for change," both the Bosnian Croat and Bosnian Serb ruling nationalist parties largely managed to hold on to their positions.

The OSCE, together with OHR, drafted a new electoral code to replace the election regulations formulated in the DPA, which had been criticized for encouraging ethnic clientelism. However, the draft was criticized for a number of reasons, and subsequently some provisions were amended, while discussion of the most contentious issue, the election of the three-member presidency, was deferred to a later date. Even this amended draft could not count on parliamentary support, and it seemed unlikely to be passed without delay.

The OSCE's Human Rights Department, with officers throughout the country, continued its important work in monitoring human rights abuses in the field and working on policies to curb such abuses.

Council of Europe

In May 1999, the Council of Europe rapporteurs for Bosnia announced a list of conditions to be fulfilled for Bosnia's accession to the Council of Europe. New rapporteurs Laszlo Surjan and Anneli Jaatteenmaki, appointed in late 1999 and early 2000 respectively, like the high representative took a prudent approach, stressing that far too many of the conditions had not been met. In a worrisome development, however, Petritsch and the rapporteurs for accession seemed to have identified three "priority" conditions: the functioning of the common institutions, adoption of a new election law, and progress on some human rights issues. Emphasizing these conditions at the expense of others previously identified risked squandering the opportunity for change represented by the conditions for Council of Europe membership.

European Union

The European Union's policy was based on the idea of the eventual integration of Bosnia and Hercegovina into Europe. The Stability Pact for Southeastern Europe, which uses the prospect of integration into Europe to foster good neighborly relations and accelerate transition into stable democracies in the Balkans, was launched in mid-1999. A concrete step toward integration was taken in March when the E.U. commissioner for external relations, Chris Patten, handed the Bosnian authorities a "road map" of conditions for a feasibility study for E.U. membership, which largely overlapped with the Council of Europe's conditions for Bosnia's membership. The prospect of closer ties with the E.U. represented a possibly strong incentive for the authorities to meet these conditions as soon as possible.

The E.U. and its member states remained the biggest donors of reconstruction aid in Bosnia. At the Regional Funding Conference held in March, the E.U. and its member states pledged over one billion euro in aid, of which a substantial part was targeted for projects involving Bosnia. In 2000, the European Commission invested around 100 million euro in programs in Bosnia, mostly for returns projects. However, the withdrawal of the European Commission Humanitarian Office (ECHO) strongly affected return programs, because ECHO's large budget (56 million euro in 1999) had been very flexible and able to follow developing return patterns. There was a need for other donors to fill this void: since most of this year's return was spontaneous, there was an increased need for flexible funding that would follow return movements as they developed.

United States

The United States, which forged the Dayton Peace Agreement that ended the war in Bosnia, continued its close involvement in Bosnia, although it let the E.U., and in particular High Representative Petritsch, take the lead role. Secretary of State Madeleine Albright visited Bosnia and Hercegovina in March this year to attend the official inauguration of the Statute for the Brcko District, which was imposed by Petritsch. During the visit, Secretary Albright also announced U.S. $7 million in budget support for the R.S. government of Prime Minister Dodik, the recipient of continuous political and financial backing by the United States despite his government's often disappointing record on crucial human rights issues.

United States assistance focused on four issues: private business development, democratic reform, economic transformation, and municipal infrastructure and services. The municipal infrastructure program was increasingly geared toward enhancing minority return, and its successor, the U.S. $70 million Community Reintegration and Stabilization Program (CRSP), was designed to focus exclusively on reconstruction of public infrastructure in return areas. Continued debates in the U.S. Congress over the ongoing U.S. military presence in Bosnia raised concern that support for the peace process might be waning, just as the investment was beginning to pay off.

Relevant Human Rights Reports:

Unfinished Business: Return of Displaced Persons and Other HR Issues in Bijeljina, 5/00

BULGARIA

Human Rights Developments

Abuses against Roma and restrictions on Islamic practitioners, and trade in arms in violation of a U.N. embargo offset improvement in other fields in Bulgaria, notably in freedom of expression.

Roma were victims of police brutality and violent attacks by private citizens who acted with impunity. Numerous cases of police ill-treatment include the beating of two young Roma, Marin Ivanov and Marin Gheorghiev, in the police station in Silistra, on November 18, 1999. Sixteen-year-old Tsvetalin Perov suffered third-degree burns on April 29, 2000, in police detention in Vidin, after being beaten and losing consciousness. On 5 July Traicho Liubomirov, a nineteen-year-old Rom, was shot dead upon arrest on suspicion of car theft in Sofia. The authorities acquiesced in the harassment and discrimination against Roma by private citizens. Ethnic Bulgarian residents in a neighborhood of Burgas signed a petition on November 4, 1999, calling for the expulsion of Roma and the demolition of Roma houses. Villagers in Mechka refused to allow Roma in public places and threatened them with ex-

pulsion after an unresolved murder on April 4, 2000.

The Parliament failed to adopt legislation of any kind to prevent discrimination against Roma in education, health care, regional, urban planning, or other areas, although such changes were envisaged by the Framework Programme for the Integration of Roma in Bulgarian Society, adopted by the government in April 1999.

On February 29, the Constitutional Court banned the Macedonian minority-based OMO Ilinden-Pirin party, which had been registered in the winter of 1999. The Bulgarian Helsinki Committee criticized the move and rejected the court's allegation that the group was advocating the secession of Pirin.

On January 8, six Islamic preachers were expelled for preaching without a permit under articles 22 and 23 of the Denominations Act (1949), despite a 1992 ruling by the Constitutional Court that these articles were unconstitutional. On August 9, Ahmad Naim Mohammed Musa, a citizen of Jordan and permanent resident of Bulgaria, was expelled from the country for allegedly preaching "radical" Islam. The chief mufti denied that Musa carried on any religious activities, and human rights groups stated that the government's accusation was based upon claims that a foundation Musa headed had provided assistance to the chief mufti's office, helping the office obtain financial independence from the state.

On January 12, the Bulgarian Parliament abolished the penalty of imprisonment for libel or slander, but replaced it the following day with heavy fines. President Stoyanov vetoed the bill providing for the fines. On June 1, 2000, a company owned by media tycoon Rupert Murdoch was awarded a license for the first private nationwide television channel. License applications by two Bulgarian companies were pending as of September.

In a report published in March, a U.N. Security Council committee investigating violations of sanctions against Angola's UNITA rebel movement found that Bulgaria had supplied weapons and training to the rebels. Bulgaria set up a commission of inquiry into the charges; on May 9 the commission announced that it had found no evidence of a violation of the embargo. (See Arms chapter.)

Defending Human Rights

Local nongovernmental organizations continued to report vigorously on human rights abuses in Bulgaria. The Bulgarian Helsinki Committee (BHC) covered a wide range of issues. The Human Rights Project addressed freedom of conscience and religious freedom, while the Tolerance Foundation focused on the situation of Roma. Women's human rights activists continued to press for state action to protect women from domestic violence, advocating for changes in the penal code to criminalize domestic violence. On November 9, 1999, four members of the parliament submitted a draft Denominations Act prepared by leading human rights groups. The parliament rejected the draft on February 2, 2000.

The Role of the International Community

United Nations

On December 8, 1999, the U.N. Committee on Economic, Social and Cultural Rights welcomed Bulgaria's extensive efforts to comply with its obligations under the covenant. It expressed concern, however, with continued discrimination against the Roma in education, social benefits, access to land, and other areas. The committee also criticized restrictions on the right to strike and the lack of opportunities for minorities to receive education in their own languages.

Organization for Security and Cooperation in Europe (OSCE)

OSCE High Commissioner on National Minorities Hans Van der Stoel delivered a report on the situation of Roma and Sinti in the OSCE area in March 2000. The high commissioner criticized employment discrimination in Bulgaria and pointed out that fourteen Romani men reportedly died in police custody between 1992 and 1998. Although the report noted that disproportionate numbers of Romani children are sent to "special schools" for mentally disabled children, it concluded that the practice is less prevalent than in the Czech Republic, Slovakia, and Hungary.

Council of Europe

On January 26, the Council of Europe's Parliamentary Assembly ended a three-year monitoring procedure for Bulgaria, on the grounds that the country was committed to democratic reform and made major steps forward on the road to democracy. A final report by the Council of Europe rapporteurs acknowledged democratic achievement in Bulgaria but also called for improvements in the independence of the judiciary and the media, the rights of minorities, the functioning of local self-government, and for additional efforts to combat corruption and police brutality. In the case of *Velikova v. Bulgaria*, regarding the 1994 police beating and death of a Roma man, Slavcho Tsonchev, the European Court of Human Rights ruled on May 18 that Bulgaria had violated the right to life and the right to an effective remedy.

European Union

In December 1999, the European Council opened negotiations for Bulgarian accession to the European Union. On July 5, the European Parliament recommended to the E.U. council that Bulgaria be taken off the list of countries whose citizens need a visa to enter the E.U. border-free territory. President Stoyanov expressed concern on July 6 that Bulgaria was regarded as an outsider in the E.U. enlargement process.

United States

During a November 1999 visit, President Clinton encouraged Bulgaria to persist in building a free society and, in apparent disregard of ongoing abuses, hailed the country's tolerance toward various ethnic groups, but he also raised arms trade concerns with the Bulgarian prime minister. Prior to the visit, the United States extended a U.S. $25 million grant to Bulgaria to mitigate the effects of the Kosovo crisis and to ease the social burden of economic reform.

CROATIA

Human Rights Developments

The election of a new government and president in Croatia at the start of 2000, following the death of President Franjo Tudjman, marked a turning point in Croatia's post-independence respect for human rights. Attempts in late 1999 by the then-ruling Croatian Democratic Union (Hrvatska Demokratska Zajednica, HDZ) to affect the outcome of the vote through control of electronic media, redistricting, and curbs on freedom of assembly led many observers to fear that President Tudjman was unwilling to relinquish power to the opposition. With the death of Tudjman on December 11, 1999, two weeks prior to the parliamentary elections, those fears remained untested, and the opposition coalition captured a large parliamentary majority in the January 3 vote. The resultant change in political culture was so swift that both candidates in the second round of voting for president on February 7 were from opposition parties.

The new government headed by Prime Minister Ivica Racan, and the incoming president Stipe Mesic, moved quickly to demonstrate their commitment to human rights and respect for Croatia's international obligations. On January 28, Foreign Minister Tonino Picula acknowledged that the International Criminal Tribunal for the former Yugoslavia (ICTY) had jurisdiction over Operation Storm, the controversial 1995 action against rebel Serbs that left several hundred thousand Croatian Serbs as refugees. On February 8, the government unveiled its legislative program, committing itself to reform state television, to uphold minority rights, and to carry out the legislative and administrative changes necessary to facilitate the return of Serb refugees. In a newspaper interview two days later, President Mesic invited all Serb refugees to return to Croatia. The new government submitted a U.S.$55 million proposal on February 21 to facilitate the return of 16,500 Croatian Serb refugees.

The government's human rights rhetoric was soon followed by concrete actions, notably in the area of cooperation with the ICTY, previously among the thorniest issues in Croatia's relations with the international community. On March 2, the ICTY deputy prosecutor announced that Croatia had acceded to its request to provide documentation related to Operation Storm and Operation Flash (another 1995 offensive against rebel Serbs). The transfer of Bosnian Croat war crimes suspect Mladen Naletilic, alias "Tuta," followed on March 21. In April, the government permitted ICTY investigators to examine the site of an alleged 1991 massacre of Serb civilians in the town of Gospic. By June, the ICTY prosecutor indicated that the organization had "full access" in Croatia. Further moves followed the August murder of Milan Levar, a Croatian veteran from Gospic present during the 1991 killings who had assisted the ICTY investigation. In early September, Croatian police arrested two Croatian army generals and ten others in connection with war crimes committed in Croatia and Bosnia. Ten suspects in Levar's murder were also arrested.

Considerable progress was made in legislative reform during the first session of the parliament. Key reforms included the April annulment of article 18 of the law on internal affairs, which gave the police wide powers of surveillance over citizens, new laws on minority languages and education on April 27, and the mostly positive changes to the constitutional law on human rights and the protection of minorities on May 11. The long-awaited amendments to the reconstruction law on June 1 and to the law on areas of special state concern on June 14, for the first time offered the prospect of equal treatment for displaced and refugee Serbs seeking to return to their homes in Croatia. At the time of writing, necessary amendments to reform the telecommunications law and a new bill to reform the state broadcaster were pending before the parliament.

Doubts about the composition of the

new Constitutional Court were allayed by three important rulings in its first months. The court's decisions in February and April to strike articles on defamation and libel from the law on public information and the penal code greatly reduced the state's ability to suppress critical reporting. (Amendments to bring the penal code into line with the ruling passed their first parliamentary reading on June 1). In February the court revoked further provisions of the law on association upholding the previous court's stance on the law. In a crucial ruling for the restitution of tenancy rights, in May the court reversed a civil court decision that stripped a Montenegrin of his tenancy rights on the grounds of alleged wartime activities, a justification used to deprive Croatian Serbs of their tenancy rights in the early 1990s. Most former tenancy right holders seeking restitution continued to lack any legal recourse, however.

Improvements to the situation of Serbs in Croatia were not confined to government statements and legislative reform. In April, the government replaced the much-criticized Commission on Return with a new high-level body to oversee refugee return. On June 6, refugees associations in Croatia and Bosnia's Republika Srpska agreed to cooperate on the two-way return of Bosnian Croats and Croatian Serbs. A month later UNHCR announced an significant increase in return requests from Croatian Serbs in Republika Srpksa. By September, more than 10,000 Serbs had returned through organized programs with several thousand more returning unassisted.

The legacy of official discrimination against Serbs proved hard to erase, despite the commitment of the new government in Zagreb. Reports from Organization for Security and Cooperation in Europe monitors indicated that many returning Serbs did not remain in Croatia. Administrative discrimination by the HDZ-dominated local authorities and local courts against Serbs continued, with little progress made on the restitution of property to Serb owners. Progress on the depoliticization of domestic war crimes trials was mixed: despite a recommendation by the

Ministry of Justice that all pending war crimes cases be reviewed by local prosecutors (and repeated international requests that such cases be reviewed first by the ICTY), a Vukovar court convicted eleven Serbs of war crimes on May 22, ten of them in absentia. In addition, more Serbs were arrested on war crimes charges, including several who had recently returned from Serbia with clearance from the Croatian government. The July decision by an Osijek court to acquit five prominent Serbs previously convicted on dubious war crimes charges was a more hopeful sign.

The depth of mistrust between the Croat and Serb communities was underscored by the murders in March of a recently returned Serb man and an elderly Serb woman by local Croats, although the police made prompt arrests in both cases. Confidence among returning Serbs was undermined by the defacing of a monument to Serbs killed during the Second World War on May 17, and a poster campaign in Karlovac, Petrinja, and Sisak listing local Serbs alleged to have committed war crimes. The demolition of 300 war-damaged Serb homes by local authorities in Gospic on June 5 sent a similar signal.

Improvements in the treatment of Serbs stood in contrast to the continuing difficulties faced by Croatia's Roma population. Many of the estimated 30,000 to 40,000 Roma in Croatia lacked access to education and employment, faced discrimination in the provision of state assistance and housing, and had difficulty obtaining citizenship, as well as suffering racist attacks. The experience of the 420 Roma in Strmec Prodravski illustrated the wider problems facing Roma communities: In May, local authorities in Varazdin country ordered the Roma to move from their settlement in the village after refusing to allow them to build more permanent dwellings and a water and electricity supply.

Defending Human Rights

There were no reports of restrictions on the freedom to monitor by international or local nongovernmental organizations in Croatia. The confidence and professionalism of Croatia's local NGOs was exemplified by their participation in the presidential and parliamentary elections, including the voter registration and education campaign by the Glas (Voice) 1999/2000 coalition and election monitoring by GONG (Gradjani Organizirano Nadgledaju Glasanje Citizens Organized to Monitor Elections). The improved situation permitted an increased focus on training and development by human rights groups, including the Croatian Helsinki Committee.

The Role of the International Community

After years of conditioning improved relations on progress in Croatia's human rights record, the international community moved quickly to reward the new authorities in Zagreb for their reform agenda with closer political and economic ties. Croatia was granted admission to the North Atlantic Treaty Organization's Partnership for Peace on May 25 and to the World Trade Organization on July 18, and its U.S. $55 million refugee return proposal was fully funded through the Stability Pact in March.

United Nations

At its annual review of human rights in the former Yugoslavia on April 18, the U.N. Commission on Human Rights adopted a resolution recommending that Croatia be dropped from the mandate of its special rapporteur provided that it made continued progress by its next session. The U.N. high commissioner for human rights maintained her field office in Croatia. The mandate of the U.N. observer mission in the disputed Prevlaka region was renewed by the Security Council until January 2001.

Organization for Security and Cooperation in Europe (OSCE)

Croatia's greatly improved relations with the OSCE were evidenced by the request of its foreign minister on March 23 that the mandate of the OSCE mission to Croatia be extended until the end of 2000, and by the positive tone of the mission's July 3 progress

report, as well as the upbeat assessment of the OSCE high commissioner on national minorities during his May 25 visit. At time of this writing, the OSCE police monitoring group in the Danube region in Croatia was to cease operations on October 31.

Council of Europe

During a June 21 visit to Zagreb, Lord Russell-Johnston, president of the Parliamentary Assembly of the Council of Europe (PACE) indicated that Croatia had now met most of its outstanding membership requirements. On September 26, PACE voted to terminate the monitoring procedure for Croatia.

European Union

The European Union signaled its major support for the Croatian government's efforts in March by upgrading its office in Zagreb into a permanent delegation. Even more significant was its decision in June opening the way for negotiations on a stabilization and association agreement with Croatia in October, with a view to eventual integration into the E.U. Croatia also received 23 million euro (approximately U.S. $23.2 million) in E.U. financial assistance, including 13.5 million euro (U.S. $16.6 million) to support refugee return.

United States

The United States moved to strengthen its already close ties to Zagreb following the elections, supporting Croatia's admission to the Partnership for Peace (PFP) and sponsoring the resolution at the U.N. Commission on Human Rights, following visits to Croatia by U.S. Secretary of State Madeleine Albright in January and February. In a long awaited move, U.S. President Bill Clinton invited the Croatian president and prime minister to Washington on August 9, announcing U.S. $30 million of support, including U.S.$5 million pledged earlier to support return.

Relevant Human Rights Watch Reports:

Croatia's Democracy Deficit: A Pre-Electoral Assessment, 12/99

CZECH REPUBLIC

Human Rights Developments

The Czech government announced the formation of a Human Rights Council in January to prepare legislative proposals and advise the government on human rights issues. The council submitted proposals to counter discrimination in education, housing, and employment in May. Despite these positive steps, increasing racial violence against the ethnic Roma minority demonstrated an alarming pattern of neglect on the part of police and legal authorities in failing to investigate and prosecute hate crime. This pattern included lenient sentences for perpetrators of hate crimes, incompetent and protracted investigations, and little recourse for victims who in many cases feared reprisals.

On February 5, "skinhead" thugs allegedly physically attacked and shouted racist insults at five Roma and one non-Roma in the town of Nachod. The victims identified some of the attackers to the police but later said the police had neither made arrests or even taken down the suspects' names. Local officials claimed that there was no evidence indicating a racially motivated attack. As of August 1, the investigation remained open.

In a July ruling, a Czech soldier who attacked an American teacher in November 1998 in Hodinin was found guilty of "hooliganism and assault" and sentenced to a suspended two-year prison term. The victim was beaten after defending a group of Roma, whom the soldier had insulted; nevertheless, the judge ruled out any racial motivation.

On April 18, the parents of eighteen Romani children from the city of Ostrava lodged an application with the European Court of Human Rights (ECHR) in Strasbourg accusing the Czech state of practicing "discrimination" and "segregation" by channeling disproportionate numbers of Romani children into special schools designed for children with mental disabilities. Although Romani children represent less than 5 percent of primary school students in Ostrava, they constitute over 50 percent of the special school population. Nationwide, 75 percent of Romani children attend special schools, comprising over half of the population of all special schools. Last October, the Czech Constitutional Court dismissed the case, arguing that it lacks the authority to rule on societal discrimination as a whole and can consider "only particular circumstances of the individual cases." In January, the Parliament eliminated a 1984 Schools Law provision that had barred students attending special schools from enrolling in secondary schools. The applicants charge that this amendment only served "to remove the formal—but not the practical—prohibition against admission to non-vocational [secondary] schools" and failed to address de facto discriminatory policies.

In January, the Ministry of the Interior responded to E.U. accession demands to tighten border controls by setting new restrictions on asylum and procedures for foreigners to establish legal residence, introducing visa requirements for certain visitors and requiring them to show proof of secured accommodation, financial resources, and health insurance. The new policy came under attack from human rights organizations for making unreasonable demands on asylum applicants by forcing them to apply for visas in their home country rather than upon arrival in the Czech Republic. The Czech Helsinki Committee (CHC) observed that the law singles out people from so-called problem countries—among them, all of South America, Africa, and the Ukraine—for especially tight restrictions. An amendment to the January law that relaxes some of these restrictions was approved by the cabinet in July and sent to the Parliament; critics of the earlier law argue that the proposed changes fail to address several key issues.

The Czech Republic's position as a country of origin, transit, and destination for trafficking in women drew attention from the press and international bodies. In January, Ukrainian and Czech police successfully broke a gang trafficking women into forced prostitution in the Czech Republic. Unfortunately, law enforcement's efforts to curb trafficking tended to disregard the legitmate fears of retaliation and needs expressed by trafficking victims. Similarly, legislators failed to adopt legal protections to facilitate victims' cooperation as witnesses in cases against traffickers. La Strada, a local NGO, struggled to provide protection for victims and educate women on the dangers of trafficking.

Attention focused on Czech police conduct in September when Prague hosted the annual IMF and World Bank meetings, along with an estimated 9,000 protestors. On September 26, protesters clashed violently with police, leading to some six hundred injuries and more than eight hundred arrests. Following the meetings, the Czech Helsinki Committee undertook an investigation into accusations of police brutality and abuse of power against detained protestors. Its initial investigation had found that many detainees were denied access to the telephone, legal assistance, interpreters, and food or water for many hours after their arrest, and some complained of physical abuse by the police. The Interior Ministry announced that it would conduct an internal investigation into police actions; the police denied the charges of systematic abuse while refusing to rule out misconduct by individual officers.

Defending Human Rights

Human rights groups operated relatively freely, despite efforts by Prime Minister Milos Zeman's government to deflect media criticism. The Counseling Center for Citizenship/Civil and Human Rights (CCC/CHR) issued recommendations on reducing discrimination. The Czech Helsinki Committee released reports on the protection of children, the police and prison system, and the new asylum and foreigners legislation. A coalition of gay and lesbian activists organized "Aprilfest," a series of discussions and events on gay and lesbian issues. With the support of Commissioner for Human Rights Petr Uhl and the Human Rights Council, the festival urged legislators to support a new bill authorizing partnership registration, although the Parliament had rejected a similar bill in December 1999.

The Role of the International Community

United Nations

In its August concluding observations, the Committee on the Elimination of Racial Discrimination (CERD) praised the Tolerance Project, a public awareness campaign to curb racial discrimination. However, the report voiced concern over the continued subjection of Roma to discrimination and violence and urged the government to implement existing hate crime legislation and eradicate racial segregation in education and housing.

European Union

The Czech Republic remained in the forefront among states in line for accession to the E.U. In its September review of the Czech Republic's preparation for accession, the E.U.-Czech Republic Association Council noted that while the Czech Republic continued to fulfill the Copenhagen political criteria, progress was still needed in reforming the judiciary and improving the human rights situation of Roma. Although the E.U. accession process proved a positive incentive on most human rights issues, it pressured Czech authorities to introduce worrisome restrictions on asylum.

Council of Europe

The European Commission on Racism and Intolerance's (ECRI) "Second Annual Report on the Czech Republic" expressed concern about the continuation of racist violence directed toward Roma. The report recommended that Czech authorities take further actions to combat racism and intolerance by enacting anti-racist legislation in education and employment.

United States

At a June hearing before the United States Commission on Security and Cooperation in Europe (CSCE), witnesses testified that current laws to protect Roma fall short of their intended goals. These concerns were echoed in the State Department's annual report on human rights practices.

Organization for Security and Cooperation in Europe (OSCE)

The high commissioner on national minorities' March report on the situation of Roma and Sinti in the OSCE area criticized the Czech government for failing to enforce laws proscribing racially motivated violence, despite having the largest number of skinhead attacks reported in the region. It called on the government to adopt affirmative action measures in employment and to address the persistent negative stereotyping of Roma in the media and in statements.

GEORGIA

Human Rights Developments

President Eduard Shevardnadze won reelection on April 9, 2000, to a second five-year term. The elections were marred by irregularities. Georgia's already poor human rights record deteriorated, as economic and social conditions worsened. Legal reforms unraveled and the government failed to take steps to reign in widespread corruption among senior government officials closely linked to President Shevardnadze.

An OSCE international election monitoring mission concluded in its final report that "considerable progress is necessary for Georgia to fully meet its commitments as a participating state of the OSCE" and that "steps should be taken to restore the confidence of opposition parties and voters in future elections."

Nontraditional religious minorities were harassed, attacked, and subjected to baseless charges during the run up to the election. The police and other authorities actively partici-pated in some of the attacks, while in other instances they failed to investigate and to bring to justice the violent adherents of a nationalist group led by a defrocked Georgian Orthodox priest known as Father Basili. Lower courts failed to rule inadmissable a suit filed by Guram Sharadze, an extreme nationalist member of Parliament, which sought to annul the registration of the Jehovah's Witness church. A lower court's favorable ruling to annul the registration was on appeal to the Supreme Court.

Violent attacks on nontraditional religious groups escalated in the months following the elections. On August 16, several journalists were beaten by members of Father Basili's organization as they were covering a trial involving adherents to the Jehovah's Witness faith at Guldani District Court. Two defendants on trial had been victims of a previous assault in October 1999, yet had themselves been charged for the attack by the authorities. On August 17, about forty members of Father Basili's organization assaulted human rights defenders and a journalist as they left the trial and court security officers failed to intervene. On August 20, Tianeti District police destroyed a meeting place of the Baptist Evangelical Church and briefly detained and threatened its pastor. On September 8, masked police officers wielding clubs forcibly dispersed a Jehovah's Witness gathering in Zugdidi. Almost seven hundred members of the Jehovah's Witnesses were forced to flee, and several were beaten by police. On September 17, Father Basili and a large group of his followers, accompanied by police from Marnueli District, looted a meeting site built for a gathering of Jehovah's Witnesses. Several Jehovah's Witnesses were dragged off buses and beaten, while others were robbed of their personal belongings. On September 28, police officers from Guldani and Nadzaladevi arrived without a warrant at an ashram belonging to followers of the Hare Krishna organization, and attempted to confiscate literature from the group.

Georgian nongovernmental organizations said that the attacks were intended to distract public attention from the government's failure to meet its social obligations, including months-long arrears in the payment of wages and pensions.

Prisoners in the Republican Prison hospital, and at Ortachal and other corrective labor colonies, went on hunger strikes in February and March to demand the release of political prisoners and a government reevaluation of the ouster of former President Zviad Gamsakhurdia. In late September, twelve prisoners escaped from the hospital, among them Loti Kobalya and Guram Absandze. Absandze had been one of the defendants in the highly publicized ongoing trial of fourteen individuals accused of participation in the February 1998 assassination attempt on President Shevardnadze. Human Rights Watch monitored the trial, noting numerous complaints from defendants regarding lack of access to lawyers and other irregularities in the pretrial period.

President Shevardnadze was quoted on national television as stating that the escapes indicated that Georgia had acted prematurely when it transferred some of its detention and postconviction prison facilities from the Ministry of Internal Affairs to the Ministry of Justice. The transfer was an important commitment made to the Council of Europe as a condition of Georgia's accession in April 1999. Some detention facilities, notably lockups located inside police stations, remained under the interior ministry, and reports of torture and abuse in these facilities continued unabated, including reports of the use of electric shock torture in the Tbilisi Main Police Department. Reports of deaths in custody included that of Tbilisi resident Davit Vashakmadze, who died after being severely beaten by members of a Tbilisi-based police unit. He and a companion were brutally beaten shortly after being stopped for a traffic violation on the evening of November 13, 1999.

In May 1998, the U.N. Human Rights Committee, after a thorough investigation, found that four individuals, supporters of former President Gamsakhurdia, had been tortured and denied fair trials, and ruled that they were entitled to an effective remedy, including their release. For the second year running, Georgia flouted the committee's recommendation, and at the time of this writing, two of the defendants whose release was recommended, Petre Gelbakhiani and Irakli Dokvadze, remained imprisoned. Repeal of legal reforms in May and July 1999 underscored the government's lack of commitment to due process guarantees. This was especially troubling as it undermined the long term development of legal institutions capable of peacefully resolving grievances involving Georgia's multiethnic and diverse religious communities, while eroding democratic control and accountability for the actions of the police and other security forces.

The minister of justice resigned in early October, shortly after the high profile prison escapes, and a new minister, Mikhael Saakashvili, assumed office. Saakashvili stated that he would put renewed focus on reform of the court system and of the procuracy. Freedom of the press suffered several blows, as the government attempted to stifle increasing public criticism of widespread corruption and police brutality. For over a year, Akaki Gogichaishvili, investigative reporter and producer of "60 Minutes," was subjected to threats and harassment by unknown individuals. The Sunday evening television program, which was among the highest rated in the nation, systematically investigated corruption among senior government officials. The harassment campaign came to a head in May, after Gogichaishvili reported receiving death threats from the deputy prosecutor general. Meanwhile, the only independent television station in the autonomous region of Adjara, TV-25, located in Batumi, was subject to a forced sale in mid-February after it began to increase its local news coverage. Owners claimed that the forced sale came at the behest of individuals linked to strongman Aslan Abashidze, who held the title of president of the Adjar Supreme Soviet and ruled the region.

Defending Human Rights

An innovative project adopted in 1998 by the Tbilisi City Council, the City Lawyer program, was shut down in March by the Ministry of Internal Affairs. The project, designed and administered in cooperation with nongovernmental organizations, had stationed lawyers hired by the city in police stations to provide twenty-four-hour-a-day legal consultations free of charge to those detained in police lockups in the metropolitan area.

The Role of the International Community

United Nations

In July, the U.N. Security Council extended the mandate of the U.N. Observer Mission in Georgia (UNOMIG) until January 31, 2001. The U.N.-led peace process, intended to achieve a negotiated political solution to the festering conflict in the breakaway region of Abkhazia, achieved no tangible solution. In July, UNOMIG reported an increase in violent incidents related to the activities of organized crime on both sides, which it said limited the activities of humanitarian organizations. It urged the parties to demonstrate the political will to engage in intensified negotiations on the issues of Abkhazia's status, the right of return of refugees, and on security and economic rehabilitation.

In August, a prominent member of the Abkhaz opposition, Zurab Achba, was assassinated by unknown individuals in Sukhumi. Achba had worked as consultant to the joint human rights office maintained by UNOMIG and the OSCE. The assassination was linked by some to those opposed to the increasingly organized and vocal opposition to Abkhaz leader Vladislav Ardzinba.

Meanwhile, in June, the U.N. Committee on the Rights of the Child, reviewing Georgia's initial report, expressed concern regarding the large number of children living and working on the streets, recommended that Georgia establish a code of standards to ensure adequate care and protection for institutionalized children, and noted the absence of adequate legislation on juvenile justice.

Organization for Security and Cooperation in Europe (OSCE)

Observers from the OSCE continued to monitor portions of the Georgian border affected by the conflict in Chechnya. The international community expressed concern regarding spillover of the conflict into Georgia.

Council of Europe

In May, members of the Council of Europe monitoring committee visited Tbilisi to assess Georgia's progress in meeting conditions stipulated when it joined the organization in April 1999.

European Union

In early September, members of a visiting E.U. parliamentary delegation, much to their credit, issued an unequivocal and timely public statement urging religious tolerance and condemning violent attacks on journalists, nongovernmental organizations, and religious minorities. In early October, the Cooperation Council between the E.U. and Georgia recommended further work by the Georgian government to ensure citizens an effective and impartial judicial system that would also ensure basic individual freedoms, including religious freedom. The council also urged Georgia to pursue more actively resolution of its internal conflicts.

United States

The United States and United Kingdom embassies in Tbilisi issued a joint public statement on September 15 condemning attacks on religious minorities, but the statement was shamefully late. Despite violent incidents throughout the year that gave ample early warning of the escalation of violence, as well as calls by Georgian nongovernmental organizations, the statement was issued only after a large scale violent attack occurred on September 8. The reluctance of the U.S. and U.K. governments to issue public statements even as human rights and economic conditions in Georgia deteriorated appeared indicative of the U.S. and European focus on securing and maintaining agreements on transportation routes through Georgia for oil and gas from the Caspian Sea region.

Relevant Human Rights Watch Reports:

Backtracking on Reform: Amendments Undermine Access to Justice, 10/00

GREECE

Human Rights Developments

Discrimination against Roma in Greece took center stage in 2000 as Roma rights were considered in a special session at the United Nations and in European institutions. Harassment and discrimination against ethnic and religious minorities remained issues of concern as the government's plan to remove the bearer's religion from state-issued identity cards focused public attention on entrenched intolerance of religious minorities. Criminal prosecutions of journalists continued under Greece's draconian libel laws.

Greece's Policy Framework for Roma failed to meet most of its objectives, according to a 2000 implementation review by the government. Illegal evictions and police abuse against Roma continued unabated. Citing police raids on settlements near Athens, rights groups charged the government with "cleansing" greater Athens of Roma to build sports facilities for the 2004 Olympics. In July, a municipal bulldozer, accompanied by the mayor and police, demolished numerous Roma huts in the Athens Aspropyrgos suburb. Greek and Albanian Roma families in the settlement—situated on a garbage dump— were ordered to leave within three days. The Greek ombudsman, tasked with investigating complaints of human rights abuses, contacted Aspropyrgos Municipality questioning the eviction's legality, but his communication was ignored. The eviction of Roma tent dwellers in the upper part of the dump occurred prior to the Aspropyrgos operation when the mayor of Ano Liosia offered Roma families 100,000 drachmas (U.S.$266) to leave and then leveled their huts.

Municipal councils continued to issue orders for the eviction of Roma communities. In October 1999, the Rio council voted to evict all Roma for alleged criminality, poor hygiene, and trespassing. A December 1999 meeting spearheaded by rights groups resulted in a halt to evictions until prefecture authorities could provide satisfactory alternative housing. In May 2000, the municipal council in Nea Kios decided to evict all Roma in the area. On May 25, armed police raided local Roma settlements and ill-treated residents, including the beatings of two teenage boys and the denial of medical treatment to their ill father. The family, along with three nephews and an ailing elderly Roma woman, was accused of "stealing electricity" and detained. The detainees were not informed of their rights or permitted to make phone calls, and were denied food and blankets offered by family members. The ombudsman lodged a complaint with municipal authorities.

Human rights activists and politicians were denied access to Nea Kios on June 8 by "citizen brigades" that blocked the streets in the presence of police officers and harassed journalist Panos Lambrou of *Epochi*. Subsequently, non-Roma citizens torched a Roma hut and shot a Roma youth. Protests by rights groups led to a June 16 Ministry of Justice decision to investigate allegations of police abuse in Nea Kios. The police raided a Roma settlement by the River Gallikos in Salonica on July 6 in search of drugs, weapons, and criminal suspects. One hundred Roma were detained but no drugs or weapons were found. The Prefecture of Salonica denounced the racist character of the police operation. In May and August respectively, the councils of Nea Tiryntha and Midea called for the eviction of all Roma from their municipalities.

Police continued to enjoy impunity for abuses targeting Roma. In March, a Salonica court dismissed charges against three police officers for the April 1998 killing of Angelos Celal, holding that the officers acted in legitimate self-defense. Celal was unarmed and shot from behind. Human rights groups lodged an unsuccessful appeal requesting that the prosecutor challenge the court's ruling.

In May 2000, the government decided to remove from state-issued identity cards the bearer's religion, a labeling that has facilitated the discriminatory treatment of religious minorities. Human rights groups hailed the decision as a step toward eliminating entrenched religious discrimination. In October 1999, a mob led by the mayor attempted to halt construction of a Jehovah's Witness building in Kasandra. Two journalists were beaten, and representatives of the ombudsman's office and the Jehovah's Witnesses were harassed. Subsequently, the mayor was indicted for incitement to religious hatred but was never arrested or tried. Mehmet Emin Aga, mufti of Xanthi, was convicted in May for "pretense of authority" for assuming the leadership of a minority Muslim group, despite a December 1999 European Court of Human Rights decision against Greece in a similar case (see below).

In November 1999, two journalists for *Eleftherotypia* were indicted for defamation under Greece's libel laws for allegations that the Lesvos police were associated with smugglers. An Athens court convicted Dimitris Rizos, publisher of *Adesmeftos Typos*, in December 1999, on a charge of aggravated defamation of the publisher of another newspaper with the same name. In March 2000, a renowned violinist and a composer were given prison sentences for defamation based on statements made during newspaper interviews.

Defending Human Rights

Most human rights groups operated without interference, although incidents of harassment were reported. Aysel Zeybek, a stateless woman member of Greece's Turkish minority and human rights activist associated with the Greek Helsinki Monitor, complained to the ombudsman detailing harassment she suffered at the Greek-Turkish border in December 1999 when she was the only person on her bus targeted for an intrusive search and verbally harassed about her association with rights groups. At the time, Zeybek, a resident of Greece, possessed official travel documents issued by the Greek

government. The ombudsman revealed that Zeybek's "inspection" was conducted by the National Information Service (EYP), Greece's intelligence agency. A letter from the EYP stated that Zeybek's inspection was conducted within the EYP's "competence....in intelligence gathering on matters of national security." Rights groups, including the International Helsinki Federation, lodged protests with the government.

The Role of the International Community

United Nations

The Committee on the Elimination of All Forms of Racial Discrimination (CERD) held a thematic discussion on Roma in August 2000 and released a statement that included information from Greek nongovernmental organizations that Roma communities near Athens were being evicted to clear land for facilities for the 2004 Olympics.

Organization for Security and Cooperation in Europe (OSCE)

A March 2000 report by the OSCE high commissioner on national minorities on the situation of Roma and Sinti criticized Greece for evictions of Roma, noting that lack of political will at the highest levels of government resulted in inadequate Roma policy implementation by mid-level policy makers and at the local level.

Council of Europe

The European Commission Against Racism and Intolerance's (ECRI) "Second Report on Greece (June 2000)" stated that problems of exclusion and discrimination against Roma, immigrants, and Muslims persisted; it encouraged the government to raise public awareness of the "multicultural reality" of Greek society. Rejecting the recommendation, the government denied that Greece is a multicultural society.

In December 1999, the European Court of Human Rights found Greece in violation of religious freedom for convicting the mufti of Komotini of "pretense to authority." The court stated that punishing the religious leader of a group that willingly followed him was incompatible with the religious pluralism required by a democratic society.

The Greek government had not, as of this writing, published the European Committee on the Prevention of Torture report on its 1999 visit.

United States

The U. S. State Department's *Country Reports on Human Rights Practices for 1999* noted persistent discrimination against immigrants, religious and ethnic minorities, and Roma, but in an apparent contradiction asserted that "most" minorities are "integrated fully into society."

HUNGARY

Rampant discrimination was at the forefront of human rights concerns as a group of Hungarian Roma took grievances to the European Court of Human Rights, drawing attention to the government's failure to address discrimination against Roma as required by its European Union accession agreement. The ill-treatment and detention of refugees remained a serious concern. Progress on religious freedom suffered a setback as Hungary promulgated a tax law that threatened to marginalize further minority religious groups.

Human Rights Developments

Most of the objectives in the Hungarian government's medium term plan for Roma rights were unmet at the end of 2000, resulting in continued discrimination in employment, housing, and education and police abuse of Hungarian Roma. In July 2000, a group of Roma families from Zamoly traveled to Strasbourg seeking political asylum in France. The Roma also lodged a complaint with the European Court of Human Rights seeking compensation for human rights abuses suffered in Hungary, including persecution and discrimination. The complaint charged that families' homes had been destroyed illegally

by the Zamoly municipal government. The families were evicted from temporary accomodation in the local cultural center after six months, and although new homes were built for them in 2000, the Roma said they did not occupy them because they feared racially motivated attacks. In August, Roma representatives from Ozd traveled to Strasbourg to consult with the Zamoly Roma. The Ozd Roma said that fifteen families from that region wanted to emigrate as well due to persecution suffered in Hungary. On August 9, 2000, the European Roma Rights Center (ERRC) sent a letter to Hungarian prime minister Viktor Orban protesting a spate of discriminatory Roma evictions in Ozd. The ERRC also expressed concern that new legislation, in effect since May 2000, permitting a notary public to order evictions expands the power of local officials to remove Roma from their homes. Although judicial review of a notary's eviction order is possible, injunctive relief is not provided by the new law, leaving families homeless while they challenge evictions.

In January 2000, the government established the Office for Immigration and Naturalization (OIN)—a central authority for asylum and immigration matters. The OIN began drafting substantial amendments to the laws dealing with asylum and aliens in June but did not invite consultation with nongovernmental organizations. In December 1999, the U.N. high commissioner for refugees warned third countries against the indiscriminate return of asylum seekers who had previously transited Hungary, noting deficiencies in the Hungarian asylum system—in particular, poor conditions of detention for asylum seekers. Hungary continued to deny refugee status to conscientious objectors from the Federal Republic of Yugoslavia (FRY) who fled to Hungary to avoid military service in the Kosovo conflict. Many of the conscientious objectors were granted "authorization to remain" status, valid for one year and renewable annually. Refugee advocates claimed that such status created a high degree of insecurity in the group and prohibited them from full integration into Hungarian society. In a March

2000 judgment on an appeal lodged by a FRY conscientious objector whose application for asylum was rejected, the Budapest Central Court ruled that OIN's decision was not "well-founded" and ordered the authority to recommence an assessment of the individual's claim. The court held that OIN did not consider the evidence that the claimant could face persecution based on his political opinions and conscientious objector status if returned to FRY. In August 2000, the OIN denied the claimant refugee status once again, but he was granted authorization to remain.

A May 2000 amendment to Hungary's tax laws threatened to newly marginalize minority religions. The amendment confirmed sales tax exemption only for Hungary's six "historical" churches and for nonprofit organizations, thus preventing 98 percent of registered churches (for example, Methodists, Adventists, Evangelicals, Pentecostals, and all Eastern religions) from reclaiming sales tax, although most of them sponsor charitable programs of "public utility." Human rights groups charged that the law signaled an increasing tendency in Hungary to privilege certain religions over others.

Defending Human Rights

Most human rights groups in Hungary operated without interference. Recognizing the disproportionate representation of Roma in Hungarian prisons, the Hungarian Helsinki Committee implemented a 2000 pilot project designed to assess the degree and scope of discrimination against Roma in criminal sentencing and began a prison monitoring program in association with the National Prison Administration.

The Role of the International Community

United Nations

In May, U.N. secretary-general Kofi Annan presented Hungary with the Franklin Delano Roosevelt International Disability Award for legislative work to raise awareness and promote access for the disabled "from a human rights perspective."

Organization for Security and Cooperation in Europe (OSCE)

In March 2000, the OSCE high commissioner on national minorities issued a report on the situation of Roma and Sinti in the OSCE area. In addition to over-representation in prisons and police abuse of Roma in Hungary, the report highlighted the high rate of Roma unemployment, overt discrimination in employment advertisements, and Hungary's failure to provide employment discrimination victims with an effective remedy.

Council of Europe

The European Commission on Racism and Intolerance's (ECRI) "Second Annual Report on Hungary (June 2000)" expressed concern over continuing discrimination and police abuse of Roma and immigrants. The report stated, among other things, that a large proportion of Roma children are tracked into "corrective" (i.e., remedial) schools, many teachers discriminate against Roma, and teaching materials are prejudiced against Roma.

European Union

In October 1999, the European Commission proposed that updated agreements for candidate countries seeking to join the European Union, including Hungary, make the improvement of the situation of Roma a short and medium term priority. A December 1999 European Union Enlargement Briefing reiterated that Roma in many candidate countries, including Hungary, continued to face deep-rooted prejudice and focused on E.U. support for candidate countries' action plans for integrating Roma into society.

Hungary was co-chair of the Southeast European Stability Pact's Working Table on Democratization and Human Rights from January-June 2000 during which time the working table focused on, among other things, projects promoting the human rights of national minorities, refugee return, and women's rights.

United States

The United States State Department's

Country Reports on Human Rights Practices for 1999 noted that Roma and foreigners in Hungary were subject to discrimination and violent police abuse. The report detailed criticisms by nongovernmental organizations that conditions of detention for asylum seekers were "inhuman."

KAZAKHSTAN

Human Rights Developments

Harassment of opposition political activists continued in 2000, after 1999 elections that were far from free and fair secured another term in office for President Nursultan Nazarbaev and a compliant Parliament. Suppression of independent and opposition-affiliated media remained routine in 2000, a year when massive corruption allegations against President Nazarbaev and other high government officials came to light.

Despite President Nazarbaev's pledge at the November 1999 Operation for Security and Cooperation in Europe (OSCE) Summit in Istanbul to implement the organization's post-election recommendations, the government has yet to publish full election results of the October 1999 primary vote or to account for the many complaints of violations submitted to electoral commissions. The parliament in June granted Nazarbaev lifetime privileges after his second term in office ends in 2006 (though he has indicated that he may run again), including the right to address parliament and state institutions and the public at will.

The government continued to use legal action to harass opposition figures. Madel Ismailov, a leader of the Worker's Opposition Party who served a year in prison on charges of "offending the honor and dignity of the President," was sentenced in April to fifteen days of administrative detention for his participation in a nonviolent demonstration in January.

In February, the government charged former prime minister Akezhan Kazhegeldin—Nazarbaev's one-time rival and leader of the Republican National People's Party (RNPK) after his dismissal in 1997—with illegal weapons possession, and in April, the tax police filed new charges against him. In May, Kazhegeldin's press secretary Igor Poberezhskii was stabbed by an unknown assailant outside of his Moscow apartment. In July, just after details of the international investigation into payments allegedly made to both President Nazarbaev and his former prime minister by foreign oil companies emerged, Italian police acting on a request filed by Kazakhstan with Interpol briefly detained Kazhegeldin at a Rome airport. Kazhegeldin's former bodyguards, Satzhan Ibraev and Petr Afanasenko, were each sentenced to three and one-half years in prison on weapons charges, a move widely seen as political retribution for their connection to Kazhegeldin.

Other members of the opposition were also affected, including political scientist and RNPK member Nurbulat Masanov, who in March awoke to find that he had been sealed into his apartment in advance of a March 30 demonstration. The apartments of RNPK leader Amirzhan Kosanov and Seidakhmet Kuttykadam, leader of the Orleu movement, were also sealed. On September 14, police detained Karishal Asanov, a writer, long-time dissident, and recipient of the Human Rights Watch Hellman-Hammett prize, in his home and held him for three hours. Asanov, who had recently published an article criticizing Kazakhstan's president, was ordered to appear for questioning on September 20.

In July, the Supreme Court upheld the administrative regulations mandating, on grounds of public security, that police had the right to attend any and all meetings of nongovernmental organizations, without providing for any judicial or other review of these police actions. This ruling was sure to have a chilling effect on freedom of assembly, already restricted by Kazakh authorities, who continued to fine members of the pensioners' movement Pokolenie (Generation) for their monthly public demonstrations. The Almaty city government granted permission for opposition forces to hold a demonstration on

March 30, although attacks on the homes of the rally's leaders suggested state-sponsored interference.

The independent print and broadcast media continued to face intense government repression. The government continued to use libel suits, confiscation of print runs and equipment, and pressure against printing houses and distribution agencies to harass media it found too critical. President Nazarbaev threatened several times over the course of the year to investigate unspecified media outlets for supposed antistate crimes. Opposition-affiliated journalists also ran the risk of physical assault: Lira Baisetova, editor of the opposition newspaper *Respublika-2000*, was beaten by an unidentified man outside her apartment on September 15 who warned her against continuing her activities. The government blocked broadcast of Russian television programs for several days in November 1999, after one program broadcast news that Swiss bank accounts linked to President Nazarbaev had been frozen. After reporting on the sealing of opposition leaders' doors in late March, editor-in-chief Tatiana Deltsova of the news program on Almaty's private T.V. Channel 31 was dismissed from her job. In May, court executors enforcing a libel judgment seized the property of the newspaper *Nachnem s Ponedel'nika* (Let's Begin on Monday), forcing it to fold; the papers' editors began a new venture, *Do I Posle Ponedel'nika* (Before and After Monday). In June, unidentified men seized the entire print run of that paper and forced one of its employees to set it on fire. Two newspapers, the *Azamat-Times* (Citizen Times) and *Karagandinskii Vestnik* (Karaganda Gazette), were also the subject of libel suits. After its printing press refused under government pressure to print the fiftieth issue of the Kazakh-language opposition paper *SolDat* (the name is a play on that of the banned *Dat*, in Kazakh, "let me speak", which was closed last year) in July, the issue was produced across the border in Russia, but then detained at the border for several days. The State Security Committee (KNB, formerly the KGB) had reportedly begun investigating the paper on charges of "impugning the honor and dignity of the President" on grounds that it published a translation of an article on the investigation of illegal payments by oil companies to high government officials, including the president, from U.S.-based *Fortune* magazine. *Vremia P.O.'s* printing house refused to publish the paper after it ran an article critical of the prime minister in August. Kazakhstan continued to censor the Internet, blocking access to the newsite eurasia.ru from within the country in September and October.

Kazakh NGOs and international organizations such as the OSCE have helped focus government attention on Kazakhstan's horrendous prison conditions. Inmates in three separate penal institutions this year carried out mass self-mutilations to protest conditions; the largest incident, in Kostanai Province in June, involved forty-four prisoners. The government made public statements deploring the widespread use of torture in criminal investigations and police brutality, but declined to take action against perpetrators. In a case documented by the Kazakhstan International Bureau for Human Rights and the Rule of Law (KIBHRRL), documentary filmmaker Dmitrii Piskunov was left in a coma after a beating by a KNB officer after a traffic dispute in July; while charges have been filed, the investigation has languished.

Government intolerance for non-traditional religious groups was evidenced by the seizure in June of religious literature from a group of Jehovah's Witnesses and the barring of a protestant missionary from the United States from entering the country. Tensions surfaced in Kazakhstan's Islamic community as well, leading to the sudden resignation in June of Kazakhstan's chief mufti, the head of the Spiritual Directorate of Kazakhstan's Muslims. In September, Kazakhstan's Foreign Ministry reportedly ordered all young men from Kazakhstan studying at religious institutions in Islamic countries to return.

Defending Human Rights

In November 1999, fire swept through the offices of the Kazakhstan International

Bureau for Human Rights and the Rule of Law in an as yet unexplained incident. No incidents of harassment of human rights monitors in Kazakhstan were reported this year.

The Role of the International Community

Organization for Security and Cooperation in Europe (OSCE)

In January, the OSCE Office for Democratic Institutions and Human Rights Election Observation Mission issued its final report on parliamentary elections held in October 1999, outlining seventeen recommendations. The OSCE center in Almaty attempted to monitor whether these recommendations, including changes to the election law, have been implemented. To that end, on September 2 the center sponsored the first in a series of round table discussions on the question of elections, which included representatives of the government and pro-government groups as well as opposition political parties and nongovernmental organizations.

European Union

President of the European Commission Romano Prodi and External Relations Commissioner Chris Patten met with President Nazarbaev in June and reportedly stressed the need for further progress towards democracy; a textile agreement was also signed. In July, the E.U./Kazakhstan council met for the second time, one year after the Partnership and Cooperation Agreement came into force. Their public statement indicated that the Cooperation Council discussed political and human rights issues.

Council of Europe

The Political Affairs Committee of the Parliamentary Assembly of the Council of Europe (PACE) continued to consider Kazakhstan's application for observer status this year.

United States

The December 1999 meeting of the U.S.-Kazakhstan Joint Commission, chaired by Vice President Al Gore, reportedly obtained President Nazarbaev's commitment to work closely with the OSCE on implementing democratic reform. Visits to Kazakhstan by the head of the CIA, the head of the FBI, NATO commander Wesley Clark, and Secretary of State Madeleine Albright in the spring came as the U.S. struggled to preserve its influence in the region. The harshest U.S. criticism came not on human rights issues, but in response to the illegal sale of fighter aircraft to North Korea in 1999 involving high Kazakh government officials. The U.S. proffered U.S.$3 million in additional assistance for counterterrorism, as well as a U.S. Trade and Development Agency (TDA) grant of U.S. $600,000 for a survey of natural gas resources.

KOSOVO

Human Rights Developments

Despite the efforts of the United Nations civilian administration and a massive North Atlantic Treay Organization (NATO) presence, human rights in Kosovo frequently remained an abstraction during 2000. Ethnic minorities were hardest hit, with continuing violence against the province's Serb, Roma, Muslim Slav, Gorani, and Turkish populations, and the Albanian minority living in northern Mitrovica town. At the time of this writing, municipal elections were scheduled for October 28, despite the absence of conditions for their free and fair conduct and against a backdrop of rising political violence among Albanian Kosovar parties and a Serb boycott. Efforts to establish rule of law and to end impunity were hampered by shortcomings in the nascent justice system, and inadequate and incompetent policing. The NATO-led Kosovo Force (KFOR) and its member governments were reluctant to take decisive action against elements of the former Kosovo Liberation Army (KLA) linked to attacks on minorities and political opponents. Despite progress in identifying the fate of missing persons, more than 3,000 remained unaccounted for from last year's armed conflict, most of them ethnic Albanians.

For the most part confined to mono-ethnic enclaves and unable to travel without KFOR escorts, the situation of minorities in Kosovo remained extremely precarious. Few of the more than 150,000 non-Albanians who fled from Kosovo since June 1999 attempted to return. Roma and especially Serbs continued to bear the brunt of much of the violence. Ethnic Croats, Muslim Slavs (including Torbesh), Gorani, and Turks also faced attacks, harassment, and pressure to leave their homes. Although far fewer murders and kidnapings took place in 2000 than in 1999, minorities continued to be disproportionately affected. On February 2, Josip Vasic, a prominent doctor and moderate member of the Serb National Council, was shot dead in a Gnjilane street by unknown assailants. On April 3, Metodije Halauska, an eighty-six-year-old ethnic Czech man, was kidnaped from his home in Pristina, beaten, and shot in the back of the head. A seventy-year-old Bosniak woman in Pec was hospitalized the same month after being beaten in the street by fifteen Albanian men. On May 15, the body of twenty-five-year-old Serb translator Petar Topoljski was found in the village of Rimaniste, near Pristina. Topoljski had gone missing a week earlier from his job with the United Nations Mission in Kosovo (UNMIK), after his name and movements were published in the Kosovo daily newspaper *Dita*, together with allegations that he was a Serb paramilitary who had participated in the mass expulsions of Albanians from the province.

The weeks surrounding the first anniversary of NATO's entry into Kosovo on June 12 saw an upsurge in violence against minorities in the province. A series of grenade and landmine attacks and drive-by shootings targeting Serbs left eleven dead and more than a dozen wounded. Valentina Cukic, an editor of a Serbian-language program of the multi-ethnic Radio Kontakt, was shot and badly wounded in Pristina June 20, together with her companion, while wearing her KFOR press identification. On July 12, a Serbian Orthodox priest and two seminary students were wounded in a drive-by shooting near the village of Klokot. In a sinister development in August, minority children were targeted: on August 18, a grenade was thrown from a moving car into a group of children at a basketball court in the Serb village of Crkvena Vodica leaving ten wounded. On August 27, an Albanian man drove his car into a group of children in the same village before fleeing the scene, killing one child and wounding three. An eighty-year-old Serb farmer from the same village was shot dead later the same day. On September 14, a forty-five-year-old Serb woman was shot dead at her home in Kamenica. A sixty-year-old Serb shepherd reported missing was discovered dead near Strpce on October 4, with gunshot wounds to the body.

The international community struggled to balance free expression against curbs on speech inciting hatred and violence. The practice of publishing the names of alleged Serb war criminals in Kosovo newspapers, redolent of the notorious lists published in the Croatian region of Eastern Slavonia, drew condemnation from UNMIK and the OSCE, but international efforts against hate speech, including the appointment of a temporary media commissioner with wide powers and the temporary closure of *Dita* after it repeatedly published inflammatory allegations against Serbs, were criticized by Kosovo Albanian journalists and international press freedom groups as an attack on free speech.

The divided town of Mitrovica remained a flash-point for inter-ethnic conflict. Some of the worst violence in the town followed a February 2 rocket attack on a UNHCR bus under KFOR escort traveling to Mitrovica from the Serb village of Banja in which two elderly Serbs were killed and three wounded. The attack sparked a wave of tit-for-tat inter-ethnic violence in northern Mitrovica that left eight non-Serbs dead and led 1,700 Albanians, Turks, and Muslim Slavs to flee their homes. The prospects for a lasting solution to the town's status remained dim. Violence against Albanians was not confined to Mitrovica. The murder of two Albanians in the village of

Cubrelj by a group of Serbs on June 12, the first anniversary of the end of war, echoed the persecution of Albanians a year earlier.

Much of the violence against Albanians, however, occurred at the hands of other Albanians. The murder of a politician from the Democratic League of Kosovo, the party headed by Ibrahim Rugova and known by its Albanian acronym, LDK, and the kidnaping and interrogation of another in the Drenica region in November 1999 was followed by a spate of execution-style killings of prominent KLA fighters. Although the killings were frequently attributed to rivalries among organized crime figures, some of the murders, including the killing in May of a politically moderate former KLA commander, Ekrem Rexha (known as Commander "Drini"), had a political dimension.

Political violence increased over the summer. On June 15 Alil Dresaj, a senior LDK politician, was shot dead by persons wearing insignia of the former KLA. On July 7, Ramush Haradinaj, a politician and former senior KLA commander, was wounded in the village of Streoce during what appears to have been a shootout. On July 12, a close aide to Haradinaj was murdered. The burned corpse of Shaban Manaj, a senior LDK official, was discovered on August 6 in a remote village. He had been kidnaped on July 27. Attacks directed against the LDK continued in August. On August 1, an LDK activist was shot and wounded in Podujevo. The head of the LDK in Srbica was wounded in a shooting the following day. The wife of an LDK official died in an explosion at their home in Dragash on August 9. Several LDK offices were attacked during the same month. Political motives were also suspected in the September murders of Shefki Popova and Rexhep Luci, two prominent Albanians with close ties to the LDK. Popova, a veteran journalist with Albanian-language daily *Rilindija* and Luci, head of Kosovo's housing and reconstruction department, were gunned down on consecutive days.

Despite the absence of "an atmosphere free of violence and intimidation" (an OSCE condition for free and fair elections), the international community pressed ahead with its plans to hold municipal elections, at the time of writing, scheduled for October 28. While most eligible Albanians registered to vote, Serbs, Muslim Slavs, and other minorities boycotted registration, citing lack of security, thus rendering them ineligible to vote. As if to confirm their reservations, a bomb exploded on August 18 in a Pristina building housing the offices of smaller Albanian, Turkish, and Bosniak political parties, as well as the Yugoslav representation in Pristina. Despite the violence and concerns that conditions were inadequate for free and fair elections, the body set up by the OSCE to enforce standards during the election was weak and lacked effective sanctions.

The International Organization for Migration in Kosovo reported that traffickers had lured dozens of women to Kosovo with offers of lucrative jobs; the women found themselves trapped in forced prostitution in brothels around the province.

Defending Human Rights

Restrictions on freedom of movement, inter-ethnic animosity, and the legacy of a decade of repression and armed conflict impaired human rights work by local nongovernmental organizations in Kosovo. The Humanitarian Law Center largely restricted its activities to monitoring the issue of missing persons and prisoners. Reports by the Council for the Defense of Human Rights and Freedoms were frequently politicized and sometimes limited to abuses against Albanians and those committed by Serbs. International human rights groups were mostly able to carry out investigations unhindered, although the highly variable security situation in Mitrovica and some minority enclaves sometimes limited or preventd access. Local organizations protested freely and often about the fate of Kosovo Albanian prisoners in Serbian jails.

The Role of the International Community

Kosovo remained a de facto international protectorate during 2000, administered by UNMIK, with security provided by NATO-led KFOR peacekeepers and United Nations police and financed primarily by the European Union and United States governments and the World Bank. Yugoslavia had little influence on events in the province outside the Serb-dominated municipalities north of Mitrovica. The international community's policies toward Kosovo pulled in contradictory directions: expected municipal elections aimed to increase local self-government for Kosovo's population, while in the area of the courts and media, international involvement increased. Despite an ongoing security gap for minorities, political violence, and growing crime, with elements of former KLA and Kosovo Protection Corps clearly implicated, NATO and the U.N. remained unable or unwilling to confront the perpetrators in a decisive and consistent manner.

United Nations

UNMIK made some progress in establishing transitional power structures and persuading most leading Albanian politicians and some moderate Serb leaders to participate in them. Its international civilian police, tasked both with policing the province and establishing a local Kosovo Police Service, remained under-equipped and often poorly trained and faced difficulties obtaining cooperation from local communities, judges, and prosecutors, and in some cases KFOR, with most cases left unsolved or dropped before reaching the courts. A case involving a Kenyan aid worker wrongly accused of fraud highlighted concerns about due process violations by U.N. police. The establishment in August of a special U.N. police unit for the protection of Serbs was a more positive development. Evidence of bias and intimidation in the nascent local court system, and a lack of serving judges from minorities led UNMIK to acknowledge that, as with the police, a greater degree of initial international supervision would be necessary. Following the model of Mitrovica, UNMIK appointed international judges to some courts and transferred some sensitive cases involving minority or political

violence to those courts. On August 14, the Polish human rights lawyer appointed by the special representative of the secretary-general in July as Kosovo's first ombudsman made his first working visit to the province. The ongoing detention of some 1,200 Kosovo Albanians in Serbia, as well as the lack of information about the fate of some 3,300 missing persons from Kosovo, including 400 Serbs and one hundred Roma, was highlighted by U.N. High Commissioner for Human Rights Mary Robinson's appointment, on September 1, of a special envoy on persons deprived of liberty. In an April resolution, the U.N. Commission on Human Rights emphasized the need for an independent judiciary and an end to inter-ethnic violence in Kosovo. The International Criminal Tribunal for the Former Yugoslavia continued its investigations in Kosovo into crimes committed by government forces and the KLA.

Organization for Security and Cooperation in Europe (OSCE)

Charged with institution building, the OSCE Mission in Kosovo performed well in the area of human rights training and monitoring, producing accurate and public periodic reports with UNHCR on the difficulties faced by Kosovo's minorities. Its lead role in organizing municipal elections was less positive, with lessons from Bosnia regarding the need for basic conditions for free and fair elections and enforcement of standards seemingly ignored. The OSCE's efforts to tackle hate speech also drew criticism from press freedom groups and Kosovo Abanian journalists.

North Atlantic Treaty Organization

The NATO-led KFOR remained the most important security actor in Kosovo. Despite some improvements, including a more mobile approach to protecting minorities pioneered by the British contingent, a reduction in the murder rate, more aggressive pursuit of illegal weapons, and an acknowledgment that attacks on minorities were organized, KFOR remained reluctant to confront the armed elements responsible for many of the attacks. An uneven response to violence among KFOR's various national contingents, an inadequate response to attacks on Roma, and complaints about cooperation with U.N. police also cast a shadow on KFOR's record.

Council of Europe

The Council of Europe and particularly its Congress of Local and Regional Authorities continued its support for democratic institution building and human rights in Kosovo through the council's office in Pristina. In July, the newly established council observation mission began monitoring preparations for the municipal elections scheduled for October 28.

European Union

European Union governments generally showed a reluctance to move beyond the condemnation of violence against minorities and toward tackling its causes. While showing more equivocation on early municipal elections than the U.N. or U.S., leading E.U. states were nonetheless unwilling to call publicly for postponement. The European Union continued to finance much of the international effort in Kosovo, although there were renewed criticisms of delays in the disbursement of promised aid by the European Commission.

United States

The United States was willing to condemn violence against minorities and even in June to acknowledge that such violence was systematic, but despite organizing a June conference of Albanian and Serb leaders outside Washington, it showed far less willingness to expend the political capital or deploy its troops in KFOR in the manner necessary actually to improve security in the province. The laissez-faire approach of U.S. policy to Kosovo was most clearly manifest in its strong support for early elections in the province, its unwillingness to acknowledge publicly the involvement of KLA members in ethnic and political violence, and in the trial of the Momcilovic brothers, where the U.S. army withheld evidence that an Albanian man

involved in an attack on the Momcilovic home had in fact been shot by U.S. troops and not by the Serb defendants, who spent a year in pretrial detention.

Relevant Human Rights Watch Reports:

Kosovo: Rape As A Weapon of "Ethnic Cleansing," 3/00

KYRGYZSTAN

Human Rights Developments

In 2000, President Askar Akaev's actions shattered the illusion of Kyrgyzstan as an "island of democracy" in a repressive region. Armed clashes on the country's border, manipulated polls for parliament and for the presidency, and restrictions on free speech, press and association, minority rights, and religion fostered an ongoing crisis, with dire implications for human rights.

The government of Kyrgyzstan attempted to limit access to the southern border with Tajikistan after armed clashes between fighters of the Islamic Movement of Uzbekistan (IMU) and Kyrgyz government troops resumed in August. Reports emerged of civilian deaths from mines laid by the Kyrgyz military in mountainous border areas; over one thousand civilians had been relocated from the conflict zone at the time of writing, in what was claimed to be a voluntary process. The IMU, whose stated goal was to move into Uzbek territory from its reported redoubts in Tajikistan and Afghanistan, once again took several sets of hostages, some of whom were released and some of whom escaped. Kyrgyz warplanes launched bombing raids on border areas in Kyrgyzstan and Tajikistan; thirty Kyrgyz were officially acknowledged to have been killed.

In elections to the parliament in February and March 2000, and for president on October 29, 2000, the government blatantly violated citizens' rights. Though fifteen "parties" participated in the parliamentary vote, courts barred four, including the three most popular opposition parties—El-Bei Bechora (the People's Party) and Ar-Namys (Dignity), and later the Democratic Movement of Kyrgyzstan—from advancing a slate of candidates, based on two provisions of the electoral law hastily passed in 1999. The government also erected significant barriers for individual opposition candidates to register. International and domestic observers noted widespread instances of fraud.

The boldness with which the Kyrgyz government attacked Akaev's potential presidential rivals, including former vice president Gen. Felix Kulov, shocked even the most jaded observers. Kulov was tried by a closed military tribunal after being arrested in March and charged with abusing his official powers when he served as minister of national security. Although the tribunal acquitted him of any wrongdoing in August, state prosecutors appealed the verdict, and a retrial was ordered in September. A Supreme Court judge, Akynbek Tilebaliev, who was said to have influenced the first court's decision to acquit, was allegedly forced by the government to resign.

In May, a Bishkek court convicted Danier Usenov, then leader of the Kyrgyz People's Party (El-Bei Bechora), and another challenger for the presidency on a four-year-old assault charge in which the plaintiff had withdrawn his original complaint, sentencing him to two years of probation. Kyrgyz law permanently bars persons with criminal convictions from standing for election to public office.

Long-time political activist, human rights defender, and founder of Kyrgyzstan's nongovernmental Guild of Prisoners of Conscience Topchubek Turgunaliev was convicted in August of plotting an attempt on President Akaev's life and overthrow of the state's constitutional system. Turgunaliev and six of his eight codefendants were sentenced to from sixteen to seventeen years in prison. The seventh man charged in the case, an officer of the MNB (Ministry for National Security, formerly the KGB) and the state's lone witness, was given a suspended sentence and immediately released.

The government introduced mandatory Kyrgyz language testing for potential presidential candidates in 2000. Seven potential opposition candidates were excluded under this provision. Citizens wishing to gather signatures to support opposition candidates faced threats and harassment, including dismissal from jobs. According to local human rights groups, provincial governors appointed by the president compelled teachers and other civil servants to support Akaev.

Authorities dealt harshly with demonstrators, casting a chill over the rights to freedom of speech and association. In March, police beat demonstrators in Kulov's home base of Kara-Bura, injuring several.

Independent newspapers' vigorous reporting during the election spawned an intense government backlash. On January 13, the Supreme Court upheld a court decision finding the popular private newspaper *Res Publica* guilty of defaming a government official; under threat of closure, the paper paid the damage award, but government harassment continued. In August, the Ministry for State Security questioned three members of the editorial board of the paper *Delo No* (Case Number) in an investigation of alleged "disclosure of state secrets," following an article on the case against Felix Kulov. KNB officials searched the homes of *Delo No* journalists in September. A Bishkek court began to consider the libel suit brought by parliamentary deputy and former Kyrgyz Communist Party First Secretary Turdakun Usubaliev against the independent newspaper *Asaba* (the Standard) in late August. Tellingly, Usubaliev was seeking to have publication suspended during the trial, as well as 50 million soms (approximately U.S. $1.06 million) in damages. The paper's owner, People's Party leader Melis Eshimkanov, was challenging President Akaev in the October 29 election. Journalist Moldosaly Ibraimov, from the southern region of Jalal-Abad, was jailed for five weeks after being charged with libel for an article he wrote about corruption during the run-up to the parliamentary elections. Media restrictions also raised minority rights questions when the government attempted to strip the private station Osh TV, which broadcasts in Uzbek, of its broadcasting license. In the face of local and international protests, the State Commission for Radio Frequencies postponed a decision until the end of the year.

The government of Kyrgyzstan also engaged in Internet censorship, shutting down the independent news site "Politika KG" from late August until October 29, the date of the presidential elections.

Kyrgyzstan intensified repression against the Islamic group Hizb ut-Tahrir (Party of Liberation), mainly active in the southern Osh province, arresting tens of the group's followers and sentencing them to prison terms on charges of inciting religious and racial hatred.

Kyrgyzstan flouted its obligations as a signatory to the 1951 refugee convention and the Convention against Torture and Other Cruel, Inhuman or Degrading Treatment or Punishment in April by its forcible deportation of Jeli Turdi, an ethnic Uighur, back to the People's Republic of China, where he risked mistreatment including torture.

Defending Human Rights

In March, prosecutors formally warned NGO Coalition for Democracy leader, Toletan Ismailova, Lidia Fomova of the Association for Social Protection of the Population, and other NGO leaders that they faced arrest under Criminal Code article 233, which punishes "destabilizing the social order," for their human rights activities. In May the Ministry of Justice refused to register the nongovernmental Guild of Prisoners of Conscience, stating that the Kyrgyz constitution precluded any arrests on political grounds.

The Kyrgyz Committee for Human Rights (KCHR) and its chairman, Ramazan Dyryldaev, faced increasingly serious harassment, as state officials attempted to confiscate the group's property, after court decisions revoked its registration. Facing arrest on criminal charges in late July, Dyryldaev, his son, and one other KCHR activist fled the country, and they remained abroad as of this writing.

The Role of the International Community

United Nations

The U.N. Resident Coordinator Office in Bishkek monitored the situation of internally displaced persons (IDPs) in connection with the Uzbek rebel incursion in August.

Kyrgyzstan submitted several reports to United Nations treaty bodies in 1999-2000. The United Nations Committee on the Rights of the Child concluded that the government was not making the necessary effort to comply with the treaty's provisions in May. In July, the Human Rights Committee reviewed and found lacking Kyrgyz compliance with its obligations under the International Covenant on Civil and Political Rights.

Organization for Security and Cooperation in Europe (OSCE)

The OSCE announced at the end of January that it would send a full observer mission to the parliamentary elections in February, shortly before the Kyrgyz government disallowed the participation of several opposition candidates. The final report of that mission thoroughly summarized election abuses and issued a series of recommendations on improving the electoral process, but the OSCE did not insist that they be implemented as a condition to its observing the October presidential poll. It announced on September 14, that it would do so, while issuing several statements critical of the arrest and harassment of opposition figures. In the aftermath of the parliamentary poll, the OSCE pressed the government to hold roundtable discussions with the opposition, which was largely excluded from the new parliament, but the government has refused to do so. In April, the OSCE opened a field office in the southern city of Osh.

European Union

The European Union held the second meeting of its Cooperation Council with Kyrgyzstan in July, which, though it noted the importance of democratic reforms, "concluded that cooperation in 2000/2001 should focus in particular on the improvement of the business climate." After the August incursion, the E.U. delegation to the OSCE Permanent Council issued a statement recognizing that "the strengthening of civil societies, progress in democratization and the rule of law as well as the improvement of economic and social conditions are essential in the fight against extremism and fundamentalism."

United States

During her April visit to the region, Secretary of State Madeleine Albright criticized the Kyrgyz retreat from democracy and extracted a promise from President Akaev to follow OSCE recommendations for improvements in advance of October's presidential election; Albright then extended U.S.$3 million in supplementary counterterrorism assistance. The administration requested $37 million in assistance for Kyrgyztan in 2001, an $8 million increase over estimated 2000 expenditures, and prefaced its January 2000 request by stating that "Kyrgyzstan's commitment to democratization and economic reform stand out as an example of the successes that can be achieved in Central Asia." After first inviting Kyrgyzstan to the June conference of democratic states in Warsaw, in May the convening states, including the United States, suggested to Kyrgyzstan that it would be best if its delegation did not make an appearance.

MACEDONIA

Human Rights Developments

Although the international community continued to view Macedonia as a model of stability and democracy in the region, its human rights record remained patchy in 2000, with police brutality and the treatment of minorities continuing areas of concern. Events leading up to the election of Macedonia's second president at the end of 1999 typified the country's mixed record: after a generally well-conducted first round of elections on October 31, 1999, the November 14, 1999,

run-off was flawed by serious irregularities in some districts. When the state electoral commission ordered a new round of voting on December 5 in 230 polling stations, irregularities were again reported, marring the victory of Boris Trajkovski, the candidate of the ruling coalition, who took office on December 15.

The killing of three police officers outside the Albanian village of Aracinovo on January 11, 2000, sparked some of most serious cases of police abuse in Macedonia since the riots and subsequent crackdown in Gostivar and Tetovo in 1997. During raids on Aracinovo by police units during the three days after the killing, Aracinovo's ethnic Albanian residents reported widespread beatings at the hands of police, as well the destruction of property and the use of tear gas. One of the three suspects arrested in connection with the murders of the police died in police custody, and at the time of this writing, the autopsy report had yet to be released. Nine other suspects were arrested and beaten in custody and some claim to have been forced to sign confessions. At time of this writing, the murders of the police officer remained unsolved.

An investigation by the office of the ombudsman in Macedonia found that the police had used excessive force in Aracinovo and recommended an internal investigation. Although some families were compensated for damage to their property, the government did little to tackle police abuse in the wake of the incident. The suspicious death in custody of another ethnic Albanian man in a Skopje prison on May 14 did little to improve confidence in policing among the Albanian community. In the three months following the Aracinovo killings, three police stations in predominantly ethnic Albanian areas were attacked with explosives, although it was not clear if the incidents were linked.

Macedonia's Roma community also suffered at the hands of the police during 2000. On April 21, a married couple of "Egyptian" ethnicity (Macedonia's so-called Egyptians consider themselves distinct from Roma) was reportedly beaten by police on the road to Ohrid after a traffic stop. The husband, a taxi driver, was arrested for lacking necessary permits (which he later claimed he had presented), was allegedly beaten in custody and sentenced to eight days in jail. On May 14, a sixteen-year-old Roma boy from Negotino Municipality was taken to the police station there, where he was reportedly beaten and forced to confess to various crimes. A further incident occurred on May 26 in the village of Stip, when six Roma men illegally removing firewood from a forest in a nearby village were apprehended by a group of police and village residents. The six men were beaten before being taken to a nearby police station where the beatings continued. The difficulties faced by Roma in Macedonia were further highlighted in June when five Roma houses in the village of Stip caught fire under suspicious circumstances. One of the houses was completely destroyed and the other four badly damaged. Police suspected arson. Roma houses in Stip has been the target of arson attacks in 1992.

A new draft law on information, introduced by the Macedonian government on May 12, drew criticism from local journalists and international press groups. Although there was consensus on the need for a new law to replace existing regulations from the communist era, free speech advocates were concerned that ethical standards for journalists were being transformed into legal provisions regulated by the government. They were also concerned about the requirement that local journalists obtain government-issued press accreditation. The law remained pending. Free expression took a blow in June with reports of widespread confiscations of the Tirana-based daily newspaper *Bota Sot* in the towns of Tetovo and Gostivar, and a five-day shut-down of its production by a local printer, ostensibly on technical grounds. *Bota Sot* was generally critical of the government.

In July, the government adopted legislation to resolve the long-standing question of Tetovo University, a private Albanian-language institution that Macedonian authorities refused to accredit as an educational institution. The passage of the law on educa-

tion on July 25 established a new multilingual tertiary institute offering training in business, education, and public management. The internationally funded institution, intended as a replacement to Tetovo University, would allow Albanians to study in their own language, although a proficiency test in Macedonian would be required before their diplomas were officially recognized. Despite receiving the backing of the Albanian party in the ruling government coalition, the new institute did not receive unequivocal support from the country's ethnic Albanian population, many of whom wanted nothing less than the recognition of Tetovo University itself.

The overall standard of September's municipal elections in Macedonia was lower than that of the 1999 presidential elections, with the vote in both rounds marred by irregularities including violence and intimidation in some districts. International monitors pointed to problems with the election law and the fact that administrative measures were selectively applied to media critical of the government. Fewer problems were observed during the second round, although ballot boxes were destroyed in fourteen polling stations.

Despite government promises to reform Macedonia's overly exclusive 1992 citizenship law in line with Council of Europe standards, the law remained unchanged. Drafted at the time of its independence from the Socialist Federal Republic of Yugoslavia, Macedonia's citizenship law never adequately resolved the status of the significant number of Yugoslav citizens who were long-term residents in Macedonia but who were neither born in Macedonia nor ethnic Macedonian. Large numbers of ethnic Albanians, Turks, and Roma who knew no other home than Macedonia remained effectively stateless as a result of the law.

Defending Human Rights

There were no reports of government restrictions on the right to monitor by local human rights organizations, such as the Helsinki Committee for Human Rights in the Republic of Macedonia, or from visiting international human rights organizations.

The Role of the International Community

United Nations

The U.N. Committee on the Rights of the Child considered Macedonia's initial report on its compliance with the Convention on the Rights of the Child in January. Among the committee's recommendations to the Macedonian authorities was a call to focus on improving school enrollment rates for minority children, particularly Roma. The difficulties faced by Roma in Macedonia were also noted at a special three-day session in August of the Committee on the Elimination of Racial Discrimination.

Organization for Security and Cooperation in Europe (OSCE)

The OSCE continued to pay close attention to events in Macedonia during 2000. In addition to the long-standing Spillover Monitor Mission to Skopje, set up in 1992 to monitor the Macedonian-Yugoslav border, the OSCE was also active in monitoring the presidential elections in October and November 1999 and local elections in September 2000 through its Office for Democratic Institutions and Human Rights (ODIHR). Although the first round of presidential elections was deemed acceptable, ODIHR's election observation mission found irregularities in the second round, and in both rounds of the local elections. The resolution of the status of Tetovo University in July owed much to efforts by the OSCE high commissioner on minorities, who also issued a comprehensive report in March on the difficulties faced by Roma and Sinti in OSCE member states, including in Macedonia.

Council of Europe

On May 5, the Council of Europe's Parliamentary Assembly decided to end its monitoring procedure for Macedonia. The decision followed a March report from its monitoring committee commending Macedonia's progress in meeting its membership obligations and commitments. The report encouraged Macedonia to bring its citizenship law into line with the European Convention on Nationality.

European Union

In March, the way was opened for negotiations between the European Union and Macedonia on an Agreement on Stabilization and Association, offering the promise of closer economic and political ties. The upgrading in relations was symbolized by the change of the E.U.'s office in Macedonia to a Permanent Delegation. During a June visit, E.U. External Relations Commissioner Chris Patten noted Macedonia's progress and indicated that the agreement was likely to be concluded before the end of 2000. E.U. financial assistance to Macedonia included 25 million euro (approximately U.S. $30.8 million) through the PHARE program and infrastructure support through the OBNOVA program.

United States

U.S. policy continued to support Macedonia's role in the NATO partnership for peace program and to emphasize its role in regional stability. The focus on security cooperation was underscored by a visit from Chairman of the U.S. Joint Chiefs of Staff Gen. Henry H. Shelton in July and visits by two teams of U.S. military experts in June. That the U.S. remained reluctant to criticize human rights abuses in Macedonia was reflected in the overly positive State Department report on Macedonia in its annual review of human rights practices and its silence over irregularities in the September municipal elections.

ROMANIA

Human Rights Developments

Romania strove to meet the requirements for accession to the European Union, making slow but steady progress in human rights. However, discrimination against Roma continued, and many sought refuge outside the country. Police brutality remained a problem. Freedom of press and thought and the right to a fair trial remained threatened. Fallout from the NATO-Yugoslav conflict, including restriction of access to shipping on the Danube, created economic hardship in its already shaky economy, driving some Romanians into the hands of traffickers and forced labor abroad. The pattern of blaming or prosecuting the victims of crimes, particularly Roma and trafficked women, continued. Minority religious groups continued to experience discrimination with limits placed on the licensing of groups and the building of places of worship.

Romania hosted the twenty-second annual International Lesbian and Gay Association (ILGA) European Conference in October 2000. ACCEPT, the local organizing NGO for ILGA's conference, monitored progress in legislative efforts to decriminalize same-sex relations. In June the lower house of Parliament, the Chamber of Deputies, repealed article 200, but article 201, proscribing "sexual perversions," remained. At this writing, only the Chamber of Deputies has voted to decriminalize gay sex; the upper Senate has yet to vote the bill into law. On August 31, the Romanian government passed an ordinance on "Preventing and Punishing all forms of Discrimination," which explicitly included sexual orientation as a protected state of identity, to take effect within sixty days of publication. Local NGOs hailed this decision as further incentive to the Senate to modify the penal code. After the October conference, ILGA released a statement urging the repeal of article 200 as a precondition for Romania's E.U. accession.

Roma continued to be subjected to ethnic and racial discrimination. On March 12, 2000, the European Roma Rights Center (ERRC) lodged applications against Romania with the European Court of Human Rights regarding cases of violence and destruction of property in Casinul Nou, 1990, and in Plaiesii de Sus, 1991, which had been ultimately denied in Romanian courts in part because the statute of limitations had expired before they could initiate final appeals, due to the slowness of the court system. Police in both cases failed to conduct on-site investigations, and in both cases the Romanian courts found that the offenses in which Roma were beaten and their homes destroyed had been committed "due to serious provocative acts of the victims."

The number of inmates of Romanian penitentiaries and police lockups who were in pretrial detention dropped in 2000 from one-third in 1997 to one-fifth. Amnesty International documented several cases of the use of excessive force, some of them including minors, and also reported that Romanian law currently allows police officers to use firearms in circumstances prohibited by international standards, such as allowing them to shoot when apprehending a suspect. APADOR-CH, the Romanian Helsinki Committee, received numerous complaints from individuals claiming that they had been tortured or ill-treated by the police. By law, such accusations were investigated by the Military Prosecutor's Office, which also decided whether an investigation was warranted, with the burden of proof on the victim.

Freedom of the press continued to be threatened under 1996 modifications to the penal code, which provided harsh sentences for critical reporting on state bodies or state-owned businesses. The Chamber of Deputies voted to eliminate or reduce the punishments under several articles of the penal code that restricted the freedom of expression. However, these revisions had not been passed by the Senate, and journalists continued to be harassed by the police. On May 26, Valentin Dragan of the newspaper *Cugetul liber* was severely beaten while attempting to recover a colleague's camera. Since August 30, 2000, a draft of a Law on Free Access to Information of Public Interest in Romania has been circulating. Several claims arising from libel cases involving public officials were brought to the European Court of Human Rights.

The Committee on the Elimination of All Forms of Discrimination Against Women (CEDAW) observed that while Romania made progress toward protecting and equalizing women's rights, few women held leadership positions in their field, and placed high priority on the adoption of proposed legislation on equal opportunities, domestic violence, and trafficking in women. Women who dared to press charges against their traffickers faced prosecution themselves for evading border controls and for engaging in prostitution. According to Romanian NGOs working on trafficking, police corruption only exacerbated the danger to trafficking victims and facilitated impunity for traffickers. Moreover, they were often coerced by police into becoming informers. In August, Cambodian police and U.N. human rights officers rescued seven women from Romania and Moldova who had been trafficked and forced into prostitution there.

The National Agency for Child Protection was created in order to accelerate efforts to reform the child welfare system in Romania. Romania signed the optional protocol of the Convention on the Rights of the Child, concerning the Involvement of Children in Armed Conflict.

Defending Human Rights

Human Rights Watch was not aware of any attempts to hinder the work of rights groups in 2000.

The Role of the International Community

United Nations

UNHCR reported that Romania had become a country of asylum for many refugees from around the world, and remained in the process of bringing its national refugee legislation into line with the 1951 Convention relating to the Status of Refugees, to which it acceded in 1991.

Operation for Security and Cooperation in Europe (OSCE)

Romania was to assume the year-long chairmanship of the OSCE in January 2001. In a report released in April on the situation of Roma and Sinti in the OSCE area, the high commissioner on national minorities emphasized the need for educational reform in Ro-

mania, particularly for ethnic minorities.

Council of Europe

In June 2000 a delegation of the Advisory Committee on the Council of Europe's Framework Convention for the Protection of National Minorities visited Bucharest. The committee expected to publish its views early in 2001.

European Union

Formal negotiations for Romania's E.U. accession began in February. Romania proposed 2007 as the date of its accession. In its October 1999 progress report, the E.U. reaffirmed that Romania met the Copenhagen political criteria for membership, but cautioned that "this position will need to be re-examined if the authorities do not continue to give priority to dealing with the crisis in their child care institutions." The report also said that "much still remains to be done in rooting out corruption, improving the working of the courts and protecting individual liberties and the rights of the Roma. Priority should also be given to reform of the public administration."

United States

The U.S. continued to cultivate close ties with Romania, including through military assistance, to prepare the country for NATO membership. In May, Secretary of State Madeline Albright and Prime Minister Mugur Isarescu pledged to continue the strategic partnership between Romania and the U.S. Romania was to receive U.S. $14 million in assistance from U.S. Agency for International Development (USAID) for development programs.

RUSSIAN FEDERATION

Human Rights Developments

The year was dominated by Russia's brutal war in Chechnya and fears of an impending crackdown on civil and political rights. Russian soldiers and police committed war crimes and other serious violations of the rules of human rights and humanitarian law in Chechnya. Following Vladimir Putin's election as Russia's new president in March, the political climate changed as officials' public statements showed increased intolerance to criticism and a general trend toward a new information order, of which the crackdown on the media conglomerate Media Most was the most emphatic. Abuse in the criminal justice system and army continued unabated, prisons remained severely overcrowded, the situation in many orphanages remained desperate, the state continued to be indifferent to cases of domestic violence and rape, and religious freedoms were further eroded. The government once more failed to introduce the structural reforms required to improve human rights observance in these areas.

Vladimir Putin, the acting president following Boris Yeltsin's surprise resignation on December 31, 1999, entered the March 26 presidential elections as a clear favorite and won in the first round with just over 50 percent of the vote—but not without widespread election fraud. Putin quickly moved to solidify his power by reigning in powerful regional leaders and attacking the "oligarchs," Russia's very wealthy new economic elite. He created seven administrative regions led by representatives responsible to the president alone and forced legislation through parliament to strip regional leaders of their seats in the Federal Council.

Putin's background as a KGB official sparked fears of an impending crackdown on human rights. Despite numerous public assurances of support for democratic values, Putin's reactions to critical media coverage and some of his actions fuelled these fears. The appointment of former KGB officer Vladimir Cherkesov as Putin's representative for the Northern Russia administrative region was another troubling sign; Cherkesov was known for his participation in persecuting dissidents in Soviet times and more recently in the prosecution of environmentalist Alexander Nikitin.

The war in Chechnya continued through-out the year. After taking Chechnya's capital Grozny in early February, Russian troops exercised nominal control over most of the republic's territory. Rebel forces retreated into the mountains to fight a guerrilla war, staging surprise attacks on Russian positions and convoys and murdering Chechens working in the new pro-Russian administration. Both sides showed scant respect for international law, but the far larger force of Russian troops backed by air power and artillery committed the lion's share of violations.

In an attempt to limit casualties among its soldiers, Russia relied heavily on air attacks. Villages and towns were "softened up" by prolonged aerial bombardments and shelling before Russian troops moved in. This strategy led to large numbers of casualties among civilians and destruction of civilian property on a horrific scale. In many of the aerial or artillery attacks Russian officers did not differentiate between military and civilian objects. When targeting military objects, Russian forces frequently used force that was clearly excessive compared to the military gain to be expected.

The city of Grozny, bombed for three straight months, from November 1999 to early February 2000, was essentially treated as one enormous military target. Though the vast majority of civilians had left the city before the assault started, an estimated twenty to forty thousand civilians, many too poor, sick, or infirm to leave, remained. These people were given little thought as the Russian military machine obliterated the city. The only hospital that functioned throughout these months—though heavily damaged—treated 5,600 people (including Chechen fighters) for injuries sustained from the bombing campaign; according to estimates this was only about half the total number of injured. Many thousands of civilians were believed to have died in Grozny alone.

On January 31 and February 1, rebel forces abandoned Grozny. An estimated two thousand Chechen fighters quit the city and stumbled into a minefield that claimed the lives of three field commanders and at least one hundred regular fighters; hundreds more suffered serious injury, including notorious commander Shamil Basaev. Russian artillery and aviation tracked the fighters' flight from Grozny to the mountainous south, destroying the villages through which the fighters passed with total disregard for the civilian population. One of the worst hit villages was Katyr-Yurt. On February 4, up to twenty thousand civilians desperately fled an intense bombardment there that commenced following the arrival of large numbers of fighters in the village. At least two hundred civilians died while many more were injured. Russian soldiers then systematically looted the village and destroyed civilian property. The village of Gekhi-Chu was given similar treatment on February 7. Russian forces summarily executed at least seven people. On March 4, up to a thousand Chechen fighters entered the village of Komsomolskoye, apparently seeking food and shelter. Russian forces surrounded the village and then, as civilians sought to flee, subjected the village to a withering assault, totally flattening it. At least one hundred civilians were unable to leave the village and were believed killed during the shelling. Hundreds of fighters also reportedly died in the attack. Russian forces refused to provide exit routes to civilians fleeing from fighting and attacked convoys of displaced persons on several occasions. Displaced persons recounted numerous tales of perilous escapes under constant fire and shelling along roads that had been declared safe exit routes. On October 29, 1999, Russian planes fired multiple rockets at a convoy of Chechen civilians, including five clearly marked Red Cross vehicles, on the road between Grozny and Nazran, leaving at least fifty dead. The convoy, consisting of hundreds of cars, was travelling from the Ingush border back to Grozny after Russian forces had refused to open the border to Ingushetia. The attack took place in excellent weather conditions and it appeared inconceivable that the pilots were not aware that they were targeting civilians. The Russian military claimed it destroyed two trucks with rebel fighters in the attack.

Russian forces showed scant respect for medical neutrality. Russian bombs partially or fully destroyed many of Chechnya's main health care facilities, including every single hospital in Grozny. Russian forces detained and ill-treated several medical professionals who had treated Chechen fighters. Chechen rebels threatened to kill at least one Chechen doctor for treating wounded Russian soldiers.

After moving into villages and towns left by rebel fighters, Russian forces carried out "mopping up" operations. These operations, meant to check for remaining rebels, frequently turned into rampages during which soldiers and riot police looted and torched homes, detained civilians at random, and raped women. Just three such operations, in Alkhan Yurt, and in the Novye Aldy and Staropromyslovskii districts of Grozny, resulted in the confirmed summary executions of more than 130 civilians. Human Rights Watch received over one hundred more allegations of summary executions, many of which it was unable to verify.

In Alkhan Yurt, Russian soldiers went on a two-week rampage after entering the village on December 1, 1999. After first temporarily expelling hundreds of civilians, soldiers systematically looted and burned the village and killed at least fourteen civilians. In the Staropromyslovskii district of Grozny, Russian soldiers killed at least fifty-one civilians between late December 1999 and early February 2000; some were simply shot, others were first tortured. On February 5, Russian forces summarily executed at least sixty civilians in the Novye Aldy and Chernorechie suburbs of Grozny, including a one-year-old baby and a woman who was eight months pregnant. Soldiers pillaged and deliberately torched numerous houses.

Looting was rampant throughout Chechnya. Soldiers systematically stripped bare civilian homes after taking control of villages. Soldiers took not only valuables, money, and electronic equipment but often also food, mattresses, windows, and even floorboards. Many civilians reported seeing soldiers load looted goods onto trucks that were subsequently driven out of the republic. Soldiers deliberately burned thousands of homes throughout Chechnya.

Russian soldiers were believed to have raped numerous Chechen women. Considering the great cultural stigma attached to rape in Chechnya's predominantly Muslim communities, allegations received by Human Rights Watch were believed to represent no more than a small fraction of the total. There was evidence that Russian servicemen raped three women in Alkhan Yurt and six in Novye Aldy. A woman from the village of Tangi-Chu was raped and murdered by a Russian officer.

Russian forces detained tens of thousands of Chechens, often arbitrarily, on suspicion of belonging to rebel forces or assisting them. Many of these Chechens faced beatings and torture at detention centers throughout Chechnya. Many of those detained were released only after relatives paid a "ransom" to police or prison guards.

Large scale arrests started in January 2000 after Gen. Viktor Kazantsev blamed "groundless trust" in Chechen civilians for setbacks in Russia's military campaign. He stated that "only children up to ten and men over sixty, and women, will henceforth be regarded as refugees." By late May, the Russian Ministry of Interior announced that over ten thousand people had been detained in Chechnya since the beginning of the year. At the time of writing, Russian forces continued to detain large numbers of Chechen civilians.

Large scale torture and ill-treatment took place in Chernokozovo in January and early February. Upon arrival, detainees were forced to run through a gauntlet of guards wielding rubber batons and rifle butts. Thirty-two-year-old Aindi Kovtorashvili, detained on January 11, had a serious shrapnel wound to the head when he arrived at Chernokozovo, but guards made him "run the gauntlet" anyway. He collapsed under the blows and died. Guards brutally beat detainees whenever they were taken out of their overcrowded cells for questioning and sometimes during interrogations. Several detainees described methods of torture, including injections, electric shock and beatings to the genitals, beatings on the soles of the feet, and rape of both men and women.

As Chernokozovo attracted international attention, the Russian government "cleaned up" the detention center and torture and ill-treatment continued unabated at other locations. Some of the most serious abuses then took place at the so-called internat in Urus-Martan, a former boarding school for girls. Allegations of ill-treatment also came from temporary police precincts throughout the Russian controlled territory of Chechnya.

Many of those who were released from detention were "bought" out by relatives. Extortion demands made upon prisoners' relatives were so common that in many cases it appeared that the detention itself was motivated solely as a money-making enterprise. Ransom varied from 2,000 rubles (approximately U.S. $80) to U.S. $5,000. Extortion was also rampant at hundreds of Russian checkpoints throughout Chechnya.

Those displaced by the conflict faced difficult conditions in refugee camps in Ingushetia and Chechnya itself. The Russian government's efforts to provide the displaced with food, medical care, and shelter were insufficient, leaving the brunt of the burden to humanitarian organizations. On various occasions, the government pressured displaced people to return to Chechnya by depriving them of food rations or simply attempting to drive the train carriages, the temporary homes of some, back into Chechnya.

Chechen rebels also showed little respect for international humanitarian law. They summarily executed at least some captured Russian soldiers and murdered numerous Chechens who worked in the new, pro-Russian administration. Chechen rebels frequently endangered civilians by placing headquarters and garrisons in densely populated areas or by firing at federal positions from such places. On several occasions, rebels reacted violently when villagers asked them to leave in order to spare their villages from bombardments. Chechen criminal groups kidnapped one Russian and one French journalist in October 1999. Both were later released. Unknown Chechens summarily executed Vladimir Yatsina, a Russian photographer, in February after kidnapping him in Ingushetia in the summer of 1999.

The Russian government did not hold those guilty of violations accountable. By September, not a single Russian soldier or police officer had been charged with or detained in connection with the massacres in Alkhan Yurt and in the Staropromyslovskii and Novye Aldy districts of Grozny. In Staropromyslovskii district, prosecutors were investigating only one killing out of the fifty-one that were documented. Officially announced investigations into other incidents lacked credibility. In response to allegations of abuses, President Putin appointed Vladimir Kalamanov as his special representative for human rights in Chechnya in February. The special representative's office provided important services to Chechens but did not significantly contribute to the accountability process.

Chechens in Moscow faced very serious abuses in the aftermath of the bombings of two Moscow apartment buildings in September 1999. Federal and local authorities took a series of draconian administrative measures against non-Muscovites as a result of which many children could not go to school while adults had trouble finding work, getting married, or receiving passports. At the same time, Moscow police were given carte blanche to terrorize ethnic Chechens living in the city. Police dragged more than twenty thousand Chechens to police stations, photographing and fingerprinting many of them. According to the Russian human rights organizations Memorial and Civic Assistance, police prosecuted at least fifty Chechens after planting drugs and ammunition in their clothes or their apartments. Moscow courts found most of these Chechens guilty despite overwhelming evidence that the charges were trumped up. Members of other ethnic minorities also faced increased harassment by police.

When Moscow mayor Yuri Luzhkov spoke of a possible "Chechen connection" following another bombing in Moscow in August 2000, Chechens appeared to be in for a repeat performance. However, the dramatic sinking of a Russian submarine diverted attention from the bombing and police apparently abandoned the crackdown, though not before detaining and seriously beating at least some Chechens.

Moscow authorities used the August explosion to defend Moscow's longstanding *propiska*, or residency permit, system. Federal prosecutors had earlier ordered Moscow to get rid of the system to bring regional legislation in line with federal laws. At the time of writing, Moscow maintained its *propiska* system.

Media freedom was another casualty of the Chechnya campaign as Russia's leadership severely limited access to the war zone and became increasingly intolerant to criticism. Most Russian media voluntarily supported the government's campaign. Those which did not often faced sanctions. Andrei Babitsky, a Radio Liberty correspondent, was reporting from Chechnya without official accreditation when he was detained by Russian forces in mid-January and taken to Chernokozovo detention center, where guards beat him several times. In early February, the Russian government announced that Babitsky had been handed over to a group of Chechen rebels, in exchange for captured Russian soldiers. Several weeks later he resurfaced in Dagestan and was immediately arrested for carrying falsified identity papers. He was released in Moscow on February 29. A court hearing was still pending at the time of writing.

Media freedom was also under threat outside the Chechen context. On May 11, heavily armed commandos of the procuracy and federal security service raided the offices of Media Most, a media holding that owns Russia's independent television station NTV, radio Ekho Moskvy, and *Segodnia* newspaper, forcibly holding dozens of employee in the building a full day. The law enforcement officers eventually confiscated part of Media Most's records. Law enforcement agencies denied a political context but the heavy handedness with which the raid was carried out gave it the appearance of a warning to independent media. On June 13, Vladimir Gusinsky, president of Media Most, was arrested. He was released several days later after being charged with large-scale embezzlement. In late July, these charges were dropped when Gusinsky agreed to transfer control over Media Most to the state-owned gas giant Gazprom.

The clumsy response by officials to the sinking of a nuclear submarine in the Barents Sea, which resulted in the deaths of 118 sailors, provoked a wave of criticism in the media, directed against President Putin and other state officials. Non-state media pointed out inconsistencies in officials' accounts and questioned President Putin's decision not to interrupt his vacation. Putin responded aggressively, accusing the media of "lying" and "ruining Russia's army and fleet."

No measures were taken to combat rampant police torture or to reform the judicial system. Police continued to torture detainees in order to secure confessions, using methods like beatings, asphyxiation, electric shock, and suspension by the arms or legs, as well as psychological intimidation. Police also gave privileges to certain detainees to pressure others into confessing. Prosecutors used coerced confessions in court, often as the primary evidence of a defendant's guilt. The procuracy failed to investigate torture complaints promptly and adequately and they rarely led to formal criminal investigations. On October 11, the Moscow City Court stripped Sergei Pashin, an outspoken opponent of torture practices and a leading judge, of his status for criticizing a judgment of a colleague and giving out his work telephone number in a radio program.

On September 13, the Presidium of the Supreme Court dismissed the prosecution's appeal against the December 29, 1999, acquittal of environmentalist Alexander Nikitin. With that decision, the criminal case, in which Nikitin was accused of espionage for the Norwegian environmental organization Bellona, finally came to an end as the prosecution had no further appeal options.

Defending Human Rights

Human rights organizations working on Chechnya faced problems of access to Chechnya and to official information, and petty harassment. Despite oral assurances that Human Rights Watch would be granted access to Chechnya, this was not the case. Memorial, a leading Russian rights group, also continued to face difficulties working inside Chechnya. Human rights workers faced occasional harassment from police and the Federal Security Service (FSB). Numerous appeals by Human Rights Watch for information from the Russian authorities went unanswered.

Other human rights activists also faced occasional problems with authorities. For example, on August 28 masked police commandos stormed the office of a human rights organization, the Glasnost Foundation, without any apparent reason. The police carrying out the raid taunted Sergei Grigoriants, the head of the organization, with the knowledge that he was a former dissident who had spent time in prison for his political activities in Soviet times.

The Role of the International Community

United Nations

In December 1999, Human Rights Watch called on the Security Council to establish a commission of inquiry to investigate violations of the laws of war in Chechnya. The Security Council, however, never formally discussed Chechnya.

In late March, U.N. High Commissioner for Human Rights Mary Robinson travelled to the area after an earlier refusal of her request for a visit sparked an international outcry. Robinson became the first senior international official to acknowledge receiving evidence of summary executions, torture, and rape. Although Foreign Minister Igor Ivanov at the end of the trip told Robinson she was welcome to visit Chechnya again in a few months, a formal invitation had not yet been extended at the time of writing.

The U.N. Commission on Human Rights adopted a resolution criticizing Russia for violations of human rights in Chechnya—the first time a resolution was adopted regarding a permanent member of the Security Council. The resolution, among other things, called on the Russian government to establish "according to recognized international standards" a national commission of inquiry and mandated five special mechanisms of the Human Rights Commission to visit Chechnya and report to the commission and the General Assembly. At the time of the General Assembly session in the fall, none of the special mechanisms had been able to visit. The Russian failure to implement the resolution was raised at a one-day commission session in September but no public record of the discussion was issued.

Organization for Security and Cooperation in Europe (OSCE)

At the November 1999 Istanbul summit, OSCE member states, including Russia, confirmed the mandate of the OSCE Assistance Group to Chechnya. The Russian government, however, subsequently refused to allow the Assistance Group to function in Ingushetia and created administrative obstacles to its return to Chechnya. As a result, the Assistance Group was unable to fulfill its functions in a meaningful way.

In other OSCE developments, its Office for Democratic Institutions and Human Rights (ODIHR) provided ad hoc technical and training assistance to the staff of Kalamanov's office. The office did not respond to evidence of widespread fraud during the March presidential elections, other than to characterize the elections as "a benchmark in the ongoing evolution of the Russian Federation's emergence as a representative democracy."

Council of Europe

A number of Council of Europe delegations visited the North Caucasus to assess the situation, including the European commissioner for human rights, members of the Parliamentary Assembly of the Council of Europe, and the Committee for the Prevention of Torture.

Chechnya figured prominently on the agenda of all Parliamentary Assembly sessions in 2000. After its January recommendations went unheeded, a majority of parliamentarians voted in April to strip Russia's parliamentary delegation of its voting rights.

The assembly also recommended that member states file an interstate complaint against Russia with the European Court of Human Rights and that the Committee of Ministers start proceedings to exclude Russia from the Council of Europe.

The Committee of Ministers brushed aside all of the recommendations of the Parliamentary Assembly without serious discussion and said that Russia's response to international pressure was satisfactory.

The secretary general of the Council of Europe invoked a seldom used mechanism to require Russia to explain the application of the European Convention on Human Rights with regard to the conflict. When Russia's response was unsatisfactory, the secretary general deferred further action to the Committee of Ministers, which remained silent.

The Council of Europe sent three experts to the office of Vladimir Kalamanov starting in June. Although the presence of these experts no doubt contributed to the efficiency of the office, the experts were not in a position to make a meaningful contribution to the accountability process.

European Union

In the early months of the war, the European Union (E.U.) under the Finnish presidency took a fairly tough stance on Russia, consistently criticizing its military operation and abuses and freezing some technical assistance funds. After Boris Yeltsin resigned as president and it became apparent that Vladimir Putin would become Russia's next president, the E.U. toned down its criticism and backed away from any tougher action.

To its credit, the E.U. introduced the resolution on Chechnya at the U.N. Commission on Human Rights. However, the E.U. itself undermined the importance of this step. As Russia openly defied all international criticism and refused to recognize or implement the resolution, the E.U. and its member states started a series of bilateral and multilateral summit talks to establish good relations with Russia's new president.

E.U. member states refused to take

Russia to the European Court of Human Rights over abuses in Chechnya. In response to an appeal from more than thirty leading human rights and humanitarian NGOs, the E.U. claimed that such a step was unnecessary as Russia was making progress toward accountability. The E.U. also refused to use political and economic levers, such as suspending the Partnership and Cooperation Agreement or support for international lending, to convince Russia to change its conduct in Chechnya.

In sharp contrast to its conduct in Kosovo in 1999, the E.U. failed to gather information independently on abuses in Chechnya. No E.U. diplomats visited Chechnya or even Ingushetia independently to interview victims of human rights abuses, although a December 1999 declaration of the E.U. foreign ministers requested that they do so.

United States

The United States limited itself to a rhetorical response to the violations in Chechnya. It criticised Russia consistently over its actions in Chechnya but was unwilling to use any stronger political or economic levers. The United States was unwilling to suspend its support for international lending to Russia or to use bilateral economic assistance to convince Russia to change its conduct. It actively pursued good relations with Putin despite the war. At times, even the rhetoric was flawed. Testifying before Congress in May, Deputy Secretary of State Strobe Talbott went to great lengths to avoid using the words "war crimes" to describe the serious violations of humanitarian law that Russian forces have committed in Chechnya.

The United States also failed to collect first hand information independently on abuses by regularly sending diplomats to the region.

Financial Institutions

The World Bank did not condition disbursement of loans to Russia on its actions in Chechnya, releasing U.S. $450 million in structural adjustment loan payments to Russia since the outbreak of the conflict in 1999.

Linked to various industrial reforms, these payments went directly to the Russian government for unfettered general budgetary spending. Bank officials stated that they would monitor the impact of the conflict but this scrutiny was apparently limited to economic concerns.

International Monetary Fund (IMF) financing for Russia remained frozen, officially because of the slow pace of economic reforms, but Russian officials claimed the IMF decision was linked to the Chechnya conflict.

Relevant Human Rights Watch Reports:

Civilian Killings in Staropromyslovski District of Grozny, 2/00

February 5: A Day of Slaughter in Novye Aldi, 6/00

"No Happiness Remains:" Civilian Killings, Pillage, and Rape in Alkhan-Yurt, Chechnya, 4/00

"Welcome to Hell:" Arbitrary Detention in Chechnya, 10/00

SLOVAKIA

Human Rights Developments

Slovakia made significant progress in human rights protection, but incidents of employment discrimination, skinhead (racist youth) violence, and police brutality and weak antidiscrimination legislation and enforcement threatened the Slovak Roma minority. The governing Slovak Democratic Coalition (SDK), in office for two years, faced criticism for failure effectively to implement legislation such as the September 1999 Resolution and Measures Concerning the Roma National Minority.

Slovakia continued its movement toward European Union accession, took the first step toward NATO membership by signing a joint statement calling for membership by 2002, and became a member state of the Organization for Economic Cooperation and Development (OECD).

Racially motivated attacks on Roma or foreigners are not subject to special sanctions under Slovak law, which provides no express protections against discrimination by reason of ethnic origin or nationality. Deputy Prime Minister for Human and Minority Rights Pal Csaky announced in May his plan to draft an antidiscrimination law. In November 1999 the Slovak National Labor Office director, despite criticism from rights groups, defended his office's policy of marking files of persons regarded as Roma with the letter "R"; he said the practice was implemented because of the "complicated social adaptability" of the group.

During a violent police raid in the Romani settlement Zehra on December 2, 1999, police shot a thirteen-year-old boy in the leg, and officers reportedly used ethnic insults and threatened to rape Roma women. Both the criminal complaint against the involved officers and the appeal were rejected.

On December 17, 1999, a skinhead in Car assaulted a twenty-one-year-old Romani man. A police spokesperson described the incident as one of "youthful imprudence" and ruled out a racial motive. On February 7, 2000, two Roma were run down and killed while walking with their son. Rather than arrest the suspect, a well-known Slovak, police threatened family members, beating some of them, the family said. On February 20, four assailants wielding baseball bats attacked Roma in a bar in the town of Velke Kapusany; two Roma sustained serious injuries.

On August 20, three men shouting racial epithets beat Anastazia Balazova, a fifty-year-old Roma woman, and two of her daughters. She died from her injuries two days later. Deputy Prime Minister Csaky called the crime "deplorable," but the chief investigator said that police had no evidence that the crime was racially motivated. On August 24, the Slovak parliament observed a minute of silence in memory of Anastazia Balazova.

In August Justice Minister Jan Carnogursky announced his opposition to the registration of homosexual partnerships, which supporters framed as a potential E.U.

accession issue since four member countries of the E.U. recognize homosexual partnerships.

Protecting Human Rights

Slovak and international NGOs monitored threats to freedom of the media. In April the New York-based Committee to Protect Journalists, in a letter to President Schuster, protested defamation charges brought against Vladimir Mohorita, a journalist from the Slovak far-right nationalist weekly *Zmena.*

The European Roma Rights Center (ERRC) continued active monitoring and advocacy on behalf of Slovak Roma at home and abroad. The ERRC provided legal expertise in a case of skinhead violence; the second court decision ordered the first instance court to widen its interpretation of race in accord with international standards, declaring the incident a racially motivated crime.

Slovakia earned praise among rights advocates for ratifying the Second Optional Protocol to the International Covenant on Civil and Political Rights (ICCPR), which calls for abolition of the death penalty.

The Role of the International Community

United Nations

In August the U.N. Committee on the Elimination of Racial Discrimination received Slovakia's periodic report on combating racial bias and adopted its concluding observations and recommendations. The committee stated its concern about allegations that Slovak police and prosecutors have failed to investigate acts of racially-motivated violence promptly and effectively and about the socioeconomic status of Roma citizens. It noted Slovakia's recognition of the committee's competence to receive discrimination claims from Slovak citizens.

Organization for Security and Cooperation in Europe (OSCE)

The OSCE high commissioner for national minorities issued a report on the situation of Roma and Sinti in the OSCE area in

March, citing unemployment rates of up to 80 percent among Slovak Roma, the absence of Romani representatives in the 150-member Slovak Parliament, and disadvantages Romani children face in schools.

Council of Europe

European Court of Human Rights president Luzius Wildhaber ranked Slovakia among the countries flooding the court with high numbers of complaints; currently there are 250 registered complaints from Slovakia, the majority of which are likely to be accepted. Almost all of the complaints filed allege unfounded delays in court proceedings. A visit to Slovakia by the European Committee to Prevent Torture in 2000 was announced, but the findings had not been released at this writing. The Advisory Committee on the Framework Convention for the Protection of National Minorities visited Slovakia in February. In June the European Commission Against Racism and Intolerance published its second report on Slovakia, acknowledging recent positive steps taken by Slovakia but recommending full adoption and implementation of antiracist legislation and of measures to combat discrimination against the Roma community.

European Union

In February the European Union (E.U.) opened membership talks with a group of six candidate nations including Slovakia. At the sixth meeting of the E.U.-Slovakia Association Council in June, the E.U. recognized progress in the protection of minorities, particularly the 1999 adoption of the minority language law. The E.U. urged implementation of the law and particular attention to improving the situation of the Roma.

Some E.U. countries retained visa regimes, imposed in 1999 when a flood of Slovak Roma sought asylum. Belgium suspended its visa requirement on August 1. Norway lifted visa requirements for Slovak nationals on August 15.

United States

During U.S. Secretary of State Madeleine Albright's November 1999 Bratislava visit, a sign of dramatically improving relations with Slovakia, Albright called for better treatment of the Roma minority. In February 2000, the U.S. State Department, in its annual report on human rights, noted considerable improvement in Slovakia but said that the status and police treatment of the Roma remained problems.

TAJIKISTAN

Human Rights Developments

The Rakhmonov government sought legitimation through flagrantly fraudulent parliamentary elections in 2000. The elections marked the last major step of the transitional process outlined in the June 1997 government-United Tajik Opposition (UTO) peace accord, but important provisions of the agreement were not implemented. Demobilization of troops and reform of government power structures remained incomplete, the 30 percent quota of government posts to be awarded to UTO representatives was never met, and national reconciliation stalled, with next to no representation of Uzbeks or Pamiris either in government or in the parliament. Instead, members of the president's Kuliabi regional group retained nearly all important government posts, and the presidential People's Democratic Party (PDP) dominated the parliament. Human rights protections were also compromised by the government's increasingly authoritarian rule, and by disorder within law enforcement agencies and internal power struggles among government military and political leaders.

In the leadup to the February 27 parliamentary elections Human Rights Watch as well as a joint U.N.-OSCE observer mission witnessed state interference in the electoral process that included the obstruction or exclusion of opposition parties, a wholly arbitrary candidate registration process and flagrantly biased coverage by the state media. On election day there were numerous and grave irregularities in the voting. Of sixty-three seats, the ruling PDP gained thirty, and eighteen seats went to candidates who are mostly PDP members or widely acknowledged to be solidly pro-government, although they ran as independents. The Communist Party won thirteen seats and the Islamic Renaissance Party two. A joint U.N.-OSCE observer mission noted that the elections failed to meet minimum democratic standards, but calls for the vote to be annulled in some districts or for a recount of the vote went unheeded. Largely uncontested elections to the upper chamber held in March resulted in the election of an overwhelming majority of presidential party members.

Wanton violence by members of law enforcement and other security agencies contributed to overall lawlessness and a precarious personal security situation for most civilians. Human Rights Watch documented numerous cases of extortion, kidnapping, and beating of ordinary civilians by Ministry of Internal Affairs, Ministry of Defense, and Ministry of Emergency Situations personnel. Members of these units were also responsible for unlawful killings of civilians during operations to locate and confiscate illegal arms. The government made several limited attempts to improve security through these arms recovery operations and the arrest of members of the armed forces for common criminal offenses. The failure to meet two objectives of the peace accord—demobilization and reform of government power structures—continued to aggravate the security situation. One positive result was a somewhat improved security climate in Dushanbe, where by June many fewer armed persons and cars with blackened windows were visible, and where residents for the first time since 1992 dared to stay outside into the late evening hours. Nonetheless, sporadic explosions and shootouts continued to occur in the capital. A May presidential decree resulted in the release of approximately 1,000 *kontraktniki* (contract servicemen) from service, but many reportedly remained in service.

Former UTO commanders, based in the Karategin Valley and neither demobilized nor awarded government posts, continued to head independent armed forces, and clashes between these renegade forces and government troops in Darband in late August led to the reported burning of civilian houses and killing of livestock by government forces. Islamic insurgents who invaded Uzbekistan and Kyrgyzstan in August were accused of maintaining bases in northeastern Tajikistan, and former UTO combatants were accused of participating in the incursion.

Violence continued to characterize the political scene. In Dushanbe on February 16 a bomb exploded in a car carrying Dushanbe mayor Mahmadsaid Ubaidullaev and deputy security minister and parliamentary candidate Shamsullo Jabirov, fatally wounding the latter. On May 20, Saifullo Rahimov, chairman of the State Committee on Radio and Television, was assassinated in Dushanbe by unidentified gunmen. The politico-military climate in the Karategin Valley deteriorated on June 3 when the chairman of the district of Garm, Sergei Davlatov, was shot down with his bodyguard and driver. International organizations temporarily evacuated the area after the killing, and at the time of writing, as in the months previous, the Karategin Valley remained off-limits for most staff of international organizations. The year also saw firefights in public venues between the heads of several Kuliabi-headed security units.

The authorities arrested hundreds of alleged members of the banned Islamic movement Hizb-ut-Tahrir on charges of possession or distribution of anti-state literature and a wide range of criminal activities. In August seven members were sentenced to terms of imprisonment of from five to twelve years on charges of membership in illegal criminal groups and anti-state activities, while another thirty-seven were on trial in Leninabad on identical charges at the time of this writing. International organization staff and local sources reported that these arrests and trials were accompanied by incommunicado detention and physical mistreatment.

Electronic media remained under government control, and independent radio stations remained off the air, as their wait for a license from the government entered its third year. In May, Khorog-based state radio employee Umed Mamadponoev was detained by police and "disappeared" after producing a locally aired program on the army mistreatment of soldiers from Gorno-Badakhshan. Local and international sources fear Mamadponoev was drafted by authorities for military service in retaliation for his broadcast, but as of early September, his whereabouts remained unknown.

Defending Human Rights

As in previous years there was little human rights monitoring by local groups, but a victory of sorts was shared by local women's NGOs when an unfair death sentence imposed on twenty-one-year-old Dilfuza Numonova was commuted in July. The move to commute her sentence had been spearheaded by international organizations, but many local women's organizations signed petitions to the government in her support. The OSCE mission gained access to several of the country's prisons and shared its findings with international medical humanitarian organizations, one of which subsequently implemented an assistance program. The International Committee of the Red Cross (ICRC) continued to be denied access to prisoners in accordance with its standard procedures.

The Role of the International Community

In the face of systematic corruption, a politically influenced judiciary, and rampant security force abuse, senior representatives of international and humanitarian organizations working in the country and regional specialists called frequently for human rights conditions to apply for funding from the Bretton Woods institutions and other financial bodies.

The World Bank conducted a major poverty assessment in 2000, with an aim to establish a poverty reduction program and provided credits totaling close to U.S. $200 million. The Asian Development Bank gave U.S. $120 million for agricultural, education, and health care reform, while Islamic Devel-

opment Bank representatives and the Coordination Group of Arab Foundations committed funds for health and infrastructure projects. China contributed some U.S. $700,000 for military technical support.

United Nations

In spite of grievously flawed elections, the unfulfilled peace agreement, and a precarious security situation, the United Nations Mission of Observers to Tajikistan (UNMOT) terminated its mandate on May 15. UNMOT's support for rushed elections at the expense of human rights goals and long-term political stability seemed at least partially designed to justify the peacekeeping mission's premature exit from the country. This haste to withdraw was illustrated by the closure of its field offices, whose personnel had been tasked with overseeing and monitoring the parliamentary elections, even before the runoff votes had been held. UNMOT was replaced by a U.N. Tajikistan Office of Peace Building (UNTOP), manned in Dushanbe by only a handful of international staff members.

Organization for Security and Cooperation in Europe (OSCE)

In 2000 a Khujand field office was added to those already in place in Shaartuz, Dusti, and Kurgan-Tiube, while an OSCE presence was maintained in Garm by a local staff member. The mission led a joint U.N.-OSCE election observation team for the February parliamentary elections and produced a comprehensive report which noted that the elections failed to meet minimum democratic standards. Noteworthy initiatives included a high-profile intervention on behalf of a prisoner facing capital punishment, a sentence later commuted to imprisonment, and access to prisons by the mission.

The Republic of Uzbekistan

The first official service flight in nine years flew once between Dushanbe and Tashkent in August but was canceled when later in that same month Uzbek-Tajik relations soured following clashes between Islamic insurgents and government troops in

Uzbekistan and Kyrgyzstan. Uzbekistan subsequently sealed its borders with Tajikistan, and a visa regime between the two countries became effective in September.

Russian Federation

Russia kept a firm military presence in Tajikistan through its 201st Motorized Rifle Division, the thousands-strong Russian Border Forces, and a permanent Russian military base in Khujand, and through support for antiterrorist and anti-drug trafficking activities. Russia threatened to conduct air strikes against alleged Chechen training bases in Afghanistan. Russia failed to use its military ties to encourage measures to curb the lawless and abusive practices of the Tajik security forces.

United States

Although United States Embassy international staff were relocated in September 1998 to Almaty for security reasons, the "suspended operations" status of the U.S. embassy was lifted in late 1999, and United States embassy personnel based in Almaty traveled regularly to Dushanbe. The U.S. Agency for International Development's budget for Central Asia suffered close to a 30 percent cut, and the agency elaborated a strategy to collaborate mainly with in-country NGOs and local government, particularly in the areas of health and environment. The State Department's *Country Reports on Human Rights Practices for 1999* provided an unbiased and in general accurate review of the sorry state of human rights in Tajikistan.

Relevant Human Rights Watch Reports:

Freedom of Expression Still Threatened, 11/99

TURKEY

Human Rights Developments

The Turkish government made almost no progress on key human rights reforms in 2000, and failed to take advantage of the opportunity presented by a marked reduction in armed violence by illegal organizations. This was in spite of the strong incentive coming from the European Union, which offered long-awaited recognition to Turkey as a candidate for membership, subject to its meeting human rights conditions. While the government procrastinated, politicians and writers were prosecuted and imprisoned for expressing their nonviolent opinions, and detainees in police custody remained at risk of ill-treatment, torture, or death in custody. A reduction in political violence contributed to a decrease in the overall volume of abuses. There were fewer deaths in custody, suggesting that public and international pressure may have had some inhibiting effect on police interrogators.

The military, still an overriding force in politics, was a factor in holding back change, particularly with regard to freedom of expression. The army publicly aired its views on a wide range of non-military issues, including the selection of presidential candidates, and justified these intrusions by reference to its purported role as guardian of the republic against separatism and religious fundamentalism.

The government, trapped between powerful conservative elements within the state and demands that Turkey fulfil its human rights commitments, equivocated, trying to please both sides. In late 1999, for example, it temporarily released Akin Birdal, imprisoned for a speech he gave while president of the Turkish Human Rights Association, and issued an amnesty for imprisoned and prosecuted journalists; both actions seemed designed to avoid official embarrassment at the E.U. Helsinki Summit in December. Akin Birdal was rearrested in early March, and prosecutions of journalists resumed and continued throughout 2000.

In December 1999 Turkey was finally recognized as an E.U. candidate, but the opening of formal negotiations was conditional on satisfaction of human rights criteria. Apparently inspired by this, an excellent program of urgent reforms was announced in January by the then State Minister with

Responsibility for Human Rights Mehmet Ali Irtemcelik, but little of the program was actually implemented. In August Turkey signed the International Covenant on Civil and Political Rights (ICCPR) and the International Covenant on Economic, Social and Cultural Rights (ICESCR), but the government indicated that significant reservations might be attached to Turkey's ratification of the covenants.

Six provinces in the southeast of Turkey remained under state of emergency legislation. In 1999 the Kurdistan Workers' Party (PKK) declared that it would abandon armed activities in Turkey, thus reducing the armed turbulence, particularly in the southeast, although some units of the PKK continued sporadic attacks, and there were some clashes between security forces and PKK groups withdrawing to Northern Iraq. Other illegal organizations, including the Workers and Peasants' Army of Turkey (TIKKO), the Islamic Raiders of the Big East-Front (IBDA-C) and the Revolutionary People's Liberation Party/Front (DHKP/C), continued their armed activities. Nevertheless, the number of clashes diminished considerably. The Anatolia News Agency reported in May that armed incidents had decreased from 3,300 in 1994, to 1,436 in 1995, to 488 in 1999, to eighteen in the first five months of 2000.

Bülent Ecevit, leader of the Democratic Left Party (DSP) and prime minister since November 1998, continued in office, leading a coalition of the extreme right wing National Action Party (MHP) and the center right ANAP (Motherland Party). In May, Ahmet Necdet Sezer was elected president of the republic, replacing Suleyman Demirel, who was nearing the end of his term. Sezer, a judge and former president of the Constitutional Court, had made a series of speeches calling for the constitution and legal system of Turkey to be "cleansed" of their repressive features. He sustained this theme in his inaugural speech in which he said the Turkey could not "meet the demands of a modern society without abandoning the structure and regulations that bring to mind a police state."

Unfortunately, government ministers who applauded his speech took no steps to dismantle the battery of laws that restrict freedom of expression and inhibit political life. Political parties risked closure if they conflicted with the official line on the role of religion and ethnicity in politics. At this writing, the religious Virtue Party (Fazilet) and the mainly Kurdish People's Democracy Party (HADEP) were both subject to pending actions for closure in the Constitutional Court. Local HADEP organizations were subject to harassment with members being arbitrarily detained and frequently ill-treated. In February, Feridun Çelik, mayor of Diyarbakir; Selim Özalp, mayor of Siirt; and Feyzullah Karaaslan, mayor of Bingöl, were detained and ill-treated during five days of incommunicado detention. They were remanded to prison but released after four days in response to international pressure.

Although Turkish media and politicians furiously debate many issues and openly criticize the government, those who contradict the official line on the role of ethnicity, religion, or the military in politics risk prosecution and imprisonment. In July a one-year sentence imposed on former prime minister Necmettin Erbakan for a speech he made in March 1994 was confirmed by the Supreme Court. Erbakan was charged under article 312 of the Turkish Criminal Code with "incitement to hatred on grounds of race or religion" although his speech contained no advocacy of hatred or violence. Criticism of the government's exclusion from higher education of women who wear the Islamic headscarf resulted in a one-year prison sentence for Hasan Celal Guzel, former Education Minister and leader of the Rebirth Party.

Such convictions under article 312 of the Turkish Criminal Code also triggered bans on participation in politics or civil society. Government efforts to reform or abolish article 312 were blocked by the military: Minister of Justice Hikmet Sami Türk explicitly acknowledged the chief of general staff's opposition to amendment of article 312.

Article 312, however, was only one of many laws that inhibited freedom of expression. Prison sentences were also handed down under article 155 for "alienating the people from the institution of military service," article 159 for "insulting state institutions," and article 8 of the Anti-Terror Law for "separatist" statements.

The campaign to restrict the wearing of headscarves for religious reasons in educational settings or on state premises continued unabated, strongly supported by the Office of the Chief of General Staff. This campaign, waged in the name of secularism, resulted in thousands of devout Muslim women being temporarily or permanently denied access to education, while others were suspended or discharged from employment in teaching or health care.

Many cases of torture and ill-treatment were reported by detainees accused of theft and other common criminal offenses as well as those interrogated under the Anti-Terror Law. Blindfolding continued to be routine. Incommunicado detention, condemned by U.N. and Council of Europe specialists as a major factor in torture, was not abolished. There was one reported death in custody.

In recent years, reports by the European Committee for the Prevention of Torture (CPT) and the U.N. special rapporteur on torture have confirmed the widespread nature of torture in Turkey. In May 2000 the Human Rights Commission of the Turkish Parliament issued six long and detailed reports documenting the persistence of torture. A seventh was published in October. Based on hundreds of interviews conducted during unannounced visits to police stations in the provinces of Istanbul, Batman, Erzincan, Erzurum, Sanliurfa and Tunceli, the commission's work was a model of parliamentary supervision.

In March 2000 the Human Rights Commission interviewed a number of juveniles at the Bakirkoy Prison for Women and Children who had been held at various police stations in Istanbul in the preceding weeks and who described being stripped naked and subjected to electric shocks, hosing with cold water under pressure, beating with a truncheon, *falaka* (beating on the soles of the feet), and being forced to stand for hours in a chest-high barrel of water. One fourteen-year-old described being interrogated under torture for eight days at Kadikoy Yeldegirmeni Police Station, and told the commission where they could find pickaxe handles used for beating the soles of detainees' feet. When the commission later went to the police station, the instruments were found just as the youngster had indicated.

On the basis of leads given by young people interviewed at Bakirkoy Women and Children's prison, the commission went to Istanbul's Kucukkoy Police Station, located an apparatus used to suspend detainees by the arms, photographed it, and handed the photographs over as evidence for judicial proceedings. At the same police station the commission was told that a room with a locked door was "an unused storage room" to which the key had been lost. The commission members broke a panel of the door and peered through to find "all of the walls, including the door, were covered with yellow sponge, in order to give sound insulation.... Almost all of the children who had told the Commission that they had been tortured at this police station had described this room covered in yellow foam." There were "lost keys" and soundproofed interrogation rooms in other police stations and provinces as well.

There were no verified reports of "disappearance," but the authorities continued to ignore demands for investigation of the pattern of "disappearances" from the mid-1990s. The European Court of Human Rights continued to investigate outstanding cases. In June the court found the Turkish government responsible for the 1994 "disappearance" of Abdulvahap Timurtas after his detention by gendarmes in Silopi, Sirnak Province.

Tension increased in the prison system as Sincan F-Type Prison, the first of a new generation of high security facilities, reached completion. The new prisons consisted of one- and three-person cells rather than the large wards that were traditional in the Turkish prison system. Prisoners held under the Anti-Terror Law were alarmed that they were about to be moved into a regime of intense isolation under article 16 of that law. A number of prisoners at Kartal Special Type Prison in Istanbul are already held in small group isolation characterized by a limited and monotonous physical and social environment with no out-of-cell time, in clear violation of international prison standards.

In June, in the wake of protests by rights groups, including Human Rights Watch, lawyers were told that clients held at Kartal Special Type Prison would be allowed access to the library and sports facilities in groups of five or ten, but this was not implemented. In July the CPT visited Turkey and examined Sincan F-Fype Prison, but as of October its findings had not been published.

In October, the Ministry of Justice published a draft law abolishing mandatory solitary or small-group isolation for prisoners held under the Anti-Terror Law.

In July a group of prisoners at Burdur Prison refused to attend court hearings in protest against the planned implementation of F-type prisons. Gendarmes who entered the prison to suppress the protest beat and injured male and female prisoners. Medical reports issued by Burdur State Hospital indicated that prisoners were suffering from burns and broken limbs and ribs, and that female prisoners had complained of being raped with objects. The arm of one prisoner, Veli Sacilik, was torn off by an excavator used to break into the ward. The Ministry of Justice made a public statement that prisoners had resisted security forces who "took care to apply only such force as was necessary to break the resistance, using modern equipment rather than firearms, and to end the riot without causing any damage."

Although Turkey retained the death penalty and courts continued to hand down death sentences, the sixteenth successive year passed without judicial executions. In June the prime minister and the minister of justice expressed personal opposition to the death penalty and called for its abolition, regretting that there was not unanimity on this issue within the coalition government.

By retaining a geographic limitation to its ratification of the 1951 U.N. Convention relating to the Status of Refugees, Turkey refuses to recognize any asylum seekers as refugees unless they come from Europe and therefore continued to be a hazardous destination for asylum seekers, most of whom are Iranian and Iraqi. In May nine Bangladeshi, Afghan, and Pakistani asylum seekers were shot dead by Turkish security forces as they crossed the border at Dogubayazit, near Agri in eastern Turkey.

Although illegal armed organizations carried out fewer attacks on civilians, in three separate incidents in August, Bektaþ Kaya and Sadik Kaya, both village officials, and Hamdi Sahin, a villager, were abducted and killed in Tokat province. The Workers and Peasants' Army of Turkey (TIKKO) was believed to be responsible for the killings.

Defending Human Rights

In a policy paper prepared as part of the E.U. accession process, the Turkish government's Special Committee on Turkey-E.U. Relations made the welcome suggestion that "the constructive function of nongovernmental organizations in raising human rights awareness should be encouraged and there should be closer cooperation and communication with them." This intention was not well reflected in practice, as members of Turkish human rights organizations were obstructed in their work in various ways ranging from ill-treatment to prosecution. Public demonstrations and press conferences on human rights issues were repeatedly prohibited by local officials or broken up by police, sometimes violently.

The Diyarbakir and Van branches of the Human Rights Association (HRA) and the Malatya branch of the Association of Human Rights and Solidarity for Oppressed Peoples (Mazlum-Der) were closed for much of the year by order of local governors or the governor of the Emergency Region.

The governor of the Emergency Region prevented a delegation of the Diyarbakir Democracy Platform, a group of civil society organizations, from crossing the border with northern Iraq where they hoped to investigate the killing of an estimated forty civilians during the Turkish armed forces' bombing of

Lolan, Kendakor region, in northern Iraq in August.

The Role of the International Community

Council of Europe

The Council of Europe monitored Turkey through its political, investigative, and judicial bodies.

The European Court of Human Rights found Turkey responsible for "disappearance," extrajudicial execution, death in custody, torture, and suppression of freedom of expression in twelve new decisions.

No report on the CPT's July mission to Turkey had been published as of October 2000. This mission's stated priority was to examine the current changes in the prison system. Reports on visits could only be published with the consent of the government in question, and in Turkey's case, reports on eight visits remain unpublished.

European Union

The development of an Accession Partnership Agreement proved an unparalleled opportunity for domestic and international pressure for positive change. Consequently, the European Commission and the European Parliament were in close contact with Turkish authorities and Turkish civil society and followed human rights developments with intense interest. For most of the year the E.U.'s public and private commentary mainly consisted of expressions of frustration at the loss of momentum and the sluggardly pace of reform. In April E.U. Enlargement Commissioner Günter Verheugen told the Turkish foreign minister: "With some concern, we have unfortunately noted that not much progress has been made since Helsinki." The Turkish-European Joint Parliamentary Commission echoed this observation in its June statement.

The particular emphasis that the European Union places on minority rights in Turkey was a cause of friction. In September, the Turkish Foreign Ministry expressed irritation that the European Parliament on releasing an aid package of 135 million euros (U.S. $117 million) to Turkey had proposed linking the funds to progress on Kurdish cultural rights and the economy in the southeast.

United States

The State Department's *Country Report on Human Rights Practices* for Turkey in 1999 fully reflected the scale of violations and official interference in political and public life. The report detailed many cases of people imprisoned for expressing their nonviolent opinions, and of torture and arbitrary killing, and accurately documented the impunity that protected the perpetrators of violations. Senior government officials publicly called for progress on human rights. In January, in response to a congressional letter, President Clinton expressed support for language rights and an interest in the Kurdish minority. Consistent with this, there was a strong reaction to the arrest of the HADEP mayors in March.

In July, the Turkish government announced that U.S. helicopter manufacturer Bell Textron won the contract for 145 attack helicopters, a sale worth an estimated four billion dollars. This class of equipment has been used to commit human rights violations in Turkey, including "disappearances" and arbitrary killings, and the sale is subject to congressional approval. A congressional debate was not expected before 2001. Rights groups protested the pending sale and pressed the U.S. government to ensure at least that effective systems be put in place to ensure end-use monitoring of this equipment.

Relevant Human Rights Watch Reports:

Human Rights and the European Union Accession Partnership, 9/00

Small Group Isolation in Turkish Prisons: An Avoidable Disaster, 5/00

TURKMENISTAN

Human Rights Developments

As his cult of personality soared to new heights, President Saparmurad Niazov continued to crack down on political and religious dissidents, to restrict freedom of the press and of movement, and to eliminate even the trappings of democracy.

Turkmenistan defaulted upon its international commitments on political reform when at the end of 1999 its Parliament voted to remove term limits for the presidency, opening the way for Niazov to remain in the presidency indefinitely. Parliamentary elections, held in November, were neither free nor fair.

In August, police prevented two hundred village women from entering the capital where they intended to take their grievances directly to the president, according to the Moscow-based Information Center for Human Rights in Central Asia.

At the end of 1999, Turkmenistan abolished the death penalty, in one of several measures promoted by President Niazov to further human rights protection. In May, a law was passed "on banning searches in the homes of Turkmenistan's citizens" without judicial authorization. Niazov said the law responded to a reality in which law enforcement officials "could plant one or two grams of drugs or other things in some of those houses they were searching in order to take vengeance on people, and many people are being harmed in this case." Another decree reaffirmed the inviolability of private property, despite a continuing spate of official confiscations of private homes. Niazov also established a special "commission for ensuring legality."

Security forces arrested longtime political activist Nurberdi Nurmamedov, leader of the banned opposition political party Agzybirlik (Unity), on January 5. Nurmamedov was sentenced in February to five years in prison on fabricated charges of "hooliganism." Faced with the threat of a prison sentence for his son, who was also arrested, Nurmamedov was forced to make a televised request for the president's forgiveness. The KNB (State Security Committee, formerly the KGB) officials demanded that Nurmamedov's family state publicly that his case was not political, but "a purely criminal matter." The Information Center for Human Rights in Central Asia reported that Nurmamedov and two fellow political prisoners, Mukhametkuli Aimuradov and Pirikuli Tangrykuliev, underwent severe beatings in September.

Minority rights suffered in 2000 when the president issued new restrictions on the use of Russian for official business. Reportedly, the number of Russian speakers seeking to leave Turkmenistan increased significantly this year. The output of Uzbek language print and broadcast media for Turkmenistan's sizeable Uzbek minority in the east of the country also reportedly shrank.

An ominous June decree ordered the National Security Committee and other state agencies to maintain "strict control" over the movements of foreigners in the country. At least one foreign journalist was questioned by the KNB. In August, KNB officials contacted Radio Liberty stringer Saparmurad Ovezberdiev, whose activities had already been closely monitored, to tell him that he could no longer report for RFE/RL because he lacked accreditation, despite the permission granted by the Ministry of Foreign Affairs for RFE journalists to work there.

Turkmenistan became one of the world's strictest censors of the Internet when on May 29, the country's communications ministry unilaterally revoked the licenses of all five private internet service providers (ISPs), forcing all Internet use to run through the state monopoly provider.

The 1997 amendments to the Law on Religion, which effectively ban religious denominations aside from Sunni Islam and Russian Orthodoxy remained in force, though Turkmenistan bowed to international pressure and promised to halt police raids on prayer meetings conducted in private homes. Turkmenistan continued to imprison religious believers, dismiss them from their jobs, confiscate religious materials, and destroy houses of worship. On November 13, 1999, Turkmen security forces bulldozed Ashgabat's Seventh-Day Adventist Church. Also in November, authorities rejected the application of the Turkmen Bible Society for registration, though the group reportedly met all of the official requirements.

In December, police and security officials detained Dmitrii Melnichenko and Mikhail Kozlov and beat, threatened, and tortured them in order to obtain information about the whereabouts of two Baptist pastors who were later deported. Police the same month raided Baptist churches in Turkmenabad (Chardjou), Mary, Turkmenbashi, and Ashgabat. Repression of protestant Christian groups appeared to have intensified in February, when the KNB raided several religious meetings held by protestant groups in private homes, and several in the congregation were subsequently fired from their jobs, according to the Keston Institute. Also in February, police sealed the premises of a building bought by Baptists for use as a house of worship in the town of Mary, and confiscated all of the religious literature inside. In October, local KNB arrested Seventh Day Adventist pastor Pavel Fedotov at a bible reading in Chardjou, charging him with holding an unsanctioned meeting and confiscating videotapes and other articles. He was released several days later.

By early in the year, Turkmen police had reportedly expelled the last remaining Russian Baptist missionaries in the country. Authorities forced the family of imprisoned Turkmen Baptist pastor Shahgildy Atakov into internal exile, while his brother was imprisoned on trumped-up administrative charges for fifteen days in March.

Muslim as well as Christian religious dissidents fell victim to persecution this year. In February, Turkmen authorities arrested Khoja Ahmed Orazgylych and charged him with unspecified economic crimes, in retaliation for his broadcast criticism on Radio Liberty's Turkmen service of the president's pronouncements on religion. While in custody, a letter purportedly signed by Orazgylych that begged the forgiveness of the president was published in the newspapers. The president publicly threatened to imprison the seventy-two-year-old Islamic scholar for twenty-five years, but on March 3, the president "commuted" Orazgylych's punishment to internal exile for an undefined term (no evidence is publicly available that any judicial proceeding ever took place). That very day, security forces removed Orazgylych and his family to the provincial town of Tejen and bulldozed his Ashgabat home and the mosque he had built on its grounds. President Niazov ordered all copies of Orazgylych's Turkmen translation of the Koran to be burned. In April, Niazov decreed that all Muslim religious schools, save for a select few schools run directly by the state-controlled religious authority, the Muftiat, should be closed, in effect banning private Muslim religious education. As many as three hundred foreign Islamic preachers had reportedly been deported from Turkmenistan this year.

Academic freedom and recognition of the right to education reached a new low. The president called for three-generation "background checks" to determine potential university students' "moral character" before they are admitted to study. Niazov also abolished his country's World Languages University, ordered that the entire printing of a new Turkmen history textbook be burned, and decreed that foreign languages should no longer be taught in schools.

Defending Human Rights

Turkmenistan allows no domestic non-governmental human rights organizations to exist. Nina Shmeleva, fifty-seven, a journalist and activist of the unregistered Russian Community of Turkmenistan who had attempted to assist ethnic Russians trying to emigrate from Turkmenistan, was forced to confess to "financial fraud" and was sentenced in May to five years in prison (her sentence was later reduced to a six-year probation).

The Role of the International Community

Organization for Security and Cooperation in Europe (OSCE)

The OSCE pointedly refused to send even a scaled-down mission to observe Turkmenistan's parliamentary elections in December, and denounced the arrest of Nurberdi Nurmamedov. Its representative on freedom of the media criticized the life-presidency. Chairman-in-Office Benita Ferrero-Waldner visited Turkmenistan in May for talks on security, economics, the environment, and human rights, and invited Turkmenistan to participate in a multilateral project on resolving disputes over water use in the region, sponsored by the OSCE's Office of Democratic Institutions and Human Rights (ODIHR), the European Community, and the World Bank, an offer President Niazov promptly rejected. For the third year in a row, Turkmenistan refused to sign a substantive Memorandum of Understanding with the ODIHR, one of the conditions under which the OSCE had agreed to establish its Ashgabat office.

European Union

In November 1999 the European Union (E.U.) signed an Interim Agreement, extending full trade benefits to Turkmenistan, rendering almost meaningless the continued suspension on human rights grounds of the Partnership and Cooperation Agreement ratification process. The E.U. also praised Turkmenistan's abolition of the death penalty, though its statement at the U.N. Commission on Human Rights session in March noted that human rights observance was "deteriorating."

United States

While the U.S. criticized high profile abuses, such as the arrest of Nurmamedov, statements were frequently delayed or downplayed so as not to interfere with negotiations on Turkmenistan's participation in the planned TransCaspian natural gas pipeline. The Clinton Administration ignored the recommendations of the U.S. government's Commission on International Religious Freedom to designate Turkmenistan as a country of particular concern, a step that could have triggered sanctions.

European Bank for Reconstruction and Development (EBRD)

After President Niazov refused to meet a visiting EBRD delegation, the bank announced in April that it would halt all public sector lending to that country, citing Turkmenistan's refusal to implement "principles of multi-party democracy, pluralism and market economics," as required by the bank's charter. The bank had earlier cancelled a planned U.S. $50 million investment to upgrade one of the country's main highways.

UNITED KINGDOM/ NORTHERN IRELAND

Human Rights Developments

In accordance with the 1998 Multi-Party Agreement, the British parliament devolved power to the new executive and assembly for Northern Ireland in December 1999. In February 2000, these institutions were suspended and direct rule by Westminster was reimposed when disagreements among political parties and paramilitary groups stymied the process of decommissioning weapons. After a favorable subsequent report by a decommissioning panel, the executive and assembly were reinstated in May. The agreement was threatened again during July and August when internal feuding among loyalist paramilitary organizations led to three killings, putting the loyalist cease-fire into question. Despite political setbacks, reforms dealing with human rights under the agreement—including police reform and a criminal justice system review—proceeded, albeit with some disappointing outcomes. Other issues of concern included new antiterrorism legislation; government stalling on establishing independent judicial inquiries into the murders of two human rights lawyers; and impunity for police abuse.

The draft legislation to implement the 1999 Patten Commission report on police reform failed to incorporate several key provisions of the report, in particular Patten's call for a policing service with human rights protections at its core. As of October 2000, the draft bill departed significantly from the recommendations addressing the crucial issue of police accountability mechanisms and the creation of a new name and symbols for the Royal Ulster Constabulary (RUC), Northern Ireland's police force. These departures threatened future recruitment of traditionally excluded groups—primarily Nationalists and Catholics—to the service.

Patten called for the police ombudsman—which replaced the ineffective Independent Commission for Police Complaints—to have the power to investigate and comment upon police policies and practice and have access to past reports on police conduct. The ombudsman's remit was limited to the investigation of individual complaints only and access to government documents was restricted. In a separate move to hold the chief constable accountable, the Patten Commission envisioned a civilian Police Board with authority to establish inquiries and to call for reports on policing matters. The proposed bill placed several important restrictions on the board's authority, however. In May 2000, Thomas Constantine, former head of the U.S. Drug Enforcement Agency, was appointed oversight commissioner for police reform. While the report envisioned a proactive commissioner with a key role in setting objectives in the reform process, the delay in Constantine's appointment and the bill's provisions suggested that the U.K. government saw a much narrower role for the post. The bill also failed to incorporate the recommendation that the name of the force be neutralized to Police Service of Northern Ireland. The bill proposed that the force's name be changed to "Police Service of Northern Ireland (incorporating Royal Ulster Constabulary)" on all title documents, causing nationalist and republican political parties to accuse the British government of bad faith. The bill went back to the House of Commons in the late fall for a final reading.

The Criminal Justice Review in its March 2000 report failed to address the effect of emergency laws on the criminal justice system; to consider new judicial arrangements, or the limited capacity of existing ones; to address human rights issues arising from passage of the 1998 Human Rights Act and the proposed Bill of Rights; and to include an independent oversight element, relying solely on the government for the report's implementation. The report recommended the establishment of a Judicial Appointments Commission; a bench more "reflective" of Northern Ireland's population; the creation of a new prosecution service; and the appointment of an attorney general. Human rights groups criticized the report for avoiding an accountability mechanism for past and pending cases.

In October 2000, the 1998 Human Rights Act, incorporating the European Convention on Human Rights (ECHR), went into force throughout the U.K. with a derogation from article 6 (fair trial standards) intact.

The Terrorism Act 2000—permanent, U.K.-wide, anti-terrorism legislation replacing emergency laws concerning political violence—became law in July and will come into force in spring 2001. The act extended, for up to five years, most of the emergency powers that applied in Northern Ireland, including retention of non-jury Diplock courts for certain political offenses; a lower standard of admissibility for confession evidence than in the criminal courts; the admissibility of statements by a senior police officer coupled with a suspect's remaining silent as evidence that a suspect belonged to an illegal organization (for example, a paramilitary group); and police and army powers of arrest, entry, search, and seizure without a warrant.

The Human Rights Commission Bill became law in the Republic of Ireland in June 2000. The Irish commission's creation, coupled with the March 1999 inauguration of the Northern Ireland Human Rights Commission, paved the way for the future establishment of a joint committee of representatives from the two commissions, tasked by the Multi-Party Agreement with the consideration of human rights concerns in all of Ireland.

In September, the family of murdered Belfast lawyer Patrick Finucane met with Prime Minister Tony Blair to press for an independent public inquiry into his killing by loyalist paramilitaries in 1989. The family stepped up efforts to establish an inquiry since new evidence was presented to the British and Irish governments in February 1998 and in an updated report in February 2000. The Finucane family and rights organizations accused the British government of using the June 1999 arrest and pending prosecution of William Stobie—charged with aiding and abetting the Finucane murderers—to stall the establishment of an inquiry.

No person was charged with the March 1999 loyalist paramilitary car bomb murder of human rights lawyer Rosemary Nelson. Citing earlier police intimidation of Nelson, human rights organizations continued to call for an independent judicial inquiry into the killing. The director of public prosecutions (DPP) decided in January 2000 not to prosecute criminally the police officers that harassed Rosemary Nelson. In May 2000, the Independent Commission for Police Complaints (ICPC) decided not to take disciplinary action against any of the officers.

The coroner for Greater Belfast decided in June 2000 not to hold an inquest into the death of Robert Hamill, who was brutally assaulted by a loyalist mob in Portadown in April 1997 and subsequently died from his injuries. Hamill's assault occurred twenty yards from a Land Rover containing four armed RUC officers. One person was convicted of "causing an affray" in the incident, but no person had been convicted of the murder, despite an investigation by the ICPC and consideration by the DPP. The coroner concluded that concerns for the safety of witnesses outweighed the imperative for an inquest. In June, the Irish government backed the call by human rights groups for an inquiry.

The Bloody Sunday Inquiry—a new tribunal of inquiry into the British army killings of fourteen men in Derry on January 30, 1972—opened in March. The original tribunal, finding the army not liable for any of the deaths, was discredited.

In December 1999, Castlereagh Holding Centre, notorious for the physical and psychological ill-treatment of political suspects, was closed.

David Adams' application for judicial review—which sought to challenge the DPP's decision not to prosecute the police officers responsible for brutally assaulting Adams in Castlereagh Holding Centre in 1994—was denied in June 2000. The application also sought judicial review of the DPP's failure to give Adams reasons for the decision not to prosecute, particularly as the decision came after a civil court judgment supporting Adams' version of the attack. In September, it was reported that one officer would face a minor disciplinary charge of "willful or careless falsehood."

Defending Human Rights

In July 2000, the police informed civil rights lawyer, Padraigin Drinan, that she was under threat from loyalist paramilitaries. Drinan succeeded Rosemary Nelson as the lawyer for the Garvaghy Road Residents Association. After significant delays, the government provided Drinan with assistance to fortify her home and protect her person.

The Role of the International Community

United Nations

In a February 2000 report, the U.N. special rapporteur on freedom of expression urged the U.K. to repeal emergency laws that had a "chilling effect" on the right to free expression; protect journalists' confidential sources; amend the Official Secrets Act to allow penalties for disclosure only when a legitimate national security interest is implicated; and disclose classified information to the public—in particular, the findings of the Stalker/Sampson and Stevens inquiries into collusion.

The U.N. special rapporteur on the independence of judges and lawyers reiterated his call for an independent judicial inquiry into the murder of Patrick Finucane. Noting inconsistencies regarding the murder's previous investigation, the special rapporteur stated that "such inconsistencies... generally arise in cases where there have been cover-ups by interested parties, including State organs."

Council of Europe

In April, the European Court of Human Rights (ECHR) ruled admissible four cases against the U.K. The cases of Gervaise McKerr, Patrick Shanaghan, the Loughgall eight, and Pearse Jordan charged violations of the right to life, the inadequacy and partiality of mechanisms to investigate killings by state agents or where collusion is alleged, and discrimination.

A June 2000 ECHR decision in the case of Gerard Magee found the U.K in breach of fair trial standards for denying Magee access to a lawyer for the first forty-eight hours of detention, holding him virtually incommunicado, and creating a "psychologically coercive" interrogation environment that forced Magee to make incriminating statements against himself.

United States

On September 13, President Clinton met with First Minister David Trimble and Deputy First Minister Seamus Mallon in the first visit to the U.S. by the leaders of Northern Ireland's new government. Clinton expressed his ongoing support for the peace process.

The U.S. House of Representatives International Relations Committee recommended in September a congressional resolution demanding the full implementation of the Patten recommendations on police reform.

The Commission on Security and Cooperation in Europe (CSCE) held a hearing in March on the protection of human rights defenders in Northern Ireland and called for independent inquiries into the Finucane and Nelson murders. The CSCE held another hearing on policing in Northern Ireland in September.

The U.S. State Department's *Country Reports on Human Rights Practices for 1999* provided a fair assessment of human rights concerns in Northern Ireland, noting police abuse and impunity; intimidation of defense lawyers; emergency laws and abuse of special powers; and calls for a ban on plastic bullets.

Relevant Human Rights Watch Reports:

Northern Ireland: A New Beginning to Policing? The Report of the Independent Commission on Policing, 11/99

UZBEKISTAN

Human Rights Developments

The government of President Islam Karimov continued its unrelenting campaign against pious Muslims who practiced their religion outside state controls. State authorities punished independent Muslims with discriminatory arrest, incommunicado detention, torture, and prison sentences of up to twenty years for violations of strict laws on religion and alleged "anti-constitutional activity." Police regularly threatened and harassed relatives of independent Muslims. Sham parliamentary and presidential elections deprived citizens of their right to political participation. When conflict broke out between armed insurgents opposed to the Karimov regime and the governments of Kyrgyzstan and Uzbekistan, civilians were displaced by the fighting, kidnapped by the armed opposition forces, and killed by landmines placed by Uzbek troops. Authorities continued to impose obstacles to abused women's attempts to obtain justice for domestic abuse and were allegedly complicit in trafficking women and girls. The government retained tight control over the media.

The government branded those with

dissenting views "enemies of the state" and added hundreds of Muslims to the thousands already imprisoned for their religious beliefs. Members of the Islamic organization Hizb ut-Tahrir (Party of Liberation) were arrested for unregistered religious activity, a crime in Uzbekistan, and possession or distribution of literature not approved by the state. The government expanded its fierce campaign against independent Muslims in 2000 by detaining, arresting, and torturing relatives of pious Muslims. Police regularly harassed and threatened relatives of men convicted of religious offenses, while arresting the relatives of men being sought, and threatening to hold them until the suspects turned themselves in or were captured. Police arrested twenty-three-year-old Nilufar Hokimova and twenty-one-year-old Nafisa Aboskhodjaeva, who were sentenced to six years in prison for "Wahabism" and alleged anti-state activity when they attempted to leave the country following the arrest, torture, and conviction of their husbands. Authorities compelled female relatives to sign documents attesting that they did not attend any illegal gatherings and placed many under a form of house arrest during holidays and elections. Police and local authorities also organized "hate rallies" reminiscent of the Stalin era, in which hundreds of neighbors and officials gathered to denounce publicly relatives of pious Muslims as traitors and "enemies of the state" and to demand a vow of contrition. Among those subjected to this treatment were relatives of the well-known independent Imam Obidhon Qori Nazarov, who was believed to have gone into hiding in March 1998.

Dozens of people accused of being followers of Imam Nazarov were arrested, adding to the hundreds of former attendees of his Tashkent mosque already in prison on fabricated charges.

Two former imams of official government mosques who had been linked to Nazarov, who were arrested earlier and released in 1999, were rearrested in 2000. Imam Abdurahim Abdurahmonov, a former student of Imam Nazarov who suffered from permanent injuries from torture in custody in 1998, was released under a 1998 presidential amnesty and then rearrested on charges of narcotics possession in 1999. Authorities released him in September 1999, following a successful appeal. In 2000, he was again arrested and, in a grossly unfair trial, sentenced to seventeen years in prison on charges of "association with terrorists." Fellow religious leader Imam Abduwahid Yuldashev, who was conditionally released in 1999 after police torture, was rearrested on July 24, 2000. As of October 2000, he was still being held incommunicado in a basement cell in Tashkent and, like many others this year, had been denied legal representation. A lawyer who saw him in detention reported that police beat him with a truncheon in his presence to force him to turn down the lawyer's services. Investigators were reportedly preparing to charge Imam Nazarov's former deputy with "Wahabism" and "spreading jihad ideas."

The police practice of planting narcotics and a small number of bullets on observant Muslim detainees was replaced in part by a new pattern in which police planted banned religious leaflets on independent Muslims, charging them with opposing the constitution and participating in unregistered religious activities. Some detainees were sent to prison for up to twenty years on such charges. Members of Hizb ut-Tahrir claimed some 4,000 of their co-religionists had been arrested since late 1998, the majority in 1999. Human Rights Watch and other rights groups documented the conviction of several hundred members of the group in 2000 for engaging in unsanctioned meetings, teaching religion and praying in private, and possession and distribution of literature not cleared by state censors.

Citizens of Uzbekistan were once again denied their right to endeavor to participate in the political system and to change their government peacefully. Parliamentary elections held in December 1999 and presidential elections in January 2000 were neither free nor fair. No genuine opposition political parties were registered, there was no opportunity to air views via the mass media, and no possibility to exercise freedom of assembly or association. An Organization for Security and Cooperation in Europe/Office of Democratic Institutions and Human Rights (OSCE/ODIHR) mission sent to Uzbekistan to assess the pre-election environment in the run up to the parliamentary race declared that conditions "fell short of the OSCE commitments for democratic elections," citing inadequate laws and regulations, direct government interference in the election process, and the absence of fundamental freedoms as among the obstacles. Agence France-Presse reported that President Karimov said after the vote, "The OSCE focuses only on establishment of democracy, the protection of human rights and the freedom of the press. I am now questioning these values."

In January 2000, Soviet-style presidential elections made a mockery of the democratic system. President Karimov claimed support from 91.9 percent of the electorate, which included a vote from his nominal opponent in the race. The U.S. government declared the election "neither free nor fair" and said it "offered Uzbekistan's voters no true choice." The OSCE abstained from sending observers because of the lack of competition.

A violent challenge to Karimov's rule came in early August 2000 when pitched battles erupted between armed insurgents and government troops in southeastern Uzbekistan and neighboring Kyrgyzstan. Tohir Yuldash, political leader of the so-called Islamic Movement of Uzbekistan (IMU), claimed responsibility for the attacks. The IMU demanded that the Uzbek government release what the group claimed were an estimated 100,000 wrongfully jailed Muslim prisoners and allow for the observance of Islamic law precepts, including permission for Muslim women to wear the veil.

There were credible allegations of violations of humanitarian law by all parties to the conflict. IMU militants were accused of taking foreign civilians hostage, including at least one German citizen later released and four United States citizens who escaped after six days of captivity. Armed insurgents allegedly killed at least one Kyrgyz soldier whom they took prisoner. Other Kyrgyz and Uzbek soldiers were also captured by the militants, but no reliable information was available regarding the conditions of their confinement.

Fighting continued in southeastern Uzbekistan and sporadically in areas closer to the capital until mid-September. Uzbek authorities brought in heavy artillery and initiated a campaign of aerial bombardments from helicopters. Authorities insisted that the target areas had been cleared of civilians, who were evacuated to nearby towns away from the battle zone. However, there were reports of civilians fleeing fighting in the southeastern region of Surkhandarya and concerns regarding the indiscriminate nature of the aerial bombardments. Hundreds of mountain residents were displaced by the conflict in southeastern Uzbekistan and thousands fled the fighting in Kyrgyzstan.

Landmines allegedly laid by Uzbek troops posed a danger to mountain residents. In at least one incident, two women were reportedly killed and two others injured when they stepped on a landmine that had been placed near the Uzbek-Tajik border by the Uzbek military. Tajik officials reported that landmines killed eight civilians and wounded five others in the area in September. Uzbekistan had not signed the international treaty to ban landmines.

In November 1999, a shoot-out in the forest of the Iangiabad region outside Tashkent left over a dozen gunmen and at least three security officers dead. Government authorities claimed that the armed men were terrorists who opened fire on police officers who stumbled upon their hideout. None of the gunmen survived the exchange. At least fourteen other men were tried for alleged ties to the gunmen and were charged with conspiracy to commit terrorism, participation in an illegal groups, and "infringement of the constitutional order," and were given lengthy terms in prison. Defendant Polvanazar Khodjaev, whose father died of torture in prison in 1999, was sentenced to death. Police tortured defendants in detention and arrested some of their relatives on fabricated charges as part of a stated government policy of collective punishment. Bahodir Hasanov, the brother of one defendant, was arrested on July 17 and held incommunicado in a basement cell for forty-one days, as of October.

Police held detainees incommunicado for up to six months, regularly denying suspects access to an attorney until after the state had obtained a confession. Police and courthouse guards demanded bribes from relatives who wanted to give detainees food and medicine or sought to attend their relatives' trials.

Torture remained routine and new methods of abuse were reported in 2000. In addition to hundreds of reports of beatings and numerous accounts of the use of electric shock, temporary suffocation, hanging by the ankles or wrists, removal of fingernails, and punctures with sharp objects, Human Rights Watch received credible reports in 2000 that police sodomized male detainees with bottles, raped them, and beat and burned them in the groin area. Male and female detainees were regularly threatened with rape. Police made such threats in particular against female detainees in the presence of male relatives to force the men to sign self-incriminating statements. Police also regularly threatened to murder detainees or their family members and to place minor children in orphanages. Self-incriminating testimony obtained through torture was routinely admitted by judges, who cited this as evidence, often the only evidence, to convict. Courts did not initiate investigations into allegations of mistreatment by police.

Torture and ill-treatment in prisons was rampant, and there were several shocking reports of deaths in custody from torture in prisons. In the infamous Jaslyk prison dozens of inmates reportedly died from mistreatment and disease. There were several shocking reports of torture causing the death of detainees and prisoners. Jaloliddin Sodiqjonov was among those who reportedly died in custody from abuse by prison authorities this year, as was Numon Saidaminov. Convicted independent Muslims who allegedly died of beatings by prison guards included Maraim Alikulov, Usmanali Khamrikulov, Rustam Norbaev, Nemat Karimov, and Shukhrat Parpiev. Police would not allow relatives to view Khimatullo Khudoiberdiev's body to determine cause of death. Suspicion also surrounded the deaths of Abduaziz Rasulov, whom police claimed hanged himself in his cell, and Dilmurad Umarov, whom authorities ruled died of tuberculosis but whose body showed signs of abuse.

Prison conditions were harsh, with prisoners routinely denied adequate food, medicine, and sanitary facilities. Authorities did not inform relatives of prisoners' whereabouts for months at a time, and guards demanded bribes for deliveries of food and other necessities. Prison officials often arbitrarily extended inmates' sentences on false charges of infractions. Muslim prisoners who prayed were punished with beatings and solitary confinement. Untreated illness led to the deaths of dozens of prisoners, including Usman Inagamov, a member of Hizb ut-Tahrir who died of cancer in custody after reportedly being turned into police by official islamic authorities. Authorities continued to deny international monitors access to prison and detention facilities.

An amnesty decree issued by President Karimov in September 2000 provided for the release of certain categories of prisoners, but excluded persons convicted of "anti-constitutional activity," a charge systematically levied against observant independent Muslims. In a positive move, higher courts commuted the death sentences of several persons convicted of nonpolitical crimes. However, government officials acknowledged that they carried out executions of several Muslims convicted of involvement in a February 1999 bombing incident. The government did not release statistics on the total number of people executed.

The September 1999 release of six Christian prisoners was viewed by some outside policy makers as a sign of liberalization in Uzbekistan's treatment of Christian groups. However, the end of the year and following months saw several brutal and dramatic attacks on Christian believers. In October 1999, police in the city of Karshi raided a church meeting held by an unregistered group of Baptists. Officers detained participants in the Baptist harvest celebration, including minor children. Police beat and tortured participants in detention and sentenced two of them to ten days in prison and payment of a fine. Despite assurances that such violations would not be repeated, police continued to harass and detain Christians, and none of the officers involved in the Karshi incident were disciplined. On May 14, 2000, Tashkent police temporarily detained ten Baptists in Tashkent for conducting a private prayer meeting.

Christians who engaged in what was perceived as missionary activity, including distribution of imported literature, were reportedly detained and mistreated by police, who carried out the government's harsh law criminalizing proselytism. State authorities put Uzbeks who convert under particularly severe pressure. Several foreign nationals accused of proselytism were denied permission to return to the country. Police reportedly subjected members of the Jehovah's Witnesses to arbitrary harassment, including repeated interrogations and fines for illegal religious activity.

Despite the fanfare over his release from prison in 1999, Pentecostal pastor Rashid Turibayev from the Autonomous Republic of Karakalpakstan in Uzbekistan was reported in September 2000 to have gone into hiding from state authorities.

In early July, Uzbek law enforcement authorities reportedly violated a verbal agreement with representatives of the United Nations high commissioner for refugees when they used a confidential list of Afghan refugees awaiting placement in a third country to track the refugees down and demand that they sign a document agreeing to leave the country within five days or else face arrest and deportation. At least ten individuals were threatened in the first days of the door-to-door campaign. One man who feared torture if returned to Afghanistan reportedly went into hiding after police threatened him. UNHCR later reported that twelve refugees were placed under house arrest for one week, but that the "misunderstanding" was resolved with yet another verbal agreement between the agency and the government. Uzbekistan had not signed the 1951 Convention relating to the Status of Refugees, but is still bound by obligations under international customary law not to return refugees to a country where their life and freedom could be threatened.

Research conducted by Human Rights Watch in 2000 revealed that police discouraged women who were abused by their husbands or other family members from filing reports and failed to investigate and punish abusers when reports were made. Local authorities pressured women to remain in abusive households and attempted to dissuade women from pursuing divorce.

The International Helsinki Federation issued a report in June 2000 citing a lack of official concern as one of the causes for the growth of trafficking of women in Uzbekistan. The report noted that Uzbek law did not specifically refer to trafficking of humans as a crime and that the abduction of girls often went unreported. A U.N.-sponsored conference held in March 2000 in Tashkent cited trafficking in humans as one of the sources of instability in the region.

Children's advocates reported that the trafficking of minor children for work in the sex industry abroad continued. According to one local NGO, girls thirteen and fourteen years old were provided with false passports and sent to countries including the United Arab Emirates. The traffickers who arranged for the girls' travel and placement in prostitution in the foreign location typically paid large bribes to Uzbek law enforcement officials who agreed to look the other way.

Child victims of sexual and other physical abuse by their families were reportedly placed in state-run facilities together with juveniles accused of committing crimes. Authorities reportedly failed to provide for children's basic needs, such as clothing and soap, at the facilities. There were unconfirmed reports that guards at children's facilities raped some of the children. Police denied minors accused of violations of the state's religion law access to legal representation.

Authorities continued to deny access to

secular education for observant Muslim students who were expelled from schools and universities since 1997 for wearing religious dress. Efforts at reinstatement were unsuccessful in 2000. A student expelled from the Women's Medresseh (Islamic school) in Tashkent was detained just days later and beaten by police to force her to abandon her religious attire.

Freedom of expression continued to be severely restricted, with essentially no independent press. All but two newspapers were government-owned and required approval from the Committee for the Control of State Secrets for all published news articles. The two private newspapers primarily published advertisements and horoscopes and did not cover news. Media watchdog Internews reported increased pressure on privately owned television and radio stations from local and national authorities. Government authorities closed or blacklisted stations that covered religion or politics and prevented them from obtaining licenses.

While the majority of the country still lacked access to the Internet, the Uzbek government nevertheless placed restrictions on its use, aiming to connect all Internet service through government servers in 2000, thereby eliminating access to content the state deemed unacceptable and enabling the government to monitor citizens' communications.

Defending Human Rights

Authorities again refused to register independent rights organizations, the Human Rights Society of Uzbekistan (HRSU) and the Independent Human Rights Organization of Uzbekistan (IHROU). The Supreme Court failed to hear the appeals of rights defenders Mahbuba Kasymova and Ismail Adylov, members of IHROU, who were jailed over a year ago for their human rights activities. Adylov, who was released from the hospital with a chronic kidney ailment just one week before authorities took him into custody, was reported to be in poor physical condition. The human rights defender was missing in custody for over thirty days in early 2000

when officials transfered him to a distant prison facility without notifying his family, depriving them of the opportunity to give him needed food and medicine.

Over a year after police illegally detained and beat IHROU chairman Mikhail Ardzinov, law enforcement officials refused to return his passport to him and continued to deny him means of redress. His repeated complaints and requests that a case be opened against his abusers was finally referred not to the state prosecutor, but to the police station that houses the officers who detained and beat him in 1999.

The head of the HRSU, Tolib Iakubov, also reported that there were no known results from the Polish government's investigation of a 1998 attack on him in Warsaw during the OSCE's annual implementation meeting. The men who beat Iakubov in broad daylight, sending him to the hospital with severe injuries, have not been brought to justice.

Human rights activists in regions outside the capital reported being subjected to police interrogation, threats, and extortion, as were victims of human rights abuse with whom they spoke. In one instance, the Akhmedov family of Andijan in the Ferghana Valley was threatened after meeting with Human Rights Watch and police forcibly confiscated a copy of the *Human Rights Watch World Report 2000*. Copies of the report were also confiscated by police from a Human Rights Watch representative outside a Syrdarya courthouse.

The activities of local and international rights defenders were seriously limited by authorities' arbitrary denial of access to nominally open judicial hearings.

The Role of the International Community

United Nations

Despite a scathing review from a team of independent consultants hired to assess the work of the United Nations Development Programme (UNDP) in Uzbekistan, that U.N. agency did not change course and refused to implement the consultants' recomendations, including a suggestion that the agency issue a formal apology to the independent human rights community in Uzbekistan for excluding it from projects. The consultants also called on UNDP to publish the report, showing the agency's past errors in order to avoid repetition. Finally, the team called on the UNDP to make good on its earlier pledge to fund the country's first Legal Aid Society. UNDP had contributed approximately U.S. $2 million since 1997 to the Uzbek government's human rights initiatives, including the Authorized Person for Human Rights in the Parliament (ombudsman) and the National Human Rights Center.

Other U.N. agencies, including the special rapporteur on torture and the working group on arbitrary arrests and disappearances, sent communications to Uzbekistan regarding individual cases.

A U.N. representative from Tashkent monitored the appeals trial of Komoliddin Sattarov, but no public comment came from the U.N. regarding the young man, who was beaten and tortured with electric shock and then sentenced to nine years in prison, partly on the grounds that he wrote a complaint to the U.N. Human Rights Committee on behalf of his arrested brother. An Uzbek municipal court had listed the complaint as part of the incriminating evidence against Sattarov. During retrial, a district court made no mention of the complaint but sentenced him to fifteen years.

European Union

After having lauded a coveted Partnership and Cooperation Agreement (PCA) as a means to push for progress in human rights, the E.U. failed to use the instrument for that purpose in 2000. There were no human rights concessions in return for financial and trade benefits awarded under the agreement. More than a year after the PCA was signed, the E.U. and Uzbekistan had failed to set up a working group on human rights and democracy, succeeding only in organizing a subcommittee on finance and economy. As of October 2000, the E.U. had suspended indefinately the meetings of the Cooperation Council under the PCA. No explanation was given for this move.

Despite its failure to use the PCA for progress in human rights, the E.U. did go on the record with its dismay over Uzbekistan's abysmal rights record. In January 2000 the E.U., in keeping with its opposition to the death penalty, issued a press release condemning the execution of six men accused of terrorism following a grossly unfair trial. During the meeting of the U.N. Commission on Human Rights in Geneva, the E.U. spoke out against ongoing repression in Uzbekistan. The E.U. also used the forum of the OSCE Permanent Council to voice dissatisfaction with the presidential elections in Uzbekistan.

Organization for Security and Cooperation in Europe (OSCE)

After finding that earlier OSCE recommendations had not been implemented and that conditions for a pluralist and competitive parliamentary race had not been met, the OSCE withheld the assignment of formal election observers but dispatched a limited assessment mission to examine the pre-election environment that condemned the parliamentary elections as falling below OSCE standards. The organization abstained from monitoring presidential elections on the grounds that conditions for a free and fair election were absent.

In apparent reaction to criticism from the Karimov government regarding OSCE activities on human rights issues, the organization emphasized economic and security interests, sometimes to the seeming exclusion of rights advocacy. The new OSCE chair, Austrian Foreign Minister Benita Ferrero-Waldner, visited Uzbekistan in June and was able to meet with representatives of local or international human rights groups or leading local rights defenders. Human rights were reportedly not given high priority in her discussions with government officials, which were concluded with the signing of a bilateral investment agreement between Austria and Uzbekistan. When some seventeen OSCE ambassadors and representatives of delegations visited Uzbekistan in July, the officials spent the majority of their time in the ancient city of Samarkand and did not meet with rights defenders during their half-day stay in the nation's capital. Meetings with the government reportedly focused on security and economic cooperation.

The OSCE/Central Asia Liaison Office (CALO) actively engaged authorities on the subject of prison access for international monitors. Staff members continued their program of trial monitoring in the country and reported their findings internally. On several occasions authorities barred CALO staff from attending nominally open court hearings.

The OSCE/CALO sponsored several training workshops in Uzbekistan. A human rights training seminar was offered for experienced activists from human rights groups, members of other nongovernmental organizations, and employees of the government's human rights bureaucracy. Another training session held by the OSCE/CALO aimed at introducing members of the judiciary, including prosecutors, judges, and lawyers, to international human rights standards.

United States

In April 2000, Secretary of State Madeleine Albright visited Uzbekistan and urged President Karimov to make a distinction between peaceful Muslim believers and terrorists. During her visit, Secretary Albright stated, "It's necessary that the government of Uzbekistan distinguishes very carefully between peaceful devout believers and those who advocate terrorism." Before she left Uzbekistan, however, Secretary Albright awarded the government with some U.S. $3 million in counterterrorism and border security assistance.

Just months later, as respect for religious freedom further deteriorated and hundreds more Muslims were sent to jail for their beliefs and practices, Secretary Albright failed to name Uzbekistan as a country of particular concern in the area of religious freedom under the 1998 International Religious Freedom Act. The State Department's *Annual Report on International Religious Freedom*, issued pursuant to the act, emphasized minor improvements in the treatment of Christians, although Christians suffered violent government attacks and continued police harassment, and characterized the crackdown on Muslims as political and not religious repression, leaving the U.S. government free to give Uzbekistan a relatively positive rating in one of the most shockingly poor areas of its rights record.

Some members of Congress took a tough stand against the flagrant abuses by Uzbekistan and sharply criticized its rights record.

Relevant Human Rights Watch Reports:

Leaving no Witnesses: Uzbekistan's Campaign Against Rights Defenders, 3/00

FEDERAL REPUBLIC OF YUGOSLAVIA

Serbia and Montenegro

Human Rights Developments

Efforts by indicted Yugoslav President Slobodan Milosevic to remain in power decisively shaped the human rights situation in 2000. The Milosevic-dominated federal parliament amended the Yugoslav constitution in July to restrict Montenegro's autonomy and allow another presidential term for Milosevic. In the September 24 federal elections, which the Montenegrin government boycotted, the opposition candidate Vojislav Kostunica defeated Milosevic in the presidential contest. By manipulating the federal election commission and federal constitutional court, Milosevic attempted to force a second round of the election. The opposition responded with a series of mass rallies. On October 5, opposition supporters stormed the parliament and occupied Serbian state television. Two days later Milosevic conceded electoral defeat, and Kostunica was inaugurated.

Leading opposition politicians faced harassment and persecution throughout the year. In February, the public prosecutor indicted Dusan Mihailovic, president of the New Democracy Party, for "spreading false information" when he publicly criticized a Milosevic speech. On February 29, Belgrade police detained and interrogated Ivan Kovacevic, the Serbian Renewal Movement spokesman and member of Serbian parliament. Zarko Korac, leader of the Social Democratic Party, was beaten by unknown assailants in early March. Jan Svetlik, opposition councilor in Zrenjanin constituency, was abducted on April 5 by two unknown assailants and kept out of town during an important local parliamentary vote before being released unharmed. Momcilo Perisic, retired Yugoslav Army Chief of Staff and an opposition leader, was stripped of his military rank in August.

On June 15, unknown persons shot at Serbian Renewal Movement leader Vuk Draskovic from the terrace outside his apartment in Budva, Montenegro. One bullet grazed Draskovic's head. In the ensuing investigation, the Serbian Ministry of Interior refused to surrender two key witnesses to the Montenegrin police. Two weeks before the assassination attempt in Budva, the police at Belgrade Airport had arrested and disarmed Draskovic's entire security staff. Vuk Draskovic had survived a car accident on October 3, 1999, which many believe was staged by the Serbian Security Service.

Unidentified groups of men, apparently State Security agents or thugs employed by the government, beat and harassed regime opponents on a number of occasions. On February 26, in Belgrade, they beat student Milos Dosen who they found taking down a poster attacking Otpor (Resistance), an antigovernment group mostly comprised of university students; on April 11, in Novi Sad, two unidentified men beat Radoje Cvetkov, secretary for urbanism in the Novi Sad Executive Council, which is controlled by the op-

position; persons in civilian clothes raided Otpor headquarters in Belgrade on September 9, forcing Otpor activists to the floor while searching the office. There was no indication that police investigated any of these cases.

The authorities prevented the opposition from staging rallies or used force to disperse them. On November 9, 1999, police forces in Belgrade used excessive force to disperse some 2,500 students demanding early parliamentary elections in Serbia. Police stopped buses with opposition supporters traveling to rallies in Belgrade (April 14) and Pozarevac (May 9). On May 17-18, the police used excessive force to disperse Belgrade street protests and beat protesters and passersby for hours after the protests.

Beginning in June 2000, in the run-up to the September elections, police were increasingly involved in the beating of opposition activists and members of Otpor. Thirty beating incidents were reported between June and August and ten more in the first week of September. In one case, the police in Vladicin Han tortured six Otpor activists for three hours, hitting them in their genitals, head, kidneys, and feet. In May and June, the police detained and interrogated 500 Otpor activists on the unfounded charge of "terrorism."

In purges of the judiciary carried out in December 1999 and July 2000, the authorities removed from their posts two judges of the Supreme Court of Serbia, one judge of the Constitutional Court, and seventeen judges of district, municipal, and commercial courts. Presidents of the courts in Serbia, elected by the government-dominated Serbian parliament, assigned politically sensitive cases to "politically reliable" judges who were expected to render decisions favorable to the authorities, and did so.

Most victims of unfair trials were Kosovars, taken from the columns of fleeing civilians during the war with NATO and charged after the war with seditious conspiracy and terrorism. In most cases courts based the convictions on confessions extorted through police torture or on the notoriously unreliable paraffin test for gunpowder, allegedly showing that the person had used arms. In one such case, the district court in Nis collectively sentenced 143 ethnic Albanians from Djakovica to sentences of between seven and thirteen years of imprisonment. Flora Brovina, poet and physician from Pristina, was accused of providing medical supplies to members of the Kosovo Liberation Army and sentenced in December 1999 to twelve years in prison for "terrorism." On July 10, the district court in Belgrade sentenced six Albanian Belgrade University students to harsh prison sentences on a charge of "preparing terrorist acts." The verdict was based on apparently planted evidence and confessions extorted by beating, the threat of murder, and mock executions.

The authorities have continued to use penal sanctions since the 1999 war to prevent public debate on war crimes committed by security forces against ethnic Albanians. On July 26, a closed-door Yugoslav military court sentenced journalist Miroslav Filipovic to seven years in prison for publishing articles on the Internet in 2000 about the crimes. In August, the Yugoslav Army threatened Natasa Kandic, a leading Yugoslav human rights activist and director of the Humanitarian Law Center, with prosecution and trial because of her August 2000 statements about war crimes committed by the security forces.

Misdemeanor judges, appointed and controlled by the government, continued imposing the payment of heavy financial penalties on numerous independent media for "libelous" statements or reports, on the basis of the Public Information Act. In almost all cases, those recovering damages were members of the three ruling parties in Serbia—the Socialist Party of Serbia (SPS), the Yugoslav Left (JUL), and the Serbian Radical Party (SRS). Belgrade authorities closed down or disrupted the signals of a number of independent and opposition-controlled television and radio stations. Police removed relay links and essential transmission equipment from the transmission facilities of radio and television stations in Pozarevac, Cuprija, Pozega, Pirot, Kraljevo, Mladenovac, and Cacak. After disrupting its signal for eight months, the government took over the Belgrade Radio-Television Studio B. Radio B2-92, which broadcast from the Studio B premises, was also taken off the air.

With the focus of repression shifting to the Serbian opposition, the Milosevic regime's harassment of ethnic minorities subsided slightly. Yet tensions in Bujanovac, Medvedja, and Presevo, municipalities bordering Kosovo and inhabited mostly by ethnic Albanians, remained high during the year. Elsewhere in Serbia, incidents against Roma received most attention. On June 7, police leveled Roma homes in a Belgrade settlement built in breach of zoning laws; during the action, the police hurled racial insults at the Roma and slapped and kicked some of them. Roma were not allowed to enter the swimming pool in Sabac, owned by the president of the local branch of the ruling Serbian Radical Party. Romani men working for a street cleaning company in Belgrade were frequent victims of attacks by racist "skinhead" youth.

The presence of some 230,000 persons displaced after the Kosovo conflict and 500,000 refugees from Croatia and Bosnia continued to strain the resources of Serbia and Montenegro. UNHCR announced in August that it would decrease aid to provide accommodation for refugees and the displaced from U.S. $65.6 million to $58.6 million.

Defending Human Rights

Nongovernmental organizations in Serbia were extraordinarily active in 2000, and the regime responded with unprecedented harassment. The Humanitarian Law Center and Yugoslav Committee for Human Rights represented numerous individuals in political trials. These groups, along with Group 484, Women in Black, and the Belgrade Center for Human Rights, also developed a network of trial monitors who reported extensively about the trials of ethnic Albanians and other victims of government repression. Government representatives and media repeatedly accused human rights groups of working for foreign intelligence agencies. In a campaign of intimidation, initiated in May, financial inspectors accompanied by regular and secret police visited the offices of six leading organizations for a purported financial inspection. The police interrogated numerous activists about their daily activities and confiscated documents unrelated to financial matters. On July 7-8, State Security Police tortured Bojan Aleksov, a human rights activist and conscientious objector who had been studying in Budapest for two years and was arrested while visiting Belgrade. In August the police banned the Council for Human Rights, a prominent human rights group from Leskovac, justifying the move on the basis of the council's "engagement in political activities."

The Role of the International Community

United Nations

The Commission on Human Rights, in a resolution passed in April, expressed grave concern at the ongoing serious violations of human rights by the Serbian and Yugoslav authorities, as well as at the failure of Belgrade to cooperate with the International Criminal Tribunal for the Former Yugoslavia. The commission welcomed positive trends in Montenegro toward democratic and economic reforms. U.N. Special Rapporteur for Human Rights in the Former Yugoslavia Jiri Dienstbier repeatedly protested the repression against the opposition, students, and the independent media in Serbia. He also called for the lifting of international sanctions against FRY. Dienstbier visited the country in March and June and during the election crisis in September and October. The commission extended the special rapporteur's mandate for one year.

Organization for Security and Cooperation in Europe (OSCE)

Efforts by the OSCE to monitor the human rights situation were unequivocally rejected by the Federal Republic of Yugoslavia, which was suspended from OSCE membership in July 1992. OSCE Representative on Freedom of Media Freimut Duve defended independent media, but his activities were branded "terrorism and a crime against sover-

eign state" by Federal Information Minister Goran Matic, and Duve was accused of being a "German agent" by Minister of Telecommunications Ivan Markovic.

The OSCE Office for Democratic Institutions and Human Rights (ODIHR) in Montenegro monitored the June 11 early municipal elections in Podgorica and Herceg Novi and found that the elections were well conducted and generally in line with OSCE commitments. In a report released on August 30, ODIHR concluded that the legislation governing the September 24 elections did not accord with international standards or OSCE commitments. Yugoslav authorities announced earlier that they would not permit ODIHR experts to observe the elections. On October 19, OSCE Chairperson-in-Office, Benita Fererro-Waldner invited the Federal Republic of Yugoslavia to join the OSCE as a participating state.

European Union

The E.U. took some steps to alleviate the impact of economic sanctions against Serbia on ordinary citizens opposing the Milosevic's government. Between November 1999 and April 2000, the European Commission conducted the program, "Energy for Democracy," delivering 17,513 tons of fuel oil to seven cities governed by the Serbian opposition. The Belgrade authorities initially blocked delivery of the E.U. assistance to opposition towns, but Belgrade eventually abandoned the unpopular measures. In July, however, Yugoslav authorities denied import licenses to a number of firms exempted from the E.U. trade and investment embargo. The commission also provided urgent aid to the media and nongovernmental organizations harassed by the government. The E.U. continued to support the democratic transition in Montenegro. On May 22, 2000, the General Affairs Council committed 20 million euros (U.S. $19.2 million) in assistance to the Montenegrin government. On October 9, the E.U. lifted the oil embargo and the ban on international flights to and from Yugoslavia. Financial and trade restrictions against firms and individuals connected to the Milosevic regime remained in place, along with the visa ban and freeze of assets belonging to these individuals.

Council of Europe

The Federal Republic of Yugoslavia's application for admission to the Council of Europe remained suspended from consideration. Council of Europe officials issued condemnations of the crackdown on independent media and the opposition and called for free and fair elections. In July the Council of Europe secretary general appointed Eva Tomic as his special representative to be based in the OSCE Office for Democratic Institutions and Human Rights in Podgorica. Tomic was tasked to provide expert assistance to the Montenegrin authorities in reforming education, local self-administration, and the judicial system and in drafting legislation.

United States

On June 29, 2000, U.S. Ambassador to the U.N. Richard Holbrooke announced a campaign to exclude FRY from membership in the U.N. Although to a lesser extent than the E.U., the United States tried to alleviate the impact of sanctions on some sectors of the Serbian population. After an April 7 meeting in Washington, D.C., with the mayors of eight major Serbian municipalities controlled by the opposition, Secretary of State Madeleine Albright announced that the U.S. would approve aid for improving health care, public services, education, and environmental protection in cities run by the democratic opposition. The U.S. exempted Montenegro from sanctions and provided an estimated $77 million in aid during the year. On October 12, the U.S. lifted its oil embargo and flight ban to the Former Yugloslavia.

Relevant Human Rights Watch Reports:

Curtailing Political Dissent: Serbia's Campaign of Violence and Harassment Against Government's Critics, 4/00
Kosovo: Rape as a Weapon of "Ethnic Cleansing,"
3/00

HUMAN
RIGHTS
WATCH

MIDDLE
EAST
AND
NORTH
AFRICA

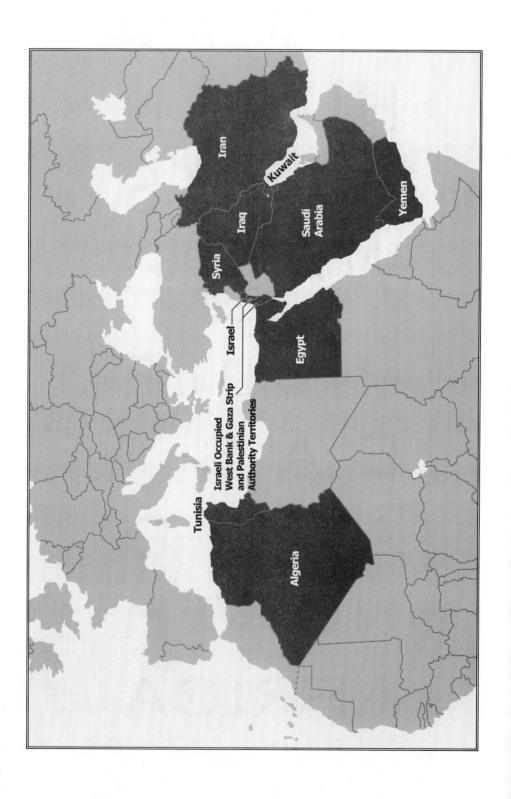

Human Rights Developments

Positive developments in some countries in the region were overshadowed by a continuing pattern of human rights abuses, political violence, and a faltering Arab-Israeli peace process. At this writing clashes unprecedented in their lethality had erupted between Palestinian demonstrators and Israeli security forces in Gaza, the West Bank, East Jerusalem, and inside Israel itself. Serious abuses including arbitrary arrest, torture, and unfair trials' were pervasive, as emergency rule or laws suspending constitutional protections were applied in many countries and the death penalty remained in force in all except Oman, Qatar, and Tunisia. Against this sobering backdrop, local activists and human rights organizations challenged these policies, though they often paid a high price for their courage. The rulers of Saudi Arabia and Bahrain made statements and authorized initiatives that suggested they might be ready to take human rights issues more seriously than in the past. The year also saw a potentially significant transition as Bashar al-Asad took power in Syria, joining the new generation of rulers in Morocco, Jordan, and Bahrain.

The status and rights of women were a key issue in many countries. In Morocco the issue of remedying the discriminatory provisions of the personal status law and a "national action plan" to give women more rights gave rise to large demonstrations for and against in March. Jordanian women and men joined together in a campaign to eliminate laws condoning "honor killings" of women, and women in Kuwait campaigned vigorously for the right to vote and stand for public office. Saudi Arabia in September ratified the Convention on the Elimination of Discrimination against Women (CEDAW). But in all these countries as in others in the region, women continued to suffer from severe forms of institutional and societal discrimination in nearly every aspect of their lives, particularly in the form of unequal personal status laws

and the lack of legal redress in cases of domestic violence. Despite some positive initiatives, tens of millions of women throughout the region continued to be denied full equality, a fact that was reflected in high rates of illiteracy and maternal mortality and low rates of political participation and was justified in terms of religion, culture, and tradition.

The issue of refugees, internally displaced and stateless persons was prominent throughout the year. Palestinian activists in the region and beyond initiated a right-of-return campaign that was well-grounded in international human rights law, but the problem of statelessness for Palestinian refugees in host countries in the region, Syrian-born Kurds, and Bidun in Kuwait and Bahrain was largely unaddressed or addressed in unsatisfactory ways. The region as a whole accounted for millions of refugees—officially acknowledged and otherwise—and internally displaced persons who, along with similarly high numbers of migrant workers, endured violations of basic rights at the hands of indifferent or worse government officials and abusive private employers. Serious anti-Moroccan immigrant violence erupted in Spain in February. The government of Iraq continued to force Kurds and other minorities out of the Kirkuk region into the autonomous three northern governorates. At least 200,000 Iraqis were illegal residents in Jordan, vulnerable to pressure from Iraqi and Jordanian intelligence services and to involuntary return to Iraq. Thousands of Iraqis desperately seeking refugee protection have turned up in Europe, Australia, and the U.S. Many Iranians and Iraqis fleeing to Turkey were denied protection there and forcibly returned to the countries they were fleeing. Iran hosted an estimated half a million Iraqi refugees and 1.4 million Afghan refugees, making it, according to the United Nations High Commissioner for Refugees, the leading refugee host country in the world. Egypt continued to be host to an estimated two million or more Sudanese, although most did not have formal refugee status.

Morocco began to come to terms with the legacy of human rights abuses under King Hassan II, who died in July 1999. His powerful and feared interior minister, Driss al-Basri, was sacked in November 1999 by the king's son and successor, Mohamed VI. In October, Moroccan activists protested at the infamous Tazmamert prison, carrying candles and red roses to commemorate those who died under horrific conditions at the secret facility in the 1970s and 1980s. The demonstrators were not permitted access to the prison itself, which reportedly was ringed by dozens of paramilitary forces. They called for the trial of those responsible for "disappearances," deaths in custody, and arbitrary detention, and the return to the families of the bodies of those who perished.

This year saw another potentially important generational transition of power when the reign of Syrian President Hafez al-Asad came to an end with his death in June, but the carefully orchestrated succession of his son Bashar left no doubt that the apparatus of the ruling Ba'th party was still firmly in place. Nevertheless, supporters of political reform broke the ice with bold public statements that would have been unimaginable under the rule of the new president's father. In Iran, expectations that the election of a new parliament with the majority composed of reformers would lead to substantive progress in human rights were thwarted when hardline conservatives fought back by closing down some thirty independent newspapers and magazines, effectively destroying what had been a vital element of the reformists' power base, and dealing a severe setback to freedom of expression. Prominent reformists also faced intimidation, detention, and prosecution throughout the year.

The year also saw important reminders, positive and negative, of the potentially constructive role of an independent judiciary in creating an environment of legal protection of basic rights. In Israel the high court issued important rulings outlawing common interrogation techniques that amounted to torture and the practice of hostage taking. In Egypt, the Constitutional Court struck down the restrictive associations law of May 1999 and the Court of Cassation ruled that parliamentary elections had to be supervised by the judiciary rather than representatives of the executive branch. The absence of an independent judiciary was unfortunately more apparent throughout the region. In Tunisia, the judiciary continued at the service of the state to harass and convict human rights activists and other peaceful dissidents. Egypt and Bahrian continued to try political critics and protestors before state security courts. In Iran President Khatami and his allies spoke eloquently about the importance of rule of law, but his conservative adversaries used revolutionary courts and special clergy courts to deliver unfair verdicts, persecute citizens peacefully advocating political reforms, and close down the country's freewheeling print media.

Military operations claimed civilian lives in Algeria, Iraq, Lebanon, Yemen, Israel, the occupied West Bank and Gaza Strip, and the Palestinian Authority territories. Several hundred persons were killed each month in Algeria as civilians were killed in indiscriminate attacks, and clashes continued between armed groups and security forces. U.S. and British air forces continued to enforce the "no-fly zone" over northern Iraq from Incirlik base in Turkey and southern Iraq from bases in Saudi Arabia, although according to press reports the number of overflights and use of missiles and bombs was considerably lower than in the previous year.

The Israeli occupation of the West Bank, Gaza Strip, and south Lebanon generated civilian casualties and damage, as well as regional tension, as U.S.-brokered peace negotiations faltered repeatedly. Israel bombed Lebanon's electricity infrastructure twice during the year, targeting on February 8 the Jamhour plant supplying Beirut as well as facilities in Baalbek and Deir Nbouh near Tripoli, and the Bsalim station in Beirut and the Deir Ammar station in Tripoli on May 5. It appeared that the Israeli Air Force used U.S.-manufactured helicopters and U.S.-supplied AGM-114 Hellfire laser-guided missiles in the Bsalim attack, which completely destroyed three of the facility's six large transformers. In a previous Israeli attack on Bsalim on May 16, 1996, U.S.-built F16 fighter planes dropped laser-guided bombs on the plant.

Israel's unilateral military withdrawal from south Lebanon in May, followed by the rapid collapse of the Israeli-backed militia—the South Lebanon Army (SLA)—marked the abrupt end of over two decades of occupation for the civilian population. Families who had fled violence, intimidation and impoverishment in the occupied zone began to return as well as those whom the SLA had summarily expelled from their homes. On May 23, local residents stormed the notorious Khiam prison, which since its opening in 1985 had been a joint enterprise of Israel and the SLA. They routed the SLA jailers without violent incident and freed about 130 detainees, some of whom had been held without charge for fifteen years. Within days, the facility was transformed into an informal museum, drawing thousands of Lebanese who toured the cramped cells and solitary confinement rooms, and read the names of torturers which were prominently posted on a large handwritten list near the entry gate.

At this writing, the death toll from Palestinian clashes with Israeli police, border police, and IDF that began on September 29 had risen to some 120, almost all of them Palestinians. More than 4,800 were injured. Human Rights Watch's investigations in Israel, the West Bank, and Gaza Strip in early October revealed a pattern of excessive, and often indiscriminate, use of lethal force by Israeli security forces in situations where demonstrators were unarmed and posed no threat of death or serious injury to the security forces or to others. By mid-October the IDF had expanded its use of tanks and helicopter gunships armed with both missiles and medium-caliber machine guns in Palestinian residential areas in the West Bank and Gaza Strip. On October 7, Hizballah guerrillas captured three Israeli soldiers on the south Lebanon-Israel border, announcing that they

were being held hostage in exchange for nineteen Lebanese in Israeli jails and possibly other Arab prisoners. A fourth Israeli was in Hizballah custody as of this writing; the Lebanese group alleged that he was a spy but the Israeli government said he was a businessman and army reservist. Successive Israeli governments have long maintained that two of the Lebanese prisoners, Shaykh 'Abd al-Karim 'Obeid and Mustafa al-Dirani, captured in Lebanon in Israeli commando operations in 1989 and 1994 respectively and held without charge ever since, were bargaining chips in exchange for Ron Arad, the Israeli navigator who went missing after his plane was shot down over Lebanon in 1986.

Comprehensive international economic sanctions remained in place on Iraq. High oil prices and a Security Council resolution in December 1999 that removed limits on the amount of oil Iraq could sell meant that the oil-for-food humanitarian relief program no longer faced cash constraints. As a short-term emergency assistance program limited to commodities, however, the oil-for-food program could not provide the extensive investment and development efforts needed to address the overall humanitarian situation, which remained grave. The Security Council resolution provided for the "suspension" of non-military sanctions in the event that Iraq cooperated satisfactorily with a new arms inspection regime, but Iraq insisted that it had fully complied with earlier resolutions and that sanctions should therefore be lifted without qualification or delay.

In the region and around the world, advocacy and demonstrations increased on behalf of Palestinian refugees and their right of return under international law. On October 7, Israeli troops opened fire at a crowd of 500 demonstrators in Ramieh on the Lebanese side of the Israel-Lebanon border. The protesters, carrying Palestinian flags and demanding the right to return, reportedly threw stones at a nearby Israeli outpost. Two Palestinians, residents of Lebanon's Shatila and Bourj al-Barajneh refugee camps, were killed and twenty-three wounded, two critically, according to press reports. Some 25,000 people participated in funeral processions for the victims the next day in Beirut. On October 24, security forces dispersed forcibly thousands of Jordanians who marched from Amman to the Allenby Bridge connecting Jordan and the West Bank to press for the right of return. The BBC reported that the demonstrators "were beaten into retreat by Jordanian police with baton, water cannon and tear gas, as helicopters hovered overhead." Among the protestors were Jordanian parliamentarians and members of professional associations.

The rights to freedom of expression and association were trampled across the region. There were no independent and critical local media in Saudi Arabia, Libya, Iraq, and Syria. In Tunisia and Egypt, the state-run broadcast and major print media were not open to independent or critical perspectives. Journalists were harassed, arrested, or imprisoned in Egypt, Iran, Morocco, Tunisia, Yemen, and areas under the control of the Palestinian Authority (P.A.), and the independent weekly *La Nation* remained suspended in Algeria. P.A. authorities ordered the closure of five radio and television stations between May 5 and June 2, and arrested Samir Qumsiah, chair of the Council of Private Radio and Television Stations, after he called for a thirty-minute broadcasting halt to protest the closures.

In Morocco, despite positive developments in other areas, foreign and local journalists faced harassment and threats during the year, and newspapers were banned or seized because of critical commentary about the current and former king, and interviews with Islamist and Polisario (*Popular Front for the Liberation of saguia el Hamra and rio de Oro*) leaders. Three journalists from France 3 were placed under house arrest for three days in October, the Paris-based press freedom organization Reporters without Borders said, after they had filmed the October 7 protest march to Tazmamert prison, and authorities confiscated their material before they left Morocco. The Moroccan government's relations with Qatar soured in July in part because of the content of programming by the emirate's regionally popular *al-Jazeera* satellite television station. Moroccan Prime Minister Abdel Rahman al-Youssoufi charged that the station "led a campaign against Morocco, against its democratic evolution, its institutions and image." Qatar's foreign minister, Sheikh Hamad bin Jassim bin Jabr al-Thani, said that "today's world does not fear the press" and press freedom "should not be a reason for tension in relations between states."

The trials of Capt. Mustafa Adib, including a prison hunger strike, attracted considerable attention in Morocco. Adib, 32 years old, had written in 1998 to then-Crown Prince Mohamed, in his capacity as head of the armed forces, to inform him of corruption and racketeering among the high command at the airbase where he served in the southeastern province of Errachidia. An initial inquiry led to the dismissal of those involved and cleared Adib of any wrongdoing, but he subsequently faced arbitrary transfers and retaliatory disciplinary measures. After failing to get relief inside the army, he filed a complaint in a civil court about his treatment, also to no avail. He was arrested on December 17, 1999, the day after he was quoted about the situation in the French daily *Le Monde*. A trial in February led to his conviction and a five-year prison term on charges of "violating military discipline" and "insulting the royal armed forces," despite objections by his lawyers that they were not allowed to call witnesses and that one of the judges had been among his commanders at the air base at the time of his original complaint. After Adib went on hunger strike in May the Supreme Court finally acted on his appeal, overturning the February sentence and returning the case to the Rabat military court. In what Adib's defense lawyer called "a parody of justice," the court on October 6 sentenced him to two-and-one-half years of imprisonment after again finding him guilty of the same charges. In late September, Transparency International, the global anti-corruption organization, named Captain Adib as one of four winners of the group's Integrity Awards at its annual general meeting.

Intellectuals, including prominent novelists, poets, and songwriters in Egypt, Kuwait, Lebanon and Yemen were prosecuted for the content of their work, sometimes based on complaints from self-appointed private guardians of the Muslim faith. In December 1999, Lebanese musician Marcel Khalifa was tried in a Beirut court for singing a song viewed as blasphemous of religious values because its text included a short verse from the Koran. The song was adapted from a poem written by Palestinian poet Mahmoud Darwish. In his testimony, Khalifa, who faced a maximum sentence of three years in prison, said "Could you imagine that Lebanon would bring its artists to court? When a country brings its artists to court, it brings itself before the court." The court acquitted Khalifa of the charges on December 15, 1999.

In Yemen, conservative clerics and political groups targeted Samir al-Yusufi, editor of the weekly *al-Thaqafiya*, for serializing *Sana'a is an Open City*, a novel by Mohammed Abdulwali. He was charged in a criminal court in July with "insulting Islam," and the case was pending as of mid-October. Egyptian author Salahuddin Muhsin was arrested in March because prosecutors found two of his books, *A Night Talk with Heaven* and *Trembling of Enlightenment*, offensive to Islam. He was tried in a state security court and received a six-month suspended sentence in July. Earlier in April, violent clashes reupted between protesters and security forces in Cairo after an Islamist newspaper charged that *A Banquet of Seaweed* by Syrian author Haidar Haidar was blasphemous. A panel of literary experts appointed by the Ministry of Culture held that the novel was not blasphemous but authorities said that it would be withdrawn from circulation.

A Kuwaiti appeals court in March banned a novel and a collection of poetry by prize-winning novelist and short-story writer Laila al-'Othman and Kuwait University philosophy professor Dr. 'Aliya Shu'ayb and fined them both. While the court did not specify which references in the works constituted illegal expressions, during pre-trial questioning prosecutors focused on a description of an apple in feminine terms in Dr. Shu'ayb's collection of poetry and a description of the "lustful" coming together of sea waves in al-'Othman's novel.

Palestinians who publicly criticized P.A. policies were arbitrarily arrested and detentained. Security forces arrested eight prominent personalities who signed a November 27, 1999, petition criticizing P.A. "tyranny and corruption." Six were released on JD50,000 (U.S. $70,000) bail on December 19, but Ahmad Dudin and 'Abd al-Sattar Qassem were held until January 6, 2000. Qassem was re-arrested on February 18 and detained until July 28, despite a July 11 high court order for his release.

The tightening of restrictions on freedom of opinion and expression extended to scholars and universities. The Tunisian government in January summarily dismissed and later expelled Jean-Francois Poirier, a French philosophy teacher at the Institute for Social Sciences, in retaliation for his association with Tunisian human rights activists, and in late July dismissed Moncef Marzouki from his post as professor of community medicine at the University of Sousse after he spoke out publicly in Paris and Washington about the government's human rights record. In late June, Egyptian authorities arrested Saadeddin Ibrahim, professor of sociology at the American University in Cairo, in connection with his efforts to mobilize students and others to monitor the country's parliamentary elections in October and November. The government held him without charge for forty-five days and subsequently filed charges against him before the Supreme State Security Court for allegedly receiving foreign funding without permission and disseminating information harmful to Egypt's reputation.

Palestinian academic Jawad al-Dalou of the Islamic University in Gaza was suspended in November 1999, along with two students, for writing in a student newspaper that many beggars in Gaza came from a particular district. Yemeni authorities closed a women's studies center at Sana'a University in December 1999 in the wake of conservative objection to a conference the center had sponsored. The pervasive presence of Yemeni security personnel on campus led some faculty to request parliamentary legislation barring them from such a role, and Iran's parliament was reportedly considering similar legislation. On August 5, Iranian authorities arrested Hojatoleslam Hassan Youssefi Eshkevari, a leading independent religious scholar, after his return from Berlin where he had presented a paper on "Dictatorship and its History." He was held in solitary confinement for two months and put on trial in October before a Special Court for the Clergy on charges of apostasy and "being corrupt on earth," which carry the death penalty. As of this writing no verdict or sentence had been announced.

Peaceful freedom of assembly, virtually non-existent in several counries including Iraq, Syria and Saudi Arabia was still a sought-after right throughout much of the region. Tunisian authorities closed down a publishing house after it had hosted a meeting on freedom of the press in that country. Palestinian Police Chief Ghazi al-Jabali in February issued new regulations prohibiting processions, demonstrations, or public meetings without prior approval from the district police commander. Offenders faced up to two months of imprisonment or a maximum JD50 (U.S. $70) fine. The high court suspended their implementation on April 29, but as of September had not acted to revoke these or other regulations limiting freedom of assemby.

The Lebanese government in April suppressed peaceful, student-led protests against the Syrian role in Lebanon and prosecuted demonstrators in the military court. At an April 17 demonstration, dozens assembled at the Ministry of Justice in Beirut to protest the arrest of two students on April 13 for distributing leaflets calling for Syria's withdrawal of milittary forces. On April 18, demonstrators gathered near the National Museum and some put tape over their mouths to underscore the government's attempts to silence them. When this crowd refused to disperse on the order of a Lebanese army officer, security forces forcibly dispersed the demonstrators, and in an ensuing clash, several were reportedly injured. Eight demonstrators received sentences ranging from ten days to six weeks in prison. In the wake of these two incidents, some one thousand students peacefully rallied on three university campuses on April 19 to cries of "The Israeli army out, the Syrian army out," and "Lebanon first." Although the campuses were surrounded by security forces and army troops, there were no arrests and the rallies did not spill out onto the streets.

Following serious clashes on October 6 between police and demonstrators protesting Israeli policies in the occupied Palestinian territories, the Jordanian government announced a complete ban on public demonstrations and detained hundreds of people. Clashes developed after Friday prayers, with the worst incidents taking place in Palestinian refugee camps. Police responded to crowds calling for an end to Jordan's peace treaty with Israel with baton charges, tear gas, and live ammunition. At least one demonstrator at the Baqa'a refugee camp near Amman was killed and scores were injured. Demonstrators and their supporters claimed that the police had used excessive force in quelling the protests.

Shaikh Hamad Bin Issa Al Khalifa, Bahrain's ruler, announced on October 2 that he envisaged "a new organizational and constitutional concept of our state," but it was not clear if he intended to institute such changes through mechanisms specified in the constitution of 1973, whose provisions for a partially elected parliament were suspended by decree in 1975. The government continued to hold without trial five opposition activists arrested in January 1996 in connection with their campaign to reinstate the 1973 constitution. One of the five, Abd al-Wahab Hussain, was released on March 17 following an order by the High Court of Appeal but was rearrested after spending about an hour at home. Others who had been released in 1999, including Shaikh Abd al-Amir al-Jamri and Shaikh Ali Ashoor, had been compelled as a condition of their release to refrain from speaking out or engaging in political activities. On April 3, Peter Hain, the British foreign minister responsible for the Middle East, responding to a query from a member of parliament, said that Abd al-Wahab Hussain was being held in "a flat on Ministry of Interior property" and that "the decision to renew the detention order was again made on public security grounds."

In Bahrain, individuals as well as associations and organizations with views critical of government policy continued to face severe restrictions. According to the London-based Bahrain Freedom Movement (BFM), for example, in late December 1999 the authorities intervened to prevent a planned meeting at the prestigious Uruba Club on the subject of human rights. On August 8 security officials intervened to force the cancellation of a long-scheduled public speech that evening at the Al-Ahli Club by Hassan Radhi, a leading defense lawyer, on the subject of constitutional rights. The BFM also reported that on July 4 speakers at the Al-Ahli club publicly criticized the ruling family's refusal to revive the partially elected National Assembly.

Bahrain's government maintained its policy of providing no information concerning the numbers or identities of persons arrested, tried, convicted, acquitted, or released under the State Security Law or brought before the State Security Court, where procedures do not meet basic fair trial standards and verdicts were not subject to appeal. The government announced the release of several hundred prisoners during the year, but the opposition BFM charged that there were numerous new arrests and state security court trials.

Women in the Middle East and North Africa continued to suffer from severe forms of discrimination in nearly every aspect of their lives and women's rights continued to be one of the most contested areas for reform. Institutionalized discrimination in personal status laws and the lack of legal redress for violence against women characterized the majority of women's human rights abuses. The year 2000 was declared by the Arab Parliamentarian Union as the year of the Arab woman. Instead of governments adopting reform policies that would address discrimi-

nation and violence against women, women's rights became a chip in political negotiations between conservative and liberal forces in society, and inaction on the part of the governments unfortunately prevailed. Countries that have signed or ratified the Convention on the Elimination of all Forms of Discrimination against Women (CEDAW)—Iraq, Israel, Egypt, Jordan, Kuwait, Lebanon, Morocco, Libya, Algeria, Tunisia, Yemen, and Saudi Arabia—maintained national laws that contradicted the spirit and letter of CEDAW.

Workers rights were limited or nonexistent, particularly in Gulf states that employed large numbers of foreign workers. According to the annual report of the International Labour Organization released in May, Oman, Saudi Arabia, and the United Arab Emirates were among the few countries anywhere that prohibited outright any type of labor organization, while Bahrain and Qatar allowed only committees or councils "whose freedom of action is tightly constrained and which therefore do not have attributes of independent workers' organizations."

Governments in the Gulf continued to use legislation to promote employment of their own nationals and to discourage the use of foreign workers. In Kuwait, over one million foreign workers enjoyed little legal protection against abusive practices of employers, and women domestic workers were excluded from the labor law, increasing their vulnerability to physical and sexual abuse. In March, the Indian government stopped issuing immigration clearances for domestic workers in Kuwait due to reported abuses.

In Saudi Arabia, 69 percent of the workforce of 7.2 million was composed of foreigners, many of them Asian. Nongovernmental organizations in Indonesia pressed the government of President Abdurrahman Wahid for a three-month hiatus in sending women workers to Saudi Arabia. In August, twenty-two groups demonstrated at the Manpower Ministry in Jakarta, demanding that the government educate women about their rights prior to leaving the country, and reach an agreement with Saudi authorities that would ensure the workers' protection against abuse and the availability of legal remedies. On June 19, an Indonesian domestic worker, Warni Samiran Audi, was beheaded in al-Ahsa in eastern Saudi Arabia. The Saudi interior ministry said she had been convicted of killing the wife of her employer. Indonesia's Manpower Ministry director general for labour, Din Syamsuddin, said the next day that the Indonesian embassy had not been officially informed of the execution, although the government had been seeking the woman's release or a reduced sentence for three years.

In the United Arab Emirates (UAE), foreigners comprised about 70 percent of the population of 2.76 million and 90 percent of the labor force. Workers did not have the right to organize trade unions, to strike, or to bargain collectively, and faced deportation if they carried out such activities. Domestic and agricultural workers were excluded from protection under the labor law, and reports continued of the physical abuse of women domestics and withholding of their wages. Migrant workers also faced corporal and capital punishment following unfair trials. An Indonesian domestic worker, Kartini binti Karim, was handed over to the police in 1999 when her employer discovered that she was pregnant and her husband was not in the country. The Fujairah Sharia court in February convicted her of adultery and sentenced her to death by stoning, while it acquitted in their absence the Indian national who was the woman's accused partner. Commenting on the trial, Sulaiman Abdulmanan of the Indonesian Foreign Ministry said that Kartini "did not understand Arabic, and it seems she was just trembling and saying yes to everything." Though she did not refute the adultery charges during the trial, she later testified that her pregnancy was the result of a rape. Kartini was never informed of her right to communicate with the Indonesian embassy or her right to a translator, and the embassy was not notified in advance of her trial. The harsh and inhumane sentence attracted international attention, and on April 25 the appeals court reduced the sentence to one year in prison and deportation. In September, the *Sharia* court in the emirate of Ras al-Khaimah found a Bangladeshi man and woman guilty of adultery and sentenced them to three months in jail and 150 lashes each. UAE Labor and Social Affairs Minister Humaid al-Tayer said the same month that employment visas would be issued "only to those who possess at least secondary education." The new measure was expected to affect adversely mainly South Asians, who comprised the largest number of unskilled wokers in the emirates.

In Bahrain this year labor activists made an effort to win the right to establish an independent trade union body. The International Center for Trade Union Rights, an independent London-based nongovernmental organization, reported in August that the executive committee of the General Committee of Bahraini Workers (GCBW), set up by the government in 1981 as an alternative to independent trade unions, requested government permission to reconstitute itself as an independent union in accordance with ILO and Arab Labor Organization principles. Shaikh Khalifa bin Salman Al Khalifa, prime minister and uncle of the amir, reportedly summoned the executive committee to a meeting where he rejected the request and said that there would be grave consequences if they persisted with such demands. The minister of labor and social affairs subsequently instructed the committee to postpone GCBW general assembly elections scheduled for November 2000 to choose a new executive committee.

Foreign workers were violently attacked in Libya, where hundreds of thousands of Africans reportedly migrated over the past several years in search of work. On September 21-22, there were clashes between African immigrants and Libyans in az-Zawiyah, a town near Tripoli, in which approximately fifty Chadian and Sudanese migrants were killed, according to the daily *al-Hayat* (London). Dozens of others reportedly were injured, according to the Libyan media and Sudan's foreign ministry. The Reuters news agency reported from Lagos on October 5 that some three thousand Nigerians returned home from Libya on Nigerian-government-organized flights and that state television featured the migrants "describing killings and beatings as ordinary Libyans had set upon alleged illegal immigrants."

Governments in the region continued gradually to embrace some of the language of human rights discourse and to establish what they said would be rights-monitoring bodies. There were welcome developments in the Algerian government's decision to permit four international human rights organizations to visit the country; the invitation that Saudi authorities extended to the U.N. special rapporteur on judicial independence; and the launching in Rabat of a human rights center co-funded by Morocco's ministry of human rights and the U.N. to provide training for judges, police officers, prison administrators, and teachers.

Information about human rights developments in Bahrain remained difficult to access but there were several indications from high government officials that they were taking human rights issues more seriously. In October 1999 the amir announced the formation of a human rights committee comprising six members of the Shura Council, an appointed advisory body with no legislative or other authority. According to *Bahrain Brief*, a London-based pro-government newsletter, the committee's duties were to "scrutinize legislation," investigate reports of abuses, and "raise awareness within society that the government considers the protection of human rights a priority." *Bahrain Brief* also reported that in February the committee was asked to examine the treatment of foreign workers. As of October, no further information was available regarding the committee's activities or the results of any investigations it may have carried out. On August 2 the amir told Cable News Network (CNN) that he was ready to allow international human rights groups free access to the country. "I am ready to carry them on my private aircraft and they can meet any group," he said. A two-person delegation from the office of United Nations High Commissioner for Human Rights Mary Robinson visited Bahrain in late October to discuss technical assistance and human rights teaching. The delegation reportedly met with the ministers of education, justice, and the interior as well as the chairman of the Shura Council's human rights committee and the president of the University of Bahrain.

On a less positive note, however, the government deferred once again a visit by the United Nations Working Group on Arbitrary Detention that was initially planned for 1999 and most recently scheduled for October 2000; the visit was rescheduled for February 2001. On October 28, according to the Bahraini daily *Al-Akhbar al-Khalij*, the minister of labour and social affairs denied the August 8 written request of eighteen Bahraini citizens for permission to set up an independent human rights committee.

There were conflicting signals from the government of Saudi Arabia in response to the launching of Amnesty International's worldwide campaign—"End Secrecy, End Suffering"—that focused on the kingdom's human rights practices. The Ministry of Foreign Affairs stated in March that the government had a "keen interest and commitment to the cause of human rights." Interior minister Prince Nayef in April dismissed as "merely nonsense" the allegations of human rights abuses in the kingdom, and added: "We welcome anyone to see for himself the facts in the kingdom as it has nothing to conceal." But Foreign Minister Prince Saud al-Faisal appeared to rule out access to the kingdom for Amnesty representatives. He told the leading Spanish daily *El Pais* in April: "If Amnesty International was seeking the truth and if it informed itself honesty of the truth, we would consider" a visit. He continued: "But so long as it continues to use erroneous information as its basis without taking into account our responses," the visit would have "no sense."

In October, Jordan signed a memorandum of understanding with the International Labor Organization that was designed to address the problem of child labor in the kingdom through actions of state ministries and NGOs. The ministry of labor said that the memorandum represented the initial step for Jordan's participation in the ILO's International Program on the Elimination of Child Labor. Jordan was the first West Asian country to ratify ILO Convention 182 Concerning the Prohibition and Immediate Action for Elimination of the Worst Forms of Child Labor, which calls for immediate measures to eliminate child slavery, debt bondage, child prostitution, trafficking, and other forms of hazardous and exploitative child labor.

There were also positive developments with respect to international justice. On September 8, Morocco and Kuwait signed the Rome Treaty for the establishment of an International Criminal Court, joining Jordan, which signed in October 1998.

Defending Human Rights

The region's vibrant and growing community of human rights activists persevered, despite widely differing local environments. At this writing, three Syrians remained in prison, serving long sentences that the state security court imposed in 1992 following an unfair trial. In Bahrain, government-controlled Iraq, Libya, Oman, Qatar, Saudi Arabia, and the United Arab Emirates severe internal restrictions meant that it was impossible for human rights activists to speak and meet openly. Elsewhere, defenders variously faced surveillance, official harassment, arrest and detention, threats of criminal prosecution, and the inability to register human rights groups under the law. In an increasingly worrying trend, the issue of foreign funding was used in Egypt and Jordan, and by the Palestinian Authority, to disparage the intentions of committed individuals and independent, locally based organizations. For example, in September the Jordanian Press Association suspended Nidal Mansour, chief editor of *al-Hadath* weekly, for receiving foreign funding for a local branch of a press freedom organization, the Center for Defending Freedom of Journalists.

In Tunisia, government efforts to monopolize human rights discourse and smother independent activists were challenged repeatedly by human rights defenders on the ground, who faced job dismissals, judicial proceedings, intensive surveillance, and sometimes physical assault at the hands of police. The Kuwaiti cabinet's 1993 order dissolving

all unlicensed human rights and humanitarian organizations remained in force and local advocates were forced to meet informally or under the auspices of organizations that enjoyed legal status. In Yemen, local groups were allowed to function although some were threatened with closure.

Activists were particularly at risk when they undertook efforts to expose corruption and gross human rights abuses. In Iran, the independent press that had been playing an increasing role in exposing human rights violations and promoting human rights principles was dealt a crippling blow with the enforced closure by hardline religious and political conservatives of thirty newspapers and the imprisonment and prosecution of leading journalists and writers. Palestinian Authority security forces in December 1999 detained eight signatories of a November 27, 1999, petition criticizing P.A. "tyranny and corruption" for periods between three weeks and seven months.

In Algeria, security forces in May detained Mohamed Smain, head of the Relizane office of the Algerian League for the Defense of Human Rights (LADDH), after he attempted to document evidence at a grave site connected with the case of two former mayors implicated in mass killings in the area. Egypt's large and sophisticated human rights community was under attack throughout the year. The controversial 1999 Law on Civil Associations and Institutions overturned on procedural grounds by the Supreme Constitutional Court had been strongly criticized by local human rights activists since it allowed the government undue interference in the internal affairs of NGOs and criminalized any activity that authorities deemed political. The Egyptian Organization for Human Rights (EOHR) was informed in late July that its application for official registration under the previous law had been granted. However, several days later the EOHR was notified that a final decision had been deferred upon the request of security officials. Due to criticism by the government and in some of the media of NGO reliance on foreign funding, several rights groups were facing the possibility of cutting back on their activities since they were largely dependent on this form of financial support.

Women's rights defenders in the region continued to address legal discrimination and violence against women. In Morocco, Egypt, Jordan, and Kuwait, they were castigated by parliamentarians, conservative parties, and the media, who alleged that their actions were destroying the family, the unity of the nation, imposing "immoral" values on society, and that they were agents of the West. The Permanent Arab Court to Resist Violence Against Women, established in December 1999 in thirteen Arab countries, launched the Feminine Rights Campaign, which called for equality between men and women especially with respect to divorce. The one-year campaign's main objective was to achieve equality in the right of divorce and its consequences; unify laws and juridical procedures; ensure equal rights as to the custody of children, marital property and all other marital rights; and establish government funding to guarantee the payment of alimony.

Human rights defenders also continued initiatives to promote joint work in the region. In October 2000 a follow-up conference to the April 1999 First International Conference of the Arab Human Rights Movement was organized by the Arab Working Group for Human Rights in coordination with five human rights organizations. The meeting, held in Rabat, Morocco, and attended by over 60 participants and observers from 43 local and international human rights organizations focused its discussions on some of the recommendations from the earlier conference. The conference called for improved coordination among Arab human rights groups and activists and more effective use of international human rights protection mechanisms. It recommended the setting up of a coordinating and representative office in Geneva, Switzerland to assist in this purpose. It called for an end to restrictions on funding sources for human rights work and recommended establishing a fund for human rights defenders. Discussions also covered ways of improving the tools available for regional human rights

protection and the role of the movement in facilitating democratic and constitutional reforms.

Also in October the Cairo Institute for Human Rights Studies organized the Second International Conference of the Arab Human Rights Movement around the theme of human rights education and dissemination. Over one hundred Arab and international experts and activists from human rights groups and governments—including artists, writers, media experts—examined the political and cultural obstacles to the dissemination of human rights in the region and sought to identify ways and to develop strategies for overcoming them. The conference adopted the Cairo Declaration on Human Rights Education and Dissemination setting out principles and standards for human rights education in the region and establishing an agenda for the 21st century. It called on Arab governments to draw up national plans for human rights education and to urgently revise existing educational curricula to ensure their consistency with human rights values.

The Work of Human Rights Watch

Staff and other representatives of Human Rights Watch's Middle East and North Africa division travelled during the year to Algeria, Egypt, Iran, Israel and the occupied Palestinian territories, Jordan, Kuwait, Lebanon, Morocco, and Yemen. The missions were multifocused, involving research, coordination and cooperative work with local human rights activists and lawyers, and dialogue with government officials wherever possible. Thematically, the major concerns of Human Rights Watch included violations of freedom of expression and association, women's rights, the absence of due process in legal proceedings in civilian and military courts, and minority rights and statelessness. In Algeria and Lebanon, the focus included accountability for past human rights abuses, including "disappearances" and extrajudicial executions at the hands of state agents and armed militia groups. Human Rights Watch covered from the field the Israeli military withdrawal from occupied south Lebanon and closely monitored and publicized subsequent developments, including the kidnapping of Lebanese civilians by Hizballah operatives. In Israel, the West Bank, and Gaza Strip Human Rights Watch investigated excessive and indiscriminate use of force by Israeli security services in clashes with Palestinian civilians, failures to protect civilians by Palestinian security forces, and attacks on civilians by civilians.

Human Rights Watch's requests for access to Saudi Arabia, Bahrain and Syria, some of them longstanding, were all pending with their respective governments at this writing.

Human Rights Watch representatives presented concerns to governments in the region, and met with senior government officials in Algeria, Egypt, Iran, Israel and Kuwait, as well as with officials in the Palestinian Authority. In Egypt and Israel, Human Rights Watch brought its concerns about detention, torture, and prison conditions to the ministries of justice. In Iran, a Human Rights Watch researcher met with the judge presiding over the trial of thirteen Iranian Jews in Shiraz to discuss due process and fair trial issues: It was the first time since 1979 that a revolutionary court judge had accepted to meet with a representative of an international human rights organization. In Kuwait, Human Rights Watch met with Ministry of Interior officials to discuss that ministry's discriminatory treatment of the Bidun, Kuwait's stateless long-term residents, and met with parliamentarians to express concerns about proposed legislation which discriminated against women and Bidun, and restricted freedom of expression. Human Rights Watch observed the military court trials in Lebanon of former South Lebanon Army soldiers and officers as well as civilians who were charged with criminal offenses under Lebanese law for contact with Israel, and collected information from Lebanese families whose relatives were known or believed to be "disappeared" in Israel or Syria.

In January 2000 Human Rights Watch wrote to the U.N. Security Council urging that the sanctions in force against Iraq be radically restructured to remove restrictions on non-military trade and investment while tightening controls on Iraq's ability to import weapons-related goods. The letter was accompanied by a memorandum addressing the impact of the sanctions on the humanitarian situation in Iraq. Human Rights Watch also called on the Security Council to set up an international tribunal to try top Iraqi leaders for war crimes and crimes against humanity. The letter acknowledged the high degree of responsibility of the Iraqi government for the unfolding humanitarian emergency, but insisted that the United States and other powers also face up to their share of the responsibility and take action to improve conditions.

Together with five other international organizations and religious groups, Human Rights Watch in March and August again urged the Security Council to address the grave humanitarian consequences of the sanctions, and in September Human Rights Watch wrote to both the Security Council and the government of Iraq setting out urgent steps necessary to alleviate the humanitarian crisis.

Human Rights Watch did not forget that other war crimes or crimes against humanity had been committed in the region and that to date no one has been held accountable in courts of law with local or international jurisdiction. It was eighteen years ago, in September 1982, that at least 700 to 800 Palestinians, and possibly as many as several thousand, were slaughtered in the Sabra and Shatila refugee camps in Beirut by the Israeli-armed and -allied Lebanese Phalange (Kata'eb) militia while nearby Israel Defense Forces (IDF) personnel looked on and did nothing to stop the sixty-two-hour indiscriminate carnage. In December 1999, we wrote to Israeli Prime Minister Ehud Barak to condemn the appointment of Maj. Gen. (Reserves) Amos Yaron as director-general of Israel's Ministry of Defense and urge his immediate dismissal from public service. While serving as an IDF division commander during Israel's invasion of Lebanon in 1982, his actions and omissions facilitated the massacre in the camps. By all accounts, the perpetrators of this indiscriminate slaughter were members of the Phalange (or *Kata'eb*, in Arabic) militia, a Lebanese force that was armed by and closely allied to Israel since the outbreak of Lebanon's civil war in 1975, but the killings were carried out in an area under IDF control. An IDF forward command post, commanded by Amos Yaron, was situated on the roof of a multi-story building located some 200 meters southwest of the Shatila camp.

Human Rights Watch noted in the letter that the Sabra and Shatila massacre was a grave violation of international humanitarian law and a crime against humanity, and urged that General Yaron—as well as the other Israelis and Lebanese with direct or indirect responsibility for the killings—should face criminal investigation and prosecution. Human Rights Watch also sent a letter to Lebanese president Emile Lahoud that raised the same point and inquired about legal or administrative measures that the government of Lebanon initiated or was contemplating with respect to investigation and prosecution of Lebanese citizens who are known or suspected to have had direct responsibility for the killings in Sabra and Shatilla. Human Rights Watch did not receive replies from either government.

In the lead up to the February parliamentary elections in Iran, Human Rights Watch issued a short briefing on current human rights conditions. Noting that the atmosphere surrounding the election campaign was notably freer than at the time of the last elections in March 1996, Human Rights Watch pointed to a number of human rights issues as still impeding a free and fair election in the Islamic Republic, and said little had changed in the legal framework relating to the enjoyment of rights in Iran.

In March, Human Rights Watch published the findings of international observers who attended the trial of Tunisia's outspoken human rights lawyer, Radhia Nasraoui, and twenty co-defendants, most of them students, on charges related to membership in or activities on behalf of an unauthorized left-wing political association, the Tunisian Communist Workers Party (Parti

Communiste des Ouvriers Tunisiens, PCOT). The trial dramatized many aspects of Tunisia's human rights situation. In addition to government measures to harass and impede the work of human rights defenders like Nasraoui, the case illustrated the use of repressive laws to imprison Tunisians who engage in peaceful political activity deemed critical of the country's present government. It also demonstrated the commonplace nature of torture during interrogations in Tunisia and the judicial system's disregard of this abuse and its failure to provide defendants with basic guarantees of a fair trial.

In advance of the Israeli withdrawal from occupied south Lebanon, Human Rights Watch disseminated a briefing paper that identified the human rights issues that were largely being neglected by the international media, and briefed Israeli and international journalists in Jerusalem.

In its 38-page report, "Promises Betrayed: Denial of Rights of Bidun, Women, and Freedom of Expression," released in October, Human Rights Watch detailed Kuwaiti laws and practices that systematically discriminate against women and stateless Bidun, and that criminalize free expression by journalists, academics, and writers. Human Rights Watch called on Kuwait to amend its Penal Code and Printing and Publications Law to protect freedom of expression and to revoke laws that discriminate against women and long-term non-citizens of Kuwait.

Also in October Human Rights Watch published the results of a week-long fact-finding investigation into the unlawful use of force against civilians by security and police forces in Israel, the West Bank, and the Gaza Strip. The organization condemned a pattern of repeated Israeli use of excessive lethal force during clashes between its security forces and Palestinian demonstrators in situations where demonstrators were unarmed and posed no threat of death or serious injury to the security forces or to others. In cases that Human Rights Watch investigated where gunfire by Palestinian security forces or armed protesters was a factor, use of lethal force by the Israel Defense Forces (IDF) was indiscriminate and not directed at the source of the threat. Human Rights Watch also documented a pattern of IDF disregard for and targeting of Palestinian medical personnel and ambulances evacuating or treating injured civilians in the West Bank and Gaza Strip In the report, Human Rights Watch also criticized the failure of the Palestinian police to act consistently to prevent armed Palestinians from shooting at Israeli Defense Forces (IDF) from positions where civilians were present and thus endangered by the Israeli response.

In a six-page briefing published in October as the first round of People's Assembly elections were getting underway in Egypt, Human Rights Watch noted several factors not conducive to a free and fair election. These included restrictions on freedom of association and assembly, including the ability to form political parties and to hold public rallies as part of an electoral campaign; arrests and prosecution before military and state security courts of political opponents, in particular members of the Muslim Brotherhood; restrictions on freedom of expression, including banning of books and newspapers and the use of criminal charges against journalists; and harassment of human rights activists and others preparing to monitor the elections.

Throughout the year Human Rights Watch sought to defend those who were persecuted for their human rights work and to protect and enlarge the political space in which independent institutions of civil society could express diverse—and dissenting—views. In the case of Tunisia, Human Rights Watch spoke out repeatedly in opposition to the government's systematic efforts to intimidate that country's human rights activists and to silence its most outspoken writers. In Egypt, Human Rights Watch intervened to criticize a restrictive NGO law and to condemn threatened prosecution of activists under military orders. Following the Palestinian Bar Association's decision to remove the names of Palestinian lawyers associated with human rights groups from its list of practicing lawyers, Human Rights Watch intervened to urge the Palestinian Authority to ensure that human rights lawyers did not face threats, intimidation or professional sanctions because of their human rights activities. In Iran, Jordan, Kuwait, Lebanon, and Yemen Human Rights Watch wrote to the governments to protest arrests or harassment of journalists, writers, artists and academic, and to urge that the fundamental right to freedom of expression be respected.

The division also devoted time and resources to advocacy efforts within the United Nations. For example, in July Human Rights Watch attended the U.N. Human Rights Committee's review of Kuwait's implementation of the International Covenant on Civil and Political Rights, where we briefed committee members on the results of our investigation into violations of women's rights, rights of Bidun residents, and freedom of expression. In October, we called for the creation of an independent panel of experts to investigate human rights violations committed during clashes between Israelis and Palestinians that began on September 29, and urged the creation of a standing body of independent international criminal justice investigators to be available for deployment by the U.N. at short notice whenever the need arises for independent, impartial investigations of a criminal justice nature.

In our continuing efforts to maximize communication with activists and others throughout the region, we translated public statements and press releases into Arabic and made these widely available. The Arabic section of Human Rights Watch's web-site continued to grow and provided access to key documents produced by the organization in its global coverage of human rights violations. Traffic to this section tripled during the year, up from about 650 page-views per day during 1999 to about 2,000 pages per day in September 2000. During September close to 250 users each day visited this section of the web-site.

The Role of the International Community

European Union
Human rights abuses in the Middle East

did not occasion much in the way of public diplomacy by the European Union or member states, despite visits to European capitals by Algerian President Abdelaziz Bouteflika, Iranian President Mohamed Khatami, King Mohamed VI of Morocco, and Shaikh Hamad bin Issa Al Khalifa of Bahrain, and visits to the region by Chris Patten, the European Union's commissioner for external affairs, Javier Solana, the E.U.'s high representative, and the foreign ministers of France, the United Kingdom, and other European countries. The E.U. at the U.N. General Assembly in October sponsored resolutions on the human rights situation in Iraq and Iran. The E.U. speech on October 26 on "the human rights situation in the world" mentioned Syria as a country "where the expression of opposition or dissidence is systematically repressed" and expressed concern about the human rights situation in Saudi Arabia, "in particular by restrictions on fundamental freedoms." The speech welcomed Algeria's invitation to several international human rights organizations but said that the E.U. "remain[ed] concerned by the persistence of violence and by the fate of missing persons."

The year also saw little movement in the "Barcelona process" of establishing a Euro-Mediterranean free trade and cooperative security zone. The European-Mediterranean Association Agreement between the E.U. and Israel, signed in 1995, went into force in June 2000 after completion of ratification by all E.U. member states. Israel thus joined Tunisia and Morocco as countries with operational association agreements. A draft agreement with Egypt was completed in July 1999, but as of this writing Egypt had not yet taken steps to sign it. There was no public discussion of how the human rights practices of these countries, especially Tunisia and Israel, could be reconciled with the stipulation in article 2 of each agreement that the agreement was premised on "respect for human rights and democratic values." There were no indications that the year had seen progress regarding negotiations over association agreements with Algeria, Lebanon, and Syria. Signed agreements with Jordan and the Palestinian Authority remained to be ratified by some E.U. member states before coming into force.

External relations commissioner Patten, speaking in Cairo in early April on the E.U.'s Mediterranean policy pointed to human rights along with drugs, terrorism, immigration, and conflict prevention as areas where "we need some practical results." "Our handling of these crucial topics needs to be sufficiently flexible to allow the partners who wish to advance ahead of others to do so without prejudicing the right of all Barcelona partners to participate in the discussions," he said.

In his Cairo speech Patten observed that Europe "now" accounted for 47 percent of total "Mediterranean imports," amounting to 30 billion euros (U.S. $25.1 billion). E.U. countries took 52 percent of all "Mediterranean exports," he said, worth 63 billion euros. (U.S. $52.7 billion). Europe, he said, "is by far the largest donor of non-military aid in the region, " amounting to 9 billion euros (U.S. $7.5 billion) in grants and loans.

According to a U.S. Congressional Research Service study of transfers of conventional arms released in August and covering the 1996-1999 period, 85 percent of United Kingdom arms deliveries to developing countries were to the Middle East, while the comparable figures for France, Germany, and Italy were 43 percent, 40 percent, and 12.5 percent respectively. European countries accounted for just over 48 percent of all arms deliveries to the region in this period. According to the study, the bulk of the sales comprised tanks and self-propelled guns, other armor, supersonic aircraft, and naval vessels.

United States

The Middle East—especially Israeli-Palestinian negotiations and conflicts and Iraq—occupied much of the Clinton administration's diplomatic energies over the year. In a June speech to the American-Arab Anti-Discrimination Committee devoted to Israeli-Palestinian negotiations and Iraq, Under Secretary of State for Political Affairs Thomas Pickering identified the components of U.S. policy in the region as achieving a comprehensive Arab-Israeli peace, ensuring regional stability, stemming the proliferation of weapons of mass destruction, creating free market conditions, encouraging sustainable development, and "expanding political reform and adherence to international norms for human rights."

In his presentation to Congress in March of the Near East segment of the Administration's foreign operations budget for fiscal year 2001, Assistant Secretary of State Edward S. Walker, Jr. said, "Advancing vital U.S. political and economic interests in the Middle East is complicated by a legacy of ethnic conflicts, border disputes, economic dislocations, ecological disruptions, and human rights abuses—all of which have contributed to terrorism and violence." Walker also stated that the Administration was "pursuing a strong program for developing civil society in a region that often lacks the most rudimentary institutions for peaceful transition of leadership, freedom of expression, or respect for women's rights."

In its budget presentation the Administration requested military and economic assistance grants of U.S. $2.8 billion for Israel, nearly U.S. $2 billion for Egypt, and U.S. $228 million for Jordan. The request for democracy programs in the region, "particularly in Algeria, Morocco, Yemen, and Oman," was $4 million. In requesting allocations for individual countries, Walker's presentation mentioned human rights or support for democratic institutions as issues of concern in Algeria, Egypt, Morocco, and Yemen, though there was no such mention in the presentations for Bahrain or Jordan. Surprisingly, Tunisia was characterized without qualification as "a stable democratic country," raising serious question about the ability of the U.S. government to recognize, let alone encourage or support, democracy in the region. The U.S. was a key convener of a conference of foreign affairs ministers in Warsaw in June entitled Towards a Community of Democracies, to which Tunisia, Algeria, Egypt, Israel, Jordan, Kuwait, Morocco, Qatar, and Yemen were invited. In a press briefing on June 19, Assistant Secretary of State for Democracy, Human Rights, and Labor Harold Koh said that the list of countries invited "was an inclusive one which included not just countries that were established democracies, but those that were striving for democracies and those that had made a commitment on the democratic path." He added that "those countries that have experienced backsliding, we hope that the conference will itself be an occasion to engage them and press them aggressively on the extent to which we found their recent progress to be lacking."

Koh visited Tunisia in June—the first visit to any country in the region by him or his predecessor since 1993 (see Tunisia chapter below). In October 1999, Koh's deputy, Bennett Freeman, visited Israel and also met with Palestinian officials and human rights activists.

The State Department's *Country Reports on Human Rights Practices for 1999*, released in February 2000, continued to provide comprehensive coverage of the human rights situation in each country in the region. Koh's introduction to the report, however, which set the tone for much of the media coverage, avoided citing abuses by Middle Eastern allies of the U.S., with the exception of Saudi Arabia regarding religious freedom, and Egypt, Oman, and Yemen with regard to the practice of female genital mutilation. Inexplicably, the introduction referred approvingly to Tunisia's presidential election, where President Ben Ali won with an official 99.4 percent of the vote, as "a modest step forward," and pointedly failed to include Tunisia in a discussion of Middle Eastern countries where dissidents and human rights defenders face arbitrary arrest, unfair trials, and intensive surveillance.

In September, the State Department released its second annual congressionally-mandated report on international religious freedom, which also included chapters on each country in the region. The report cited Iran, Iraq, and Saudi Arabia for intolerance towards religious minorities, and Egypt, Israel, and Jordan for discriminatory policies. The report also noted limited improvements in Egypt, Iran, Israel, Qatar, and Saudi Arabia.

According to the report, Assistant Secretary of State for International Organizations David Welch met with Saudi Arabia's foreign minister, Prince Saud al-Faisal, to discuss religious freedom and human rights issues. In the Saudi Arabia chapter, the report's authors wrote that "the overwhelming majority of citizens support an Islamic state and oppose public non-Muslim worship," without any indication of how this conclusion was reached concerning a country where freedom of expression is severely restricted.

The Congressional Research Service report on arms transfers released in August noted that "the high value of U.S. arms transfer agreements with developing nations is attributable to major purchase by key U.S. clients in the Near East, and to a lesser extent in Asia, together with a continuation of well-established defense support arrangements with such purchasers." For the most recent period covered, 1996 to 1999, Middle East countries accounted for more than 65 percent of total deliveries of U.S. arms to developing countries, and the U.S. accounted for nearly 50 percent of all arms purchase agreements by Middle East states. The principal Middle East purchasers of U.S. arms in this period were Egypt ($5.8 billion), Saudi Arabia ($5.5 billion), and Israel ($4.2 billion). The report listed tanks and self-propelled guns, armored vehicles, naval vessels, supersonic aircraft, helicopters, surface-to-air missiles and anti-ship missiles as the main categories of weapons systems purchased.

The U.S. signed a wide-ranging free trade agreement with Jordan on October 24 similar to agreements already concluded with Canada, Mexico, and Israel. U.S. and Jordanian officials expressed hope that the agreement would attract international investment to Jordan. The Clinton Administration promoted the agreement with Jordan as a model for future trade pacts on the grounds that its provisions mandated compliance of both parties with international labor and environmental standards.

ALGERIA

Human Rights Developments

President Abd al-Aziz Bouteflika's "civil harmony" initiative achieved only partial success in bringing an end to the political violence that has ravaged the country for most of the last decade. Although the violence was on a lesser scale than in earlier years, brutal and indiscriminate attacks on civilians and clashes between government forces and armed groups continued to claim an estimated 200 lives per month. There were very few reports of perpetrators being caught and brought to justice. The generally improved public security situation, especially in major cities, was reflected in fewer reported incidents of arbitrary arrests, "disappearances," and torture, but the lack of progress in resolving thousands of cases of "disappeared" persons remained a blight on the government's human rights record. The government failed also to institute reforms to prevent a possible resurgence of systematic human rights violations by the security forces.

The Civil Harmony Law, adopted in July 1999 and endorsed overwhelmingly in a national referendum the following September, set a deadline of January 13, 2000, for members and supporters of armed groups to surrender to the authorities. The law offered immunity from prosecution for persons who had not themselves committed killings or bombings or other serious crimes, and significantly reduced sentences to persons who acknowledged responsibility "for causing death or permanent injury of a person or for rape, or for using explosives in public places or in places frequented by the public." In principle, individuals wishing to take advantage of the law were required to surrender their arms and make a full disclosure of their actions to the authorities. According to officials, the law's probation or reduced sentence provisions became applicable once the information in such disclosures had been verified by local and national security offices.

The issue of whether or not to accept the terms of the Civil Harmony Law reportedly created considerable dissension within the armed groups, in particular the Islamic Salvation Army (Armée Islamique du Salut, AIS), which had, in practice, observed a cease-fire with the army since October 1997. Some reportedly held out for terms that included a political role for the Islamic Salvation Front (Front Islamique du Salut, FIS), banned since 1992. On November 22, 1999, Abdelkader Hachani, the top-ranking FIS official not in detention, was assassinated in Algiers. In December 1999, the authorities announced the arrest of his alleged murderer, but as of October 2000 no information concerning any investigation into the killing had been made public.

On January 10, three days prior to the expiry of the Civil Harmony Law's six-month grace period, President Bouteflika issued a decree granting a "pardon with the force of amnesty" (*grâce amnistiante*) to "persons belonging to organizations which voluntarily and spontaneously decide to put an end to acts of violence, which put themselves entirely at the disposal of the state and whose names appear in the annex to [this] decree"—namely, the AIS. This decree exempted all persons covered from having to make any declaration of the acts that they had committed and from imprisonment or other sanction. It also exempted them from the ten-year deprivation of civil and political rights, such as the right to vote or stand for office, that had been applied to persons "repenting" under the terms of the Civil Harmony Law. It was, in effect, a blanket amnesty for all crimes no matter how heinous. The next day, January 11, AIS commander Madani Mezrag formally announced the group's dissolution. Two days later, the Islamic League for Preaching and Holy War (Ligue Islamique de la Daâwa et du Djihad, LIDD), which had broken from the Armed Islamic Group (Groupe Islamique Armé, GIA) and, with the AIS, observed the cease-fire with the army, also dissolved itself under the terms of the pardon.

GIA elements led by Antar Zouabri and Hassan Hattab's Salafist Group for Preaching and Combat denounced President Bouteflika's overtures and continued to mount attacks on civilians as well as security posts and military patrols.

The government claimed widespread public support for the Civil Harmony Law, citing the September 1999 referendum, yet the law made no provision for transparency, or for involving the victims of crimes or the general public. Many Algerians, most vocally groups representing families of victims of attacks by armed groups, contended that investigations of "repentis"—those accepting amnesty under the law—were cursory and that many were cleared before the veracity and thoroughness of their confessions could be established. They also charged that the January 10 pardon betrayed the spirit of the Civil Harmony Law by amnestying all crimes, however grave, enabling perpetrators of killings and rape to return to the communities they had formerly terrorized.

Reflecting this lack of official transparency, accurate information about the law's implementation and the numbers of persons who benefitted from it was difficult to obtain and often contradictory. Algerian and French press reports suggested that some 1,500 fighters had turned themselves in under the law, and estimated that the January 10 amnesty covered at most between two and three thousand AIS adherents. The Algiers daily *El Watan*, citing "sources close to the security services," wrote on July 13 that those remaining with the armed groups numbered more than nine hundred, operating in small units away from the main populated areas. Interior Minister Yazid Zerhouni, in a January 20 press conference, asserted that "eighty percent of the terrorists" had surrendered their arms. However, when pressed as to how these estimates were calculated, he stated "I can't give you the numbers for the simple reason that we are presently at the stage of identification and census." Ministry of Justice officials told Human Rights Watch in May that the total number of beneficiaries of the Civil Harmony Law and the January 10 pardon was about 5,600, of whom some 330 were serving reduced sentences for crimes of violence. Murad Zoughir, the public prosecutor for the *wilaya* (province) of Algiers, told

Human Rights Watch that the probation committee he headed had dealt with approximately one hundred "repentis," of whom about thirty had been sentenced to jail terms, forty exonerated, fifteen placed on probation, and fifteen of whom remained under investigation. The failure of the government to provide precise information about those benefitting from the Civil Harmony Law or the full pardon, the offenses to which they confessed or with which they were charged, and the disposition of their cases fueled considerable suspicion that perpetrators of grave abuses were being cleared and given immunity with little scrutiny or accountability.

There was virtually no progress in efforts to resolve some 4,000 documented cases of alleged "disappearances" in previous years at the hands of security officials. Throughout the year Algerian human rights lawyers and organizations of relatives continued to receive and document further cases. In an interview in *Middle East Insight*, a Washington, D.C.-based bi-monthly, President Bouteflika said, "As to disappeared individuals, Algerian justice will spare no effort, conducted in the framework of the law, to seek solutions to cases fully documented with verified evidence." In response to repeated requests by Human Rights Watch in May, however, as well as requests by other international organizations and families of the "disappeared," government officials declined to provide names or information in cases they claimed to have resolved.

Such limited information as was made available by different ministries and official sources was inconsistent, and the government made no apparent effort to reconcile the discrepancies evident in the different accounts. Interior Minister Zerhouni, at his January 20 press conference, said that of 4,600 complaints of "disappearances" known to his ministry, "among them 2,600 or 2,700 have been cleared up. It includes persons who have gone back to the *maquis* (lit. "the bush"), and others who have been killed by their comrades, some who've been incarcerated, and still some who were found in the camps of the AIS." Minister of Justice Ahmed

Ouyahia told the government daily *El Moudjahid* on May 21 that his ministry had opened files on 3,019 cases of missing persons and that "a large number of the so-called disappeared were in fact in the ranks of terrorist groups," while two hundred were "alive and well either in prison or among the beneficiaries of the Civil Harmony Law."

Ministry of Justice officials told Human Rights Watch that of these 3,019 cases, 833 were persons being sought by the security forces, ninety-three had been killed in clashes with security forces, eighty-two were in detention, nine had been killed in clashes among armed groups, forty-nine had been released from detention and "may have joined the terrorists," and seventy-four were at their homes. Human Rights Watch requested the names of individuals in any of the categories mentioned, to determine to what extent they corresponded to those compiled by lawyers and human rights groups. The officials declined to provide them, however, on the grounds that they were all still "under investigation."

Kamel Rezzag-Bara, head of the quasi-official National Human Rights Observatory (Observatoire National des Droits de l'Homme, ONDH), told Human Rights Watch in May that the ONDH had 4,146 "disappeared" files open, 70 percent of which dated from the 1993-1995 period, and none of which were more recent than 1998. He declined to provide a list of names of missing persons, insisting that to do so would be "not useful," but provided oral summaries of several cases in which individuals reported as being "disappeared" had allegedly been killed in clashes with security forces or had turned up at home.

Ministry of Interior officials, reflecting the lack of seriousness with which they have addressed the issue of the "disappeared," told Human Rights Watch in May that the problem of three thousand "disappearances" and missing persons out of a population today totaling thirty million did not compare adversely with Algeria's independence war, which had left some fifty thousand individuals out of a population then of around nine million unaccounted for.

Women, as well as men and children, continued to be killed by armed groups (see WRD section). The Algerian press, reflecting official estimates, reported that 2,600 women had been sexually assaulted or raped during the conflict, mostly in the 1995 to 1998 period, but some women's rights activists estimated the number at some 5,000. Government officials, when meeting Human Rights Watch in May, pointed to the high proportion of women engaged in professions, such as medicine and the judiciary, as an indication of sexual equality, but they were unable to indicate progress in dealing with the discriminatory Family Code of 1984, which institutionalized the unequal status of women in matters of personal status, marriage, divorce, property, and inheritance. President Bouteflika, at a March 2000 conference organized by several women's rights groups, asserted that changes regarding women's rights had to take into account a society's religious beliefs and traditions.

Several individuals were detained and held incommunicado by security forces, at least one of whom remained unaccounted for in late October 2000. Seventy-three-year-old El Hadj M'lik was arrested at his home in central Algiers on the evening of April 13, several hours after security officials had visited his house seeking his son. His family reported that by mid-September they had had no contact with him nor received any clarification from the authorities concerning his whereabouts.

Ali Mebroukine, a law professor at the National School of Administration in Algiers and former advisor to President Liamine Zeroual, was arrested in Algiers on May 27 on his return from Paris. According to *Algeria-Interface*, a Paris-based information website, he was seen once by his wife in mid-June when he was brought along by police who searched their home and seized documents. His wife, Insaf, was later taken to a secret location and questioned, then released after being instructed to "be quiet" about her husband. On June 28, the military investigating magistrate overseeing the case confirmed

to Mebroukine's lawyer that he was being held in Blida military prison but did not divulge any charges or other information about his detention.

Ministry of Justice officials assured Human Rights Watch in May that the government treated allegations of human rights abuses by government officials seriously, and stated that 348 persons associated with the security forces, including members of "self-defense" militias (Groups for Legitimate Defense, GLD) organized and armed by the interior ministry, had been prosecuted for human rights abuses since 1992. Of these, they said, 179 were cases of physical abuse and fifteen concerned arbitrary detention or torture. The officials declined, however, to disclose names or other details, but noted that the numbers included several police officers punished for their involvement in a well-publicized incident in December 1999 in the town of Dellys. There, after a bomb explosion, the authorities had indiscriminately rounded up some one hundred persons and beaten many of them. Officials told Human Rights Watch that there had still been no prosecutions, however, in the case of two mayors and GLD leaders in the Relizane area who had been briefly detained in April 1998 for allegedly carrying out a series of abductions and executions, although the case was still "under investigation."

The authorities appeared to make little effort to establish an effective process to ensure that basic forensic work was carried out in order to help identify homicide victims and suspects, and so to help establish whether those found buried in unmarked graves included persons reported to have "disappeared" in the custody of the security forces in previous years. During a visit to Canada in April, President Bouteflika reportedly dismissed the question of undertaking credible and independent inquiries into responsibility for "disappearances" and massacres in Algeria as "intellectual coquetry."

The government maintained the state of emergency proclaimed in 1992, and on several occasions acted to prevent public gatherings by human rights groups as well as critics of its policies. On March 22, for example, police in

Oran forcibly dispersed a demonstration of relatives of the "disappeared" and subsequently charged several women with participating in an unauthorized gathering in a public place. On June 25, police clashed with demonstrators at an unauthorized rally in Algiers held to mark the second anniversary of the murder of Kabyle singer and rights activist Lounes Matoub.

Several human rights organizations told Human Rights Watch that government policies curtailed their right to freedom of association. The National Association of Families of "Disappeared" (ANFD) held weekly demonstrations outside the offices of the ONDH to demand that the government provide information about missing relatives, but it was not able to obtain official authorization to function. The Association of Families of "Disappeared" in Constantine faced a similar problem, and said that the authorities had interfered several times with their regular demonstrations outside government offices. Ali Mrabet, a founder of Sumoud (Steadfastness), which advocates investigation of killings and kidnapings, said that the Ministry of Interior had ignored its three-year-old application for registration, without which the group could not obtain permits to hold meetings or open a bank account. Similarly, Rassemblement Action Jeunesse (RAJ), a national youth association, produced documentation from recent years showing numerous refusals by local authorities to their applications to hold meetings, conferences, exhibitions, or film showings in Algiers and Tizi Ouzou. RAJ Secretary General Hakim Addad told Human Rights Watch that the authorities had continued to interdict RAJ or other organizations' gatherings, though no longer in written form.

The governments commitment to freedom of association was called into question by its response to efforts begun in December 1999 to register a new political party, the Movement for Fidelity and Justice (WAFA), under the leadership of former foreign minister and 1999 presidential candidate Ahmed Taleb Ibrahimi. WAFA was seen by some as representing a segment of the banned FIS. The

political parties law allowed the government sixty days to reject WAFA's application, but it did not do this. However, the interior minister refused to publish notice of the party's registration in the Official Gazette, a step that requires his signature, and without which the party could not get permits for meetings and conferences. The minister declared on May 10 that he "would not be the one to sign the decision to return the banned party." The Algerian League for the Defense of Human Rights (LADDH) and the Algerian Human Rights League (LADH) both called on the government in July to register WAFA in compliance with the law, but ONDH head Rezzag-Bara asserted to Human Rights Watch that WAFA did not need an official response to function.

FIS leader Abbasi Madani remained under house arrest and the party's number two, Ali Belhadj, remained in prison but was allowed to receive family visits. When questioned about their status by the pan-Arab daily *Al-Hayat* in an interview published on September 13, President Bouteflika replied, "The FIS was disbanded by court order before I came to power. The new constitution doesn't provide for FIS's existence at all. So don't talk to me about this subject because to me FIS doesn't exist." He said that Belhadj "is now being kept in better conditions than he has ever been," and that "If Ali Belhadj disavows all those who use violence, then I will help him."

Algeria's privately-owned print media covered many politically sensitive issues in a critical fashion, although some topics, such as the political role of the military leadership, remained the off-limits. Press accounts of security operations continued to rely almost exclusively on official sources, depicting raids and clashes that resulted in the deaths of unnamed "terrorists" but seldom their apprehension. No journalists were prosecuted for publication of "security-related information," but Reporters without Borders (Reporters Sans Frontières, RSF) reported that several publishers were subject to libel suits, including some brought by army officers or directors of state companies. The independent weekly *La Nation* remained suspended, ostensibly for failing to pay outstanding invoices to the Société d'Impression d'Alger (SIA), one of the state printing houses that effectively monopolize newspaper printing. According to RSF, which visited the country in June, the directors of several newspapers suspended in 1992 had been unable to secure the official authorization required by state-owned printing companies to resume publication. Broadcast media remained a government monopoly. Journalists working for the Paris daily *Libération* and Radio France International were unable to get visas to visit Algeria immediately prior to President Bouteflika's state visit to Paris in June. (See below.)

Defending Human Rights

In March, the government invited four international human rights organizations to visit the country after having barred visits by the groups for several years. Human Rights Watch, Amnesty International, the International Federation of Human Rights (FIDH), and RSF visited the country in separate ten-day missions in May and June. Amnesty International and RSF subsequently said that they had been able to move around the country without restriction. The FIDH, however, "strongly deplored" the "continuous tight surveillance" it said it had experienced and the "misinformation and unfounded attacks" of "certain organs of the so-called 'independent' private media." The Human Rights Watch delegation was able to travel freely and meet with officials, lawyers, nongovernmental organizations, and victims and families of victims of abuses by the government and by armed groups.

The government ignored requests by the U.N. special rapporteurs on torture and on extrajudicial, summary, or arbitrary executions to visit the country. Foreign ministry officials and ONDH head Rezzag-Bara told Human Rights Watch that Algeria considered the rapporteurs as "secondary mechanisms." They contended that official reports to the U.N. Human Rights Committee and other treaty bodies, and cooperation with international human rights organizations, adequately discharged the country's obligations with regard to U.N. human rights mechanisms.

Several lawyers and other human rights defenders continued to document abuses, and women's and victim's rights organizations were active. The government imposed limits on the activities of some groups (see above), however, and activists complained to Human Rights Watch that the authorities were often unresponsive when they requested investigations or information on cases. On May 27, security forces detained Mohamed Smain, head of the Relizane office of the LADDH, after he attempted to document evidence at a grave site connected with the case of the two former mayors implicated in mass killings in the area (see above). He was released the next day but authorities confiscated his videotape of the site. Rachid Mesli, a human rights lawyer who had been released from prison in July 1999 after serving all but a few days of a three year sentence on trumped up charges, was stopped at the airport and questioned in June after returning from Geneva after attending a meeting about the future of Algeria. Mesli left Algeria with his family in August and requested political asylum in Switzerland. He told Human Rights Watch that following his return from Geneva surveillance of his activities had intensified and that a prison acquaintance had been tortured in an effort to elicit, among other things, damaging information about Mesli, leading him to fear that he would be arrested and returned to prison.

The International Committee of the Red Cross, after a seven-year absence, conducted prison visits in October-November 1999 and March-May 2000, in which they visited seventeen places of detention administered by the Ministry of Justice and interviewed 763 prisoners of their choosing. They did not, however, have access to persons who may have been held in military barracks or police facilities.

The Role of theInternational Community

European Union

The states of the European Union publicly supported what political leaders termed the reconciliation policies of President Bouteflika but said little about human rights violations or the problem of impunity. An E.U. ministerial "troika" comprising External Affairs Minister Chris Patten, Common Foreign and Security Policy High Representative Javier Solana, and Finnish Foreign Minister Tarja Halonen, visited Algiers in November 1999. A fifth round of negotiations on the E.U.-Algeria Association Agreement took place in July, but there were no signs that a final agreement was near.

President Bouteflika made his first foreign visit as president to Italy in November 1999. According to Radio Algiers, when asked at a press conference about investigations into responsibility for killings, he replied that, "politics are one thing and history another. Now I am extinguishing a fire and tackling political issues, with priority given to the present." He visited France in June 2000, the first official visit by an Algerian head of state for seventeen years and only the second since Algeria's independence in 1962. France agreed in principle to a debt-for-equity exchange which would convert a small portion of Algeria's U.S. $3.4 billion debt—Ffr400 million (U.S. $58 million)—into private investments by French companies. French and Italian warships paid official visits to Algeria over the course of the last year.

During Spanish Prime Minister José María Aznar's visit to Algiers in July, the Spanish daily *El Pais* reported that Madrid was inclined to look favorably on Algeria's request for help in training its security forces. The newspaper reported also that Algeria had requested action be taken against Islamist "fundamentalists" residing in Spain.

Qatar confirmed British media reports in July that £4.6 (U.S. $6.65) million worth of British military equipment that it had purchased was destined for Algeria. The Qatari purchase order to BAe (formerly British Aerospace) had specified that, as directed by its ruler, Shaikh Hamad bin Khalifah Al Thani, Qatar would forward the equipment freely as a gift "to the armed services of the state of Algeria." The equipment included Landrover Defender rapid deployment vehicles and night vision equipment.

According to a U.S. Congressional Research Service study of arms transfers released in August, Algeria took deliveries of U.S. $600 million worth of arms from European countries other than the U.K., France, Germany, and Italy in the 1996-1999 period. During that same period, Russia delivered U.S. $400 million and China sent U.S. $100 million worth of arms to Algeria.

United States

The United States quietly but publicly supported President Bouteflika's political initiatives and his efforts to privatize the state-dominated economy. Commenting on the Civil Harmony Law in late January, Ambassador Cameron Hume told the *Chicago Tribune* that "Algerians are the ones who have to forgive and forget. Every country has to find its own way. We allowed the people of Northern Ireland, and Turkey and South Africa to do this." He added, "If it [the law and the pardon] works for them, I'll respect it," but failed to make clear that grave offenses such as crimes against humanity should not be covered by an amnesty. Hume was quoted in the Algiers daily *El Watan* on June 21 as saying that "the United States is in the best position to encourage positive change in Algeria, together with and not in competition with its European allies."

Signs of growing U.S. economic interest in Algeria included visits by leading private U.S.-based international banks and investment houses such as Chase Manhattan to Algiers in June 2000, a month that also saw a visit by Under Secretary of the Treasury Stuart Eizenstat. U.S. private investments in Algeria were estimated at between U.S. $3.5 and $4 billion, almost entirely in oil and gas exploration and production. Many of these investments were backed by the U.S. Export-Import Bank, whose chairman, James

Harmon, visited Algiers in December and whose $1.6 billion exposure in Algeria was by far the bank's largest in any Middle Eastern or North African country. Following Harmon's visit the bank announced that it had eliminated the previous U.S. $2 billion ceiling on Export-Import financing in Algeria. According to Algerian press reports, Eizenstat told Algerian officials and heads of companies that U.S. private investments outside of hydrocarbon industries would depend on the creation of a North African free trade area with Tunisia and Morocco.

The U.S. also pursued closer military ties with Algeria. There were several visits by high-level military officers following the September 1999 visit of Vice-Admiral Daniel Murphy, commander of the U.S. Navy's Sixth Fleet. Admiral Charles Abbot, deputy commander of U.S. armed forces in Europe, met with President Bouteflika and army chief of staff Maj. Gen. Mohamed Lamari on April 24 and reportedly discussed setting up a permanent joint military program. Maj.Gen. Randall Schmidt, director of aerospace operations for the U.S. Air Force in Europe, met with Algerian military and defense officials in late July in Algiers.

Deputy Assistant Secretary of State Ronald Neumann, commenting on the text of President Bouteflika's remarks on human rights at a cabinet meeting in mid-March, wrote to Algerian ambassador Idriss Jazairy on March 24 expressing support for the president's "determination to strengthen the rights of individuals in detention and in preventive custody" and "his proposals to reinforce control by the judiciary of the criminal investigative branch of the police services." The text of the letter appeared in the May 7 edition of the government daily *El Moudjahid*.

EGYPT

Human Rights Developments

The government of President Husni Mubarak intensified its efforts to exercise control over civil society institutions, harassing and restricting the activities of political parties, human rights and other nongovernmental organizations (NGOs), professional associations and the press. Infringements of freedom of expression, association and assembly, particularly in the run up to the People's Assembly elections scheduled for October and November 2000, raised doubt about the government's stated commitment to fair and free elections. State security forces continued to commit grave human rights violations with impunity, including the detention without charge or trial of political detainees and torture, and political opponents continued to be sentenced after unfair trials.

In May, the state of emergency was extended for a further three years. In force almost continuously since 1967, the emergency laws gave the authorities extensive powers to arrest suspects at will and detain them without trial for prolonged periods, and to refer civilian defendants to military courts or to exceptional state security courts whose procedures fall far short of international standards for fair trial.

Elections for the People's Assembly, initially scheduled to start in mid-November, were brought forward to October 18, 2000 and spread out over three rounds to allow judicial supervision of both principal and auxiliary polling stations. The change came as a result of the Supreme Constitutional Court ruling on July 8 that legislation governing parliamentary elections was unconstitutional due to the absence of full judicial supervision. In two extraordinary sessions on July 15 and 16, the People's Assembly and the *Majlis al-Shura* (consultative council, the upper house of the parliament) approved three presidential decrees that amended the legislation governing the elections. The principal amendment was to Article 24 of the Law on the Exercise of Political Rights (Law 73 of 1956), which had provided for judicial supervision of principal polling stations only, while auxiliary stations were supervised by civil servants.

On May 20, the Political Parties Committee of the *Majlis al-Shura* froze the activities of the Islamist opposition Labor Party and banned its publications, ostensibly because of a leadership dispute within the party. This action, widely perceived as part of an attempt to silence government critics ahead of the elections, followed violent street demonstrations in early May over the publication of a novel alleged to be offensive to Islam. The Labor Party's bi-weekly newspaper, *al-Sha'ab*, had denounced the novel (see below). Despite several court rulings in favor of the party, the ban on its publications remained in force as of October.

In another legal move on July 24, the Political Parties Committee formally requested the Labor Party's dissolution by referring the case to the Political Parties Tribunal, an exceptional court established by the Law on Political Parties (Law 40 of 1977). This followed a decision by prosecutors to charge nine Labor Party figures with having links with the banned Muslim Brotherhood, receiving unauthorized funding and "working against national unity," among them Labor Party secretary general 'Adel Hussain. In April, he and three other Labor Party figures were convicted for slandering Deputy Prime Minister Yusuf Wali. Hussain was fined and the others sentenced to between one and two years in prison.

In keeping with past practice of referring civilian political suspects to military courts, the government brought twenty defendants allegedly linked to the Muslim Brotherhood to trial before the Supreme Military Court on December 25, 1999. The defendants faced incitement and other charges under articles 30, 86, and 88 of the Penal Code, including membership of, and recruiting others to, an illegal organization and attempting to control the activities of professional associations. None of the charges involved the use or advocacy of violence. The defendants, mostly lawyers, university professors, and other professionals had been arrested in October 1999 and detained at Mazra'at Tora Prison. The 2000 announcement of the verdicts, due in July, was deferred first to October 3 and then to November 7. Many Egyptians saw the prosecutions as an attempt by the authorities to prevent the defendants from running as independent candidates in elections for the People's Assembly and for the boards of their respective professional associations. Mukhtar Muhammad Nouh, for example, a former member of parliament, had been expected to stand as a candidate in the Egyptian Lawyers' Association's board elections due to be held on July 1 but postponed by the authorities pending a court ruling in a dispute over election procedures. This was resolved on September 5 when the Supreme Administrative Court rejected a government appeal against a lower court decision that board elections be held solely on the premises of the Egyptian Lawyers' Association and its branches. By October 2000 no new date had been set for these elections.

In the absence of official figures, it was not possible to specify the number of political detainees being held without trial, but the authorities freed at least several hundred between January and July. They also made scores of new arrests, mostly of suspected members of the Muslim Brotherhood, and thousands of other political detainees, the vast majority of them actual or suspected membership of banned groups, in particular *al-Gama'a al-Islamiyya* (Islamic Group) and *al-Gihad* (Holy Struggle), continued to be held in administrative detention under emergency legislation. They included some who had completed prison sentences and others who had been held without charge or trial for prolonged periods, in some cases for over ten years. Many detainees successfully challenged the legality of their continued detention in the courts, but Ministry of Interior officials routinely ignored the courts' rulings and continued to hold the detainees in harsh conditions at prisons such as al-Fayyum, Wadi Natrun I and II, and Abu Za'bal al-Sina'i, where detainees were deprived of all contact with the outside world for long periods. In a positive development, at least sixty-eight detainees held in these prisons were allowed family visits in September.

Security forces tortured and ill-treated detainees, and there were reports that as many as fifteen detainees died in custody due to poor conditions and lack of medical care, and, in at least one case, due to torture. Again, however, the authorities' failure to disclose information on such cases, or whether official investigations were held to determine the causes of such deaths, hampered efforts to assess the true scale of the problem in Egypt's prisons and detention centers. One case, however, did lead to official action. The authorities charged six police officers following the death of Ahmad Muhammad 'Issa, beaten to death on February 10 in Wadi Natrun prison, and their trial was continuing in October.

In a positive development, Interior Minister Habib al-Adli announced on September 17 that the practices of flogging and caning as disciplinary measures in prisons would be banned.

Egyptian courts sentenced as least sixty-six people to death, and the authorities carried out eighteen executions between February and September, according to Amnesty International. Most death sentences were imposed for ordinary criminal offences, but two of those executed had been sentenced in their absence for membership of an armed illegal group after an unfair trial.

The controversial Law on Civil Associations and Institutions (Law 153 of 1999), condemned by Egyptian and international human rights groups for excessively restricting the activities of NGOs and facilitating undue government interference in their internal affairs, was overturned by the Supreme Constitutional Court on June 3. Issued shortly after the 1999 law's registration deadline for NGOs, the court ruled the law unconstitutional on procedural grounds because it had not been presented to the *Majlis al-Shura*. Egyptian human rights activists welcomed the ruling, which also noted that administrative courts, not the courts of first instance, should hear cases arising from disputes between NGOs and the authorities. The day after the ruling, the Ministry of Social Affairs announced that Law 32 of 1964, which the 1999 law had been intended to replace, would remain in force, but that NGOs that had been granted registration under the overturned law would retain that status, giving rise to confu-

sion as to which law governed their activities. On September 3, Deputy Justice Minister Fathi Naguib told Human Rights Watch that the overturned law would be revised in light of the constitutional court decision and then submitted again to the People's Assembly after the elections. He said there would be no further consultations with NGO representatives regarding the provisions of the law, which he asserted was "fair and democratic."

The government prosecuted at least one writer for his exercise of freedom of expression. On March 10, police arrested author Salahuddin Muhsin, charging him with writing books deemed offensive to Islam. Prosecutors cited two of his books, *A Night Talk with Heaven* and *Trembling of Enlightenment*, when he appeared before the State Security Court for Misdemeanours in Giza on June 17. On July 8, the court imposed a six-month suspended sentence, rendering Muhsin liable to certain imprisonment should he be convicted of a similar offence in future.

The November 1999 decision of the Ministry of Culture to authorize the re-printing of *A Banquet of Seaweed* by Syrian author Haidar Haidar, first published in Lebanon in 1983, led to widespread protests in Cairo following an April 28 article in the Islamist *al-Sha'ab* newspaper, which denounced the book as blasphemous. Several thousand demonstrators, many of them al-Azhar University students, staged a series of protests from May 7, and students at 'Ain Shams and Cairo universities held similar protests. As the protests became increasingly violent, police reportedly used rubber bullets and tear gas to disperse the demonstrators, and several police officers and tens of students were injured. Police also arrested scores of students, prompting further demonstrations calling for their release, and all were freed without charge within days. Although a panel of literary experts appointed by the Ministry of Culture cleared the novel of the charge of blasphemy, the authorities announced that the book would be withdrawn from circulation. On May 12, the prosecutor-general's staff interrogated two Ministry of Culture employees about the re-printing of the novel but no formal charges were brought.

The right to freedom of conscience and religion also came under attack in other ways, involving both Muslims and Christians. On September 5, the Emergency State Security Court sentenced Manal Wahid Mana'i to five years in prison under Article 98(f) of the Penal Code for denigrating Islam. She was arrested, together with fifteen others, in December 1999 as the alleged leader of a Sufi sect and accused of "claiming prophecy and using the Islamic religion to propagate extremist ideas." Twelve of her co-defendants, among them her husband 'Abd al-Hamid Muhammad Kamel, received sentences ranging from six months to three years of imprisonment. Two other defendants were fined. Another died in custody, reportedly of natural causes before the verdict.

In another case, the Sohag Criminal Court sentenced Sourial Gayed Ishaq, a Coptic Christian, to three years in prison under articles 160 and 161 of the Penal Code for insulting Islam. He had reportedly made offensive remarks in public about Islam after sectarian violence broke out between Muslims and Christians in his village, al-Kusheh, on December 31, 1999. A financial dispute between a Muslim and a Christian had led to three days of rioting and the deaths of some twenty-three victims, most of them Christians. Security forces imposed a curfew and arrested scores of villagers to end the bloodshed, and both the government and local human rights groups, including the Egyptian Organization for Human Rights (EOHR) and the Centre for Human Rights Legal Aid (CHRLA), launched their own investigations. On March 11, Prosecutor-General Maher 'Abd al-Wahed announced that those responsible would be tried on murder, attempted murder, incitement to violence, robbery, and other charges, and two trials involving 135 defendants began before criminal courts in Sohag and Dar al-Salam in the first week of June. On September 5, the Sohag court sentenced four defendants tried in their absence to ten years of imprisonment and sixteen others to prison terms of between six-

teen others to prison terms of between six months and two years. The court acquitted nineteen others. The trial of the remaining defendants before the Dar al-Salam criminal court was still continuing in October 2000.

Defending Human Rights

The government closely monitored the activities of human rights organizations and restricted their work. Official investigations brought against targeted activists were kept pending, in some cases for years. The case against Hafez Abu Sa'da, secretary general of the EOHR, who had been detained for fifteen days in December 1998, remained ambiguous. The government had charged him and other EOHR members with accepting funds from a foreign donor—the British embassy in Cairo—to harm to Egypt's national interests. On February 13, several days before the EOHR was due to issue a report on renewed sectarian violence in al-Kusheh (see above), the Prosecutor-General's Office announced that it had referred the case to the Emergency Supreme State Security Court. In March, however, Prosecutor-General 'Abd al-Wahed told Human Rights Watch that the British ambassador had confirmed that the funds in question were intended to support a women's legal aid project, and that in light of this information Abu Sa'da's "file was closed." By October 2000, however, the authorities had still not informed Abu Sa'da officially that the case was closed.

The EOHR and other local human rights groups condemned the government's extension of the state of emergency. The EOHR was among a number of human rights groups that applied for official registration under the 1999 NGO law in the first half of the year but of these, only CHRLA had been granted registration before the law was overturned by the constitutional court. Applications by other human rights groups had not as yet been fully processed. The Arab Organization for Human Rights (AOHR) was granted legal status as a regional organization in early May under a separate agreement with the Ministry of Foreign Affairs. After the 1999 law was declared invalid, the Ministry of Social Affairs informed the EOHR on July 24 that its application for registration would be considered under the 1964 law and requested that it provide the necessary documentation. Several days later, ministry officials told the EOHR verbally that its registration had been granted, and gave a registration number, but on July 30 the ministry informed the EOHR in writing that the decision on its application had been deferred upon "a request from security officials."

Human rights activists preparing to monitor the People's Assembly elections also came under attack. On the night of June 30, State Security Intelligence (SSI) officials arrested Sa'adeddin Ibrahim, sociology lecturer at the American University of Cairo and director of the Ibn Khaldun Center for Development Studies. The SSI raided both his home and the center and confiscated documents, computers and other belongings. The authorities also arrested the center's chief accountant, Nadia 'Abd al-Nur, and her assistant, Usama Hammad, and they, together with Ibrahim, were interrogated by officials of the prosecutor-general. The authorities issued renewable, fifteen day detention orders against Ibrahim and 'Abd al-Nur under Military Decree No. 4 of 1992. Abd al-Nur went on hunger strike for two days to protest the conditions in which she was being held at the Womens' prison. During her first two weeks in detention, the authorities interrogated her without the presence of a defense lawyer. Prosecutors initially accused Ibrahim of receiving foreign funding without the authorities' permission, forgery of election documents, fraud and the dissemination of false information damaging to Egypt's interests, but failed to specify the legal basis for these or later accusations. The authorities questioned at least fourteen others in connection with the case, some of whom they detained for several weeks.

In early July, the authorities detained and interrogated staff of the Women Voters' Support Center, a NGO cooperating with the Ibn Khaldun Center on educational programs for voters. They included Warda 'Ali Bahi and Magda al-Bey, detained without charges for six days and one month respectively. The authorities then released Sa'adeddin Ibrahim and Nadia 'Abd al-Nur on bail on August 10, and others in the ensuing days, but took further action on September 24 after Ibrahim announced that he intended to monitor the parliamentary elections. The prosecutor general formally referred the case to the Supreme State Security Court, naming twenty-eight defendants, including ten who were not in custody and would be tried in their absence. Both the Ibn Khaldun Center and the Women Voters' Support Center remained closed. The trial was set for November 18.

The Role of the International Community

United Nations

The U.N. Working Group on Arbitrary Detention, in an opinion issued on September 15, 1999, requested the government to remedy the situation of Mahmoud Mubarak Ahmad, a medical doctor held without charge or trial since January 1995, in contravention of Egypt's international legal obligations. The working group had raised the case with the government in June 1998 but received no response. In its December 1999 report, the U.N. Working Group on Enforced or Involuntary Disappearances stated that it had submitted new information to the government on seven cases, and had received a response on one case.

The U.N. Committee on Economic, Social and Cultural Rights on May 2 and 3 considered Egypt's initial report on the implementation of the International Covenant on Economic, Social and Cultural Rights. In its concluding observations, adopted on May 12, the committee noted improvements in the educational system and the reduction of illiteracy, granting divorce rights to women, and improvements in the public health system. However, it criticized the state of emergency for limiting "the scope of implementation of constitutional guarantees for economic, social and cultural rights," and expressed concern about infringements of workers' and women's rights, child labor, media censorship, and freedom of association. The committee recommended, among other things, that the Law on Civil Associations and Institutions (Law 153/1999) be repealed or amended to conform with Egypt's constitution and its international obligations, noting that the law "gives the government control over the rights of NGOs to manage their own activities, including seeking external funding." The committee further recommended that the new Personal Status Code be reviewed to remove provisions that discriminate against women, and that new labor laws be promulgated "to protect children from abusive working conditions" and to eradicate child labor.

European Union

The European Parliament, in a January 20 resolution, expressed concern about "sectarian clashes between Copts and Muslims in Egypt, which resulted in the deaths of more than 20 Egyptian citizens in several villages in Upper Egypt on 1 and 2 January 2000." The resolution called on Egypt to "raise awareness about religious tolerance and respect for human rights and minority freedoms by launching a campaign on sectarian hatred and violence," and to consider the abolition of the death penalty. It also expressed support for the stated efforts of the Egyptian government to investigate the clashes and to compensate those injured.

The E.U. Commissioner for External Relations Chris Patten visited Egypt on April 1 for talks with Prime Minister Atef Obeid and senior cabinet members focusing on E.U.-Egypt relations, the Middle East peace process and the Euro-Mediterranean Association Agreement. Negotiations over the Association Agreement were concluded in June 1999 but as of October 2000 Egypt had not signed it. On September 6, the European Commission adopted a series of recommendations in preparation for the Fourth Meeting of Euro-Mediterranean Foreign Ministers, scheduled to be held in Marseilles on November 16 and 17. These urged Egypt to sign the Association Agreement and, referring to E.U. economic assistance mechanisms, advocated "greater emphasis on human rights issues," in order to make financial assistance programs "more dependent on substantial progress in these areas."

United States

The U.S. remained Egypt's largest provider of foreign aid, with military assistance in fiscal year 2000 estimated at U.S. $1.3 billion and U.S. $727 million in economic support funds, but U.S. criticism of Egypt's human rights record remained muted. For fiscal year 2001 the Clinton Administration requested U.S. $1.3 billion in military assistance and U.S.$695 million for economic support funds, describing Egypt as "a key supporter of the Mideast peace process ... [and] an indispensable ally in the region." The administration's budget document stated that 10 percent of the economic support funds were for educational and health programs, as well as to "support democracy by assisting civil society organizations' role in public decision-making."

In the case of Sa'adeddin Ibrahim (see above), who held dual Egyptian-U.S. citizenship, the State Department several times called on the Egyptian government to press formal charges or release him from detention.

In its Country Reports on Human Rights Practices for 1999, the State Department said that Egypt "continued to commit numerous human rights abuses, although its record improved somewhat over the previous year, mainly due to a decrease in terrorist activity by Islamic extremists." In its Annual Report on International Religious Freedom for 2000, released on September 5, the State Department claimed to observe "a trend toward improvement in the Government's respect for and the protection of the right to religious freedom."

President Mubarak visited Washington, D.C., in late March, and President Clinton stopped briefly in Cairo on August 29 to discuss Israeli-Palestinian negotiations. In neither case was there any indication that human rights issues were on the agenda. Prior to President Mubarak's March visit, the U.S. Commission on International Religious Freedom as well as several U.S. legislators publicly urged President Clinton to raise the issue of sectarian violence and alleged discrimination against the Coptic Christian community.

IRAN

Human Rights Developments

There was continued struggle between reformists and conservatives over the political direction of the Islamic republic leading to new human rights abuses, notably violations of freedom of expression. Reformist candidates supporting President Khatami won a significant victory in February's parliamentary elections, hailed as the fairest in Iran's history, but hopes that this would lead quickly to institutionalized gains for the legal protection of human rights proved misplaced. Conservatives used their control over powerful state institutions, most importantly the judiciary, to intimidate and silence supporters of greater political freedom. Twenty-five independent newspapers and magazines were closed, and leading publishers and journalists were imprisoned on vague charges of "insulting Islam" or "calling into question the Islamic foundation of the republic." The prosecution and conviction, after an unfair trial, of ten Iranian Jews from Shiraz on charges of espionage for Israel highlighted serious due process shortcomings in Iran's judicial system and raised fears that religious minorities would face greater persecution. The government continued to make frequent use of the death penalty after trials which failed to comply with international standards. Some executions were carried out in public.

The early part of the year was dominated by elections for the sixth *Majles* (Islamic Consultative Assembly). Parliamentary elections in 1996 had been marred when the Council of Guardians vetoed more than 44 percent of the candidates. This year the council, a government-appointed body of twelve senior clerics and legal experts, vetoed less than 10 percent of the candidates. Of 6,083 candidates who stood for election to the 290 seats, 576 were disqualified. Despite the exclusion of representatives of parties opposed to, or openly critical of, clerical rule, Iranians were presented with a choice of candidates representing a range of views.

Conservatives maneuvered, however, to limit the extent of the reformist victory, and blocked high-profile reformists from running as candidates in a variety of ways. Abdullah Nouri, the impeached former minister of the interior, publisher of the prominent daily newspaper *Khordad*, and reformist candidate for speaker, was brought to trial in November 1999 before the Special Court for the Clergy.

However, he used his trial as an opportunity to advocate reform, reminding his conservative accusers that they could not impose their own interpretation of Islam and challenging the religious and legal authority of the court, which he likened to an inquisition. Nouri's statements, which included favorable reference to Ayatollah Montazeri's criticisms of the *velayet-e faqih* (rule of the supreme jurist) were widely reported in the opposition press. Nevertheless, Nouri was convicted, sentenced to five years of imprisonment, and disqualified from standing in the election.

In January, the Council of Guardians removed other prominent reformists from the list of candidates, including Abbas Abdi, a leader of the 1989 seizure of the U.S. embassy in Tehran, which occasioned the hostage crisis, who had since then taken public steps to reconcile with his former captives. Candidates from the opposition Iran Freedom Movement, including its leader Ebrahim Yazdi, were again banned from participating in the elections.

Mahmoud Ali Chehregani, an advocate of the rights of the Azeri minority, was prevented from registering as a candidate for the election in Tabriz by being detained by local police until after the registration deadline had passed.

On March 12, a gunman shot and severely wounded Saeid Hajjarian, a director of *Sobh-e Emrouz*, the reformist newspaper that had taken the lead in exposing the involvement of state officials in extrajudicial executions of dissident intellectuals. He was also a leading political advisor to President Khatami, and regarded as the architect of the reformists' February electoral triumph. His assailant escaped from the scene of the shooting on a motorcycle of the type reserved for use by security forces and police at the scene made no attempt to apprehend him, raising suspicion that he was acting in collaboration with members of the security forces. However, the assailant was arrested soon afterwards and, together with four co-conspirators, tried, and sentenced to fifteen years of imprisonment.

The attempt on Hajjarian's life heightened fears that paramilitary death squads were at work within the state apparatus. A group of police officers charged with an attack on a Tehran University student dormitory in July 1999 (see World Report 2000) went on trial in March, but they did not include uniformed paramilitaries who witnesses said were responsible for the worst of the violence, in which at least four students were killed. In July, a senior police officer among those charged was acquitted. Scores of students who were detained during demonstrations and in the raid on the dormitory remained in prison.

State officials accused of involvement in the murder of dissidents and intellectuals at the end of 1998 have not yet been tried in public. In September, a statement from the judiciary, published in the press, announced the beginning of court proceedings against eighteen former ministry of information officials accused of involvement in the killings. Only two of the accused were in detention. Lawyers for the victims' families, who were granted access to prosecution files, complained that the files were still incomplete and raised questions about what had happened to material gathered during two years of investigations.

Conservatives mounted a concerted campaign to close independent newspapers in order to weaken the reformists' influence. In the absence of formal political parties, newspapers were key agents for mobilizing popular support for the reformist cause, with many leading reformists publishing their own newspapers, which acted as forums for wide-ranging discussion of issues confronting the country. The press had been a major factor in the reformists' electoral success and, increasingly, was exposing corruption within the ruling conservative elite and its involvement in gross human rights violations, including extrajudicial executions of dissidents. The conservatives' action against the press dealt a devastating blow to what had been one of the few visible achievements of the reform movement, a vibrant, independent print media.

The reformist movement was far from monolithic. It included both Islamist democrats, who advocated a more responsive political system, and others who more directly challenged the clergy's central role in politics and the notion that the supreme leader of the Islamic Republic should have absolute power to determine divinely ordained policy.

In April, conservative elements within the judiciary began to close down independent newspapers and magazines, and to imprison leading journalists and editors. On April 10, Mashallah Shamsol-Vaezin, a pioneer of independent media and editor of a succession of banned titles, was imprisoned for thirty months on the grounds that an article he had published criticizing the death penalty defamed Islam. On April 22, Akbar Ganji, a leading investigative journalist for *Fath* newspaper, was imprisoned by the Tehran Press Court for defaming the security forces in articles he had written about official involvement in political killings and the attack on Saeid Hajjarian. On April 23, Shamsol-Vaezin's publisher, Latif Safari, was imprisoned for two and a half years by the press court. The same day, eight daily and three weekly newspapers were ordered closed. Other prominent publishers or editors, some of whom were also politicians, were indicted for press offenses or summoned to appear before the press court. In August, Ahmad Zeidabadi, Massoud Behnoud, Ebrahim Nabavi, all journalists for independent newspapers, were taken into detention without charge or explanation.

Supreme Leader Ayatollah Khamenei,

while endorsing "the free flow of information," openly condoned the action taken against the press accusing some un-named titles of being "bases of the enemy." Following this lead, conservatives redoubled their attacks on reformists as agents of hostile alien forces, and the last remaining major independent daily, *Bahar*, was closed down in August. Ayatollah Jannati, a member of the Council of Guardians, remarked that closing down the newspapers was "the best thing the judiciary had done since the revolution."

In April, leading Iranian reformist politicians attended an international conference on Iran in Berlin, which was also attended by banned, exiled political activists. This allowed conservatives to portray the reformists as linked to hostile foreign powers, and many were prosecuted for participating in what the state-controlled media portrayed as an anti-Iranian, anti-Islamic event. Veteran independent politician, Ezzatollah Sahabi, now more than seventy years of age, spent more than six weeks in detention under interrogation before being released on bail. Three participants in the Berlin conference remained in prison at the end of the year. Five others are awaiting trial, but free on bail.

With the reformist press suppressed, conservatives were emboldened to tamper with the election results. In May, the Council of Guardians nullified the results in eleven constituencies and canceled 726,000 of the more than three million votes cast in the Tehran constituency, without explanation. For the clerical establishment, the most embarrassing outcome of the election was former President Rafsanjani's failure to gain enough votes to win a seat in the new Majles. Revised results several months later placed Rafsanjani higher in the poll but, rather than face humiliating criticism that the vote had been rigged, the powerful former president stood down from his seat.

When the new *Majles* convened in late May the reformists controlled some 150 of the 290 seats, but it was unclear whether the diverse factions of the reformist bloc would be able to operate as a unified voting group. Many reformists appeared chastened by the conservative backlash and anxious to reassure conservatives that change would not undermine the foundations of the state. Mehdi Karroubi, a cleric with a long history of senior government service, was elected speaker as a candidate acceptable to all factions.

The new parliament promised to amend the repressive press law passed in the closing months of the previous parliament. The law required applicants for new newspaper licenses to obtain prior approval from the judiciary, closing a previous loophole that had enabled banned newspapers to reopen days later under a new name. The law also facilitated the closure of newspapers on vaguely worded charges of "insulting Islam" or "undermining the religious foundation of the republic," leaving the press court with wide discretion to censor titles of which it disapproved. Reformists drafted a new bill that would better protect press freedom but this was vehemently attacked by conservatives as un-Islamic and likely to spread corruption in society. On August 6, Ayatollah Khamenei ordered the parliament to drop its consideration of a new press law. This unprecedented intervention in the legislative process by the supreme leader was accepted by Speaker Karroubi, averting open conflict between the parliament and the Council of Guardians, which was anyway expected to veto the proposed new law.

Other early actions by the new parliament indicated a pragmatic approach. New legislation to facilitate access by foreign investors to the Iranian market passed unanimously, indicating a shared recognition that the country's severe economic problems needed government attention. Reformist pledges to carry out public inquiries into the attack on student dormitories remained unfulfilled, however. On a positive note, a parliamentary commission carried out an investigation into prison conditions, visiting prisons in different parts of the country. The publication of the commission's findings, scheduled for mid-October, was delayed, reportedly because of their critical tone and exposure of torture.

Former detainees, arrested after the student disturbances in July 1999, informed Human Rights Watch that they were tortured and sexually abused while in prison in 1999 and early 2000. Ahmad Batebi, a student sentenced to thirteen years of imprisonment, wrote a letter to the head of the judiciary that was published in the international press, protesting beating and lashing that he had suffered while in detention.

Unfulfilled expectations were the cause of several clashes between demonstrators and hardline conservative supporters and the security forces. On the anniversary of the student demonstrations of July 1999, students marched and were joined by other demonstrators expressing their frustration at poor economic conditions. The protesters in Tehran were beaten by the self-styled partisans of the party of God, *ansar-e hezbollahi*, and forcibly dispersed.

More serious clashes occurred in the provincial town of Khorramabad in West Azerbaijan province in late August. Two leading reformist thinkers, Abdol Karim Soroush and Mohssen Kadivar, were prevented by *hezbollahis* armed with clubs and knives from attending a student convention in the town at which they were due to give speeches. There followed a week of street clashes between students and hardline vigilantes in which a police officer was killed and dozens of people were injured, requiring hospital treatment. Townspeople joined in the protests on the side of the students. One hundred and fifty protesters, mostly students, were detained after these disturbances.

Hardline vigilantes were less active in the early part of the year, partly because the judiciary was more actively targeting reformists. On April 14, the supreme leader condoned "legal-violence" against the "bases of the enemy" and "centers of corruption," suggesting that the vigilantes should act only when the judiciary and the legal authorities were not doing enough to maintain order. His remarks at Friday prayers contained a barely veiled threat that citizen violence to protect Islam was justified if the state was failing in its obligation to protect the faith. As demonstrations of popular discontent mounted to-

wards the end of the year, the vigilantes resumed their usual activities of assaulting reformists, breaking up demonstrations, and provoking disorder designed to discredit the reformist cause. In September, a group of vigilantes attacked a book exhibit in Esfahan, claiming that the titles showed disrespect for Islam. After the extreme vigilante violence of July 1999, Minister of Information Ali Younessi declared that such violence would no longer be permitted, but one year later he could only acknowledge that "they have their own leadership network and do as they please." The activities of the shadowy paramilitary supporters of conservatism, and the identities of the leaders behind the violence, had been favorite topics of the independent press. With suppression of this media, hardliners were able to intimidate political opponents free from the threat of public exposure.

A former vigilante, Amir Farshad Ebrahimi, stated in a videotape that vigilantes had received payments from senior clerics in order to carry out attacks on reformist personalities and to disrupt public events. He was sentenced in October, after a closed trial, to two years of imprisonment for defamation of public officials. His lawyer, Shirin Ebadi, and another lawyer, Mohssen Rahami, who had received a copy of the tape, were given suspended prison sentences and banned from practicing law for five years. False allegations were made by the conservative press that a Human Rights Watch researcher had been involved in the production and dissemination of the tape, but no formal charges were made against her.

The April trial in Shiraz of thirteen Iranian Jews accused of spying for Israel was conducted against this background of factional conflict. The factual basis of the case against the accused remained shrouded in mystery even after ten of them were convicted of forming an illegal organization and maintaining contacts with Israel, a hostile foreign power. While the trial was in progress, defendants gave interviews on state-controlled television in which they confessed to espionage. These confessions were contested by their lawyer, however, and appear not to have formed part of the court proceedings.

The trial, before a revolutionary court, was unfair. It was conducted in closed session, and observers, including a representative of Human Rights Watch, were denied access to the proceedings. Before trial, the defendants were held incommunicado for many months, during which the statements that formed the basis for their conviction were taken from them by the judge in his dual role as prosecutor as well as judge. The defendants, three of whom were acquitted at trial, were allowed access to legal counsel only once they had confessed.

Yet, in some respects, the trial of the Jews was uncharacteristically transparent by the standards of Iran's revolutionary courts. The trial judge met with journalists, diplomats, and human rights observers and answered questions about the case. Whereas most defendants tried before such courts are denied all access to legal counsel, in the Shiraz trial, principal defense lawyer Esmail Naseri openly challenged the validity of his clients' confessions, made while they were denied access to their lawyer, and pointed out the absence of other incriminating evidence. After the July sentencing of ten of the defendants to prison terms of between two and thirteen years, Naseri commented that, by law, they should be released pending an appeal because of the many procedural violations in the prosecution process, but that he feared political interference would rule this out. Then, in September, days before the result of the appeal was due to be announced Naseri told a press conference that he had been pressured to withdraw his objections to his clients' confessions and told that they would choose new lawyers if he refused to do so. He said that the thirteen had been held in prolonged solitary confinement until they were disorientated and willing to incriminate themselves, and that he would reveal the source of the pressure and threats against him if his clients' confessions were upheld. In September, the appeals court upheld the convictions but reduced the sentences to between two and six years. In October, the defendants allowed the deadline for filing an appeal to the Supreme Court to pass, and dismissed their defense lawyers without explanation.

While all Iranian leaders took exception to international criticism of the case, stressing that the judicial process should be allowed to take its course, President Khatami repeatedly emphasized that the Jewish community formed an integral part of Iranian society. In August, he received leaders of the Iranian Jewish community and relatives of the Shiraz defendants.

Other minority religious communities continued to be subjected to persecution. In February, three Bahais, Sirus Zabihi-Moghadam, Hedayat Kashefi-Najafabadi and Manouchehr Khulusi, were sentenced to death, apparently because of their religious activities. Two of the three had been detained since 1997 for violating the ban on Bahai religious gatherings. The details of the third man's detention were not known.

The Iraq-based armed opposition group, the People's Mojahedine Organization of Iran, continued to carry out attacks against targets inside Iran. Although the organization claimed to be targeting officials, several civilians were killed or injured in incidents, such as a mortar attack on the presidential office in downtown Tehran in February.

Defending Human Rights

The closure of independent newspapers was a major blow to public awareness of, and discourse on, human rights, but some steps were taken towards the creation of independent local human rights organizations. An Iranian Committee for the Protection of Journalists continued to promote and protect international standards on freedom of expression, but most of the organization's leaders were subsequently imprisoned or facing prosecution for their journalism. The nongovernmental Writers Association publicly criticized attacks on the press and restrictions on freedom of expression, and the Islamic Commission on Human Rights, an official body based within the judiciary, also spoke out against the closure of newspapers and prosecutions of editors and journalists. Mehrangiz

Kar, a lawyer and women's rights activist, was arrested in April after making a speech advocating women's rights at the Berlin conference. She was freed on bail after a month. In August, Hassan Youssefi Eshkevari, a religious scholar, was imprisoned on his return from Germany for his advocacy of liberal interpretations of Islam supportive of human rights principles. He had delayed his return from the Berlin conference. He was charged as an apostate and with being corrupt on earth, charges which carry the death penalty.

Access to the country by international human rights observers remained restricted and the U.N. special representative on Iran continued to be denied entry. However, a Human Rights Watch researcher in possession of an Iranian passport was able to visit in April and to meet with officials, but other Human Rights Watch representatives and those of other nongovernmental organizations were generally not issued visas. The government allowed representatives of a French legal association to visit Iran at the time of the Shiraz trial of Iranian Jews.

The Role of the International Community

United Nations

The U.N. Commission on Human Rights, while welcoming a number of positive developments such as the February elections, "expressed concern" about Iran's human rights record in a resolution in April. The resolution called on the government to resume cooperation with the U.N. special representative on Iran, Maurice Copithorne of Canada, and it extended his mandate. The resolution also expressed concern over the Jews' trial, discrimination against the situation of religious minorities, and the prevalence of the death penalty. In his report to the General Assembly in October, Copithorne was more critical, singling out the "accelerating attack on the press" as the most dramatic development, but also noting the lack of progress in judicial reform and the execution of 130 people between January and July.

European Union

The prospect of lucrative Iranian trade and investment contracts for European corporations was a high priority for E.U. leaders, but the Shiraz trial of Iranian Jews strained the improving relations between E.U. members states and Iran. In France and other European countries, demonstrations called for the severing of diplomatic relations with Iran if the defendants were convicted, and in April the European Parliament passed a resolution urging the Iranian authorities to guarantee a fair trial, allow access to international observers, and introduce a moratorium on the death penalty. Many E.U. leaders, while condemning continued violations of human rights, publicly expressed support for the reformist policies of President Khatami, and he made state visits to France and Germany during the year.

United States

There was a continued slow warming of relations between the United States and Iran. The U.S. commented favorably on the February elections, but continued to express concern over Iran's alleged support for international terrorism and efforts to develop nuclear weapons. President Clinton and other U.S. leaders publicly criticized the Shiraz trial. Restrictions were eased on the import to the U.S. of certain goods, but restrictions on U.S. corporations investing in Iran remained in place, to the increasing displeasure of corporations who saw contracts being awarded to their European competitors.

A delegation of Iranian parliamentarians led by Speaker Karrubi attended an Inter-Parliamentary Union conference in New York in August, and met several members of the U.S. Congress at a reception. During President Khatami's visit to New York for the U.N. Millennium Summit, President Clinton and Secretary of State Madeleine Albright conspicuously attended his speeches. The State Department's *Country Report on Human Rights Practices for 1999*, issued before the post-election crack-down on the reformist movement, gave some credit for improvements in the freedom of expression field, while remaining critical of a wide range of violations. The *Annual Report on International Religious Freedom*, issued by the State Department in early September identified Iran as "a country of concern," because of its persecution of religious minorities.

IRAQ AND IRAQI KURDISTAN

Human Rights Developments

The Iraqi government continued to commit widespread and gross human rights violations, including arbitrary arrests of suspected political opponents, executions of prisoners, and forced expulsions of Kurds and Turkmen from Kirkuk and other districts. Known or suspected political opponents living abroad were reportedly frequently targeted and threatened by Iraqi government agents.

Relations between the two opposition groups, the Kurdistan Democratic Party (KDP) and the Patriotic Union of Kurdistan (PUK), that retained control over most of the northern provinces of Duhok, Arbil and Sulaimaniya, remained strained despite a 1998 U.S.-brokered peace agreement and continued mediation efforts by the U.S. In the north, the year was punctuated by clashes between these and other Kurdish parties, resulting in casualties and some arrests, and human rights abuses were committed by the KDP, PUK and opposition groups. Municipal council elections were held in PUK-controlled territory in February, the first in the region since May 1992.

In the area under Iraqi government control, elections were held on March 27 for a new four-year term National Assembly, in which 220 of the 250 parliamentary seats were contested. The other thirty, reserved for the Kurdish population, were filled by presidential appointees.

Economic sanctions imposed on Iraq by the United Nations Security Council in August 1991 remained in force. The Security Council adopted a resolution expanding the "oil-for-food" program and setting up a new weapons inspection system, proposing the suspension of the sanctions for a limited period following compliance by Iraq with the provisions of the resolution. The Iraqi government rejected the proposal, stating that none of the Security Council's resolutions provided for such suspension, and continued to demand the total lifting of sanctions. International consensus over the sanctions was further eroded following several "humanitarian flights" by Russia, France, Syria and Egypt, among others, following the reopening of Baghdad's Saddam International airport in mid-July.

Human Rights Developments in Government-controlled Iraq

Five Republican Guard officers were reportedly executed on December 29, 1999, after being accused of complicity in the alleged attempted murder of President Saddam Hussein's younger son, Qusay. Among them were Lieut. Col. Ibrahim Jassem and Capt. 'Umar Abdul Razzaq. In April, a number of Republican Guard and Special Security Forces personnel were reportedly arrested following an alleged coup attempt. Some forty Republican Guard members were reportedly among those taken to Radhwaniyya prison, including Staff Lieut. Col. Hashem Jassem Majid and Lieut. Col. Shawqi Shraishi. Further arrests and executions were reported in May of four officers belonging to the Special Security Forces, among them staff colonels Kadhim Jawad 'Ali and 'Ali Muhammad Salman.

Numerous executions of political prisoners as well as those convicted for criminal offences were apparently carried out as part of the government's "prison cleansing" campaign involving several prisons, including Abu Ghraib and Radhwaniyya. In March, the opposition Iraqi Communist Party's Center for Human Rights submitted to the U.N. special rapporteur on Iraq details on 223 executions that it said were carried out between October 12, 1999, and March 9, 2000. They included twenty-six political detainees executed on November 26, 1999, and a further twenty-six executed on January 27, all in Abu Ghraib prison near Baghdad. The majority were Shi'a Muslims from Basra, al-Samawa, al-Nasiriyya, al-Diwaniyya, al-Hilla, al-'Amara and Baghdad, some of whom had been held without judicial due process since 1991 on suspicion of having participated in the March 1991 uprising. The bodies of the victims were reportedly buried in mass graves near the prison.

Iraqi security forces continued to target suspected supporters of Ayatollah Muhammad Sadeq al-Sadr, a leading Shi'a cleric who was assassinated in al-Najaf in February 1999 together with his two sons. In March, scores of Shi'a Muslims who had fled Iraq earlier in the year and in 1999 told Human Rights Watch that they had been repeatedly interrogated and in some cases detained and tortured. Some of those detained were relatives of prominent clerics or of Ayatollah al-Sadr's students who had been arrested shortly after his assassination. Twenty-two of those arrested soon after his murder were tried by a special court attached to the Mudiriyyat al-Amn al-'Amma (General Security Directorate) in Baghdad on charges including carrying out armed attacks on military and Ba'th Party personnel, membership of a prohibited organization, and sheltering supporters of Ayatollah al-Sadr who were being sought by the authorities. On May 13, at least six, all students of religion in al-Najaf, were sentenced to death and their homes demolished. They included Shaikh Salim Jassem al-'Abbudi, Shaikh Nasser al-Saa'idi and Sa'ad al-Nuri. Other defendants received sentences of life imprisonment or lesser terms. By October 2000 it was not known whether the death sentences had been carried out. Some of their relatives were also arrested and tortured.

Iraqi intelligence agents targeted political opponents who had fled Iraq, threatening and intimidating them or arresting and torturing family members still in the country. On June 7, Staff Lieut. Gen. Najib al-Salihi, former chief of staff of the Iraqi army's Sixth Armoured Division who had fled to Jordan in 1995, received a videotape showing the rape of a female relative by intelligence personnel. The rape or threat of rape has long been used in Iraq as a punitive measure against opponents to extract confessions or information or to pressure them into desisting from anti-government activities. Shortly afterwards, Salihi received a telephone call from his brother in Baghdad, asking him to cease all opposition activity. Iraqi political exiles living in Europe and elsewhere consistently reported being threatened with the arrest or execution of their relatives if they did not return to Iraq or abandoned opposition activity, and asylum seekers in Jordan, Syria and other countries reported being under surveillance by Iraqi intelligence agents.

The government continued its forced expulsion of Kurds and Turkmen from Kirkuk, Khaniqin, Makhmour, Sinjar, Tuz Khormatu, and other districts as part of its 'Arabization' program. Those expelled included individuals who had refused to sign so-called "nationality correction" forms, introduced by the authorities prior to the 1997 population census, requiring members of ethnic groups residing in these districts to relinquish their Kurdish or Turkman identities and to register officially as Arabs. The Iraqi authorities also seized their property and assets; those who were expelled to areas controlled by Kurdish opposition forces were stripped of all possessions and their ration cards were withdrawn. A smaller number, mostly Turkmen, were forcibly expelled to central and southern Iraq, including al-Ramadi, and were allowed to take some of their possessions. In both cases, the Iraqi authorities frequently detained heads of households until the expulsions were complete. Over 800 people were reportedly expelled between January and June, bringing the total number of those expelled since 1991 to over 94,000, according to Kurdish opposition sources.

Press freedom and the right to information remained severely restricted. The government maintained tight control on all media outlets, including television, radio, and newspapers, most of which were state-owned. Satellite dishes and modems remained under ban, and the installation of facsimile machines continued to require special permission. Plans announced by the authorities in November 1999 to allow Iraqis to tune into selected satellite television channels through a paid service had not materialized by October 2000. Internet services, provided solely by the Ministry of Culture and Information, became available to Iraqis for the first time on July 27 when an Internet café opened in Baghdad. The authorities announced that additional centers would be opened in other cities in the future. Minister of Transport and Communications Ahmad Murtada Khalil reportedly said that customers could browse those Web sites that did not violate "the precepts of the Islamic religion" or offend "morals and ethics." However, users were reportedly banned access to unmonitored Web-based electronic mail systems.

On June 28, two staff members of the United Nations Food and Agriculture Organization (FAO) were shot dead in Baghdad and seven others wounded, reportedly by an Iraqi identified by the authorities as Fowad Hussain Haidar. He said he had carried out the attack in protest at the U.N.-imposed embargo.

The overall humanitarian situation in Iraq remained dire despite the expanded "oil-for-food" program. In his March 10 report to the Security Council on the operation of the program, U.N. Secretary-General Kofi Annan noted that "an excessive number of holds" continued to impede the relief program. These included holds on contracts in the water and sanitation and electric power sectors, which he stated were a major factor impeding progress in the area of public health. In his most recent report of September 8 to the Security Council, the Secretary-General noted some improvements in this area, but said that "infrastructural degradation" of the water and sanitation sector was being exacerbated by "the absence of key complementary items currently on hold and adequate maintenance, spare parts and staffing." As regards the electricity sector, the report stated that the "entire electricity grid is in a precarious state and is in imminent danger of collapsing altogether." The overall provision of health care and services was said to be in "steep decline." This assessment was supported by the findings of U.N. and other humanitarian agencies. In a report published in December 1999, the International Committee of the Red Cross (ICRC) said the sanctions have had a "devastating effect on the lives of civilians," and that while the "oil-for-food" program has alleviated their plight, "it has not halted the collapse of the health system and the deterioration of the water supplies, which together pose one of the gravest threats to the health and well-being of the civilian population." In a report published on September 13, the FAO said that while existing food rations, combined with market food purchases, have "halted further deterioration in the nutritional situation, they have not by themselves been able to reverse this trend." It concluded that acute malnutrition among children under five had decreased only slightly from the 12 percent recorded in 1995, and that at least 800,000 children under five were chronically malnourished.

Human Rights Developments in Iraqi Kurdistan

The two major Kurdish opposition groups in Iraqi Kurdistan, the KDP and the PUK, retained control over most areas in the three northern provinces of Arbil, Duhok and Sulaimaniya. Despite mediation efforts by U.S. government officials, little progress was made towards the implementation of the provisions of the 1998 Washington Accord. Both sides pledged to normalize relations but continued to maintain separate administrative, legislative and executive structures in areas under their control. On October 22, senior officials from the two parties agreed on a series of measures, including prisoner exchanges, the gradual return of internally displaced people to their homes, and arrangements for the organization of free movement of people and trade between their respective areas. Most of these measures were not implemented. In December 1999, the PUK announced that it would set up a separate court of cassation to serve areas it controlled, and on February 3 held municipal council elections. One prisoner exchange took place on March 6, the PUK releasing five KDP prisoners and the KDP releasing ten PUK prisoners. Both sides continued to grant regular access to their prisons to ICRC representatives who, as of April, were visiting an estimated 500 detainees held by both parties.

In March, the KDP broadcast on its television channel, Kurdistan TV, statements by five detainees in its custody who had apparently admitted to carrying out acts of sabotage in the Arbil region in previous months. The five were allegedly members of the opposition Islamic Unity Movement of Kurdistan (IUMK), whose leaders denied these allegations in a statement issued on March 15, saying that Iraqi government agents were likely to be responsible for these acts. They also said the five detainees had been denied judicial due process and their confessions extracted under torture, which KDP officials denied in an April 2 statement. Acts of sabotage continued, however, with two bomb blasts occurring in June in both Arbil and Sulaimaniya amid reports of the Iraqi government's deployment of additional troops to the northern region, apparently with the aim of launching armed attacks on Kurdish-controlled territory.

KDP security forces attacked the headquarters of the opposition Iraqi Turkmen Front (ITF) in Arbil on July 11, killing Abdullah Adil Hursit and Feridun Fazil Mehmet, both guards. The immediate reason for the attack was unclear, but relations between the two sides had deteriorated since an earlier incident in April, when several ITF members staged a sit-in at their headquarters in protest at what they stated was undue interference by the KDP in the Turkmen community's internal affairs. The KDP denied these charges.

PUK forces arrested members and supporters of the opposition Iraqi Workers Communist Party (IWCP) in July and August in an apparent attempt to pressure them into leaving PUK-controlled areas. Thirteen demonstrators protesting the cutting of water and electricity supplies to IWCP bases were arrested on July 13 outside the PUK's Ministry of Interior building in Sulaimaniya. Others were arrested in the ensuing days, including three IWCP leaders who were reportedly negotiating a settlement with PUK officials at the time. The premises of two organizations affiliated to the IWCP, the Centre for the Protection of Women in Kurdistan and the Independent Womens' Organization, were raided on July 21. Twelve women sheltering at the center, a shelter for abused women, were taken away and their whereabouts remained unknown. Most of the IWCP detainees were released by late September.

A number of people were killed and attempts made on the lives of others by unknown assailants in apparently politically motivated acts. Among them was Farhad Faraj, a political activist and founder of a trade union organization, the Union for the Unemployed in Kurdistan, who was killed outside his home in Sulaimaniya city on October 17, 1999. In another incident, Hawjin Mala Amin, a researcher at the anthropology department of Sulaimaniya University, was shot outside his home in the city on December 9, 1999. He survived and later stated that he may have been targeted because of his outspoken views on Islam. In a speech on December 23, 1999, PUK leader Jalal Talabani condemned the attack and stated that "perpetrators of terror" who were targeting writers and artists would be punished. On July 17, a parliamentarian in the Kurdistan Regional Government (KRG), Osman Hassan, was shot dead by a group of armed men near Arbil. He had represented the PUK prior to 1996, and had elected to remain in Arbil when PUK forces were ousted from the regional capital that year and withdrew to their strongholds in Sulaimaniya province. The KDP initiated an investigation into his death, but its outcome was not known by October 2000.

There were repeated military incursions by Turkey's armed forces into northern Iraq in pursuit of members of the opposition Kurdistan Workers' Party (PKK) of Turkey. Several thousand troops were deployed in September and November 1999, with the Turkish airforce targeting PKK positions in both KDP and PUK-controlled areas. Further incursions were carried out in April, May, and August 2000, resulting in one case in the killing of thirty-eight Iraqi Kurdish civilians. (See Turkey). In July, armed clashes broke out between PKK and KDP forces, lasting several days and reportedly resulting in forty casualties, most of them PKK fighters. In mid-September, fierce fighting broke out between PKK and PUK forces, which continued intermittently for over two weeks in several areas, including Qala Diza, Rania, and Zeli, with scores of casualties reported on both sides. The fighting ended on October 4 when the PKK declared a unilateral ceasefire.

The Role of the International Community

United Nations

Policy toward Iraq continued to cause divisions within the Security Council and the international community generally, exacerbated by mounting evidence that U.N. sanctions were having a devastating humanitarian impact in Iraq. As evidence of this, the Security Council was able to adopt Resolution 1284 on December 17, 1999, only after three permanent members, France, China, and Russia agreed to abstain. The resolution established, as a subsidiary body to the council, the U.N. Monitoring, Verification, and Inspection Commission (UNMOVIC) to carry out weapons inspections in Iraq authorized by Resolution 687 (1991). Its predecessor, UNSCOM, was disbanded following the withdrawal of its staff from Iraq in December 1998. The resolution proposed the suspension of sanctions for a 120-day period, renewable by the council, made contingent upon Iraq's cooperation with UNMOVIC. It also removed the dollar ceiling on Iraqi oil exports, allowing increased funding of the "oil-for-food" humanitarian relief program authorized under Resolution 986 (1995). However, it did not incorporate fully the March 1999 recommendations of the council's "humanitarian panel" addressing Iraq's urgent humanitarian needs, notably the infrastructure planning and investment required to meet basic civilian needs. Iraq's Deputy Prime Minister, Tariq Aziz, condemned the resolution and said that no weapons inspectors would be permitted into the country.

On February 14, the Secretary-General appointed Yuli Vorontsov as high-level coordinator for the return of missing property and missing persons from Iraq to Kuwait, as required by Resolution 1284. An estimated 605 Kuwaiti and third-country nationals remained unaccounted for since the withdrawal of Iraqi forces from Kuwait in February 1991.

On June 8, the Security Council adopted Resolution 1302, extending the "oil-for-food" program for a further six months, introducing accelerated procedures for the approval of water and sanitation equipment, and instructing the secretary-general to appoint independent experts to conduct a comprehensive assessment of the humanitarian situation in Iraq. In his September 8 report to the Security Council on the operation of the "oil-for-food" program, the secretary-general reported that the Iraqi government had refused to issue visas to the experts he had appointed. It also refused to discuss how a "cash component" to the "oil-for-food" program could allow U.N.-controlled funds to be used to purchase locally produced goods and services. The report also cited serious problems stemming from protracted holds by the Security Council's sanctions committee on key infrastructure repair items affecting public health, emphasizing that humanitarian relief alone cannot address the overall impoverishment of ordinary people.

U.N. Humanitarian Coordinator for Iraq Hans von Sponeck left Iraq on March 31 after resigning in protest at the effect of sanctions on the Iraqi population, and was succeeded by Tun Myat. On August 15, Benon Sevan, executive director of the U.N. Office of the Iraq Program (OIP), urged the Security Council to adopt a "fresh approach and more flexibility" following a 17-day visit to Iraq.

In a resolution adopted on December 17, 1999, the General Assembly strongly condemned Iraq's human rights record, including widespread and systematic torture, summary and arbitrary executions, widespread use of the death penalty, and "the suppression of freedom of thought, expression, information, association, assembly and movement." It called on the government to "cease its repressive practices" and to "bring the actions of its military and security forces into conformity with the standards of international law." It also urged cooperation with U.N. human rights mechanisms, "in particular by receiving a return visit by the Special Rapporteur to Iraq."

In November 1999, Max van der Stoel, special rapporteur on Iraq since 1991, resigned. He was succeeded by Andreas Mavrommatis, who said in a preliminary report to the Commission on Human Rights in March that he had received numerous communications alleging human rights violations by the Iraqi government, including arbitrary detentions, executions, torture, "disappearances," and discrimination against religious and other minorities. While expressing concern about the grave humanitarian situation in Iraq, the special rapporteur also noted that serious violations of human rights and fundamental freedoms could not be justified under any circumstances. He added that he had made a formal request to the government to visit Iraq to "study, in situ, the human rights situation." The special rapporteur's mandate was extended for a further year in a resolution passed on April 18, in which the commission strongly condemned the "systematic, widespread and extremely grave violations of human rights and of international humanitarian law" in Iraq. It urged the government to abide by its international legal obligations and to cooperate with the U.N. human rights mechanisms, including by granting the special rapporteur access to the country. In a report to the General Assembly, issued in August, the special rapporteur presented additional information he had received about human rights abuses in Iraq, including arbitrary arrests, torture, and the harrassment of political opponents. By October, the special rapporteur had not been invited to visit Iraq.

On August 18, the U.N. Subcommission on the Promotion and Protection of Human Rights adopted a resolution calling on the Security Council to lift the embargo provisions affecting the humanitarian situation of the population of Iraq. The resolution also appealed to all governments, including that of Iraq, to alleviate the suffering of the Iraqi population, in particular by facilitating the delivery of food and medical supplies to meet their basic needs.

On June 14, the Committee on the Elimination of Discrimination against Women considered Iraq's combined second and third periodic reports submitted under article 18 of the Convention on the Elimination of Discrimination against Women. The committee noted that the advancement of women and their socio-economic well-being had been adversely affected by the ongoing sanctions, but stressed Iraq's obligations under the convention to implement the relevant anti-discriminatory measures. The committee criticized, among other things, discrimination against women under Iraq's nationality law and violence against women perpetrated through honor killings.

European Union

The E.U. remained the largest donor of humanitarian aid to Iraq, with 8.6 million euros allocated for the year through the European Community Humanitarian Office (ECHO). It was intended to fund operations in central and southern Iraq run by U.N. specialized agencies and NGOs related to health care, water and sanitation, food, and education

The European Parliament, in a January 20 resolution, criticized Iraq for failing to clarify the cases of 605 Kuwaiti and third-country nationals taken prisoner during Iraq's occupation of Kuwait, calling for their immediate release and for the names of those who may have died in captivity to be revealed; demanding a review of all cases submitted through the ICRC over the past six years; and urging Iraq to resume participation in meetings of the Tripartite Commission, which was set up in April 1991 under ICRC chairmanship to ascertain the fate of missing military personnel and civilians after the 1991 Gulf

War. In an April 13 resolution, the parliament observed that "sanctions are penalizing the civilian population but, in nine years, have not succeeded in weakening the Iraqi regime," and called on the E.U. to take action to ensure that the Security Council "clarifies the terms of Resolution 1284 by specifying precisely what is expected of the Iraqi government." The resolution also called for the lifting of sanctions "as a matter of urgency" once Iraq agreed to cooperate in implementing relevant U.N. resolutions. In a further resolution on July 6, the European Parliament reiterated its call for the lifting of economic sanctions on Iraq "while maintaining a strict arms embargo," and proposed sending a fact-finding parliamentary delegation to Iraq to assess ways of extending the "oil-for food" program as a means of improving living conditions in Iraq. The resolution also proposed that the E.U. play a role in bringing about "a lifting of the no-fly zone, together with a formal renunciation by the Iraqi Government of the use of military force in dealing with the demands for autonomy of the Kurdish people."

The report of an all-party inquiry by the International Development Committee of the U.K. House of Commons entitled *The Future of Sanctions* concluded in January that the heavy responsibility of the Iraqi government for the humanitarian crisis in the country did not "entirely excuse the international community from a part in the suffering of Iraqis." "A sanctions regime which relies on the good faith of Saddam Hussain is fundamentally flawed," the report said.

British policy on Iraq remained closely aligned with that of the United States, although there were reports that U.K. officials were pushing their U.S. counterparts on some aspects of policy, especially Security Council "holds" on contracts under the "oil-for-food" program. In a July 17 letter to Church of England representatives following a mission to Iraq, Peter Hain, the minister of state with responsibility for the Middle East, wrote that "this is an area in which we continue to press the U.S. for greater flexibility." On the question of "smarter sanctions," Hain wrote that "the regime in place against

Iraq is already targeted as far as it can be on the government."

United States

The U.S., together with the U.K., maintained its policing of the "no-fly zone" over northern Iraq from Incirlik base in Turkey, and that of southern Iraq from bases in Saudi Arabia. Scores of civilians were reportedly killed as a result of air strikes carried out by the coalition forces in these zones. In response to information released by Iraq on August 15 that since December 1998, U.S. and U.K. forces had flown over 18,500 sorties killing 311 Iraqis and wounding 967 others, a State Department spokesman said on August 28 that air strikes in the no-fly zones "are only taken in self-defense in response to Iraqi threats to our forces," and that "we make every effort to avoid civilian casualties and damage to civilian facilities."

The U.S. continued to insist on the maintenance of comprehensive sanctions on Iraq, including full compliance with Security Council resolution 1284, despite mounting evidence from U.N. specialized agencies and NGOs working in Iraq that the ongoing sanctions have caused a humanitarian crisis. In a statement before the Security Council on March 24, Deputy Permanent Representative to the U.N. James Cunningham noted that the sanctions " have never targeted the Iraqi people and have never limited the import of food and medicine." He placed full responsibility on the Iraqi government, "due to both its failure to meet its obligations under Security Council resolutions and its cynical manipulation of civilian suffering in an effort to obtain the lifting of sanctions without compliance."

On August 2, the tenth anniversary of Iraq's invasion of Kuwait, the State Department's Ambassador-at-Large for War Crimes issues, David Scheffer, announced the administration's intention to declassify a number of Iraqi government documents captured by U.S. forces in Kuwait in 1991. He said this would contribute to efforts to bring Iraqi officials to justice for war crimes. The documents would be released through the Iraq

Foundation, a U.S.-based NGO, providing evidence which "justifies an international tribunal like what exists for the former Yugoslavia and Rwanda."

Ambassador Scheffer also confirmed that the Clinton administration was providing financial assistance to six NGOs to gather the necessary documentation for that purpose. On September 28, the State Department entered into a $4 million grant agreement with the opposition Iraqi National Congress (INC) for programs in the areas of information, advocacy, and humanitarian relief. The sum was the first part of a U.S. $8 million package allocated to the INC by Congress from the Economic Support Fund for fiscal year 2000 independently of the $97 million allocated to INC under the 1998 Iraq Liberation Act.

In its *Country Reports on Human Rights Practices for 1999*, released on February 25, the State Department described Iraq's human rights record as "extremely poor." It said that the government was responsible for numerous summary executions of suspected opponents, "disappearances," arbitrary detention, torture, and the denial of the basic right of due process. In its *Annual Report on International Religious Freedom for 2000*, released on September 5, the State Department noted that the government "for decades has conducted a brutal campaign of murder, summary execution, and protracted arbitrary arrest against the religious leaders and followers of the majority Shi'a Muslim population, and has sought to undermine the identity of minority Christian (Assyrian and Chaldean) and Yazidi groups."

ISRAEL, OCCUPIED WEST BANK, GAZA STRIP, & PALESTINIAN AUTHORITY TERRITORIES

Human Rights Developments

Within three weeks, more than 120 Palestinians were killed and over 4,800 injured in clashes with Israeli security forces that began on September 29. Most of the deaths were the result of excessive, and often indiscriminate, use of lethal force by Israel Defense Forces (IDF) soldiers, police, and border police against unarmed civilian demonstrators, including children. The casualties were disproportionately on the Palestinian side, but two Israeli soldiers were beaten to death by a Palestinian mob. The large number of deaths and injuries in the clashes and the resulting deteriorating relationship between Israel and the Palestinian Authority and neighboring states greatly overshadowed and put into question certain human rights improvements, notably, an apparent decrease in the use of torture by Israeli interrogators, a reduction in the hostages and administrative detainees Israel held, and fewer revocations of Jerusalem residency permits. In several cases the Israeli government also actively sought to thwart court rulings supporting human rights by supporting initiatives to legalize torture and hostage-taking, and by delaying the enforcement of court rulings against discrimination. On July 24, the Knesset voted to extend the fifty-two-year-old state of emergency until January 26, 2001, to allow the government time to enact similar powers into statute law.

Discrimination in law and practice against ethnic and religious minorities and other societal groups, especially on issues of employment, social benefits, and personal status, remained a major problem. While court challenges to discrimination were sometimes successful, the process often took years, and court rulings frequently were not applicable to other cases or were not fully implemented by the government. For example, on March 8 the High Court of Justice ruled on an October 1995 petition brought by a Palestinian couple who, though Israeli citizens, were barred from purchasing a home in a Jewish neighborhood built on state-owned lands. More than 90 percent of land in Israel is state land, much of it expropriated from Palestinians. The court ruled that the authorities could not allocate land to citizens solely on the basis of their religion, though it noted that discrimination between Jews and non-Jews might be acceptable under unspecified "special circumstances." The ruling ordered the government to take such "special circumstances" into consideration when determining "with deliberate speed" whether it would allow the couple to settle in the neighborhood, and stated that its ruling in this case would not affect previous discriminatory land allocations.

Women faced discrimination in employment, access to education and health care, and personal status, including marriage, divorce, inheritance, and child custody. (See Women's Human Rights.) Palestinian women and foreign women workers faced additional discrimination that made them especially vulnerable to abuses. A number of well-publicized cases of trafficking in women for prostitution, domestic violence, and sexual harassment and assault helped increase public awareness, but women suffering from such violations still had little recourse. As of this writing, the Defense Ministry had taken few steps to address an enduring pattern of sexual harassment of women in the military, despite a number of high-profile cases involving ministry officials. The Knesset voted on July 5 to lift the immunity of Transportation Minister Yitzhak Mordechai, a former defense minister who had served in the IDF for thirty-three years, after he was accused in March of sexually assaulting three women under his supervision beginning in 1992. By the end of July the Civil Service Commission had received fifty-five complaints of sexual harassment in the Defense Ministry, five more than in all of 1999.

On May 22, the High Court of Justice set a six month deadline for the government to establish procedures for women to pray "according to their custom" at the Western Wall in Jerusalem. The case was brought in 1989 after conservative Jews violently attacked Jewish women who were attempting to pray alongside men according to the customs of Reform Judaism. Despite a 1994 High Court of Justice ruling upholding the women's right to worship at the Western Wall, they were not permitted to do so. On March 31, a draft law punishing such prayer with up to seven years of imprisonment passed its preliminary Knesset reading, and in early June the government asked to have the May 22 court judgement reviewed by an expanded panel of judges, on the grounds that it failed to adequately address "the affront to the feelings of those who pray at the wall" that would ensue if women were allowed to pray with men.

The rate of revocation of permanent residency permits of Palestinian residents of East Jerusalem declined following Minister of Interior Natan Sharansky's October 17, 1999, announcement that he had ended the so-called "center of life" policy. (See *Human Rights Watch World Report 2000*). After repeated legal challenges led by the Jerusalem-based Center for Defense of the Individual (Hamoked), the High Court of Justice ordered Sharansky to clarify the terms of the new policy, and on March 15 he stated in an affidavit before the High Court of Justice that Palestinian Jerusalemites living abroad would not lose their permanent residency if they visited Jerusalem and maintained valid Israeli-issued travel documents. Those who acquired foreign nationality or permanent resident status elsewhere continued to lose residency rights in Jerusalem, and Minister Sharansky did not clarify the status of Palestinian Jerusalemites living in the West Bank. According to Hamoked, persons who sought to reinstate their residency status under the new policy frequently faced serious administrative obstacles. Some 11,000 Palestinians were estimated to have lost their residency rights between 1996 and 1999.

Labor conditions for foreign and Palestinian workers remained poor. Palestinians faced widespread discrimination in employment, while foreign workers were especially vulnerable to exploitation by employers and labor contractors. On August 22, Ha'aretz reported that Prime Minister Ehud Barak had ordered an increase in deportations of undocumented foreign workers and set a quota of 50,000 work permits per year. The move was opposed by workers' groups and even the Public Security Ministry, which preferred a policy of targeting labor importers. The government had temporarily halted deportations in December 1999 following allegations of abuses of foreign workers, including prolonged detention of persons awaiting deportation; their detention together with criminal prisoners; and the detention of victims of crimes while awaiting to testify in criminal cases. In May, the Interior Ministry acknowledged that it had prevented labor organizations such as Kav La'oved from handing out pamphlets on labor rights to workers arriving at Ben-Gurion airport.

On September 29, Israeli security forces used lethal force to disperse thousands of Palestinians attending Friday prayers at al-Aqsa Mosque in East Jerusalem after some of those present threw stones at police and at Jewish worshipers at the Western Wall. An unusually large number of Palestinians were present at the mosque to protest a visit the previous day by Knesset Member Ariel Sharon, interpreted by many as an assertion of Israeli sovereignty over the area. Israeli forces killed five Palestinians and wounded over 200. Violent clashes between Israeli security forces and Palestinians then spread to other parts of the West Bank, Gaza, and Israel. Within three weeks, more than 120 Palestinians were killed and 4,800 injured, many as result of excessive, often indiscriminate, use of lethal force by Israeli security forces against unarmed civilians. In a number of cases IDF soldiers appeared to target

Palestinian medics, at least one of whom was killed and twenty-seven were injured by mid-October. At this writing, the IDF had significantly expanded its use of tanks and helicopter gunships armed with both missiles and medium-caliber machine guns in Palestinian residential areas.

Israel retained extensive control over, and placed restrictions on, the freedom of movement of all West Bank and Gaza Strip Palestinians. These policies obstructed Palestinian economic activity and access to health care, schools and universities, places of worship, and family members in other parts of the territories or in Israeli prisons. On October 25, 1999, Israel opened a "safe passage" allowing some increased movement between the Gaza Strip and the West Bank, but the arbitrary nature of the criteria for issuing travel permits and their indiscriminate imposition on an entire population assured that the restrictions remained a form of collective punishment. Following September 29 Israel increased restrictions on movement into, out of, and within the West Bank and Gaza Strip.

Palestinians passing through Israeli checkpoints were frequently subjected to harassment, physical abuse, and even torture by Israeli soldiers and police. For example, in a well-publicized incident on September 6, three Palestinian laborers required hospital treatment after being beaten by border police at a checkpoint. During the attack the police photographed themselves with their victims, and the unit commander later told Ha'aretz, "What we did was not special. Everybody does it." Other incidents resulted in deaths, as on July 9 when soldiers fired on a taxi carrying Atidal Muammer, killing her and injuring her husband, two children, and other passersby. Following an investigation, the IDF said the killing was "a terrible mistake," and stated that its soldiers were responding to shots from a different vehicle. However, no such vehicle was recovered and no spent cartridges were found at the scene of the shooting.

According to government figures, settlement construction in the Israeli-occupied West Bank and Gaza Strip increased by 96 percent in the first half of 2000, with 860 of the 1,067 new starts in the Jerusalem area. At the same time, demolitions of Palestinian homes built without permits in the Israeli-occupied territories and in Israel continued, as did forced expulsions and expropriation of Palestinian land. In October and November 1999, Israeli authorities expelled some seven hundred Palestinian cave dwellers from the Mount Hebron area of the West Bank, and destroyed or confiscated their homes and their personal property, including livestock. The government alleged that the area where the cave dwellers had lived for decades was a "closed military zone." An investigation by the Israeli human rights group, B'Tselem, concluded, however, that the area had not been used for military exercises, and the expulsion was more likely intended to placate Jewish settlers whom the government had recently removed from a nearby illegal settlement outpost. On March 29 the High Court of Justice ruled that the cave dwellers could return to the area, pending a final determination in the case.

Close to one thousand Palestinian prisoners participated in a month-long hunger strike in May, protesting arbitrary treatment by prison officials, substandard prison conditions, prohibitions on family visits, use of solitary confinement, poor medical care, and Israel's refusal to release all the categories of prisoners specified in its agreements with the Palestine Liberation Organization (PLO). The strike was called off on May 31 after prison authorities promised to review complaints and ease some restrictions on visitors. According to Ha'aretz, a government report issued in June on conditions in Shatta prison described living conditions as "particularly harsh" in the wing where Palestinian prisoners from the Israeli-occupied territories were held, and concluded that the exposed tents used to house prisoners and filthy bathrooms at the prison were unfit for human use.

Several deaths in custody were reported. On August 11 Ramez Fayez Mohammed Rashid Elrizi died in al-Nafha prison. His father said that he had been in relatively good health during an August 9 visit. The family

of Lafi al-Rajabi told the nongovernmental Palestinian Society for the Protection of Human Rights and the Environment (LAW) that he had contacted them on January 14, shortly before he died in an Israeli detention center near Nablus, saying his life was in danger. His body reportedly was returned to the family bearing cuts, bruises, and with wire marks on the neck. A third detainee, Sami As'ad, reportedly hanged himself in Kishon prison on June 19, seven weeks after being arrested. According to Ha'aretz, a psychiatric evaluation had found him to have personality disorders, and he had previously attempted suicide. As of this writing, Human Rights Watch is not aware of official findings regarding the causes of any of these deaths being made public.

On April 12, the High Court of Justice ruled that Israel could not continue to administratively detain Lebanese nationals solely as "bargaining chips" for the return of its soldiers missing in action. Five such hostages had been released in December 1999, and a sixth hostage, reported to be mentally ill, was released on April 5. Thirteen more hostages were released on April 19, but Israel continued to hold Shaykh `Abd al-Karim Obeid, kidnapped in July 1989, and Mustafa al-Dirani, kidnapped in May 1994, despite repeated court challenges. Both men were held in solitary confinement at an undisclosed location, and on March 13 a lawyer for al-Dirani filed a civil case against the Israeli government seeking NIS6,000,000 (U.S. $1,473,900) in compensation for torture, including rape, that al-Dirani had allegedly suffered while in Israeli custody. On June 11 the Israeli Cabinet approved draft legislation to legalize hostage-taking which was specifically intended to facilitate al-Dirani and Obeid's continued detention, and the bill passed its first Knesset reading on June 21.

Israel also continued to detain Palestinians for long periods without charge or trial. According to the IDF, as of September 12 Israel held five Palestinians as administrative detainees, including Khaled Hussein Jaradat, who had been held continuously since August 21, 1997.

Following a September 6, 1999, High Court of Justice ruling that General Security Service (GSS) officers were not authorized to use "physical means"—torture—during interrogations, reports of incidents of torture decreased significantly. However, according to the nongovernmental Public Committee against Torture in Israel (PCATI), the GSS continued to employ interrogation techniques including beatings, sleep deprivation, prolonged periods handcuffed to chairs, placing detainees with "collaborators" who beat, tortured, and threatened them to obtain confessions; and long periods of incommunicado detention. In February, the government made public the summary of a 1995 state comptroller report showing that high-ranking GSS officers had condoned "serious and systematic violations" by GSS interrogators between 1988 and 1992, and had lied to judges. No actions were taken, however, to prosecute individuals who had been responsible for torture, and the Knesset continued to consider draft legislation to legalize torture in cases where a suspect was believed to have information that could stop an imminent attack.

Palestinian Authority

Palestinian security services continued to operate with impunity, despite recurring cases of torture, arbitrary arrests, and prolonged detention without charge or trial. An overwhelmed judiciary was further weakened by repeated executive branch interference in its work. Critics of these and other Palestinian Authority (P.A.) abuses were frequently subject to harassment, arrest, and in some instances, violent attacks. Military and state security courts issued death sentences after grossly unfair trials, which were not subject to appeal.

While individuals alleged to have affiliations to political organizations critical of P.A. policy were frequently targeted for arbitrary arrest, there were also reports of mass arrests, as when some thirty students were detained after a demonstration at Birzeit University on February 26. In June, the non-governmental Palestinian Human Rights

Monitoring Group (PHRMG) reported that despite seventy-three High Court of Justice orders to release detainees that had been issued since January 1997, only four had been implemented. For example, as of this writing Wa'il 'Ali Faraj, arrested on April 25, 1996, remained in detention despite a February 20, 1999, court order for his release.

The security forces' impunity extended to torture and ill-treatment of both political and criminal detainees. According to LAW, when questioned on August 7 about specific cases of torture, Police Commander Major Kamal al-Shaykh asserted that "the thief who does not confess must be beaten as a last resort to force him to confess." Such attitudes may have contributed to the June 6 death in custody of thirty-five-year-old Khalid Mohammed Yunis Bahar. According to the Palestinian human rights group Law in the Service of Man (al-Haq), P.A. police arrested Bahar on May 25, apparently without a warrant, and his family was prevented from visiting him. Earlier, on December 6, 1999, Mahmud Mohammed Khalil Hassan al-Bajjali, age thirty-three, died in Ramallah prison. Both men were reported to have been in good health. As of this writing the P.A. had not released autopsy reports in these and twenty-one cases of deaths in custody that occurred in previous years.

During clashes between Palestinians and the IDF that began on September 29 (see above), Palestinian security forces failed to act consistently and effectively to prevent armed civilians from opening fire on IDF soldiers or positions from places where civilians were present. This failure endangered the Palestinian civilian population when the IDF responded, often excessively and indiscriminately.

The judiciary suffered from a severe lack of resources and executive branch interference, and trials fell far short of international fair trial standards. P.A. President Yasser Arafat refused to ratify the Judicial Authority Law, passed by parliament on November 25, 1998, and instead issued ad hoc decrees, including a June 1 decree creating a Supreme Judicial Council with poorly defined powers, and a November 1, 1999 decree creating the post of "attorney general for state security courts." The new post was filled by Khaled al-Qidra, the disgraced former attorney general who had been removed from his post in 1997 following complaints of corruption and protests by human rights organizations.

Fair trial violations were particularly egregious in state security courts, which, along with "regular" military courts, had the power to try civilians and were responsible for the majority of death sentences passed. Trials in these courts were not subject to appeal, and sentences were sometimes issued only hours after arrest, as in the case of Raji Saqir. A state security court sentenced Saqir to death on July 3, having convened on the night of July 2, the day after the crime was committed. Security court jurisdiction was expanded in June to include drug trafficking cases, including those punishable by death.

The P.A. continued its efforts to control and restrict freedom of expression. Broadcast media were frequently subject to closure, and journalists and commentators to arrest, in retaliation for reporting criticism of P.A. policies. Five radio and television stations were ordered suspended between May 5 and June 2, and on June 2 Samir Qumsiah, chair of the Council of Private Radio and Television Stations, was arrested after calling on stations to halt broadcasts for half an hour to protest the closures. Security forces also arrested eight prominent personalities who signed a November 27, 1999, petition criticizing P.A. "tyranny and corruption." Six were released on JD50,000 (U.S. $70,000) bail on December 19, but Ahmad Dudin and 'Abd al-Sattar Qassem were held until January 6. Qassem was rearrested on February 18 and detained until July 28, despite a July 11 High Court of Justice order for his release.

Academics risked punishment when their published views challenged social conventions. On November 24, 1999 the Islamic University in Gaza suspended Dr. Jawad al-Dalou and two students for publishing a student newspaper article that noted that many beggars came from the Nezla district in Gaza. A statement issued by the university said the suspensions were "in respect of the wishes of the dignified local personalities of the district of Nezla in the Jabalia camp."

On February 29 Chief of Police Ghazi al-Jabali issued new regulations limiting freedom of assembly, in contravention of existing law. The regulations prohibited organizing processions, demonstrations, or public meetings without prior approval from the district police commander, on penalty of up to two months of imprisonment or an up to JD50 (U.S. $70) fine. The High Court of Justice suspended their implementation on April 29, but as of September had not acted to revoke these or other regulations limiting freedom of assembly issued by President Arafat in his capacity as minister of interior on April 30.

Defending Human Rights

Israel and the Occupied West Bank and Gaza Strip

Israel permitted human rights organizations to collect and disseminate information in areas under its control. However, according to PCATI, lawyers for Palestinian detainees frequently had difficulty gaining access to their clients, and even after filing legal challenges against such denials sometimes waited weeks or months before being able to meet their clients. Closures often kept Palestinian human rights workers and lawyers, including those with Israeli citizenship or Jerusalem identity cards, from traveling freely within the West Bank, the Gaza Strip, and Israel. Palestinians who had previously been detained were also refused access to prisons and detainees.

Palestinian Authority

Palestinian NGOs and activists continued to be subjected to police harassment and threats by P.A. officials because of their criticism of P.A. abuses. These actions may have contributed to violent attacks on activists, including the December 1, 1999, shooting of Palestinian Legislative Council member Mu'awwiya al-Masri by masked men; the December 11, 1999, stoning by unknown persons of Hanan Elmasu, director of Birzeit

University's Human Rights Action Project, which knocked her unconscious; and the December 16, 1999, beating of Palestinian Legislative Council member 'Abd al-Jawad Saleh by General Intelligence officers. All three attacks were apparently in retaliation for support of a November 1999 petition campaign. In February staff members of the PHRMG received threatening letters and phone calls warning them to resign and threatening to include their names in a public campaign against the organization.

On April 19 the Ministry of Interior improperly closed the Gaza-based Civic Forum Institute, established in 1998, on the grounds that it was not a registered organization under NGO Law 1/2000. The law set a nine-month deadline for NGOs to comply with the regulations or be considered illegal. Government officials also continued to attack Palestinian human rights organizations and activists in the press. In February, the Palestinian Center for Human Rights (PCHR) filed a complaint with the attorney general against Khalil al-Zaben, coordinator of the government-appointed NGO council, for defamatory statements in the semi-official *al-Nashra* magazine. As of this writing no action had been taken on that case or previous defamation cases against al-Zaben.

Police detained Khalil Abu Shamala, director of Addameer, a Gaza-based human rights organization specializing in prisoners' rights, on April 16, immediately after he had issued a press release protesting Chief of Police Ghazi al-Jabali's ban on Addameer's rally scheduled for that afternoon to commemorate Palestinian Prisoners' Day. He was released on April 17. On August 8, al-Jabali ordered LAW and its director, Khader Shkirat, banned from "visiting prisons, detention centers, police command centers, and police locations" because of his "continuous attacks on the [Palestinian] Authority." The order followed an incident the previous day, when Shkirat was violently removed from the Ramallah police headquarters after he raised cases of police torture of detainees and protested against official interference in LAW's lawyers' access to certain detainees.

The Role of the International Community

United Nations

U.N. bodies made a number of urgent interventions in an effort to end the violent clashes that began on September 29. The Commission on Human Rights, in a resolution issued at the end of a special session held October 17-19, "strongly condemn[ed] the disproportionate and indiscriminate use of force in violation of international humanitarian law by the Israeli occupying Power against innocent and unarmed Palestinian civilians...which constitutes a flagrant and grave violation of the right to life and also constitutes a war crime and a crime against humanity." The resolution established an independent inquiry commission to investigate Israeli human rights violations and grave breaches of international humanitarian law. It also requested several U.N. bodies—the commission's special rapporteurs on extrajudicial, summary or arbitrary executions; torture; violence against women; religious intolerance; racism, racial discrimination, xenophobia and related intolerance; and the right to housing; its Working Group on Enforced or Involuntary Disappearances; and the representative of the Secretary-General for internally displaced persons—to conduct immediate investigations and report the findings to the Commission on Human Rights at its fifty-seventh session and, on an interim basis, to the General Assembly at its fifty-fifth session. The commission also requested High Commissioner for Human Rights Mary Robinson to undertake an urgent visit to the occupied territories and to facilitate the mechanisms of the Commission in the implementation of the resolution.

From October 18 to October 20 the General Assembly (G.A.) reconvened its emergency special session on illegal Israeli actions in Occupied East Jerusalem and the rest of the Occupied Palestinian Territory, originally convened in April 1997 under the assembly's "Uniting for peace" resolution. The G.A. "condemn[ed] acts of violence, especially the excessive use of force by the

Israeli forces against Palestinian civilians," demanded that Israel fulfil its obligations and responsibilities under the Fourth Geneva Convention, and "strongly support[ed] the establishment of a mechanism of inquiry." The Security Council adopted a resolution on October 7 that condemned "acts of violence, especially the excessive use of force against Palestinians," and called upon Israel to "abide scrupulously by its legal obligations and its responsibilities under the Fourth Geneva Convention."

Secretary-General Kofi Annan met with Israeli and Palestinian leaders in Paris on October 4, and then on October 9 began nine days of intensive meetings in Israel, the Palestinian Authority territories, Lebanon, and Egypt.

The special rapporteur on extrajudicial, summary, or arbitrary executions on October 5 urged the government of Israel to investigate all incidents of alleged killings by government forces without delay, to ensure that those responsible were brought to justice, and to ensure that its security forces respected international human rights standards.

Israel continued to refuse to cooperate with the special rapporteur of the Commission on Human Rights on the situation of human rights in the Palestinian territories occupied since 1967. Giorgio Giacomelli replaced Hannu Halinen in that post in December 1999. His first report, presented on March 15, found widespread Israeli violations of international human rights law and humanitarian law. A second report, presented to the Special Session of the Commission stated that during the clashes that began on September 29, the IDF and Israeli police had used deadly force "without warning, and without employing deterrence or gradual measures consistent with the minimum standards and methods of crowd control or management of civil unrest."

On May 26 the Western European and Others Group (WEOG) offered Israel temporary membership in its regional grouping of U.N. member states. Full participation in many U.N. bodies, including the Security Council, is organized through regional groupings, and the Asian Group's unwillingness to admit Israel to that grouping had made it ineligible for many U.N. bodies. The U.S. credited its own high-level lobbying for the WEOG decision.

European Union

The European Union expanded its relationship with Israel, while continuing its role as intermediary in bilateral negotiations between Israel and its neighboring states and the Palestine Liberation Organization (PLO), including a January visit to the region by then-E.U. President Jaime Gama and repeated trips by E.U. Council Secretary-General and High Representative for Common Foreign and Security Policy Javier Solana. E.U. member states voted against the Commission on Human Rights' October 19 resolution. The French representative to the commission said that while the E.U. supported convening the special session, provisions of the resolution went beyond the role of the commission and threatened the realization of agreements recently signed by Israel and the PLO.

The Euro-Mediterranean Association Agreement between the European Union (E.U.) and Israel came into force on June 1. In a statement following the Association Council's first meeting on June 13, the E.U. said it had "discussed human rights in Israel, in accordance with the provisions of the Association Agreement, which indicate that respect for human rights and fundamental freedoms and strengthening democracy are essential elements of the Agreement itself."

The E.U. remained the largest single donor to the P.A. During a January 24 E.U. General Affairs Council meeting with President Yasser Arafat, the council said it would welcome the PA announcing a moratorium on the death penalty.

United States

Israel remained the largest recipient of U.S. aid which included U.S. $949 million in economic aid and $3.12 billion in military assistance—including a one-time grant of $1.2 billion in military aid pursuant to the October 1998 Wye River Memorandum between Israel and the PLO. The Palestinian Authority received no military aid and $485 million in economic aid, including a one-time grant of $400 million pursuant to the Wye River Memorandum.

In 2000 the U.S. significantly stepped up efforts to broker a negotiated settlement between Israel and the PLO, including hosting multiple high level trips to the region and hosting a July 11-24 meeting between the Israeli and Palestinian leaders. In an agreement reached during the October 16-17 emergency summit held at Sharm al-Shaykh, Egypt, the U.S. agreed to head a trilateral U.S.-Israeli-Palestinian fact-finding committee to look into the sources of the violent clashes that began in Israel, the West Bank, and Gaza Strip on September 29, and to facilitate security cooperation and consultation between the two parties. On July 27, U.S. President Bill Clinton announced plans for "a comprehensive review" of U.S.-Israeli relations "with a view toward what we can do to ensure that Israeli maintains its qualitative edge," and a memorandum of understanding on U.S. assistance to Israel "with a goal of making a long-term commitment to the necessary support to modernize the IDF." Clinton also stated that he would issue a decision by the end of the year on whether to move the U.S. embassy to West Jerusalem.

U.S. criticism of P.A. human rights violations continued to pay deference to perceived Israeli interests, as when State Department Spokesman James P. Rubin responded to a November 29, 1999 question about the P.A.'s arrests of signatories to a petition critical of its policies. While Rubin expressed concern "about any actions that limit the freedom of expression and peaceful dissent in the Palestinian Authority," he also stated that "Incitement to violence, however, would be another matter and does require a vigorous response," despite the lack of any evidence linking the petitioners to violence. In contrast, criticism of Israeli abuses, including torture of American citizens of Palestinian descent, was decidedly muted. When asked on December 3, 1999, if Secretary of State Madeleine Albright would raise torture in her meetings with Israeli officials, Rubin said, "with respect to the legislation authorizing the use of physical force, we try not to interfere with the internal Israeli public debate on this and political debate on this issue," but that the U.S. would welcome any actions that are consistent with internationally recognized human rights standards.

Relevant Human Rights Watch Reports:

Investigation into Unlawful Use of Force in the West Bank, Gaza Strip, and Northern Israel, 10/00

KUWAIT

Human Rights Developments

In the aftermath of the 1990-1991 Iraqi occupation, Kuwaiti officials promised major human rights improvements. Almost ten years later, enduring violations far outweighed incremental improvements. Kuwait's ratification of five major human rights treaties had not been accompanied by significant changes in law or practice. The government had still not investigated or punished those responsible for hundreds of cases of extrajudicial execution, torture, and "disappearance" in custody, which took place during the February to June 1991 post-liberation martial law period. Forty-two persons remained in prison serving sentences imposed after grossly unfair martial law court trials.

More than 100,000 long-term residents of Kuwait faced widespread and systematic discrimination, and tens of thousands more were prevented from returning to Kuwait. Known as Bidun, they had lived in Kuwait for decades, even generations, unable to obtain Kuwaiti nationality, and without effective nationality elsewhere. Kuwait severely restricted their rights to leave and return to Kuwait, to marry and found a family, and to work, and their children's rights to education, to be registered immediately after birth, and to acquire a nationality. Bidun also suffered disproportionately from discrimination on the basis of sex, particularly with regard to issues of nationality and naturalization, marriage, divorce, and family reunification. According to the Ministry of Interior, some 37,000 Bidun became eligible to apply for naturalization following amendments to the Nationality Law on May 16. However, the law limited the number who would be granted nationality in any given year, raising concern that even those eligible could continue to face discrimination for many years to come. The government also said that Bidun not eligible for naturalization would face prosecution and potential deportation if they did not register as foreigners. Prosecutions began immediately following June 27, when the Ministry of Interior ended a nine month program in which it issued five year residency permits and other benefits to Bidun who signed affidavits admitting to a foreign nationality and renouncing claims to Kuwait nationality. The government tolerated a trade in forged foreign passports, raising concerns that significant numbers of those who presented passports purporting to have been issued by countries such as the Dominican Republic, Colombia, and Nigeria when applying for the program may not have had effective nationality in those countries.

Despite repeated government promises to amend labor laws and to crack down on the illegal trade in work visas, more than one million foreign workers faced serious restrictions on their ability to organize and bargain collectively, and had few legal remedies against abuses by employers. Female domestic workers, who were excluded from the labor law, were particularly vulnerable to physical and sexual abuse by employers. In March, India announced that it had stopped issuing immigration clearances to Indian nationals wishing to work as domestics in Kuwait because of abuses there. In October 1999, army and national guard units were deployed to halt two days of rioting by thousands of Egyptian migrants. According to Kuwaiti newspapers, many of those rioting had paid Kuwaiti brokers thousands of dollars in return for what they believed were legal work visas, only to find no jobs awaiting them.

Women faced widespread discrimination in both law and practice. The Personal Status Law discriminated against women in inheritance rights, the weight given to their testimony in court, and rights in contracting marriage, during marriage, and at its dissolution. The Penal Code reduced or eliminated punishments for violent crimes committed by men against women, and criminalized abortion even when it was necessary to save a woman's life. Women were prohibited from voting and standing for election, and discriminated in relation to the passage of nationality to their spouses and children. In November 1999, the National Assembly twice rejected legislation granting voting rights for women, and on July 4 the Constitutional Court rejected four legal challenges to the ban on women voting. As of this writing, the National Assembly had yet to vote on several draft amendments to the election law, including amendments granting women voting rights but not the right to stand for office. On June 26 the National Assembly passed legislation requiring gender segregation in private universities. As of this writing, however, a similar law passed in 1996 requiring public universities be segregated within five years had not been implemented.

Vaguely worded provisions in the Penal Code and Printing and Publications Law were repeatedly used against writers and journalists deemed to have offended religion, morality, the head of state, or national security. Punishments included imprisonment, fines, and confiscation and closure of periodicals. On March 26, an appeals court fined prize-winning novelist and short story writer Laila al-'Othman and publisher Yahiya al-Rubay'an KD1000 (U.S. $3260) each for distributing al-'Othman's novel, *al-Rahiil* (The Departure), despite provisions in the Penal Code exempting works "published according to the accepted rules of science or art." The court also fined al-Rubay'an and Kuwait University philosophy professor Dr. 'Aliya Shu'ayb KD100 (U.S. $326) each for distributing Shu'ayb's collection of poetry, *'Anakib Tarthi Jurhan* (Spiders Bemoan a Wound), without a permit. In January, a lower court had sentenced all three to two months in prison. Both books were ordered banned, although *al-Rahiil* had been published and had circulated legally in Kuwait since 1984, and *Anakib Tarthi Jurhan* had been in circulation since 1993.

On February 7, Kuwait executed Matar al-Mutairi, a Kuwaiti national convicted of murder. As of this writing, at least twenty-eight persons were awaiting execution. Many had been convicted of drug offences following Kuwait's expansion of the death penalty in 1995. Others included 'Ala Husayn, the Iraqi-imposed prime minister during its occupation of Kuwait. Husayn, who had been granted political asylum in Norway, was sentenced to death after he returned to Kuwait to face trial in January.

Defending Human Rights

Kuwait continued to deny formal recognition to all human rights nongovernmental associations and to restrict their ability to organize public meetings and events. The Council of Ministers had ordered the dissolution of all unlicensed human rights and humanitarian organizations in August 1993, but more recently had tolerated some informal gatherings by human rights activists, including members of the unlicensed Kuwaiti Society for Human Rights (KSHR), an affiliate of the Arab Organization for Human Rights. Some human rights activists were able to meet under the auspices of registered associations, such as the University Graduates' Society.

On May 9, the Interior Ministry's director general of punitive institutions prevented National Assembly Human Rights Committee members from making a prearranged visit to the Central Prison, despite the committee's parliamentary mandate to visit and receive complaints from prisoners. The minister of interior later called the decision "a misunderstanding." However, the ministry had interfered with past visits, including confiscating prisoners' written complaints to the committee in January 1996.

A Human Rights Watch delegate met in April with government officials, lawyers, activists, and victims in Kuwait, and in February delegates from Amnesty International sponsored a joint conference with the Kuwaiti Bar Association titled "Justice and Human Dignity."

The Role of the International Community

United Nations

The United Nations Human Rights Committee reviewed Kuwait's first periodic report on its implementation of the International Covenant on Civil and Political Rights (ICCPR) on July 18 and 19, 2000. Kuwait had submitted the report in May 1998, almost a year after it was due. The Human Rights Committee identified twenty-three "principal subjects of concern," including discrimination against women and Bidun; unfair trials, "disappearances," and abuses by security personnel; and restrictions on freedom of opinion, expression, and association. The committee also found that Kuwait's reservation to articles 2(1) and 3 of the ICCPR "contravenes the State party's essential obligations" and "is therefore without legal effect." Kuwait's second periodic report is due by July 31, 2004. Six other state reports due to four other human rights treaty monitoring bodies were overdue and had yet to be submitted at the time of this writing. They included Kuwait's initial and second periodic report on the Convention on the Elimination of All Forms of Discrimination against Women, which were due on October 2, 1995, and October 2, 1999.

Kuwait signed the Rome Statute of the International Criminal Court on September 8.

Relevant Human Rights Watch Reports:

Promises Betrayed: Denial of Rights of Bidun, Women, and Freedom of Expression, 10/00

SAUDI ARABIA

Human Rights Developments

"It is absurd to impose on an individual or a society rights that are alien to its beliefs or principles," Saudi Arabia's deputy premier and effective head of state Crown Prince Abdullah bin Abdul Aziz told the U.N. Third Millenium summit in New York on September 6. He warned of "the ramifications of unbridled globalization and its use as an umbrella to violate the sovereignty of states and interfere with their internal affairs under a variety of pretexts, especially from the angle of human rights." The kingdom's fourteen million citizens and six to seven million foreign residents thus continued to be denied a range of basic rights guranteed under international law.

Freedom of expression and association were nonexistent rights, political parties and independent local media were not permitted, and even peaceful anti-government activities remained virtually unthinkable. Infringements on privacy, institutionalized gender discrimination, harsh restrictions on the exercise of religious freedom, and the use of capital and corporal punishment were also major features of the kingdom's human rights record.

There were some encouraging developments, however, such as greater official sensitivity to international criticism of the country's human rights practices, recognition of international standards with respect to women's rights, and public pledges to establish human rights monitoring bodies. On September 7, Saudi Arabia became a party to the Convention on the Elimination of All Forms of Discrimination Against Women (CEDAW), although on August 21 the Council of Ministers, in announcing the government's intention to sign the treaty, said that it would not comply with "any clause in the agreement that contradicts Islamic sharia [law]."

Freedom of expression remained strictly circumscribed and there was no independent press. The eighth Arabic-language daily newspaper in the kingdom, *al-Watan*, was launched in September, joining other Saudi newspapers and media bankrolled by the royal family, including the influential pan-Arab daily *al-Hayat*. The Royal Decree for Printed Material and Publications, promulgated in 1982, contained a list of prohibited topics covering any material that was printed, published, or circulated in the kingdom. Violations of the law were criminal offenses, punishable with up to one year of imprisonment and/or fines.

The number of independent licensed Internet service providers (ISPs) in the kingdom increased to about thirty, with some 100,000 subscribers. Capacity reportedly could not meet demand, and there was evidence that the kingdom continued its efforts to monitor and restrict Web access in the country. "The Saudi government has a right to protect its society," Saudi Telecommunications Company (STC) president Abdel Rahman al-Yami said. "We would like to be not open, but selective in what content comes in....[T]he fast growth in the customer base has created challenges for the network." The STC was responsible for the backbone network inside the country while the King Abdul Aziz City for Science and Technology (KACST) controlled content as the sole gateway to the Internet. In August, KACST blocked the Yahoo "Clubs" site, which contained some 250 Saudi clubs with over 60,000 members. "The Clubs site was blocked because most of the material was against the kingdom's religious, social and political values," said KACST official Khalil al-Jadaan. In April, the government closed an Internet cafe in Mecca that was popular with university students. The action came as a result of a court complaint that the women-only cafe was being used for "immoral purposes," the BBC reported, citing *Arab News*. "What was uncovered was against both our religion and our traditions," charged Brigadier Yousef Matter of the civil police, adding that the court had empowered him to shut down other cybercafes in Mecca.

Capital punishment was applied for crimes including murder, rape, armed robbery, drug smuggling, sodomy, and sorcery. In most cases, the condemned were decapitated in public squares after being blind-folded, handcuffed, shackled at the ankles, and tranquilized. By late September 2000, at least 104 Saudis and foreigners had been beheaded, exceeding in nine months the total of 103 that Amnesty International recorded in 1999. Two of the foreigners beheaded in 2000 were women: a Pakistani in July for heroin smuggling, and an Indonesian in June for murder.

Saudi courts continued to impose corporal punishment, including amputations of hands and feet for robbery, and floggings for lesser crimes such as "sexual deviance" and drunkenness. The number of lashes was not clearly prescribed by law and varied according to the discretion of judges, and ranged from dozens of lashes to several thousand, usually applied over a period of weeks or months. A court in Qunfuda sentenced nine Saudi alleged transvestites in April. Five drew prison terms of six years and 2,600 lashes, and the other four were sentenced to five years and 2,400 lashes. The floggings reportedly were to be carried out in fifty equal sessions, with a fifteen-day hiatus between each punishment. In August, the daily *Okaz* reported that a court had ordered the surgical removal of the left eye of an Egyptian, Abd al-Muti Abdel Rahman Muhamed, after he was convicted of throwing acid in the face of another Egyptian, injuring and disfiguring his left eye. The operation was performed in a hospital in Medina. In addition to this punishment, Abdel Rahman was reportedly fined U.S. $68,800 and sentenced to an undisclosed prison term.

The inherent cruelty of such sentences was heightened by due process concerns about the fairness of legal and administrative procedures. Under the 1983 Principles of Arrest, Temporary Confinement, and Preventative Regulations, detainees had no right to judicial review, no right to legal counsel, and could be held in prolonged detention pending a decision by the regional governor or the minister of interior. Suspects had no right to examine witnesses, or to call witnesses of their own, and uncorroborated confessions could constitute the basis for conviction and sentencing.

Hani 'Abd al-Rahim Hussain al-Sayegh, a Saudi citizen deported from the United States on October 11, 1999, after the U.S. Attorney General's Office stated that it lacked sufficient evidence to charge him in connection with the 1996 Khobar Tower bombing in Dhahran that killed nineteen American troops, was held in virtual incommunicado detention without charges and without access to legal counsel for at least three months after his arrival in the kingdom. The U.S. did not make public guarantees it claimed to have sought and received from Saudi Arabia prior to his deportation that he would not be maltreated and would receive a fair trial.

The government heavily restricted religious freedom and actively discouraged religious practices other than the Wahhabi interpretation of the Hanbali school of Sunni Islam. Officially, non-Muslims were free to worship privately but in October 1999 and January 2000, according to the U.S. State Department, two Filipino Christian services were raided by the *mutawwa'in*, the state-financed religious police known as the Committee to Promote Virtue and Prevent Vice. Thirteen people were arrested the first time and another sixteen persons in January; all were deported. Saudi officials reportedly said that the services had too many participants to be considered private.

The *mutawwa'in* also policed public display of religious icons and public worship or practice of religions other than Wahhabi Islam, and had the authority to detain Muslims and non-Muslims for up to twenty-four hours for offenses such as indecent dress and comportment. Official intolerance extended to alternative interpretations of Islam, and members of Saudi religious minorities continued to be harassed or detained for the peaceful practice of their faith. Shia Muslims, who constitute about eight percent of the Saudi population, faced discrimination in employment as well as limitations on religious practices. Shia jurisprudence books were banned, the traditional annual Shia mourning procession of Ashura was discouraged, and operating independent Islamic religious establishments remained illegal. At least seven Shi'a religious leaders—Abd al-Latif Muhammad Ali, Habib al-Hamid, Abd al-Latif al-Samin, Abdallah Ramadan, Sa'id al-Bahaar, Muhammad Abd al-Khidair, and Habib Hamdah Sayid Hashim al-Sadah—reportedly remained in prison for violating these restrictions.

Several incidents during the year punctured the kingdom's stability. These included violent clashes between Ismaili Shiites and security forces in the southwest province of Najran in April; the August 9 shooting by a Saudi university student at a housing complex for foreign defense workers in Khamis Mushayt near the King Khalid air base in southwest Asir province in which authorities said one Saudi Royal Air Force police officer was killed and another two seriously injured; a two-day uprising at al-Jawf prison in the north, also in August; and the hijacking of a Saudi Arabian Airlines plane flying from Jeddah to London on October 14 by two armed Saudis whom the government identified as first lieutenants in the security forces.

There were conflicting accounts about the unrest in the southwest city of Najran where Ismaili Shiites confronted security forces and the provincial governor in April. The unrest was variously attributed to public Shi'a observance of Ashura for the first time in many years, the closure of an Ismaili mosque, the arrest of an Ismaili cleric, and tensions along Saudi's border with Yemen, where Ismailis have strong links. Between April 14 and 16, according to the London-based Committee to Protect Legitimate Rights in the Arabian Peninsula, three Isma'ili religious scholars, Haythim al-Sayyid Muhammad al-Shakhs of al-Ahsa, Abdullah al-Sayyid Hussain al-Nahwi of al-Mabraz, and Jud Juwwad al-Nahwi of al-Mabraz, were arrested for their involvement with the outlawed Islamic Action Movement. The same source named eleven religious scholars forbidden from preaching and religious activities, and another twelve scholars who remained imprisoned for such activities, some for as long as five years. Ahmad bin Muhammad al-Khayat, a Shi'a Isma'ili cleric

and according to Saudi authorities an illegal Yemeni immigrant, was arrested on April 23 for "practicing sorcery" while teaching in al-Mansura mosque in Najran. No details were available on the precise nature of his alleged offense, or whether his activities were connected with Isma'ili religious practices deemed idolatrous by Wahhabi doctrine. An associate of al-Khayat reportedly shot and injured a policeman who was searching the cleric's home.

By some accounts, Saudi religious police raided an Isma'ili mosque, closed it down, and confiscated its books. Protesters then assembled in front of the home of Najran's provincial governor, Prince Masha'al bin Saud bin Abd al-Aziz. According to Agence France-Presse, the Interior Ministry deployed forces overnight amidst warnings that the protesters were liable to be "arrested, questioned, and tried in keeping with Islamic law." According to the Saudi Press Agency, citing the Interior Ministry, security forces raided not a mosque but the home of an "illegal resident" who was practicing "sorcery." During the search and after the sorcerer was arrested, the SPA said, one member of the security forces was shot and injured. At a demonstration at the governor's headquarters calling for the release of the alleged sorcerer, protesters fired guns and burned vehicles, killing one member of the security forces and injuring others. There was no independent confirmation of the numbers killed, injured and arrested in the days that followed, and official government statements clearly sought to downplay the incident.

On August 11, some 400 inmates at the central prison in al-Jawf went on a two-day rampage. According to an unnamed Saudi security official cited in press reports, the prisoners attacked a guard, burned bedding in their cells, and then rioted, causing extensive damage. Calm was reportedly restored the next day, after police and special security forces were airlifted to the area to assist the guards. The inmates reportedly were frustrated at the lack of response to repeated complaints about prison conditions and sought a meeting with the provincial governor. According to the Saudi official, demands included the provision of newspapers, doors on bathrooms, and improved food, sanitation and recreation.

Saudi women continued to face severe discrimination in all aspects of their lives, including the family, education, employment, and the justice system. Religious police enforced a modesty code of dress and institutions from schools to ministries were gender-segregated. This year a princess and distant cousin of the king was appointed assistant under secretary at the Ministry of Education—the highest position ever held by a Saudi woman—in charge of girls' education. Saudi businesswomen continued to be active through their own associations, including the Businesswomen's Forum in the Eastern Province. According to one report, of the 76,000 members of the Jeddah, Riyadh and Eastern Province chambers of commerce, some 5,500 were women.

Interior Minister Prince Nayif bin Abdelaziz said in August that the kingdom's high population growth rate and the large number of job-seeking graduates presented "an economic, social, security and cultural problem." Unemployment among Saudi citizens was an estimated 14 percent, and 20 percent among workers aged twenty to twenty-nine years old, according to the chief economist at the Saudi American Bank in Riyadh. The government therefore continued to take steps to reduce its reliance on foreign workers, a process described as "Saudiization," which Prince Nayif declared a "top priority."

The large population of foreign workers included some 1.2 million Egyptians and 1.2 million Indians, according to the U.S. State Department. Undocumented workers included those who remained after entering the country to perform the *haj* or *umra*, and those who stayed after the expiry of their work visas. Migrants have long been subjected to restrictions such as the surrender of passports to Saudi sponsors, limitations on freedom of movement, prohibitions on trade union organizing, and lack of access to legal representation in cases of arrest. Overstayers

and violators of the *iqama* (residency permit system) were given a July 2 deadline to obtain the proper authorizations or leave the country, which authorities later extended to August 29, after which date all penalties were to be "firmly implemented," the Interior Ministry said. Prince Nayif said that *iqama* violators included those who left or fled their Saudi sponsors or who were carrying out business activities on their own. Anyone without a residence permit after the deadline faced fines of over U.S. $25,000, prison sentences of six months, and deportation. Special police squads searched work places and homes for violators, including both foreign workers and their Saudi employers. Thousands of foreigners left or were expelled. For example, the Nigerian press reported on July 20 that 1,000 Nigerians had already been rounded up and deported, and Pakistani media said on September 27 that 2,441 Pakistani workers had been deported, in addition to thousands of undocumented workers who left the country voluntarily. In September, the Ministry of Labor and Social Affairs reportedly wrote to private firms with over twenty employees, instructing them to increase by 25 percent the number of Saudis on their payrolls.

Saudi Arabia continued to provide refuge and financial support to Idi Amin, the exiled Ugandan leader whose regime was responsible for a reign of terror that left an estimated 300,00 dead in the 1970s. After fleeing Uganda in 1979, Amin arrived in the kingdom at the invitation of the late King Faisal and reportedly has since been protected by government-paid Saudi guards. A journalist with Uganda's *New Vision* newspaper interviewed Amin in Jeddah in 1999 and reported that he had moved from his home in the city center "to a more exclusive area...mainly occupied by powerful oil sheikhs."

Defending Human Rights

Saudi restrictions on access to the country, coupled with the lack of freedom of association and expression, made it extremely difficult to obtain detailed information about human rights conditions, and there were no independent human rights organizations operating from inside the country either overtly or clandestinely. Surveillance of telephone, the Internet, and postal communications made it risky for persons inside the kingdom to provide information. Saudis abroad were reluctant to speak of sensitive matters for fear of repercussion on family members or future employment prospects. As of October 2000, there were no indications that the new rights bodies announced by the government in April had been set up or begun operation. It was also unclear if the cabinet's August decision to ratify CEDAW, albeit with reservations, would enable independent women's rights groups to organize and function freely inside the kingdom.

Amnesty International launched a worldwide campaign focused on Saudi Arabia—"End Secrecy, End Suffering"—and published reports about the kingdom in March, May, and October. The campaign provoked repeated public responses from Saudi government officials that ranged from welcoming invitations to intense criticism. On March 27, the Saudi Ministry of Foreign Affairs issued a detailed statement saying that the kingdom had a "keen interest and commitment to the cause of human rights," there were no political prisoners, and the criminal justice system was "properly administered." Harsh words followed from senior Saudi officials. For example, Defense Minister Prince Sultan bin Abdul Aziz charged on April 11 at a joint press conference with British Defense Minister Geoff Hoon that "all that has been said against Saudi Arabia is motivated by hate." He added: "Those who have the slightest doubt over human rights in Saudi Arabia should come to the kingdom to see for themselves. We have six million non-Saudis who work in all fields and enjoy their rights." Saudi newspapers on April 15 quoted Interior Minister Prince Nayef, who dismissed as "merely nonsense" the allegations of human rights abuses in the kingdom. The interior minister was also quoted the same day as saying: "We welcome anyone to see for himself the facts in the kingdom as it has nothing to conceal."

But Foreign Minister Prince Saud al-Faisal appeared to exclude Amnesty International from the interior minister's invitation to visit the kingdom. In an interview with the Spanish daily *El Pais*, reported by Agence France-Presse on April 16, he said: "If Amnesty International was seeking the truth and if it informed itself honesty of the truth, we would consider a visit." He continued: "But so long as it continues to use erroneous information as its basis without taking into account our responses," the visit would have "no sense." As of this writing, neither AmnestyInternational nor Human Rights Watch have received positive responses to requests for access to the kingdom.

After the release of Amnesty International's second report, which concerned the justice system, the criticism continued. For example, Minister Abdullah al-Sheik said on May 9 that critics of the kingdom's rights record "have misled many people with lies and fallacies which they spread through the media." And on May 20 the daily *al-Riyadh* quoted Prince Turki bin Muhamed, deputy foreign minister for political affairs, charging: "The target of Amnesty's campaign against Saudi Arabia is Islam."

The Role of the International Community

United Nations

Saudi Arabia for the first time was elected as one of the fifty-three members of the U.N. Commission on Human Rights for the 2001-2003 term. On April 6, Prince Turki bin Muhammad Saud al-Kabir told the commission that "the Kingdom of Saudi Arabia and the other members of the Organization of the Islamic Conference are jointly seeking to promote the universality of human rights." The prince stated that the kingdom prohibited any form of torture, and that his government did "not prohibit exercise of freedom of expression and assembly provided that this is neither prejudicial to public order nor detrimental to public morals," and that all laws applied "to both sexes without distinction or exception."

Prince Turki also told the commission that the government would set up "a national governmental body, reporting directly to the Prime Minister and headed by a high-level official, vested with authority to look into all human rights issues." He added that "an independent non-governmental national body" would also be established " to help to publicize and protect human rights, to affirm the need for compliance with the regulations pertaining thereto and to advocate the punishment of offenders." He stated that "human rights sections" would be created in various government agencies, including the Ministry of Justice, the Ministry of the Interior, the Ministry of Foreign Affairs and the Ministry of Labor, "to emphasize the vital need for compliance with human rights regulations and principles," and that new regulations would be adopted to govern the legal profession and legal counseling.

The prince extended an invitation to the U.N. special rapporteur on the independence of judges and lawyers to study the Saudi court system. In July, the Consultative Council, an advisory body, deliberated over a new draft law for regulation of legal procedures.

On September 7 Crown Prince Abdallah signed at the U.N. the Convention on the Elimination of all Forms of Discrimination Against Women (CEDAW), although it was too early to assess the practical effect on women's rights in the kingdom.

On October 25, Secretary-General Kofi Annan announced the appointment of Thoraya Ahmed Obeid, a Saudi woman who has served in U.N. posts since 1975, as executive director of the U.N. Population Fund. "Today, all the Saudi women are recognizing that you broke the ceiling one more time for Saudi women, and we thank you for that," she told Annan. She also was quoted as saying: "Once you talk about human rights, you talk about women, you talk about freedom. It is a process the country is going through," adding that she hoped it would "impact on my sisters in Saudi Arabia and make a difference in our lives."

European Union

The European Commission continued to negotiate with the Gulf Cooperation Council (of which Saudi Arabia is the leading member) for a free trade agreement. The Joint Communique of the E.U.-GCC Ministerial Meeting issued November 2, 1999, said that "The GCC Ministers, while noting the diversity of systems of values, which should be taken fully into consideration, joined the E.U. in reiterating their continuing commitment to the promotion and protection of human rights." European countries, along with the U.S. and Japan, have called for Saudi admission to the World Trade Organization.

According to the Saudi government, Western-based multinational oil companies were committed to investing some U.S. $100 billion in the kingdom's natural gas and petrochemical sectors over the next two decades. In July, it was revealed that twelve corporations had been shortlisted to prepare detailed project proposals, including four based in Europe: Royal Dutch/Shell Group, BP Amoco, ENI, and Total Fina Elf.

United Kingdom

Noting that in 1999 Saudi Arabia was the nineteenth largest export market in the world, the British government reported that the kingdom was its largest market in the Middle East, with exports of £1.5 billion. The United Kingdom maintained a hefty arms trade with Saudi Arabia, although exports declined in 1999 to £131 million sterling from £803 million in 1998.

Foreign office minister of state Peter Hain noted in a speech on June 20 at the Investing in Saudi Arabia conference in London that Britain was the second largest investor in Saudi Arabia with investments totalling U.S. $3.5 billion. He noted that some 30,000 Britons resided in the country, and there were more than ninety joint ventures between British and Saudi companies. He reported that top British corporations in Saudi included GlaxoWellcome, Shell, Rolls-Royce, BAE Systems, Tate & Lyle, and Unilever.

Hain added: "Saudi Arabia is important. We all know why. It remains the economic powerhouse of the region. Saudi Arabia is one of the few countries that can still dictate business on its own terms, sometimes against all the odds of the economics textbooks. Who else could have the international banks lending so readily? Who else could have the international oil companies queuing-up to invest billions of dollars?"

United States

U.S. Defense Secretary William Cohen was asked at an April 9 joint press briefing in Jeddah with his Saudi counterpart Prince Sultan bin Abdulaziz al-Saud to discuss areas of disagreement between the United States and Saudi Arabia. "That's a very easy answer," he replied. "There are no points of disagreement between his Royal Highness and myself or between the kingdom of Saudi Arabia and the United States."

Saudi Arabia was the largest market in the region for American products, and the U.S. once again was Saudi Arabia's number one trading partner, with military and civilian exports of U.S. $7.9 billion in 1999, according to an April 2000 report of the U.S. embassy in Riyadh. The kingdom was among the world's top ten military spenders, the State Department said in its August 2000 report, World Military Expenditures and Arms Transfers 1998, and the number one recipient of U.S. arms exports in the period 1995-1997, with $13.7 billion in sales.

About 4,000 U.S. troops were stationed at Prince Sultan air base. Minister of Defense Prince Sultan said on April 9 that rumors of a reduction of U.S. forces in Saudi Arabia were "not correct." He visited Washington, D.C., on November 1-4, 1999 at the invitation of Secretary of Defense Cohen, and had meetings with President Clinton, Secretary of State Albright, Secretary Cohen and other senior officials. The State Department issued a joint statement on November 5, saying that topics of discussion included "the close cooperation of the two governments, particularly military and economic cooperation," and that the two countries "agreed that continuing high-level military contact and joint military training enhance[d] preparedness

help[ed] sustain security and peace in the Middle East and throughout the world." On July 20, the Defense Department announced a proposed $475 million military sale to Saudi Arabia for 500 AIM-120C Advanced Medium Range Air to Air Missiles and other logistical and program support.

At a press conference in Riyadh on February 26, U.S. Energy Secretary Bill Richardson termed Saudi Arabia "a good friend and strong ally" of the U.S., and noted that ties were cemented by "a strong trade relationship, a significant investment relationship, a valued strategic partnership and a long-standing energy relationship." He also said that the U.S. welcomed the kingdom's decision to "revise the foreign capital investment law to make it more attractive for foreign investors to do business in Saudi Arabia," and that U.S. companies were "very pleased with the prospect of participation in the gas upstream sector and other potential foreign investment opportunities."

Saudi officials stressed the importance of U.S. support for the kingdom's entry into the World Trade Organization (WTO). At a banquet on September 5 in New York hosted by the Saudi-American Business Council, Crown Prince Abdullah said: "We expect that official U.S. agencies and the U.S. business community will support our efforts to complete the procedures to win WTO membership." The U.S. embassy in Riyadh noted in an April report that accession to the WTO was "the keystone of Saudi Arabia's economic reform program." It was reported in September that Crown Prince Abdullah would be meeting in New York with representatives of the eight U.S.-based oil companies selected in August to further pursue energy development projects in Saudi Arabia: Chevron, Conoco, ExxonMobil, Marathon, Phillips, Texaco, Enron, and Occidental.

The State Department once again issued a critical written assessment of Saudi Arabia's human rights practices in its annual country report, issued in February, but Clinton administration officials once again did not raise rights issues publicly. In a scathing indictment of the kingdom's practices, the U.S.

Commission on International Religious Freedom wrote to Secretary of State Albright recommending that Saudi Arabia be added to the list of "countries of particular concern," pursuant to the 1998 International Religious Freedom Act, for "particularly severe violations of religious freedom." The commission stated that "the government brazenly denies religious freedom and vigorously enforces its prohibition against all forms of public religious expression other than that of Wahabi Muslims. Numerous Christians and Shi'a Muslims continue to be detained, imprisoned and deported."

SYRIA

Human Rights Developments

One chapter of Syrian history came to a close with the death on June 10 of President Hafez al-Asad, in power since 1970. The Ba'th Party then quickly orchestrated the political and military elevation of his thirty-four-year-old son, Bashar, allowing citizens only the choice of voting yes or no in a one-candidate presidential referendum held on July 10. The Syrian constitution also was expeditiously amended to lower the minimum required age of the president, and Bashar al-Asad was elected with 97.27 percent of the vote. The British-trained opthamologist had already been designated commander-in-chief of the armed forces and elected leader of the Ba'th Party. Amidst grumbling about the possible onset of dynastic rule in Syria by the Alawite minority, many nevertheless hoped that the new president would eventually breathe life into the country's civil society, stagnant from decades of one-party rule. Prior to his father's death, Bashar al-Asad's action-oriented enthusiasm about computer-based information technology (he headed the Syrian Computer Society) and his campaigns against endemic official corruption were well publicized in Syria, raising expectations that as president he might tackle political as well as economic reform.

In neighboring Lebanon, opponents of Syria's long-term domination of the country had their own hopes, calling repeatedly for reassessment of the lopsided bilateral relationship and return of full sovereignty. It was not only Asad's death but Israel's earlier military withdrawal from occupied south Lebanon in May that prompted and emboldened Lebanese critics and activists, particularly university students, to press directly and publicly for the withdrawal from their country of all Syrian troops and security forces.

With Israeli-Syrian peace negotiations again stalled, the Golan Heights, which Israel annexed in 1981, remained under occupation and Israeli settlement activity there continued.

Despite the presidential succession, Syrians continued to be denied civil and political rights. Freedom of expression, association, and assembly were strictly limited in law and practice; the local media and access to the Internet remained state-controlled; and the pervasive powers of the security forces under the country's long-standing emergency law, in force since 1963, were intact. There were no effective safeguards against arbitrary arrest and torture; civilian and military prisons, including the infamous Tadmor in the Palmyran desert, remained off-limits to independent observers; and the Kurdish minority continued to be denied basic rights, including the right to a nationality for tens of thousands. No one inside the country dared to advocate justice and accountability for current and former government officials responsible for gross human rights abuses, including the massacre of possibly as many as 1,100 unarmed prisoners at Tadmor in 1980, and the military assault on the city of Hama in 1982 in which thousands were killed.

Numerous Syrians lived in political exile abroad. The children of some of those blacklisted from returning were deprived of Syrian nationality and in some cases were technically stateless because they lacked passports. Human Rights Watch continued to receive information about Syrian exiles who were arrested, detained, and subsequently forced to leave countries where they resided and worked because they carried, of necessity, forged passports. As of this writing, there were no reported public initiatives by the government to address this major political and humanitarian issue, which affected entire families, including women and children.

Hundreds of Syrian, Palestinian, and other political prisoners continued to be held, but the government provided no official figures. In a June 27 letter to President-elect Bashar al-Asad, Amnesty International estimated the number of political prisoners at 1,500 — of whom approximately 800, mostly members or sympathizers of the Muslim Brotherhood but also supporters of the pro-Iraqi Ba'th Party and communists, were believed to be in Tadmor prison. Another 560 prisoners were held in Sednaya prison, and two hundred in other detention centers and in Duma women's prison, Amnesty International said.

In a welcome development, releases of political prisoners, including human rights activists, took place before and after the death of Hafez al-Asad. Two members of the Communist Action Party, Fateh Jamus and Abd al-Karim Aslan, who had served sixteen and eighteen-year terms, respectively, were reported released prior to Hafez al-Asad's death. There were reports that sixteen Jordanian political detainees were freed in March, and another seventeen during the next several months, and three members of the Muslim Brotherhood were released in May. Syrian political exiles confirmed that "dozens" of political detainees were released in June and July, including thirty members of the Muslim Brotherhood; three Jordanians, including Khalid Awad who had served twelve years on political charges; journalist Faisal Allush from the Communist Action Party, who was released after fifteen years in prison; and two members of the Tawhid movement, military commander Samir al-Hassan and Lebanese Sunni activist Hashim Minkara, freed after serving fifteen years.

An anti-corruption campaign launched by Hafez al-Asad and continued by his son resulted in arrests and convictions of senior officials and one alleged suicide. On May 10, former Prime Minister Mahmud Zu'bi was expelled from the Ba'th Party based on allegations of corruption. He had been removed from office on March 7 amid accusations of mismanagement and was banned from leaving the country. The interior ministry said on May 21 that Zubi killed himself when the Damascus police commander went to his house to deliver a summons. His funeral was not attended by the president or members of the cabinet.

A group of three dozen Syrian opposition figures in exile, calling itself the Committee of Coordination for Democracy in Syria, criticized the anti-corruption campaign in a June 10 statement published in *al-Quds al-Arabi*, the London-based pan-Arab daily. The exiles, including Sarkis Sarkis, Adib al-Hurani, and Yusif Abadlaki, charged that the real purpose of the campaign was to eliminate potential opponents of Bashar al-Asad. The group also called for the canceling of emergency law, an accounting for the "disappeared," freedom of expression, and political pluralism.

Another call for political reform and human rights came in a September statement signed by ninety-nine prominent intellectuals, artists, and others residing in Syria and abroad that appeared in the Lebanese daily *al-Safir*. The statement called on the authorities to cancel emergency law, issue a general amnesty for all political prisoners, allow political exiles to return, and recognize the rights to freedom of assembly, press, and opinion. The signatories included novelist Abdel Rahman Munif, poet Adonis, and philosophy professor Sadiq al-Azm. Earlier appeals included a June editorial in the pan-Arab daily *al-Hayat* for intellectual and press freedoms, and a July request from Ibrahim Abu Daqqah, human rights advisor to Palestinian Authority leader Yaser Arafat, for the release of Palestinian detainees. From Beirut, a Lebanese member of parliament, Boutros Harb, called for an "opening of the files" on some two hundred Lebanese known or suspected of being imprisoned in Syria, some of whom had been detained without trial for over fifteen years. The Jordanian branch of the

Arab Organization for Human Rights also called for the release of sixty-nine Jordanians, as well as Lebanese and Palestinian prisoners.

In other welcome developments, some seventy-five foreign journalists were allowed greater freedom than previously to report from Damascus during Hafez al-Asad's funeral. Bashar al-Asad also decreed measures that provided greater Internet access through connections in offices, at least two private Internet cafes in Damascus, the Asad National Library, and Damascus International Airport. The Syrian Telecommunications Establishment (STE), the country's only Internet service provider, still blocked access to Israeli materials and Syrian opposition Web sites—such as the London-based Syrian Rights Committee—and censored electronic mail. "In Syria we have 5,000 subscribers," Ghassan Lahham, vice-president of the Syrian Computer Society, told a press conference in Beirut on April 15. "These are mainly companies and government institutions. We are working to increase to 20,000 by the end of the year," he said, adding that STE would remain the country's only Internet provider. Beirut's *Daily Star* reported on April 17 that it cost SL2,400 (about U.S. $50) for Internet subscribers in Syria to receive fifteen hours of access monthly, and that a committee had been created "to consider allowing a private company to study applications from people seeking Internet access in Syria."

Against the backdrop of the impending Israeli withdrawal from the occupied south, Lebanese citizens used various tactics to protest Syrian domination of their country. On March 23, for example, journalist Gebran Tueni, managing director and chairman of the board of the independent daily *an-Nahar* (Beirut), wrote as an editorial an extraordinarily frank open letter addressed to then Col. Bashar al-Asad, who had been assigned responsibility for Syria-Lebanon relations by his father. He wrote that "many Lebanese are neither at ease with the Syrian policy in Lebanon, nor the Syria 'presence' in Lebanon....[T]hey resent the way Syria deals with Lebanon, they detest it and reject it....We are not a Syrian province." Tueni also criti-

cized "direct Syrian interference in Lebanese politics," and said that Lebanese "refuse the principle of pre-fabricated voting lists in Damascus" and "reject arresting Lebanese in Syrian prisons." He went on: "There are some Lebanese fears that are getting deeper. There are people who believe that Syria is an enemy. You have to face this reality to be able to solve the problem." Two days later, Lebanese president Emile Lahoud condemned such writing as a "broken record ... played with pro-Israeli motivations." He added: "We all know that such calls and their timing do not reflect interest in protecting Lebanon's sovereignty and independence."

The next month, Lebanese authorities got tough with anti-Syria protesters and referred eight of them to the military court. On April 14, Lebanese authorities arrested two students, Naim Semaani and Mark Choucair, and a lawyer, Maroun Nasrani, and accused them of distributing pamphlets critical of the Syrian presence in Lebanon. They were tried on April 17 in the military court and fined for "distributing pamphlets harmful to the government and to its ties with a sisterly country." On the day of the trial, several dozen student protesters at the Justice Palace clashed with police and five were arrested and referred to the military court. The *Daily Star* reported that the demonstrators "struck at police with their fists and chanted anti-Syrian slogans. 'Syria get out of here,' they shouted."

In June, Tueni penned another editorial, this time directed at Syrian foreign minister Farouq Shara' who had said that pressure from media campaigns and foreign governments would not lead to the withdrawal of Syrian troops, which he contended prevented the eruption of sectarian strife in Lebanon. "Allow us to completely reject your words and the words of some Lebanese trumpets that use the same justification to defend the presence of Syrian troops in Lebanon," Tueni wrote. He added that it was "natural for Minister Shara' to believe journalism does not have the right to claim it represents the views of citizens because in Syria, as in similar regimes, journalism does not represent public opinion but talks with the tongue of the ruling regime."

By September, the Council of Maronite Bishops, led by Patriarch Nasrallah Sfeir, was openly calling for the withdrawal of Syrian troops, whose presence it said "embarrasses the Lebanese." In a September 20 statement the council charged that Syria's "hegemony covered all Lebanese institutions, administrations and government departments." The patriarch pledged that the efforts would continue: "We are not going to be frightened into silence. Nothing will bring this campaign to a halt especially after the Israeli occupation of south Lebanon has ended."

Defending Human Rights

There were no locally based human rights nongovernmental organizations (NGOs) allowed to operate freely and openly with the protection of legal status as NGOs. But activists with the lone independent watchdog group, the Committees for the Defense of Democratic Freedoms and Human Rights in Syria (CDF), including several former detainees, convened "publicly" in Damascus on September 15 for the first time in eleven years. Their purpose, they said, was to underscore their hope for a democratic transformation in Syria. They elected a new board of trustees, including eight persons living in Syria and three in Europe. Aktham Naisse, an attorney who was released in 1998 because of poor health, was elected president of the organization.

Ten CDF activists, including Naisse, had been tried in the state security court in 1992 and sentenced to terms ranging from five to ten years of imprisonment. Thabet Murad and Bassam al-Shaykh were released from Sednaya prison after their sentences expired in early 2000. Three others —journalist and writer Nizar Nayouf, Muhammad Ali Habib, and Afif Muzhir—remained imprisoned, Nayouf reportedly in solitary confinement in Mezze military prison. The World Association of Newspapers denied reports that Nayouf had been released in April, and said that he "adamantly refused" an offer of release in exchange for signing a statement that he would relinquish all human rights awards

and refrain from future political activity. Nayouf, disabled years earlier by torture under interrogation and at Mezze and Tadmur military prisons, suffered from serious medical problems. Syrian authorities continued to deny reports that Nayouf suffered from Hodgkin's disease, a form of lymphatic cancer.

In Lebanon and France, independent human rights groups actively campaigned for the release of several hundred Lebanese they knew or suspected were being held in Syria prisons. While confirming reports that dozens of political prisoners had been released by late July, CDF's Paris-based spokesman Ghayath Naisse said that the "prisoner release is partial, not the comprehensive one we were hoping for." Representatives of eighteen human rights organizations from Palestine and Morocco, Tunisia, Egypt, and other Arab countries wrote in June to the Ninth Regional Congress of the Syrian Ba'th Party calling for an end to emergency law. The letter said that hundreds of political prisoners released from "grisly detention centers" were "still deprived of their civil rights by order of the Supreme State Security Court. They are prevented from traveling, their movements are restricted, and many have lost their jobs." The letter called on the authorities "to make the brave and historic decision to do away with political detention once and for all, release all political prisoners, and restore to them their full civil rights as guaranteed by the Syrian Constitution."

Syrian authorities continued to be unresponsive to letters from Human Rights Watch, and did not respond positively to a long-standing request to visit the country to carry out research.

The Role of the International Community

United Nations

The United Nations Educational, Scientific and Cultural Organization (UNESCO) called attention on May 3, World Press Freedom Day, to the plight of imprisoned Syrian human rights activists by awarding Nizar

Nayuf, who was serving a ten-year prison term despite poor health, the Guillermo Cano World Press Freedom Award.

European Union

Once again, human rights were not a dominant concern in European relations with Syria. The European Union continued to hold talks with Damascus with the aim of concluding an Association Agreement by the year 2010, according to Marc Pierini, head of the European mission in Damascus. Prior to two days of talks in Damascus in November 1999, Pierini told Agence France-Presse that human rights would be "an important part of the agreement" and would be discussed in these meetings as well. But he seemed to mute the message with the following words: "The European Union, whose declared objectives are to strengthen Syria's stability and prosperity, must take into account the legitimate concern of the Syrian authorities not to bring social troubles in the wake of the reforms."

In a July 17 speech in London to the Council for the Advancement of Arab-British Understanding, British foreign office minister Peter Hain noted the "very smooth" transition to power of Bashar al-Asad. He added: "I believe that, over the past year, Britain and Syria have laid the foundations for a new relationship between our countries. I welcome President [Bashar] Asad's commitment to social and economic reform, and to the strategic choice of peace. Britain will, as an old friend, seek to help Syria in both."

United States

U.S. relations with Syria remained lukewarm at best, although Clinton administration efforts to broker a peace deal with Israel continued, including a meeting in Geneva on March 26 between President Clinton and President Hafez al-Asad that was widely viewed as unsuccessful. Syria remained on the U.S. list of "terrorist" countries, although bilateral trade in 1999 totalled $172.67 in U.S. exports to Syria and $94.9 million in Syrian exports to the U.S., according to the Foreign Trade Division of the U.S. Census Bureau.

The U.S. State Department both criticized and praised Syria in its *Patterns of Global Terrorism 1999* report, released in April 2000: "Syria continued to provide safehaven and support to several terrorist groups, some of which maintained training camps or other facilities on Syrian territory. Ahmad Jibril's Popular Front Liberation of Palestinian-General Command (PFLP-GC) and the Palestinian Islamic Jihad (PIJ), for example, were headquartered in Damascus. In addition, Syria granted a wide variety of terrorist groups—including HAMAS, the PFLP-GC, and the PIJ—basing privileges or refuge in areas of Lebanon's Bekaa Valley under Syrian control." The report also noted, however, that the Syrian government "continued to restrain their international activities, instructing leaders of terrorist organizations in Damascus in August to refrain from military activities and limit their actions solely to the political realm."

On December 8, 1999, President Clinton announced that Prime Minister Barak and President al-Asad had agreed to resume Israel-Syria negotiations from the point that they were suspended in January 1996. The talks commenced at a meeting on December 15, 1999, between President Clinton, Prime Minister Barak and Syrian Foreign Minister Farouq al-Shara', followed by talks in Shepherdstown, West Virginia, on January 3-11, 2000.

Secretary of State Madeleine Albright said on January 17: "At the end of the last round, it was agreed that the Israeli-Syrian talks would resume on January 19. Both sides have since been reviewing the status of the talks and the draft working document. Presently, their approaches to the next round differ, and as a result, there is going to be a delay. In the meantime, each side has agreed to send experts to Washington to meet us and provide their comments on the draft."

There were no breakthroughs at the March 26 meeting between Clinton and Asad in Geneva and it appeared that from the American side at least none were expected. En route to the meeting, U.S. National Security Advisor Samuel Berger said in a March 25 press briefing aboard Air Force One that the purpose of the meeting was "not to try to reach an agreement between Israel and Syria." He also noted that "if nothing else happens [in Geneva] other than that Asad and Barak and the President have a better sense that their interests are either reconcilable or irreconcilable, that will be, I think, useful; they'll each make decisions based on that." On the flight, an unnamed senior Clinton administration official provided additional background about the U.S. view: "I think it is important for the Syrian government to convey and demonstrate to the people of Israel that if, in fact, they give up some or all of the Golan Heights. . . .they will gain from that a qualitatively different relationship with Syria, which involves genuine dialogue exchange, at a people-to-people level as well a commercial level and otherwise." The White House released these remarks as part of the official transcript of the press briefing.

In a May 8 speech in Washington to the Anti-Defamation League, Assistant Secretary for Near Eastern Affairs Edward Walker made clear the U.S. and Israeli approach to the negotiation. He stated: "Despite difficulties, we have not given up on the Syrian track. But negotiating the future of the Golan Heights is risky business for Israel. We recognize that only an agreement that enhances Israel's security will be acceptable to Israelis and the United States. At the same time, a way must be found to meet the needs of the Syrian side as well. It would be a great mistake to assume that the Syrians do not, in their own way, face significant risks in approaching peace. Therefore, as long as both Israelis and Syrians are still interested in finding a way forward, and we believe that continues to be the case, the United States will persist in our efforts to help them."

There was evidence that Israel was preparing to lobby for U.S. aid to Syria if a peace treaty was concluded. The diplomatic correspondent for the respected Israeli daily Ha'aretz reported on March 26 from Geneva that the Israeli embassy in Washington was "exploring the possibility of U.S. aid to Syria following the signing of a peace agreement between Syria and the Jewish state." He said

"diplomats assessed that the White House could convince Congress to grant Syria an aid package, but doubts exist about the possibility of American military aid for Syria." He wrote that it was expected "that if an agreement with Syria is signed, Israel will seek assistance from Jewish groups in the United States in pushing an aid package for Syria through Congress," and that "[s]ources involved in securing congressional aid said that a combined aid package for both Israel and Syria would be approved because it will be difficult for members of Congress to oppose such a package." The article noted that Israel had requested $17 billion in U.S. military assistance to finance its withdrawal from the Golan Heights.

Except for a reference in an October 14, 1999, speech by Secretary of State Madeleine Albright to human rights defender Nizar Nayuf being "near death after years of solitary confinement, torture, and neglect," the Clinton administration did not raise Syria's human rights practices publicly and expressed satisfaction at the peaceful transition to power of Bashar al-Asad. Asked before she departed for Hafez al-Asad's funeral if she would raise human rights concerns, Albright suggested that such a message would be inappropriate. "I think that it's important for Dr. Bashar Asad to ... take on the mantle and for the transition process to be pursued," Albright said. "From what we've seen in the past twenty-four hours ... it looks like a peaceful transition. It is important that it be peaceful."

Albright did, however, comment about the continuing Syrian military presence in Lebanon in the wake of the Israeli withdrawal in May. For example, on June 7 in Cairo she noted the "bold move Prime Minister Barak took in withdrawing his forces from Lebanon and doing it according to [U.N. Security Council] Resolution 425," and said it was "very important for all parties involved in that to carry out their obligations vis-à-vis 425. I would hope very much that the Lebanese army would begin to move into Southern Lebanon and that the Lebanese would take control over their own territory and all foreign forces would depart." She added that Lebanon would be discussed in her meeting that day with Syrian Foreign Minister Farouq Shara':

"We're going to talk about Lebanon and I think about making sure that everybody fulfills their obligations according to 425. As I've said, the Syrians have been cooperative and I think it is very important that all parties do in fact follow through on their obligations—these are international obligations—the Israelis have lived up to them, I think it would be good if everybody else did also."

TUNISIA

Human Rights Developments

The struggle of Tunisian activists to exercise their rights to meet and speak about human rights abuses in the country was in the forefront of developments this past year. Public confrontations, including several high profile hunger strikes by political prisoners and by activists under judicial restraints, contributed to the release of some prisoners and a government decision to restore passports and the right to travel to leading human rights lawyers and activists after years of denial. The government, however, remained hostile to any public criticism and criminalized "unlicensed" political activities. The lack of political pluralism was evident from President Zine al-Abidine Ben Ali's reelection for a fourth term on October 24 with 99.4 percent of the votes and by the ruling Democratic Constitutional Rally's (Rassemblement Constitutionnel Democratique, RCD) capture of 94 percent of the vote in the May 28 municipal elections. The increase in protests during the year reflected not any increase in official tolerance but rather a new defiance spurred by frustration over the lack of basic rights.

There was also dissatisfaction with the government's performance on the economic front. The first serious breakdown in labor relations for a decade occurred in early February, when taxi and truck drivers held a three-day strike to protest the introduction of a new driving code and the potential it offered for increased arbitrary abuse and extortion of bribes by the police under the guise of enforcing the new system. The following week, secondary school and university students and unemployed youths demonstrated on the streets of several southern cities and towns, including Gabes, Jebeniana, El Amra, Medenine, Jerba, Douz, Gafsa, and Sfax, amid rumors that bread prices were to rise. For more than a week, they demonstrated against the rise in basic food prices and unemployment, and government corruption. Police arrested hundreds of demonstrators, many of whom alleged that they were ill-treated in custody, but most were released uncharged or received suspended sentences. More than forty, however, were sentenced to between three and eight months in prison.

On November 7, following President Ben Ali's reelection and on the twelfth anniversary of his assumption of power, the authorities released more than 1,000 prisoners, including some 600 political prisoners, on certain conditions as part of a reported amnesty. Many of those freed were sympathizers or low-ranking adherents of al-Nahda (Renaissance), a proscribed Islamist movement, who had been imprisoned for offenses such as attending meetings of an "unauthorized" organization or making donations to the families of imprisoned members. The authorities also released five accused members of the banned Tunisian Communist Worker's Party (Parti Communiste des Ouvrier Tunisiens, PCOT)–Ali Jellouli, Nejib Baccouchi, Noureddine Benticha, Chedli Hammami, and Taha Sass–who they had sentenced in July 1999 after an unfair trial on political charges. A sixth, Fahem Boukaddous, who had been badly tortured in 1999, remained in prison until June 2000. All senior imprisoned al-Nahda members continued to be held, serving long terms under harsh conditions.

Released political prisoners faced a range of punitive measures, some court sanctioned, such as "administrative controls" requiring them to present themselves, often daily, at local police stations and others arbitrary, including restrictions on travel and having their telephone communications cut. Some were dismissed or excluded from their public-sector jobs and private sector employees were pressured not to hire them. Most were subjected to heavy and intimidating police surveillance. On August 28, Hamadi Romdhane was arrested for refusing to submit to administrative controls. A former prisoner, the authorities first told him that administrative controls on those released in accordance with the November 1999 amnesty, had been released but later that they had been reinstated. He was required to sign in on a daily basis at a police station twelve kilometers from his home. Fearing that he could not earn a living under these circumstances, he refused to comply.

The authorities remained determined to quash efforts aimed at developing associations that might be independent and critical of the government. They continued to deny legal status to the nongovernmental Rally for an International Development Alternative (Rassemblement pour une Alternative Internationale de Developpement, RAID) and National Council on Liberties in Tunisia (Conseil Nationale pour les Libertés en Tunisie, CNLT), a human rights monitoring group, thus rendering these associations' supporters liable to arrest and imprisonment on charges of belonging to "unauthorized" organizations. In April, police detained Fathi Chamkhi, president of RAID, together with RAID member Mohamed Chourabi and photocopy shop owner Iheb el-Hani, for possessing RAID and CNLT documents and charged them with "spreading false information liable to disturb public order, defamation of the authorities, inciting fellow citizens to violate the laws of the country, and belonging to an unauthorized association." The two were released on bail on May 8 but their files remained open, leaving them vulnerable to future harassment.

Throughout the year, local human rights activists were summoned before prosecutors or judges, or detained for brief periods and then released. As of mid-October, those under investigation and facing trial included human rights lawyer Nejib Hosni, Mustapha Ben Jaafar, secretary general of the Democratic Forum for Labor and Liberties, another "unauthorized" association, and PCOT activist Mohamed Hedi Sassi.

The government demonstrated particular intolerance when those associated with the CNLT refused to submit to official efforts to silence them. The security forces in December 1999 twice ransacked the offices of Editions Aloés, a publishing house established by CNLT founding member Sihem Ben Sedrine, wife of the CNLT's secretary-general Omer Mestiri, and seized computers and archives. On January 13, Editions Aloés' co-founder and literary director, Jean-Francois Revel, a French national, was summarily dismissed from his position as assistant professor of philosophy at the Institut des Sciences Humaines in Tunis. On February 13, he was ordered to leave the country after he traveled with Ben Sedrine and journalist Taoufik Ben Brik to document the February demonstrations in the south of the country.

Ben Brik, also a founding member of the CNLT, began a hunger strike on April 3 to protest the government's confiscation of his passport a year earlier, repeated police harassment of his family, and Tunisian media blacklisting of his work. On April 10, he was charged with "spreading false information" and "defaming the authorities." The charges, which carried a penalty of up to nine years of imprisonment, were brought in response to Swiss newspaper articles he had written, including one on police harassment of Ben Sedrine. Also on April 10, police forcibly evacuated and closed down Sihem Ben Sedrine's Editions Aloés publishing house, where Taoufiq Ben Brik was conducting his hunger strike, on the grounds that a meeting held there the previous day to discuss freedom of the press, and attended by foreign journalists, had constituted "a threat to public order." On April 26, police detained and badly beat Ben Sedrine, Ben Brik's brother Jalal Zoughlami, and 70-year-old lawyer Ali Ben Salem after a confrontation in which police prevented foreign journalists and Tunisian supporters from visiting Ben Brik at home. On May 3, a court convicted Zoughlami of "verbally and physically abusing" a police officer who was kicking Ben Salem and sentenced him to three months of imprisonment. The authorities shortly afterwards dropped the charges against Ben Brik and returned his passport, allowing him to travel to France were he continued his hunger strike in protest at his brother's imprisonment. An appeal court reduced Zoughlami's sentence to take account of time served awaiting trial and he was released on May 15.

In a televised cabinet meeting on May 15, President Ben Ali defended "the inalienable right of every citizen" to a passport and travel abroad. Despite the welcome return of passports to a number of well-known activists, however, the authorities continued to deny them to less prominent critics as well as to family members of political prisoners and expatriate activists. Other forms of harassment, including routine and intensive police surveillance and house searches at all hours, continued unabated. Mehdi Zougah, a dual French/Tunisian national, returned to Tunisia in August after his Tunisian passport was restored after six years. Despite receiving apparent assurances that he could return safely, he was arrested upon arrival and held in secret detention for twelve days. It was then revealed that he had been convicted in his absence in 1998 for membership in an illegal organization and sentenced to twelve years imprisonment. As of this writing he remains in detention and is due to appear in court on January 8, 2001 on the charge of membership in an illegal organization.

For a number of political activists and their families the year saw no respite. On June 28, seventeen-year-old Nadia Hammami and Najoua Rezgui, daughter and wife, respectively, of convicted PCOT activists Hama Hammami and Abdeljabbar Maddouri, launched hunger strikes to demand an end to state harassment. Nadia and her sisters, Oussaima, eleven years old, and Sarah, eleven months, continued to be denied passports, presumably because of the political activities of their father and their mother, human rights lawyer Radhia Nasraoui. Hama Hammami, a

nonviolent political activist, had suffered torture and ill-treatment during previous prison terms and remained in hiding after he was convicted in his absence and sentenced in July 1999, to more than nine years in prison on several charges, including "defamation of the public order," "spreading false information," and "holding unauthorized meetings." Nadia ended her hunger strike after 13 days on the advice of doctors. Najoua Rezgui, whose husband was also in hiding after he received a similar sentence in the same July 1999 trial, had herself been arrested on several occasions. Rezgui ended her hunger strike after 20 days.

Prisoners conducted hunger strikes demanding improved treatment and prison conditions. Most of the approximately 1,000 political prisoners in Tunisia were serving sentences for "membership of an unlicenced organization," mostly al-Nahda, or related nonviolent offenses such as distributing tracts or attending meetings. Reports by the CNLT in October 1999 and by the nongovernmental International Federation of Human Rights (FIDH) and the Committee for the Respect of Liberties and Human Rights in Tunisia (CRLDHT) in June 2000 documented overcrowded prisons with poor hygiene, inadequate medical care, cruel and degrading disciplinary measures, and regular beatings of prisoners by guards. Several al-Nahda leaders had been held in solitary confinement for months or years. On April 9, prisoners Fahem Boukaddous and Abdelmoumen Belanes, both convicted of membership of the PCOT and suffering from medical conditions, began hunger strikes. They were joined in May by Sadok Chorou , Samir Diallo, and Fathi al-Ouraghi, all convicted of links with al-Nahda, to demand adequate medical care. Lawyer Taoufik Chaieb, imprisoned since 1996 for links with al-Nahda, began a near two-month hunger strike on July 11. After his condition deteriorated seriously, President Ben Ali released him under a presidential amnesty on September 5.

At least three persons died in custody in suspicious circumstances. On May 10, El-Id Ben Saleh was reportedly attacked and killed by fellow detainees in Gafsa prison. On July 22, Chaker El-Azouzi was reportedly beaten to death by police in Hammamet after being taken into custody. On September 17, Ridha Jeddi died in Menzel Bourguiba police station; his body reportedly bore marks of torture when returned to his family. The independent Tunisian League for Human Rights (LTDH) called for investigations into all three cases but at this writing there was no information that they had taken place.

In a meeting with private newspaper publishers on May 3, International Press Freedom Day, President Ben Ali told the media: "Write as you wish. Be critical as long as what you say is true," stating that, "If somebody bothers you about this you have only to contact me." There was no noticeable change, however, in the deferential tone of Tunisia's privately-owned print media, which continued to ignore domestic human rights issues and contributed to the climate of intimidation by printing scurrilous attacks on persons in disfavor with the government. On May 23, Riad Ben Fadel, editor of the Arabic-language edition of the Paris-based monthly *Le Monde diplomatique,* was wounded by gunfire two days after he criticized the authorities' handling of the Ben Brik affair. President Ben Ali met with Ben Fadel after the shooting and promised an investigation.

In June, President Ben Ali took Tunisia's state-run television service to task for not "being more responsive to the preoccupations and expectations of citizens" and for not promoting "pluralism of thought and diversity of opinion." Radio, also state-run, and television remained government mouthpieces, however, and gave no air time to political critics or human rights activists.

Defending Human Rights

Human rights activists faced restrictions ranging from no coverage of their activism in the government- controlled press and banned gatherings to job dismissal and judicial proceedings with the threat of imprisonment. Surveillance extended to phone tapping, disconnecting phone lines, and interception of mail and faxes. By the end of the year, the government had restored the passports of most prominent activists, but maintained travel restrictions on some.

The experience of CNLT spokesman Moncef Marzouki was typical. In November 1999, following publication of several communiqués by the CNLT, the authorities brought him before an investigating judge to answer charges that included maintaining an "unrecognized" association and "spreading false information aiming to disturb the public order." In May, his passport was returned to him and his phone line restored after a four year interruption, but in July, following a short trip to Paris and Washington, he was dismissed from his post as professor of community medicine at the University of Sousse on grounds that he had traveled without permission. On October 19, The authorities prevented him from leaving Tunis airport to attend a meeting in Spain.

Marzouki's university dismissal followed by one day a speech by President Ben Ali to cadres of the ruling RCD party in which he threatened to prosecute unnamed citizens whose criticisms of Tunisia while abroad "amount[ed] to treason." In an unmistakable reference to the CNLT, Ben Ali said, "It is out of the question that in the name of public liberties illegal structures are set up claiming for themselves the status of associations, organizations, or committees." The CNLT continued to issue strongly-worded critiques of human rights abuses despite the government's steadfast rejection of its application for legal recognition. In October 1999, it published a report on prison conditions and in March 2000, a detailed overview of human rights violations in the country.

The Tunisian League for Human Rights (LTDH), the Young Lawyers' Association, and the Tunisian Association of Democratic Women (AFTD), all legally recognized, also spoke out against rights violations despite government pressure and obstacles to holding public meetings.

In April, police prevented the Tunisian section of Amnesty International (AI) from holding a public meeting on the human rights situation in Saudi Arabia. Security officers prevented Mahmoud Ben Romdhane, chair of the organization's international board, and other members and guests, including foreign diplomats, from approaching the organization's Tunis office, and lawyer Hachemi Jegham, former president of AI's Tunisia section, was physically dragged from the building. In July, Donatella Rovera and Hassina Giraud from AI and Patrick Baudouin from the FIDH were barred from entering the country at Tunis-Carthage airport.

The Role of the International Community

United Nations

The United Nations special rapporteur on freedom of opinion and expression visited Tunisia in April 1999 and issued his report on February 25, 2000. The report concluded that Tunisia "still has a long way to go to take full advantage of its favourable economic context and adopt measures designed to strengthen the protection of human rights and, in particular, the right to freedom of opinion and expression." It expressed particular concern over the reported punishment and harassment of families of persons under arrest, state control of broadcasting and major print media, and "inadequate" government efforts to remove "unnecessary constraints" on journalists. The special rapporteur recommended revision and amendment of laws governing the press, political parties, and associations, and called on the government to abolish "all direct and indirect forms of censorship" and "to put an end to the alleged intimidation and harassment of persons seeking to exercise their right to freedom of opinion and expression." The report also called on the government to respond positively to the standing requests of the special rapporteur on torture and the special rapporteur on the independence of judges and lawyers to visit the country.

European Union

The confrontation between the Tunisian government and human rights groups received considerable media coverage in France and other E.U. countries, especially the hunger strike of journalist Taoufik Ben Brik (see above). Swiss Foreign Minister Joseph Deiss said in Tunis on May 2 that he had handed his Tunisian counterpart a memorandum "that contains Switzerland's hope for a solution to this question in accordance with the principles of law that are defended by our two countries." French Foreign Minister Hubert Vedrine, in a speech the same day to the French National Assembly, said that "we attach a great value to press freedom" and that "we have asked the Tunisian authorities a number of times and in different ways to find a humane and rapid end to this deplorable situation." Ben Brik continued his hunger strike in Paris after the Tunisian government returned his passport on May 1.

The European Parliament on June 15 adopted an emergency resolution urging Tunisia to "establish a true multiparty system" and "guarantee the exercise of fundamental rights and freedoms." The resolution called on the E.U.-Tunisian Association Council, set up by the E.U.'s Association Agreement with Tunisia, to conduct a "joint evaluation of respect for human rights in Tunisia," and asked the European Commission to report to parliament "on the evolution of the human rights situation in Tunisia."

United States

A visit by President Ben Ali to Washington, D.C., scheduled for mid-July was postponed because of President Clinton's engagement in Israeli-Palestinian negotiations at Camp David and was not subsequently rescheduled.

U.S. Assistant Secretary of State for Democracy, Human Rights, and Labor Harold Koh, made a three-day visit to Tunisia in June, where he met with human rights advocates, journalists, and government officials. At a press conference on June 14, Koh commended the government's record on social and economic progress and said that "this is an important moment to match those steps with steps in the area of civil and political rights." He identified greater political pluralism, judicial transparency and independence, and media censorship as key concerns. He also said that "further progress would be welcomed" in government steps "to ensure the ability of all Tunisians to travel freely, to speak openly, and to gather together independent associations, including human rights organizations."

Assistant Secretary Koh's candid assessment of Tunisia's human rights record was not matched elsewhere in U.S. public diplomacy over the year. In the State Department's official Congressional Budget Justification released on March 15, Assistant Secretary of State for Near Eastern Affairs Edwin S. Walker, Jr. characterized Tunisia, without qualification, as "a stable, democratic country." The administration requested U.S. $2.5 million in military aid and almost U.S. $1 million for military training for Tunisia for fiscal year 2001. Tunisia was invited to participate in the Community of Democracies ministerial conference in Warsaw, Poland, in late June, a meeting that enjoyed high-level U.S. support. The Tunisia chapter in the State Department's *Country Reports on Human Rights Practices for 1999* provided a comprehensive overview of the human rights situation, but the introductory paragraphs muted this criticism by characterizing the government's human rights performance as "uneven," a term it appeared to justify by referring to the October presidential and legislative elections as "mark[ing] a modest step toward democratic development." Assistant Secretary Koh's introduction to the *Country Reports* was inappropriately indulgent to Tunisia. It failed to mention that country in discussing repression of dissidents and human rights defenders by Middle Eastern governments, and went on to commend the government for releasing on early parole Tunisian Human Rights League Vice-President Khemais Ksila, repeating uncritically and without qualification the government's bogus charges that kept Ksila in jail for two years in the first place.

Relevant Human Rights Watch Reports:

The Administration of Justice in Tunisia: Torture, Trumped-Up Charges and a Tainted Trial, 2/00

YEMEN

Human Rights Developments

Yemen's poor human rights record showed little improvement in 2000. While the government set up several committees to monitor abuses, it signally failed to implement basic human rights protections in most areas. There were credible reports of torture in state prisons as well as in private jails and illegal detention facilities, and the courts continued to impose death sentences and cruel punishments such as floggings for a wide range of offenses. The authorities detained political opponents and ignored court orders for their release or trial, and threatened to dissolve a main opposition party. Government harassment of the independent press and restrictions generally on freedom of expression worsened. Women continued to face institutionalized discrimination, especially in personal status and criminal law. Yemenis and foreign nationals remained prey to kidnaping by criminal or disaffected groups, provoking government responses that were often marked by excessive and indiscriminate use of lethal force by security forces and the imposition of collective punishment. A draft law presented to parliament in April would allow police to open fire at any "dubious" gathering of more than five persons.

Investigations into the October 12 bombing of the USS Cole, a naval destroyer refueling in the port of Aden, were conducted on the Yemeni side by the Political Security Organization (PSO), an agency that reported directly to President Ali Abdallah Salih and operated without any judicial or other formal authorization. According to press reports, some 1,500 persons were picked up for questioning and about sixty were reportedly being held at the end of October. The U.S.

Federal Bureau of Investigation (FBI) dispatched several score of agents to assist in the investigation, but were not allowed to participate in interrogations. The PSO contributed to a general atmosphere of political intimidation through its routine recourse to harassment, beatings, and arbitrary detention. PSO plainclothes agents in past years infiltrated the independent press, syndicates, and civic organizations, in some cases forcing those organizations to cease their activities. Persons seeking to work for government institutions, including the university, required PSO clearance.

Yemeni human rights activists told Human Rights Watch that torture and ill-treatment of detainees was less frequent than in recent years, but the local press did carry reports of abusive treatment of detainees and prisoners by the authorities. Muhammad Ali Talib of Lahj governorate, for example, was arrested several times without warrant and severely beaten, according to the Aden-based Organization for the Defense of Human Rights and Democratic Liberties, and the *Yemen Times* reported on April 24 that police officers had beaten to death detainee Amin Abdullah al-Samti in al-'Udain district, Ibb governorate.

According to local press reports and human rights organizations, mistreatment and torture occurred in private as well as in official detention facilities. On April 1, the governor of al-Hodeida removed the al-Mansuriya district security director, Ahmad Ali Naji, and had him charged with using the district's detention facilities to mistreat prisoners and extort bribes. In July, lawyer and parliamentarian Muhammad Naji al-Alaw discovered a freight container at Sana'a University's law faculty being used by administrators as a detention facility for holding students and employees accused of minor violations. On April 11, three people died of suffocation and thirst after being detained in a container in Jabal al-Sharq in Dhamar governorate. Their deaths were widely attributed to two tribal leaders but in a letter to the Aden-based independent daily *al-Ayyam*, one of these denied allegations that his family operated a private jail.

In a move to crack down on private jails and prisons, the government dispatched forces to a number of districts in Ibb governorate in late October 1999. Facilities in al-'Udain were blown up, and twenty-four detainees were transferred to state facilities for investigation. In general, however, the government seemed reluctant to take legal measures against those operating private prisons, most of whom were prominent tribal and regional leaders.

Although a presidential decree issued in 1998 made kidnapping of foreigners a capital offense and set up a special court in Sana'a to try those accused of the crime, Yemenis, as well as foreign tourists and diplomats, continued to be kidnapped by diverse groups, often inhabitants of marginalized northern and eastern regions seeking economic or political concessions from the government. Most victims were released unharmed after payment of a ransom, but on June 10, Norwegian diplomat Gudbrand Stuve and his nine-year-old son were victims of a kidnap attempt on a busy street in Sana'a. Stuve, however, was killed in a shoot-out between the four kidnappers, tribesmen from al-Jawf, and the occupants of another car, apparently members of the security forces.

On several occasions, the government deployed military and paramilitary units to areas where kidnappers were suspected of hiding with their captives and used excessive force against local inhabitants. In early July, for example, according to the London-based *al-Sharq al-Awsat* daily, government forces surrounded the Sirwah area in the eastern governorate of Mareb after six Republican Guard officers were kidnapped by people seeking the release of a man convicted of hijacking a car. Even after the release of the hostages, government troops continued to bombard the area, killing at least three people and injuring others, and destroying houses, according to Sana'a's English-language weekly *Yemen Times*.

In September, security forces surrounded Kud Qarru village, near Aden, where citizens had prevented a contractor from extracting gravel and stones from what they regarded as their properties, and put down the protest by force, injuring several people and detaining 135, according to *al-Ayyam*. Lawyer 'Arif Ahmad al-Halimi, detained in this incident on September 9 and released on September 26, alleged that the security forces carried out further detentions, used torture, and refused to comply with judicial orders to release detainees. In mid-October, fifteen people from the area were brought to trial for "forming an armed gang to appropriate state property," charges they denied.

Several journalists were questioned by security forces and detained without charge, and opposition or independent newspapers were the targets of defamation suits brought by the Ministry of Information. In September 1999, the appeals court in Sana'a ordered the suspension of *al-Shura*, the weekly newspaper of the opposition Union of Yemeni Popular Forces; the paper remained suspended for nearly a year and only resumed publication in August 2000. On February 22, a Sana'a court suspended *al-Wahdawi*, publication of the opposition Nasserist Unionist Party, for thirty days and fined journalist Jamal 'Amer YR 5,000 (U.S. $30) in connection with an article on Yemeni-Saudi relations. Also in February, the head of security forces in Aden threatened Hisham Basharahil, editor of the independent thrice-weekly newspaper *al-Ayyam*, with arson or physical harm for an article published in 1999 reporting the destruction of a Aden synagogue by security forces. On May 10, Basharahil was charged in an Aden court with spreading false information about the government, instigating the use of force and terrorism, and threatening the republican system in Yemen by publishing an interview with a London-based militant, Abu al-Hamza al-Masri, on August 11, 1999.

Assaults on freedom of expression came from sources outside the government as well. Mosque preachers and conservative political groups in Sana'a, Aden, Tai'zz, and al-Hodaida waged a campaign in June against Samir Rashad al-Yusufi, editor of the Ta'izz-based weekly *al-Thaqafiya*, over its serialization of *Sana'a is an Open City*, a novel by Mohammed Abdulwali that they alleged was blasphemous. In July, al-Yusufi was brought to trial on charges of apostasy before the criminal chamber of a Sana'a court. According to local human rights defenders, the judge handling the case, Mohammed Mahdi al-Raimi, had been among those involved in the campaign against al-Yusufi. Al-Raimi prohibited all reporting about the trial, and summoned to court two newspapers, *al-Nas* and *al-Ihya' al-'Arabi*, for violating this order. At this writing, the Supreme Court was deliberating on the question of whether the Sana'a court's jurisdiction covered a Ta'izz-based newspaper.

The authorities detained persons suspected of possessing publications banned in Yemen, among them bookshop owner Ayoub Nu'man and Faisal Sa'id Far'a, director of al-Sa'id Cultural Establishment in Ta'izz. Jarallah 'Omar and Ali Salih 'Ubbad, leaders of the opposition Yemeni Socialist Party, were briefly held on the same charge at Sana'a airport in late April. The government suspended international and mobile phone service and pagers for a number of days at the time of the tenth anniversary of Yemen's unification in May. Internet access, available only through a government company, continued to be extremely slow and expensive, and access to some websites containing political content was reportedly blocked.

Academic freedom came under attack on December 3, 1999, when the Sana'a University administration closed its Empirical Research and Women's Studies Center. Despite a complaint by students, the closure was upheld in court. This followed conservative outrage over certain presentations made at a September 1999 conference on "Challenges for Women's Studies in the 21st Century." In particular, *al-Sahwa*, the Yemeni Congregation for Reform's (*al-Islah*) weekly newspaper, criticized the conference, the center's curriculum, and its staff. So fierce was the condemnation from this and other quarters that the center's executive director, Ra'ufa Hasan al-Sharqi, felt obliged to employ personal bodyguards. In April 2000, a new Center for the Study of the Woman was opened at the university but gender studies had been purged from the curriculum.

The autonomy of the university was also violated by the regular presence of security personnel on campus, leading some faculty members to request the parliament to ban the security forces from campuses.

In late April, the authorities closed the Yemeni Socialist Party (YSP) center in Ja'ar, a town in Abyan governorate, and detained between fifty and one hundred supporters and party members who they suspected of planning a rally to commemorate two victims of police killings in April 1998 in Mukalla. In late August, five leading YSP members were detained in Aden on charges of meeting without a permit. Delegates to the YSP's Fourth General Congress, held in Sana'a from August 30 to September 1, decided to reinstate to the central committee forty-two exiled leaders, four of whom had been sentenced to death in 1998 in their absence. The authorities claimed that this proved the party's "separatist" leanings. In an interview in al-Sharq al-Awsat on September 9, Foreign Minister Abd al-Qadir Ba Jammal suggested that the YSP "should be given the coup de grace." Al-Sharq al-Awsat reported on September 21 that the government had set up a special committee to consider the legal aspects of the possible dissolution of the YSP, although Sultan al-Barakani, a leading member of the ruling General Peoples's Congress (GPC), repeatedly denied this possibility, calling it "inconceivable." At this writing, YSP members claimed that some U.S. $14-18 million in party funds remained frozen by the government.

President Saleh and a group of 144 members of parliament put forward two sets of proposals for constitutional changes on August 23. The president proposed lengthening the parliamentary term from four to six years, and so postponing elections planned for April 2001. The parliamentarians proposed extending the presidential term from five to seven years, effectively paving the way for Saleh, in power since 1978 but directly elected for the first time in September 1999, to remain in office, subject to reelection,

until 2013. This proposal would also empower the president to dissolve parliament, and to amend aspects of the constitution without holding a referendum, and grant the president-appointed Consultative Council legislative powers, thus marginalizing the role of the elected parliament. Such changes would significantly offset the impact of the proposed abolition of the president's authority to make law by decree when parliament is in recess, and were expected to be passed by the parliament, which is dominated by the president's party, before the end of 2000. At this writing, however, it was not clear whether the government would submit the proposed amendments to a national referendum, as required by the 1994 constitution.

Despite the president's stated commitment in September 1999 to stand down as chair of the Supreme Judicial Council, the parliament had not passed the necessary amendments to Law 1/1991 on Judicial Authority as of this writing.

Although women enjoyed the same "general rights and obligations" as men under the constitution, they faced discrimination in national legislation. Under Law 20/1992 on Personal Status, as amended in 1998 and 1999, women were required to sue for divorce although men could divorce at will, and divorced mothers, unlike fathers, lost custody of their children upon remarriage. Sisters and daughters inherited half the share of brothers and sons. In 1999, the minimum marriage age of fifteen for women, rarely enforced, was abolished; the onset of puberty, interpreted by conservatives to be at the age of nine, was set as a requirement for consummation of marriage. The law was silent on procedures to enforce this provision. Penal legislation forbade the testimony of women in criminal matters and compensation to be paid for assault or murder of a woman was half that of a man. Prison conditions for women and their children were harsh. Children were reportedly detained in facilities with adults, and women prisoners were vulnerable to sexual exploitation by prison guards. Without any basis in current legislation, women prisoners who completed their sentences were only released to the custody of a male guardian who agreed to take responsibility for them, with the result that many women remained incarcerated after their terms had expired.

According to a United Nations Children's Fund (UNICEF) study released in 1999, there were four hundred so-called honor killings in 1997. This was probably a conservative assessment, since such crimes often went unreported and uninvestigated. Only since 1999 have the Yemeni press and human rights and women's groups reported on violence against women on a regular basis.

Law 12/1994 imposed the death penalty for murder, kidnapping, adultery, apostasy, and a range of other crimes. These sentences, as well as flogging for premarital sexual relations and consumption of alcohol, were often carried out in public. At least twenty-two executions of persons convicted of murder were reported between January 1999 and April 2000.

Defending Human Rights

Local human rights groups were able to operate, but were under some pressure from the Ministry of Insurance and Social Affairs. On April 9, the ministry ordered all nongovernmental organizations to submit reports on their activities and budgets as well as general information and details of their internal elections, as required by Law 11/1963 on Charitable Societies, passed by by the former Arab Republic of Yemen. Except for the Aden-based Organization for the Defense of Human Rights and Democratic Liberties, which regularly publicizes human rights abuses, most human rights organizations concentrated on training or awareness-raising workshops for journalists and legislators. Local chapters of Amnesty International operated in the major cities. International human rights monitors were able to visit Yemen.

The Role of the International Community

United States

The U.S. reportedly trained Yemeni special forces in small-unit combat and counter-terrorism skills over the past year. The administration's budget request to Congress for fiscal year 2001 included $4 million in economic support funds and $1.6 million for training a small number of officers in the U.S. as well as for demining and counter-narcotics programs.

President Salih visited the United States in April and August. On the occasion of his meeting with President Clinton in Washington in April, the U.S. commended Yemen "for its democratic achievements, including guaranteeing through its constitution women's right to full political and economic participation." The United States also publicly welcomed the degree of religious tolerance in Yemen, and "the right accorded to Yemeni Jewish communities....including those in Israel, to visit Yemen." Yemen was among more than one hundred countries invited to the U.S.-supported Towards a Community of Democracies ministerial conference in Warsaw on June 25-26.

The State Department's *Country Reports on Human Rights Practices for 1999* assessed the government's human rights record as "poor," citing the PSO's "broad discretion over perceived national security issues," prolonged pretrial detention, and restrictions on freedom of expression as among the most serious problems.

HUMAN
RIGHTS
WATCH

UNITED
STATES

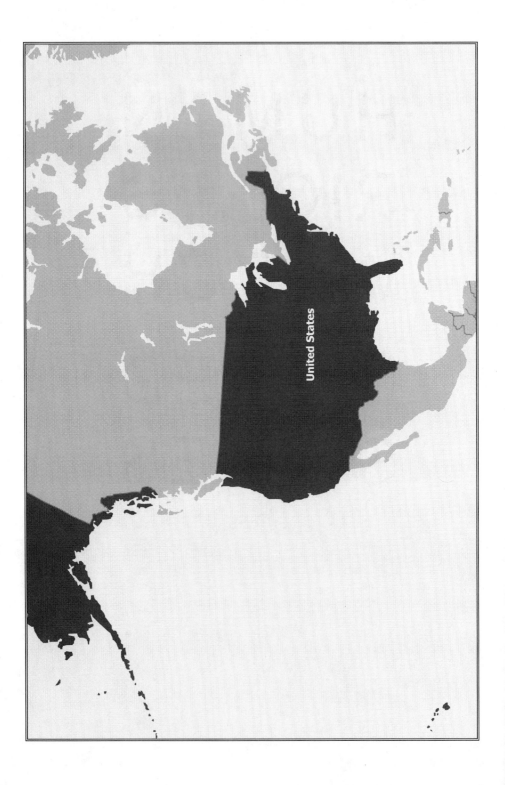

As the Clinton Administration's second term ended in 2000, evidence of its domestic human rights legacy was scant. The country made little progress in embracing international human rights standards at home. Most public officials remained either unaware of their human rights obligations or content to ignore them.

As in previous years, serious human rights violations were most apparent in the criminal justice system—including police brutality, discriminatory racial disparities in incarceration, abusive conditions of confinement, and state-sponsored executions, even of juvenile offenders and the mentally handicapped. But extensively documented human rights violations also included violations of workers' rights, discrimination against gay men and lesbians in the military, and the abuse of migrant child farmworkers.

The United States in 2000 submitted reports on its compliance with two international human rights treaties—the Convention on the Elimination of All Forms of Racial Discrimination and the Convention against Torture and Other Cruel, Inhuman or Degrading Treatment or Punishment—to the respective treaty monitoring bodies. Both reports acknowledged significant abuses of the rights affirmed in those treaties.

The initial report of the U.S. to the United Nations Committee against Torture—produced four years after it was due—acknowledged areas of "concern, contention and criticism" with regard to police abuse, excessive use of force in prison, prison overcrowding, physical and mental abuse of inmates, and the lack of adequate training and oversight for police and prison guards. Nevertheless, the initial report was incomplete and misleading in several important aspects. It failed to acknowledge crucial weaknesses in laws and mechanisms to protect the right to be free of torture and cruel, inhuman or degrading treatment or punishment, as well as the serious obstacles abuse victims face in securing legal redress. It failed also to confront forthrightly the prevalence of abuses against detained and incarcerated men, women and children throughout the United States.

The report also glossed over the impact of the reservations, understandings, and declarations the United States made when it ratified the convention. The United States redefined torture, as prohibited by the convention, to include only conduct already prohibited under the U.S. Constitution and to exclude, with few exceptions, mental torture that is not accompanied by physical torture. It also declared the treaty to be non-self-executing, and then failed to enact implementing legislation, with the result that U.S. residents cannot turn to the courts to seek protection of the rights affirmed under the treaty. The U.S., in effect, declined to change its laws to bring them up to international standards.

In May, the U.N. Committee against Torture issued a statement of conclusions and recommendations highlighting a range of U.S. practices that contravened the convention. The committee's concerns included: ill-treatment by police and prison officials, much of it racially discriminatory; sexual assaults upon female detainees and prisoners and degrading conditions of confinement of female prisoners; the use of electro-shock devices and restraint chairs; the excessively harsh regime of super-maximum security prisons; and the holding of youths in adult prisons. The committee urged the U.S. to enact legislation making torture a federal crime; to withdraw its reservations and declarations to the convention; to take the necessary steps to ensure those who violate the convention are investigated, prosecuted, and punished; to prohibit stun belts and restraint chairs; and to ensure that minors are not incarcerated in adult facilities.

In September, the U.S. produced—five years late—its initial report to the United Nations Committee on the Elimination of Racial Discrimination. With unprecedented and welcome candor, the report acknowledged the persistence of racism, racial discrimination and de facto segregation in the United States. The tenor and content of the report signaled the Clinton Administration's recognition that despite decades of civil rights legislation and public and private efforts, the inequalities faced by minorities remained one of the country's most crucial and unresolved human rights challenges.

One of the report's most significant weaknesses was in its consideration of the role of race discrimination in the criminal justice system. It acknowledged the dramatically disproportionate incarceration rates for minorities, noted the many studies indicating that members of minority groups, especially blacks and Hispanics, "may be disproportionately subject to adverse treatment throughout the criminal justice process," and acknowledged concerns that "incidents of police brutality seem to target disproportionately individuals belonging to racial or ethnic minorities." But it did not question whether the ostensibly race-neutral criminal laws or law enforcement practices causing the incarceration disparities violated CERD, nor did it acknowledge the federal government's obligation, under CERD, to ensure that state criminal justice systems (which account for 90 percent of the incarcerated population) were free of racial discrimination.

The report did acknowledge the dramatic, racially disparate impact of federal sentencing laws that prescribe different sentences for powder cocaine versus crack cocaine offenses, even though the two drugs are pharmacologically identical. The laws impose a mandatory five year prison sentence on anyone convicted of selling five grams or more of crack cocaine, and a ten year mandatory sentence for selling fifty grams or more. One hundred times as much powder cocaine must be sold to receive the same sentences. By setting a much lower drug-weight threshold for crack than powder cocaine, the laws resulted in substantially higher sentences for crack cocaine offenders. Although the majority of crack users were white, blacks comprised almost 90 percent of federal offenders convicted of crack offenses and hence served longer sentences for similar drug crimes than whites. While recounting the Clinton Administration's unsuccessful effort to secure a limited reform of the cocaine sentencing laws (a reform which, in any event, would still have left black drug defendants disproportionately vulnerable to higher sentences), the report did not venture an assessment of whether the current laws violate CERD. Nor did it consider whether the striking racial differences in the incarceration of drug offenders at the state level was consistent with CERD, reflecting the Administration's general reluctance to subject the U.S. war on drugs to human rights scrutiny.

As reflected in the report, the Administration also mistakenly believed that U.S. constitutional prohibitions on race discrimination meet its obligations under CERD. Under state and federal constitutional law, racial disparities in law enforcement are constitutional as long as they are not undertaken with discriminatory intent or purpose. But CERD prohibits policies or practices that have the effect of discriminating on the basis of race regardless of intent. By requiring proof of discriminatory intent, U.S. constitutional law erects a frequently insurmountable obstacle to obtaining judicial relief from criminal justice policies that have an unjustifiably discriminatory impact. Instead of championing reforms that would reduce striking racial disparities in, for example, the rates at which blacks and whites are arrested and incarcerated on drug charges, the Clinton Administration expressed pride in constitutional protections that do not, in fact, meet international standards.

The U.S. maintained its failure to become party to important human rights treaties, including the International Covenant on Economic, Social and Cultural Rights and the Convention on the Elimination of All Forms of Discrimination against Women (CEDAW). It was one of only two countries in the world—with Somalia, which has no internationally recognized government—that had not ratified the Convention on the Rights of the Child. In addition, little progress was made toward signing and ratifying core International Labour Organization conventions intended to protect basic labor rights, though the Clinton Administration did sign ILO Convention No. 182, the Convention concerning the Prohibition and Immediate Action for the Elimination of the Worst Forms of Child Labour in December of 1999. It also submitted an ILO Convention concerning employment discrimination to the Senate for ratification, but the Senate did not act.

Death Penalty

An important and positive human rights development was the heightened criticism of the death penalty. The increasing debate over unfairness in capital cases and the high risk of executing the innocent caused public support for the death penalty to decline to its lowest point in years (60 percent). In September, a bi-partisan group of congressmen released a national opinion poll indicating that 80 percent of Americans supported reforming the death penalty, with 64 percent supporting a moratorium on executions until issues of fairness in capital punishment were resolved.

Debate about the death penalty was fueled by the record number of executions (145 at the time of this writing) in Texas under Gov. George W. Bush, the Republican presidential nominee; the publication of important national reports; and the first-ever imposition of a moratorium on executions by a state governor. Governor Bush's complacency with the high number of executions in Texas, his refusal to acknowledge the extensively documented lack of adequate legal representation for capital defendants in Texas, and his refusal to oppose the execution of even mentally handicapped defendants or youthful offenders generated widespread media attention and criticism.

A comprehensive review of capital cases over a twenty-three year period by a team of university professors revealed that more than two of every three death penalty sentences were overturned on appeal. The study found that capital trials were persistently and systematically fraught with error and injustice, including poor legal representation of capital defendants by incompetent attorneys and prosecutorial misconduct.

Although racial disparities in the application of the death penalty among the states have long been documented, a new study by the U.S. Department of Justice found dramatic racial and geographic imbalances in the administration of the federal death penalty as well. The study found, for example, that 80 percent of federal defendants who faced capital charges, and 74 percent of convicted defendants for whom prosecutors recommended the death penalty, were members of minorities. The study increased public concern that race plays an impermissible role in death penalty decisions.

Driven by the exoneration of thirteen death row inmates—compared to the twelve executed in the state since the death penalty's reinstatement in 1977—Illinois Gov. George Ryan, a Republican, imposed a state-wide moratorium on executions at the end of January. In New Hampshire, the state legislature passed a bill abolishing the death penalty, but the state's governor, Jeanne Shaheen, a Democrat, vetoed the measure. In the U.S. Congress, legislators introduced the Innocence Protection Act, which would require that competent, experienced attorneys be appointed to represent capital defendants and that capital defendants have access to DNA testing, among other reforms. The bill's chances for passage appeared slim as the 106th Congress wound down, but its reintroduction during the next Congress seemed likely.

Despite these positive developments, as of October 24, the United States had put seventy persons to death in 2000, and eighteen more persons were scheduled for execution before the end of the year. The vast majority of executions in 2000 occurred in the Southern states, with Texas accounting for nearly half of all executions. Among those executed were individuals who were mentally impaired and four juvenile offenders—persons below the age of eighteen when the crimes for which they were sentenced were committed. Approximately 3,682 persons were on death row as of July 1. The U.S. continued to be one of only five countries in the world that executes juvenile offenders.

Police Abuse

Each year, thousands of allegations of police abuse are filed across the country. While videotaped police actions—such as those documenting Philadelphia police officers beating a man after a vehicle chase, Miami-Dade officers kicking a man in the face after a vehicle pursuit, and Los Angeles police officers using excessive force to disperse political protesters during the Democratic National Convention—displayed the problem vividly in 2000, most incidents of alleged police abuse took place away from public scrutiny. Because of inadequate investigative and disciplinary systems, relatively few police officers who violate departmental rules, or the law, are held accountable. Victims seeking redress faced obstacles that ranged from overt intimidation to the reluctance of local and federal prosecutors to take on police brutality cases. During fiscal year 1999, approximately 12,000 civil rights complaints, most alleging police abuse, were submitted to the U.S. Department of Justice, but over the same period just thirty-one officers were either convicted or pled guilty to crimes under the civil rights statute stemming from complaints during 1999 and previous years.

In a positive development, the Department of Justice stepped up efforts to check police abuse through "pattern or practice" inquiries and agreements. These inquiries, authorized in 1994 legislation, allow the Justice Department to conduct civil investigations into law enforcement agencies to determine whether there is a pattern or practice of civil rights violations. Two of the country's largest police departments, the New York City Police Department (NYPD) and the Los Angeles Police Department (LAPD), were investigated by the Justice Department under these powers and, along with city officials, were negotiating agreements to avoid being sued by the Justice Department and possible, direct Justice Department oversight and court-imposed reforms. At this writing, progress was slow in talks between Justice Department and New York City officials. In Los Angeles, city officials had accepted, in theory, a "consent decree" that addresses some of the reforms required. The legally binding agreement should ensure that an effective, computerized tracking system to identify officers in need of enhanced supervision is created and utilized; the civilian board of commissioners

that oversees the police is strengthened; and that a special unit to investigate shootings and use of force by officers is created. Other police departments have also been investigated under these powers.

Several high-profile incidents involving the New York City police, including the assault on Abner Louima in August 1997, the February 1999 shooting death of Amadou Diallo, who was unarmed, and the March 2000 shooting death of Patrick Dorismond, also unarmed, raised concerns that the city's police officers were not adequately trained, supervised, or disciplined. Following the assault on Louima, the Justice Department initiated an inquiry into the NYPD's management. A separate Justice Department investigation focused on the Street Crime Unit and allegations of racial profiling by its officers; Diallo was shot and killed by officers assigned to the unit.

In Los Angeles, the Justice Department's inquiry focused primarily on the origins of the Rampart scandal. The anti-gang unit based in the LAPD's Rampart Division brutalized residents and framed suspects. The officer at the center of the scandal, Rafael Perez, provided information about his and other officers' misconduct after he was caught stealing cocaine from a police evidence room and sought a lighter prison sentence.

In one LAPD case, Javier Ovando was shot, allegedly by Perez's partner, and paralyzed and then served three years in prison. The officers allegedly framed him and placed a gun at the scene to make it appear Perez had been armed. Approximately one hundred other convictions were overturned as a result of the officers' tainted testimony and evidence that had sent individuals to prison. The expense facing the city and county of Los Angeles arising from civil lawsuits for excessive force, false imprisonment and other violations, as well as investigating and reviewing all cases related to the expanding number of officers implicated in the scandal, was predicted to cost in the hundreds of millions of dollars.

The wide-ranging Rampart scandal revealed poor management and practices by

LAPD officials and the district attorney's office, and lax oversight by the civilian police commission. It also demonstrated that many of the key Christopher Commission reforms from 1991 had yet to take hold, leading to ineffectual monitoring of officers' behavior. In a May 2000 letter to the Los Angeles city attorney, the Justice Department stated that it had found, as a result of its investigation, "serious deficiencies in City and LAPD policies and procedures for training, supervising, and investigating and disciplining police officers foster and perpetuate officer misconduct."

The issue of racial profiling by police received increased attention. Legislation to require the compilation of statistics on vehicle stops and searches, and the race of vehicle occupants, was under consideration in the U.S. Congress. Several police departments, in response to pressure from activist groups and concerned political and community leaders, started to compile these statistics voluntarily. The purpose of the data compilation was to document and end the discriminatory and illegal practice by police of stopping and searching vehicles based on the race of the driver or passengers.

Overincarceration, Drugs and Race

The world's largest prison population continued to grow because of punitive criminal justice policies that mandated harsh prison terms even for minor nonviolent offenses and increased the length of sentences, and because of increases in the number of inmates returned to prison for parole violations. In August, the U.S. Department of Justice revealed that the number of men and women behind bars in the U.S. at the end of 1999 exceeded two million and the rate of incarceration had reached 690 inmates per 100,000 residents—a rate Human Rights Watch believed to be the highest in the world (with the exception of Rwanda). The Department of Justice also revealed that approximately 1.5 million children—2 percent of the country's children—had a parent in state or federal prison.

Prison was not reserved for notably dangerous or violent offenders: approximately 70 percent of all new admissions to state prison in 1998 (the most recent year for which data was available) were people convicted of nonviolent property, drug or public order offenses. The unrelenting war on drugs continued to pull hundreds of thousands of drug offenders into the criminal justice system: 1,559,100 people were arrested on drug charges in 1998; approximately 450,000 drug offenders were confined in jails and prisons. According to the Department of Justice, 107,000 people were sent to state prison on drug charges in 1998, representing 30.8 percent of all new state admissions. Drug offenders constituted 57.8 percent of all federal inmates.

Racial minorities comprised a strikingly disproportionate percentage of the prison population. African Americans constituted 46.5 percent of state prisoners and 40 percent of federal prisoners, although they constituted only 12 percent of the national population. Nationwide, black men were eight times more likely to be in prison than white men, with an incarceration rate of 3,408 per 100,000 black male residents compared to a white male rate of 417 per 100,000. But in eleven states, black men were incarcerated at rates that were between twelve and twenty-six times greater than those of white men. The Department of Justice estimated that 9.4 percent of all black men in their late twenties were in prison in 1999 compared to 1 percent of white men in the same age group.

Female incarceration rates, though much lower than male, reflected similar racial disparities, with black women eight times more likely to be in prison than white. Racial disparities were also pronounced in the incarceration of youths: although juveniles belonging to minority groups constituted one-third of the adolescent population in the United States, they comprised two-thirds of the juveniles confined in local detention and state correctional systems. Minority youths were transferred to adult courts and sentenced to incarceration more frequently than white youths charged with similar offenses.

Drug law enforcement practices that disproportionately target black Americans contributed to wide disparities in black and white incarceration rates. Nationally, black men were admitted to state prison on drug charges at a rate relative to population that was 13.4 times greater than that of white men. Black youths with no prior admissions were admitted to public correctional facilities for drug offenses at forty-eight times the rate of white youths. In some states the racial disparities were even worse: in seven states, blacks constituted between 80 and 90 percent of all drug offenders sent to prison and, in at least fifteen states, black men were sent to prison on drug charges at rates that were from twenty to fifty-seven times greater than those of white men. The concentration of drug law enforcement in low income minority neighborhoods and higher arrest rates for black drug offenders than white were primarily responsible for the remarkable racial disparities in drug offender incarceration.

Political timidity by legislators meant scant progress in reducing the inordinately high sentences for drug and other nonviolent offenses required under mandatory minimum sentencing laws. In New York, for example, the legislature once again adjourned without reforming twenty-five year old drug law legislation that required the same length of prison sentence for first-time offenders convicted of selling two ounces of cocaine as for murderers—a minimum of fifteen years to life.

A growing number of citizens were unable to vote because of laws that disenfranchise people convicted of felonies who are in prison, on probation or parole—and even, in one quarter of the states, who have finished serving their sentences. An estimated 3.9 million U.S. citizens were disenfranchised, including over one million who had fully completed their sentences. Black Americans were particularly hard hit by disenfranchisement laws: 13 percent of black men—1.4 million—were disenfranchised; in two states, almost one in three black men was unable to vote because of a felony conviction. Legislative efforts and local initiatives across the country to reform disenfranchisement laws proliferated, but most were blocked by conservative opposition. Lawsuits challenging disenfranchisement laws were proceeding in Florida, Pennsylvania and Washington.

Conditions of Confinement

Prisons remained overcrowded: twenty-two states and the federal prison system operated at 100 percent or more of their highest capacity. Overcrowding contributed to the growth of private prisons: according to the Department of Justice privately-operated facilities held 5.5 percent of all state prisoners and 2.5 percent of federal prisoners.

Most inmates had scant opportunities for work, training, education, treatment or counseling because of taxpayer resistance to increasing the already astonishing U.S. \$41 billion spent annually on corrections and because of the prevailing punitive ideology that applauds harsh prison conditions. Idle inmates with long sentences, little hope of early release (and hence little incentive for good behavior) and jammed into poorly equipped facilities, sometimes became violent: in 1998 (the most recent year for which data was available), fifty-nine inmates were killed by other inmates, and assaults, fights, and rapes left 6,750 inmates and 2,331 correctional staff injured seriously enough to require medical attention. Rivalry and tension between race-based prison gangs lay behind many individual assaults and sometimes escalated into violent riots.

Men in prison were subject to prisoner-on-prisoner sexual abuse, whose effects on the victim's psyche were serious and enduring. Inmate victims reported nightmares, deep depression, shame, loss of self-esteem, self-hatred, and considering or attempting suicide. Victims of rape, in the most extreme cases, were literally the slaves of the perpetrators, being "rented out" for sex, "sold," or even auctioned off to other inmates. Despite the devastating psychological impact of such abuse, few if any preventative measures were taken in most jurisdictions, while perpetrators were rarely punished adequately by prison officials.

Over twenty thousand prisoners were confined in special super-maximum security facilities. They typically spent all their waking and sleeping hours locked alone or with a cellmate in small sometimes windowless cells from which they were released for only a few hours each week for solitary recreation or showers. Super-max prisoners had almost no access to educational or recreational activities or other sources of mental stimulation and were handcuffed, shackled and escorted by officers whenever they left their cells. Although super-max confinement was ostensibly designed to control incorrigibly violent or dangerous inmates, many inmates so confined did not meet those criteria. An inmate committed suicide at the super-max in Ohio in April, the third suicide since it opened in 1998, while draconian rules and restrictions prompted a prolonged hunger strike at the super-max in Illinois. Inmates at Wisconsin's new super-max prison filed a lawsuit challenging the constitutionality of the conditions to which they were subjected, including round-the-clock confinement in isolation, constant fluorescent lighting in their cells, twenty-four hour video monitoring that permitted female staff to watch prisoners shower and urinate, and inadequate recreation.

Reports of frequent incidents of physical abuse, racial harassment and excessive use of force continued at Virginia's two super-maximum security prisons. Between January and June 2000, two inmates—who had both been transferred from Connecticut—died at one of these prisons, Wallens Ridge State Prison. One of the deaths was a suicide; the other occurred after the inmate had been stunned several times with a 50,000 volt electronic stun device and left in five-point restraints. New Mexican inmates transferred to Wallens Ridge in 1999 complained of gratuitous and malicious physical abuse by prison guards, including beatings and shocks from electric stun devices. In January 2000, the Federal Bureau of Investigation initiated a preliminary investigation into their claims at the request of the New Mexico attorney general.

According to the Virginia Department of Corrections, between January 1999 and June 2000, prison guards at Red Onion State Prison,

Virginia's first super-max, fired 116 blank rounds and twenty-five stinger rounds of rubber pellets and discharged hand-held electronic stun devices 130 times. Most other prison systems controlled inmate fights without recourse to firearms or electric shocks. In June, three inmate bystanders at Red Onion were injured by rubber pellets when guards fired shotguns to break up an inmate scuffle. Inmates at the prison complained in 2000 of an apparently new staff practice of placing inmates in five point restraints for as long as forty-eight hours because they masturbated or displayed their genitals in front of female staff. In September, the U.S. Department of Justice announced that it was opening a formal investigation to determine whether inmates' constitutional rights were being violated at Red Onion.

A fourteen month long Department of Justice investigation of conditions at Nassau County Jail resulted in a scathing report released in September. The report said the jail had an "institutional culture that supports and promotes abuses." The documented abuses included brutal beatings by officers and officers paying inmates to beat other inmates, especially targeting sex offenders.

Hampered by lack of counsel, inadequate access to legal materials and legal restrictions on inmate litigation, prisoners rarely obtained judicial relief against abusive officers, though some did. In March, a county jail in Oregon paid $1.75 million to settle an excessive force lawsuit brought by an inmate who had been strapped into a restraint chair, doused with large amounts of pepper spray and subjected to choke holds. He lapsed into a coma for 71 days and suffered permanent brain damage.

Criminal prosecution of brutal correctional officers was rare, and convictions in such cases even rarer. In February, four guards from Florida State Prison were indicted on murder charges in connection with the July 1999 beating death of Frank Valdez. An autopsy revealed that all his ribs had been broken and there were boot marks imprinted on his body. The guards contended that Valdes injured himself. They were awaiting trial at this writing. In California, eight prison guards were acquitted in June of federal charges that they staged gladiator-style fights among inmates at Corcoran State Prison. Similarly, in November 1999, four Corcoran guards were acquitted of setting up the rape of an inmate by a notoriously violent prisoner. Independent investigations and state legislative hearings in 1998 confirmed a pattern of brutality at Corcoran and the failure of the Department of Corrections to investigate abuses and discipline those responsible. In both court cases, the authorities faced the daunting tasks of breaking through officer solidarity and a code of silence, and of prosecuting prison guards before juries drawn from the rural communities in which the guards lived—and in which prisons were a major source of employment.

Over 100,000 children in the United States were confined in juvenile facilities. Many of them faced appalling conditions of abuse and neglect. In South Dakota, a class action suit was brought challenging widespread physical abuses against girls detained at the State Training School. The suit charged that guards routinely shackled youths in spread-eagled fashion after cutting off their clothes, sprayed them with pepper spray while naked, and routinely placed them in isolation for twenty-three hours each day for extended periods. Although the state government conducted an investigation of juvenile detention facilities in 1999, it did not implement any reforms to end abusive policies and practices.

After twenty-seven years of litigation, the state of Louisiana agreed in September to significant changes in its juvenile detention system to protect youth from the extensively documented physical, sexual, and mental abuse that had been prevalent, and to provide youth with rehabilitative services and medical, dental, and mental health care. In May, the Louisiana Department of Public Safety and Corrections moved the last remaining detainees out of the Jena Juvenile Justice Center, a for-profit institution run by the Wackenhut Corrections Corporation. The move came four months after the U.S. Department of

Justice's mental health expert reported that "Jena's environment is unsafe, violent and inhumane for the juveniles incarcerated there."

The trend toward trying more children in the adult criminal system continued in 2000, depriving those affected of the variety of rehabilitative dispositions available in juvenile proceedings. In California, for example, voters approved a measure in March that made transfer to the adult system mandatory in some cases and gave prosecutors the final word in many others; before the measure's passage, juveniles were transferred to the adult system only after a judicial hearing.

In Maryland, a public outcry over the treatment of children in adult jails, prompted in part by a Human Rights Watch report released in November 1999, led to some improvements in the education provided the incarcerated children. The Baltimore City Detention Center's school appointed additional teachers and began to offer a full school day to juveniles in the general and protective custody sections, but those held in the segregation and other sections continued to be deprived of regular classroom instruction. In Prince George's County—where youths were receiving no education at the time of Human Rights Watch's July 1998 visit—the Department of Corrections and the county board of education began to provide educational services in September 2000.

In October, the Civil Rights Division of the U.S. Department of Justice notified Maryland that it would investigate conditions of detention at the Baltimore City Detention Center. The Justice Department planned to examine whether youths were subjected to excessive periods of isolation. The investigators were also to determine whether all detainees, including youths, received adequate medical and mental health care and whether they were protected from harm.

Minority youths in the United States were significantly more likely to be sent to adult courts than their white counterparts. Compared to white youths, children of color in California were 2.8 times more likely to be charged with violent crimes, 6.2 times more likely to be tried in adult court, and seven times more likely to be sentenced to prison when they were tried as adults.

Sexual abuse against women by correctional officers remained widespread despite new laws prohibiting it and greater public awareness of the problem. A U.S. government study in December 1999 found pervasive allegations of sexual abuse and misconduct by corrections officers. Criminal prosecutions of abusive staff appeared to increase. Cases since December 1999 included, for example, eleven former guards and a prison official who were indicted on charges of sexually assaulting or harassing sixteen female prisoners at a county jail operated by a private corrections company; the conviction of a New Mexico jail guard on federal civil rights charges stemming from the sexual assault of jail prisoners; the sentencing of a New York jail guard to three years of probation after pleading guilty to sodomizing two female prisoners; and the sentencing of an Ohio jail officer to a four year prison term for sexually assaulting three female prisoners. In Michigan, however, legislators passed a law that took effect in March that exempted prisoners from the protection of the state civil rights act, which prohibits discrimination based on race and gender. Through this legislation, Michigan suppressed prisoners' efforts to seek redress for sexual abuse through lawsuits against the Corrections Department. In California, although a law went into effect in January that increased the criminal penalties for sexual misconduct, the state failed to ensure that women could safely report abuse. Women prisoners in one California prison, for example, claimed that their cells were ransacked and personal items damaged or taken after they reported abuse. Others reported being held in "protective" custody pending investigation of their "allegation."

A federal circuit court upheld federal legislation, the Prison Litigation Reform Act, that bars lawsuits by inmates seeking damages for mental or emotional injury suffered while in custody where there is no proof of significant physical injury. Georgia inmates had filed a lawsuit alleging that in 1996 prison

officers had made them remove their clothes in front a female guard, tap dance while naked and shave with an unlubricated razor. Under the court's ruling, inmates cannot sue for humiliation, mental torture or non-physical sadistic treatment by guards unless, in effect, they have broken bones or blood to show for it. This restriction on the ability of inmates to vindicate their rights in court was one of many ways in which U.S. laws and judicial mechanisms failed to meet the standards mandated by the Convention against Torture.

Labor Rights

In August 2000, Human Rights Watch published a ground-breaking, 200-page report on violations of workers' rights to freedom of association in the United States. The report was based on field research undertaken during 1999-2000 in California, Colorado, Florida, Illinois, Louisiana, New York, North Carolina, Michigan, Washington, and other states. The report, the first comprehensive analysis of workers' rights in the United States under international norms, detailed widespread labor rights violations across regions, industries and employment status.

Each year thousands of workers in the United States are spied on, harassed, pressured, threatened, suspended, fired, deported or otherwise victimized by employers in reprisal for their exercise of the right to freedom of association. In the 1950's, victims numbered in the hundreds each year. In 1969, the number was more than 6,000. By the 1990's, more than 20,000 workers each year were dismissed or otherwise victims of discrimination serious enough for the government-appointed National Labor Relations Board (NLRB) to issue a reinstatement and "back-pay" or other remedial order—nearly 24,000 in 1998, the last year for which official figures were available when the Human Rights Watch report was published.

Loophole-ridden laws, paralyzing delays, and feeble enforcement have created a culture of impunity in many areas of U.S. labor law and practice. Employers intent on resisting workers' self-organization can drag out legal proceedings for years, fearing little more than an order to post a written notice in the workplace promising not to repeat unlawful conduct.

Human Rights Watch found that millions of workers, including farm workers, household domestic workers, and low-level supervisors, were expressly excluded from protection under the law guaranteeing the right of workers to organize. In Washington and North Carolina, Human Rights Watch found evidence of campaigns of intimidation against migrant workers.

Other findings included: one-sided rules for union organizing that unfairly favor employers over workers, allowing such tactics as "captive-audience meetings" where managers predict workplace closures if workers vote for union representation; workers being caught up in a web of labor contracting and subcontracting that effectively denied them the right to organize and bargain with the employers holding the real power over their jobs and working conditions; employers having the legal power to permanently replace workers who exercise the right to strike; and harsh rules against "secondary boycotts" that frustrate worker solidarity efforts.

In another investigation into labor rights in the United States, Human Rights Watch found that the rights of migrant domestic workers with special temporary visas were often violated. The special visas allowed such workers, most of whom are women, to be employed in the U.S. by foreign diplomats, officials of international organizations, and others. Because the domestic workers' visas are employment-based, they lose their legal immigration status in the U.S. if they flee abusive employers, and may face deportation. These workers were especially vulnerable to abuses by their employers because they live and work in virtual isolation and often without basic knowledge regarding their rights or the American legal system. Meanwhile, the U.S. government has failed to establish procedures to monitor employer compliance with employment contracts, humane treatment of workers, and other mandatory terms of these workers' special visas.

In a report describing the treatment of child farmworkers in the United States, Human Rights Watch found that over 300,000 children worked as hired laborers on commercial farms, frequently under dangerous and grueling conditions. The child farmworkers worked long hours for little pay and risked pesticide poisoning, heat illnesses, injuries, and life-long disabilities. They accounted for 8 percent of working children in the United States but suffered 40 percent of work-related fatalities.

Children working on U.S. farms often worked twelve-hour days, sometimes beginning at 3:00 or 4:00 am. They reported routine exposure to dangerous pesticides that cause cancer and brain damage, with short-term symptoms including rashes, headaches, dizziness, nausea, and vomiting. Young farmworkers became dizzy from laboring in excessive temperatures without adequate access to drinking water, and were forced to work without access to toilets or hand washing facilities. Long hours of work also interfered with the education of children working in the fields, causing them to miss school and leaving them too exhausted to study or stay awake in class. Only 55 percent of farmworker children in the United States completed high school.

Even to the limited extent that U.S. laws did protect farmworker children, they were not adequately enforced. The U.S. Department of Labor, charged with enforcement of the child labor, wage and hour provisions of federal labor law, cited only 104 cases of child labor violations in fiscal year 1998, even though an estimated one million child labor violations occur in US agriculture every year. Compounding the problem, penalties were typically too weak to discourage employers from using illegal child labor.

Gay and Lesbian Rights

The July 1999 murder of Private First Class Barry Winchell at Fort Campbell, Kentucky, by a fellow soldier who believed Winchell to be gay brought overdue attention to the problem of anti-gay harassment in the military. Six years after the Clinton Administration's "Don't Ask, Don't Tell" policy was codified as law and implemented, the military's own surveys and investigations found that training on how to implement the law was deficient and that anti-gay harassment remained pervasive in the military. Many military personnel who faced verbal or physical harassment and feared for their safety made statements acknowledging they were gay, knowing that it would mean the end of their careers but also that if they complained officially about anti-gay harassment they would probably themselves face an intrusive inquiry and discharge. They also knew that harassers were rarely punished.

Although the "Don't Ask, Don't Tell" policy was ostensibly intended to allow gay, lesbian, and bisexual service members to remain in the military, discharges increased significantly after the policy's adoption. From 1994 to 1999, a total of 5,412 service members were removed from the armed forces under the policy, with yearly discharge totals nearly doubling, from 617 in 1994 to 1,149 in 1998. In 1999, the number of such separations dropped slightly, to 1,034; nevertheless, the discharge rate was still 73 percent higher than it had been prior to the implementation of the policy. Women were discharged at a disproportionately high rate, while the policy provided an additional means for men to harass women service members by threatening to "out" those who refused their advances or threatened to report them, thus ending their careers.

The U.S. was increasingly out of step internationally in maintaining restrictions on homosexuals serving in the military. Most of its NATO and other allies either allowed homosexuals to serve openly or had no policy on the issue. In September 1999, the European Court of Human Rights rejected a United Kingdom ban on homosexuals serving in the military based on similar grounds as the "Don't Ask, Don't Tell" policy.

In U.S. schools, lesbian, gay, bisexual, arrd transgender students were frequently targeted for harassment by their peers, according to initial findings of a Human Rights Watch investigation. They were nearly three times as likely as their peers to have been involved in at least one physical fight in school, three times as likely to have been threatened or injured with a weapon at school, and nearly four times as likely to skip school because they felt unsafe, according to the 1999 Massachusetts Youth Risk Behavior Survey. Most alarmingly, the survey found that those who identified as lesbian, gay, or bisexual were more than twice as likely to consider suicide and more than four times as likely to attempt suicide than their peers.

Efforts to provide a safe, supportive environment for these students were hampered by discriminatory legislation in several states. For example, a South Carolina statute provided that health education in public school "may not include a discussion of alternate sexual lifestyles from heterosexual relationships including, but not limited to, homosexual relationships except in the context of instruction concerning sexually transmitted diseases." Similarly, a measure on the November ballot in Oregon would provide that "the instruction of behaviors relating to homosexuality and bisexuality shall not be presented in a public school in a manner which encourages, promotes, or sanctions such behaviors."

Several states had legislation or programs in place to address harassment and violence toward lesbian, gay, bisexual, and transgender youth. California, Connecticut, Massachusetts, and Wisconsin explicitly prohibited harassment and discrimination against teachers or students on the basis of sexual orientation. Massachusetts and Vermont, the only states to include questions relating to sexual orientation on statewide, youth risk behavior surveys, had state programs to provide support to gay, lesbian, and bisexual youths. Challenges remained in implementing these programs and statutory protections and in preventing their erosion; in Vermont, for example, a backlash against civil union legislation enacted in April threatened funding for the state's youth program.

Immigrants' Rights

In September 2000, the number of detainees held in the custody of the Immigration and Naturalization Service (INS), on average per day, reached a record high of 20,000. In 1995, there was a daily average of 6,700 detainees. The dramatic increase stemmed from the 1996 Illegal Immigration Reform and Immigrant Responsibility Act, which broadened the criteria that require detention and eventual deportation.

The increasing numbers of detainees strained the ability of the INS to provide humane and safe conditions in its detention facilities, and the influx of detainees led to a space crisis. More than half of all INS detainees were held in prisons or local jails intended for criminal inmates, exposing them to treatment and conditions inappropriate to their administrative detainee status and hampering their access to legal assistance. Asylum-seekers continued to be detained as the rule, rather than the exception, as the INS continued to ignore international standards relating to the treatment of asylum-seekers. In its own facilities, the INS implemented some standards, but INS detainees assigned to jails were under the direct control of jail officials and INS monitoring of such jails was minimal. In late October, the INS planned to issue additional detention standards that would apply to its own facilities and to jails, but they had not been made public at this writing. Congress, however, failed to fund the monitors requested by the INS to ensure that the standards prescribed for its own facilities and the jails with which its contracts were upheld.

The INS continued to detain unaccompanied children for lengthy periods before releasing them to family members or appropriate guardians. Human Rights Watch was particularly concerned that more than a third of the children in INS custody—nearly 2,000 children during the year ending in September 1999—were held in juvenile detention centers and county jails. Of the nearly 1,300 children held in secure confinement for more than three days, 58 percent were waiting to be transferred to a shelter care or similar facility or were held in such confinement simply because the INS lacked any alternative for them. By failing to place children in the least restrictive setting appropriate to their circumstances, the INS violated international standards, its own regulations, and the terms of a legal settlement.

During the year, the INS reportedly released more than a thousand long-term detainees who had orders of deportation but could not be repatriated for political or other reasons to countries such as Cuba, Vietnam, Cambodia, and Laos. The INS plan put in place during 1999 required mandatory reviews for detainees who were ordered deported but who could not actually be sent to their home countries, and who were thus facing indefinite detention. Those who were released had to meet certain criteria, such as having community sponsors, evidence of rehabilitation, and proof that they would not pose a danger to society.

The 1996 Illegal Immigration Reform and Immigration Responsibility Act's expedited removal proceedings, intended to process and deport individuals who enter the United States without valid documents with minimum delay, imperiled genuine asylum seekers and resulted in immigrants' being detained in increasing numbers. Asylum seekers with questionable documents were sent to "secondary inspection" where they had to convey their fears regarding return to their country of origin. The expedited process was characterized by excessive secrecy, making it virtually impossible to monitor the fairness of INS officials' decisions at each stage of the initial review.

The size of the U.S. Border Patrol continued to grow rapidly to number approximately 8,000 agents, double the 1993 total, raising concerns about the quality, training, and supervision of its agents. In particular, the agency's capacity to investigate complaints of abuse against its agents, and to take disciplinary actions in appropriate cases, was in question. Little information was made public relating to the investigation and discipline stemming from such allegations.

Yet, Border Patrol agents shot border-crossers in questionable circumstances and were accused of sexual assaults, beatings, and reckless vehicle pursuits that caused injuries.

Border Patrol agents said they shot at some border-crossers because they reached for, or attempted to throw, rocks at the agents. Border Patrol agents are not required to wear protective gear even though this would reduce the risk to agents and the stated justification for resorting to deadly force.

Revelant Human Rights Watch Reports:

Fingers to the Bone: United States Failure to Protect Child Farmworkers, 6/00
No Minor Matter: Children in Maryland's Jails, 11/99
Out of Sight: Super-Maximum Security Confinement in the United States, 2/00
Punishment and Prejudice: Racial Disparities in the War on Drugs, 5/00
Unfair Advantage: Workers' Freedom of Association in the United States Under International Human Rights Standards, 8/00

HUMAN RIGHTS WATCH

WOMEN'S HUMAN RIGHTS

The year 2000 marked the fifth anniversary of the U.N.'s Fourth World Conference on Women in Beijing, China, an event that heralded respect for women's human rights as a central part of any and all efforts to improve women's status around the globe. Five years later, what gains did women see in government efforts to protect their rights? Activists welcomed important signs of progress, including greater awareness of abuses of women's human rights; stronger international standards for prosecuting violence against women, particularly in conflict situations; and some initial efforts by governments and international actors to implement programs to support women's rights. Still, these steps forward seemed few and far between, especially when contrasted with the scale and scope of ongoing violations of women's most fundamental human rights.

One of the most striking developments in the past year—evident in June 2000 in the negotiations at the special sessions of the U.N. General Assembly for the Beijing + 5 Review (Beijing + 5) to assess progress in improving women's status—was how actively some governments were willing to work to thwart recent gains in protecting women's human rights. They set out to master the language of women's human rights while they at the same time sought to undermine the power of the idea and the movement. Perhaps a sign that they had started taking women's rights activists seriously, governments' resistance to further progress on women's human rights took several forms, although most of the obstructionist tactics at the U.N. meeting and elsewhere relied on the age-old strategy of divide and conquer.

First, and perhaps most threatening, was the refusal of governments to accept that for women to truly enjoy their human rights, they must be treated with dignity in all aspects of their lives. Instead, government actions reflected the belief that women are not entitled to full enjoyment of their human rights. Hence, while governments condemned some forms of violence against women, they readily excused others and defended laws that denied women their legal rights. In Morocco, for example, a reformist government pledged to pursue programs to measure and respond to violence against women, but allowed proposed reforms to the country's family code—which continues to subject female decision-making to male authority—to languish. In other countries, laws that recognized men as the legal heads of households remained in place, denying women's rights to decide for themselves, freely, whether and whom to marry, whether to work outside the home, or even when to seek medical attention. Laws requiring female obedience or subservience were often key to making women dependent on men and tied to abusive relationships.

Some governments failed to attack not only certain forms of violence, but also the many laws and practices that either rendered women vulnerable to attacks or made it difficult for them to escape or redress abuse. A government survey in Japan showed that 15.4 percent of women polled had been physically assaulted at least once by their husbands, but police remained reluctant to intervene in such cases and some women reported that police tried to dissuade them from pursuing their claims. In Khartoum, Sudan, a senior government official tried to enforce women's dependency by banning them from jobs in restaurants, gas stations, and similar institutions. When women demonstrated in protest, police set upon them, using tear gas and batons, and arresting over twenty of the demonstrators.

Certain governments also acted to deny rights that might protect women's autonomy in their sexual and reproductive decision-making. In the negotiations at Beijing + 5, some governments argued that women do not—and should not—enjoy rights in this fundamentally personal part of their lives, the right, for example, to make decisions about whether and with whom to have intimate relations free from discrimination, coercion, and violence. They further claimed that such rights were not universal, and defended practices such as those that discriminated against single women or resulted in forced marriage for reasons of culture or tradition. Rather than tackling those problems as violations of women's human rights, some governments asserted that concern with women's reproductive and sexual autonomy represented the "radical" agenda of "Western" activists and did not merit further attention. They preferred instead to limit the debate to addressing women's reproductive and sexual health needs, and to avoid discussion of government obligations to respect women's rights. Even those governments that claimed the mantle of leadership in promoting women's rights—Canada, the United States, and some European countries—failed to challenge this onslaught at Beijing + 5.

By suggesting that some of women's human rights are not universal, some governments raised the prospect that certain violations could be excused as culturally specific practices and, indeed, that situations of profound inequality could be found acceptable internationally. This was particularly the case with regard to women's enjoyment of their rights in the context of the family. Thus, many governments in South Asia, the Middle East, and Africa, appeared content to leave unchallenged the assumption that men have the right to discipline their wives as they see fit. In Pakistan, for example, women accused by their husbands of "inappropriate" or "immoral" behavior could be assaulted, maimed, or killed with effective impunity in the name of family honor. Activists maintained that such violence—over eight hundred women died in 1999 in such attacks—would persist so long as the country's laws enshrine male superiority. Activists in India, where on average reportedly fourteen women are murdered each day by their husbands' relatives, also called for a stronger government response to violence against women in the family.

Governments often used the cultural-specificity argument to justify using a separate standard to evaluate their performance in promoting the human rights of women. For example, in Saudi Arabia, press reports in April 2000 indicated that the Interior Minister refused to even discuss lifting a discriminatory ban on women's driving until "after

society accepts the idea."

The wide-ranging resistance to protecting women's human rights could be attributed in part to a desire to curb women's effectiveness in joining forces across national borders and turning the attention of the human rights system to abuses of women's human rights and government obligations to prevent and remedy such problems. Despite obstacles, women's human rights activists set new international standards for how women should be treated, and sometimes changed the situation in their local communities. In Jordan, for example, local activists successfully pushed their governments to introduce legislation to improve women's rights. In Russia, crisis centers mounted a national campaign against domestic violence and helped women bring cases to court. In Tanzania, the office of the U.N. High Commissioner for Refugees (UNHCR) implemented programs to protect women from sexual and domestic violence. In two cases brought in U.S. courts, fugitive former Bosnian Serb leader Radovan Karadzic was ordered to pay billions of dollars for atrocities, including rape and other sexual violence, committed by his soldiers. And, the Optional Protocol to the Convention on the Elimination of All Forms of Discrimination Against Women (CEDAW) was set to enter into force in December 2000, after Italy became the tenth country to ratify the instrument, thus creating a new mechanism for enforcing women's human rights.

The following section provides an overview of key developments, positive and negative, for women's human rights in 2000. Our investigations and monitoring throughout the year showed that violence and discrimination against women as committed and tolerated by states remained the norm in the countries in which we worked. Reports from activists and the news media in other countries confirmed the pattern of abuse of women's rights and underscored the need for urgent attention to the problem.

Human Rights Developments

In 2000, governments further mastered the rhetoric of respect for women's human rights. Often, however this rhetoric was unmatched by meaningful action. When they took steps to support women's rights, those steps were often cursory and uncoordinated. Although governments committed themselves to protecting women's human rights, in practice they were generally unwilling to protect *all women's human rights* in *all spheres of women's lives*. (Emphasis added.) Thus, the South African government, for example, could proudly declare its commitment to women's rights at Beijing + 5, yet thousands of South African women farmworkers had no ability to establish work contracts independently of their husbands. Similarly, the government of Peru condemned violence against women, while obliging domestic violence victims to undergo mandatory conciliation sessions with their abusers; the Uzbekistan government maintained constitutional guarantees of women's equality but women wishing to divorce their husbands faced major, gender-specific obstacles; the Taliban administration in Afghanistan shrouded its denial of women's rights in the rhetoric of protection but its forces raped ethnic Hazara and Tajik women with impunity; and Japan's government treated trafficked women not as victims of abuse but as criminals.

As the cases below illustrate, in most cases governments committed themselves to protecting only some rights, in only some instances, and only when funds were readily available to do so, and, most important, only when minimal political or social capital would be expended. The stark consequence of this for millions of women was that they lived with daily violence and discrimination from infancy to old age. The universality of women's rights, and the indivisibility of those rights, for all practical purposes, was for most women little more than a dream.

Violence against Women

In September 2000, the United Nations Population Fund (UNFPA) reported that across the world, one in three women had been physically assaulted or abused in some way, typically by someone she knew, such as her husband or another male member of her family. In response, governments publicly condemned violence against women and committed to show political will and provide financial resources for its eradication, but their performance, in practice, failed miserably to meet women's needs. Whether in Peru or Jordan, the U.S. or South Africa, or other states, men who beat or raped women in their homes or in state custody, or who murdered female family members to restore "family honor," or sexually assaulted female students, all too often were able to do so with impunity. Too often, states' response to this violence was perfunctory and short-sighted. At times officials did not bother to respond at all.

Governments' commitment to stopping violence against women was tested and failed in the area of violence against women in the family. Pakistan was a case in point. There, successive civilian and military-led governments alike have treated violence against women as a low priority. Under the former civilian government, the officially-appointed Commission of Inquiry for Women reported in 1997 that domestic violence was one of the country's most pervasive human rights problems. Yet, the government totally ignored the commission's findings and recommendations. Pakistan's military leaders also performed poorly. After seizing power in October 1999, the new military government condemned violence against women and identified it as a national problem. In March 2000, Pakistan's Human Rights Commission reported that, on average, at least two women were burned every day in domestic violence incidents. However, rather than explicitly criminalize all forms of family violence against women or provide clear guidelines for police intervention and protection in such cases, in August 2000, Pakistan's military government formed yet another commission to make yet more recommendations. Moreover, like the civilian administration before it, the military government resisted removing violence against women in the family from its perch of impunity. At Beijing + 5, Pakistan, along with several other obstructionist countries, lobbied successfully to delete language that identified customary laws and practices —such as early marriages, polygamy, female genital mutilation (FGM), and honor killings as violations of women's human rights—from the final conference document that outlined future initiatives and actions to implement the Beijing Declaration and the Platform for Action.

As with Pakistan, the Jordanian government's commitment to fighting violence against women stopped at women's front doors. From January to late-October, at least thirteen women were killed in Jordan in the name of "family honor." Nevertheless, for a second time (the first vote was in November 1999) in January 2000, the lower house of parliament, with a sweeping majority, refused to pass legislation to revoke article 340 of the Jordanian Penal Code, which effectively prescribes minimal punishment for males who kill female family members if they can demonstrate that their motivation was to uphold or restore family honor. Lower house parliamentarians sought to justify their veto of the proposed reform by asserting that they were protecting Jordan's traditional and moral values against Western influences. However, as it had previously done in October 1999, in February 2000 the parliament's upper house voted to approve the repeal of article 340, and a joint session of the two houses was awaited to finally decide the issue. Despite such setbacks on the parliamentary front, Jordanian civil society activists continued their nation-wide campaign to amend article 340. Between August and November 1999, the Jordanian National Committee to Eliminate the So-Called Crimes of Honor gathered over 15,000 signatures for a petition that called for abolition of laws that protect perpetrators of so-called honor crimes, and presented the petition to the speaker of the lower house of the parliament in November 1999. In 2000, the committee and other women's human rights activists continued to gather signatures, raise awareness on the issue, and make honor crimes a national concern.

In 1999, Russian police reported that, as of 1997, they had registered over four million men as potential abusers of members of their families. Their figures were based on recorded reports of prior abuse or threats. This startlingly high number of reports was received despite the existence of significant barriers which deterred women from reporting domestic violence. The Women's Alliance, a women's crisis center in Siberia, for example, reported that eighteen of the thirty-five women who called its hotline between May 1999 and May 2000 to report instances of violence against them, told counselors that police officers had refused to take a statement about their abuse. In six other cases, police had refused to respond to emergency calls from women being subjected to domestic violence. Official indifference to both domestic violence and sexual violence left women throughout Russia at risk and without recourse.

Yet, Russia did not pass legislation specifically criminalizing domestic violence and did not provide federal funding for crisis centers to assist their work. Despite the lack of such support, however, the Russian Association of Crisis Centers for Women, a nationwide alliance of nongovernmental crisis centers, pressed ahead to implement a public education campaign on violence against women. Television commercials and radio spots spread the anti-violence message throughout the country. Meanwhile, with a congressional mandate to do so, the U.S. government provided some aid to the crisis centers, making available U.S. $500,000.

Even in countries where domestic violence was explicitly illegal, women's lives remained in jeopardy. In Peru, one local women's rights group, DEMUS, estimated that nine out of ten Peruvian women were subjected to some kind of abuse in their intimate relationships. Nonetheless, the Peruvian Congress failed to reform its family violence legislation in a way that would afford women the greatest level of protection. Following a consultative process that some local nongovernmental organizations (NGOs) characterized as more promotional than productive, Congress modified the Law for the Prevention of Family Violence in July 2000. The amended law has a significantly improved definition of domestic violence, which includes sexual violence, provides a more complete definition of psychological violence, and broadens the scope of the law's application to include intimate partners not living together at the time of the violence. However, in a move that activists warned could severely undermine the gains of the amended law, Congress left standing the requirement that women who report domestic violence undergo a mandatory conciliation session with their alleged abusers. In a memorandum to members of the congressional Commission on Women in March 2000, Human Rights Watch challenged this and other shortcomings of the law, arguing that conciliation sessions imposed inappropriate obligations on the victims, obstructed women's access to justice, and endangered women's lives.

In South Africa, women confronted violence in the street and in school. South African women's rights activists reported that the country suffered from one of the highest levels of violence against women in the world. Not even schools provided safe havens from violence. Human Rights Watch research in April 2000 found that male students and teachers sexually assaulted female students on a regular basis, but abusers were seldom apprehended and punished. There existed only few and inadequate mechanisms to refer these cases out of the school system for investigation and prosecution. Instead, school officials preferred to resolve such cases internally, with the result that girls who were assaulted had no access to justice and found themselves continuing to attend school with those who had raped or abused them, and who remained at liberty to inflict similar abuse on others.

Governments frequently did not afford women protection against violence and were reluctant to investigate and punish those responsible, even when their own agents were the alleged perpetrators. In some cases, they even sought to limit prisoners' right to seek redress for abuse. For example, in the United States, a major government study released in December 1999 found that the substantiation rate for allegations of sexual abuse and misconduct by corrections officers averaged about 18 percent in the federal prison system and in the California and Texas state systems. However, in Michigan state, a law went into effect in March 2000 that excluded prisoners from the protections provided under the state civil rights act, which prohibits discrimination based on race and gender. Through this legislation, Michigan effectively eliminated the possibility that women prisoners could seek redress for sexual abuse in prison through lawsuits against the corrections department.

The same U.S. government study reported that the number of women incarcerated in state and federal prisons had climbed to approximately 85,000 by the start of 1999, an increase of more than 500 percent over 1980. The steady rise in the population of women prisoners, and NGO monitoring and reporting on violence against women in custody, sparked greater public awareness about custodial sexual violence and misconduct, and underscored the need to implement reforms to prevent and effectively respond to these abuses. However, adoption of laws was not enough, as California demonstrated. Human Rights Watch research showed that, although a California law went into effect in January 2000 that increased the criminal penalties for sexual misconduct against women in custody, California nevertheless failed to ensure that women could safely report these violations without risking retaliation. During an investigation in 2000, Human Rights Watch found that retaliation by prison guards was perhaps the most critical factor in women's reluctance to report abuse. Corrections personnel exercised enormous power over prisoners and had wide scope for retaliation. Women prisoners told Human Rights Watch that their cells were ransacked and personal items were damaged or taken after they reported abuse. Others reported being held in "protective" custody pending investigation of their allegation. Increased surveillance of inmates also meant that women had less privacy and were more likely to be the victims of prurient viewing by corrections officers, male and female, while they showered, undressed, or used the toilet.

Women in Conflict and Refugees

Soldiers, militia, and their sympathizers continued to sexually assault women with impunity in armed conflicts around the globe, including in Sierra Leone, Chechnya, East Timor, the Democratic Republic of Congo, Afghanistan, Indonesia, Kosovo, Bosnia, and Angola. Despite international recognition of rape and other sexual assault in armed conflict as crimes, governments and the international community rarely responded vigorously to investigate and punish such violence. In fact, they typically went no further than rhetorical condemnation. In addition, women faced rampant violence and discrimination in their post-conflict lives. Women refugees, in their countries of refuge, continued to be sexually and otherwise physically attacked by armed groups and civilians. Women returning to their communities post-conflict found negligible protection from domestic violence or state-tolerated sex discrimination.

For example, in Sierra Leone, under the guise of bringing an end to the human suffering caused by the conflict, the fragile July 1999 Lomé peace accord granted a blanket amnesty to Revolutionary United Front (RUF) rebels for their atrocities, including sexual violence. From the signing of the peace accord to its collapse in May 2000, RUF rebels never stopped raping women. A hellish cycle of rape, sexual assault, and mutilation continued, perpetrated by all sides, including the Westside Boys rebel faction and pro-government Civil Defense Force militia. Sexual violence often took the form of individual and gang rape; sexual assault with objects such as firewood, umbrellas, and sticks; and sexual slavery. Despite egregious attacks on women, the Sierra Leonean police and the U.N. Mission in Sierra Leone (UNAMSIL) did very little to protect women from further attacks and investigate cases to ensure that perpetrators were captured and punished.

Similarly, Russian soldiers raped women with impunity in Chechnya. Testimonies collected by human rights activists showed that women, men, and girls detained by Russian authorities were tortured, beaten, and raped. Witnesses spoke of brutal rapes in Russian-controlled areas of Chechnya, such as the villages of Alkhan-Yurt and Shali. Despite compelling and overwhelming evidence that Russian soldiers raped women during the Chechen conflict, Russian authorities managed to arrest only one alleged perpetrator, a colonel, on March 29, 2000. Charged with the sexual assault and murder of a Chechen woman, as of late October, the colonel was eligible for amnesty.

In Algeria, armed Islamist groups continued to target women in a conflict that has ebbed and flowed since 1992, when the government suspended elections Islamists were expected to win. Although threatening and assaulting women was part of their basic mode of operation of many of these groups well before the suspension of the 1992 elections, armed Islamist groups adopted violence against women as a more overt strategy between 1993 and 1998. Between 1993 and 1994, they killed women for expressing their opinions and for working in certain professions, such as hairdressers and writers. They also forcibly took women as wives in "temporary marriages." From 1995 to 1998, they treated women who lived in villages that opposed their rule as spoils of war, raping, abducting, and killing them. Disputing official government figures of two thousand six hundred, Algerian women's rights activists estimated that these groups raped five thousand women between 1995 and 1998. They criticized as severely deficient government programs and assistance to victims of sexual violence.

In Afghanistan, as the twenty-year civil war continued, the Taliban, which controlled 90 percent of the country, continued to violate women's rights with unabated severity. In addition to severe restrictions on women's access to paid work, health care, and secondary and higher education, the U.N.'s rapporteur for Afghanistan reported that Taliban members had abducted and raped ethnic Hazara and Tajik women with impunity. Such sexual violence by the Taliban undermined its leaders' claim that their policies toward women were intended to protect them from violence and abuse.

Violence against women continued to be a constant feature in the complex conflict in the eastern Democratic Republic of Congo. In March 2000, Human Rights Watch documented dozens of cases of rape and other human rights violations in areas controlled by the Goma-based Congolese Rally for Democracy (*Rassamblement Congolais pour la Democratie, RCD*) and its Rwandan allies. The RCD raped and otherwise attacked civilians to deter them from supporting its opponents. In one particularly gruesome incident, RCD soldiers beat, stripped, and raped five women who had been detained, reportedly because a RCD soldier's wife accused them of sorcery. The soldiers then put hot peppers in the women's vaginas, put them in a pit, and buried them alive. Despite its claim to be the legitimate local authority, the RCD failed to prevent or punish rape and other violence committed by its soldiers or civilians.

Similarly, in East Timor, pro-Indonesian militia and some Indonesian soldiers raped many women during the weeks of violence surrounding the referendum on East Timor's status in August 1999. At this writing, over 100,000 refugees remain under militia control in West Timor, where violence, including sexual violence, by militia continued. The Indonesian government's failure to disarm and disband the militia undermined its claim that it would bring perpetrators of violence to justice. However, the attorney general's office, in cooperation with U.N. civilian police, conducted an investigation into the violence and in September 2000 published a list of nineteen suspects whom they plan to charge with various crimes, including rape.

The ranks of refugees, internally displaced persons (IDPs), and asylum seekers continued to swell in 2000, as large numbers of people fled conflict and persecution at home and sought refuge elsewhere. The UNHCR reported that, in 2000, twenty-two million refugees and displaced persons were under their protection or receiving assistance from them. Women who fled their homes in search of sanctuary from violence too often found themselves confronting yet more sexual and physical violence as refugees. For example, numerous Sierra Leonean and Liberian refugees living in Guinea were physically and sexually attacked by police, military, and civilians, following an inflammatory address by President Lansana Conte of Guinea. On September 6, 2000, the president accused the refugees of supporting rebels responsible for cross-border attacks on Guinea's territory. Thousands of refugees in the capital, Conakry, were then rounded up and many women and adolescent girls as young as fourteen years old were sexually abused, often by multiple attackers. As of late-October, the Guinean authorities had neither acknowledged nor investigated the attacks on refugees.

Even in post-conflict periods, women's human rights were not protected. Kosovar women confronted discrimination and a steep rise in domestic violence, rape, trafficking, and abductions following the war. The government ignored blatant discrimination against women. Women widowed by war feared the loss of their children due to an Albanian custom requiring the children to be handed over to the deceased father's family. Women's rights activists throughout the province fought to draw attention to discrimination against women in the postwar environment and sought political representation in the interim government. Women's efforts did yield a U.N. regulation mandating that at least 30 percent of each political party's top fifteen candidates must be women. But most activists felt that little had been done to combat discriminatory practices that relegated women to the traditional homemaker role.

Labor Rights

Women contended with discriminatory laws and practices in the labor force in 2000 that obstructed and conditioned their participation and denied them their human rights. For example, even though across the globe women were entering the formal workforce in record numbers, in Sudan women's very right to work was under fierce attack. On September 3, 2000, the Governor of the State of Khartoum, citing Islamic law, imposed a ban on women working in public places. Only days later, on September 9, 2000, however, amid international and local outrage, the Sudanese Constitutional Court suspended the ban, pending review of an appeal lodged by three women's rights groups.

In addition to statutory discrimination, women faced practical discrimination. Even as the International Labor Organization (ILO) adopted a new international Convention on Maternity Protection in May 2000 and estimated that 50 percent of the labor force was female, in some countries women's participation in the workforce was determined by their reproductive status. Not only were women's reproductive functions perceived to be in the way at work, but their bodies were also at risk at work. Women workers faced sexual harassment and violence on the job, with little hope of redress. Employers often considered women's reproductive and productive roles to be incompatible, and governments did little to challenge them. In Mexico, Guatemala, and South Africa, for example, governments failed to enforce international and national laws to protect women from discrimination and violence during the hiring process and on the job.

In 2000, women's right to exercise reproductive autonomy in the workforce continued to be under attack in Mexico. Thousands of women working in maquiladoras (export-processing factories) faced frequent discrimination based on their reproductive status. Many transnational corporations regularly required women to undergo pre-employment pregnancy testing, with the aim of denying pregnant women work. Other corporations went even further, creating unbearable work conditions for pregnant workers to provoke their resignation. Activists complained that, although some corporations had renounced such discriminatory practices, others continued them without sanction by the Mexican government.

As in past years, in 2000 the Mexican government continued to undertake merely cosmetic action and to use North American Free Trade Agreement (NAFTA) fora to spread misinformation about its policies. The Mexican government actively used these meetings to undermine women's rights to reproductive autonomy, equality, and privacy in the work sphere by disseminating information—especially designed for and targeted at female workers—that represented an arbitrary government policy with no basis in the labor code as law. In one such example, government pamphlets stated that women workers had an obligation to inform their employers of their pregnancy status. The Mexican government also used the latest NAFTA-related outlet (a meeting in Puebla, Mexico, on May 30, 2000) to contend that the labor code allowed for postemployment pregnancy testing of working women when that testing was intended to protect the well-being of the woman worker or her fetus.

Working women in neighboring Guatemala suffered similar rights violations, in which their participation and equal rights in the labor force were limited by statutory discrimination and government inaction. In an investigation conducted in 2000, Human Rights Watch found that discrimination on the basis of reproductive status was an inescapable fact for both maquiladora line operators and domestic workers in Guatemala. This discrimination took the form of questions about pregnancy status and pregnancy testing as a condition for employment in maquiladoras, post-hire penalization of pregnant workers in factories and private households, and failure to comply with maternity protections in both sectors. Live-in domestic workers, many of whom were young indigenous women who migrated to the capital from rural villages, were subjected to special regulations in the labor code that excluded all domestic workers from key labor rights protections, such as the eight-hour workday. Often isolated in private households, domestic workers were particularly vulnerable to sexual harassment. Government response to gender-specific labor rights violations was negligent at best. While government officials recognized discrimination on the basis of reproductive status as illegal, they did not take any proactive steps to combat it. Despite being lobbied by women's rights groups and community associations, as of late October the government had not adopted legislation on sexual harassment, nor had it revised provisions in the labor code that accorded domestic workers lesser rights than other workers.

In the agricultural sector, women were likely to fare equally poorly. Human Rights Watch research in 2000 found that women farmworkers in South Africa were discriminated against and sexually and otherwise physically abused by their coworkers and employers. Some discrimination was based on marital status. Married women farmworkers, for example, were denied employment contracts in their own names, such that their jobs were dependent on those of their husbands. Often, women farmworkers' access to housing was also determined by their relationship to a man. Because the majority of farmowners offered housing only to permanent male employees, single women farmworkers were generally not able to live on the farm. In addition, women were also paid less than their male counterparts for the same type of work or work of equal value. By denying women's agency and reinforcing their economic dependency on men, these discriminatory practices made women more vulnerable to violence in their homes and the workplace on farms.

Despite laws prohibiting sex discrimination in the workplace, the South African government did little to protect women's rights in the agricultural sector. In a landmark April 1999 ruling, the Land Claims Court held that a woman farmworker could not be evicted from the farm where she worked following the dismissal of her husband and that the right to family life afforded the female farmworker the right to allow her husband to continue living in her home on the farm. Yet, in 2000 the government took no active steps to ensure that this important precedent was enforced. Many women continued to face unfair evictions because their husbands had been dismissed, and few knew about their rights or how to enforce them.

Trafficking

Around the world, governments continued to allow trafficking of women and girls for forced labor and servitude to flourish with near impunity. Lured with fraudulent promises of lucrative opportunities, women migrated within and across borders for work. A U.S. Department of State trafficking report released in 2000 found that crime rings and loosely connected criminal networks trafficked between 45,000 and 50,000 women and children into the U.S. annually. Trafficking did not occur in a vacuum. Violations of women's human rights in countries of origin—including state-tolerated sex discrimination, domestic violence, and rampant sexual violence—contributed to women's vulnerability to abuse. Whether the women traveled voluntarily, found themselves tricked into migrating, or were sold into the sex industry or sweatshops, trafficking victims suffered horribly similar human rights violations. Stripped of their passports, often unable to speak the local language, sold as chattel, and terrified of local law enforcement authorities and their traffickers, many women and girls struggled to pay off the enormously inflated debts owed to traffickers; others attempted to escape. In the countries of destination, women encountered violence, state complicity, detention, and deportation.

For example, Nigerian women's rights organizations reported that hundreds of Nigerian women and girls hoping to escape poverty and discrimination at home voluntarily migrated to Europe in response to job offers as domestic workers or waitresses. Upon arrival, many found themselves trapped in forced prostitution, saddled with exorbitant debts, and forced to work under brutal conditions. Like other trafficked women around the world, Nigerian women struggled to pay off their "debt." Forbidden to refuse any customer, women who dared to resist encountered harsh punishment from their employers, including physical assault. Some clients also sexually and physically attacked the women; other clients robbed them. Their status as "illegal migrants" made the women particularly vulnerable to attacks by customers and traffickers alike. The Women's Consortium of Nigeria (WACON), a Nigeria-based advocacy group that provides support for victims of trafficking, reported that some employers denounced trafficked women to immigration officials as "illegal aliens." The result was deportation for the victims, often under inhumane conditions. In May 2000, WACON used the trafficking cases it documented to advocate within Nigeria for, among other things, repatriation procedures guaranteeing victims safety and respect for their human rights, as well as health care and counseling services. Activists reported that the Nigerian government had arrested several men in connection with the sale of girls to Europe and the trafficking of them to West Africa.

The Israeli government also failed to take even minimal steps to protect trafficked women trapped in that country. In July, after the publication of a blistering report on trafficking by Amnesty International, and after years of lobbying by Israeli women's organizations, the Knesset amended the criminal code to make the buying and selling of human beings for prostitution a criminal offense. The law had little impact, however, on the lives of dozens of women still detained in prison in Israel and awaiting deportation. Despite the new legislation, the Israeli government continued to treat trafficked women not as victims, but as criminals and "illegal aliens," housing women in prisons and making them particularly vulnerable to human rights abuses. Nor was the law particularly dissuasive to traffickers, who continued to bring hundreds of women and girls from the countries of the former Soviet Union and Eastern Europe into Israel for forced labor in the sex industry. Although Israel yielded to international pressure and began prosecuting a small number of traffickers, its efforts were undermined by its failure to provide minimal guarantees for victims of trafficking, including witness protection, legal assistance, relief from deportation, or third-country resettlement.

Danger also plagued undocumented Thai women working in the Japanese sex industry. As in Israel, Japanese government authorities failed to consider the coercive and deceptive circumstances of trafficked women's arrival and employment in Japan. Instead, they treated the women as criminals or undocumented workers.

Although high-ranking Japanese and Thai officials publicly condemned trafficking in women and exhibited some understanding of the slavery-like nature of the abuses involved, women in these countries still lacked any meaningful legal redress. Japanese officials failed to enforce even the minimal available legal protections. For example, the Japanese government identified an amendment to the Law on Control and Improvement of Amusement Businesses as its primary effort to address trafficking. But the narrowly-written law proved wholly inadequate to provide relief for trafficking victims. Most glaringly, the law lacked criminal penalties: revocation of an establishment's license stands as the only punishment for violations. In March 2000, the police admitted that the new amended provision had not yet been used. Furthermore, labor officials told Human Rights Watch that officials in the Employment Security Office, as local offices charged with monitoring enforcement of the labor code are called, failed to understand the laws that could be used to prosecute traffickers, and thus rarely enforced them.

Likewise, in Bosnia and Herzegovina, traffickers continued to abuse and exploit women from the former Soviet Union and Eastern Europe with impunity. In 1999, Human Rights Watch uncovered brothels filled with women trafficked from Ukraine, Moldova, Bulgaria, Belarus, and Romania scattered throughout Bosnia. In interviews with Human Rights Watch, women in the brothels reported that they had been sold from brothel owner to brothel owner, placed in debt bondage, threatened, and beaten. Trafficking showed no signs of abating. One year after Human Rights Watch completed its research, a United Nations report on trafficking into Bosnia confirmed the widespread abuses. The May 2000 report documented significant local police, international police, and some Stabilisation Force (SFOR) complicity. Between March 1999 and March 2000, the U.N. intervened in forty cases involving one hundred and eighty-two women, five of whom were under the age of eighteen. In fourteen of those cases, the U.N. found compelling evidence of complicity by SFOR, local, or international police. In one case, an SFOR civilian paid seven thousand Deutsche Marks (U.S.$3057) to purchase two women from a brothel owner. NATO declined to waive the SFOR member's diplomatic immunity; he left Bosnia and Herzegovina without legal repercussions. With growing awareness of the surge in trafficking, U.N. officials initiated a "trafficking project" in Bosnia in 1999 in cooperation with local nongovernmental organizations and the International Organization on Migration to provide shelter, legal aid, and protection for women who sought to escape their traffickers. After one year in operation, the program appeared to provide women trafficked into Bosnia with some concrete support. However, the Bosnian government and international community made little progress on prosecuting those responsible for the abuses.

Women's Status in the Family

The family remained one of the most contested sites for progress on women's rights. During Beijing + 5 at the U.N. in June, governments congratulated themselves on their efforts to ensure equality for women in all spheres of life. Some governments did, in fact, change national legislation to guarantee women's equality in the family. For example, according to a September 2000 United Nations Population Fund (UNFPA) report, both the Czech Republic and Cape Verde enacted new family codes that guaranteed women equality. Nevertheless, many other governments were unyielding in their resistance to reform personal status laws that discriminated against women. Governments justified their inaction as preserving their societies' morals, unity, religion, culture, and tradition. Countries like Morocco, Rwanda, Algeria, Israel, and Egypt maintained laws and practices that blatantly discriminated against women in marriage, access to divorce, child custody, and inheritance, among other issues. These laws and practices relegated women to a subordinate status in the family and restricted their autonomy to make decisions about their lives.

In Morocco, the Family Code granted different rights to women and men and consistently rendered women's autonomy subject to male guardianship and authority. The introduction by Prime Minister El-Yousoufi of a national plan for the integration of women in development in March 1999 raised hopes that women's status would improve in critical areas. However, by late 2000, the government had made negligible progress toward implementing the plan, as a result of resistance by conservative and Islamist factions to the plan's section on reforming the Family Code. The section on the reform of the personal status code calls for, among other things, raising the age of marriage for girls and women from fifteen to eighteen, canceling the guardianship requirement for adult women, outlawing polygamy except in certain cases, giving women the right to half of their husbands' property after a divorce, and allowing divorced women to maintain custody of their children if they remarry. In March 2000, conservative and Islamist factions organized a march in Casablanca in opposition to the plan, while progressive factions organized a march in Rabat in support of it. In May 2000, in response to the intense public debate around the proposed legal reforms, the prime minister appointed a committee of scholars and religious authorities to consider the controversial aspects of the plan and make recommendations to King Mohamed VI. As of late October 2000, this committee had not met. Moroccan women's rights activists argued that, since the plan addresses only a minimum of their demands, a self-described progressive government should have no problem meeting them.

In Israel, an amendment to the Equal Rights for Women Law was passed in March 2000. The amendment deals with, inter alia, equal social rights for women in all spheres of life: the right of women over their bodies, protection against violence and trafficking, and representation for women in the public sector. The equality proposed by this law extended to all spheres of life except family life. Issues of marriage and divorce continued to be exclusively within the jurisdiction of the religious courts, be they Jewish, Christian, Muslim, or Druze. These courts controlled women's lives and their right to administer their lives. For example, under these religious courts, women did not have equal access to divorce. According to the Israel Women's Network, thousands of Jewish women continued to be a *gunot*, "chained" women whose husbands refused to divorce them. *Mevoi Satum* (Impasse), an Israeli organization dedicated to helping a *gunot*, estimated that over 97 percent of men who deny their wives a divorce were physically abusive.

In January 2000, the Egyptian parliament passed a new law on divorce. The *Khole'* law opened the possibility for the first time for women unilaterally to request divorce on grounds of incompatibility, while requiring women to forgo alimony and to repay their husbands any dowry. Many women's rights activists acknowledged that the new law facilitated women's access to divorce, but noted that it is too early to assess its full impact.

In Uzbekistan, despite the constitutional guarantee of full legal equality between men and women, in practice, women continued to face discrimination in their access to divorce and to marital property. Privileging "protection of the family," over women's equality and autonomy, the Uzbek government erected legal and administrative barriers to divorce. Courts refused to grant women divorce without permission from local authorities. Also, a husband's refusal to divorce barred his wife's legal claim to marital property, although he, relying on the lax enforcement of laws against bigamy, could re-marry at will.

On a positive note, the Rwandan Supreme Court, which by law must approve all new legislation before it becomes binding and enforceable, finally approved the inheritance bill adopted by parliament in June 1999. The new inheritance law became applicable to all Rwandans in November 1999, reversing decades of inequality women faced in the area of inheritance. Women had encountered barriers in reclaiming their property after the 1994 genocide, mainly due to discriminatory customary law. By law, Rwandan women can now inherit property from their parents or husbands. The law enables widows whose deceased husbands' male relatives had already inherited their property to reclaim it. Rwandan women's rights activists cautioned, however, that without a nation-wide campaign to educate women and society at large about the new law, the daily reality of discriminatory land inheritance practices would continue to dominate most women's lives.

The Role of the International Community

Although women's human rights received much attention from the international community in the year 2000, states and intergovernmental organizations failed to take the substantive actions necessary to prevent and redress violations of women's human rights. In a variety of fora, states tried repeatedly to abdicate responsibility for ending violence against women and other violations. Some states disclaimed responsibility for violations in the so-called private sphere. Some states argued that they were responsible for redressing only gender-based violence, not gender-based discrimination. And finally, some states tried to attack women's human rights activists in ways designed to divide the movement. Although women's rights activists were able to withstand most of these attacks, the progress that many had hoped for, especially within the Beijing + 5 review process, simply did not happen.

United Nations

In June 2000, the United Nations General Assembly held a special session, "Women 2000: Gender Equality, Development and Peace in the 21st Century," to review the Beijing Platform for Action. Delegates from more than 180 states were charged with reviewing the progress made during the previous five years in implementing the Beijing Platform, which was drafted and signed by 189 governments at the U.N. Fourth World

Conference on Women held in Beijing, China, in 1995. What should have been a moment for states to reflect on progress made in advancing the status of women, to identify obstacles to their advancement, and to renew their commitment to ensuring that women enjoy their human rights and fundamental freedoms quickly deteriorated into a struggle to prevent states' backtracking. A small group of obstructionist governments, including Algeria, Nicaragua, Syria, Pakistan, and the Holy See, used Beijing + 5 to attack the very principles of equality underlying the Platform for Action. Unfortunately for women, the majority of states, while not participating in the attack, failed to mount a vigorous defense of the commitments made in Beijing. For example, governments such as the U.S., Canada, Australia, and member states of the European Union could have taken the initiative by immediately and publicly condemning efforts to downplay abuses of women's rights. They could have countered with proposals to strengthen the language of the Platform for Action and called for concrete measures and benchmarks to assess progress. Instead, these so-called leaders kept a low public profile and allowed much of the debate to be set by the reactionary minority. As the special session drew near to an end, with the outcome document still unfinished, there were widespread fears among NGOs that this session would be remembered as "Beijing - 5." States finally adopted an outcome document that reaffirmed the Platform for Action and included some advances, but largely failed to call for concrete actions which would move states beyond rhetoric to action.

The strategies and arguments used by the obstructionist minority at Beijing +5 were familiar to those who had been involved in the Cairo +5 review in 1999 and the ongoing negotiations on the International Criminal Court (ICC). First, some representatives claimed that states do not commit human rights abuses against women; they argued that gender-specific and gender-based forms of violence against women are perpetrated solely by individuals, not state actors. This argument failed to take into account the experi-

ences of women who face persecution by the state because of their political opinions or because they fail to conform to gender-based stereotypes, or, in some cases, such as under the Taliban in Afghanistan, simply because they are women. This argument also failed to address the well-documented obstacles women encounter when seeking redress after experiencing violence. Not only are women denied redress through the criminal justice system, but in some countries, like Pakistan, women risk being attacked by the police if they dare to file a complaint.

Another strategy used in the attack on the Platform for Action involved attempting to separate the issue of violence against women from other violations. Many countries were willing to condemn violence against women but were insistent that the violence was unconnected to violations of other rights. Many delegates spoke about the need to end domestic violence, but avoided agreeing to specific actions such as ensuring that their criminal codes prohibit violence by an intimate partner; requiring that police, forensic medical personnel, prosecutors and judges be trained to handle effectively domestic violence cases; and implementing effective protection for victims of domestic violence. In Jordan, for example, the government has condemned so-called honor killings, but its only means of offering protection to women threatened with murder is to incarcerate them, in violation of their rights to liberty and freedom of movement.

More generally, these states ignored how women's vulnerability to violence is connected to a wide range of violations of civil, cultural, economic, political and social rights. For example, even as delegates condemned domestic violence, the concern was too often presented without context. In particular, governments failed to recognize that in many countries women are denied access to public life, to paid work, to education, to credit, to custody of their children, and to inherit land and property. These human rights violations make women particularly vulnerable to domestic violence by making it almost impossible for them to leave abusive relationships.

This strategy of refusing to recognize more than a few rights was evident in the fight at Beijing + 5 over whether human rights protect individual autonomy when it comes to decision-making about sex. Women's rights advocates pressed governments to recognize sexual rights in the outcomes document, but states refused, opting instead to call for attention to women's sexual health. States repeatedly refused to recognize that when women cannot negotiate, on equal terms, if, when and with whom to have intimate relationships, they are more vulnerable to sexual and other forms of violence. In the effort to exclude the language of sexual rights from the document, states also resorted to attacks aimed at driving a wedge between women's rights activists by insisting that only "Western" women want sexual rights.

Even as the highly-politicized Beijing +5 review process was taking place, numerous U.N. programs and agencies released their own reports highlighting the pervasiveness of violence against women, the extent to which women suffer from discrimination in many contexts, and the correlations between poverty and gender. The United Nations Development Fund for Women (UNIFEM) reported that 70 percent of the world's 1.3 billion people living in poverty are women. And, despite the pledges made by governments at Beijing, the situation for women is getting worse in certain areas. For example, the number of rural women living in absolute poverty, i.e. life-threatening poverty, has risen by 50 percent over the last two decades as opposed to 30 percent for men. UNIFEM further reported that although women work two-thirds of all hours worked, they earn one-tenth of all income and own less than one-tenth of the world's property. In April, at the World Education Forum in Dakar, Senegal, Secretary-General Kofi Annan noted that two-thirds of the 110 million children who are not receiving an education are girls.

The UNIFEW report and a UNICEF report on domestic violence reinforced the argument that human rights are indivisible and, specifically that for women to truly enjoy the right to freedom from violence, they must be able to enjoy their rights in other spheres as well. First the UNIFEM report showed that women remain economically disadvantaged in most countries, and that their second class status makes them both vulnerable to violence and unable to escape violence. The UNICEF report addressed not only the pervasiveness of domestic violence against women and girls, but also the social, economic and health costs both to individuals who suffer the violence and to society. This correlation between gender and poverty is a problem for developed countries as well as developing countries. For example, in the U.S., women represent 57.2 percent of people living in poverty.

The search of women's human rights activists for an end to impunity for gender-based violence was not limited to the domestic sphere. At meetings held at the U.N. in New York in March and June 2000, states wrapped up their negotiations on the elements of crimes, and rules of evidence and procedures for the International Criminal Court (ICC). Women's ability to seek redress for sexual violence through the ICC came under fire when a small group of states proposed that all the crimes of sexual violence enumerated in the ICC treaty be exempted if they were committed by a family member or pursuant to religious or cultural practices. The proposal was ultimately rejected, but not before it was used to undermine the reach of the court by raising the threshold required to establish crimes against humanity.

At the International Criminal Tribunal for Rwanda (ICTR), Alfred Musema, director of the Tea Factory in Gisovu, was found guilty of genocide, extermination, and one count of rape. He was found not guilty of other inhumane acts, including the allegations that he repeatedly incited others "to have fun" with Tutsi women by raping them and, in one case, ordered a woman to be raped and have her breast cut off and fed to her son. In a separate opinion, Judge Navanethem Pillay dissented. She did not agree with the factual findings of her fellow judges that Witness M was credible in all of his accounts except for his testimony that Musema ordered rapes. Pillay argued that there was no basis on which to find that Witness M was not also credible on this one specific issue. The case raised concerns that investigators for the ICTR may not have conducted sufficiently thorough investigations to compile evidence of the widespread use of rape and other forms of sexual violence during the genocide. Women's rights activists in Rwanda cited lack of information and trust that the court will actually take the measures necessary to protect them from being publicly identified as two significant reasons that victims of sexual violence have not come forward to speak with investigators about their experiences. The ICTR opened an outreach center in Kigali in September 2000 to facilitate communication and cooperation between the court and Rwandans.

At the International Criminal Tribunal for the former Yugoslavia (ICTY), victims of sexual violence came under attack when an expert witness for the defense in the case of The Prosecutor of the Tribunal against Dragan Gagovic, Gojko Jankovic, Janko Janjic, Radomir Kovac, Zoran Vukovic, Dragan Zelenovic, Dragoljub Kunarac, and Radovan Stankovic (or Foca case) argued that in the absence of corroborating medical evidence, "it is as if the rape did not happen." This testimony highlighted two significant issues for the ad hoc tribunals. First, in cases of sexual violence, the difficulties of obtaining convictions using the high evidentiary standards required by the tribunal, such as corroborating medical evidence. Second, the tribunals need to assist survivors of sexual violence in getting medical attention. In situations of armed conflict, it is unlikely that women will have timely access to medical attention, including the possibility of collecting medically-relevant evidence for a rape investigation. But, as with other survivors of torture, women should get medical attention as soon as possible and a well-trained medical professional may be able to document other evidence of sexual violence.

These issues must be addressed immediately, as credible reports of sexual violence perpetrated against women in conflict poured in throughout the year from Chechnya, Sierra Leone, Guinea, East and West Timor, Afghanistan, and elsewhere. In this regard, the U.N. failed again to learn from its past mistakes and to ensure that investigators hired by U.N. civilian police to investigate war crimes and crimes against humanity were experienced in documenting and investigating crimes of sexual violence. The United Nations Transitional Administration for East Timor (UNTAET) initially not only failed to include investigators with expertise in investigating crimes of sexual violence, but in several cases, when they did attempt to interview women in East Timor, failed to conduct the investigations in a confidential manner to protect the women's identity. Where the alleged perpetrators remained at large, women's rights groups who had collected this evidence refused further cooperation with UNTAET until an effective witness protection program was put in place. These problems, however, appeared to have been partly rectified by September 2000.

U.N. High Commissioner for Human Rights Mary Robinson visited East Timor and met with many women survivors. However, human rights activists were disappointed that, in her January 2000 report on the situation in East Timor, she failed to press for immediate action to improve the situation of women victims, for example, by calling for the rapid deployment of women civilian police with expertise in investigating cases of sexual violence, for the active investigation of leads in specific cases, and for increased efforts to get suspects detained and returned to East Timor.

UNHCR faced the ongoing challenge of meeting the protection and humanitarian needs of refugees in increasingly hostile environments. In Tanzania and Guinea, politicians accused refugees of causing economic hardship and instability in their countries. As a result, refugees were threatened with violence in Tanzania and attacked by police, solders, and civilians in Guinea. These attacks included rape of women. The deliberate targeting and murder of UNHCR workers in West Timor and Guinea raised the specter of people charged with protecting refugees being left unprotected and exposed to attack, in part because of a lack of political will by the international community to ensure their safety and that of the refugees that they seek to protect.

The pilot program in the Tanzanian camps funded by the U.N. Foundation continued to address sexual and domestic violence within the camps. The program received generally favorable reviews for tackling domestic violence, a problem that had been largely unaddressed in the camps, although there remained problems with consistent monitoring and follow up of individual cases. Similar programs were introduced in camps in Kenya, Liberia, Guinea and Sierra Leone. However, all these programs were at risk of being shut down because of the lack of financial support from donor governments.

UNHCR revised its guidelines on women refugees to reflect the understanding that its protection duties include preventing and addressing both sexual and domestic violence against refugees in and around the camps. The revised guidelines were scheduled to be submitted to the NGO community for comments in early 2001. UNHCR also continued its work to elaborate the Executive Committee's position on gender-related persecution by examining both procedural and substantive elements of how to determine asylum claims by women. UNHCR finally filled the long - vacant position of Senior Coordinator for Refugee Women.

For the women of Afghanistan, the U.N. was a desperately needed ally in their struggle to survive and enjoy some semblance of their most fundamental human rights, but here the U.N. sent mixed messages. On the one hand, the U.N. played an important role in protesting a Taliban edict closing down female-run bakeries in the summer, and two human rights rapporteurs strongly condemned the Taliban's treatment of women. On the other hand, UNHCR continued repatriation efforts, often to areas where women's rights were severely restricted and where their physical well-being was at risk. This raised questions about whether refugees choosing to repatriate

were fully informed by UNHCR of the security issues women face in Afghanistan and who in the household was making the decision.

At regular intervals since January 1999, 102 countries have met at the United Nations in Vienna to draft a new Convention Against Transnational Organized Crime. The purpose of the convention is to define areas of law enforcement cooperation, legal procedures, and other measures between States relating to all forms of transnational crime. Three "Additional Protocols" were also being drafted including one to address Trafficking in Persons, Especially Women and Children. A major concern was to ensure that the treaties recognize that victims of trafficking have suffered a variety of human rights abuses and that they have access to redress.

At the annual session of the U.N. Commission on Human Rights, the U.N. special rapporteur on violence against women, Radhika Coomaraswamy, whose mandate was extended for another three years, issued a timely report on trafficking against women that explored the complexity of the issue, but strongly called on states to recognize that women who were trafficked are neither criminal nor illegal migrants and should be given the opportunity to seek redress for violations they experienced in the course of being trafficked. Her report was aimed, in part, at states negotiating a U.N. protocol on trafficking in Vienna.

The commission also adopted, for the first time, a resolution on "Women's Equal Ownership of, Access to and Control over Land and the Equal Right to Own Property and to Adequate Housing." The commission also appointed a special rapporteur on the right to food and the right to housing, signifying increased attention by the commission to violations of economic rights. If the special rapporteur successfully integrates a gender-based analysis into the work, this could be a substantial step toward recognition of the relationship between gender-based discrimination and gender-based violence.

The Committee on the Elimination of All Forms of Discrimination against Women

(CEDAW) raised concerns about the caste system during its February review of India's initial report under CEDAW. CEDAW expressed concern over extreme forms of physical and sexual violence against women belonging to particular castes or ethnic or religious groups, and over customary practices such as dowry, sati, and the devadasi system, all of which contribute to a higher incidence of gender-based violence in the country.

United States

Given its self-proclaimed role as a vigorous defender of women's human rights around the world, the U.S. missed several opportunities in 2000 to live up to this claim. Although 166 countries, including all industrialized nations, had ratified CEDAW, the U.S. still had not. Despite pressure from women's rights groups, constituents, and colleagues, Senator Jesse Helms continued to resist demands that CEDAW be put to a vote by the Senate Foreign Relations Committee, which he chaired. On International Women's Day, Senator Helms redoubled his efforts against CEDAW ratification and publicly vowed never to allow a Senate vote on CEDAW; instead, he promised to leave it in the "dustbin" for several more "decades." In May, Senator Helms introduced a resolution calling for the Senate to reject CEDAW.

The U.S. government also missed an opportunity to demonstrate its commitment to women's human rights at home when it again failed to take action to prevent sexual abuse of women incarcerated in state and federal prisons. Legislative and remedial measures were either stalled or failing. For example, in late 1999, Delegate Eleanor Holmes Norton introduced a bill in the House of Representatives to withhold federal funds from states that failed to implement five specific safeguards to prevent sexual abuse. Although the bill was sent to a judiciary subcommittee in November 1999, as of mid-October 2000 the bill was buried, apparently due to lack of support.

It was not just the legislative branch that failed women in U.S. prisons. After the Department of Justice settled its case against the Michigan Department of Corrections (MDOC) alleging widespread sexual abuse, retaliation, and privacy violations, the federal judge presiding over the federal and parallel state cases allowed the state case to continue, expressing his concern that the settlement was not strong enough to protect the women. The Justice Department failed to monitor its agreement, and even basic provisions such as counseling for women victims of sexual abuse were never provided. A settlement between the private litigants and MDOC was agreed in September. Michigan agreed to pay several million dollars in damages and to provide significant injunctive relief.

Nonetheless, leadership on women's human rights did emerge elsewhere. In 2000, the U.S. Senate passed landmark legislation to protect trafficked victims' rights in the U.S. and abroad. The new legislation, among other things, acknowledged that people are trafficked around the world for all types of work; dedicated resources to prosecuting and preventing trafficking in the U.S. and elsewhere; and established a visa that allows trafficked victims to remain in the U.S. to pursue civil or criminal claims against their traffickers.

In June, Congressman Jerrold Nadler presented a resolution condemning "honor killings" and urging, among other things, that the Department of State, in its yearly report on human rights, should include information on incidences of honor crimes and on what steps the respective governments are taking to address this problem. U.S. women's rights groups welcomed this effort as a consciousness raising device, but warned that it was insufficient on its own and called for greater commitment by the U.S. government to raising concerns about violence against women in its bi- and multilateral meetings with other governments.

While the U.S. Congress was starting to remove violence against women from the cloaked secrecy of the family, at the special session of the U.N. General Assembly for the Beijing + 5 review, the U.S. failed to take a leadership role and rally opposition when several governments sought to exempt violence to which women were exposed in the context of the family, or under the guise of religious or cultural practices, from being considered a human rights abuse. In a further failure of its purported leadership on women's rights, at Beijing + 5 the U.S. vigorously opposed and had removed from the final document reference to the rights of incarcerated women, arguing that this subject was not in the 1995 Beijing Platform for Action.

Nor did the U.S. play a strong leadership role on women's human rights in some key bilateral fora. For example, the U.S. government maintained only a nominal commitment to holding Mexico accountable for failing to enforce its labor code with regard to protecting women from sex discrimination based on their reproductive status. In 2000, the U.S. government was content to let the NAFTA review process proceed without intervening in any meaningful way to influence or direct it. As in past years, the U.S. government missed critical opportunities to strengthen the NAFTA review process. The U.S. failed to register an official complaint when Mexico used a National Agreement on Labor Cooperation (NAALC) meeting in Puebla, Mexico, to disseminate misinformation about employers having the right to test women workers for pregnancy if such testing is to protect the well-being of the woman or her fetus. The U.S. also failed to initiate any in-country monitoring to determine the veracity of Mexico's claims, and failed to ensure that concerned NGOS were kept informed in a timely manner about basic developments, such as the holding of public meetings to discuss women workers rights in Mexico. The final U.S. National Administrative Office report was more than a year overdue as of late October 2000.

European Union

The European Union evidenced some commitment to women's human rights, launching a U.S. $29.2 million community "action program" to combat violence against women and children. The grant program, a continuation of the DAPHNE program initiated in 1997, provided assistance to public institutions and NGOs fighting trafficking, domestic violence, and violence against minority groups and migrants. Open to states applying for membership in the community as well as member states, the mechanism provided funding to dozens of organizations working for women's human rights, including one group created to prevent violence against lesbians.

Council of Europe

The Council of Europe continued its efforts to combat the trafficking of women and children with Recommendation No. R. (2000) 11, adopted by the Committee of Ministers in May 2000. The recommendation encouraged Council of Europe member states to, inter alia, allow victims of trafficking to press charges with the benefit of witness protection, compensate victims with perpetrators' assets, grant temporary residence status with access to medical and social assistance, and support the creation of a NGO anti-trafficking network. Regrettably, the document focused only on trafficking into the sex industry, ignoring the phenomenon of trafficking for other forms of forced labor.

Organization for Security and Cooperation in Europe (OSCE)

Critics questioned the OSCE's commitment to women's human rights as the institution abruptly downgraded the position of gender adviser from the Office of the Secretary General to the personnel office. Several member states spearheaded an effort in 1997 to create a permanent position of gender adviser to monitor OSCE policies on women's human rights and combat gender discrimination within the institution. The arbitrary decision to remove the gender adviser from a policy-making role undermined the Vienna-based gender adviser's ability to press for progress on issues ranging from sexual harassment to improved monitoring of women's human rights violations in the field. The much-vaunted internal sexual harassment policy, created in 1999, met with skepticism from staff members, who doubted the organization's commitment to the correct handling of complaints and feared negative consequences for using the mechanism. And for the third year in a row, the OSCE leadership refused to make public statistics on women's representation inside the OSCE's institutions, thwarting calls for transparency. While the OSCE adopted a substantive and ambitious gender action plan, the political will to implement the policy appeared to be sadly lacking.

The OSCE's backsliding on women's human rights internally contrasted with the new programs it initiated to combat trafficking and to train women political leaders in the field. The OSCE's Office for Democratic Institutions and Human Rights (ODIHR) funded a range of anti-trafficking projects in the Balkans, Central Asia, Central and Eastern Europe, and the former Soviet Union— many carried out in coordination with local NGOs with special expertise on trafficking. In addition, the Austrian government, acting as the OSCE chair in 2000, seconded its former minister for women's affairs, Dr. Helga Konrad, to ODIHR to chair the Stability Pact Task Force on Trafficking in Human Beings. OSCE offices in Central Asian countries provided training programs on human rights documentation and leadership skills to women human rights activists.

Relevant Human Rights Watch Reports:

Democratic Republic of the Congo: Eastern Congo Ravaged: Killing Civilians and Silencing Protest, 5/00

Japan: Owed Justice: Thai Women Trafficked into Debt Bondage in Japan, 9/00

Kuwait: Promises Betrayed: Denial of Rights of Bidun, Women, and Freedom of Expression, 10/00

Russian/Chechnya: "No Happiness Remains:" Civilian Killings, Pillage, & Rape in Alkhan-Yurt, 4/00

Tanzania: Seeking Protection; Addressing Sexual and Domestic Violence in Tanzania's Refugee Camps, 10/00

Federal Republic of Yugoslavia: Kosovo: Rape As a Weapon of "Ethnic Cleansing," 3/00

HUMAN RIGHTS WATCH

SPECIAL

ISSUES AND

CAMPAIGNS

ACADEMIC FREEDOM

The pursuit and dissemination of knowledge remained disproportionately dangerous activities as educators and their students were frequent targets of violence and repression sponsored or countenanced by regimes bent on stifling critical analysis and dissent. In the worst cases, these governments used intimidation, physical abuse, and imprisonment to punish campus-based critics, and, by example, to repress civil society. More commonly, governments pursued the same ends by silencing academics and censoring their teaching, research, and publication on important subjects. Many countries also continued to deny equal access to educational institutions to women and members of disfavored minority groups. Ten years after the landmark World Conference on Education for All held in Jomtien, Thailand, a similar gathering held in April in Dakar, Senegal, found that despite some improvements in literacy rates and access to education, in many countries buffeted by political instability or financial downturns, education remained out of reach of significant portions of the population.

Repression of Academics

Due to their role in addressing controversial questions and shaping public debate, educators and researchers in many countries faced imprisonment, torture, and even murder. These attacks were more broadly aimed at discouraging other academics from pursuing politically sensitive lines of inquiry and ultimately at blocking social debate and dissent.

Separatist violence in Aceh, Indonesia, was the context for the murder of Afwan Idris, rector of the Ar Raniry State Institute of Islamic Studies (IAIN), who was shot on September 16 at his home in Banda Aceh, Aceh's capital. Idris was considered a strong candidate for the province's governorship and served as a member of the independent commission set up by former Indonesian president Habibie to investigate past grave human rights abuses in Aceh. Under Idris' tenure, IAIN became a center for debate and discussion on Aceh's political status for a number of nongovernmental groups. Although at the time of writing no arrests had been made in connection with the murder, Acehnese NGOs reported that the motorcycle used by the gunmen was seen shortly after the shooting on the grounds of the Mobile Brigade (Brimob) police complex.

The Egyptian government conducted a campaign of intimidation against academics, apparently alarmed by the possibility of critical analysis of the country's October parliamentary elections. Authorities closed the Ibn Khaldun Center for Development Studies, a leading political science research center, on June 30, and detained sixteen of its staff, including Saad El-Din Ibrahim, chair of the Sociology Department at the American University in Cairo, for over five weeks without bringing any charges. The detainees were released on bail in mid-August, but several were rearrested on September 25 pursuant to various charges, ranging from accepting foreign funding without government approval (related to the Ibn Khaldun Center's financing by the European Union) to issuing negative statements about Egypt's internal situation. Ibrahim blamed the arrests on the Ibn Khaldun Center's documentation of widespread fraud during the previous Egyptian parliamentary elections.

As part of its broad pattern of attacks on academics, in March, the Egyptian Education Ministry docked the pay of thirty-six teachers and a headmaster, all from Qena in Upper Egypt, for having attended a training program aimed at promoting civic education. The teachers were fined amounts ranging from nineteen days' to two months' salary. At least one teacher was transferred to an administrative post. The training sessions were organized by the Group for Democratic Development, a leading Egyptian NGO, whose earlier academic seminar on transforming Islamicist groups into legitimate political groups was cancelled by government order in January. This harassment placed Egyptian academics and NGOs in a defensive position prior to the elections and prompted several NGOs to return grants from foreign funders, thus scaling back or altogether stopping their support of critical academic research.

The Chinese government also continued to control academic life and in some areas increased pressure on educators whose work touched on sensitive issues of religious and ethnic identity, for instance in Tibet and in Xinjiang, a western province with a predominantly Moslem Uighur population. On May 25, the head of a part-time Uighur school was detained in Urumqi and, because he conducted classes in Arabic that drew Moslem students, accused of opening a religious school, although the bulk of the school's activity consisted of literacy classes and courses in Chinese, English, Russian, and Japanese.

Censorship and Ideological Controls

The freedom of academics to research and teach was constrained in various countries either directly, through government control of faculty appointments, or indirectly, under stifling censorship laws. Events in 2000 demonstrated that regardless of the means used, constriction of scholarship drove away qualified academics and coarsened the quality of public debate.

Academics in Serbia chafed under government limits on their work. The University Act of 1998, imposed under pressure from former Yugoslav president Slobodan Milosevic, subjected faculty members to political oversight and deprived them of the right to select their administrators. At the time of writing, the act was still in force despite student demonstrations demanding its rescission. As a result of this law Belgrade University alone lost some 180 instructors and professors. One prominent example was Obrad Savic, a professor for twenty-two years and a leading proponent of democratic reform and academic freedom. On May 16, the university terminated his contract after not paying his salary since May 1998. The decision to terminate Savic came shortly after he had published and distributed a publication entitled "In Defense of the University," in which he criticized the Milosevic government's efforts to strangle free inquiry on university campuses. He postponed his most recent project, a series of international seminars on democracy organized in conjunction with the New School University in New York, fearing government retaliation against seminar participants. Savic told Human Rights Watch that he was given no opportunity to contest the university's decision to terminate his employment.

Tunisian authorities also sought to stifle political dissent when they dismissed prominent human rights activist Dr. Moncef Marzouki on July 29 from his post as professor of medicine at the University of Sousse. Marzouki, a former president of the Tunisian League for Human Rights (LTDH), was the spokesperson for the National Council on Liberties in Tunisia (CNLT). Marzouki received a notice of dismissal from the Ministry of Health one day after President Zine el-Abidine Ben Ali denounced critics of his government as "mercenaries" and "traitors." Marzouki's dismissal followed years of persecution: In 1993, the Tunisian government prohibited him from carrying out any medical research and closed down the Center for Community Medicine, which he had founded; in June 1999, he was abducted by plainclothes security officials and held incommunicado for several days.

Kuwaiti academics faced legal attacks against their exercise of freedom of expression instigated by religious conservative groups using vaguely worded articles in Kuwait's Penal Code and Press Law. These laws allow for sentences of up to one year in prison and a fine of up to 1,000 KD (U.S. $3,260) for disseminating "opinions that include sarcasm, contempt, or belittling of a religion or a religious school of thought, whether by defamation of its belief system or its traditions or its rituals or its instructions." Using these laws, on October 4, 1999, Kuwait's Misdemeanor Appeals Court sentenced

Ahmad al-Baghdadi, then chair of Kuwait University's Political Science Department and an expert in Islamic law and history, to one month in jail for a 1996 article in a Kuwait University student newspaper (*al-Sho'ula*). The article discussed popular acceptance of some religious notions in the context of a wider social debate regarding gender segregation in Kuwaiti universities. One day after being imprisoned, Baghdadi went on a hunger strike and had to be hospitalized four days later due to heart problems. On October 18, Amir Sheikh Jaber al-Ahmad al-Sabah, Kuwait's ruler, pardoned Baghdadi, who has since returned to teaching. Another instructor at Kuwait University, philosophy professor 'Aliya Shu'ayb, had her two-month prison sentence reduced to a 100 KD (U.S. $326) fine after she was found guilty of defaming religion in her collection of poetry, although the book had been in circulation since 1993. Shu'ayb contended that the charges against her stemmed from her studies of sexuality among students at Kuwait University.

A controversy in Hong Kong highlighted the precarious position of universities there as they faced the encroachment of central control by the territory's Beijing-appointed administration. Chung Ting-you, a prominent pollster and director of the Public Opinion Program at Hong Kong University (HKU), claimed on July 7 that HKU Vice-Chancellor Cheng Yiu-chung had pressured him on behalf of Chief Executive Tung Chee-hwa to cease polling popular support for the chief executive. Chung's surveys, which had revealed deteriorating popular support for Tung, had been attacked by pro-Beijing administrators and media as suffering from a "pro-democracy" bias. In a welcome move, HKU responded to intense student and public demands for an inquiry by convening an independent panel of three prominents jurists and academics to investigate the matter. The panel found on August 29 that Vice-Chancellor Cheng and Pro-Vice-Chancellor Wong Siu-lun had indeed pressured Chung. The two resigned as a result of the findings. Despite these resignations and the panel's inquiry,

several professors stated that the incident had signalled the academic community to avoid politically sensitive research.

India, too, witnessed a deterioration in its academic freedom as Muslim and Christian educational facilities came under attack in states governed by the Hindu nationalist Bharatiya Janata Party. At the institutional level, the BJP and its allies continued to implement their program of "Hinduizing" education by mandating Hindu prayers in certain state schools and revising text books to include anti-Islamic and anti-Christian propaganda. On April 9, police searching for two suspects attacked the Jamia Millia Islamia, a Muslim institution of higher education in Delhi, and ransacked the dormitories and vandalized the campus mosque.

Muslim educational facilities also remained under pressure in Turkmenistan, where the government of Saparmurad Niazov banned all private Muslim religious education unless provided by the officially sanctioned Muftiat. Niazov's educational plan also called for three-generation background checks of potential students' moral character and the abolition of the teaching of foreign languages in the country.

Suppression of Student Activism

Student groups constituted an important element of political life in many countries. While at times their actions took them far outside of academic concerns, more often students were subjected to scrutiny and repression because of their exposure to critical ideas and their ability to mobilize in the relative shelter of university campuses.

In Yugoslavia, students played a critical role in the electoral defeat of Slobodan Milosevic, whose government had increasingly targeted students in response to the development of a loosely-structured, student-led opposition movement known as Otpor (Resistance). Numerous university professors, human rights activists, artists, church representatives, and members of the Serbian Academy of Science and Arts publicly supported or joined the group. On May 16, Ivan Markovic, the former Yugoslav minister of telecommunications and a high official of the Yugoslav Left (JUL), one of the parties in Milosevic's ruling coalition, accused Otpor of being a "terrorist organization." Authorities soon dropped this charge after it proved untenable, but continued to harass Otpor. In May and June, the police detained and interrogated some 500 Otpor activists. Authorities stepped up their attacks in August as the September national elections approached and Otpor launched a campaign calling for a high turnout of young voters. Otpor claimed that police detained hundreds of its members in August alone and beat at least ten who were in custody. Furthermore, police refused to investigate attacks on Otpor activists by plainclothes thugs believed to have worked for the Milosevic government.

Iranian students also remained active in the ongoing struggle between reformists and conservatives. Repeated calls for self-restraint under the doctrine of "active calm" by students prevented a reprise of the bloody riots that engulfed several campuses in July 1999, although attacks on student activists by mobs reportedly connected to government security forces continued. In the worst such incident, on August 26 a mob attacked the seventh annual gathering of the largest student pro-reform organization, the Office for Consolidating Unity (Daftar Tahkim Vahdat), in the city of Khoramabad, and prevented prominent government critics Abdolkarim Soroush (a philosophy professor) and Mohsen Kadivar from addressing the group. Government forces at the scene were reportedly unable or unwilling to protect the students. Over the next several days of violence, dozens were injured and one police officer was killed.

In a troubling development, in Lebanon, which had enjoyed a relatively open academic environment in the Middle East, students demonstrating peacefully in Beirut for the withdrawal of Syrian military forces from Lebanon faced an unduly forceful reaction from Lebanese security forces. On April 17 and 18, army and security troops forcibly broke student-led demonstrations in Beirut, injuring thirteen people, two of them seriously. Military tribunals sentenced at least ten students to prison terms ranging from ten days to six weeks for distributing leaflets.

Access to Education

Equal access to education is one of the most widely recognized principles of international human rights law, enshrined in article 26 of the Universal Declaration of Human Rights and the subsequent international conventions implementing it, including the Convention against Discrimination in Education, article 13 of the International Covenant on Economic, Social, and Cultural Rights, and article 28 of the Convention on the Rights of the Child. The unfortunately broad catalogue of failures in achieving this ideal reflected the global prevalence of discrimination, especially when aggravated by conditions of poverty, conflict, and war.

On April 26, U.N. Secretary-General Kofi Annan launched a ten-year initiative on girls' education at the opening of the World Education Forum in Dakar, Senegal. Forum participants pledged to ensure that all children, especially girls, have access to quality basic education by 2015. Nevertheless, reports submitted by 180 countries regarding their educational systems showed that women and girls remained the most widespread victims of educational discrimination.

Information gathered by Human Rights Watch mirrored these findings on the range of obstacles blocking equal access to education by girls and women. These vary from the blatant discrimination by the Taliban in Afghanistan, which continued to bar females from all public educational institutions, to other less obvious though equally pernicious forms of discrimination around the globe. Human Rights Watch's research in South Africa confirmed reports that sexual violence in schools against girls created a culture of violence that discouraged girls from continuing their education. Turkey, Turkmenistan, and Uzbekistan continued to prohibit female students from wearing religious attire, thereby effectively blocking these students' access to educational facilities.

Discrimination on other grounds also was widespread. In the United States, lesbian, gay, bisexual and transgender students faced discrimination by their peers and, in some instances, public administrators. As set out more fully in the chapter on Children's Rights, these students were part of a large number of students around the world who were denied their right to education because of discrimination based on race, gender, religion, ethnicity, or nationality.

Ethnic discrimination against Roma continued on an institutional level in Eastern Europe and the Balkans, as Croatia, Macedonia, Bulgaria, Slovakia, Hungary, and the Czech Republic failed to provide equal access to educational facilities to Romani students and, in the latter two countries, channelled them toward corrective programs designed for mentally handicapped or learning disabled children in disproportionately high numbers.

Relevant Human Rights Watch Reports:

Tunisia: The Administration of Justice in Tunisia: Torture, Trumped-Up Charges and a Tainted Trial, 3/00
Turkey: Human Rights and European Union Accession Partnership, 9/00
United States: Fingers to the Bone: United States Failure to Protect Child Farmworkers, 5/00
Federal Republic of Yugoslavia: Curtailing Political Dissent: Serbia's Campaign of Violence and Harassment Against government Critics, 4/00

BUSINESS AND HUMAN RIGHTS

Introduction

The recognition that business and human rights were inextricably intertwined continued to grow throughout the year and moved beyond a simple debate over the need to adopt codes of conduct. Those companies that previously stated a commitment to human rights continued to develop programs to implement their policies. As in previous years, the apparel and footwear industry and the energy industry were the focus of scrutiny because of their long-standing problems.

However, the issue of business and human rights moved beyond the sole focus on corporations. Increasingly, governments—either individually or through multilateral institutions—became part of the effort to ensure that human rights were not sidelined by commercial considerations. Through court cases, scrutiny over the corrupting influence of oil revenues, or because of multilateral institutions' efforts to address these issues, governments emerged as a crucial actor in the debate over business and human rights.

The Apparel and Footwear Industry

As the U.S. and European apparel and footwear industry continued to develop and implement monitoring and compliance programs—principally through the development of the White House-sponsored Fair Labor Association (FLA), the Council on Economic Priorities (CEP) Social Accountability 8000 program (SA-8000), and the new Workers' Rights Consortium (WRC)—to ensure the rights of workers in the industry were respected throughout the world, controversies emerged about the effectiveness of the various initiatives. At the same time, litigation emerged as another method of ensuring corporate respect for workers' rights.

Controversy on College Campuses

Throughout the year, university students in the United States stepped up efforts to ensure that their schools did not sanction abusive labor practices through their apparel licensing agreements. Unlike previous years, however, the students focused their efforts on two key demands: that universities withdraw from the FLA, a monitoring body made up of corporations and human rights organizations, and instead join the newly formed Workers Rights Consortium (WRC), a monitoring body made up of student organizations, university officials, and labor organizations. These demands led to a heated debate over the quality of various voluntary monitoring organizations and was best epitomized by the actions of Nike in 2000.

On April 24, Phil Knight, Nike's chairman and chief executive officer, announced that he would not donate any more money to his alma mater, the University of Oregon, because the school had joined the WRC instead of the FLA, where Nike is a founding member. Previously, Knight donated approximately U.S. $50 million to the university and planned to donate millions more until the university joined the WRC. A few days later, on April 28, Nike terminated negotiations with the University of Michigan over the renewal of a six year multimillion dollar licensing agreement because of the university's support for the WRC.

On July 2, university professors stepped into the fray. Under the auspices of the Academic Consortium on International Trade (ACIT), more than 200 scholars wrote an open letter to universities stating concerns about the way decisions to join either the FLA or the WRC were made by universities and suggested that both initiatives may actually be detrimental to the cause of workers' rights. ACIT also urged universities to consider other initiatives such as SA-8000, to undertake more research and consultation before joining any particular monitoring group, and warned that raising wages of workers further may have detrimental effects because "the net result would be shifts in employment that will worsen the collective welfare of the very workers in poor countries who are supposed to be helped" by these initiatives. The FLA criticized ACIT, arguing that it had unfairly compared the FLA to the WRC. The WRC attributed ACIT's criticism to an effort to undermine the credibility of these initiatives since ACIT was not part of the decision-making process. While it was too early to assess whether any of these initiatives was completely adequate since none of them had been fully implemented, the controversies surrounding factory monitoring strongly suggested that these internecine disputes would continue in the absence of enforceable legal standards requiring corporations to respect workers' rights.

Litigation Against Apparel Companies

On June 2, the U.S. Ninth Circuit Court of Appeals overturned a lower court decision and ruled that twenty-three garment workers in Saipan could anonymously sue garment manufacturers because disclosing their identities could subject them to retaliation by employers, the Chinese government, and third-party "recruiting companies" since they had paid agents recruiting fees to migrate from China in order to work in Saipan; and allowed the case to be heard in Hawaii rather than in Saipan. The workers had filed a class action suit against twenty-two companies for violations of the Fair Labor Standards Act and accused apparel companies of conspiracy under the Racketeering Influenced Corrupt Organizations Act (RICO). Earlier, on March 28, eight defendants in the lawsuit: Calvin Klein Inc., Jones Apparel Group, Liz Claiborne Inc., The May Department Stores Company, Oshkosh B'Gosh Inc., Sears Roebuck and Company, Tommy Hilfiger USA Inc., and Warnaco Inc. agreed to a U.S. $5.7 million settlement with the plaintiffs that would be used to fund a rigorous independent monitoring program to monitor working conditions in Saipan. Previously, in 1999, Bryland L.P., Chadwick's of Boston, Cutter & Buck, The Dress Barn, Donna Karan Inc., Gymboree Corp., J. Crew Inc., Nordstrom Inc., Phillips Van-Heusen, and Polo Ralph Lauren also settled with the plaintiffs in exchange for funding an independent monitoring program. At this writing, Abercrombie & Fitch Inc., Associated Merchandising Corp., Brooks Brothers Inc., Gap Inc., J.C. Penney Co., Lane Bryant Inc., Levi-Strauss Inc., the Limited Inc., Talbots Inc., and Woolrich Inc. were among the companies that had yet to settle with the plaintiffs. Barring a comprehensive settlement, the trial was expected to begin in February 2001.

The Energy Industry

Oil prices rose sharply in 2000 to levels more than three times that of 1997-98 largely due to an imbalance between global supply and demand. As energy companies and energy exporting countries profited from the price rise, the energy industry increasingly recognized that these large revenue streams could negatively impact prospects for good governance, fiscal and political accountability, and human rights. In particular, large revenue streams generated by oil development provided an incentive for corrupt governments to subvert democratic processes and limit freedom of expression in order to evade public accountability. Two examples of this phenomenon were developments in Kazakhstan and Angola.

Kazakhstan

A corruption scandal involving President Nursultan Nazarbayev and his associates, coupled with a deteriorating human rights situation, strongly suggested that Nazarbayev was seeking to consolidate political and economic control over this oil-rich country—a key player in the development of Caspian pipelines—at the expense of good governance and human rights.

For example, on June 12, 2000, the United States Department of Justice (DOJ) requested information from the Swiss authorities regarding the "alleged use of U.S. banks to funnel funds belonging to certain oil companies through Swiss bank accounts and shell companies in Switzerland and the British Virgin Islands for ultimate transfer to present and former high-ranking officials of Kazakhstan," in order to determine whether these transactions violated the Foreign Corrupt Practices Act and the Racketeer Influenced and Corrupt Organizations Act (RICO) as well as U.S. money laundering and extortion statutes.

The DOJ cited transactions totaling U.S. $114,822,577 from March 1997 to September 1998, which were transferred from several international oil companies including Amoco Kazakhstan Petroleum Company, Amoco Kazakhstan (CPC) Inc. (both companies are now part of BP), Phillips Petroleum Kazakhstan, and Mobil Oil Corporation (now part of ExxonMobil), to James H. Giffen, a close associate of Nazarbayev and financial advisor to the Kazakh government. Giffen subsequently transferred U.S. $55,869,000 of these funds to accounts belonging to Akezhan Kazhegeldin, a former prime minister of Kazakhstan, Nurlan Balgimbaiev, another former prime minister and current president of the powerful state-owned KazakhOil company, and President Nursultan Nazarbayev, or their families. At this writing, Giffen, as a U.S. citizen and the conduit for these transfers, was the primary focus of the DOJ investigation. The DOJ had not determined whether any of the U.S. oil companies acted illegally.

During the period that these transactions took place (March 1997 to September 1998), the Nazarbayev government took action to undermine freedom of speech, assembly, and association in Kazakhstan to prevent independent media reporting of such activities, and to deny Kazakh citizens the right to express their opinions and change their government.

The government used six main methods to harass the independent media: it filed criminal charges of engaging in "criminal speech" against individuals and publications; confiscated publications for alleged violations of the Law on the Mass Media; bankrupted publications through the awarding of large libel damages to government officials; disrupted publications' activities through harassment by the tax inspectorate or the customs authorities, and by denying access to state printing and distribution networks; and through informal and formal censorship of reporters.

One particularly illustrative case concerned the independent newspaper *Dat*. On September 10, 1998 an Almaty district court found *Dat* guilty of criminal libel and ordered to pay 35 million tenge (approximately U.S. $457,000) to the head of the state-funded Kazakhstan-1 television channel. *Dat* routinely published articles on government corruption and in this case, reprinted an account of a July 7, 1997 press conference in which a former employee of Kazakhstan-1 claimed that the station misused government funds. After the decision, police seized *Dat's* computer equipment and other property, and froze its bank accounts. Five days after the court's decision, Phillips Petroleum Kazakhstan Ltd. transferred U.S. $30,000,000 into a Swiss account for its legitimate participation in the Caspian Offshore Oil Consortium. From these funds, U.S. $20,519,000 was then transferred to Giffen, who then transferred the funds to accounts in the British Virgin Islands belonging to companies registered to Nazarbayev and Balgimbaiev, according to the DOJ. The juxtaposition of these two events—the government's closing of *Dat* and the transactions involving Nazarbayev and Balgimbaiev—underscored the linkages between human rights and corruption.

The electoral process was also undermined. In May 1998, the Kazakh parliament adopted amendments to the Law on Elections requiring that potential candidates for elected office submit documents to the Central Electoral Commission certifying their mental health and barred from election any candidates who had been found guilty by a court of any administrative violations or of corruption. On October 7, 1998, less than a month after the last financial transaction, Nazarbayev, then fifty-eight, signed constitutional amendments that eliminated the sixty-five year age limit on officeholders, increased the president's term from five to seven years, and removed the 50 percent minimum public participation threshold for presidential elections that were part of the 1995 constitution. On October 8, 1998, Nazarbayev announced that presidential elections would be held on January 10, 1999—two years earlier than scheduled. Opposition candidates did not fare well. Three were barred from running, including former prime minister Kazhegeldin, because they had either violated administrative provisions regulating public meetings or participated in unregistered public organizations—laws that severely curtailed freedom of assembly and association. Kazhegeldin had left the government in 1997 after a dispute with Nazarbayev and emerged as the leading opposition political figure. Ultimately, Nazarbayev won the election with more than 79 percent of the vote and secured the presi-

dency until at least 2006. However, the Organization for Security and Cooperation in Europe (OSCE) refused to send observers because the election so clearly fell far short of international standards for free and fair elections.

On July 17, 2000, Swiss authorities confirmed that they had frozen accounts connected with the DOJ and their own investigations. The Swiss investigation began in 1999 following a request by the Kazakh government to seize the accounts of former prime minister Kazhegeldin, whom it accused of tax evasion, money laundering, and abuse of office. When investigating the allegations, the Swiss found far greater sums of money held in accounts controlled by Nazarbayev. They froze those accounts and identified an account controlled by Kazhegeldin's son-in-law that held approximately U.S. $6 million. Kazhegeldin said that he had originally tried to return the money to Nazarbayev, but could not, and left it undisturbed. Kazakh government officials denied that they held foreign bank accounts altogether and denounced reports that such accounts had been identified and frozen by U.S. and Swiss authorities.

These requests underscored the Kazakh government's hostility to political opponents and its ongoing efforts to harass the most visible opposition politician, Kazhegeldin, in particular. Kazakh authorities also requested Kazhegeldin's arrest and extradition to Kazakhstan to face money laundering and abuse of office charges while he was traveling through Moscow and Italy in September 1999 and July 2000, respectively. On both occasions, Kazhegeldin was briefly detained, but released after strong protests by the international community because the charges were believed to be politically motivated and improperly used the international police system (INTERPOL). Nevertheless, questions remained about the U.S. $6 million account linked to Kazhegeldin.

In addition to pursuing political opponents abroad, Nazarbayev signed a law on July 21 to grant himself lifetime powers, including rights to remain on the powerful Kazakh Security Council, to head the parliamentary assembly of Kazakh peoples, to make national addresses on television and before parliament, to attend government meetings, to advise any future president on policy matters, and to immunity from prosecution. Opposition parliamentarians strongly criticized the law and suggested that Nazarbayev was moving towards making himself president-for-life, like his counterpart Sapurmurad Niyazov in gas-rich Turkmenistan.

Angola

On April 3, 2000, as part of a larger agreement on economic reform, the International Monetary Fund (IMF) and the Angolan government reached an agreement to monitor oil revenues, known as the "Oil Diagnostic," that would be supervised by the World Bank and implemented by KPMG, an international accounting firm that also had the Angolan central bank as a client. It was an effort by the international financial institutions to assess the percentage of government oil revenues that were deposited in the Central Bank. The Angolan budget had previously been opaque, raising concerns among multilateral financial institutions, NGOs, companies, and governments that oil revenues were being used secretly to finance arms purchases and that future oil production was mortgaged for immediate oil-backed loans. Some oil revenues bypassed the Ministry of Finance and the Central Bank and went directly to the state-owned Sociedade Nacional de Combustiveis de Angola (Sonangol) company, or to the Presidency to procure weapons. These payments being secret, they also sparked allegations of official corruption. More such allegations emerged in June 2000 when André Tarallo, former Africa director of France's Elf Aquitaine (now TotalFina-Elf), testified to French authorities investigating corruption charges against the company that the Elf Corporation had paid large sums (up to U.S. $0.40/barrel) to African leaders, including Angolan President José Eduardo dos Santos, primarily through a slush fund the company held in Liechtenstein. Dos Santos and TotalFina-Elf vigorously denied the allega-

tions.

In this context, Angolan government attacks on the rights to freedom of expression and association undermined these and other rights and targeted journalists' efforts to ensure governmental accountability. Gustavo Costa, of the Portuguese-language newspaper *Expresso*, for example, was charged with defamation and slander for writing about cabinet corruption in April 1999, and on December 24, 1999 received a suspended prison sentence, was fined U.S. $508 and ordered to pay U.S. $2,000 compensation for "defaming the Chief of the Civil Office of the President, Jose Leitao." Costa's trial was closed to the public and the media, and he complained that he was pressured to reveal his sources. His lawyer lodged an appeal to the Supreme Court, but it had yet to be heard.

In September 2000, the Angolan government introduced a new press law that severely restricted freedom of expression. It prescribed sentences of two to eight years of imprisonment for any journalist who impugns the president's honor or reputation; allows the authorities the right to determine who can work as a journalist; empowers them to seize or ban publications, including foreign publications, at their discretion; and allows the arrest and detention of journalists for thirty days before charges are filed. The law also removed truth as a defense against libel involving the president or office of the president, enabling the authorities to imprison journalists who write accurate reports if these are deemed to impugn the president's honor or reputation. The law was reportedly intended to curtail increased domestic press questioning of the government following the publication of a report by a U.K.-based NGO, Global Witness, exposing the links between oil and high levels of government corruption involving President Dos Santos and his associates.

Despite such censorship, however, public dissatisfaction over government mismanagement grew in Angola; and the *Economist Intelligence Unit* (EIU), reported in August 2000 that "public criticism of the government has grown noticeably, particularly focusing on official corruption.... The resurgent peace movement has also been active in articulating growing exasperation with the country's political leadership over the impression that the country's enormous, and growing, oil wealth has failed to produce any tangible benefits to the general population."

The IMF/World Bank Oil Diagnostic, scheduled to run from September 2000 until late 2002, was a partial response to questions about the government's use—or misuse—of oil revenues. The success of the oil diagnostic would hinge on the quality of information provided to KPMG by the government and informed third-parties, such as the international oil companies. Yet, several weaknesses limited the agreement's effectiveness. Rather than agree to a full-scale audit of its oil revenues, Angola's government agreed to a basic agreement that would only compare projected oil revenues with the actual amount of money deposited in the central bank. The oil diagnostic would not have the capacity to trace the flow of funds out of the central bank, nor to investigate the use of any funds that were generated by oil revenues that were not deposited in the central bank, such as those previously funnelled through the Presidency or Sonangol for covert arms purchases. Further, the terms of reference and the reports of the oil diagnostic—a baseline report conducted in September, followed by quarterly updates, and a final report in late 2002—were not to be made publicly available, despite the agreement's purported aim to increase transparency and government accountability.

The Role of the International Community

Two key developments within multilateral institutions highlighted a growing awareness that these institutions must address business and human rights: the launch of the U.N. Global Compact and a decision by the European Bank for Reconstruction and Development (EBRD) to suspend public sector lending to Turkmenistan because of its refusal to move to a multiparty democracy. These efforts sent a strong message that the multilateral institutions supported corporate responsibility and good governance, but they did not show that these institutions would consistently apply strong standards to ensure adherence. At the same time, U.S. courts began to address the parameters of corporate liability for human rights violations.

United Nations Global Compact

On July 26, U.N. Secretary-General Kofi Annan convened a meeting with the heads of U.N. agencies, corporations, labor unions, and NGOs to launch the U.N. Global Compact, a voluntary initiative to promote corporate responsibility and cooperation between companies and the U.N. Comprising a set of nine principles that supporting corporations were required to endorse, coupled with minimal reporting requirements, and supporting guidelines that were intended to ensure that corporations "complicit" in human rights violations would not be allowed to partner with the U.N. The Global Compact was hailed by the U.N. as a major step forward in pushing corporations to respect human rights, including labor rights, and environmental protection, and to promote "partnerships" between the U.N., corporations, labor unions, and NGOs. However, it was criticized by NGOs, including those that participated in the July 26 meeting, because it did not contain any independent monitoring mechanisms to assess the conduct of corporations; the guidelines were too vague and did not adequately ensure that companies complicit in human rights violations would be barred from partnership with the U.N.; and that the weaknesses in the compact could enable companies to garner favorable publicity, or "bluewash" their image by securing the use of the U.N. logo, without having to adequately improve their human rights, labor rights, or environmental performance. In addition to highlighting these shortcomings, Human Rights Watch called on the U.N. to begin the process of developing binding standards on corporations, rather than solely relying on the voluntary Global Compact.

European Bank for Reconstruction and Development and Turkmenistan

In a stunning rebuke of the dictatorship under Turkmenistan's president-for-life, Sapurmurad Niyazov, the European Bank for Reconstruction and Development (EBRD) indefinitely suspended lending to the government on April 19 while continuing private sector lending. The EBRD justified its decision because of the government's failure to implement economic reforms and because "[t]here has been no progress towards a pluralist or democratic political system, as President Niyazov retains a firm grip on power, not properly balanced by the country's legislature or judiciary. Most disturbingly, President Niyazov was made President for life in December 1999."

Events leading up to the EBRD decision were almost comical. Earlier in April, an EBRD delegation tried to meet with Niyazov to discuss economic and political reforms and future lending by the bank. Niyazov rebuffed their requests and then told the media that, "[t]he issue put by the European Bank is as follows: You have to increase the price of petrol and do things as they are done in Europe, and the second issue is to establish a multiparty system in your country and that is one of our conditions. I said that they were bank clerks. I have not received them. I said that I did not want to discuss such things with them." Following this snub, Charles Frank, then acting president of the EBRD, announced that "[t]he President's refusal even to discuss the question of political reform suggests that the Government of Turkmenistan is not committed to one of the basic principles upon which the EBRD was founded," and promptly cut off public sector lending. While the decision sent a clear message that the EBRD could act strongly on the issue of multiparty democracy, it remained to be seen whether the bank would take the same approach with other client governments that were hostile to democracy, such as Azerbaijan and Kazakhstan.

Doe v. Unocal

On August 31, U.S. District Judge Ronald Lew ruled on a summary judgement motion in the closely watched Doe v. Unocal case that was originally filed in 1997. The plaintiffs argued that Unocal, a California-based oil company, was liable under the Alien Tort Claims Act (ATCA) for human rights violations, including forced relocations, forced labor, rape, and torture "perpetrated by the Burmese military in furtherance and for the benefit of the pipeline." This arose from the company's participation in the joint-venture that constructed and operated the Yadana gas pipeline that runs from Burma to Thailand. Security for the project was provided by the Burmese military, who committed human rights abuses while fulfilling their security role. Although Judge Lew found that the "evidence does suggest that Unocal knew that forced labor was being utilized and that the Joint Venturers benefitted from the practice," he dismissed the suit because of insufficient evidence that Unocal had actively participated in or conspired with the Burmese military to commit human rights violations, and because Unocal's joint-venture with the Burmese government did not make it legally liable for human rights violations committed by the Burmese military. At this writing, the plaintiffs planned to appeal the decision to the Ninth Circuit Court of Appeals. The other joint-venture partners: Total of France (now TotalFina-Elf), the Myanma Oil and Gas Enterprise, and the Petroleum Authority of Thailand, were not defendants in this case because the court ruled that it did not have jurisdiction over foreign companies.

CHILD SOLDIERS CAMPAIGN

Seventeen-year-old Abubakar (not his real name) was one of thousands of children abducted by the Revolutionary United Front (RUF) during the recent conflict in Sierra Leone. Abubakar took part in fighting and was often forced to commit abuses. In one instance, he and others were ordered by their commander to burn down an entire town after a counterattack on the RUF by government helicopters. "It was not my wish to go fight, it was because they captured me and forced me," he told Human Rights Watch. "There was no use in arguing with them, because in the RUF if you argue with any commander they will kill you."

Like Abubakar, an estimated 300,000 girls and boys under the age of eighteen were fighting in armed conflicts in approximately thirty countries. These young combatants served in government forces, pro-government militias, and armed opposition groups. Their ranks included children as young as eight recruited into Colombia's paramilitaries, teenaged boys forcibly taken from their villages in Myanmar to serve in the national army, and young girls kidnapped by the Lord's Resistance Army in Northern Uganda for use as soldiers and sex slaves.

In a breakthrough in efforts to end the use of child soldiers, six years of negotiations led to agreement on January 21 on a new optional protocol to the Convention on the Rights of the Child. The protocol established eighteen as the minimum age for direct participation in hostilities, for compulsory recruitment, and for any recruitment or use in hostilities by nongovernmental armed groups.

Agreement on the protocol was a tremendous achievement for the Coalition to Stop the Use of Child Soldiers, which had aggressively campaigned for a global ban on the use of children as soldiers. The coalition was founded by Human Rights Watch and five other international organizations in 1998 and subsequently grew to encompass national partners and campaigns in more than thirty countries.

The protocol marked a significant advance over previous international standards, which permitted children as young as fifteen to be legally recruited and sent to war. The new protocol established a clear standard that any use of children in war was unacceptable, and provided a critical new basis for exerting public and political pressure against governments and armed groups that use children in armed conflict.

The biggest weakness of the protocol was its failure to establish eighteen as the minimum age for voluntary recruitment into government armed forces. The protocol required states to raise the minimum age for voluntary recruitment from the previous minimum of fifteen, and to implement certain safeguards when recruiting under-eighteens including parental permission and proof of age. States were also required to deposit a binding declaration at the time of ratification stipulating the state's minimum age for voluntary recruitment.

The coalition, along with U.N. agencies and the International Committee of the Red Cross, had consistently campaigned for a prohibition of any recruitment or participation in hostilities by children under the age of eighteen, arguing that the only way to ensure that children do not participate in war is to not recruit them in the first place. But many governments based their positions during the negotiations on their existing military recruitment practices, and insisted on the right to continue recruiting under-age volunteers. The resulting provision created an unfortunate double-standard, allowing governments to recruit under-eighteens, but prohibiting nongovernmental armed forces from doing so.

The negotiations on the protocol were marked by a significant shift in the United States position. After six years of vigorous opposition to eighteen as the minimum age for participation in armed conflict, the U.S. reversed itself and agreed for the first time to end the deployment of U.S. troops who were under eighteen into combat and to support the protocol. This was the first time that the United States had ever agreed to change its practices in order to support a human rights standard.

The protocol was formally adopted by the U.N. General Assembly on May 25, and opened for signature in early June. By the close of the U.N. Millennium Summit, held in New York from September 6-8, sixty-eight countries had signed the new protocol, and three (Canada, Bangladesh, and Sri Lanka) had ratified it.

The coalition announced that it would

campaign for universal ratification of the protocol and urge states to deposit binding declarations upon ratification setting a minimum age of at least eighteen for voluntary recruitment. It set an initial target of one hundred signatures by the first anniversary of the protocol's adoption on May 25, 2001, and fifty ratifications by the time of the September 2001 U.N. General Assembly Special Session on Children.

During the Millennium Summit, the coalition drew attention to the use of child soldiers and the new protocol by unveiling a special "children's war memorial" during a ceremony attended by more that twenty governments. The memorial was inscribed with the name, age, and country of scores of child soldiers killed, wounded, missing, or detained in armed conflicts around the world. Those attending the ceremony included the president of Mali, the prime ministers of New Zealand and Sweden, the first ladies of Ecuador and Norway, and representatives from fifteen other governments.

The coalition also held the fourth in a series of regional conferences on the use of children as soldiers, following previous conferences in 1999 for Africa, Latin America, and Europe. The Asia-Pacific conference was held from May 15 to 18 in Kathmandu, Nepal. Representatives of twenty-four governments (including Australia, Bangladesh, Cambodia, China, Japan, North Korea, South Korea, India, Indonesia, Kazakhstan, Laos, Nepal, Pakistan, the Philippines, Sri Lanka, and Thailand) and more than one hundred delegates from NGOs across the region attended the conference, together with representatives of UNICEF and other agencies.

The coalition released a new report at the conference on the use of children as soldiers in the region, estimating that at least 75,000 children under the age of eighteen were participating in conflicts in Asia and the Pacific, placing the region second only to Africa in the use of children as soldiers. The report named Burma as one of the largest users of child soldiers in the world, and Afghanistan, Cambodia, and Sri Lanka as some of the other worst affected countries.

The conference concluded with a strong declaration in support of the new Optional Protocol, calling on states to ratify it without reservations and specify at least eighteen years as the minimum age for voluntary recruitment. Delegates called on government armed forces and armed groups to immediately demobilize or release into safety child soldiers. They also urged tight controls on the availability of small arms, including the sanctioning of those supplying forces using children in this way.

Human Rights Watch, which had chaired the coalition since its inception, continued to play a leadership role in the global campaign to end the use of child soldiers. Human Rights Watch participated in briefings for the press, representatives of the Organization of American States, and members of the U.N. Security Council. It spoke at numerous events, including the Asia-Pacific regional conference in Kathmandu, and the International Conference on War-Affected Children, held in Winnipeg, Canada in September 2000. Human Rights Watch's Brussels office took the lead in the coalition's advocacy with the European Union, European Parliament, and the OSCE, and lobbied OSCE member states in favor of a strong ministerial decision on children and armed conflict.

Human Rights Watch also maintained a strong role with the U.S. Campaign to Stop the Use of Child Soldiers. It helped influence the United States' change of position regarding the Optional Protocol and the age of deployment for U.S. troops, and worked with the Clinton administration and Congress to support U.S. ratification of the protocol. Congressional resolutions were adopted by the Senate in June, and the House of Representatives in July, urging the United States' signature and swift consideration for ratification. President Clinton signed the protocol on July 5 at the U.N., and submitted it to the Senate later that month; at the time of this writing, the Senate Foreign Relations Committee had taken no action.

HUMAN RIGHTS WATCH INTERNATIONAL FILM FESTIVAL

The Human Rights Watch International Film Festival was created in 1988 to advance public education on human rights issues and concerns using the unique medium of film. Each year, the festival exhibits the finest films and videos with human rights themes in theaters and on cable television throughout the United States and elsewhere—a reflection of both the scope of the festival and its increasing global appeal. The 2000 festival featured thirty films (twenty-two of which were premieres), from twelve countries. The festival included feature-length fiction films, documentaries, and animation. In 2000, selections from the festival were presented in four countries and within the U.S. selected films showcased in ten cities.

In selecting films for the festival, Human Rights Watch concentrates equally on artistic merit and human rights content. The festival encourages filmmakers around the world to address human rights subject matter in their work and presents films and videos from both new and established international filmmakers. Each year, the festival's programming committee screens more than 500 films and videos to create a program that represents a range of countries and issues. Once a film is nominated for a place in the program, staff of the relevant division of Human Rights Watch also view the work to confirm its accuracy in the portrayal of human rights concerns. Though the festival rules out films that contain unacceptable inaccuracies of fact, we do not bar any films on the basis of a particular point of view.

The 2000 festival was first presented over a two-week period in New York, as a collaborative venture with the Film Society of Lincoln Center, and then selections from the festival were presented at the Northwest Film Center in Portland, Oregon and several other cities throughout the U.S. The 2000 festival reached out to a broader audience by co-presenting selected films with five important New York festivals (the African Film Festival, the Margaret Mead Film Festival, and the New York Latino Film Festival, The New Festival/New York Lesbian and Gay Film Festival, the Urban World Film Festival) and several independent media organizations (the Educational Video Center, Free Speech TV, Paper Tiger TV and POV/The American Documentary). A majority of the screenings were followed by discussions with the filmmakers, media activists, and Human Rights Watch staff on the issues represented in each work.

Two documentaries featured in this year's festival had dramatic effects in their countries of origin. Following the recent theatrical release and television airing of Irit Gal's documentary *Harmed Forces*, the Israeli Parliament re-categorized Israeli Defense Force veterans with post-traumatic stress disorder (PTSD)) as "military disabled" rather than "mentally ill," which enabled these veterans to receive Israeli disability benefits and Social Security Insurance. "Harmed Forces" is an intimate documentary portral of two former Israeli soldiers who still suffer from post-traumatic stress disorder following their military service in Israel's 1982 campaign in Lebanon. The Argentine documentary *Spoils of War*, which chronicles the ongoing courageous efforts of the "Grandmothers of the Plaza de Mayo" from the early 1970s until today, helped several families reunite with relatives who were "disappeared" during that country's dirty war.

The 2000 opening night celebration presented the New York premiere of the screen adaptation of Anna Deveare Smith's *Twilight: Los Angeles,* her one-woman/multi-voiced portrait of the violence triggered in Los Angeles by the acquittal in 1992 of four police officers in the beating of Rodney King. Acclaimed documentary filmmaker Marc Levin directed Smith's tour-de-force performance.

As part of the opening night program, the festival annually awards a prize in the name of cinematographer and director Nestor Almendros, who was also a cherished friend of the festival and Human Rights Watch. The award, which includes a cash prize of U.S. $5,000 goes to a deserving and courageous filmmaker in recognition of his or her contributions to human rights through film. The 2000 festival awarded the Nestor Almendros Prizes to Randa Chahal Sabbag, for her stunning feature debut, *A Civilized People* (*Civilisees*). The film is a tragicomic story of the experiences of a diverse group of characters during the Lebanese civil war. Currently, the Lebanese government has asked Chahal Sabbag to cut forty-seven minutes of this film, claiming that these sections are offensive and inflammatory. Chahal Sabbag refuses to cut (re-edit) her film and to date the film has still not been allowed to screen in Lebanon.

In 1995, in honor of Irene Diamond, a longtime board member and supporter of Human Rights Watch, the festival launched the Irene Diamond Lifetime Achievement award, which is presented annually to a director whose life's work demonstrates an outstanding commitment to human rights and film. Previous recipients have included Costa Gavras, Ousmane Sembene, Barbara Kopple, and Alan J. Pakula. This year, the award was presented to American filmmaker Frederick Wiseman. Wiseman, one of the greatest living documentary filmmakers, has created an exceptional body of work consisting of thirty full-length films devoted primarily to exploring American institutions—from the armed services to hospitals, from welfare to the high school system, from public parks to whole cities and public housing projects. Wiseman is an unflinchingly honest filmmaker, who has repeatedly stared down painful truths that many artists either can not or will not address. Throughout his work, Wiseman has told the story of his country's idiosyncracies, flaws, strengths, and tragedies.

Highlights of the 2000 festival included two films dealing with the plight of those "disappeared" under Argentina's military dictatorship: David Blausetein's extraordinary documentary *Spoils of War,* which we described in the preceding pages, and *Garage Olimpo*, the dramatic feature by formerly exiled Argentinean Marco Bechis. *Garage Olimpo* tells the story of a young woman kidnapped and tortured in a clandestine Buenos Aires prison and her efforts to survive no matter what the costs. Other highlights included, *Made in the YoUth S.A.* and *ICC: A Call for Justice*, two short films conceived and produced by youth producers in consultation with Human Rights Watch. Both short video had their world premieres at this year's festival and played to sold-out audiences. This year's closing night screening included the New York premiere of Jens Meruer's *Public Enemy*, a fascinating look at the Black Panther movement through the recollections of four of its most outspoken members: co-founder Bobby Seale, law professor Kathleen Cleaver (the highest ranking female Panther), prisoner-turned-playwright Jamal Joseph, and musician and record producer Nile Rodgers.

Each year the festival holds a series of special film screenings for high school students and their teachers in an effort to encourage dialogue about human rights in the classroom. Daytime screenings are followed by discussions among the students, their teachers, visiting filmmakers, and Human Rights Watch staff. In 2000, the program included a special collaborative screening of short films from Africa with the New York African Film Festival.

In 1996, the festival expanded to London. The 2000 London festival produced with the Ritzy Theater in Brixton showcased the United Kingdom premiere of David O. Russell's *Three Kings*, an ironic and powerful drama about the involvement of United States soldiers in the Gulf War.

The festival overall was extremely successful with a timely screening of *A Cry from the Grave*, about the massacre in the Bosnian town of Srebrenica in July 1995 and the major effort by the International War Crimes Tribunal to find and prosecute the perpetrators. The festival closed with a special screening of Norman Jewison's *The Hurricane,* starring Academy Award winner Danzel Washington as Rubin "Hurricane" Carter, a man wrongly accused and sentenced to three life terms of imprisonment.

In a further effort to expand the festival's scope, the Global Showcase, a selected package of traveling films from the festival, was created in 1994. The Global Showcase is presented annually in a growing number of sites and cities around the world. The 2000 showcase traveled internationally to Sydney and Melbourne, Australia; Lodz, Poland; Cairo, Egypt; and Beirut, Lebanon. In the United States the showcase has been presented in Houston, Texas; St. Louis, Missouri; Albuquerque, New Mexico; Boulder, Colorado; Amherst, Massachusetts; Chicago, Illinois; Memphis, Tennessee; Salt Lake City, Utah; Portland, Oregon; Seattle, Washington; and Rochester, New York. The traveling festival plans extensive expansion in Boston, Massachusetts and San Francisco, California in January of 2001.

INTERNATIONAL CAMPAIGN TO BAN LANDMINES

The International Campaign to Ban Landmines (ICBL), launched in 1992 by Human Rights Watch and five other nongovernmental organizations, brought together over 1,400 human rights, humanitarian, children's, peace, disability, veterans, medical, humanitarian mine action, development, arms control, religious, environmental, and women's groups in over ninety countries who worked locally, nationally, regionally, and internationally to ban antipersonnel landmines. The ICBL was coordinated by an international committee of fourteen organizations, including Human Rights Watch, which remained one of the most active campaign members. The ICBL and its then coordinator Jody Williams (a member of the Advisory Committee of the Human Rights Watch Arms Division) were jointly awarded the 1997 Nobel Peace Prize.

Progress toward the complete eradication of antipersonnel mines continued at an impressive pace, and the ICBL continued its intense global activity. Perhaps most notable were the further development of the ICBL's groundbreaking Landmine Monitor system, and the ICBL's extensive involvement in the intersessional work program of the 1997 Mine Ban Treaty.

Campaign priorities were universalization of the Mine Ban Treaty—convincing recalcitrant nations to accede to the treaty—and ensuring effective implementation of the treaty. Particular targets were states of the former Soviet Union and the Middle East/North Africa, as well as the United States. Key issues of concern included: how to respond to violations of the ban treaty; antivehicle mines with antihandling devices which are prohibited by the treaty; joint military operations between States Parties and nonsignatories using mines; and continued stockpiling and transit of mines by nonsignatories in the territory of States Parties. Other priorities included: promoting increased funding for sustainable and appropriate mine action programs; promoting increased funding for comprehensive victim assistance programs and greater involvement of mine victims and mine-affected communities in the planning and implementation of such programs; and exploring ways to encourage non-state actors to commit to the banning of antipersonnel mines.

Four permanent working groups and one ad hoc working group of the ICBL led these efforts to address the various aspects of the humanitarian landmines crisis. They were the Treaty Working Group (chaired by Human Rights Watch), the Working Group on Victim Assistance, the Mine Action Working Group, and the Non-State Actors Working Group, as well as the ad hoc Ethics and Justice Working Group.

Regional and thematic conferences were held to continue to build public awareness and further various aspects of the ban movement. Regional conferences, either held by ICBL members or where ICBL members participated, were held in Azerbaijan, Belarus (on stockpile destruction), Croatia, Egypt, Georgia, Malaysia, and Slovenia. National seminars or workshops were held in India, Iran, Japan, Nepal, Nigeria, and the U.S. As for thematic conferences, members of the ICBL held a follow-up conference in Germany to continue to develop the Bad Honnef concept of mine action and development, while others held a conference in Switzerland to engage non-state actors in the landmine ban.

New campaigners in countries including Cameroon, Côte d'Ivoire, Chile, Iran, Nigeria, Poland, Sierra Leone, Slovenia, Syria, and Togo began activities, as did a new group, Refugees Against Landmines, among Chechen refugees in Georgia; new work was also being carried out in Nagorno-Karabakh. The second anniversary of the opening for signature of the Mine Ban Treaty galvanized campaigners into action worldwide, as on December 3, 1999, activities were held around the globe, from theater and basketball games between disabled teams in Angola, to exhibits in South Korea and special hockey matches in the U.S. Similarly, the first anniversary of the entry into force of the treaty on March 1, 2000, further spurred action worldwide. A concerted ratification campaign included a coordinated letter-writing campaign with other partners, embassy visits, and various activities and media events in thirty-three countries around the world.

Additionally, ICBL members undertook a number of advocacy and awareness-building missions, including traveling to Kosovo, Korea, the United Arab Emirates, and Belgium (for the European Council and Parliament). The ICBL sent letters to heads of state and engaged in other advocacy activities on the occasions of international events such as the Francophone summit in Moncton, New Brunswick; the U.N. General Assembly in New York; the Special Summit of the European Council on the establishment of an area of Freedom, Security, and Justice in Finland; the Helsinki Summit of the European Union; the Organization of American States Summit; the Organization of African Unity Summit; the Inter-Parliamentary Union; and the As-

sembly of African Francophone Parliamentarians. Letters to heads of state were also sent on the occasions of the December 3 and March 1 anniversaries urging governments to accede to or ratify the treaty, destroy their stocks, submit their transparency report as required under the treaty's article 7, and increase funding for mine action and victim assistance. The ICBL also issued regular action alerts.

The campaign committed to significant ICBL participation in the intersessional work program established in May 1999 at the First Meeting of States Parties. ICBL Working Groups took the lead in liaising with the five Standing Committees of Experts (SCEs). The intersessional work program was aimed at consolidating and concentrating global mine action efforts and highlighting the role of the Mine Ban Treaty as a comprehensive framework for mine action. The five SCEs served to facilitate the implementation of provisions of the Mine Ban Treaty, with extensive input, recommendations, and action points from NGOs. The five Standing Committees of Experts on Victim Assistance, Socio-economic Reintegration and Mine Awareness; Mine Clearance; Stockpile Destruction; Technologies for Mine Action; and the General Status and Operation of the Convention each met two times in the intersessional period between the first and second meetings of States Parties. The intersessional work proved to be an important mechanism to both spur and measure progress made in the full implementation of the Mine Ban Treaty. In September 2000 the Second Meeting of States Parties was held in Geneva, resulting in an extensive action program for the coming year.

Just prior to the Geneva meeting, the ICBL released the 1,100-page *Landmine Monitor Report 2000*, the second annual report to emerge from the Landmine Monitor system. The Landmine Monitor network grew to 115 researchers in ninety-five countries, and the system and the annual report were widely recognized as a crucial element in addressing the landmine crisis.

Between November 1999 and October 2000, the number of nations ratifying the

Mine Ban Treaty grew from eighty-seven to 107, and a total of 139 countries had signed, ratified, or acceded to the treaty. But notable states such as the United States, Russia, and China continued to stay outside of the emerging international norm against the antipersonnel mine.

INTERNATIONAL JUSTICE

Introduction

The emerging system of international justice was further strengthened in 2000. Despite the British government's release of General Augusto Pinochet from custody in March, the litigation surrounding the requests for his extradition produced important additional consequences. The four states that had sought his extradition from London, Belgium, France, Spain, and Switzerland all successfully challenged, before a British court, the decision by Jack Straw, the home affairs minister, not to disclose Pinochet's medical records. In an illustrative example of the synergy between justice at the international level and increased access to national courts, the Chilean Supreme Court in August lifted Pinochet's parliamentary immunity and opened the way to his trial before the courts there. This synergy took another form in West Africa. In February, Senegalese authorities arrested former Chadian leader Hissène Habré on charges of torture in Chad during the 1980s. While a court dismissed the indictment in July, the decision was appealed in Dakar. Inspired by the litigation in the Senegalese court, Chadian victims moved to bring cases against Habré's accomplices to court in Chad. In August, reflecting greater international cooperation on these justice issues, Mexican authorities, responding to a request from a Spanish judge, arrested Ricardo Cavallo, an Argentinian accused of torture during the "Dirty War."

Meanwhile, the International Criminal Tribunal for Yugoslavia (ICTY) obtained custody of senior indictees, including Momcilo Krajisnik, the wartime president of the Bosnian Serb assembly and the highest ranking politician arrested so far. With the fall of the Milosevic government in Belgrade in October, the possibility increased that Slobodan Milosevic, Ratko Mladic, Radovan Karazdic, and other senior indictees from Yugoslavia would be apprehended and held to account in The Hague. During 2000, the new government of Croatia undertook to cooperate more closely with the ICTY by transferring a Croatian indictee to the tribunal and allowing it to carry out investigations on Croatian territory of alleged crimes against Serbs in 1991. The International Criminal Tribunal for Rwanda convicted three defendants of genocide as it took measures to reform its procedures to facilitate greater efficiency. The jurisprudence and judicial practice of the ad hoc tribunals enriched the work of the Preparatory Commission for the International Criminal Court as it drafted the Rules of Procedure and Evidence and Elements of Crimes for the ICC. In response to horrific crimes, new, mixed judicial mechanism were established. The United Nations Security Council authorized the creation of a mixed national-international tribunal to prosecute human rights criminals in war-torn Sierra Leone. In Cambodia, the United Nations continued negotiations with the Hun Sen government to ensure that the mixed national-international tribunal being established there to try Khmer Rouge leaders adhered to international standards for fair trial. Momentum for the early establishment of the International Criminal Court (ICC), a cornerstone of a strengthened system of international justice, grew dramatically. The process of ratifying the ICC Treaty highlighted another aspect of the intersection of justice on the international plane and the national level. As states began adopting the implementing legislation necessary to make cooperation with the permanent international court meaningful, they seized the opportunity to amend domestic criminal law to strengthen prosecution of genocide, crimes against humanity, and war crimes by national courts.

Human Rights Watch was encouraged by these and other developments, but recognized the serious challenges ahead. Prosecuting human rights criminals on the basis of universal jurisdiction regardless of a territorial or nationality nexus required a solid commitment of political will and the process was subject to corruptive political interference. States lacked appropriate domestic legislation to allow them to pursue these cases, while others were reluctant to invoke universal jurisidiction even for the most egregious human rights crimes. While the two existing ad hoc tribunals, with a limited geograhical mandate, continued to deepen the jurisprudence of international humanitarian law and practice, their work was hampered by inconsistent support for apprehension of indictees. The balance shifted away from the impunity so often associated with these crimes, but further steps were needed to reinforce the trend toward accountability.

Prosecutions

Hissène Habré

In February 2000, a Senegalese court indicted Chad's exiled former dictator, Hissène Habré, on torture charges and placed him under house arrest. It was the first time that an African had been charged with atrocities against his own people by the court of another African country.

Habré ruled Chad from 1982 until he was deposed in 1990 by current president Idriss Deby and fled to Senegal. Since Habré's fall, Chadians have sought to bring him to justice. The Chadian Association of Victims of Political Repression and Crime (AVCRP) compiled information on each of 792 victims of Habré's brutality, hoping to use the cases in a prosecution of Habré. A 1992 truth commission report accused Habré's regime of 40,000 political murders and systematic torture. With many ranking officials of the Idriss Deby government, including Deby himself, involved in Habré's crimes, however, the new government did not pursue Habré's extradition from Senegal.

In 1999, with the Pinochet precedent in mind, the Chadian Association for the Promotion and Defense of Human Rights requested Human Rights Watch's assistance in bringing Habré to justice in Senegal. Researchers visited Chad twice, where they met victims and witnesses and benefited from the documentation prepared in 1991 by the Association of Victims. Meanwhile, Human Rights Watch quietly organized a coalition of Chadian, Senegalese, and international NGOs to support the complaint, as well as a group of Senegalese lawyers to represent the victims. Seven individual Chadians and one Frenchwoman, whose Chadian husband was killed by Habré's regime, acted as private plaintiffs, as did the AVCRP.

In a criminal complaint filed in Dakar Regional Court, the plaintiffs, several of whom came to Senegal for the event, officially accused Habré of torture and crimes against humanity. The torture charges were based on the Senegalese statute on torture as well as the 1984 Convention against Torture which Senegal ratified in 1987. The groups also cited Senegal's obligations under customary international law to prosecute those accused of crimes against humanity.

In the court papers presented to the Investigating Judge, the groups provided details of ninety-seven political killings, 142 cases of torture, and one hundred "disappearances," most carried out by Habré's dreaded DDS (Documentation and Security Directorate), as well as a 1992 report by a French medical team on torture under Habré, and the Chadian truth commission report. The organizations presented the sworn testimony of two former prisoners who were ordered by the DDS to dig mass graves to bury Habré's opponents. Two of the plaintiffs described being subjected to a torture method called the "Arbatachar," in which a prisoner's four limbs were tied together behind his back, leading to loss of circulation and paralysis.

On the eve of the filing, the NGOs and the plaintiffs met with the Senegalese minister of justice, who assured that there would be no political interference in the work of the judiciary. The case, brought as a private prosecution, moved with stunning speed. The judge first forwarded the file to the prosecutor for his non-binding advice. The prosecutor, made aware of the need to act quickly so that Habré did not flee the country and so the victims could be heard before returning to Chad, gave his favorable advice within two days. The next day the victims gave their closed-door testimony before the judge, something they had waited nine years to do. The judge then called in Habré on February 3, 2000, indicted him on charges of complicity with torture, and placed him under house arrest. He also opened an investigation against persons still to be named for "disappearances, crimes against humanity, and barbarous acts," meaning that he can later indict Habré or others on these charges.

Unfortunately, politics then entered the picture. In March 2000, Abdoulaye Wade was elected president of Senegal. Habré's attorney was one of Wade's closest aides and became a presidential adviser while continuing to defend Habré. When Habré filed a motion to dismiss the case, the state prosecutor, reversing the previous position, supported the motion. President Wade also headed a panel that removed the Investigating Judge who was handling the case and promoted the chief judge before which the motion to dismiss was lodged. Habré also reportedly spent lavishly to influence the outcome of the case.

On July 4, 2000, the court dismissed the charges against Habré, ruling that Senegal had not enacted legislation to implement the Convention against Torture and therefore had no jurisdiction to pursue the charges because the crimes were not committed in Senegal.

The victims appealed the dismissal to the Cour de Cassation, Senegal's highest court. In the meantime, public opinion increasingly questioned Senegal's moves. The United Nations special rapporteurs on the independence of judges and lawyers, and on torture, made a rare joint and public expression of their concern to the government of Senegal over the dismissal and the surrounding circumstances.

Cavallo

On August 24, Mexican authorities arrested Ricardo Miguel Cavallo, accused of having been a torturer in the Navy Mechanics School during Argentina's 1976 to 1983 military government. Cavallo was allegedly implicated in hundreds of cases of kidnapping, "disappearence," and torture. An order for Cavallo's arrest, and then a formal extradition request, later came from the same Spanish judge, Baltasar Garzon, who sought to extradite Augusto Pinochet. The case was pending at the time of this writing.

The Cavallo case could potentially extend the "Pinochet precedent" to a country, Mexico, that was once considered a haven of impunity. In addition, by targeting a lower-ranking official, the arrest spoke to police officers and soldiers around the world telling them that if they committed torture today, they could be apprehended tomorrow, and not only in Europe.

Montesinos

Human Rights Watch actively opposed impunity for Vladimiro Montesinos, the Peruvian intelligence chief and close ally of Peruvian President Alberto Fujimori, who had fled to Panama to seek political asylum. Human Rights Watch had documented Montesinos' involvement in human rights abuses in Peru. Evidence linked him to kidnappings and murders carried out by a death squad belonging to a Peruvian intelligence agency. He was also implicated in the torture of army intelligence agents and journalists who were suspected of leaking information to the press about the agency's illegal activities. Human Rights Watch staff visited Panama in October to press the government to deny Montesinos political asylum, since he was a perpatrator, not a victim, of political persecution. Human Rights Watch asked Panamamian authorities to open a judicial inquiry and prosecute Montesinos for these crimes. In late October, Montesinos left Panama and returned to Peru.

The International Criminal Court

As the number and diversity of state signatories and parties grew during 2000, momentum for the early entry into force of the International Criminal Court Treaty increased significantly. The court, which will prosecute crimes of genocide, crimes against humanity and war crimes where national courts fail to do their job, will be a cornerstone in the emerging system of international justice. The adoption of national implementing legislation for the treaty highlighted the possibilities to strengthen national enforcement of international criminal law while enhancing protections for the rights of the accused. The Preparatory Commission for the International Criminal Court, which met three times from late 1999 until mid-2000, completed its work on the Elements of Crimes and Rules of Procedure by its June 30, 2000 deadline. Governments and nongovernmental organizations (NGOs) convened regional and sub-regional conferences to accelerate ratification and the adoption of meaningful implementing legislation. Simultaneously, NGOs engaged in intensive advocacy efforts on behalf of the court. These positive developments stood in stark contrast to the continuing efforts of the United States government to re-open and weaken the treaty by carving out an exemption from prosecution for U.S. nationals.

Growing Momentum

States worldwide solidified their commitment to ending impunity through the International Criminal Court Treaty. Over the year nearly thirty states committed themselves to the objectives and purposes of the treaty by becoming signatories. As of this writing, 114 states had signed the treaty. But more than just the numbers increased. The state signatories became more diverse as well. Reflecting the increasingly universal support for the court, the Russian Federation, Mexico, Morocco, Sudan, Kuwait, Thailand, and Nigeria all signed the treaty in 2000.

One year ago four states had completed ratification. As of late October, twenty-one states, just over one-third the total necessary to trigger the treaty's entry into force, had completed their ratification processes. In 2000, more states which saw the court as providing important protection against egregious crimes drove the quickening pace of ratification. These states sought to become states parties as quickly as possible. The twenty-one states parties included a small number whose national legal systems first required the adoption of implementing legislation necessary to bring domestic law into conformity with the treaty. Their ratification represented the fruition of intensive legislative work over the past eighteen months. The group of state parties included members of the sixty-strong "Like Minded Group" of states, those that had shown the greatest commitment to an independent and effective court, as well as states not previously known for their strong support of the court. The growing regional diversity of states parties reinforced the legitimacy and credibility of a universally-supported court.

During the year, government and intergovernmental organization officials convened regional and sub-regional conferences to accelerate the process of ratification. In May, the Foreign Ministry of Spain convened the Ibero-American Meeting on International Criminal Justice in Madrid. Government officials, academics, and other experts from the region shared views on ICC ratification and implementation. In mid-May, the Council of Europe convened a Consultative Meeting for Member States in Strasbourg to exchange experience on ratification and implementing legislation. The Council of Europe circulated a questionnaire with information about progress and obstacles to ratification that led to greater awareness among the council's forty-one member states. In early June, the General Assembly of the Organization of American States met in Canada and adopted a resolution that called for ICC signature and ratification. Numerous foreign ministers there expressed their support for the court and NGOs reaffirmed their commitment to working with governments to obtain the early establishment of the court. In October, Pacific Island law ministers met in Rarotonga in the Cook Islands to attend a seminar on implementing the Rome Statute. This session addressed the importance of the court and provided a forum for South Pacific states to discuss issues they faced in implementing the treaty.

The United Nations Millennium Summit in early September showcased the mounting support for the court. Four governments deposited their instruments of ratification during the Millennium Summit and eleven signed the treaty. Twenty heads of state and government representing nations as diverse as New Zealand and Croatia cited the importance of the ICC in their formal statements. Foreign ministers repeatedly expressed their governments' support for early entry into force of the treaty at the debate opening the U.N. General Assembly session. At the opening of the session Canadian Foreign Minister Lloyd Axworthy launched Canada's campaign on behalf of the ICC. He pledged Canadian assistance for regional conferences and Canadian government lawyers to assist states in ratification and implementing legislation. During the General Assembly's Sixth Committee debate on the ICC at the end of October, delegates described the progress towards the early establishment of the court as an irresistible trend. In addition, the numerous interventions sounded a clear rejection of U.S. efforts to obtain an exemption for U.S. nationals. In a marked change from previous years, many delegations, whether they had ratified or not, called on all states to sign and ratify as quickly as possible. These developments represented a growing commitment to end impunity for genocide, crimes against humanity, and war crimes.

The Work of the Preparatory Commission

The achievements of the Preparatory Commission for the International Criminal Court's during 2000 provided another indication of the growing support for the court. As a concession that allowed U.S. participation in the drafting, the Final Act of the Rome Treaty mandated that the Preparatory Commission enumerate the Elements of Crimes for genocide, crimes against humanity, and war crimes as well as draft the Rules of Procedure and Evidence. Negotiators completed a draft of the court's Elements of Crimes and Rules of Procedure and Evidence

on schedule on June 30, 2000. With the Elements of Crimes, the negotiators specified the intent and nature of the conduct which the ICC prosecutor will have to prove in order to gain a conviction before the court. The Elements of Crimes for genocide and war crimes were, for the most part, finalized at the March 2000 session of the commission. Negotiators at the June session focused on several outstanding issues pertaining to crimes against humanity. Although the completed Rules of Procedure and Evidence for the ICC contained political compromises necessary for adoption by consensus, they maintained the important balance between the due process rights of the accused and the need to protect victims of heinous crimes from further trauma in the court. The rules retain the underlying principle that the chambers of the court maintain ultimate control over the conduct of proceedings. The Preparatory Commission's adoption of these two subsidiary instruments by consensus, unlike the treaty itself, reflected the growing acceptance of the court and contributed to the accelerating pace of ratifications.

Constitutional Challenges and Opportunity for Law Reform

The growing number of signatures and ratifications appeared even more remarkable as the domestic hurdles to ratification became clearer. In many states ratification generated debate about the compatibility of the ICC Statute with certain constitutional norms. Poland, Estonia, Brazil, Portugal, the Czech Republic, and Costa Rica, to name only a few, debated these constitutional questions. The stakes were particularly high for states with relatively new constitutions that had not previously amended their fundamental law. The debate centered on three constitutional norms: prohibitions on the extradition of nationals, provisions on immunities, and prohibitions on life imprisonment. A small number of states, including Germany and France, chose to amend their constitutions before ratifying. Others, such as Belgium, chose to amend the constitution after ratification so that the amendment procedure would not delay ratification. In other states, including Norway, Venezuela, and Argentina, interpretation of the relevant constitutional provisions led to the conclusion that initial concerns about compatibility were unfounded and that the constitution did not require amendment.

As of this writing, both Canada and New Zealand had enacted their implementing legislation. In August, the United Kingdom released its draft implementing law for public comment prior to its introduction into Parliament. While the worldwide process of amending national criminal laws to conform with the requirements of the Rome Treaty was only in its early phase, initial experience highlights the extraordinary potential the implementing process offers to reform domestic criminal law more generally. Taking the opportunity afforded by the adoption of implementing legislation, Canada and New Zealand introduced laws to give their national courts the authority to investigate and prosecute the ICC crimes on the basis of universal jurisdiction. Italy and France, among others, were considering following suit.

The locus of ICC activity had shifted decisively to the national arena. As the possibility of transforming domestic criminal law and enhancing respect for human rights domestically became evident, the potential extended benefits of the ICC process became clearer.

United States

The United States government continued to pose the greatest obstacle to the effective functioning of the court. During 2000, the Clinton administration intensified its efforts to obtain an exemption for U.S. nationals from prosecution by the ICC. Before and during each of the Preparatory Commission sessions since the end of 1999, the U.S. government campaigned hard to gain acceptance of its proposal for an exemption. At the March session, the U.S. delegation circulated a two-part proposal that contained a procedural rule and text for the Relationship Agreement between the ICC and the United Nations. By making the Relationship Agreement binding on the treaty, the proposed procedural rule provided a bridge to the exemption for U.S. nationals. The proposed Relationship Agreement text contained language that would exempt nationals of non-party states unless the Security Council had taken specified measures under its powers to maintain international peace and security.

In advance of the June session, U.S. government lobbying intensified. In mid-April, U.S. Secretary of State Madeleine Albright sent a letter to her counterparts in capitals worldwide pressing them to accept both the proposed procedural rule and the exemption text for the Relationship Agreement. In May, the Portuguese Presidency, on behalf of the European Union, convened a meeting for E.U. Members States to formulate a common position rejecting the March U.S. proposal. The European initiative galvanized more intense diplomatic activity by Washington. Following the E.U. coordination effort, U.S. officials visited European capitals to enlist acquiescence to, if not active support for, U.S. demands. Nonetheless, on May 29, the Portuguese, as E.U. president, presented an informal demarche rejecting the U.S. two-part proposal.

At the June Preparatory Commission session the U.S. introduced its proposed procedural rule, but not a text for the Relationship Agreement. The proposed rule effectively amended the treaty by qualitatively broadening the type of agreements that the court could enter into beyond the limited exception already contained in the treaty. Denying that the rule was only the first step in a two-part plan, the U.S. delegation insisted the proposed rule was a "separate and distinct proposal . . . It should not be interpreted as requiring or in any way calling for the negotiation of provisions in any particular international agreement by the Court or by any other international organization or State." Given the procedural nature of the rule, a sufficient number of European Union and "Like Minded" member states felt that it was best to "give the Americans" a concession. The commission adopted a convoluted but harmless procedural rule that essentially repeated the language of the statute of the court. Nonetheless, the United States side, contradicting previous statements about the standalone character of the rule, publicly touted the rule as the first step to the desired exemption.

Coinciding with the start of the June Preparatory Commission session, the Republican Party leadership of the U.S. Senate and House of Representatives introduced the American Servicemembers Protection Act. This bill would have eliminated U.S. military assistance for states, other than NATO members and the State of Israel, that ratified the ICC treaty until the U.S. Senate had given its advice and consent on the ICC Treaty. This politically partisan effort, intended in part to intimidate delegations into submitting to U.S. demands, clarified the congressional leadership's views on the court. As of this writing, the bill appeared to be dead.

The Work of Nongovernmental Organizations

The Coalition for the International Criminal Court continued to work intensively over the year. The coalition, composed of over one thousand civil society groups, worked on several levels. CICC staff coordinated civil society involvement in the three Preparatory Commission sessions over the year and brought activists from Latin America, Asia, Africa, the Middle East, and Europe to the Preparatory Commission meetings. The coalition organized the nongovernmental organizations to cover and report on the most important substantive issues and enabled civil society to press for stronger provisions. It took a strong principled stand in encouraging state opposition to United States government efforts to carve an exemption into the treaty for U.S. nationals. Coalition staff conducted missions to Bangladesh, Brazil, South Africa, Bulgaria, Mexico, and Argentina to name only a few.

Throughout 2000, the coalition initiated conferences on the ICC to engage officials and civil society in closer cooperation. In February, the coalition together with Mexican NGOs and academics convened a conference in Mexico City to examine the establishment of the ICC and the position of the Mexican

government. In April, the Asian NGO Network for an ICC convened a conference in Dhaka, Bangladesh on the ICC and promoted ratification by Bangladesh. In July, No Peace Without Justice, a coalition member, convened a conference in Rome to mark the second anniversary of the treaty on July 17, 2000. Parliamentarians for Global Action convened a session for Latin American parliamentarians in Buenos Aires in October.

To highlight the importance of the early entry into force of the treaty among other constituencies, coalition staff also attended conferences focusing on other substantive issues including the Accra Workshop on War Affected Children in West Africa. The conference, which brought together officials from the sixteen members of the Economic Community of West African States (ECOWAS), included a session on the International Criminal Court and in the final declaration ECOWAS states committed themselves to "ratify the Statute of the International Criminal Court . . ."

The Work of Human Rights Watch

Believing that the International Criminal Court will be a cornerstone of an emerging system of international justice and that the treaty's early entry into force will be an important practical and symbolic measure against impunity, during 2000, Human Rights Watch devoted considerable resources to the establishment of the court. Through visits to selected capitals and participation at numerous conferences Human Rights Watch staff attempted to better understand the various constitutional, legal, and political obstacles to ratification in key states. On this basis Human Rights Watch formulated its research and advocacy strategy to overcome the principal hurdles. Human Rights Watch assisted ratification by analyzing the questions of the compatibility between constitutional provisions and the Rome Treaty. At the 1999 November-December Preparatory Commission, Human Rights Watch circulated an informal paper on the compatibility of the treaty's provisions on immunities, extradition of nationals, and life imprisonment with constitutional norms. The paper summarized the diverse experience with these questions and highlighted the modes of interpretative analysis that made amendments moot. Simultaneously, and in close conjunction with its focus on constitutional issues, Human Rights Watch International Justice Program staff conducted missions to Bolivia, Costa Rica, Panama, Mexico, Argentina, Uruguay, Canada, Croatia, Slovakia, the Czech Republic, Estonia, Spain, Portugal, the United Kingdom, France, New Zealand, Australia, South Africa, Malawi, and Namibia. Human Rights Watch divisional staff included ICC advocacy on missions in Egypt, Thailand, Brazil, and Japan.

In the course of the year, as states addressed the challenge of implementing legislation, Human Rights Watch became increasingly involved in issues of national implementing law. Staff discussed and provided input on legislative proposals being considered in Canada, New Zealand, Argentina, and the United Kingdom.

LESBIAN AND GAY RIGHTS

Protection from abuse remained elusive for lesbians, gay men, and bisexual and transgender people in 2000, despite the reaffirmation in the Universal Declaration of Human Rights that "All people are born free and equal in dignity and rights." In virtually every country in the world, people suffered from de jure and de facto discrimination based on their actual or perceived sexual orientation or gender identity. Sexual minorities were persecuted in a significant number of countries and in many ways, including the application of the death penalty or long prison sentences for private sexual acts between consenting adults. In some countries, sexual minorities were targeted for extrajudicial execution. In many countries, police actively participated in the persecution. Pervasive bias within the criminal justice system in many countries effectively precluded members of sexual minorities from seeking redress.

These attacks on human rights and fundamental freedoms also occurred in international fora where states were supposedly working to promote human rights. For example, in New York in June at the five year review meeting for the Fourth World Conference on Women, many delegates refused to recognize women's sexual rights and some states continued to defend violations of women's human rights in the name of religious and cultural practices. Activists stressed the connection between the need for states to recognize women's right to control their sexuality and enjoy physical autonomy if states were serious about wanting to reduce violence against women. Many delegates refused to acknowledge that discrimination against lesbian and single women created a climate in which attacks on such women were deemed justified.

Other intergovernmental bodies played a significant role in upholding the human rights of lesbian, gay, bisexual, and transgender individuals. In July, for example, the Council of Europe's Parliamentary Assembly approved Armenia and Azerbaijan's applications for membership with the understanding that each country would repeal legislation that discriminated against lesbian, gay, bisexual, and transgender persons. In a further debate the assembly voted to support recommendations that national governments recognize persecution on the grounds of sexual orientation for the purposes of asylum and grant bi-national same-sex couples the same residence rights as bi-national heterosexual couples. In September, the Parliamentary Assembly called upon its member states to include sexual orientation among the prohibited bases of discrimination, revoke sodomy laws and similar legislation criminalizing sexual relations between consenting adults of the same sex, and apply the same age of consent for all sexual relations.

Despite the council's laudable efforts, the International Gay and Lesbian Association (IGLA) reported to the Parliamentary Assembly's Legal Affairs and Human Rights

Committee in March that "discrimination against lesbian, gay and bisexual persons remains endemic and extremely serious" in Europe and that "[h]omophobic violence is common, even in countries like Sweden which are world leaders in their support for lesbian and gay rights."

Persecution

Lesbian, gay, bisexual, and transgender individuals were vilified by officials of several states. Their claims to equal enjoyment of rights and equal protection before the law were routinely denied in many states. State-sponsored hostility and entrenched bias toward lesbian, gay, bisexual, and transgender people not only placed them at risk of violence and persecution by agents of the state, but virtually guaranteed that they would face serious obstacles if they turned to the state for protection or redress when attacked by private actors.

World Pride 2000, an international event calling attention to human rights violations of lesbian, gay, bisexual, and transgender people, held in July in Rome, came under heavy criticism from the Vatican. In the wake of the Vatican's criticism, Italy's prime minister Guiliano Amato ordered the country's minister for equal rights to cancel her ministry's official sponsorship of World Pride. The pope went on to condemn the event as "an offense to the Christian values of the city."

Leaders in Namibia, Uganda, and Zimbabwe continued to denounce lesbian, gay, bisexual, and transgender individuals during the year. Zimbabwean President Robert Mugabe continued his longstanding anti-gay campaign. At a New Year's Day celebration, he characterized same-sex marriage as "an abomination, a rottenness of culture, real decadence of culture." In Namibia, President Sam Nujoma was regularly quoted as calling lesbians and gays "unnatural" and against the will of God. State television reported in October 2000 that Home Affairs Minister Jerry Ekandjo urged new police officers to "eliminate" lesbians and gays "from the face of Namibia."

Ugandan President Yoweri Museveni appeared to back away from his September 1999 directive to Criminal Investigations Division officers to "look for homosexuals, lock them up and charge them." At a news conference in November 1999, he criticized lesbians and gays for "provoking and upsetting" society but suggested that they could live in Uganda as long they "did it quietly."

In the month after President Museveni ordered the arrest of lesbian, gay, bisexual, and transgender Ugandans, the International Gay and Lesbian Human Rights Commission (IGLHRC) received reports that several students had been expelled from schools for their involvement in same-sex relationships. The offices of *Sister Namibia,* a magazine known for its strong support of gay and lesbian rights, was set on fire on July 10 in what appeared to be a deliberate attack; the Namibian National Society for Human Rights noted, "While the motive for the attack is not yet known, the attack occurred barely a week after Namibian President Sam Nujoma launched a verbal attack on the homosexual community."

According to the Lebanese human rights organization Multi-Initiative on Rights: Search, Assist and Defend (MIRSAD), Beirut Morals Police (Police des Mœurs) officers entered the offices of Destination, an Lebanese internet service provider, in April to obtain information about the owners of a website for Lebanese gays and lesbians that was accessible to internet users in Lebanon but maintained in the United States. Later that month, officers questioned the general manager and another senior staff member at the Hobaich police station. When MIRSAD posted an urgent action message on several websites, the military prosecutor charged MIRSAD and Destination officials with "tarnishing the reputation of the Morals Police by distributing a printed flier," in violation of article 157 of the Military Penal Code; their trial was scheduled for September 25. If convicted, they would face three months to three years of imprisonment.

Gay men, lesbians, and transgender people have been subjected to a campaign of terror, violence, and murder in El Salvador over the last several years. Governmental indifference to these offenses was compounded by state agents' active participation in violence. A person who identified himself as a member of the special Presidential Battalion used his weapon to threaten a transgender person who was participating in Lesbian and Gay Pride Day celebrations in the Constitution Plaza in San Salvador. Asociación "Entre Amigos" Executive Director William Hernández repeatedly received death threats. The Salvadorean police acknowledged that Hernández and "Entre Amigos" qualified for protection due to the repeated attacks and threats to which they had been subjected. Nevertheless, the chief of the National Civil Police initially refused to appoint any officers to provide protection because officers who "do not share the sexual tastes" of those they should protect would feel uncomfortable doing their work. Hernández was placed under special police protection following an international campaign.

In August, a longstanding prohibition against the use of a public park in Aguascalientes, Mexico, by "dogs and homosexuals" became the focus of public attention after a sign announcing the ban was repaired and reposted at the park entrance. Asked for his thoughts on the gay community in interviews broadcast on the Mexican network Televisa and in the national newspaper *La Jornada,* Aguascalientes Director of Regulations Jorge Alvarez Medina stated that he was against "this type of people" and declared that he "will not allow access to homosexuals" while he remained in charge of municipal regulations. In a welcome development, however, National Action Party (Partido de Acción Nacional, PAN) National President Luís Felipe Bravo Mena denied that Alvarez Medina's remarks reflected the policy of the PAN, the governing party in Aguascalientes. Declaring that "we reject and repudiate" Alvarez Medina's remarks, Bravo Mena stated, "If any doubt remains, I can say that I feel that this is absolutely reprehensible. We do not believe in any type of discrimination and reject it."

At least four transgender persons in Valencia, in the Venezuelan state of Carabobo, were reportedly detained without judicial order by Carabobo police, according to Amnesty International. In July, police improperly detained two transgender persons for eight days; in August, officers forced two other members of Valencia's transgender community to undress in the street, beat them, and then held them for several days in August without permitting them legal, medical, or family visits.

In September, the Brazilian GLBT Pride Parade Association of São Paulo (Associação da Parada do Orgulho GLBT de São Paulo) received a letter bomb, one day after several gay and lesbian rights organizations and other human rights NGOs received letters threatening to "exterminate" gays, Jews, blacks, and persons from Brazil's northeast. There were an estimated 169 bias-motivated killings of sexual minorities in Brazil in 1999, according to a May report issued by the Grupo Gay de Bahia; the states of Pernambuco and São Paulo recorded the highest number of killings.

The Criminalization of Private Sexual Conduct

Over eighty countries continued to criminalize sexual activity between consenting adults of the same sex, according to the IGLHRC. Elsewhere, national or local legislation discriminated against lesbian, gay, bisexual, and transgender persons by imposing different standards for the legal age of consent. In addition, lesbian, gay, bisexual, and transgender persons were often targeted for arrest under provisions relating to "scandalous conduct," "public decency," loitering, and similar charges.

In Saudi Arabia, where sodomy was punishable by the death penalty, six men were executed for that crime in July. In April, nine men were sentenced to up to 2,600 lashes each for transvestism and "deviant sexual behavior"; because the sentence could not be carried out in a single session without killing the men, it was to be carried out at fifteen-day intervals over a period of two years.

Sri Lanka's Press Council fined a gay

rights activist in June for filing a complaint against a newspaper that had published a letter urging that lesbians be turned over to convicted rapists. The council declared that being a lesbian was an "act of sadism" and that the activist, rather than the newspaper, was guilty of promoting improper values.

At this writing, the Romanian Senate was considering the abolition of article 200, which criminalized all sexual relations between consenting adults of the same sex if "committed in public or if producing public scandal." The article was interpreted to include casual gestures of intimacy such as holding hands and kissing. The measure passed the Chamber of Deputies, the Romanian Parliament's lower house, on June 28. The measures under consideration did not address article 201, which continued to penalize "acts of sexual perversion" if "committed in public or if producing public scandal" with one to five years of imprisonment. A 1998 report jointly published by Human Rights Watch and the IGLHRC documented the human rights abuses suffered by lesbian, gay, bisexual, and transgender persons in Romania as a result of both provisions.

In response to a 1993 decision of the European Court of Human Rights, Cyprus amended its criminal laws in June to equalize the male age of consent, setting it at eighteen. Before the amendment, the age of consent for men engaging in heterosexual sex had been sixteen, while the age of consent for men engaging in homosexual sex had been eighteen. The age of consent for all women continued to be sixteen. Other European countries continued to maintain unequal ages of consent. A notable example was Austria, where the age of consent was fourteen for heterosexual males and eighteen for men who had sexual relations with other men.

In the United States, fifteen states retained laws prohibiting consensual sexual relations between adults of the same sex, classifying these acts as "sodomy," "sexual misconduct," "unnatural intercourse," or "crimes against nature." A Texas court overturned the state's sodomy law in June, while the highest court of the neighboring state of Louisiana upheld the state's "crimes against nature" statute in July. A challenge to Massachusetts' sodomy law was pending at this writing. Massachusetts was the only state in New England to retain legislation prohibiting sexual relations between consenting adults of the same sex.

In August, former Malaysian Deputy Prime Minister Anwar Ibrahim and his adopted brother Sukma Dermawan were both convicted of sodomy. Anwar was sentenced to nine years in prison; Sukma received six years and four lashes with a rattan cane. The prosecution of Anwar was widely viewed inside and outside Malaysia as a case of political revenge against Anwar and his supporters, who had grown increasingly critical of Prime Minister Mahathir in the months prior to Anwar's ouster and arrest. Anwar's prosecution was also seen as undermining the integrity of the Malaysian judiciary, which had already been criticized widely for its lack of independence (see Malaysia chapter).

In May, the Zimbabwe Supreme Court upheld former President Canaan Banana's 1998 conviction for sodomy and indecent assault. Banana was quoted in 1999 as describing homosexuality as "deviant, abominable, and wrong according to the scriptures and according to Zimbabwean culture."

Even in countries where the laws criminalizing private consensual conduct between adults were not enforced, the existence of these laws provided the foundation for attacks on sexual minorities. Men and women who identified as gay, lesbian, or bisexual were attacked as immoral and putative criminals. Thus, discrimination on the basis of this characterization was deemed justified.

The Military

In September 1999, the European Court of Human Rights ruled that the United Kingdom's ban on lesbian and gay service members violated the Convention on Human Rights and Fundamental Freedoms. In July 2000, the court awarded four gay British service members compensation for their discharge.

Lesbian, gay, bisexual, and transgender

individuals were not barred from military service throughout much of the rest of Europe. In remarks published in the French gay magazine *Têtu* in May, Gen. Alain Raevel declared of France's policy with regard to lesbian, gay, bisexual, and transgender service members, "The army which we are building is an extension of society . . . . We need to recruit boys and girls for 400 different types of work. The fact that they may be homosexual does not concern us." Similarly, lesbian, gay, bisexual, and transgender individuals served in Canada and Israel without official retaliation.

With most of its allies either allowing homosexuals to serve openly or having no policy on the subject they considered unrelated to job performance, the United States found itself increasingly isolated in maintaining restrictions on lesbian, gay, bisexual, and transgender servicemembers. Turkey was the only other member of the North Atlantic Treaty Organization (NATO) that continued to ban gays and lesbians from its armed forces. Six years after the U.S. military codified and implemented its "don't ask, don't tell" policy, its own investigations found that training on implementation of the law was lagging and that anti-gay comments and harassment were pervasive. Although the "don't ask, don't tell" policy was ostensibly intended to allow a greater number of gay, lesbian, or bisexual service members to remain in the military, discharges increased significantly after the policy's adoption. From 1994 to 1999, a total of 5,412 service members were separated from the armed forces under the policy, with yearly discharge totals nearly doubling, from 617 in 1994 to 1,149 in 1998. In 1999, the number of separations dropped slightly, to 1,034; nevertheless, the discharge rate was still 73 percent higher than it was prior to the implementation of "don't ask, don't tell." Women were discharged at a disproportionately high rate. In addition, the policy enabled male harassers to threaten to "out" women—and end their careers—if the women rejected their advances or threatened to report them.

Even more disturbing than the increase in the number of service members separated from the military under this policy was the continued failure of the U.S. Department of Defense to hold anyone accountable for violations of the policy. This lack of accountability spilled over to the murder case of Barry Winchell, a gay army private at Fort Campbell in 1999. A U.S. Army review, issued in July, of the circumstances surrounding the beating death of Winchell on the base, concluded that no officers would be held responsible for the killing and that there was no "climate" of homophobia on the base. This conclusion contradicted a Defense Department inspector general report issued in March which found that harassment based on perceived homosexuality was widespread in the military. It also contradicted numerous reports that Winchell was relentlessly taunted with anti-gay slurs in the months before he was murdered.

Marriage and Discrimination Based on Family Configuration

Barriers to the legal recognition of lesbian, gay, bisexual, and transgender families continued to crumble slowly in a number of countries throughout the world. In March, the European Parliament, the legislative body of the European Union, called on its member states to "guarantee one-parent families, unmarried couples, and same-sex couples rights equal to those enjoyed by traditional couples and families."

On September 13, the Dutch Parliament passed legislation permitting marriage between same-sex couples. The legislation, which was limited to Dutch citizens and to those with residency permits, also provided for adoption rights and access to the courts in cases of divorce. The law was expected to go into effect in early 2001, making the Netherlands the first country to allow same-sex couples to marry.

Denmark, Greenland, Iceland, Norway, and Sweden had provisions for registered partnerships, which did not provide all of the benefits of civil marriage—often according limited or no adoption rights, in particular—and were generally limited only to citizens or to residents who had lived in the country for several years. France's civil pact of solidarity (pacte civile de solidarité, PACS) and Hungary's cohabitation law had similar limitations. In June, Iceland expanded its registered partnership law to permit same-sex couples to adopt each other's biological children. The law was also extended to cover Danes, Swedes, and Norwegians living in Iceland; other foreigners were permitted to enter into registered partnerships after they had resided in Iceland for two years.

A comprehensive same-sex partnership bill introduced in Germany on July 5 would grant same-sex couples spousal rights in taxation, inheritance, immigration, social security, child custody, health insurance, name changes, and other areas. The plan was expected to pass the Bundestag, the lower house of the German parliament; support in the Bundesrat, necessary to enact some aspects of the proposal, was not assured.

The U.S. state of Vermont enacted legislation in April providing for civil unions between same-sex couples. The law was passed in response to a December 1999 decision of the Vermont Supreme Court holding that the state's constitution required Vermont "to extend to same-sex couples the common benefits and protections that flow from marriage under Vermont law." Although civil unions carried virtually all of the state rights and responsibilities of marriage, they were not recognized by the federal government or any other U.S. state.

Brazil granted same-sex partners the same rights as married couples with respect to pensions, social security benefits, and taxation in June. This step was achieved by decree: legislation to provide for civil unions between persons of the same sex remained pending in the federal Chamber of Deputies.

In November 1999, the Latvian Parliament's Human Rights and Public Affairs Commission rejected proposed legislation that would provide for registered partnerships for same-sex couples. In August, Slovak Justice Minister Jan Carnogursky announced that same-sex partnerships would not be registered in Slovakia, reportedly stating that such partnerships would "degrade" heterosexual families.

Israel's Interior Ministry announced in July that it allowed same-sex partners to receive immigration benefits on equal terms with heterosexual common-law spouses. Under the ministry's policy, the noncitizen partner is granted a renewable one-year tourist permit with employment authorization and may request temporary resident status after four years; eventually, the partner may seek permanent residence and then citizenship.

With the addition of Israel, at least fourteen countries offered immigration benefits to same-sex couples. Unlike most countries' immigration policies with regard to married heterosexual couples, these policies typically required same-sex couples to demonstrate that they had had a committed relationship for one to two years or more before they were eligible for any immigration benefits. Australia required same-sex couples to show "a mutual commitment to a shared life" for at least the twelve months preceding the date of application. In New Zealand, same-sex couples had to have been "living in a genuine and stable de facto relationship" for two years. The United Kingdom required applicants to show that they had had "a relationship akin to marriage" for two years or more. Belgium required a relationship of at least three and a half years' duration. The other countries that offered same-sex immigration benefits were Canada, Denmark, Finland, France, Namibia, the Netherlands, Norway, South Africa, and Sweden.

Harassment and Discrimination Against Students

Lesbian, gay, bisexual, and transgender students in the United States and elsewhere were frequently targeted for harassment by their peers. Lesbian, gay, and bisexual youth were nearly three times as likely as their peers to have been involved in at least one physical fight in school, three times as likely to have been threatened or injured with a weapon at school, and nearly four times as likely to skip school because they felt unsafe, according to the 1999 Massachusetts Youth Risk Behavior Survey. Moreover, the survey found that those who identified as lesbian, gay, or bisexual were more than twice as likely to consider suicide and more than four times as likely to attempt suicide than their peers.

Efforts to provide a safe, supportive environment for lesbian, gay, bisexual, and transgender students in the United States were hampered by discriminatory legislation in several states. In addition, many students also faced hostile school administrations. In two particularly prolonged disputes, school districts in Utah and California attempted to deny students the right to form clubs known as gay-straight alliances, in violation of the federal Equal Access Act. Both school districts began to permit the student groups to meet in September 2000, doing so only after the students who sought to form the groups filed lawsuits against the districts. (See Children's Rights).

PRISONS

The number of people incarcerated in the United States reached two million this year, a staggering figure both in absolute terms and in terms of the incarceration rate it represented. But the U.S. was not alone in holding record numbers of inmates. Prisoner numbers continued to rise in countries all over the world, resulting in severe overcrowding of prisons and other detention facilities. Although overall figures were difficult to estimate due to some countries' refusal to disclose information about their penal facilities, even such basic facts as the number of inmates held, the world inmate population was roughly eight to ten million people.

In many countries, the high levels of official secrecy that made prisoner numbers impossible to determine were equally effective in cutting off information about even the most egregious prison abuses. By barring human rights groups, journalists, and other outside observers access to their penal facilities, prison officials sought to shield substandard conditions from critical scrutiny. In extreme cases, including China and Cuba, the International Committee of the Red Cross (ICRC) was barred from providing basic humanitarian relief to prisoners.

While conditions of detention varied greatly from country to country and facility to facility, standards in most countries were shockingly low. Prisons and jails in even the richest and most developed countries were plagued by severe overcrowding, decaying physical infrastructure, a lack of medical care, guard abuse and corruption, and prisoner-on-prisoner violence. With the public primarily concerned about keeping prisoners locked up rather than about the conditions in which prisoners were confined, little progress was made toward remedying these abuses.

Abusive Treatment of Prisoners

Unchecked outbursts of violence occurred in many prisons, violating prisoners' right to life. On April 27, in what was described as the bloodiest prison conflict in Colombian history, at least twenty-five inmates were killed in Bogotá's Modelo prison. The incident, which pitted rival inmate groups against each other, was sparked by the discovery of a mutilated body stuffed in a sewer pipe.

While the body count from this incident was exceptional, the violence itself was not. As evidenced by a subsequent prison search that resulted in the discovery of two AK-47 assault rifles, eight grenades, dozens of firearms, and several thousand knives, Modelo prison was a mini-arsenal, and violence was frequent. Indeed, some 1,200 Colombian inmates were killed over the past decade, a disproportionate number of them in Modelo prison. "In the four years that I've been in the Modelo I've seen more blood and more death than in all my life of crime," said an inmate there. The combination of severe overcrowding—the prison housed some 4,700 inmates in space for 1,900—an extreme shortage of staff, and plentiful weapons made violence inevitable.

The Mata Grande Penitentiary in Rondonopolis, Brazil, was the scene of a similar killing spree in March. Thirteen prisoners were murdered when a group of inmates overpowered the handful of guards that manned their cellblock, gaining entry to a neighboring area that housed their enemies. The killings were apparently part of an effort to gain control of the prison drug trade. Although violence was common at the prison, the police were reported to have been slow to respond to the crisis, taking three hours to enter the facility and regain control over the inmates.

Mass killings such as these merited an occasional mention in the press, but the vast majority of inmate deaths went unnoticed. In some countries, including Brazil, Kenya, Venezuela, and Panama, prison homicides were so frequent as to seem routine. Inmates were usually killed by other inmates rather than by guards, but inmate-on-inmate violence was usually the predictable result of official negligence. By neglecting to supervise and control the inmates within their facilities, by failing to respond to incidents of violence, by corruptly allowing the entry of weapons into the prisons, and by generally abetting the tyranny of the strongest prisoners over the weakest, prison authorities were directly responsible for the violence of their charges.

Prisoner death rates were often far higher than corresponding rates among the populations outside prisons. While violence was a factor in some penal facilities, disease—often the predictable result of overcrowding, malnutrition, unhygienic conditions, and lack of medical care—remained the most common cause of death in prison. Food shortages in some prisons, combined with extreme overcrowding, created ideal conditions for the spread of communicable diseases.

Tuberculosis (TB) continued to ravage prison populations around the world. The spread of TB was especially worrisome in Russia, in light of the country's enormous inmate population—over one million prisoners as of September 2000—and the increasing prevalence of multi-drug resistant (MDR) strains of the disease. Approximately one of out every ten inmates was infected with tuberculosis, with more than 20 percent of sick inmates being affected by MDR strains, constituting a serious threat to public health. Nor was the tuberculosis epidemic confined to Russia; rather, it swept through prisons all over the former Soviet Union. High rates of TB were also reported in the prisons of Brazil and India, two countries with substantial inmate populations.

The HIV/AIDS epidemic ravaged prison populations, with penal facilities around the world reporting grossly disproportionate rates of HIV infection and of confirmed AIDS cases. In a positive development, Botswana's government introduced a bill in July to allow inmates in the late stages of AIDS and other terminal illnesses to return home to their families. But inmates around the world frequently died of AIDS while incarcerated, often deprived of even basic medical care.

Physical abuse of prisoners by guards remained another chronic problem. Some countries continued to permit corporal punishment and the routine use of leg irons, fetters, shackles, and chains. The heavy bar fetters used in Pakistani prisons, for example, turned simple movements such as walking into painful ordeals. In many prison systems, unwarranted beatings were so common as to be an integral part of prison life.

Women prisoners were particularly vulnerable to custodial sexual abuse. The problem was widespread in the United States, where male guards outnumbered women guards in many women's prisons. In some countries, Haiti being a conspicuous example, female prisoners were even held together with male inmates, a situation that exposed them to rampant sexual abuse and violence.

In contravention of international standards, juvenile inmates were often held together with adults. Many of Pakistan's jails and police lockups mixed juvenile and adult prisoners, as did certain detention facilities in Nicaragua, Kenya, South Africa and Zambia. Children in such circumstances frequently fell victim to physical abuse, including rape, by adult inmates.

Extortion by prison staff, and its less aggressive corollary, guard corruption, was common in prisons around the world. Given the substantial power that guards exercised over inmates, these problems were predictable, but the low salaries that guards were generally paid severely aggravated them. In exchange for contraband or special treatment, inmates supplemented guards' salaries with bribes. Powerful inmates in some facilities in Colombia, India, and Mexico, among others, enjoyed cellular phones, rich diets, and comfortable lodgings, while their less fortunate brethren lived in squalor. In Argentina, as part of an effort to combat rampant guard corruption, the government launched a purge of its prison service, dismissing numerous high-ranking officials in April. The mass firing was sparked by revelations that guards had released inmates on robbing excursions and had even sent one inmate out to kill the judge investigating these schemes.

Overcrowding—prevalent in almost every country for which information was available—was at the root of many of the worst abuses. The problem was often most severe in smaller pretrial detention facilities, where, in many countries, inmates were packed together with no space to stretch or move around. In some Brazilian police lockups, where a large proportion of the country's approximately 190,000 detainees were held, overcrowding was so acute, and floor space was at such a premium, that inmates had to tie themselves to the cell bars to sleep. In Brazil, as in many other countries, inmates often suffered long stays in these dreadful conditions.

Another common problem was governments' continued reliance on old, antiquated, and physically decaying prison facilities. Nineteenth-century prisons needing constant upkeep remained in use in a number of countries, including the United States, Mexico, Russia, Italy, and the United Kingdom, although even many modern facilities were in severe disrepair due to lack of maintenance. Notably, some prisons lacked a functional system of plumbing, leaving prisoners to "slop out" their cells, that is, to defecate in buckets that they periodically emptied.

A different set of concerns was raised by the spread of ultra-modern "super-maximum" security prisons. Originally prevalent in the United States, where politicians and state corrections authorities promoted them as part of a politically popular quest for more "austere" prison conditions, the supermax model was increasingly followed in other countries. Prisoners confined in such facilities spent an average of twenty-three hours a day in their cells, enduring extreme social isolation, enforced idleness, and extraordinarily limited recreational and educational opportunities. While prison authorities defended the use of super-maximum security facilities by asserting that they held only the most dangerous, disruptive, or escape-prone inmates, few safeguards existed to prevent other prisoners from being arbitrarily or discriminatorily transferred to such facilities.

The small group isolation regime instituted at Turkey's Kartal Special-Type Prison was one example of this trend. Beginning in 1999, the Turkish authorities began holding prisoners charged under the country's Anti-Terror Law in a new cell-based system, by which inmates remained locked in shared cells for lengthy periods of time, deprived of other human contact and lacking opportunities for exercise, work, education, or other activities. In these conditions, one detainee wrote, "Your senses of taste, smell, hearing, feeling, and sight fade. You cannot laugh at anything and you cry at the smallest thing." Penal experts, including the European Committee for the Prevention of Torture, have warned that such conditions may endanger prisoners' physical and mental health.

Fiscal constraints and competing budget priorities were to blame for prison deficiencies in some countries, but, as the supermax example suggests, harsh prison conditions were sometimes purposefully imposed. In Peru, notably, a punitive motive was evident in the decision to hold top-security prisoners in high-altitude Challapalca and Yanamayo prisons, whose remote locations and miserable conditions led the Inter-American Commission on Human Rights to declare that they were "unfit" to serve as places of detention.

Conditions in many prisons were, in short, so deficient as to constitute cruel, inhuman, or degrading treatment, violating article 7 of the International Covenant on Civil and Political Rights. Their specific failings could also be enumerated under the more detailed provisions of the U.N. Standard Minimum Rules for the Treatment of Prisoners. A widely known set of prison standards, the Standard Minimum Rules describe "the minimum conditions which are accepted as suitable by the United Nations." Although the Standard Minimum Rules were formally integrated into the prison laws and regulations of many countries, few if any prison systems observed all of their prescriptions in practice.

With few means to draw public attention to violations of their rights, prisoners around the world frequently resorted to hunger strikes, self-mutilation, rioting, and other forms of protest. The most dramatic such incident took place in Kazakhstan in July, when forty-four prisoners at Arkalyk prison reportedly attempted mass suicide in protest of conditions. The inmates used razors and broken glass to slash their necks, stomachs, and wrists. Other outbreaks of prison unrest were reported in Argentina, Brazil, Chile, Colombia, the Czech Republic, England, Greece, Israel, Italy, Mexico, Peru, Saudi Arabia, Sri Lanka, Trinidad and Tobago, Turkey, and Venezuela.

Unsentenced Prisoners

Even those unsympathetic to convicted criminals and entirely skeptical of the idea of rehabilitation had reason to be concerned about the inhuman treatment of prisoners. Although comprehensive figures were impossible to obtain, the available statistics showed that a large proportion of the world's prisoners had not been convicted of any crime, but were instead being preventively detained at some stage of the trial process. In countries as varied as Bangladesh, Burundi, Chad, the Dominican Republic, Ecuador, El Salvador, Guatemala, Haiti, India, Mali, Nigeria, Pakistan, Peru, Rwanda, Uganda, and Venezuela, unsentenced prisoners made up the majority of the prison population. Indeed, some 90 percent of Honduran, Para-

guayan, and Uruguayan inmates were unsentenced. Of the more than 125,000 prisoners jailed on charges of having participated in the 1994 genocide in Rwanda, only some 3,000 have been brought to trial.

Worse, such detainees were in many instances held for years before being acquitted of the crime with which they were charged. Prisoners also continued to be held after the expiration of their sentences in some countries.

Defending Prisoners' Human Rights

Struggling against the government's natural tendency toward secrecy and silence on prison abuses, the efforts of numerous local human rights groups around the world—who sought to obtain access to prisons, monitored prison conditions, and publicized the abuses they found—were critical. The Moscow Center for Prison Reform, for example, has done particularly important work in drawing attention to the dreadful conditions of Russia's prisons and jails, and the TB crisis afflicting the inmate population.

In some countries, government human rights ombudspersons, parliamentary commissions, and other official monitors also helped call attention to abuses. In the United Kingdom, notably, the chief inspector of prisons continued his vigorous investigation and forthright criticism of conditions in the country's penal facilities.

In France, two special parliamentary commissions issued scathing official reports in July that called for major reforms in that country's prison system. The reports noted, among other serious failings, that unsentenced prisoners made up 40 percent of the French prison population, one of the highest such rates among industrialized countries.

At the regional level as well, prison monitoring mechanisms were active. The European Committee for the Prevention of Torture (CPT) continued its important work, inspecting penal institutions in eight countries in the first nine months of 2000: Turkey, Poland, Ukraine, Cyprus, France, Italy, Lithuania, and Russia, undertaking three visits to the latter country. As of October 2000, forty-one countries were party to the European Convention for the Prevention of Torture and Inhuman or Degrading Treatment or Punishment, the treaty authorizing the CPT's monitoring.

In Africa, the special rapporteur on prisons and conditions of detention, an adjunct to the African Commission on Human and Peoples' Rights, completed his fourth year, inspecting prisons in the Gambia.

U.N. Monitoring Efforts

The vast scale and chronic nature of human rights violations in the world's prisons have long been of concern to the United Nations, as demonstrated by the 1955 promulgation of the U.N. Standard Minimum Rules for the Treatment of Prisoners. Indeed, the international community's failure to adopt these standards in practice, even while it has embraced them in theory, has inspired the United Nations' most recent prisons effort.

For nearly a decade, a U.N. working group has been hammering out a draft treaty that would establish a U.N. subcommittee authorized to make regular and ad hoc visits to places of detention in states party to the treaty, including prisons, jails, and police lockups. As described in the draft treaty—conceived as an optional protocol to the Convention against Torture—the primary goal of the subcommittee would be to prevent torture and other ill-treatment. Based on the information obtained during its periodic and ad hoc visits, the subcommittee would make detailed recommendations to state authorities regarding necessary improvements to their detention facilities, and the authorities would be expected to implement these recommendations.

The proposed monitoring mechanism held great promise, yet it also had serious potential flaws. Notable among them was the possibility that the subcommittee could be entirely barred from reporting publicly on abuses it discovers, pursuant to a strict rule of confidentiality that some countries have advocated. Although the draft treaty favored cooperation between governments and the subcommittee as a means of instituting reme-dial measures, it must, if it is to create an effective mechanism, leave open the possibility of public reporting, at least in situations where governments stubbornly refuse to cooperate with the subcommittee or to implement its recommendations.

The working group's most recent two-week session, in October 1999, ended without any progress being made toward the completion of a draft treaty. The failure of the 1999 session led the head of the working group to convene intersessional consultations to assist the drafting process. Three days of informal consultations in October highlighted the wide gap between countries on such fundamental issues as which places should be subject to visits, whether prior consent must be obtained, whether reservations to the optional protocol should be allowed, and the impact of national legislation on the nature and scope of visits.

Other U.N. bodies pressed countries to improve their prison conditions. In August and September, U.N. Special Rapporteur on Torture Sir Nigel Rodley spent three weeks visiting police stations, prisons and other detention facilities in Brazil. At the end of his mission to the country, he expressed deep concern over Brazil's treatment of prisoners, stating that they were routinely subject to subhuman conditions and severe physical abuse.

Relevant Human Rights Watch Reports:

No Minor Matter: Children in Maryland's Jails, 11/99
Out of Sight: Super-Maximum Security Confinement in the United States, 2/00
Small Group Isolation in Turkish Prisons: An Avoidable Disaster, 5/00

RACIAL DISCRIMINATION AND RELATED INTOLERANCE

We are served refreshment only in separate cups at roadside tea stalls, turned away from public swimming pools, stopped on highways as presumptive criminals, trafficked as prostitutes, denied our mother's nationality, classed willy-nilly as "mentally disabled" in schools, and abducted into slavery.

We are denied housing or burned out of our homes, refused fresh water from village wells, barred from employment or forced to perform degrading labor, and driven out of out of our communities or even our countries by terror.

We face beatings, sexual assault, wrongful arrest, or murder on a daily basis. In lieu of the birthright of equality we are marked from birth with the brand of discriminatory treatment.

These words are the distillation of testimony received by Human Rights Watch that reflect the reality of racism as a global ill. This is the experience of countless millions who are victims of racial discrimination, xenophobia, and related intolerance on a daily basis. They include minorities around the world—and some majority populations too, even in the post-apartheid era. They have in common their humanity and the denial of full equality by reason of their birth. They are the victims of the politics of exclusion, stigmatization, and scapegoating—or of targeted neglect and social invisibility.

The International Convention on the Elimination of All Forms of Racial Discrimination (CERD) defines "racial discrimination" broadly and concretely. Adopted in 1965, its definition of racial discrimination includes "any distinction, exclusion, restriction or preference based on race, colour, descent or national or ethnic origin which has the purpose or effect of nullifying or impairing the recognition, enjoyment or exercise, on an equal footing, of human rights and fundamental freedoms in the political, economic, social, cultural or any other field of public life."

The reality of racism does not turn only on the definition of the groups that are oppressed, or on the much disputed concept of race itself, but may be driven largely by the perceptions of the oppressor. Racism blights the lives of groups defined primarily by ethnicity, caste, or an identity shaped by religion. Unlike class or other indicators of social status, these are attributes by which people are instantly identified and which can not readily be shed. Even if the very idea of race is discounted, racism is a very real and deadly phenomenon.

The convention on racial discrimination requires states to guarantee to all individuals the enjoyment of rights without such discrimination—and to ensure that public policies are discriminatory neither in purpose nor in effect. In many countries, the discriminatory effect of public policy, regardless of its intent, serves to lock people away from the exercise of civil and political rights—and by doing so bars their way to the enjoyment of economic, social, and cultural rights.

International action to combat racism has long been on the agenda of the United Nations and regional intergovernmental bodies, as well as the object of campaigning by a vast constellation of nongovernmental organizations. The apartheid regime in South Africa was a focus of much of this international effort, particularly after the dismantling of legal segregation in the United States and the gradual efforts to remedy its consequences. The end of apartheid in 1994 was a landmark in this struggle, but the challenge remained. Just one month before Nelson Mandela's May 9, 1994, election to the South African presidency, Hutu extremists launched a campaign of genocide against the Tutsi minority in Rwanda.

Racism and intolerance in Africa's Great Lakes region and elsewhere persisted in many forms even where the basis of "otherness" itself was clouded. The Hutu-Tutsi divide in Rwanda and neighboring states was itself founded on a blurring over time of social strata into something approximating ethnicity. The so-called "ethnic cleansing" of the former Yugoslavia, in turn, was driven by a racism defined by ethnicity, religion, language, and national origin. In the year 2000, millions faced violence, internal displacement, the arbitrary loss of their nationality, or expulsion from their countries by reason of their descent. Millions more faced pervasive racism that was less apparent to the casual observer—but was in its effect often no less pernicious.

Human Rights Watch in 2000 brought a new focus to the issue of racial discrimination as it affects migrants and refugees and populations identified by caste. The organization's work concentrated on the discriminatory impact of state policy and practice in two areas. These were discrimination in the determination of nationality and citizenship rights, and discrimination in criminal justice and in the public administration of state institutions, services, and resources. These issues are discussed further below.

The World Conference Against Racism

The Third World Conference Against Racism, Racial Discrimination, Xenophobia and Related Intolerance will be held in South Africa from August 31 to September 7, 2001. The conference will be the first forum of its kind since the end of apartheid in South Africa (previous world conferences were held in 1978 and 1983). As such, it can build upon the lessons learned in abolishing the apartheid system, while addressing the racist effect of other policies and practices that continue to afflict whole populations. Its convening reflects both the achievements of the international community and the ongoing challenges it faced in combatting racism. It should cel-

ebrate the end of apartheid—but there will be little else to celebrate unless the conference itself catalyzes real introspection by participating governments and real mechanisms for change.

With the end of apartheid, there was some concern that in this third conference the continuing challenge of racism would be portrayed by governments as largely a matter of education, control, and punishment of ordinary people—to confront racism which was in some way inherent, spontaneous, and natural. There seemed a real risk that the international community would focus first on treating racism as a social disease, its vectors of transmission the ordinary citizen, private groups, and unscrupulous Internet service providers. In initial planning sessions, the role of governments and government officials at all levels, from education ministries to community police, in imposing and enforcing policies with racist effect went largely unvoiced. Rather, governments vied to hold themselves up as exemplars in identifying "best practices" in eliminating overt racism from public policy and private practice and in their pedagogic efforts to preach tolerance. The identification and remedying of the racist effect of government policies and practices where racist intent was not clearly present were largely off the agenda.

The preparations for the World Conference were undertaken by governments and civil society alike. Early consultations generated new nongovernmental alliances, bringing together legal reform groups, advocates for migrants and refugees, women's rights activists, faith-based organizations, civil rights activists and human rights groups, veteran campaigners of the anti-apartheid movement, a wide spectrum of minority rights groups, and other grass-roots activists. These nongovernmental organizations have already organized scores of consultative meetings in many countries, while participating in the preparatory meetings, expert seminars, and regional conferences of the United Nations' formal program. The consultative meetings and the expert seminars have already made a significant contribution to the substance of the World Conference and should go some way toward encouraging government representatives to take seriously their responsibilities to combat racism.

The Preparatory Committee for the World Conference identified five broad themes for the provisional agenda of the conference at its first session in May 2000. These were the sources, causes, forms, and contemporary manifestations of racism; the victims; measures of prevention, education and protection; the provision of effective remedies; and strategies to achieve full and effective equality. In some of these areas considerable dissent was registered by powerful governments. Two governments of countries in which caste was the focus of discriminatory treatment—India and Japan—called for the exclusion of descent-based caste discrimination from the deliberations. Despite India's massive lobbying effort toward exclusion of victims of caste discrimination, however, there was an apparent consensus that the conference would be inclusive in its identification of the victims of racism and related intolerance.

The real break in consensus emerged on the matter of remedies. A draft slate of themes prepared by the African Group of delegates had been broadly acceptable, apart from its fourth thematic point, the question of remedies. Dissent turned primarily on the reference to compensation, with former European colonial powers and the United States adamantly opposed to language that implied their acknowledgment of material obligations to remedy past abuses. This was an echo of debates within the United States on the issue of reparations to address the heritage of slavery and segregation, a context that had led the drafters to choose the less politically charged term "compensatory measures." The dissenters may also have reacted negatively to the recommendation of a U.N. expert seminar on the remedies available to victims, held in preparation for the World Conference in February, on the centrality of "reparations": "Victims of racial discrimination are entitled to reparation in its different forms, such as restitution, compensation, rehabilita-

tion, satisfaction and guarantees of non-repetition. Monetary and non-monetary forms of reparation are equally important in rendering justice to victims of racial discrimination. Non-monetary forms of reparation include measures such as verification of the facts and their public disclosure; official declarations or judicial decisions that restore dignity and rebuild reputation; acknowledgment of the facts and acceptance of responsibility; and the commemoration and the payment of tribute to the victims."

A late-night compromise placed the word "compensatory" in brackets: "The provision of effective remedies, recourse, redress, [compensatory] and other measures at the national, regional and international level," annotated by a series of explanatory statements from delegates. The Western Group reserved the right to "revisit this point." The African delegates declared their intent to support the inclusion of reference to compensatory measures as founded in general principles of international human rights law establishing the right to restitution, compensation, and rehabilitation for victims of grave violations of human rights.

The agenda of the World Conference will be discussed further at a special inter-sessional meeting to be held in January 2001 and finalized at the second session of the Preparatory Committee to be held in Geneva in May-June 2001. Regional conferences are to be held in Santiago, Chile (the Americas meeting, in December 2000), in Tehran, Iran (the Asia meeting, to include part of the Middle East, in February 2001), in Dakar, Senegal (the Africa meeting, in January 2001). The European regional meeting was held in Strasbourg, France, in October. Expert seminars were held on the protection of minorities and other vulnerable groups (Warsaw, Poland, in July); on migrants and trafficking in persons, with particular reference to women and children (Bangkok, Thailand, in September), and on preventing ethnic and racial conflicts (Addis-Ababa, Ethiopia, in October). In November a seminar on race and gender is to be held in Zagreb, Croatia.

Nationals Without Nationality

In many parts of the world people were denied citizenship and corresponding civil rights in their own countries, or stripped of citizenship, solely because of their race or national descent. In some cases this applied to populations that had been present in a country for generations, often predating their country's independence. In others, children born in their mother's country were denied that nationality because women could not transmit their nationality, rendering the children potentially stateless on gender grounds, or forced to take the nationality of a non-national father.

Denial or removal of the rights of citizenship could be a means comprehensively to deny a population a broad range of human rights. The issue was most dramatic as it concerned children's rights to a nationality and to the full exercise of human rights. Children denied citizenship in their own country were often denied a right to education, to social services, to many areas of employment as they reached adulthood, or even to documents establishing their identity. In some cases, governments informally recognized members of particular national minorities as distinct from foreigners—as in the case of Syria's large Kurdish minority, hundreds of thousands of members of Thailand's hill tribes, or Kuwait's Bidun—while according them a restrictive status short of full recognition as nationals: as if citizens without citizenship. Democratic participation in the regulation of their own community's affairs was impossible for this disenfranchised population. International conventions on statelessness were inadequate to address this denial of citizenship rights on national or racial grounds.

Arbitrary deprivation of citizenship and disputed nationality was both a cause and consequence of forcible displacement of certain populations, and proved to be a significant obstacle in seeking solutions to long-standing refugee situations. In South Asia, for example, more than 100,000 Bhutanese refugees remained in exile, the majority of them in southeast Nepal, after most of them were arbitrarily stripped of their nationality and expelled from Bhutan in the early 1990s. Ten years later, the Bhutanese government continued to block refugee return, claiming that the majority of them were not bona fide Bhutanese citizens and hence enjoyed no right to return.

Naturalization policies, by which non-nationals received citizenship, were often wholly or largely founded on discriminatory grounds. Denial was often the norm even for people with deep roots in a country who retained no connections with any other. In many regions, changing patterns of migration and catastrophic movements of refugees fleeing war or ethnic persecution had long moved large populations in an ebb and flow across national boundaries. Over decades these population movements resulted in large populations putting down new roots in countries to which they were relative newcomers, but who had no other country to which to return. The children of these upheavals were the most vulnerable to discriminatory nationality policies and practices.

In the Middle East, statelessness most frequently stemmed from the deprivation of nationality, often as a result of conflict over the composition of a state and its borders. A situation of citizens without citizenship also derived from the failure to establish nationality at crucial junctures during the process of state formation, or the redefinition of the terms of nationality that sometimes accompanied or followed international armed conflict. The denial of citizenship was exacerbated by the persistence of nationality laws that typically made it difficult for foreigners to gain nationality, even when an individual was born in a country or resident there for many years; prevented women nationals from passing their nationality to their children; and prohibited dual nationality. Taken together, these factors produced large populations whose statelessness was inherited, and often restricted their opportunity to vote, work, register marriage, births, and deaths, own or inherit property, receive government health and educational benefits, or travel.

The problem of statelessness for Palestinian refugees in host countries in the region, Syrian-born Kurds, and Bidun in Kuwait and Bahrain was largely unaddressed or addressed in unsatisfactory ways. In a report published in October 2000, Human Rights Watch criticized Kuwait's treatment of its 120,000 Bidun residents, many of whom have lived in Kuwait for decades or generations and who should be eligible for naturalization but have not been granted it. Since the mid-1980s, they have faced widespread and systematic discrimination, including violations of their right to enter and leave Kuwait, to marry and found a family, and to work. Their children's right to education, to be registered immediately after birth, and to acquire a nationality are also violated. The government of Iraq continued to force Kurds and other minorities out of the Kirkuk region and into the three northern autonomous governorates.

Particular calamities occurred when governments stripped whole ethnic or racial groups of their recognized nationality, most commonly in situations of upheaval or when new states emerged. Ethiopia summarily denationalized and expelled some seventy thousand Ethiopian citizens of Eritrean origin from their country by early 2000, after war broke out with Eritrea. Governments—and opposition groups—also seized upon the denial of citizenship to particular groups to further political aims in the absence of crisis, and in doing so sowed new crises. In the Ivory Coast, ethnic politics became a center-piece of political discourse, the questioning by high officials of who was a "true Ivorian" leading to intercommunal violence. In Cambodia, members of the ethnic Vietnamese minority faced a new wave of repression in November 1999, when authorities charged that some 600 ethnic Vietnamese residents of a floating village were illegal immigrants. The villagers were long-time Cambodian citizens, according to statements to human rights workers, and they said that local authorities confiscated their identity documents before they were forced to flee to a location near the Vietnamese border. Discriminatory nationality and citizenship policies and practices in these circumstances were frequently accompanied by racist violence. (See Cambodia.)

There was some good news. On August 29, the Thai cabinet granted citizenship to the descendants of three groups of displaced persons: Burmese who entered the country prior to March 1976, Nepalese migrants, and Chinese migrants who had migrated to Thailand since the 1960s. Members of other groups, including Thailand's ethnic minority hilltribes however, remained without a nationality or full citizenship rights. Around 300,000 such people registered with the government were permitted to reside and work in the country but faced restrictions on their movement, could not participate in elections, and could not own land. Hundreds of thousands of other hilltribe villagers remained unregistered and were officially considered as illegal immigrants. In a potentially important reform, the Thai government in May 2000 delegated decision-making on the citizenship of hilltribe children born in Thailand to district chiefs. (See Thailand.)

Migrants and Refugees

The preparations for the World Conference come in a climate of increasing xenophobia and racism in many world regions from which governments have not stood aloof. As economic globalization, regional economic crises, and political upheaval have stimulated movement of people across national borders, migrants and refugees in particular have been assailed by new measures of discrimination on an enormous scale. Migration and refugee policies are increasingly driven by xenophobic and racist attitudes. The open expression of racist views by politicians and through the media increasingly threatens the protection of refugees and migrants worldwide, with many governments indicating a greater interest in erecting barriers and keeping people out than in providing protection.

In Western Europe, the weakening of the refugee protection regime has been accompanied by both subtle and blatant forms of racist and xenophobic rhetoric. Asylum seekers and migrants—and by extension members of minorities in general—have been branded as criminals and job usurpers. This scapegoating provided tools for political mobilization by nationalist parties and even by some in the mainstream. The physical and psychological abuse of migrant workers is fueled by this racist rhetoric—and by impunity for such abuse. Women migrant domestic workers who are sexually assaulted are discouraged from seeking legal redress for sexual violence for fear of immediate detention and summary deportation. Racist abuse by private citizens, as the police stand by, is paralleled by a disturbing trend toward racist violence by the police. Some of the countries of Africa, Asia, and the Middle East that have traditionally hosted the vast majority of the world's refugees cited Western European precedents in justifying their adoption of similar restrictions, while mostly continuing to provide generous refuge to the bulk of the world's refugees.

Several U.N. bodies criticized Australia's treatment of refugees—and of its aboriginal minority—in 2000, prompting a harsh rejoinder from that country's government. In the Pacific, ethnic tensions rooted in longstanding social and economic grievances and a perception on the part of indigenous elites of dispossession by migrants or their descendants, led to a coup in Fiji in May and an attempted coup in the Solomon Islands in June.

Trends in human population movements and toward an increasingly international labor force make it particularly urgent to address racism as a factor in the generation of and response to migration and refugee flows, and in its relation to international and domestic conflict. Women migrants and girls suffered in particular, through trafficking and forced prostitution, from their lack of protection in the work place, and in constraints on family life imposed by migration and the specter of statelessness. Xenophobia, often whipped up by political or religious leaders, served to stimulate discriminatory treatment involving ever greater violence.

Foreign workers were violently attacked in Libya, where hundreds of thousands of Africans reportedly migrated over the past several years in search of work. Some fifty Chadian and Sudanese migrants were reported killed in clashes between Africans and Libyans near Tripoli in September. Thousands of other migrant workers reportedly fled the country as a consequence of the attacks.

The movement of refugees, migrants, and victims of trafficking was a major issue in Asia, with protection inevitably requiring intergovernmental cooperation. To combat trafficking of Thai women to Japan, for example, both the Thai and Japanese governments needed to reform legislation and crack down on corruption of police and immigration officials. To protect foreign migrant workers against abuse in Malaysia or Korea, countries exporting labor needed to prosecute illegal labor recruiters while the receiving countries needed to step up investigations and prosecutions of abusive employers.

Racist Impact: Criminal Justice and Public Administration

A key to the fight against discrimination was to monitor public policy which, through state action or inaction, discriminated in effect. To this end Human Rights Watch urged states to introduce transparency in governmental practices and monitor the potentially discriminatory effect of policies and practices on people within their jurisdiction. In addition to obstacles to political participation by citizens, the area of criminal justice had a particular potential for discriminatory effect, and at the national or local level involved practices—like racial profiling, in which one's race was the determining factor in falling under suspicion—with racist intent. Broader areas of public administration, notably the regulation of public health, housing, employment, and education, also required scrutiny, as alternatively constituting gateways or insuperable obstacles to the enjoyment of fundamental rights. The potential for public policies or practices to have unequal and negative consequences for particular groups required particular scrutiny.

The Committee on the Elimination of Racial Discrimination, in its General Recommendation on article 1, paragraph 1 of CERD, concluded that the convention obliges states "to nullify any law or practice *which has the effect* of creating or perpetuating racial discrimination." (Emphasis added.) As a consequence, it declared that in considering whether differentiation of treatment constituted discrimination, "it will look to see *whether that action has an unjustifiable disparate impact* upon a group distinguished by race, color, descent, or national or ethnic origin." (Emphasis added.) Such policies or practices could be expressly racist, or, while appearing race neutral, reflect a malign neglect, a refusal to take needed actions to secure equal treatment of all racial and ethnic groups. Minorities in Turkey, for example, were statistically invisible as a matter of public policy: the very existence of a Kurdish minority was denied by the state and reporting on the deprivation of this minority's rights is criminally sanctioned.

In many societies, racism was most evident in the area of criminal justice; in the administration of social services, education, and public housing; and even in restrictions of freedom of movement and the right to live in a particular area of one's own country. In the states of the former USSR, control of movement and residence continued to be exercised at the national, provincial, or municipal level. In Russia, the enforcement of these restrictions often assumed ethnic or racial dimensions, while implementation of residency controls through the *propiska* system of permits served as a pretext for the police harassment, arbitrary arrest, and extortion of people distinguished by their racial characteristics. Moscow police in September 1999 were given carte blanche in the wake of two bombing incidents there to carry out mass arrests of ethnic Chechens living in the city, taking more than twenty thousand Chechens to police stations. Administrative measures kept Chechen children out of school, while adults had trouble finding work, registering marriages, or receiving passports. (See Russia.)

In the United States, racial discrimination in the criminal justice system was increasingly the object of concern—problems the United States went some way to address in submitting its initial report to the United Nations Committee on the Elimination of Racial Discrimination in September (as required as a party to CERD). The report, although five years late, frankly acknowledged dramatically disproportionate incarceration rates for minorities in the criminal justice system and cited studies indicating that members of minority groups, especially blacks and Hispanics, "may be disproportionately subject to adverse treatment throughout the criminal justice process." It further acknowledged concerns that "incidents of police brutality seem to target disproportionately individuals belonging to racial or ethnic minorities." The report, however, did not question whether ostensibly race-neutral criminal laws or law enforcement practices causing the incarceration disparities violated CERD, nor did it acknowledge the federal government's obligation, under CERD, to ensure that state criminal justice systems (which account for 90 percent of the incarcerated population) are free of racial discrimination.

Criminal justice policies in the United States permanently stripped many of its nationals of fundamental civil rights in a manner disproportionately affecting minorities. A growing number of citizens were unable to vote because of laws that disenfranchise people convicted of felonies who are in prison, on probation, or on parole—and even, in one quarter of the states, who have finished serving their sentences. An estimated 3.9 million U.S. citizens were disenfranchised, including over one million who had fully completed their sentences. Black Americans were particularly hard hit by disenfranchisement laws: 13 percent of black men—1.4 million—were disenfranchised. In two states, almost one in three black men was unable to vote because of a felony conviction. (See United States.)

Discrimination in criminal justice and public policy was perhaps most pervasive and deep rooted where discrimination was founded on caste, or, as in the United States, where the heritage of slavery and legislated segregation remained potent factors. This sometimes embraced hidden forms of racism that had extraordinary rights-defeating consequences. In India, the emancipation by law of members of castes once known as "untouchables"—and now known as Dalits—failed to eliminate the norms and structures of India's hidden apartheid. De facto segregation continued to be enforced by government authority ranging from the police and lower courts to state and municipal officials. There are more than 160 million Dalits in India and tens of millions of others with similar caste distinctions in other South Asian countries.

The U.N. Committee on the Elimination of Discrimination against Women raised concerns about the caste system during its February review of India's initial report under the Convention on the Elimination of All Forms of Discrimination against Women. The committee expressed concern over extreme forms of physical and sexual violence against women belonging to particular castes or ethnic or religious groups India. The U.N. Committee on the Rights of the Child, in turn, concluded in January that the caste system was an obstacle to children's human rights. In Japan, the minority caste known as Burakumin also faced discriminatory treatment, despite the Burakumins' de jure equality. The Committee on the Elimination of Racial Discrimination ruled authoritatively in 1996 that the situation of India's scheduled castes, which were based on descent, fell within the scope of the convention. (See India.)

The de facto segregation of the Roma minority in many nations of Eastern Europe became increasingly visible as European political institutions raised ongoing discriminatory treatment there as a major obstacle to European integration. Harassment and violent attacks against Roma were reported in Bulgaria, Croatia, the Czech Republic, Hungary, Romania, Serbia, and Slovakia, and expulsion from homes and communities was widely reported. Roma children often lacked access to schools in Croatia, and in the Czech Republic they were disproportionately shunted into classes for the mentally disabled. In Serbia, Croatia, Hungary—and in the European Union in Greece—municipal authorities forced Roma out of their homes.

In Bulgaria, residents in a neighborhood of Burgas signed a petition on November 4, 1999, calling for the expulsion of Roma and the demolition of Roma houses; villagers in Mechka made Roma scapegoats for a crime committed in April, refusing to allow Roma in public places and threatening them with expulsion from the town. In Serbia, Roma in Sabac were turned away from a public swimming pool. In Slovakia, the head of the National Labor Office in November 1999 defended the office's policy of marking files of persons regarded as Roma with the letter "R" which he said reflected the "complicated social adaptability" of the group. The denial of nationality to Roma was also an issue in recent years in the Czech and Slovak Republics, but had been addressed by legislative reform.

The Work of Human Rights Watch

The focus of Human Rights Watch in the lead up to the 2001 conference was upon four neglected areas in which the racist effect of government policies and practices vitiated the rights of huge sectors of humanity. They included an emphasis on issues concerning two groups which required particular protection—migrants and refugees, who in their tens of millions were increasingly vulnerable as a consequence of globalization and political upheaval; and the possibly hundreds of millions of individuals who were oppressed by reason of caste. In both cases, a particular emphasis was made on the double discrimination faced by women who were victimized both by reason of their origins and their gender. The focus was also on policies and practices regarding nationality and racial discrimination in criminal justice and public administration.

Human Rights Watch took part in regular briefings of national and international bodies regarding its findings and recommendations regarding situations of racial discrimination. In August, in response to a NGO briefing organized by the International Dalit Solidarity Network—of which Human Rights Watch is a member—the U.N. Sub-Commission on the Promotion and Protection of Human

Rights passed without a vote a resolution on "discrimination on the basis of work and descent." The resolution was aimed at addressing the plight of Dalits.

Human Rights Watch delegates participated in May in the first session of the Preparatory Committee for the World Conference, in Geneva, and took part in the European conference in Strasbourg in October, the first of the five regional conferences to be held. Human Rights Watch had also participated in a series of United States regional meetings of nongovernmental organizations to plan activities around the World Conference. Human Rights Watch presented a paper to the European conference jointly with the European Council on Refugees and Exiles (ECRE) concerning the human rights of refugees and migrants, in a critique of the draft General Conclusions of the European Conference Against Racism.

Human Rights Watch explored practical measures behind which to mobilize international action to address these issues during and beyond the World Conference, including:

A call to end the deprivation of citizenship on racial and related grounds, including their intersection with gender. International agreements on statelessness should be ratified as a matter of priority; but these standards alone are inadequate to eliminate this widespread and devastating form of discrimination;

A call to develop an international program of action to make caste- or other descent-based segregation, violence, and abuse as intolerable as apartheid;

A call to ratify the International Convention on the Protection of the Rights of All Migrant Workers and Members of Their Families as a measure of protection against discriminatory treatment; to apply international refugee law to refugees without discrimination; and to improve international monitoring by which to detect and remedy discriminatory treatment of migrants and refugees.

A call for states to systematically collect and report information on law enforcement and the administration of justice, including juvenile justice, as it concerns different population groups, with a view to identifying and remedying any discriminatory purpose or effect;

A call for states to monitor the administration of public affairs in such areas as education, health care, housing, and the enforcement of labor rights, in order to identify and remedy any discriminatory purpose or effect in public policy and programs.

Relevant Human Rights Watch Reports:

Bosnia and Hercegovina: Unfinished Business: Return of Displaced Persons and Other Human Rights Issues in Bijeljina, 5/00

Burma/Bangladesh: Burmese Refugees in Bangladesh: Still No Durable Solution, 5/00

Burundi: Neglecting Justice in Making Peace, 4/00

Burundi: Emptying the Hills: Regroupment Camps in Burundi, 7/00

China: Tibet Since 1950: Silence Prison or Exile, 5/00

Democratic Republic of the Congo: Eastern Congo Ravaged: Killing Civilians and Silencing Protest, 5/00

Federal Republic of Yugoslavia/Kosovo: Rape As A Weapon of "Ethnic Cleansing," 3/00

Japan: Owed Justice: Thai Women Trafficked into Debt Bondage in Japan, 9/00

Kuwait: Promises Betrayed: Denial of Rights of Bidun, Women, and Freedom of Expression, 10/00

Malaysia/Burma: Living in Limbo: Burmese Rohingyas in Malaysia, 8/00

Russia/Chechnya: "No Happiness Remains:" Civilian Killings, Pillage, and Rape in Alkhan-yurt, Chechnya, 3/00

Russia/Chechnya: February 5: A Day of Slaughter in Novye Aldi, 6/00

Rwanda: The Search for Security and Human Rights Abuses, 4/00

Turkey: Human Rights and the European Union Accession Partnership, 9/00

United States: Fingers to the Bone: United States Failure to Protect Child Farmworkers, 6/00

United States: No Minor Matter: Children in Maryland's Jails, 11/99

United States: Punishment and Prejudice: Racial Disparities in the War on Drugs, 5/00

REFUGEES, ASYLUM SEEKERS, AND INTERNALLY DISPLACED PERSONS

50 Years On: What Future for International Refugee Protection?

How countries treat those who have been forced to flee persecution and human rights abuse elsewhere is a litmus test of their commitment to defending human rights and upholding humanitarian values. Yet, fifty years after its inception, the states that first established a formal refugee protection system appeared to be abandoning this principle, and the future of the international refugee regime was under serious threat.

The year 2000/2001 marked the fiftieth anniversary of the establishment of an international refugee protection regime, set up primarily by European states to respond to the needs of some 30 million people displaced during the Second World War. In December 1950, the Office of the United Nations High Commissioner for Refugees (UNHCR) was established and in July 1951 an international instrument to protect the rights of refugees—the 1951 Convention relating to the Status of Refugees (1951 convention)—came into effect.

At the core of the international refugee regime is the fundamental right of any individual to seek and enjoy asylum from persecution in other countries. Enshrined in article 14 (1) of the 1948 Universal Declaration of Human Rights, the principle of asylum recognizes that when all other forms of human rights protection have failed, individuals must be able to leave their country freely and seek refuge elsewhere. The availability of asylum can literally be a matter of life or death for those at risk of persecution or abuse.

A Changing Climate for Refugees

Until the 1990s most refugee movements were a consequence of Cold War politics, and refugees often had a strategic geopolitical value in the arena of superpower rivalry. Their existence was used either to discredit countries of origin, or to bolster the image of receiving countries and strengthen alliances with superpower partners, as in the case of Nicaraguan refugees in Honduras, Afghans in Pakistan, and Cambodians in Thailand.

Several factors coincided at the beginning of the 1990s to change the political environment for refugees. First, the end of the Cold War era caused refugees to lose much of their geopolitical and military value. Host countries preferred to establish good political and economic relations with their neighbors and refugees were viewed as a potential irritant. Many refugee hosting countries, affected by regional economic crises, claimed that fewer resources were available to host large, long-term refugee populations or fund lengthy and expensive asylum determination procedures. Refugees were made scapegoats for many countries' domestic problem and blamed for threatening national or regional security, draining resources, degrading the environment, and rising crime. Politicians shamelessly employed xenophobic rhetoric to win electoral support and, with the popular press, peddled images of "floods" of refugees and immigrants pouring into their countries. In the industrialized states, particularly, many governments became obsessed with erecting barriers to keep people out, rather than providing protection.

While this was occurring, the convergence of political and economic instability throughout much of the world with the increasing global accessibility of international communications and travel meant that larger numbers of people were on the move—some to escape the misery of economic privations, others to escape persecution, conflict, and gross human rights abuse. As legal channels of migration were curbed, people turned increasingly to alternative methods to reach their country of destination, including the services of opportunistic, exploitative and often dangerous human trafficking and smuggling rings that were able to circumvent routine migration controls. By the end of the 1990s, governments, particularly in industrialized states, viewed the trafficking and smuggling of persons as one of the most serious aspects of transnational organized crime and joined forces in a concerted drive to end the practice. Unfortunately, protecting the human rights of trafficked and smuggled persons was not the primary motive behind these efforts. Instead, combating human trafficking and smuggling became these governments' primary response to the asylum and migration issue. Much less attention was paid to why asylum seekers and migrants made use of such methods to reach their country of destination or to the root causes of such outflows, and even less to the need to preserve the right of all persons, regardless of their means of travel, to seek and enjoy asylum from persecution

Industrialized States: The Beginning and the End of Refugee Protection?

Western Europe

Nowhere was the retraction in protection more pronounced than in the industrialized countries of Western Europe, North America, and Australia—the very countries responsible for establishing the international refugee regime. Western European countries made particularly vigorous and visible efforts to control inflows of asylum seekers and perceived abuse of the asylum system. The pursuit of a zero immigration policy throughout Western Europe since the 1970s, and the closure of almost all alternative legal channels of immigration, coupled with the global trends described above, led to a marked increase in the number of people applying for asylum in Western European countries between 1985 (157,280 applicants) and 1992 (673,947 applicants). Governments perceived that the

asylum system was being abused by individuals who were leaving their countries for economic reasons rather than in pursuit of international protection. Racist violence rose in many countries, fueled by the anti-immigration rhetoric of politicians and the media, creating a hostile environment for refugees and migrants throughout the region.

Harmonization of European Asylum Policy

During the 1990s, European Union (E.U.) countries sought to harmonize their immigration and asylum policies. This process started in the early 1990s with various non-binding resolutions adopted by member states of the then European Community on different aspects of asylum policy. Two important treaties, the Schengen Agreement on common border controls, and the Dublin Convention establishing arrangements for identifying state responsibility for assessing asylum applications came into effect in 1997 and 1994, respectively.

The 1997 Treaty of Amsterdam, effective from May 1999, further advanced harmonization, as states determined common criteria for dealing with asylum applicants, reception of asylum seekers, family reunification, and deportation policies. A disturbing protocol to the treaty restricted the right of E.U. citizens to seek asylum in another E.U. state.

In an effort to proceed from the agenda established in the Amsterdam Treaty, in October 1999 a "Special Meeting of the European Council on the Establishment of an Area of Freedom, Security and Justice" was held in Tampere, Finland. The Presidency Conclusions of the Tampere European Council were generally viewed as a positive development by advocacy groups as they included a a reaffirmation of the right to seek asylum, and a commitment to work towards the establishment of a common European asylum system based on the full and inclusive application of the 1951 convention and to harmonize European asylum policies with "guarantees to those who seek protection in or access to the European Union." Less positive, however, was the continuing emphasis on common policies to contain and control asylum and migration movements.

In December 1998, the E.U. High Level Working Group on Asylum and Migration was set up to produce Action Plans on the root causes of migration in six major refugee and migrant producing countries. The Action Plans focused on integrated strategies to control migration outflows both from the regions of origin and into E.U. countries.

In July 2000, the French government, then holding the E.U. presidency, issued an "action plan to improve the control of immigration." Similar to other such E.U. initiatives, the French proposed an information exchange, early warning, and response system to coordinate E.U. member states' response to "waves" of immigration, characterized as a "fire-brigade policing" approach. In addition, they proposed establishing a network of E.U. immigration liaison officers in principal migration source countries to help control migration flows.

Access to Asylum Barred

Central to the right to seek asylum is the principle of freedom of movement and the right of an individual to leave any country, including their own. Yet European asylum policy systematically obstructed these rights during the 1990s. Most explicit was the introduction of visa requirements for nationals of common refugee producing countries, including those with well-documented human rights problems, such as China, Burma, Sudan, the Democratic Republic of Congo, Sierra Leone, Turkmenistan, and Rwanda. Beginning with a September 1995 Regulation, the E.U. maintained a common list of countries whose nationals were required to obtain visas before entering the territory of any E.U. state. The October 1999 Presidency Conclusions of the Tampere European Council, and a draft 2000 European Commission (E.C.) Regulation on a common visa regime, also contributed to a standardization of visa imposition across the European Union. As no would-be refugee was likely to be able to obtain a visa to come to a Western European country, this effectively forced asylum seekers either to travel on false or forged documents, or with no documentation.

At the same time, E.U. countries introduced legislation that penalized asylum seekers who traveled on forged or false documents and the companies that transported them. Carriers' liability legislation, resulting in heavy fines for airlines and shipping companies that transported undocumented or incorrectly documented migrants, became a requirement under the Schengen Agreement on border controls. Private travel companies were effectively made responsible for front-line immigration controls and they began to take proactive measures to avoid the fines, including rigorous pre-departure immigration checks by airline staff.

The E.U. adopted a new policy on border control in October 1996, establishing "airline liaison officers." By July 2000, the U.K., Danish, German, and Dutch governments were all using immigration officers in their embassies and consulates in main refugee-generating countries to assist airline staff in checking the authenticity of travel documents. In a July 2000 report, UNHCR criticized efforts to intercept potential asylum seekers at the point of departure without a substantive review of their asylum claim as an obstruction of the right to seek asylum which could amount to constructive *refoulement* if individuals were thereby prevented from leaving countries where their lives and freedom were threatened.

Those asylum seekers who did manage to evade pre-departure border controls and reach their country of destination faced punitive measures on arrival. Increasingly, asylum seekers who arrived in E.U. countries with false, forged, or no documents were immediately detained—ostensibly for short periods to allow the authorities to verify their identity, but in practice often for weeks or months. Illegal entry also impacted negatively on refugee status determination procedures. Asylum seekers who entered illegally were often given fast-track assessments, or considered as "manifestly unfounded" cases, and their means of entry contributed to negative assessments of credibility.

Article 31 of the 1951 convention explicitly exempted refugees who come directly from the territory where they fear persecution from punishment for illegal entry, provided that they present themselves without delay to the authorities and show good cause for their illegal entry or presence. Long before the virtual *cordon sanitaire* was created around Western Europe, the drafters of the 1951 convention recognized that many refugees must leave their countries under extreme circumstances and have little opportunity to obtain legal travel documents or permission to enter their country of asylum.

Containment in the Region

E.U. and other states also sought increasingly to contain refugee movements within their region of origin. This began in January 1998 with the E.U.'s "Action Plan on the Influx of Migrants from Iraq and the Neighboring Region," a panicked response to fears of a possible "mass influx" of Turkish and Iraqi Kurds into Western Europe. The proposal set the tone for Action Plans on Somalia, Afghanistan, Morocco, Iraq, and Sri Lanka prepared by the E.U. High Level Working Group on Asylum and Migration. These dealt cursorily with preventive measures such as conflict resolution, development, and poverty reduction in refugees' countries of origin, but focused primarily on exporting migration controls, such as airport liaison officers, anti-immigration information campaigns, and readmission arrangements to the source countries. While welcoming the comprehensive approach to migration that addressed root causes as well as migration policies, advocacy groups criticized the action plans for failing effectively to address human rights violations in countries of origin and the need for refugee protection for those who fled such violations. Like the first Iraq action plan, the overriding aim of the High Level Working Group action plans appeared to be containing migration in the region and preventing flows of asylum seekers and migrants to E.U. countries.

1951 Refugee Convention Under Threat

Western European governments sought to dilute their obligations under the 1951 convention and its 1967 protocol, despite reaffirming the centrality of these treaties in both the 1997 Amsterdam Treaty and the 1999 Presidency Conclusions of the Tampere European Council. In particular, they applied the refugee definition in an overly restrictive way, not intended by the drafters of the convention, thereby excluding many people at risk of persecution from international refugee protection. Those excluded included people who fled persecution by non-state agents, such as the Taliban in Afghanistan, or situations of generalized violence and civil conflict, as in Colombia. Governments also insisted that asylum seekers demonstrate actual persecution, not just a credible fear of future persecution. Advocacy groups, such as the non-governmental European Council on Refugees and Exiles, argued that these narrow interpretations were inconsistent with international refugee law.

E.U. states also introduced various alternative, or complementary, protection regimes as substitutes for 1951 convention protection. Under most of these regimes, states granted asylum seekers temporary leave to remain on humanitarian grounds, but did not extend to them the full rights and protection of 1951 convention refugee status. These alternative regimes were often highly discretionary with no consistency between E.U. states regarding the length of stay allowed or the rights afforded to the individual. Moreover, temporary protection—which was initially intended to deal with mass influx emergencies where states were unable to conduct individual refugee status determination—was increasingly applied as a subsidiary form of refugee protection.

Taken together, the overly restrictive application of the 1951 convention and the increasing use of alternative, subsidiary forms of protection resulted in states narrowing their obligations under the 1951 convention, the denial of meaningful protection for those in need, and serious erosion of the international refugee protection regime. Added to this, between 1998 and 2000 various E.U. governments proposed drastic revisions to the 1951 convention in order to make it more "relevant" to contemporary migration challenges. The Austrian government, while holding the E.U. presidency, first proposed this in a July 1998 strategy paper that depicted the 1951 convention as a product of the Cold War period that had never been intended to deal with contemporary large-scale refugee movements caused by civil war, inter-ethnic violence, and persecution by non-state agents. The Austrians proposed a comprehensive, integrated approach to migration that addressed trade and development, as well as migration policy. This proposal, particularly its reference to the need to amend the 1951 convention, was considered too radical by most E.U. states at the time.

British Home Secretary Jack Straw reopened the issue in June 2000, at a conference organized by the Portuguese E.U. presidency on a common European asylum system, launching a vigorous attack on the relevance and efficacy of the 1951 convention. He claimed that the European asylum system was massively abused by economic migrants who had no credible asylum claim and who were brought to Europe by highly organized criminal trafficking or smuggling syndicates. He characterized the 1951 convention as inadequate and never intended to deal with contemporary "massive intercontinental migratory movement."

He proposed a new approach to refugee protection whereby E.U. states would designate those countries and ethnic groups most at risk of persecution, agree on quotas of asylum seekers from these countries, and determine asylum claims within regions of origin. He also proposed a list of "safe countries" which would include "all E.U. states, the U.S., Canada, Australia and *many others*" (our emphasis) from which applications for asylum would not be considered. A third group would include "the accession states and others" where there would be a general presumption of safety and asylum claims would be considered under an acceler-

ated process.

The British proposal was a worrying return to the notion of "safe countries of origin" and highlighted yet again the lack of commitment amongst European governments to upholding the right of all individuals to leave their countries and seek asylum.

Australia: Xenophobia and Threats to Asylum

Australia also increasingly pursued a punitive asylum policy and showed little regard for either abiding or being judged by international human rights standards. Despite only receiving a tiny proportion of the world's refugees—9,450 asylum applicants in 1999, compared with 95,110 applicants in Germany—Australia reacted with disproportionate zeal to a perceived threat of being overwhelmed by "floods" of foreigners brought in through illegal people trafficking and smuggling.

Australia pursued a draconian policy of mandatory detention for all asylum seekers and other non-citizens who arrived though "illegal" channels with forged, illegal, or no documents, and who declared themselves as asylum seekers on arrival. In July 2000, the U.N. Human Rights Committee criticized Australia for its mandatory detention policies and for not informing, nor allowing , NGOs access to inform detainees of their right to seek legal advice. Asylum seekers were kept in remote detention centers thousands of miles away from major population centers.

In October 1999, Australia made amendments to its 1958 Migration Act that, according to UNHCR, seriously undermined refugee protection. Refugees arriving in an unauthorized manner were refused family reunification rights for a minimum of thirty months after they received refugee status and were not provided with travel documents in violation of article 31 of the 1951 convention; article 28 of the 1951 convention, which provides for travel documents for refugees that permit re-entry; and fundamental principles of family unity upheld in the 1951 convention, in UNHCR Executive Committee Conclusions, and in other international human rights instruments.

On August 29, 2000, the Australian government stated that it would restrict future cooperation with U.N. bodies and in particular reject treaty bodies' requests to delay the deportation of unsuccessful asylum seekers. This followed two high profile interventions by the U.N. Committee against Torture seeking a delay in the return of asylum seekers until it had considered their claims that they would face torture in the countries they had fled. The government also announced that it would undertake a comprehensive review of the interpretation and implementation of the 1951 convention and consider the need for remedial legislation.

The Global Picture

The anti-refugee policies and xenophobic attitudes of industrialized states had significant global export value. Traditionally generous hosting countries in Africa, Asia, and the Middle East referred to the example set in the West when defending their own increasingly restrictive policies and practices. Nevertheless, the world's poorer nations continued to host the vast majority of the world's refugees and in times of crisis endeavored to keep their doors open to those fleeing civil conflict and gross human rights abuse.

Africa

Traditionally one of the most generous refugee hosting regions in the world, recent years saw a significant shift in African refugee policies. The plethora of violent internal and regional conflicts that plagued so many African countries over the past decade meant that at the turn of the century few countries were immune from refugee crises. Yet the presence of militia groups within refugee settlements and the fear that mass refugee movements would result in instability and conflicts spilling over national borders made host countries increasingly wary and contributed to more restrictive refugee policies and, in some cases, lack of safe asylum. The Great Lakes refugee crisis—sparked by the Rwandan genocide in 1994 and subsequent and continuing mass movements of refugees across as many as nine countries, and the conspicuous and destabilizing presence of military and political elements in refugee camps—heralded the end of the legacy of generous asylum and open-door policies for refugees in Central and East Africa.

West Africa

By mid-2000, a similar scenario was unfolding in West Africa, where a deteriorating security situation threatened the safety of hundreds of thousands of refugees. Host to the second largest refugee population in Africa, Guinea earned a reputation as a generous country of refuge. By September 2000, there were nearly half a million refugees—330,00 Sierra Leoneans and 126,000 Liberians—inside Guinea.

This pattern of generous hospitality was seriously threatened by the deteriorating security situation in the region in 2000. A rapid influx of refugees into Guinea from Sierra Leone from May onwards and fears of infiltration by Sierra Leonean rebels, prompted the Guinean government to close its borders with Sierra Leone in early August, although "vulnerable" groups were subsequently allowed entry following interventions by UNHCR. Tensions rose between Guinea, Sierra Leone, and Liberia from late July onwards, as each country accused the other of supporting rebel activity. A series of cross-border attacks from both Liberia and Sierra Leone between August and October claimed the lives of hundreds of Guinean civilians and injured many others. Most of these attacks occurred close to the Sierra Leonean and Liberian borders in exactly the same areas where the refugee camps were located.

The attacks resulted in serious reprisals against Sierra Leonean and Liberian refugees in Guinea, both in the border camps and in the cities. On September 9, Guinean President Lansana Conte made an inflammatory broadcast in which he blamed refugees for harboring rebels and urged the Guinean population to round-up all foreigners. For several days, armed groups of civilian militias, police, and soldiers broke into the homes of Sierra Leonean and Liberian refugees in Conakry, beat, raped, and arrested them, and looted their belongings. Over five thousand people were detained and hundreds more sought refuge in the Sierra Leonean and Liberian embassies. Hundreds of refugees fled Guinea, many of them by boat back to Sierra Leone. Despite pleas for calm and assurances by government officials that Guinea would remain a safe country of asylum for refugees, President Conte made further anti-refugee statements in a speech marking the anniversary of Guinea's independence on October 2.

The situation for refugees in camps along the Liberian and Sierra Leonean borders was also critical. Several camps in the Forecariah region on the border with Sierra Leone were attacked by Sierra Leonean rebels and by Guinean civilians, forcing thousands of refugees to flee back into rebel-controlled areas of Sierra Leone. At the same time, Guinea's borders with Sierra Leone and Liberia remained closed to refugees fleeing conflict and human rights violations, and refugees in Guinea were faced with the unenviable choice of remaining unprotected in Guinea, or returning to Liberia and Sierra Leone.

Guinea in Perspective

Security versus Asylum: The Case of Thailand

The situation in Guinea exemplified two worrying trends. The first was governments' readiness to indiscriminately blame and take actions against foreigners and refugees when faced with national security threats. In Thailand, for example, the government reacted harshly when Burmese gunmen seized the Burmese embassy in Bangkok in October 1999 and took five hundred people hostage in the Ratchaburi provincial hospital in January 2000. Following these events, the authorities announced that all refugees should move to camps along the border and Maneeloy Student Center, a camp for dissident Burmese refugees, would be closed. Thai authorities deported five Burmese, four of whom had

applied for refugee status with UNHCR, to the border town of Myawaddy where they were arrested by the Burmese authorities. Provincial admission boards were set up to determine asylum claims, and refugee protection was restricted only to those fleeing fighting in Burma. All other Burmese were declared to be illegal immigrants and risked forcible repatriation to Burma. In June, the Thai authorities expelled 116 refugees from Don Yang refugee camp in Kanchanaburi Province, and in August, Thai officials returned around one hundred ethnic minority Karen from Nu Pho Camp in Rak province.

Disparity in International Response: The Kosovo Factor

The second trend highlighted by the Guinea crisis was the gross disparity in the international response to refugee crises. Despite the similarities with the situation in Macedonia during the Kosovo emergency in 1999, the difference in the international response to the two situations was striking. Unlike Macedonia, where the international community poured in resources and reacted quickly to evacuate refugees and thus relieve the pressure on Macedonia and help to keep the borders open, the international response to the crisis in Guinea was negligible. The crisis hardly touched the world media headlines, international funding was seriously lacking, and there was certainly no airlifting of refugees to safety in Western countries.

Attacks on Humanitarian Workers Threaten Refugee Protection

A major threat to refugee protection throughout 2000 was the alarming spate of attacks on humanitarian workers. The brutal murders of three UNHCR staff members in Atambua, West Timor, on September 6, and the murder of the head of the UNHCR office and abduction of another staff member in Macenta, Guinea, on September 17, highlighted the extreme dangers for humanitarian workers worldwide. The murders provoked a global protest and prompted UNHCR to withdraw all staff from West Timor, as well as from the border areas of Guinea. At the same time, they left refugees in these areas almost completely unprotected and unassisted with no outside witnesses to abuses.

West Timor

Despite the return of over 170,000 refugees to East Timor since mass forced expulsions in 1999, as many as 125,000 refugees remained in camps in West Timor where many of them had been held hostage by the same militia leaders responsible for the violence that had erupted in East Timor following the pro-independence referendum vote in September 1999. Human Rights Watch charged continuously throughout 1999 and 2000 that the Indonesian authorities and army had failed to disarm the militia or prevent attacks on refugees in the camps and on humanitarian workers assisting them. In September 2000, UNHCR reported a total of 120 incidents of attacks, harassment, and intimidation of humanitarian workers and refugees since it established a presence in West Timor a year earlier. In August 2000, UNHCR was forced to close down its operations in the camps when three of its staff members were attacked and seriously injured while delivering assistance to Naen camp, outside Kefamenaunu town. The murder of the three staff in Atambua occurred within a week of UNHCR resuming its operations.

Following the withdrawal of nearly all international staff from West Timor, the camps were largely cut off from any international assistance or protection and there was little information about conditions inside. Most critically, Human Rights Watch and local NGOs expressed serious concerns that the registration of the refugees by the Indonesian authorities without minimal safeguards to ensure freedom of choice and in the absence of international monitoring could result in the forcible relocation of refugees to other parts of Indonesia against their will. The U.N., on the other hand, insisted that they would not return staff to West Timor until credible security guarantees were in place. These included the arrest and trial of the perpetrators of the UNHCR murders and other attacks on humanitarian workers; the complete disarming and disbanding of the militias; and the restoration of law, order and security in the camps in West Timor. More than a month after the killings, although the Indonesian authorities had arrested six suspects, there was no evidence that the militias had been brought under control or that law and order had been restored to the camps.

The situations in Guinea and West Timor posed a grave dilemma for the international community. On the one hand, it was clearly unacceptable for humanitarian workers to be the targets of deliberate and vicious attacks. On the other, the withdrawal of all international staff considerably increased the vulnerability of displaced people and their exposure to attacks, forced return, and other abuses. Until governments are able to ensure the security of humanitarian workers, the protection of some of the world's most vulnerable populations will be seriously at risk.

Protecting Refugee Women and Children

Throughout the year, refugee women were victims of sexual and domestic violence. In Guinea, for example, women were targeted in the retaliatory attacks on refugees in the wake of President Conte's inflammatory anti-refugee declarations. Human Rights Watch reported on the rape of Sierra Leonean and Liberian refugee women by groups of armed civilian militia, police, and soldiers in the September attacks in Conakry. Women, some of them as young as fourteen, were raped—in many cases gang raped—sexually assaulted, and humiliated, often in the presence of family members. Many of the women had fled Sierra Leone to escape gross human rights violations, including rape and other sexual assault. Human Rights Watch charged that UNHCR and the international community were slow to publicly condemn these brutal attacks against refugee women and called on the Guinean government and UNHCR to immediately investigate the incidents of rape and bring the perpetrators to justice. In 2000, Human Rights Watch issued a report on the high levels of sexual and domestic violence against Burundian refugee women in camps in Tanzania. The situation in Guinea and Tanzania highlighted the persistent dangers for refugee women and lack of effective protection against or rapid response to sexual violence in emergency situations and to domestic violence in refugee settlements.

Protracted Refugee Crises: The Right to Return

Throughout the world, millions of refugees remained in exile unable to return to their homes either because of continuing political instability and insecurity, or because of deliberate obstructions by states unwilling to take them back. In South Asia, despite high level visits by U.N. High Commissioner for Refugees Sadako Ogata to Nepal and Bhutan in April and May 2000, and U.S. Assistant Secretary of State for Refugees, Julia Taft, to Nepal in October 1999, and to Bhutan in January 2000, more than 100,000 Bhutanese refugees were denied their legitimate right to return to Bhutan and remained in camps in southeast Nepal. The refugees, many of whom were arbitrarily stripped of their Bhutanese nationality despite having lived in Bhutan for several generations, were expelled from the country in the early 1990s during a government crack-down on Bhutanese of ethnic-Nepali origin living in southern Bhutan. Since then, the Bhutanese government has systematically blocked the refugees' return, claiming that the majority are not Bhutanese citizens, and has shunned international offers to assist in resolving the situation.

Elsewhere, in Bosnia and Hercegovina, over one million people remained displaced, the majority of them internally, and unable to return to minority areas due to bureaucratic obstructions and lack of available housing. There was, however, some progress in 2000, and by June UNHCR had registered 19,751 returns, many of them spontaneous, as compared to 7,709 during the comparable period in 1999.

Palestinian refugees remained the largest and most protracted refugee situation in the world. In 1997, UNHCR estimated that there were 6.4 million Palestinian refugees worldwide, about half of whom were believed to be stateless. In March 2000, 3.7 million Palestinian refugees were registered with the United Nations Relief and Works Agency (UNRWA) in Jordan, Syria, Lebanon, and the Israeli-occupied West Bank and Gaza. The Israeli government has made the return of Palestinian refugees both legally and practically impossible since their exodus following the 1948-49 Arab-Israeli war, and the 1967 war, thus denying Palestinian refugees their legitimate right to return to their own country. Although the resolution of the refugee crisis was a key issue on the agenda of the final status negotiations between Israel and the Palestinian Liberation Organization (PLO), little progress was made in 2000. Human Rights Watch supported a rights-based approach to the resolution of the refugee problem that upheld the right of Palestinian refugees to return to their own country, as well as opportunities for local integration in host countries or third country resettlement. Individuals should be able to choose freely and in an informed manner their preferred option. In the event that individuals are unable to return to their original homes or place of residence, they should be able to return to the vicinity and compensation should be provided according to international standards.

The Challenge of the New Millennium: Protecting the Internally Displaced

Debate over Institutional Responsibility

The plight of internally displaced persons dominated humanitarian debate throughout 2000. The year began with an impassioned statement by U.S. Ambassador to the U.N. Richard Holbrooke during a Security Council session on humanitarian assistance to displaced persons in Africa in January. Having recently returned from a trip to Angola, Holbrooke expressed dismay at the lack of an effective international response to the problem of internal displacement. He challenged the very distinction between a refugee and an internally displaced person (IDP) and made a controversial call for a single agency to take responsibility for providing protection to IDPs, citing UNHCR as the most appropriate choice.

Holbrooke's statements triggered a frenzied response within the U.N. system. While there was a general consensus that the existing system of responding to internal displacement crises was inadequate, there was widespread opposition to giving UNHCR lead agency responsibility for IDPs. To a certain extent, the debate turned into an ugly turf battle between rival U.N. agencies unwilling to yield more power and responsibility to UNHCR. But there were also more substantive reasons for the reservations to Holbrooke's proposals.

Refugee experts pointed out the dangers of collapsing the terms refugee and internally displaced person in legal and protection terms. Refugees, by definition, are unable, or unwilling, to avail themselves of the protection of their own country and have crossed an international border in search of protection. Governments have an obligation under international law to provide refugees with protection and UNHCR's mandate is to ensure that governments abide by these obligations. Internally displaced persons, on the other hand, remain, if only technically, under the protection of their own governments and do not automatically trigger an international response. Refugee advocates feared that UNHCR's involvement in providing in-country protection to internally displaced persons could provide an excuse for asylum countries to return refugees to their countries of origin. Indeed, Western European and other industrialized states were already denying asylum to refugees for whom they believed "internal flight alternatives" or "in-country" protection existed in their country of origin.

In a July 2000 address in New York, U.N. High Commissioner for Refugees Sadako Ogata also expressed reservations about eroding the distinction between refugees and IDPs, because of the specific nature of protection required by each group. Ogata also criticized the international community for focusing too much on the question of the institutional response to internal displacement, and too

little on the underlying political, economic and social root causes.

Despite Holbrooke's resolute support for a lead-agency model, the U.N. sided with a collaborative approach. A senior inter-agency network was established to review the U.N.'s response to situations of internal displacement, under the auspices of the Office for the Coordination of Humanitarian Affairs (OCHA), and a special focal point on internal displacement was created in the U.N. secretariat.

Human Rights Watch: Focus on Protecting Internally Displaced Persons

While Human Rights Watch did not take a position on specific inter-agency responsibility for internally displaced persons, the organization continued to advocate for more consistent and effective protection for IDPs and for more active adherence by governments with the Guiding Principles on Internal Displacement and other human rights and humanitarian standards pertaining to the internally displaced. Human Rights Watch monitored and reported on a wide range of situations of internal displacement worldwide. These included longstanding situations of internal displacement, such as in Sri Lanka, Turkey and Colombia, as well as new displacement crises.

The escalation of the border conflict between Ethiopia and Eritrea during May 2000 provoked massive displacements of both Eritreans and Ethiopians. Nearly 1.5 million Eritreans were uprooted by the conflict, including 90,000 who sought refuge in Sudan—more than a quarter of whom had returned to Eritrea by October 2000. In Angola, a new wave of internal displacement was sparked by the intense fighting following the governmental campaign launched in October 1999 to flush out UNITA from their traditional strongholds in the central highlands. More than 200,000 persons were displaced during the first half of 2000, and at the end of June, the total number of IDPs was estimated at 2.5 million. In Colombia, some 134,000 persons were displaced during the first part of 2000, most by paramilitaries as well as guerrillas and the armed forces, adding to the estimated total of 1.8 million IDPs and 80,000-105,000 refugees from Colombia in Venezuela, Ecuador, and Panama at the end of 1999.

The eastern part of the Democratic Republic of Congo (DRC) experienced a rapid deterioration in the humanitarian situation from the start of the year, with fighting in the South and North Kivu areas resulting in major population displacements. By July 2000, a total of 1.6 million people were displaced in the DRC. In the Moluccan islands region of Indonesia, clashes between members of Muslim and Christian communities since early 1999 left three thousand or more people dead and displaced hundreds of thousands. In Russia, hundreds of thousands of Chechens remained displaced in the neighboring republic of Ingushetia following the conflict in Chechnya in 1999.

Human Rights Watch identified a wide variety of serious protection problems facing internally displaced persons worldwide.

Access to Safety Denied

Russian authorities continued to deny displaced Chechens access to safety in Ingushetia and elsewhere in the Russian Federation. On a number of occasions between October and December 1999, Russian forces fired on convoys of fleeing Chechen civilians resulting in scores of deaths and injuries. In October 1999, for example, at least eleven people were killed when a Russian tank fired on a bus carrying displaced persons near the Russian-controlled town of Chervlyonnaya. On October 29, a large civilian convoy, including Red Cross vehicles, was attacked outside Shaami-Yurt. Serious abuses, including widespread extortion, theft, arbitrary arrests, beatings, and in some cases rape, were common at the Russian check points. Young males were particularly targeted, discouraging many from trying to leave. Russian officials also repeatedly closed the borders between Chechnya and Ingushetia, Dagestan, Stavropol, and North Ossetia. In November 1999, for example, 40,000 civilians were

stranded for days in heavy fighting when the Russian authorities closed the Ingush-Chechen border. In January 2000, the authorities announced that males between the ages of ten and sixty would not be allowed to leave Chechnya, although this policy was later retracted under international pressure.

In Sri Lanka, between May and July 2000, both the armed separatist Liberation Tigers of Tamil Eelam (LTTE) and the government imposed severe restrictions on IDPs trying to move out of areas under their control. This often meant that civilians were trapped in conflict zones and unable to flee.

Forced Round-ups and Relocation Programs

In other situations, government or rebel forces deliberately rounded-up civilians and held them in camp-like settlements. In Burundi, for example, 350,000 people had been forced into "regroupment" camps around the capital, Bujumbura, by January 2000 as part of the government's counter-insurgency program. Soldiers used force and threats to move civilians into the camps, killing and injuring dozens. Despite concerted pressure from the international community, including Nelson Mandela, it was not until June that the authorities began to systematically disband the camps. By October most of the camps around Bujumbura were closed, but officials continued using "temporary" regroupment to make it easier for soldiers to "cleanse" areas of rebels.

Restrictions on Freedom of Movement

Human Rights Watch reported on numerous situations where freedom of movement was obstructed and the movement of displaced persons manipulated by both government and rebel forces. In Aceh, Indonesian soldiers reportedly emptied IDP camps by force and prevented others from leaving their homes. Acehnese rebels, on the other hand, reportedly encouraged displacement, preventing displaced persons from staying with relatives and forcing them into large, more visible centralized camps. In Congo

Brazzaville, rebel militia groups held displaced persons hostage in camps for much of 1999 and prevented them from returning to their homes. Government authorities also restricted the return of IDPs. In May 1999, the government facilitated a mass return of IDPs from their hiding places in the forests of southern Congo back to the capital with promises to guarantee their safety. Instead, soldiers at roadblocks raped and assaulted hundreds of women and girls, and extrajudicially executed scores of young men who were randomly accused of being rebels.

Lack of Access to Humanitarian Assistance

A serious problem facing internally displaced persons everywhere was lack of access to humanitarian assistance. Infant and maternal mortality and morbidity rates amongst IDPs were, as a result, some of the highest in the world. There were three main reasons for lack of humanitarian access:

First, in places such as Chechnya, the Democratic Republic of Congo (DRC), Burundi, Congo Brazzaville, Sri Lanka, Indonesia's Moluccan islands, and Angola, the extremely dangerous security conditions, lack of security guarantees, landmines, and inaccessibility of camps prevented humanitarian workers from having access to thousands of internally displaced persons. In the DRC, for example, the U.N. estimated that only one million of the 1.6 million IDPs had access to any humanitarian assistance due to the precarious security conditions in South Kivu. As a result, infant mortality rates amongst the displaced were the highest in the region and the maternal mortality rate was the highest in the world;

Second, were deliberate obstructions to the delivery of humanitarian assistance by government authorities or rebel forces, as in Burundi, Congo Brazzaville, the DRC, Sri Lanka, Aceh, Indonesia's Moluccan islands, and Chechnya. In Aceh, for example, Indonesian authorities in some cases tried to obstruct local NGOs and student groups in their efforts to assist IDPs through physical attacks, detention, torture, and harsh treatment of volunteers, destruction of volunteer posts, and seizure of medical supplies. In Burundi, soldiers occasionally blocked international agencies trying to bring assistance to the camps, and even when access was resumed many of the camps were inaccessible to relief agencies;

Third, humanitarian assistance was limited by inadequate international response and lack of coordination. In Angola, for example, a U.N. interagency mission in March 2000 concluded that there were serious gaps in the planning, delivery, and monitoring of humanitarian assistance. And in October 1999, the relief agency, Medecins Sans Frontieres (Doctors Without Borders), decried the "unbearable silence of the international community" toward the "forgotten war" in Congo Brazzaville.

Forcible Return of Displaced Persons

Finally, Human Rights Watch reported on the forcible return of displaced persons to areas where their safety could not be guaranteed, in blatant violation of international humanitarian law and the Guiding Principles on Internal Displacement. In December 1999, for example, the Russian military compiled a list of twenty-four towns and village under Russian control designated as "safe areas" for IDP return. In a letter to the then prime minister Vladamir Putin, Human Rights Watch declared that while the armed conflict continued in Chechnya it was not safe for displaced persons to return. Documented cases of summary executions of civilians by Russian soldiers, as well as arbitrary arrests, looting, rape, beatings, and extortion in Russian-controlled villages were further evidence of this. Despite these protests, the Russian authorities took measures to forcibly return displaced persons. These included physically returning railway carriages housing displaced persons in Ingushetia to war zones in Chechnya, refusing to register displaced persons for assistance, and denial of food and shelter.

The Way Forward

As the world marked the fiftieth anniversary of an international regime to protect the rights of refugees, the largest group of forcibly displaced persons worldwide—the internally displaced—remained largely excluded from any consistent form of international protection and their rights were persistently violated. Protecting the rights of internally displaced persons, while at the same time preserving and strengthening the right to asylum for refugees, were the two critical challenges facing the international community at the end of 2000.

Relevant Human Rights Watch Reports:

Bosnia and Hercegovinia: Unfinished Business, The Return of Refugees and Displaced Persons to Bijeljina, 5/00

Burmese Refugees in Bangladesh: Still No Durable Solution, 5/00

Burundi: Emptying the Hills: Regroupment in Burundi, 6/00

Chechnya: "Welcome to Hell," 10/00

Civilian Deaths in the NATO Air Campaign, 2/00

Eastern Congo Ravaged: Killing Civilians and Silencing Protest, 5/00

Federal Republic of Yugoslavia and Kosovo: Rape as a Weapon of "Ethnic Cleansing," 3/00

Japan: Owed Justice: Thai Women Trafficked into Debt Bondage in Japan, 9/00

Kuwait: Promises Betrayed: Denial of Rights of Bidun, Women, and Freedom of Expression, 10/00

Malaysia: Living in Limbo: Burmese Rohingyas in Malaysia, 8/00

Rwanda: The Search for Security and Human Rights Abuses, 4/00

Tanzania: Seeking Protection: Addressing Sexual and Domestic Violence in Tanzania's Refugee Camps, 9/00

Turkey: Human Rights and the European Union Accession Partnership, 9/00

West Timor: Forced Expulsions to West Timor and the Refugee Crisis, 12/99

HUMAN
RIGHTS
WATCH

APPENDIX

AWARDS

Hellman/Hammett Grants

The Hellman/Hammett grants are given annually by Human Rights Watch to recognize the courage of writers around the world who have been targets of political persecution and are in financial need. Twenty-eight writers from twenty-two countries received grants in 2000. Among them are Taoufik Ben Brik of Tunisia, Mamadali Makhmudov of Uzbekistan, and Nadire Mater of Turkey, who were jailed for writings that offended their governments. Of those who were forced into exile, some like Jonah Anguka (Kenya), Kadhim-Joni Mahdi (Iraq), and Alejandra Matus (Chile) received asylum in the United States. Others were victims of bloody conflicts in the former Yugoslavia, Sierra Leone, and the Democratic Republic of Congo.

In many countries, governments use military and presidential decrees, criminal libel, and colonial-era sedition laws to silence critics. Writers and journalists are often threatened, harassed, assaulted, or thrown into jail merely for providing information from nongovernmental sources. As a result, in addition to those who are directly targeted, many others are forced to practice self-censorship.

The Hellman/Hammett grant program began in 1989 when the estates of American authors Lillian Hellman and Dashiell Hammett asked Human Rights Watch to design a program for writers in financial need as a result of expressing their views. By publicizing the persecution that the grant recipients endure, Human Rights Watch focuses attention on censorship and suppression of free speech. In some cases the publicity is a protection against further abuse. In other cases, the writers request anonymity because of the dangerous circumstances in which they and their families are living.

Following are short biographies of those recipients in 2000 whose names can be safely released.

Jonah Anguka (Kenya), writer and former government administrator, was tortured and held in solitary confinement for three years on fabricated charges that he had murdered Robert Ouko, the foreign minister. After his acquittal by the Nairobi High Court, he was dismissed from his job and put under constant surveillance by President Moi's intelligence service. Fearing for his life, Anguka fled to the United States and was granted asylum. In exile, he published a book, *Absolute Power: The Ouko Murder Mystery* in which he named people whom he believes were involved in the murder plot, examined the police role in the cover-up, and listed possible motives for the assassination.

Claudia Anthony (Sierra Leone), journalist, has contributed to many independent newspapers in Freetown and to the BBC World Service. She is best known for writing about the rights of women and children. In February 1997, she founded her own paper, *Tribune of the People.* She is also the founder and executive director of the Alliance for Female Journalists in Sierra Leone. In January 1998, the ruling junta warned her to stop filing reports to the BBC, a serious threat in the context of Sierra Leone's brutal civil war. Anthony continued reporting. One month later, after that day's paper had published a story describing a looting incident carried out by a well-known rebel commander, armed rebels stormed her office. She escaped by pretending to be someone else. During the rebel invasion in January 1999, armed men damaged and looted the offices of *The Tribune of the People,* and it was forced to close. Anthony stayed in Freetown at great risk.

Taoufik Ben Brik (Tunisia) is one of the few journalists to break the silence of self-censorship that has pervaded the Tunisian press under President Zine al-Abidine Ben Ali. As a result, Ben Brik has repeatedly been the target of government harassment. His passport was confiscated to prevent him from leaving Tunisia; he was physically assaulted by presumed state agents; his phone lines are frequently cut, and his family's property has been vandalized by suspected plainclothes policemen. On April 3, 2000, Ben Brik was summoned before a state prosecutor for questioning about articles he wrote for European newspapers about the human rights situation in Tunisia. He then began a hunger strike to protest his treatment and that of other human rights defenders. After twenty-eight days, the government dropped the charges against him and gave him a new passport. Ben Brik continued his hunger strike until his brother was also released.

Yorro Jallow (The Gambia) is the founder and managing editor of the *Independent*, a bi-weekly newspaper that strives to provide an alternative to the country's pro-government press. One month after launching the paper, Jallow and his staff were arrested, held but not charged, threatened, and released. The next day, they were told to report to the National Intelligence Agency with documents relating to the newspaper's registration. After several weeks of hassling, the paper resumed publication. Jallow suspects the harassment is due, at least in part, to an editorial that the paper ran condemning human rights abuses committed in The Gambia.

Gakoko John (Uganda-Kenya) was born to a Tutsi Rwandan refugee family in southern Uganda and escaped to Kenya in 1981 when the Ugandan army accused his family of sympathizing with the rebels and murdered them all except his cousin and himself. He lived freely in Nairobi for more than a decade until a new Kenyan policy forced him into Kakuma Refugee Camp. In the camp, he has been writing articles and poetry for the newsletter and teaching in the adult education program. In 1996, when Hutu refugees arrived in Kakuma, they started to harass him, alleging that his writing showed a Tutsi bias that made him an unwelcome neighbor. In February 1998, they set fire to his house at 2 a.m. while he slept. He narrowly escaped and has been living in fear for his life.

Mohsen Kadivar (Iran) is a legal scholar whose writing on the theology of freedom has been critical of the doctrine of Velayat-e Faqih (Rule of the Supreme Jurist), an innovation in Shi'te political thought instituted in Iran by Ayatollah Khomeini in 1979. This controversial theory places temporal and spiritual power in the hands of the most qualified religious scholar. Kadivar and an increasing number of religious scholars in Iran have questioned the religious authenticity of this form of autocratic rule. In 1999, Kadivar was convicted by the Special Court for Clergy and sentenced to eighteen months in prison on charges of having spread false information about Iran's "sacred system of the Islamic Republic" and of helping enemies of the Islamic revolution.

Zeljko Kopanja (Bosnia), editor of *Nezavisne Novine,* Bosnia's main independent paper, received numerous complaints and death threats after publication of front page articles giving detailed accounts of war crimes committed by Serbian armed forces in Bosnia. On October 22, 1999, he was seriously wounded when a bomb exploded as he opened his car door. Doctors were forced to amputate both his legs. The perpetrators have not been found, and Kopanja continues to write.

Christiana Lambrinidis (Greece) writes experimental conflict-resolution plays based on testimony of women living in areas of ethnic or political conflict. Following production of one play in Athens in 1998, she received death threats, there was a bomb scare at the theater, her women's literature seminar was canceled, government funding that had been promised was withheld, and book stores refused to stock her book.

Hamide Berisha-Latifi (Kosovo), journalist, received death threats, lost her job, was harassed, beaten, and arrested for her work as a writer. In March 1998, she discovered that her name was on a police "blacklist." Soon afterward, after taking a photo of the police beating an Albanian student at a peaceful demonstration in Pristina, she was turned over to the police by a Serbian journalist. She pretended to be a foreigner and was released. Unable to work, she went to England, where she coordinated the Alliance of Kosova Journalists and edited its magazine, *Pa Cenzure-Uncensored.* In May 2000, she returned to Kosovo.

Li Shizheng (China), a journalist and poet, is widely known under his pen name Duo Duo. In 1989, while attending an international poetry festival, he gave interviews that made it dangerous for him to return to post-

Tiananmen China. He settled in Holland and is struggling to publish.

Kadhim-Joni Mahdi (Iraq), fiction writer, was jailed in 1991 for speaking against the government and jailed again in 1994 for his involvement with a literary group. On release from prison, he fled via Jordan and Saudi Arabia to the United States where he was granted refugee status. He now lives in Phoenix, Arizona, and supports himself as a barber while trying to finish a novel.

Mamadali Makhmudov (Uzbekistan) is a poet in the traditional "dastan" style of epic verse, which typically features a hero with magical qualities. Under the Soviet government, the dastan was labeled "impregnated with the poison of feudalism" and Makhmudov was forced to repudiate his work. After the Soviet Union collapsed, his most famous work, *Immortal Cliffs,* was retroactively awarded the Cholpan Prize. In 1991, Makhmudov supported the political party of a fellow writer, Muhammad Salih. The party lost the elections and has been banned since 1993. Makhmudov was first arrested in 1994 when his house was raided and police produced a firearm as evidence that he was guilty of terrorism. This charge met with widespread disbelief and was dropped. Next he was charged with embezzlement and sentenced to four years in prison. An international campaign was mounted on his behalf, and when no evidence was produced, he was given a presidential amnesty and released. In February 1999, after a car bomb exploded in Tashkent, he was picked up and taken to an unknown location. He "reappeared" in May, was tried with little access to a lawyer, and sentenced to fourteen years in prison.

Nadire Mater (Turkey), journalist, writes about Turkish politics including the Kurdish issue. In 1999, she wrote *Mehmet's Book,* telling the stories of soldiers who fought in southeast Turkey. The book was published in April. A court banned it in June and ordered all remaining copies seized. Mater is on trial for "insulting the armed forces." If convicted, she could be sentenced to six years in prison.

Alejandra Matus (Chile), journalist, received her first death threat after recording a radio program in which she recounted stories that aimed to give a voice to the poor. In 1994, after she published a story that exposed corruption in Santiago's Military Hospital, complaints were filed against her for sedition and insulting the Chilean army. She narrowly escaped prosecution although the reports proved true. She continued political investigations, including inquiries into the "disappearance" of Chilean citizens under Pinochet and the murder of former Foreign Minister Orlando Letelier. In 1999 she published *The Black Book of Chilean Justice,* which was banned in Chile in April 1999. Facing arrest under a law that criminalizes "insulting" high government officials, she fled to the United States and was granted political asylum. At this writing, she does freelance reporting from Miami.

Tshimanga M'Baya (Democratic Republic of the Congo), journalist, is president and one of five founders of Journaliste en Danger (JED), a nongovernmental press freedom group that exposes and protests abuse and repression of journalists by the government of President Laurent Kabila. JED members have received countless anonymous telephone threats, been denounced as "traitors" in the pay of "imperialists," detained, questioned by intelligence service agents, and physically attacked.

Shannon McFarlin (United States), former reporter at the *Celina Daily Standard,* won first prize for investigative reporting from the Ohio Associated Press and a Pulitzer Prize nomination in 1991 for a year-long series on the local sheriff that resulted in his resignation and conviction on criminal charges. In 1996, a new publisher took over management of the paper. At the time McFarlin was working on a story about possible misuse of public funds by the new school district superintendent. Before writing the story, she was fired and threatened with court action if she tried to contact any school official, even as a private citizen. She was maligned in *Daily Standard* editorials by the publisher and the mayor. In an attempt to clear her name, she asked for and was denied speaking time at a local school board meeting.

Yilmaz Odaba i (Turkey), poet, writer, and journalist, is a native of southeast Turkey. Obada i was first arrested at age nineteen following the September 1980 military coup and charged with "disseminating separatist propaganda." He was held for several weeks during which he reported being tortured. In 1987, he was arrested again, prosecuted for membership in the Socialist Party, and sentenced to eight years in prison, but the sentence was overturned by the Turkish Supreme Court. In 1994, he served ten months in prison for writing about the uprising of Seihk Said. In 1998, he served six months of an eighteen-month sentence for writing *Dreams and Life,* a collection of essays on poetry and culture. In March 2000, he was returned to prison on a seven-month sentence for "insulting the court," a charge arising from comments he made while on trial.

Carlos Pulgarin (Colombia) is a journalist at *El Tiempo,* a Bogota-based national daily newspaper. Soon after Pulgarin reported on the assassination of indigenous activists by right-wing paramilitary forces, he began receiving death threats accusing him of being a front for the revolutionary Armed Forces of Colombia, Colombia's largest guerrilla movement. He spent two months in hiding, worked anonymously for three months without further harassment, and then the threats resumed. He was kidnapped and held briefly, so he fled to Peru where he made great efforts to conceal his whereabouts. But after a few weeks, he was again receiving threatening messages. The Peruvian government agreed to provide police protection for a limited period, and journalist groups arranged for him to go to Spain where he is seeking political asylum.

Reach Sambath (Cambodia), journalist for Agence France-Presse, has been on his own since the age of thirteen when his entire family except one brother was wiped out by the Khmer Rouge. In the past seven years, he has covered two elections, the death of Pol Pot, and various human rights and political issues. He has also been a volunteer journalism teacher in Phnom Penh.

Svetlana Slapsak (Serbia), university professor, has written fifteen books on semantics and literature, political essays, and a mock-adventure novel. She and her husband, a Slovenian, were active in the peace movement, and when war broke out, Slapsak was branded a traitor and fired. Unable to find work in Belgrade, she took a part-time job at the university in Ljubljana, the capital of Slovenia, where her husband is a professor. She organized a women's group, "Silence kills; Let's speak up for peace!" This caused two colleagues to denounce her as a "Serbian spy," and she lost her part-time position. In 1995, she started a feminist quarterly, *ProFemina,* in Belgrade. It has been continually attacked by the state media. Several days after the NATO bombing began, police seized the building where *ProFemina* was located and took all its papers. *ProFemina* is now registered in Montenegro.

Abdolkarim Soroush (Iran), scholar and a leading proponent of political reform within the Islamic Republic, is the author of many books on Islamic philosophy. He has been banned from teaching since 1994. He has received harassing phone calls threatening him with imprisonment if he continues to criticize the government, and has been subjected to intimidation and physical assault by religious conservatives and their supporters. He has periodically been denied permission to travel to international conferences.

Vu Thu Hien (Vietnam), writer of fiction and film scripts, was arrested in 1967 and held in prison without trial for eight years. Apparently Vu Thu Hien's arrest related to his father's disagreements with the leadership of the Vietnamese Communist Party, his father having been a high ranking party official until 1963. After Vu Thu Hien's release from prison, he wrote under a pseudonym, including a novel that won first prize from the Vietnam Writers Association in 1989. All the while, he was under surveillance by the Cultural Police. In 1993, he fled to Moscow, but word that he was writing a memoir leaked to the Vietnamese Embassy and Hanoi's secret police searched his apartment. He moved to Poland where he was warned that another attack was imminent. This forced him to flee and seek political asylum in Paris.

Pavel Zhuk (Belarus), editor of successive newspapers, has struggled to provide an independent source of news and analysis in the face of government efforts to silence all alternative views in Belarus. In November 1997, *Svaboda* was shut down by the Lukashenka regime in retaliation for coverage of the political opposition. Zhuk and his staff continued to produce an Internet version and resumed publishing in print in January 1998 under a new name, *Naviny*. In September 1999, after losing a libel suit filed by the head of Belarus' Security Council, *Naviny* was forced to close. Police raided Zhuk's home in an effort to collect the libel fine. He again continued publication via the Internet. In October the regime suspended registration of nine independent publications, including *Nasha Svaboda,* Zhuk's intended replacement for *Naviny,* which had not yet published its first issue. Zhuk's coverage of an antigovernment demonstration in mid-October prompted the regime to order tax inspectors to audit *Naviny*'s advertisers and its printer. The police issued an arrest warrant for Zhuk, who spent several weeks in hiding. International pressure caused the regime to suspend its pursuit of Zhuk and helped restore registration for *Nasha Svaboda,* which as of June 2000 was publishing five days a week and was posted on the Internet.

MISSIONS

Africa Division

Angola: Advocacy, including report release (December 1999).

Belgium: Advocacy (December 1999).

Burundi: Research; work with local nongovernmental organizations (December 1999, February-April, August-September).

Democratic Republic of Congo: Research; advocacy on government measures to demobilize child soldiers and for the release of long-term political prisoners in Kinshasa; work with local nongovernmental organizations (December 1999, February-April, May, August-September).

Guinea: Research on treatment of refugees from Sierra Leone and Liberia and attacks on Guinean civilians by suspected rebels from Sierra Leone and Liberia (September).

Malawi: Advocacy regarding ratification of the Rome Treaty to establish the International Criminal Court; work with national nongovernmental organizations on campaign plans for speedy ratification (October).

Namibia: Advocacy regarding ratification of the Rome Treaty to establish the International Criminal Court; work with national nongovernmental organizations on campaign plans for speedy ratification (October).

Netherlands: Advocacy (December 1999).

Nigeria: Research on the deteriorating situation in the Delta; and work with local nongovernmental organizations (November-December 1999).

Republic of Congo: Research, Brazzaville (May).

Rwanda: Research and advocacy; work with local nongovernmental organizations (December 1999, February-April, August-September).

South Africa: Research on sexual violence and harassment in the schools and the right to education (March-April); follow-up research and hold workshops on farm violence and the criminal justice system, in partnership with the National Land Committee, a local nongovernmental organization (September); advocacy on the International Criminal Court (October).

Swaziland: Advocacy on the International Criminal Court (October).

Uganda: Research on the northern border of Kenya on the relief effort in Sudan and work with local nongovernmental organizations (July); work with local nongovernmental organizations (December 1999, February-April, May, August-September).

Zambia: Advocacy during the World Bank's Consultative Group meeting; release of report with Afronet, a local nongovernmental organization (December 1999).

Americas Division

Brazil: Meet with government officials to discuss recent developments in policy affecting human rights (October).

Colombia: Research in the area of the Revolutionary Armed Forces of Colombia (Fuerzas Armadas Revolucionarias de Colombia, FARC) on laws of war violations (May-June).

Chile: Attended appeals court hearings on Pinochet's immunity (April); meetings with officials and human rights lawyers to discuss Pinochet case and freedom of expression concerns (June).

Haiti: Research on the post-election parliamentary situation and continued human rights abuses since the OAS/U.N.'s mission departure (June-July).

Panama: Mission to intercede with Panamanian government not to grant political asylum to former Peruvian spymaster, Vladimiro Montesinos (October).

Peru: Research election conditions (March); research conditions for run-off election (May); observer of meeting of Peruvian NGOs with OAS representative Lloyd Axworthy and OAS Secretary General Cesar Gaviria (June-July); observed election protests (July).

Asia Division

Austria: Advocacy, U.N. Crimes Commission Congress (April); research on Trafficking (June).

China: Participant in a U.N. workshop on human rights in the Asia Pacific region, Beijing (March).

Cambodia: Avocacy with Cambodian NGOs and government officials about draft legislation to try Khmer Rouge leaders and to monitor negotiations between the U.N. and the Cambodia government on establishing a tribunal (January); research on the situation of Vietnamese asylum-seekers in Cambodia and UNHCR policy towards them (March); research and networking with Cambodian NGOs working on the issue of confiscation of indigenous minority lands by the Cambodian military for a case due to go to trial in December (November, 1999).

East Timor and Indonesia: Research of continuing obstacles to justice (establishing accountability) for the terror and destruction in East Timor after the U.N.-supervised vote in September 1999 (August); research in East Timor and West Timor (October-November 1999).

India: Convened a meeting of state representatives to the National Campaign for Dalit Human Rights—a nationwide NGO coalition born out of Human Rights Watch's work on caste-based abuse and discrimination in India—on future campaign strategies; advocacy in several national-level campaign events, including a protest rally in the capital that culminated in the submission of 2.5 million signatures to India's prime minister demanding the abolishment of "untouchability"; trial observer during the Justice Mohan Commission hearings in Tamil Nadu, set up to look into allegations of excessive use of force by the police during labor protests that resulted in the deaths of seventeen lower-caste laborers on July 23, 1999, in Tirunelveli district (December 1999).

Japan: Advocacy (June).

Malaysia: Research on treatment of Burmese refugees in Malaysia (November-December).

Sri Lanka: Attended the Neelan Tiruchelvam Commemoration in Colombo, held to honor the life and work of Neelan Tiruchelvam, a renowned Tamil human rights activist who was killed in a LTTE suicide bombing in 1999 (January/February).

Switzerland: Advocacy in Geneva at the Preparatory Meeting for Beijing +5 (January); advocacy at the U.N. Commission on Human Rights (April); present at first prepcom for the U.N. World Conference Against Racism, Racial Discrimination, Xenophobia and Related Intolerance; advocacy for the inclusion of caste and other forms of descent-based discrimination on the agenda, with Dalit NGO representatives of the International Dalit Solidarity Network (May); advocacy on Malaysia refugee report through meetings with UNHCR and donor governments (July); UNHCR Executive Committee Meeting (September-October).

Thailand: Advocacy at meeting of the Asian Development Bank and People's Forum 2000 and an alternative NGO gathering convened prior to the ADB Meeting (May 2000); concerning the International Criminal Court (June); at the Asia regional Experts Meeting in preparation for the U.N. World Conference Against (September); the International Conference on Corruption, Democracy and Development.(September); the Regional Seminar on Job Discrimination Against Women (September); and participation in a meeting on Research Training on Trafficking of Women. Research on changes in Thai policy toward Burmese refugees and on forced relocation of villages in Burma (February/March).

United Kingdom: Convened London meeting resulting in the formation of the International Dalit Solidarity Network (March); advocacy to release report, *Reform or Re-pression? Post-Coup Abuses in Pakistan* (October); advocacy (October).

United States: Observer at the World Trade Organization summit December 1999 in Seattle, Washington (December, 1999); legislative Hearings on Sexual Abuse of Women in Prison (October); General Assembly Special Session on Women (June).

Europe and Central Asia Division

Austria: Attend OSCE migration seminar (September).

Azerbaijan: Research, human rights in the pre-election period (September-October); research (May).

Belarus: Research, allegations of labor rights violations in Minsk, Gomel, Mogilev, Brest, and Belarus (December 1999).

Belgium: Advocacy, meetings with the E.U. on Turkey and Central Asia (November 1999 and May).

Bosnia and Hercegovina: Research on refugee returns (March, May, October).

Croatia: Research, pre-election conditions (November 1999).

Czech Republic: Attend IMF/World Bank annual meetings (September).

Europe: Advocacy on Chechnya and Central Asia in Czech Republic, Poland, France, and Switzerland (March).

Federal Republic of Yugoslavia/Kosovo: Research on war crimes (November 1999); research on impunity and security in post-war Kosovo, particularly as they affect minorities (May).

Serbia: Research on post-election transition (October).

France: Advocacy on Chechnya at the Council of Europe (January, April, September); attended Europe regional meeting for World Conference Against Racism (September-October).

Georgia: Advocacy for release of report (September); ongoing research from Tbilisi office.

Germany: Advocacy, on the current situation in Kosovo (April).

Ireland: Attend Council of Europe Human Rights Conference (March).

Russia: Ongoing research and advocacy through Moscow office; ongoing presence in Ingushetia to research abuses in Chechnya (November 1999 to May 2000).

Switzerland: Advocacy on Central Asia at the U.N. Commission on Human Rights (March); meeting on migrants' rights issues (Sept.-Oct. 2000).

Tajikistan: Ongoing research from Dushanbe office through May 2000.

Turkey: Attended OSCE Summit (November 1999); attended Turkish Human Rights Association's conference on prison conditions and investigated conditions in small-group isolation prisons (January 2000); met with civil society and government officials regarding prison conditions and planned reform; released a report on prison conditions (May); monitored trial of journalist Nadire Mater (September).

Uzbekistan: Ongoing research and advocacy from Tashkent office. Research on violence against women (May-June).

Middle East and North Africa Division
Algeria: Research and government meetings (May).

Egypt: Government meetings (March); research (August/September).
Geneva: Advocacy (July).

Iran: Research (April-May).

Israel/PA: Advocacy (May); NGO and government meetings (June); research on recent violence (October).

Jordan: Research (February/March, August/September).

Kuwait: Research (April).

Lebanon: Research (May); trial observation (June).

Morocco: Conference-workshop on improving NGO advocacy (March).

Yemen: Advocacy and consultation with nongovernmental organizations (February).

Arms Division

Belgium: Participation in Landmine Monitor Researchers Meeting (February).

Bulgaria: Advocacy, Sofia (December).

Denmark: Advocacy, presentation on the humanitarian impact of arms flows to Africa (June).

Egypt: Participation in Landmine Monitor Regional Researchers Workshop and Regional Conference on Landmines (April).

France: Advocacy, public events on landmines, Paris, and ICBL coordination committee meeting (September).

Netherlands: Participation in Landmine Monitor Researchers Meeting (May).

South Africa: Meeting with government officials and other contacts in advance of the release of report on South Africa's arms trade and human rights (October).

Sweden: Participation in meeting on corruption in the arms trade co-hosted by Sweden's Ministry of Foreign Affairs and Transparency International (February).

Switzerland: Participation in diplomatic meeting on stockpile destruction and in first meeting of states parties to Protocol II or Convention on Conventional Weapons (CCW) (December 1999); participation in diplomatic meeting on general operation and status of mine ban treaty (January); participation in ICBL coordination committee meeting (May); participation in diplomatic meeting on stockpile destruction and on general operation and status of mine ban treaty (May); participation in the Second Meeting of States Parties to the Mine Ban Treaty (September).

Ukraine: Participation in Landmine Monitor Regional Researchers Workshop (October).

United States: Participation in U.S. Campaign to Ban Landmines events in Des Moines, Iowa (January); briefing on "Landmines in Mozambique" to conference co-sponsored by the Bureau of Intelligence and Research of the U.S. Department of State and the National Intelligence Council in Washington DC (April); participation in General Electric shareholders annual meeting in support of resolution on GE's landmine production in Richmond, Virginia (April); participation in Peacejam board meeting in New York City on behalf of Jody Williams (June); participation in U.S. Campaign to Ban Landmines events in Washington D.C. (July); participation in Carnegie Endowment for International Peace event (September); small arms seminar hosted by NISAT and the Red Cross (October).

Children's Rights Division

Canada: Participation in the International Conference on War-Affected Children (September).

Hungary: Participation in UNICEF- sponsored conference: "Children Deprived of Parental Care: Rights and Realities" (October).

Nepal: Participation in Asia-Pacific Conference on the Use of Children as Soldiers (May).

Switzerland: Advocacy at the U.N. Working Group negotiating the Optional Protocol to the Convention on the Rights of the Child on the Involvement of Children in Armed Conflict (January); participation in the Committee on the Rights of the Child day of discussion on state violence against children (September).

United States: Child Farmworkers in the United States (June 1999-April 2000); violence and Discrimination against Lesbian, Gay, Bisexual, and Transgender Students in U.S. Public Schools (October 1999-October 2000); California, Georgia, Kansas, Massachusetts, New York, Texas, Utah Discrimination Against Girls in South African Schools (March-April).

Women's Rights Division

Algeria: Research, violence against women during the armed conflict and discrimination against women in family law (May).

Guatemala: Research, labor rights of female live-in domestic workers as well as maquiladora workers (May-June).

Netherlands: Advocacy in The Hague to discuss sex crimes during the Kosovo conflict (May).

United Kingdom: Advocacy in London to discuss report on Kosovo, *Rape as a Weapon of "Ethnic Cleansing,"* and the OSCE (October).

Morocco: Research and advocacy on discrimination and violence against women in the family (June-July).

Peru: Research, violence against women in the family (December 1999).

South Africa: Research, violence and discrimination against female farm workers (March-April, September).

United States: Research on lesbian, gay, bisexual, and transgender issues in California, Georgia, Kansas, Massachusetts, New York, Texas, and Utah (October 1999-October 2000); research into sexual abuse in women's prisons (January-February).

Uzbekistan: Research, violence against women in the family (May-June).

2000 HUMAN RIGHTS WATCH PUBLICATIONS

To order any of the following titles, please call our Publications Department at (212) 216-1813 and ask for our publications catalog or visit our site on the World Wide Web at http://www.hrw.org. This listing also contains reports from 1999 that were not listed in the World Report 2000..

Bosnia/Herzegovia
Unfinished Business: Return of Displaced Persons and Other HR Issues in Bijeljina, 5/00, 77pp.

Burma/Bangladesh
Burmese Refugees in Bangladesh: Still no Durable Solution, 5/00, 29pp.

Burundi
Emptying The Hills: Regroupment in Burundi, 7/00, 38pp.
Neglecting Justice in Making Peace, 4/00, 18pp.

China
Nipped in the Bud: The Suppression of the Chineses Democracy Movement, 9/00, 36pp.
Tibet Since 1950: Silence Prison or Exile, 5/00, 184 ppp.

Colombia
The Ties That Bind:Colombia and Military-Paramilitary Links, 2/00, 25pp.

Croatia
Croatia's Democracy Deficit: A Pre-Electoral Assessment, 12/99, 20pp.

Democratic Republic of Congo
Eastern Congo Ravaged — Killing Civilians and Silencing Protest, 5/00 40pp.

Georgia
Backtracking on Reform: Amendments Undermine Access to Justice, 10/00, 64pp.

Indonesia
Forced Expulsions to West Timor and The Refugee Crisis, 11/99, 21pp.
Human Rights and Pro-Independence Actions in Papua, 1999-2000, 5/00, 42pp.

Israel, The Occupied West Bank and Gaza Strip, and The Palestinian Aurthority Territories
Investigation into Unlawful use of Force in the West Bank, Gaza Strip, and Northern Israel, October 4 through October 11, 10/00, 13pp.

Japan
Owed Justice: Thai Women Trafficked into Debt Bondage in Japan, 9/00, 228pp.

Kuwait
Promises Betrayed: Denial of Rights of Bidun, Women, & Freedom of Expression, 10/00, 43pp.

Malaysia/Burma
Living in Limbo: Burmese Rohingyas in Malaysia, 8/00, 77pp.

NATO
Civilian Deaths in the Nato Air Campaign, 2/00, 79pp.

Pakistan
Prison Bound, The Denial of Juvenile Justice in Pakistan, 10/99, 147pp.
Reform or Repression? Post-Coup Abuses in Pakistan, 10/00, 24pp.

Russia/Chechnya
"Welcome to Hell": Arbitrary Detention, Torture, and Extortion in Chechnya, 10/00, 99pp.
February 5: A Day of Slaughter in Novye Aldi , 6/00, 43pp.
No Happiness Remains:" Civilian Killings, Pillage, and Rape in Alkhan-Yurt, Chechnya 4/00, 35pp.
Civilian Killings in Staropromyslovski of Grozny, 2/00, 18pp.

Rwanda
The Search for Security and Human Rights Abuses, 4/00 30pp.

South Africa
A Question of Principle: Arms Trade and Human Rights, 10/00, 48pp.

Tajikistan
Freedom of Expression Still Threatened, 11/99, 32pp.

Tanzania
Seeking Protection: Addressing Sexual and Domestic Violence in Tanzania's Refugee Camps, 10/00, 151pp.

Tunisia
The Administration of Justice in Tunisia:Torture, Trumped-Up Charges and a Tainted Trial, 2/00, 31pp.

Turkey
Human Rights and The European Union Accession Partnership, 9/00, 31pp.
Small Group Isolation in Turkish Prisons: An Avoidable Disaster, 5/00, 15pp.

United Kingdom/Northern Ireland
Northern Ireland: A New Beginning to Policing? The Report of the Independent Commission on Policing, 11/99, 21pp.

United States
Unfair Advantage: Workers' Freedom of Association in the U.S. under International Human Rights Standards, 8/00, 220pp.
Fingers to the Bone: United States Failure to Protect Child Farmworkers, 6/00, 112pp.
Clinton's Landmine Legacy, 7/00, 44 pp.
Punishment and Prejudice—The Racial Cost of the War on Drugs, 5/00, 39 pp.
Out of Sight: Super-Maximum Security Confinement in the US, 2/00, 9 pp.

Uzbekistan
Leaving No Witnesses: Uzbekistan's Campaign Against Rights Defenders, 3/00, 37pp.

Vietnam
The Silencing of Dissent, 5/00, 38pp.

Federal Republic of Yugoslavia
Kosovo: Rape As A Weapon of "Ethnic Cleansing", 3/00, 39pp.
Curtailing Political Dissent: Serbia's Campaign of Violence and Harassment Against Government's Violence and Harassment Against government's critics, 4/00, 41pp.

STAFF AND COMMITTEES

Human Rights Watch Staff

Executive: Kenneth Roth, executive director; Susan Osnos, associate director; Jennifer Gaboury, executive assistant; Justine Mickle, consultant.

Advocacy: Reed Brody, advocacy director; Lotte Leicht, Brussels office director; Joanna Weschler, U.N. representative; Francisco Cox, international justice counsel; Leon Peijnenburg, E.U. coordinator; Jacqueline Brandner, Maura

Dundon, associates; Olivier Bercault, Camille Bonnant, Pascal Kambale, Roemer LeMaitre, consultants.

Communications: Carroll Bogert, communications director; Jean-Paul Marthoz, Brussels press director; Minky Worden, electronic media director; Patrick Minges, publications director; Jagdish Parikh, on-line researcher; Urmi Shah, press information officer; Vanessa Saenen, office and press coordinator (Brussels); Sobeira Genao, publications manager; Fitzroy Hepkins, mail manager; Evan Weinberger, Doris Joe, Jose Martinez, associates; Vania Nedialkova, Csaba Szilagyi, consultants; Areta Lloyd, Miguel Morales, assistants.

Development and Outreach: Michele Alexander, development and outreach director; Michael Cooper, deputy development and outreach director (New York Committee); Rachel Weintraub, special events director; Rona Peligal, foundation relations director; Charles Urquhart, foundation relations associate director; Pam Bruns, California Committee (South) director; Emma Cherniavsky, California Committee (South) associate director; Clint Dalton, California Committee (North) director; Marie Janson, Europe director (London Committee); Veronica Matushaj, creative services and direct response manager; Michelle Leisure, special events coordinator; Adam Greenfield, office administrator (Los Angeles); Zoe Gottlieb, Thomas Yeh, associates; Raymond P. Happy (Community Counselling Services), Rafael Jiménez, Marie-Ange Kalenga, Corinne Sevily (EuroAmerican Communications), consultants; Matthew Lieber, Jasmina Repak, assistants.

Finance: Barbara Guglielmo, finance director; Anderson Allen, office manager (Washington, D.C.); Bessie Skoures, office administrator (Brussels); Rachael Noronha, office administrator (London); Mei Tang, accountant; Abdou Seye, bookkeeper; Assie Koroma, receptionist (Washington, D.C.); Yumersis Amancio, Lateefah Bell, assistants.

Human Resources: Maria Pignataro Nielsen, human resources director; Christian Peña, office manager (New York); Gil Colon, Yanet Encarnacion, Mary Majao, Arayna Thomas, receptionists (New York); Ernest Ulrich, consultant; Josephine Mescallado, assistant.

Information Technology: Walid Ayoub, information technology director; Amin Khair, network administrator/help desk; Arturo Cabrejo, office/help desk associate; Edward Valentini, consultant; Juan Acuña,, assistant.

International Justice: Richard Dicker, director; Helen Duffy, associate counsel; Indira Rosenthal, Brigitte Suhr, International Justice counsel.

Legal Office: Wilder Tayler, Legal and Policy Director; Dinah PoKempner, general counsel; Andrew Ayers, special assistant.

Program: Malcolm Smart, program director; Michael McClintock, deputy program director; Jeri Laber, senior advisor; Peter Bouckaert, emergencies researcher; Allyson Collins, senior researcher (United States) and Washington associate director; Lance Compa, researcher (United States); Jamie Fellner, associate counsel (United States); Arvind Ganesan, business and human rights director; Rachael Reilly, refugee policy director; Saman Zia-Zarifi, academic freedom director; Jacqueline Brandner, Sam David, Rebecca Hart, Jonathan Horowitz, Gail Yamauchi, associates; Marcia Allina, Manuel Couffignal, Julia Duchrow, Bruce Goldstein, Judith Greene, Tomas Jonsson, Mavis Matenge, Jena Matzen, Rachel Rosenbloom, Sinead Walsh, consultants.

International Film Festival: Bruni Burres, director; John Anderson, associate director; Andrea Holley, traveling festival manager; Fernanda Amorim Leventhal, assistant.

1999-2000 Fellowship Recipients: Judith Sunderland, Leonard H. Sandler Fellow; Carol Pier, Orville Schell Fellow; Erika George, Alan R. Finberg Fellow; Zama Coursen-Neff, Furman Fellow; Cynthia Totten, Georgetown

Women's Law and Public Policy Fellow.

Board of Directors
Jonathan F. Fanton, chair; Robert L. Bernstein, founding chair; Lisa Anderson, David M. Brown, William D. Carmichael, Dorothy Cullman, Gina Despres, Irene Diamond, Fiona Druckenmiller, Edith Everett, Michael E. Gellert, Vartan Gregorian, Alice H. Henkin, James F. Hoge, Jr., Stephen L. Kass, Marina Pinto Kaufman, Bruce J. Klatsky, Joanne Leedom Ackerman, Joshua Mailman, Dr. Yolanda T. Moses, Joel Motley, Samuel K. Murumba, Andrew Nathan, Jane Olson, Peter Osnos, Kathleen Peratis, Catherine Powell, Bruce Rabb, Sigrid Rausing, Orville Schell, Sid Sheinberg, Gary G. Sick, Malcolm B. Smith, Domna Stanton, John J. Studzinski, Maya Wiley, Roland Algrant (*board member emeritus*), Adrian W. DeWind, (*board member emeritus*).

Members of Board Committees and Sub-Committees: Helen Bernstein, special events; Martin Blumenthal, development; Lori Damrosch, policy; Henry Everett, investment; Mike Farrell, policy; Barbara Finberg, campaign steering committee; Robert Menschel, investment; Minna Schrag, policy; Florence Teicher, policy; Maureen White, nominating.

Africa Division
Staff
Peter Takirambudde, executive director; Suliman Ali Baldo, senior researcher; Corinne Dufka, researcher; Janet Fleischman, Washington director; Juliane Kippenberg, NGO liaison; Bronwen Manby, senior researcher; Binaifer Nowrojee, senior researcher; Sara Rakita, researcher; Jemera Rone, counsel; Tony Tate, researcher; Alex Vines, senior researcher; Zac Freeman, Ethel Higonnet, Tamar Satnet, associates; Molly Bingham, Alison DesForges, Steve Ellis, Ellen Vermeulen, consultants; Marti Flacks, assistant.

Advisory Committee
Vincent A. Mai, chair; Carole Artigiani, Robert L. Bernstein, William Carmichael, Michael Chege, Roberta Cohen, Carol Corillon, Cheryl "Imani" Countess, Alison L. DesForges, R. Harcourt Dodds, Stephen Ellmann, Aaron Etra, Gail M. Gerhart, Arthur C. Helton, Alice H. Henkin, Robert Joffe, Professor E. Kannyo, Thomas Karis, Muna Ndulo, Vincent A. Mai, Samuel Murumba, James C.N. Paul, Sidney S. Rosdeitcher, Dorothy Thomas, Dirk van Zyl Smit, R. Keith Walton, Claude E. Welch, Jr., Maureen White, Aristide Zolberg.

Americas Division
Staff
José Miguel Vivanco, executive director; Joanne Mariner, deputy director; Sebastian Brett, researcher; Robin Kirk, researcher; Joel Solomon, research director; Monisha Bajaj, Tzeitel Cruz-Donat, Elizabeth Hollenback, associates; Charles T. Call, James Louis Cavallaro, Anne Fuller, Jill Hedges, consultants; Barbara Graves, assistant.

Advisory Committee
Stephen L. Kass, chair; Marina Pinto Kaufman, vice-chair; David Nachman, vice-chair; Roland Algrant, Peter D. Bell, Marecelo Bronstein, Paul Chevigny, Roberto Cuéllar, Dorothy Cullman, Tom J. Farer, Alejandro Garro, Peter Hakim, Ronald G. Hellman, Bianca Jagger, Mark Kaplan, Margaret A. Lang, Kenneth Maxwell, Jocelyn McCalla, Bruce Rabb, Michael Shifter, George Soros, Julien Studley, Rose Styron, Javier Timerman, Horacio Verbitsky, José Zalaquett.

Asia Division
Staff
Sidney Jones, executive director; Joe Saunders, deputy director; Sara Colm, researcher; Jeannine Guthrie, NGO liaison; Mike Jendrzejczyk, Washington director; Smita Narula, senior researcher; Gary Risser, researcher; Mickey Spiegel, researcher; Jan van der Made, researcher; Adam Bassine, Liz Weiss, associates; Kate Beddall, Matt Easton, Karin Deutsch Karlekar, Sebastiaan der

Kinderen, Nancy Leou, Hasan Mujtaba, consultants.

Advisory Committee

Maureen Aung-Thwin, Edward J. Baker, Harry Barnes, Robert L. Bernstein, Jagdish Bhagwati, Greg Carr, Jerome Cohen, Clarence Dias, Prof. Dolores A. Donovan, Frances Fitzgerald, Adrienne Germain, Prof. Merle Goldman, Prof. Deborah Greenberg, Jack Greenberg, Paul Hoffman, Sharon Hom, Rounaq Jahan, Virginia Leary, Prof. Daniel Lev, Perry Link, Bishop Paul Moore, Andy Nathan, Yuri Orlov, Kathleen Peratis, Victoria Riskin, Sheila Rothman, Barnett Rubin, Orville Schell, Prof. James Scott, Steve Shapiro, Dr. Eric Stover, and Maya Wiley.

Europe & Central Asia Division
Staff

Holly Cartner, executive director; Rachel Denber, deputy director; Fred Abrahams, senior researcher; Elizabeth Andersen, advocacy director; Cassandra Cavanaugh, senior researcher; Theresa Freese, researcher; Pamela Gomez, Caucasus office director; Julia Hall, researcher; Malcolm Hawkes, researcher; Bogdan Ivanisevic, researcher; Diederik Lohman, Moscow office director; André Lommen, researcher; Alexander Petrov, Moscow office deputy director; Acacia Shields, researcher; Marie Struthers, Tajikistan office director; Jonathan Sugden, researcher; Benjamin Ward, researcher; Alexander Frangos, coordinator; Liudmila Belova, Rachel Bien, Elizabeth Eagen, George Gogia, Alexandra Perina, Maria Pulzetti, Rebecca Stich, Natasha Zaretsky, associates; Johana Bjorken, Chuck Call, Erika Dailey, Max Marcus, Rebecca Morgan, Jim Ron, John Walker, consultants; Yulia Dultsina, Natalia Ermolaev, assistants.

Advisory Steering Committee

Peter Osnos, chair; Mort Abramowitz, Henri Barkey, Barbara Finberg, Frederica Friedman, Felice Gaer, Michael Gellert, Paul Goble, Alice Henkin, Stanley Hoffmann, Robert James, Walter Link, Kati Marton, Prema Mathai-Davis, Karl Meyer, Joel Motley,

Herbert Okun, Jane Olson, Kathleen Peratis, Hannah Pakula, Barnett Rubin, Collette Shulman, Leon Sigal, Malcolm Smith, George Soros, Donald Sutherland, Adele Sweet, Ruti Teitel, Mark von Hagen, Mark Walton, William Zabel, Ambassador Warren Zimmermann.

Middle East & North Africa Division
Staff

Hanny Megally, executive director; Eric Goldstein, deputy director; Clarisa Bencomo, researcher; Hania Mufti, London office director; Elahé Sharifpour-Hicks, researcher; Virginia Sherry, associate director; Joe Stork, advocacy director; Tobie Barton, Erin Sawaya, associates; Gamal Eid, Alaa Kaoud, Sheila Carapico, consultants.

Advisory Committee

Lisa Anderson, co-chair; Gary Sick, co-Chair; Bruce Rabb, vice-chair; Khaled Abou El-Fadl, Shaul Bakhash, M. Cherif Bassiouni, Martin Blumenthal, Paul Chevigny, Helena Cobban, Edith Everett, Mansour Farhang, Christopher E. George, Rita E. Hauser, Ulrich Haynes, Rev. J. Bryan Hehir, Edy Kaufman, Marina Pinto Kaufman, Samir Khalaf, Judith Kipper, Ann M. Lesch, Stephen P. Marks, Rolando Matalon, Philip Mattar, Sheila Nemazee, Jane Schaller, Jean-Francois Seznec, Charles Shamas, Sanford Solender, Shibley Telhami, Andrew Whitley, Napoleon B. Williams, Jr., James J. Zogby.

Arms Division
Staff

Joost R. Hiltermann, executive director; Stephen D. Goose, program director; Loretta Bondí, advocacy coordinator; Mark Hiznay, researcher; Ernst Jan Hogendoorn, researcher; Lisa Misol, researcher; Alex Vines, senior researcher; Mary Wareham, senior advocate (landmines); Jasmine Juteau, Hannah Novak, Charli Wyatt, associates; William M. Arkin, Robin Bhatty, Tara Magner, Monica Schurtman, Cindy Shiner, Frank Smyth, Henry Thompson, consultants.

Advisory Committee

Dr. Torsten N. Wiesel, chair; Nicole Ball, vice-chair; Vincent McGee, vice-chair; Amb. Ahmedou Ould Abdallah, Ken Anderson, David Brown, Ahmed H. Esa, Alastair Hay, Lao Mong Hay, Patricia Irvin, Michael Klare, Frederick J. Knecht, Edward Laurance, Graça Machel, Laurie Nathan, Janne E. Nolan, Josephine Odera, Julian P. Perry Robinson, Andrew J. Pierre, Eugénia Piza-Lopez, David Rieff, Kumar Rupesinghe, John Ryle, Archbishop Emeritus Desmond Tutu, Keith Walton, Jody Williams, and Thomas Winship.

Children's Rights Division

Staff

Lois Whitman, executive director; Jo Becker, advocacy director; Michael Bochenek, researcher; Vikram Parekh, researcher; Yodon Thonden, senior researcher; Shalu Rozario, associate; Rosa Ehrenreich, Clovene Hanchard, Kathleen Hunt, Amy Marx, Glenn McGrory, Marco Simons, Robert Sloane, Mark Templeton, Lee Tucker, consultants.

Advisory Commitee

Jane Green Schaller, chair; Roland Algrant, vice-chair; Goldie Alfasi-Siffert, Michelle India Baird, Phyllis W. Beck, James Bell, Albina du Boisrouvray, Rachel Brett, Bernardine Dohrn, Fr. Robert Drinan, Barbara Finberg, Sanford J. Fox, Gail Furman, Lisa Hedley, Anita Howe-Waxman, Kathleen Hunt, Eugene Isenberg, Sheila B. Kamerman, Rhoda Karpatkin, Kela Leon, Alan Levine, Miriam Lyons, Hadassah Brooks Morgan, Prexy Nesbitt, Elena Nightingale, Martha J. Olson, Marta Santos Pais, Susan Rappaport, Jack Rendler, Robert G. Schwartz, Mark I. Soler, Lisa Sullivan, William Taggart, William L. Taylor, Geraldine Van Bueren, Peter Volmink, James D. Weill, and Derrick Wong.

Women's Rights Division

Staff

Regan Ralph, executive director; LaShawn R. Jefferson, deputy director; Widney Brown, advocacy director; Kinsey Dinan, researcher; Chirumbidzo Mabuwa, researcher; Isis Nusair, researcher; Martina Vandenberg, researcher; Tejal Jesrani, Laura Rusu, Smita Varia, associates; Patti Gossman, consultant.

Advisory Committee

Kathleen Peratis, chair; Mahnaz Afkhami, Roland Algrant, Abudllahi An-Na'im, Helen Bernstein, Beverlee Bruce, Charlotte Bunch, Holly J. Burkhalter, Rhonda Copelon, Lisa Crooms, Gina Despres, Joan Dunlop, Claire Flom, Adrienne Germain, Zhu Hong, Marina Pinto Kaufman, Asma Khader, Gara LaMarche, Joyce Mends-Cole, Yolanda T. Moses, Marysa Navarro-Aranguren, Susan Petersen, Marina Pisklakova, Catherine Powell, Celina Romany, Margaret Schuler, and Domna Stanton.

HUMAN RIGHTS WATCH COUNCIL

California Committee, South

Mike Farrell, co-chair; Vicki Riskin, co-chair; Thomas Higgins, vice co-chair; Zazi Pope, vice co-chair.

Executive Committee

Jane Olson, co-founder; Justin Connolly, Jonathan Feldman, Eric Garcetti, Beth Greenfield, Thomas R. Parker, Marina Pisklakova Parker, David W. Rintels, Sid Sheinberg, Diane O. Wittenberg.

Stanley Sheinbaum, co-founder; Elaine Attias, Joan Willens Beerman, Rabbi Leonard Beerman, Terree Bowers, Geoffrey Cowan, Nancy Cushing-Jones, Peggy Davis, Stephen Davis, Chiara Di Geronimo, Mary Estrin, Danny Glover, Paul Hoffman, Paula Holt, Claudia Kahn, Barry Kemp, Maggie Kemp, Emily Levine, Roberto Lovato, Kristin Olson McKissick, Alison Dundes Renteln, Tracy Rice, Carol Richards, Lawrence D. Rose, Pippa Scott, William D. Temko, Andrea Van de Kamp, Matt Ward, Patricia Williams, Stanley Wolpert.

California Committee, North
Orville Schell, co-chair; Nancy Parrish, co-chair; Jeff Bleich, Rebecca Brackman, Stuart Davidson, Dorothy Edelman, Jack Edelman, Sherry Ferris, Elizabeth Rice Larsen, Walter Link, Steve Silberstein.

New York Committee
Domna Stanton, chair; Joel Motley, vice-chair; Robert Joffe, chair emeritus; Allen R. Adler, Henry Arnhold, Marilyn Berger, Richard Berger, Robert L. Bernstein, Martin Blumenthal, Dorothy Cullman, Adrian DeWind, Irene Diamond, Strachan Donnelley, Graham Duncan, Patrick Durkin, Jonathan F. Fanton, Barbara Finberg, Gail Furman, Jay Furman, David S. Hirsch, Joseph Hofheimer, Debbie Hymowitz, Gregg Hymowitz, Yves-Andre Istel, Robert James, Nancy Kamel, Steve Kass, Jesse L. Lehman, Douglas Liman, Jonathan Lopatin, Vincent Mai, Vincent McGee, David Nachman, Peter Osnos, James H. Ottaway, Jr., Kathleen Peratis, Bruce Rabb, Barbara Paul Robinson, Nina Rosenwald, Alice Sandler, Jeffrey Scheuer, Bruce Slovin, Francesca Slovin, Malcolm B. Smith, Thomas Sobol, Michael Steinhardt, Donald J. Sutherland, Eva Timerman, Javier Timerman, Arthur Zankel.

London Committee
John Studzinski, chair; Jenny Dearden, Tony Elliott, Steven Glick, Louis Greig, Laura Malkin, Robert Marcus, Sigrid Rausing, Alice Smith, Ingrid Wassenaar, Patricia Wilson.

Members-At-Large
Gregory C. Carr, Gina Despres, Arnold Hiatt, John Kaneb, Robin Ray, Stuart Ray.